AF608069

PRINT CULTURE HISTORIES BEYOND THE METROPOLIS

Print Culture Histories beyond the Metropolis

Edited by

JAMES J. CONNOLLY, PATRICK COLLIER,
FRANK FELSENSTEIN, KENNETH R. HALL,
AND ROBERT G. HALL

UNIVERSITY OF TORONTO PRESS
Toronto Buffalo London

Toronto Buffalo London
www.utppublishing.com

ISBN 978-1-4426-5062-6 (cloth)

Studies in Book and Print Culture

Library and Archives Canada Cataloguing in Publication

Print culture histories beyond the metropolis / edited by James J. Connolly, Patrick Collier, Frank Felsenstein, Kenneth R. Hall, and Robert Hall.

Includes bibliographical references and index.
ISBN 978-1-4426-5062-6 (bound)

1. Books and reading – History. 2. Book industries and trade – History. 3. Literature publishing – History. 4. Transmission of texts – History. 5. Popular literature – History and criticism. 6. Popular culture – History. I. Connolly, James J., 1962–, editor II. Collier, Patrick, editor III. Felsenstein, Frank, author, editor IV. Hall, Kenneth R., author, editor V. Hall, Robert G. (Robert Gaston), 1958–, author, editor

Z1003.P75 2016 028'.909 C2015-906896-7

This book has been published with the assistance of Ball State University.

University of Toronto Press acknowledges the financial assistance to its publishing program of the Canada Council for the Arts and the Ontario Arts Council, an agency of the Government of Ontario.

Canada Council for the Arts Conseil des Arts du Canada

Funded by the Government of Canada Financé par le gouvernement du Canada Canada

Contents

Illustrations and Maps

Illustrations

Tables

Map

Acknowledgments

The essays collected in this book were first written for the Print Culture Histories Beyond the Metropolis Conference, held at Ball State University in March 2013. That conference and this volume were supported with a Collaborative Research Grant from the National Endowment for the Humanities. The conference also received support from several units at Ball State University, including the Center for Middletown Studies, Ball State University Libraries, the English Department, and the History Department. The proceedings of the conference are available for viewing through the Print Culture Histories Conference Collection held in the Digital Media Repository maintained by Ball State University Libraries (http://libx.bsu.edu/).

In addition to the editors, a number of other people played vital roles in producing this volume. Melanie Cabak was instrumental in both the organization of the conference and the production of the book. Michael Smith, Erin Bretz, and Rich Usdowski provided valuable help as well. The staff of Ball State University Archives enabled us to make the conference proceedings available online and provided guidance in assembling the illustrations. Michael Hradesky of the Ball State Geography Department designed the map in chapter 2. Our thanks as well to Wayne Wiegand, Robb Haberman, Stephan Morillo, Scott Stephan, Joanne Passet, Richard Warner, Christopher Phillips, and Martin Hewitt for their contributions to the conference, which guided revisions of many of the chapters.

Siobhan McMenemy of the University of Toronto Press has patiently guided us through the publication process. Charles Stuart provided excellent copyediting of an unruly manuscript and saved us from many errors. Thanks to both and to the anonymous readers who helped us revise and improve the final product.

PRINT CULTURE HISTORIES BEYOND THE METROPOLIS

Print Culture Histories beyond the Metropolis: An Introduction

PATRICK COLLIER AND JAMES J. CONNOLLY

On 5 October 1892, the front cover of the *Illustrated London News* bore an image of two vaguely Oriental-looking women, one wearing a robe and a diadem and whose appearance is vaguely Near Eastern and the other, incongruously, wearing East Asian clothing that matches her faintly Chinese features. The two are smiling as they happily leaf through the pages of the *Illustrated London News* itself, its advertising wrapper adorned at the top with the paper's trademark flag, its title superimposed upon a silhouette of the London skyline. Below the image appears this legend: "Our conquest of egypt" (fig. 0.1). This text-image package brings together two of the selling points of the *Illustrated London News*, an extremely popular weekly newspaper that catered to middle-class readers: illustration and the empire. Started in 1842, the paper had achieved almost immediate success with its combination of illustration and news of London. Later in the century, and particularly in the 1890s, the newspaper also emphasized imperial and international news, dispatching artists and journalists to places as far-flung as Russia, Burma, and Persia to represent exotic foreign cultures and report on British interests and activities.

The image can obviously be read as an egregious product of a colonialist mindset that exoticizes and feminizes colonial peoples under a confused, conflated otherness. The women in the image are posited as objects (of commerce, of conquest, and of representation) whose ethnic differences are irrelevant before a colonial gaze that equalizes them as subjects of imperial rule. Such rule is wittily (if with ironic accuracy) equated with access to colonial markets for imperial commodities, in this case the print commodity of the *Illustrated London News*, which both represented the colonial other for readers back in London and shipped such representations

THE ILLUSTRATED LONDON NEWS

REGISTERED AT THE GENERAL POST-OFFICE FOR TRANSMISSION ABROAD.

No. 2794.—VOL. CI. SATURDAY, NOVEMBER 5, 1892. TWO WHOLE SHEETS } SIXPENCE. By Post, 6½d.

OUR OCCUPATION OF EGYPT.

0.1 *Illustrated London News*, 5 October 1892.

back to the colonies, where the paper was marketed to civil servants anxious for news of home.

But we wish to suggest a different reading of the image, as an allegory of a view that has long dominated scholarly work on the history of modern print. In this perspective, print culture and all that it entails – publishing, the trade in print objects, literary culture, the movement of political and philosophical ideas – originates from metropolitan or imperial centres and flows to provincial or colonial margins. The smiles on the faces of these exotic *Illustrated London News* readers suggest that they are eager recipients of the print culture generated in the metropole. The incongruity of their dress, which seems utterly unrelated to Egypt, speaks to the fantastic nature of the peripheral reader when viewed from the imperial centre. The image is a fantasy of easy imperial conquest, and these pictured readers are fantasy objects, creations of the imperial imagination: just as their dress bears no obvious relation to Egypt, their grateful consumption of imperial print has, we presume, no historical relation to actual, historical readers of the *Illustrated London News*. But in this they are not so different from the provincial (or colonial) reader as imagined by contemporary studies of print culture, which too frequently take an urban standpoint as their default setting. How often have book historians or literary scholars similarly imagined provincial cities, rural communities, or colonial outposts as passive recipients of a culture moving out from the metropolitan centre? How often have they, usually implicitly, embraced a quasi-imperial view of non-urban spaces and their readers as backward, behind the times, or eagerly awaiting the new and enlightening to reach them from centres of culture and learning?

Rethinking Print Culture Studies

The following pages attempt a radical shifting of this view: a provisional, local, and multi-voiced telling of the history – or, rather, the histories – of modern print culture, not from the point of view of urban and imperial centres but from that of provincial locales and imperial peripheries.[1] *Print Culture Histories beyond the Metropolis* brings together leading scholars of literature, history, library studies, and communications to explore the ways in which residents of smaller cities, provincial districts, rural settings, and colonial outposts engaged with print. The focus of the volume is the modern, anglophone world (primarily since the eighteenth century) and its unifying purpose is to examine the historical dynamics of print culture (which includes the production, dissemination, and reading of printed material, as well as the creation of meaning through print) from non-metropolitan vantage points.

Decentring print culture history makes visible the print practices of vast numbers of readers, writers, librarians, teachers, and booksellers previously absent from the history of print. An intentionally non-metropolitan perspective also avoids an excessive emphasis on the *production* of printed materials by placing equal weight on their *consumption* and on the role that the latter process plays in the creation of meanings ascribed to texts. In this respect it furthers a process, now well underway, which moves readers towards the centre of print culture history. As Jonathan Rose has argued, literary history, the history of the book, and media studies for decades reiterated the notion that the habits and responses of actual readers were "unknowable" – a gross misapprehension that said more about which archives scholars were willing to work (books, periodicals, and the private papers of leading figures) and which they tended to ignore (letters, diaries, library records, and private papers of ordinary people, many of them to be found in far-flung locales).[2] In the years since Rose's monumental study of working-class readers appeared, new online resources such as the What Middletown Read database, the Australian Common Reader, and Dissenting Academies Online have made the study of certain discrete sets of readers accessible to scholars around the world. These data sets, along with new, digitally-based analytical techniques, permit us to explore reading choices and the contexts in which they were made in greater detail and to assign those choices greater weight in historical investigations of print culture.

By paying heed to such local particularities, the essays assembled here complicate the usual core-periphery formula by assigning creative force to ordinary people and communities. Putting a peripatetic editor from upstate New York, black-run newspapers in Latin America, a clerk banished to a New Zealand sheep station, members of a Dissenting academy in rural England, or library users in Muncie, Indiana, and Lambton, Australia, at the centre of the analysis, this volume produces a more complex accounting of how printed materials circulated, a stronger sense of their impact, and a fuller understanding of how local contexts and particular forms of social interaction shaped reading experiences. Conclusions reached in these essays are broad and varied, but one key thread ties them together: they all prompt us to develop more complex explanations of how individuals, groups, and communities engaged with the modern world through print. While they acknowledge that the constantly emerging divide (or perhaps it would be better to say *dialogue*) between the country and the city shaped the experiences of readers, they also speak powerfully of the way that individuals in non-metropolitan locations were appropriating, grappling with, and taking part in modern print culture in ways indelibly marked by local conditions, affiliations, institutions, and patterns of sociability. Dualities such as core-periphery and cosmopolitan-provincial prove inadequate to explain these processes, as do standard colonial and post-colonial models of resistance, accommodation, and authority. As works of history, these essays tend to move away from theorizing and towards descriptions and assessments of print's role in cultural interactions in particular times, places, and circumstances. They demonstrate forcefully the ways in which seemingly isolated places were sites of cultural creativity and not simply settings characterized by the imitation of ideas and styles generated in metropolitan centres. Many of these essays also explore the economic and cultural networks that linked smaller cities and towns with each other and with urban centres, documenting the multiple flows of ideas, styles, and information between and among them.

Beyond Metropolitan Bias

Print Culture Histories beyond the Metropolis thus offers a corrective to investigations of print culture that display what might be termed a metropolitan bias: one strong enough to suggest, sometimes explicitly and sometimes implicitly, that modernity itself was an urban phenomenon. Distinctions between the modern, progressive urban centre and the backwards, nostalgic provinces are a staple of contemporary historical and social analysis.[3] Insofar as rural districts, smaller cities and towns, and colonial outposts have modernized, most scholars have suggested, they have done so through a process that flows outward from metropolitan centres of gestation, gradually, incompletely, and unevenly to national and, ultimately, imperial peripheries. This predisposition informs studies that view print culture from the perspective of producers (writers, publishers, periodicals) and those that study reading and reception. In the latter case, this bias is perhaps nowhere more evident than in the title of David M. Henkin's *City Reading: Written Words and Public Spaces in Antebellum New York*. While Henkin's impressive reconstruction of "the specific conditions of print's reception and consumption by a heterogeneous … population" is almost perfectly in step with the approach of *Print Culture Histories beyond the Metropolis*, its urban emphasis goes beyond method, implying an entire, metropole-centred philosophy of history that sees urban transformations as paradigmatic, indeed as virtually identical with modernity itself. This philosophy allows Henkin to claim that his study of the public nature of reading in mid-nineteenth-century New York constitutes "a glimpse at the emergence of urban modernity in the capitalist west" and to posit his own, contemporary readers as "ambivalent inheritors of the nineteenth-century urban legacy."[4] We see this same metropolitan emphasis in other recent scholarship. The contributions to Ann L. Ardis and Patrick Collier's *Transatlantic Print Culture 1880–1940* include essays on London, New York, and other urban centres, but little or nothing on print in more peripheral settings. David Finkelstein and Alistair McCleery's *Introduction to Book History* argues that "for well over five hundred years, print has been central to the shaping of western society, and to the transmission of its values outwards (whether imposed or voluntarily) into colonized and connected societies and territories." Explicitly or implicitly, many, if not most, studies of print culture adopt this core-periphery model, or the parallel framework that sets at odds the cosmopolitan and the provincial.[5]

By now there is a considerable body of scholarship, in various disciplines, that works to undo a simple core-periphery construct. Post-colonial studies emphasize the creation of hybrid identities and insist that local circumstances must be taken into account to make sense of the syncretic cultural patterns that unfolded in imperial possessions and other subservient political contexts. New scholarship in rural history presents a complex, dynamic relationship between the countryside and the city. A recent vein of urban studies focusing on smaller cities, influenced in part by theories about the significance of place, argues that the experience of life in such settings involved more than the replication of trends and patterns that began in big cities.[6]

Some literary and print culture historians, too, have begun to push the field away from a reflexive metropolitan bias. In the third chapter of his pathbreaking *Atlas of the European Novel, 1800–1900*, Franco Moretti avoids the trap of simply assuming a core-periphery pattern by assembling data from library catalogues as a means of tracing the geographic distribution of fiction in nineteenth-century Europe. Although Moretti and his collaborators sought to find variation across collections, they instead encountered remarkable uniformity among smaller catalogues located outside the metropolitan publishing centres of London and Paris. From this Moretti concludes the modern novel did in fact flow from centre to periphery; London and Paris were sites of literary ferment and variety; provincial (and, later, colonial) cities imported a narrow canon of metropolitan novels, of which their writers produced more-or-less slavish imitations.

In this analysis, Moretti writes, peripheral locales experienced "very little freedom and very little creativity." The strength of Moretti's work lies in its willingness to test the prevailing centralized model rather than to take it as a given. Yet Moretti's *Atlas* is severely limited by his data and by his perspective, neither of which are concerned with the ways in which fiction was *consumed* in these seemingly isolated locales.[7] More limiting still is Moretti's emphasis on the novel itself (as opposed to the myriad other practices of print culture, from devotional writing to daily journalism); as Moretti acknowledges, the novel is "the most centralized of all literary genres," and other forms (he names folk tales) produce a much less centralized cultural geography.[8]

Moretti thus suggests, although he doesn't pursue, the notion that close attention to local contexts and processes, as well as "non-literary" forms, reveals "provincial" environments marked by considerable literary and cultural diversity and ferment. Book history undertaken from a postcolonial perspective has, indeed, made clear the vibrancy of print culture outside metropolitan contexts. A key piece of the agenda driving Robin Fraser's *Book History through Postcolonial Eyes* is an attempt to problematize our understanding of what constitutes a book by examining the interplay of print, scribal, and oral traditions in colonial South Asia and Africa. Such settings, Fraser argues, produce distinctive print cultures that cannot be rendered simply as faint echoes of metropolitan experiences and perspectives. Fraser also emphasizes local influences on the way books are read and interpreted. He notes, for instance, the varied and strategic ways in which readers in colonial settings interpreted Marie Corelli's *The Sorrows of Satan* (1895), imbuing the popular British writer's allegorical novel with specific political meanings that served their own purposes. A scholar taking his or her cue from the dismissive reviews Corelli received in Western Europe, without venturing to consider the various contexts in which her novel was read, is blind to these interpretations. (Incidentally, *The Sorrows of Satan* was also quite popular among readers in Muncie, Indiana, and it seems certain that these American readers assigned different, equally distinctive interpretations to Corelli's tale.) As Fraser insists, when investigators ground their work in peripheral settings rather than metropolitan centres, book history becomes a more complex endeavour.[9]

Nowhere is the multifaceted character of non-metropolitan print culture more evident than in the essays Fraser and Mary Hammond collected in *Books Without Borders*. Framed around a set of theoretical concerns, pithily summarized in the question, "where does the book belong?" these two volumes of essays pay special attention to the "manufacture, distribution, transit, and integration" of printed material. Taken together, they make clear not only that one can find rich, idiosyncratic print cultures in locales far distant from the publishing and literary centres of the West, but also that ideas, literary forms, and popular tastes moved in many directions and cannot be adequately investigated in studies limited to individual nations. These conclusions characterize our volume as well, although we take a slightly different tack, seeking to explore print culture history from ostensibly peripheral vantage points in the belief that such ground-level investigations will encourage the decentred, multifocal approach to print culture history that Fraser and Hammond seek.[10]

In addition to these broader works, there has been a handful of studies examining print culture in specific settings that further demonstrate the value of concentrating on peripheral locales. Christine Pawley's *Reading on the Middle Border* provides a painstaking reconstruction of the distinctive literary life of the small town of Osage, Iowa; it demonstrates the salience of local social patterns (such as religious demographics) and such local institutions as the public library in influencing reading experiences. Lynn Hollen Lees's recent discussion of the civic life of British colonial settlements on the Malay Penninsula argues that locally generated print culture and high levels of literacy produced a hybrid identity. In a much different vein, Priya Joshi's *In Another Country: Colonialism, Culture, and the English Novel in India* describes how Indians refashioned both the reading and writing of novels in response to particular colonial circumstances.[11] What remains to be done is to consider these experiences more systematically and to incorporate such analysis into our larger understanding of print culture history.

Print Culture Histories beyond the Metropolis also seeks to amplify recent research on the circulation of printed material. It builds upon, and perhaps complicates, Robert Darnton's well-known, and thoroughly debated, model of a communications circuit by further exploring writing, printing, borrowing, and reading in peripheral locales. It also expands upon the arguments advanced by Janice Radway and Carl Kaestle, who describe print culture as "in motion" in their introduction to the fourth volume of the History of the Book in America series. They argue that although the increased production and expanded circulation of books, magazines, and newspapers in the United States during the industrial era encouraged cultural consolidation, that process was complicated by a variety of local circumstances, ranging from ethnic and racial solidarities to the practices of women's book clubs or local librarians.[12] The systematic attention to non-metropolitan contexts offered in our volume underscores the point while also extending it beyond the American experience. Localities and particularities were not simply obstacles to the centralizing impulses facilitated by industrialized print; they were founts of meaning that gave print culture, at least in the modern, anglophone world, a kaleidoscopic character.[13]

Decentred Methods and Provisional Insights

By definition, research on settings that lie "beyond the metropolis" constitutes a vast and varied field of study, and we do not aspire to comprehensiveness here. Indeed, this volume relies heavily on studies of North American communities during the nineteenth and twentieth centuries, including three essays that capitalize on the What Middletown Read database, which reproduces library circulation records in Muncie, Indiana, from 1891 to 1902. Our intent is to supply a depth of analysis that will compensate for the geographic limits inherent in this collection, as well as to present different models for exploiting increasingly accessible digital resources. We believe as well that the American emphasis in our volume complements and potentially enables work by scholars employing post-colonial perspectives to investigate print culture in Asia and Africa, by foregrounding the methodological problems and theoretical premises common to the study of print culture outside of acknowledged cultural centres.

At the same time, it is crucial to note the dramatic differences between (to cite actual locales addressed in this book) an agricultural region in twentieth century North America and a South Asian colonial possession two hundred years earlier, or between a network of Dissenting ministers in eighteenth-century England and another linking black editors during the interwar years. We do not seek to flatten or erase these differences. But we do think there is value in stripping away the geographic and cultural conceits that have shaped so much print culture history. The way to do that is to decentre the field. The studies of reading, writing, print, and publishing beyond the metropolis that are assembled here provide a model for a more dynamic understanding of print culture history as it developed in the modern, anglophone world. In sum, the essays collected here forcefully demonstrate a stunning variety and resourcefulness in the literacy practices of people living, working, writing, and reading beyond the metropolis; they also present a unique, complex set of distinct social and institutional landscapes in which reading, writing, and the circulation of ideas and printed materials took place. In so doing they testify to the existence of a rich and substantially untapped field for further research.

These studies necessarily pay heed to the particularities and peculiarities of local practices and histories and take care to avoid asserting new, overarching historical generalizations about provincial practices. It would be a mistake to replace the specious verities of the metropolitan-centred world view with a set of corresponding, hypostasized claims about non-urban literacy practices. As media historian William Uricchio has argued, there is strength and value in the heterogeneity and irreducibility of individual case studies precisely because the "mundane specificity of historical practices" serves to "disrupt and reconfigure" historical generalizations that otherwise tend to calcify and become hegemonic.[14] Nonetheless, taken together, the essays in this volume do suggest some fertile, provisional insights about the workings of print culture in the provinces – insights that, tellingly, emphasize not widespread, structural commonalities but rather difference, multiplicity, heterogeneity, and diverse strategies and adaptations to diverse conditions. To be sure, our readers will identify further threads of connection between the essays, which we offer, above all, as a spur to further print culture scholarship that ventures outside of urban centres.

As a common project, then, this volume suggests the following insights:

1 Print materials often circulated in ways independent of the commercial networks and circulation routes established by metropolitan printers, publishers, and booksellers.
2 Small cities, colonial outposts, and rural settings were sites of creative ferment, and their residents were not merely passive consumers of ideas and styles generated in urban centres.
3 Local, particular, and even at times peculiar institutions and practices were typically as important in shaping the literacy practices and self-fashioning of provincial citizens as the decisions of cultural arbiters and trendsetters in the urban centre.
4 The experiences and even identities of actual readers are not overdetermined by their status as "provincial" or "cosmopolitan"; local readers devised their own ways to access print in areas of relative scarcity and their own ways of constructing literate identities in far-flung locations.
5 The development of digital tools offers new ways of investigating print culture engagements beyond the metropolis, particularly among readers. These include the digitized library records that are primary sources for Kyle Roberts, Frank Felsenstein, Lynne Tatlock, Joel Shrock, and Julianne Lamond in this volume. In what follows we address each of these insights by drawing on the work of our contributors.

Circulation within, among, and around Peripheries

(1) *Print materials often circulated in ways independent of the commercial networks and circulation routes established by metropolitan printers, publishers, and booksellers.*

While much previous work has focused on the flow of ideas and materials from imperial and metropolitan centres to colonies and provincial locales, this volume demonstrates resoundingly the vigorous movement of print materials along the byways linking "peripheral" communities and within these communities themselves. Perhaps most strikingly, Ronald and Mary Zboray trace a set of widespread, unofficial, non-commercial practices for sharing and securing reading material in American locations where it was hard to come by during the Civil War. These resourceful, often improvisational strategies range from the mundane (the long-forgotten, free practice of mailing used newspapers by simply printing an address in a visible location and putting them in the mail) to the morbid (collecting newspapers left behind by troops after battle or retreat) to the morally objectionable (raiding the private libraries of homes seized in battle). The very notion of *scarcity* upsets one of the major premises of print culture studies, whose metropolitan bias has led scholars to emphasize the *plenitude* of print artefacts at any given historical moment. This orientation squares with the sense, common in metropolitan intellectuals from the eighteenth century on, that presses were churning out reams of mostly low-quality reading material, a flood that threatened to swamp readers and undermine public taste, discrimination, and reason.[15] The Zborays' work, however, brings home the scarcity of print facing many readers in the far-flung territories of the United States during these disrupted years, the keenly emotional and sentimental nature of their relations to printed objects, and the strategies they evolved to feed their desire to read and share printed material.

Clearly, in their transit between such locations as battlefields, soldier's home towns, and small territorial settlements, the print exchanges the Zborays trace did not flow through urban centres or rely on the commercial and managerial agents and transportation networks centred there. If the sum of the eccentric paths such objects traced can be described as a network, it was an asymmetrical network, replete with links but lacking in large clusters. In her chapter, Lara Putnam finds a similar movement of objects and ideas afoot in the imperial periphery. Again, post-colonial histories often emphasize the importance of metropolitan intellectuals as spurs to activism, suggesting that radical politics flows from and through the ideas of mobile intellectuals such as Mohandas Gandhi, with access to, and often educated in, the centre. But Putnam traces the movement of insurgent writing around the periphery, without recourse to the centre; she recounts, for instance, that ships from North Africa docked in the Caribbean en route to North America, dropping off and picking up newspapers at each stop, and that newsagents in the Panama Canal Zone gathered and distributed large-circulation papers from metropolitan centres and tiny ones from nearby islands. Thus canal labourers could read, in a Pittsburgh newspaper, the complaints of a mother whose son was imprisoned in New Iberia, Louisiana, and reports from Gary, Indiana, about fundraising to aid Ethiopia. Such exchanges, for Putnam, demonstrate that peripheral readers were not only active, but interactive in the battles against imperialism and white supremacy and that distinct sites of grassroots activism influenced one another; thus anti-imperialist agitation was fuelled as much by shared awareness generated through this kind of circulation as by the influence of a handful of prominent, cosmopolitan intellectuals.

The Zboray's work on informal or improvised means of circulation emphasizes the degree to which, in a print-oriented culture, the circulation of ideas depends upon the circulation of objects. James Raven's chapter finds still deeper grounds of interdependency between these spheres in his exploration of the history of job printing. Homely, purely functional, non-intellectual in content, the products of job printing – business ledgers, bills of lading, advertising flyers, banknotes, pre-made forms – constituted a major source of revenue for European printers from Gutenberg and Caxton through the nineteenth century. Waning and waxing in response to economic trends and evolving government restraints, provincial printing was typically oriented not to book publishing or journalism flowing from, or oriented to, urban centres but to local businesses keen to capitalize on the efficiencies offered by such functional print matter. Raven argues that job printing, virtually unstudied by historians of print culture, is nothing shy of an unacknowledged engine of modernity, as job-printers' products served to increase efficiency and to standardize practices in an emerging commercial economy.

If we are correct in insisting that the circulation of ideas relies upon the circulation of objects, Brad Evans's work here forcefully suggests that, all the same, the former is not reducible to the latter. The American literary movement focused around small, avant-garde periodicals in the late nineteenth century, which took its oppositional style and tone from the *petits revues* of Paris, managed to establish outlets in small towns in the American Midwest despite a perhaps total lack of circulation of French objects to the U.S. hinterland. What circulated between Paris and the editors of American "ephemeral bibelots," Evans argues, were not objects or, even, ideas precisely so much as a set of practices focused on citation. The bibelots cited one another obsessively, and shared a common storehouse of writers, images, genres, and motifs, which they also cited. These citations created networks of signs that linked magazines – networks that were more local than global, as the American bibelots typically cited each other rather than the publications of Paris, the putative centre. Crucially, these local citational networks gave their readers a sense of an insider's knowingness, a sense of being in on the joke, that replicated for a reader in East Lansing, Michigan, the sense of belonging to an oppositional movement that a reader in the Paris of the 1870s might have enjoyed. With minimal circulation between centre and periphery, a mindset and a set of publishing practices reconstituted itself in small clusters all over the world – a mindset that would take full flower several decades later in the emergence of modernism in literature and visual art.

Evans, the Zborays, and Raven all illuminate surprising practices of circulating print objects that exceed or circumvent more familiar circulation routes. Chapters by Kenneth Hall and Christine Pawley, discussed at greater length below, illuminate new and unexpected sites and directions for the movement of ideas (in the Indian subcontinent and the agrarian United States Midwest, respectively), while Kyle Roberts tracks the non-commercial circulation of books among the English Dissenting community. Together, these chapters constitute a substantial rethinking of circulation, freeing us from models of circulation through and from a centre (or *heart*, to evoke the bodily metaphor that is never far from the surface in such discussions) and shifting us towards the more complex, asymmetrical complex of connection and movement suggested by network theory, which, not coincidentally, powerfully informs Evans's chapter.

Creative Ferment

(2) *Small cities, colonial outposts, and rural settings were sites of creative ferment, and their residents were not merely passive consumers of ideas and styles generated in the metropole urban centres.*

It is difficult to imagine a less urbane or "cosmopolitan" setting than the sheep station at Brancepeth, New Zealand, one hundred miles from

Wellington and ten miles from the North Island's southeast coast. Yet the cultural furore over literary realism and the New Woman novel that roiled the British literary marketplace at the fin-de-siècle found itself enacted, on a smaller scale, in Brancepeth in 1898, when local librarian John Vaughan Miller burned a copy of Sarah Grand's *The Beth Book*, and assailed it in print in the local newspaper. While it would be tempting to see in this event the far-flung ripples of a wave emanating from the imperial capitol, Lydia Wevers instead finds in the episode the unique reading culture of the sheep station, where Miller exercised, or at least imagined, an outsized influence. Here Miller maintained the station library, entered his critical marginalia liberally into books (which might later be loaned out), and wrote literary criticism for the local paper, a practice at once pedagogical and pedantic, and perhaps above all oriented to displaying his erudition in a place and from a position that would seem to offer it no outlet. Miller's active if cantankerous reading and his intemperate response to *The Beth Book* undermine any notion of provincial passive reception of the literary culture of the metropole.

In an analogous fashion, Kenneth Hall complicates a simplistic sense that the cultures of colonial India were the passive object of British Orientalist scholarship and publishing, particularly in the early years of British dominion on the subcontinent. Hall reconstructs a complex welter of emerging print culture institutions there in the late eighteenth and early nineteenth centuries, institutions including company colleges set up by the English East India company to train civil servants; newspapers started by English and Indian entrepreneurs; the publishing arm of a Baptist missionary society; and the learned societies that collaborated with them to produce Bibles, lexicons of local languages, translations of Hindu legal codes, and textbooks for civil servants. Crucially, Hall notes the collaboration between South Indian and Bengali scholars and English Orientalists, the latter informed by Enlightenment notions of human equality and thus respectful of Hindu culture and open to scholarly cooperation. Such collaborations helped enable the academic recognition of the common roots of the European languages and Sanskrit, and briefly held out the possibility of more egalitarian Anglo-Indian relations, until the backlash from the Sepoy Rebellion resulted in a more iron-fisted Raj.

Hall locates the exchange of ideas between Indian and British Orientalists within the material landscape of a burgeoning print culture. He finds there a ferment that – if less equal, and finally productive of imperial rather than subversive effects – parallels the ferment of ideas within the periphery that Putnam traces a hundred years later in the Caribbean. Their work offers a riposte to the easy binary of (active) metropolitan production and (passive) colonial reception. And their tracing of the role of emerging institutions in enabling surprising cultural exchanges points to what we see as the third major insight of this volume: the inestimable importance of local institutions in enabling the engagement with print by rural and provincial people. This insight informs the work of Tatlock, Schrock, and Felsenstein – all of whom reveal surprising reading habits in the readers of the Muncie, Indiana, Carnegie library – as well as chapters by Robert Hall, Kyle Roberts, and Christine Pawley, whose work focuses on other, equally important local institutions.

Local Institutions

(3) *Local, particular, and even at times peculiar institutions and practices were typically as important in shaping the literacy practices and self-fashioning of provincial citizens as the decisions of cultural arbiters and trendsetters in the urban centre.*

Robert G. Hall demonstrates that the horizon of reading possibilities available to working people in Asthon-under-Lyne in the mid-nineteenth century was, to a great extent and in quite specific ways, conditioned by a relatively small number of local institutions. As migration and population growth overwhelmed the town's meagre educational infrastructure, and as printed material remained prohibitively expensive for the working classes, the work of providing reading instruction, practice, and material fell substantially to local institutions ranging from the Mechanics Institute – its reading offerings leavened with the middle-class ideology of moral uplift – to radically oriented Chartist reading rooms. Far from neutral sites for the encounter of individuals with the written word, these institutions enabled dramatically different reading practices and understandings of the social function of literacy. Chartist institutions placed printed material at visitors' disposal for free and fostered an "oral and collective" experience of the written word in which radical politics, sociability, and free assembly intermingled. This brew perhaps goes a ways to explaining why the Chartist reading rooms were significantly more popular with working men than the Mechanics Institutes or the village library, both of which cost money and offered working-class readers, along with their serving of print, several helpings of morally superior social pressure to, in the words of one observer, "tidy 'themselves up and to associate with better-class people'."[16]

If the Chartists offered reading practices that spoke to class identity, the Dissenting academies examined by Kyle Roberts did the same for a large and important religious subculture. Like the Chartists, the Dissenting academies fashioned non-commercial ways of circulating print, in their case to foster community among their students, faculty, and graduates. As in the non-commercial exchanges amid the disruptions of the American Civil War tracked by the Zborays, these improvised and provisional practices responded to local needs and gradually took on the status of institutional, if unofficial, practices. But these practices – gifting, loaning, and manuscript circulation among them – did more than establish a network for the distribution of print objects independent of the centralized routes for transportation and distribution based in London. They also established practices of sociability and shared responsibility that cemented the Dissenting community and allowed it to reproduce its values in successive generations.

While Hall's and Roberts's essays focus primarily on institutions tied to class or religious identity, all of the historical readers who appear in these pages relied substantially on such local institutions in their print engagement: Clara Steen, in Christine Pawley's telling, studied in the relatively new, land-grant Iowa State College and relied on her local library. Perhaps more surprisingly, the YWCA and the agricultural extension office also served as "print culture institutions" in her writing and reading life. The ad hoc Brancepeth sheep station library served a similar role for John Vaughan Miller. And the well-travelled upstate New York editor George Chandler Bragdon, as Joan Rubin explains, used semi-formal men's clubs, reading clubs, and learned societies as a self-improvement regime wherever he could find them. Their biographies illustrate our next insight: the substantial relative autonomy of local readers, whose identities and practices were determined neither by national or metropolitan values nor by a disabling sense of "provincial" status.

Real Readers, Diverse Practices

(4) *The experiences and even identities of actual readers are not overdetermined by their status as "provincial" or "cosmopolitan"; local readers devised their own ways to access print in areas of relative scarcity and their own ways of constructing literate identities in far-flung locations.*

It would be difficult to imagine three literate lives as different as those of the itinerant editor Bragdon, the station clerk and erstwhile librarian Miller, and the farmer and rural columnist Steen. But their stories, as shared by Rubin, Lydia Wevers, and Pawley here, demonstrate the degree to which the experience of reading, writing, and responding to print materials – indeed, the sense of one's self as not merely literate but *literary* – could be indispensible to the self-fashioning of modern individuals far from the purported centres of literary and cultural life. Bragdon's story, particularly, testifies to the artificiality of the metropolitan/provincial distinction, as his frenetic career as an editor was nourished at all points by a reading and writing diet that was equal parts "cosmopolitan" (in his exposure to ideas emanating from Europe, Washington, DC, and New York) and "provincial" (in his prodigious contribution to local periodicals and his immersion in literary and intellectual clubs and societies in the many towns and small cities in which he worked). Further, Bragdon's history of travel to New York and Washington involved him in networks that gained him access to substantial, national-level political power (in the person of his friend, local political boss, U.S. Representative, and later senator Roscoe T. Conkling). The sheer amount and variety of Bragdon's reading, writing, travel, and connectedness underscores the wrongheadedness of "provincial" as an adjective to describe a person: "provincial" and "metropolitan" are perhaps better understood as mutually implicated mindsets, which could (and did) coexist within individual psyches. Bragdon's history shows that his vision of himself in the world was anything but provincial.

Miller, though he was undeniably more cut off, geographically, from traditional centres, went to considerable lengths to imagine himself (and present himself to others in his immediate sphere) as literary, as a kind of local authority on matters of newsworthy importance in the imperial centre and an arbiter and provider of reading material for his local community. Even with a paucity of local institutions – he was limited to the small station library and to infrequent access to the "house library" of the landowning family – he crafted a distinctly literary sense of self. Steen benefited from a moment in history in which educational and cultural institutions were being established in the rural Midwest. Her story demonstrates the array of institutions and networks that not only enabled literate/literary practice even in a remote, rural farm community, but allowed for men and women in such places to imagine themselves as part of vital communities that cannot be adequately described as "national" or "local." By allowing Steen to envision herself as part of and, crucially, to address, distinct communities of farmers, of women, and of "middle Americans," this hodgepodge of institutions enabled a set of identities and audiences that render the categories "cosmopolitan" and "provincial" beside the point.

Even when moving beyond the experience of individual readers we can see the limitations of these terms. In his discussion of print culture in 1890s Muncie, Indiana, Frank Felsenstein accepts the practical utility of the label "cosmopolitan" but complicates our understanding of what this might mean in a small, seemingly provincial community. His consideration of "cosmopolitan trends" finds evidence that local residents imagined themselves as participants in a process of national, international, and perhaps even universal cultural development. Muncie during the final decade of the nineteenth century was a rapidly growing city with grand ambitions. Citing its cultural institutions as well as its economic development, Muncie's boosters saw their city as moving towards a "higher and better civilization." Such boasting represented more than an expression of municipal pride. It also reflected an impulse to identify with broader segments of the world that stretched beyond national boundaries. If such thinking did not constitute a full-fledged cosmopolitanism as it has been defined by various theorists, it nevertheless suggests an outlook that we cannot simply dismiss as provincial.

The local public library, as Felsenstein notes, was central to the city's cultural aspirations. Civic leaders pointed to the quality of its collections and its educational impact as evidence of the community's growing sophistication. Felsenstein also draws upon the catalogue details and circulation records available through the What Middletown Read database to document the ways that the library helped provide users such as Rosa Burmaster with an experience of the world beyond the city's limits. Through such analysis we can see how reading offered local residents with a means of imagining themselves as connected to people and places far beyond their Midwestern American hometown.[17]

Databases, Circulation, and Reading

(5) *The development of digital tools offers new ways of investigating print culture engagements beyond the metropolis, particularly among readers.*

A number of the essays contained in this volume rely upon databases constructed from library circulation records that invite new insights into print culture history. Kyle Roberts employs the Dissenting Academies Online records to trace the forces shaping the circulation of texts among Nonconforming ministers in the English Midlands during the eighteenth century. Julieanne Lamond uses data made available through the Australian

Common Reader to examine the circulation of printed materials held by the Lambton Mechanics' and Miners' Institute, in Lambton, New South Wales, Australia, during the early twentieth century. Shrock, Felsenstein, and Tatlock exploit the What Middletown Read database, which makes accessible the borrowing records of the Muncie Public Library during the 1890s and the first few years of the twentieth century. These contributions illustrate some of the ways that large samples of circulation data can open new avenues of analysis that highlight the importance of readers and their communities.

Most obviously, these resources allow us to get at the reading choices of ordinary people in new ways and, more significantly, to begin to better understand the social dimensions of reading. We see in sharper relief the interplay between networks of print distribution and local patterns of sociability. Despite the gulf of time and space that separates Dissenting ministers in eighteenth-century England from library patrons in Lambton and Muncie, the process of choosing what to read and assigning meanings to texts is shaped not only by publishers, booksellers, and librarians, but also by intimate and communal relationships. The chapters by Lamond, Tatlock, and Shrock provide especially tantalizing evidence of the ways that the interplay of market forces and local patterns of sociability shaped reading choices and collective reading patterns.

Lamond's work on the Lambton Miners' and Mechanics' Institute uses the tools of digitial humanities, including cluster analysis and other visualization tools, to tease out "zones of connection" among readers and books. Lamond take us beyond simple lists of the most frequently borrowed titles and shows us patterns within this data. Certain sets of readers shared an affinity for particular titles and certain books had higher percentages of readers in common. These relationships, Lamond suggests, can be treated as networks, and her analysis reveals a series of "densely interconnected patterns of shared reading practices." These networks represent trace evidence of the impact of social ties, market forces, and collective values that shaped reading behaviour.

The remaining challenge is to explain the sources of these zones of connection. Lamond notes that common cultural capital (such as that held by the Welsh miners who populated Lambton) and local manifestations of literary sociability may explain some of these patterns. Examining these factors will in some cases require more old-fashioned kinds of historical research, including combing through old newspapers, obscure family records, and other archival sources to flesh out the social relationships that influenced reading. Investigation of library records, such as those employed by Felsenstein to examine Muncie Public Library acquisitions, can also offer us ways of detecting the influence of marketing efforts from publishers or the impact of the burgeoning circulation of magazines on reading tastes.

Tatlock and Shrock work with the What Middletown Read database, illustrating the value of contextualizing circulation data. Tatlock's investigation into the remarkable popularity of translations of the novels of the German writer E. Marlitt (the pseudonym for Eugenia John) in late-nineteenth-century America uses the Muncie data alongside corroborating evidence such as contemporary book reviews and personal inscriptions to make sense of that appeal. Employing topic modelling and affinity analysis, she finds that Marlitt's work closely resembled in theme and substance Charlotte Brontë's classic *Jane Eyre*. It overlapped in a similar manner with other domestic romances. Tatlock suggests that the popularity of translations of Marlitt (and other similar German fiction) did not represent the kind of cosmopolitanism discussed by Rubin, Felsenstein, and others in this volume, but instead signalled a flattening out of cultural differences through marketing and translation. Nevertheless, for Tatlock, the consumption of "lightly exotic" German fiction does at least suggest that Muncie's readers possessed a modest sense of commonality that may have counterbalanced cultural differences (a conclusion in line with Felsenstein's analysis of the same city).

Where Tatlock uses Muncie data to emphasize the homogenizing influence of publishers and their marketing operations, Joel Shrock's exploration of the same records finds deviation from categories devised by the purveyors of popular fiction. He presents evidence of "crossover reading," the tendency of girls to read "boys'" books (and vice versa) as well as the propensity of adults to read material marketed for children. These patterns, which Lamond also detects in the Lambton data, suggest that efforts to use children's fiction as means of defining and sustaining gender roles, for instance, ran aground amid the appeal adventure narratives, such as those by Horatio Alger and Oliver Optic (William Taylor Adams), held for girls. While Shrock sees the selections evident in Muncie as part of a broader pattern, he also points to local influences that encouraged this form of reading behaviour, including the accommodating nature of the Muncie Public Library staff, which employed a light touch in directing patrons' choices, and the intimate ties at work in families such as the Burts. Shrock's combination of ground-level social history and data analysis points the way towards further research that highlights both readers and the social environments in which they engaged with print.

A Dynamic Approach

Despite their variety, the essays in this volume push in the same direction: against standardized, centrifugal models of print culture history. The movement of books and ideas was too complex and the creative influences at work in local contexts too strong to permit formulations that simply project outward from the centre and assume the periphery fell in line. What replaces this conventional formula is less clear. One option is to abandon any all-encompassing generalizations and settle for a plethora of ground-level particularities. But scholars in search of broader explanatory frameworks will not be satisfied with an approach that threatens to devolve into antiquarian local history or to negate entirely metropolitan influences. There are certainly regional and chronological distinctions to be made, and such differentiation will remain salient in studies of print culture history. The challenge is to generalize without erasing the agency of readers, writers, printers, and publishers even when they resided far from urban centres.

To accomplish this goal, we propose a dynamic approach that does not overcorrect for the prevailing metropolitan bias evident in print culture history. It recognizes the ferment and creativity that is so powerfully released in the big-city environment while avoiding the condescending dismissal of people and institutions found in other, less heralded settings. As this volume shows, one can find worldly editors, discriminating readers, and well-connected writers even in seemingly isolated corners of the modern world. Circulation records from such supposedly provincial locales as Muncie, Indiana, and Lambton, New South Wales, reveal an engaged readership that at times defied the marketing categories devised by publishers or the standards advanced by cultural elites. And, it is clear, print provided a means through which people could encounter the world beyond their locality. In sum, this volume demonstrates the value of a decentred perspective that gives meaningful roles to readers, editors, librarians, publishers, and printers, as well as to the communities and institutions that served them, as we write the history of print culture in the modern world.

NOTES

1 For a definition of print culture studies, see Brake (2001, 125–36). Brake traces the vogue for print culture studies over the last two decades to the increasing

popularity of Cultural Studies in humanities departments and to digitization, which has broadened the range of print materials easily available to scholars and students. The field of print culture studies emerges in an interdisciplinary nexus between the disciplines of literature, history, media studies, and journalism, and embraces the new subfield of "periodical studies," she argues.

2 Rose (2001, 1–11).

3 Franco Moretti, for instance, quotes Kenneth Clark: "The history of European art is, to a large extent, the history of a series of centres, from each of which radiated a style [...] which was metropolitan at its centre, and became more and more provincial as it reached the periphery." To this Moretti adds that "the history of the novel certainly supports Clark's thesis" (1998, 164). We discuss Moretti further below.

4 Henkin (1998, 24–5).

5 Ardis and Collier (2008); Finkelstein and McCleery (2005, 4).

6 The literature on post-colonialism and hybrid cultural formation is extensive. For an introduction see Young (1995) and Burke (2009); Riney-Kehrberg (2007, 155–8); Connolly (2008, 3–14).

7 Moretti (1998, 173).

8 Moretti (1998, 165).

9 Fraser (2008, 176–7).

10 Fraser and Hammond (2008, 3, 5).

11 Pawley (2001); Lees (2011, 35–147); Joshi (2002).

12 Darnton (1996, 181–97); Kaestle and Radway (2009, 7–21).

13 Two other studies that engage with the themes of this book warrant mention. Trish Loughran's *The Republic in Print: Print Culture in the Age of U.S. Nation Building, 1770–1870* is attuned to tensions between centralizing initiatives (what she calls "metrobuilding" because such efforts focused on urban centres) and local or regional loyalties. She gives primacy to the latter, especially during the formative years of the new United States, though the breadth of her investigation prevents sustained examination of specific localities. Benito Rial Costas's recent essay collection, *Print Culture and Peripheries in Early Modern Europe: A Contribution the History of Printing and the Book Trade in Small European and Spanish Cities,* takes a similarly decentred perspective, but its chronological and geographic focus, as well as its concentration on the book trade but not on periodicals or reading experiences, distinguish it from this volume. In different ways, both volumes highlight the value of research on print culture that escapes the gravitational pull of the metropolis. Loughran (2007); Rial Costas (2012).

14 Uricchio (2003, 23–9).

15 Patrick Leary (2007) thus addressed the tension between a historical "economy of abundance" among print artefacts and a "scholarly economy of scarcity,"

in which scholars had difficult and unequal access to these primary materials. The digitization of historical newspapers promised, he suggested, to inaugurate a new "scholarly economy of abundance," with its own attendant problems, among them the emergence of an "off-line penumbra" of works never digitized and thus unlikely to inform future scholarly work. See also Leary (2005, 72–86).

16 Elliott (1861, 677)

17 Lynne Tatlock's essay in this volume, discussed below, amplifies this point.

PART ONE

Circulation

1 Non-Metropolitan Printing and Business in Britain and Ireland between the Sixteenth and Eighteenth Centuries

JAMES RAVEN

Two neglected and related "print culture" histories reach importantly beyond the metropolis. These histories are of jobbing printing in the printing house and of jobbing printing in the economic revolution of the sixteenth to eighteenth centuries. Neither history has been given the attention it deserves, and each history illuminates a geographical range of activity that is often ignored. Local printers and stationers developed networks and circuits entirely independent of the metropolis, even if intersections between town and country also continued for particular and mutual advantage. Many country customers, however, had no need or even knowledge of items printed in the capital; nor, indeed, did customers in the many remote and more successful of country printing districts need to depend on products from large regional centers.

With a few brave but marginalized exceptions, almost every account of the development of printing with moveable type since the mid-fifteenth century elucidates, in one way or another, the production of books, periodicals, and newspapers.[1] What is almost entirely overlooked is the printer's output of job work – the myriad of rapid, unromantic, practical productions that were the basis of the printer's trade. Without their production of job work the vast majority of printers would have failed. Almost every printer from the fifteenth century to the nineteenth century depended on the regular income afforded by jobbing work. It has been a hidden history. It is also a history of the social construction of knowledge, even though jobbing printing is a subject without any book-length study devoted to it. It is now nearly forty years since Keith Maslen, having immersed himself in the eighteenth-century Bowyer printing ledgers, urged bibliographers to go beyond W.W. Greg's founding "apologia" that their proper concern is with "books as material objects."[2] Even Maslen, in his path-breaking essay, seems to have regarded the study of jobbing – indispensable as he said it was – to be principally a means of understanding better the production and reception of books (in terms of concurrent printing and printing house practices, for example). His conclusion, nonetheless, was that "jobbing printing can be used as an index of civilization," a conclusion yet to be tested by scholarly study.[3]

The neglect of the second hidden history of printing is just as significant. We have hundreds of accounts of the commercial and industrial revolution of Europe from Carlo Cippola[4] onwards (and indeed before Cipolla), but nowhere in this is the printer given due significance for lowering transaction costs by the provision of jobbing printing – or job work – that ranged from advertisements to receipts and a myriad of blank forms, legal and commercial. The economic transformation to which the printers' products and services contributed was one of astonishing range and complexity. During the seventeenth century, printers in London but also many other British towns undertook an unprecedented range and volume of jobbing work. The transformation occurred between the printing reigns of Christopher and Robert Barker (1529–99 and ?1562–1645) and of William and Andrew Strahan (1715–85 and 1750–1831), respectively the most prominent printers of their age, but it had its origins in late fifteenth- and sixteenth-century Continental Europe, and in the printing houses of the Low Countries, France, Germany, Italy, and Spain.

The interlinked histories considered here were, in varying degrees, both urban and rural. The great majority of early modern printers in Britain worked in London, but much of their output travelled widely and had a broad influence. In England and Scotland the country printer began to promote and service business from the arrival of printing presses outside London and Edinburgh in the sixteenth century. In Ireland, most printers of the seventeenth century operated in Dublin, but the expansion of printing to include almost all Irish towns and market centres is notable in the eighteenth century. Printers' contributions to commercial, financial, and even industrial expansion continued through the seventeenth century, despite the disruption of civil war, but they were curtailed in England for more than thirty years by the Restoration licensing laws. With the imposition of the licensing laws from 1662, printing in England was restricted to London, Cambridge, Oxford, and York, but the lapse of those laws in 1695 enabled the migration of printers to regional towns and cities. The migration was hesitant at first (with no guarantee that restrictive laws might not be reimposed), but by the late 1720s the expansion of country-town printing was assured. Dominated by newspaper printing, which provided the financial mainstay for the non-metropolitan printers, most of these men and women also acted as agents for London wholesale booksellers (for which the country newspaper served as important advertising vehicles). The jobbing printing of the regional printers, however, was at least as financially important, and in many cases more so, than that of London printers, and as much ignored in book trade history. From the mid-eighteenth century, the volume, quality, and location of jobbing printing was transformed. The scale of press activity was unprecedented. Nothing as potent had been seen since the arrival of the printing press across Europe in the mid- to late fifteenth century. What was even more remarkable was that printing house business accelerated despite a virtual technological standstill in the design of the common printing press.[5]

For merchants, retailers, manufacturers, and investors, the changes were nothing short of a revolution in print. We can divide up the commercial-assistance activity of the printer into three general types. The first are general treatments of the economy from extended philosophies to small essays in what would later be called political, economy. The second are items of practical guidance, including, for example, printed books and pamphlets that advanced new techniques in accounting and business management. Much other printing assisted in selling wares and advertising services. In businesses both small and large, efficiency and accuracy were aided and gauged by ready reckoners, trade-calculating tables, timetables, and charts for travel by road and water. But the third (and unlike most of the activity of the first two, not involving a bookseller) was jobbing printing proper and allied stationery sales. Booksellers and stationers supplied an unparalleled volume of ledgers and account books. Printers undertook a new and vast range of business jobbing, including printed bills, tickets, receipt forms, commercial and financial blanks, promissory notes, warrants, indentures, and authorizations.

There is, of course, some overlap between these categories and the merging of job work into something wider. For example, print raised subscriptions to public works and helped organize commercial institutions. It promoted new transport, marketing, and rating schemes, and it enabled protest against them. Many printers' and booksellers' premises became an integral part of local business development, offering a diverse range of services, including carriage, warehousing, public notification, and even banking. Print, as the surviving inventories and business ledgers of the printer-stationers show, was to be of crucial importance in the development of financial and commercial organization. Surviving examples of job work and printing house business records from many different towns and cities suggest how accuracy was aided and transaction costs lowered by a new and vast range of business and legal jobbing, including printed bills, tickets, receipt forms, commercial and financial blanks, promissory notes, warrants, indentures, and authorizations.

Jobbing printing (or just "jobbing" or "job work"), the printing of items other than books, notably comprises the earliest surviving examples of printing by moveable type in many Western countries. A small thirty-line indulgence, printed by Gutenberg in 1455, a year before his great Bible was published, has claims according to Maslen "to be the earliest product of the Western printing-press."[6] The first work known to have been printed in England, in December 1475 by Caxton at Westminster, is similarly a job work, as, much later, is the first press product in New Zealand, a single hymn sheet of 1830.[7]

Within years of the introduction of moveable type, European printing houses were supported by an increasing volume of jobbing, including institutional orders from ecclesiastical visitation articles. In Europe and Britain, the great majority of this material and its record of production are, however, entirely lost from historical sight. The four copies of the indulgence printed by Caxton and recovered by Paul Needham, cut up into strips and sewn into a composite book, represent only a tiny fraction of the thousands of lost issues from only one of the first printing houses.[8] Folke Dahl concluded that the survival rate of English newsbooks printed between 1620 and 1642 was as little as 0.013 per cent (or 1 in 10,000). Tessa Watt added that survivals of earlier, sixteenth-century English ballads represented perhaps 1 in 10,000 of the original number of copies or 1 in 10 of the original number of editions.[9] For many massive print jobs, not a single actual exemplar of the printed material itself survives.[10]

A typical example of how "jobbing" has been marginalized is the study of the eighteenth-century London printer Charles Ackers (and his extant ledgers from 1732 to 1748) by D.F. McKenzie and J.C. Ross. No one did more to redefine the scope of printing and bibliographical studies in the late twentieth century than the late Don McKenzie, and his meticulous, wide-ranging, and innovative research, which notably (in relation to our interests here) began with a pioneering micro-study of the early presswork and schedules of Cambridge University printers. Even McKenzie, however, consigned the jobbing work of Ackers to the category of "ephemera" and did relatively little to question its significance. Certainly, it is true that Ackers, with a lucrative contract for printing the *London Magazine* (in which he also had a financial share), was not as reliant on jobbing as many of his fellow printers, but even his known sales catalogues, quarter bills, fee tables, advertisements, and miscellaneous items for municipal and parochial service amounted to about a tenth of his gross income, and this is assuming that the imperfect surviving records did indeed catch all his jobbing.

Importantly, simple quantity and the proportion of overall income is not all; jobbing provided a much needed tie-over for slack periods and an indispensable provision for presses that often worked at under-capacity as well as supplying a promotional aid to demonstrate what a printer might do with skill and dedication. Standing type (i.e., type left in made-up pages) required extensive storage space, and, in any event, the high value of type precluded the keeping of much set type for very long. The only exceptions seem to have been standing type for certain items of up to a total of four sheets (which can, of course, include a very great range of productions) or occasional title pages and other special and often-repeated settings (usually stored as set pages without formes).[11] In England, between 1587 and 1637, regulations issued by the Stationers' Company also supposedly forbade formes to be kept standing and limited editions to 1,250–1,500 copies from one setting of type, or 2,500–3,000 copies for certain small publications. Exceptions were admitted in 1635 (with formes allowed to stand for a year, uniquely, for "the Psalter, the Grammar and accidence, Almanacs and Prognostications, and the primer and ABC"). Even here we have to be careful – the same 1635 decree confirmed that the regulations since 1587 had often been ignored.[12] As a consequence of these and earlier limitations, the productive capacity of most European presses, and certainly the English press, probably changed little before the mid-seventeenth century (and indeed, if the use of the presses had been maximized, over-capacity would have resulted).[13]

Many business accounts that would allow us to quantify orders for jobbing print and gauge the range of the different jobs have disappeared, both from the printing houses and from the clients. From London, the four extant printing ledgers of William Bowyer, father and son, have been painstakingly studied and reproduced,[14] but the Bowyer firm is one of only four similar collections (or second-hand records of such collections) surviving from eighteenth-century London.[15] Those few London printers whose ledgers and business accounts have survived, however, were all major firms where jobbing printing was fitted in between printing books. Dozens of other printers in the capital were offered far fewer contracts for books and pamphlets and relied almost entirely on commercial jobbing. For these, no business ledgers are now available.

Even more notably, however, print was harnessed to commercial development in the small market towns as much as in the great trading and publishing centres. A distributional network radiating from London and Edinburgh, with country storekeepers acting as the agents of London publishers, had served bookselling for two and half centuries. Here there are almost no surviving country printing ledgers, but the records of clients do survive, in a great variety of archives and collections. These records can be used in order to demonstrate how it might be possible to recover the history of non-metropolitan jobbing printing and its consequences in early modern and eighteenth-century Britain. Such records ably demonstrate the independence of local printing from metropolitan influence and the centrality of even small towns within their own market and radial distributive network. The financial stability derived from jobbing helped sustain the localized and regional print cultures described elsewhere in this volume.[16]

To 1800 and beyond, country grocers and general suppliers continued to stock ranges of popular printed material and to act as agents for booksellers in regional centres or in London and Edinburgh. In the first half of the eighteenth century, the general storekeeper was essential to sustaining the demand for print, even though surviving records of his dealings are almost entirely lost. Largely because of this, the general storekeepers have been neglected in accounts of the development of the book trade. In 1726 William Cooke petitioned the Chester corporation to set up as bookseller, "there being demand for the sale of books, for until lately there had been no bookseller there, but divers grocers had sold schoolbooks, Bibles, Common Prayer books, divinity, history and poetry books."[17] The shopkeepers' trade in printed items and stationery supplies was strengthened by the new ease with which contacts could be made and orders placed with distant manufacturers and stockists. From the late seventeenth century new postal schemes and transport services augmented the routes of the chapmen, journeymen, and the country agents of London wholesalers. Several printers in the regions also served as postmasters. Edward Ince, for example, who brought the first commercial letterpress to Chester in 1711, was also postmaster for the town. He was an especially active promoter of those trading publications that were allowed special dispensation under postal and excise regulations.[18] Another leading bookseller-postmaster was David Randie, postmaster of Edinburgh and associate of Robert Thomson, who in 1715 published the first newspaper in Glasgow, was also postmaster to the town. In the 1730s and 1740s, the *Newcastle Journal* boasted of up to eleven postmaster agents, distributing the newspaper from their offices in Carlisle, Cockermouth, Whitehaven, Penrith, Appleby, Kirkby Stephen, Brough, Bedale, Berwick, Duns, and Kelso.[19]

Regional trading circuits were further extended by the sale of news-sheets. A newspaper's distribution network ensured the successful introduction of many London wares as well as a more cost-effective circulation of local produce. In one published study of a regional trading network, Ian Maxted shows how Devon's complex communications system, with its various intermediaries, expanded significantly during the eighteenth century.[20] Another study of Suffolk charts the development of carrier services, turnpike roads, trading routes, and a distributional network of agents, newsmen, and messengers.[21] In Scotland similar development was centred around Edinburgh and Glasgow. In every county in Britain one or two towns promoted local associations between printer-stationers, booksellers, binders, and general storekeepers, linked through at least one of their number with London or major regional distributors.

Despite the broad similarities of regional book trades and printing development, those working in the trades pursued extremely varied careers. Many printers were well-travelled men, and their wanderings account for the sudden appearance and then disappearance of particular local imprints in chronological listings of printed items. Orion Adams took over his father's print shop in Manchester in 1732, sold up in 1748, reopened shortly afterwards in Chester, returned to Manchester in 1752, and moved to Plymouth in 1758, to Dublin in 1766, and to Birmingham in 1769.[22] The businesses of such country or semi-itinerant printers were modestly scaled, and certainly contrasted with the few large London firms employing many working printers, notably those of Richardson, Strahan, and the bookseller-publisher Lowndes. Most country establishments operated with one master printer and one or two journeymen or apprentices. From what evidence we have, some country printers attracted small numbers of orders for their jobbing work and must have supplemented their income by other trades and services. The account book of John Cheney, printer of Banbury, lists twenty-five orders in 1769 and forty-three orders in 1770. All are modest undertakings and nothing larger than half-sheet bills are printed.[23]

In all firms, productivity was limited by the technological constraints of the printing press. Throughout the century the maximum output of the single hand press worked by two men remained at about 250 impressions per hour. In addition, most businesses could not escape large overheads, with much capital invested in press, type, and stock. Such firms were extremely vulnerable to the larger fluctuations of the economy resulting from war, bad harvests, or the recurrent recessions that followed the advancing but imperfectly supported commercial enterprise of the second half of the century. Insecurity also increased within the trade, following the more open and cut-throat competition of the final third of the century. Bankruptcy figures in the book trades more than doubled between 1772 and 1800.

For a few, however, printing and bookselling offered handsome rewards. Successful printers, stationers, and booksellers could become rich and influential men and women. In Edinburgh Gavin Hamilton, who opened his premises in 1729, was personally never wealthy, but as "Bailie Hamilton" he took a powerful place in local government and gambled on several commercial investments.[24] In London as early as 1670 Thomas Dawks II was worth over £1,000 in estate and personalty. James Dodsley, Thomas Longman II, and Charles Dilly each left over £60,000.[25] These were astonishing fortunes, far in excess of the wealth of many early manufacturers and comparing favourably even with wealthy merchants.[26] Provincial fortunes were far more modest, but in their own terms equally impressive. Gabrill Roggers, bookseller of Shrewsbury, died in 1704 with a personal estate of £600. His local clergyman certainly deemed the achievement worthy of record in the parish register.[27] In the same town John Rogers, who had commenced printing in 1707, was made mayor four years later.[28] William Cook, printer of Thornton in Cheshire, left an impressive estate at his death in 1740.[29] In Hull, John Mace, who was issuing catalogues of books from the 1730s and acted as agent for the *York Courant*, was never a printer himself but died in 1778 worth over £1,000. James Linden of Southampton, like so many of the printers established in country towns at mid-century, was styling himself "gentleman" by the end of his life.[30] Both Thomas Lockett of Dorchester and Benjamin Collins of Salisbury died wealthy men.[31] In the Midlands William Hutton's fortune dated from his changing from selling books to setting up as a stationer to supply local business. By the 1790s his assets put him on a par with the richest Birmingham gentry – as he found out for himself when his house was one of the first to be destroyed by the mob in the riots of 1792.[32]

Connections between these changes in the printing trades and the wider expansion of trade and industry can be glimpsed in the record. Even so, much of the actual servicing of commerce by print has left very fragmentary evidence and the diversity of the printers' operations only adds to the confusion in existing sources. Business historians have, of course, faced similar difficulties with eighteenth-century commercial and industrial records. Many histories of early trade and manufacturing have also encountered the type of materials considered below. Many sources seem unpromising. A few of the original constituent contracts of the "financial revolution" survive, but they add little to company and Treasury ledgers in surveys of the development of joint stock companies or government revenue operations. The history of overseas and inland trade has been constructed from diverse records, but little could be gained from surviving printed chits of exchange. They are few in number and it is often impossible to gauge their representativeness. Accounts of local retailing are even patchier, reliant upon the survival of shop accounts and trading advertisements.[33] Nevertheless, the surviving articles of exchange between printer-stationers and traders and their customers remain the key to understanding the complementary relationship between new printing and new trade. Sources range from the well-known products of individual presses, notably newspapers and printed trade lists and catalogues, to the few surviving printers' business records and rare – but neglected – collections of jobbing work and printed ephemera. Much evidence of the functional connections between printing and commercial and financial transactions can also be retrieved from local legal and municipal administrative records. These are particularly underused resources for printing history; the examples that follow are a suggestive trawl of the riches available.

In 1721 William Craighton, bookseller of Ipswich, died unexpectedly. The resulting inventory of his goods gives one insight into the early eighteenth-century provincial book trade.[34] A tenth of Craighton's investment in his stock of books was in copybooks, shop books, and account books. Together with unbound paper and stationery, the account books amount to over a third of his total valued business assets. Craighton's son took over the business when he came of age in 1727, advertising his wares in the *Ipswich Journal* then owned by Bagnall but soon bought up and printed by the younger Craighton himself. Craighton gave notice of printing account books and copy books made up, ruled, bound, and delivered to order. The Craighton weekly newspaper was a major commercial force in East Suffolk. Each issue carried up to a hundred advertisements for goods, services, and employment. Private properties and commercial premises were sold and let, and auctions, share prices, sailings, coaches, and parcel deliveries all announced. Available by order from the shop were the latest, mostly London-printed, guides designed for the merchant, the counting-house clerk, the specialist trader, or the gentleman anxious to learn more about estate or personal financial management.

Craighton's services for local traders were repeated in every large town in Britain and Ireland. In the first half of the century towns like Bristol, Canterbury, Exeter, Cambridge, Oxford, Norwich, Dundee, Cork, and Belfast were the centres of stationery production and jobbing printing serving growing provincial trades. William and Benjamin Collins commenced book and stationery selling in Salisbury and launched and then relaunched the *Salisbury Journal* in 1729 and 1736. The newspaper was to carry thousands of traders' advertisements in the south and southwest of England. Benjamin Collins developed close trading relations with a number of London firms, and the local customer was able to obtain locally printed works as well as publications produced in partnership with a major London bookseller. By 1750 Collins had opened his "publick register" where "Masters and Mistresses may be informed of servants of all kinds; Gentlemen may likewise be informed of houses and lodgings to be lett ... [and] of estates to be bought and sold."[35] In Shrewsbury Thomas Durston advertised a wide variety of stationery for local businesses.[36] From the late 1750s William Cruttwell and Robert Goadby competed in Sherborne, Dorset, not only with their rival newspapers and political lobbying but also in the supply of stationery and jobbing printing to local traders.[37] In Tunbridge Wells Jaspar Sprange was offering similar services from the early 1770s. In a collection of 650 items printed by Sprange, mostly from the years 1794–7, 200 are playbills or advertisements for entertainments, 190 are announcements of auctions, 35 are the title pages to auction catalogues, 80 are notices for local tradesmen, and the remainder, a typically rich assortment of jobbing including trade cards, official notices, blank forms, tickets, and labels for bottles.[38] An even greater variety is seen in another collection, that of over one thousand items printed by John Soulby and son, printers at Ulverston in north Lancashire from the 1790s. In a town of just under three thousand people in 1800, John Soulby senior printed general trade cards, notices of cattle fairs and freight charges, advertisements for labourers, the letting of contracts and sales of ships and ships' parts, and notices of coach departures, services, and mail coach arrivals. Of the 497 items of Soulby jobbing held at Reading University, two-thirds were notices for public display. The majority are posters advertising sales of goods and produce and the sale or leasing of land and property. Most of these are for auction sales.[39]

With sharply increased business demands for writing materials and stationery, many customers faced frequent bottlenecks in the supply of paper and its servicing by processors and even printers. Throughout the century, most civic corporations remained anxious about the availability of paper both for their own use and for the provision of their commissioned printers.[40] The earliest newspapers were constrained as much by paper shortages and costs as they were by stamp duties or the technical limitations of the press. Even local tradesmen who came to rely upon particular suppliers of paper and bound books often found themselves the victims of regional shortages. Such frustrations could only have increased as the variety of sizes and quality of papers expanded. As early as 1712 – as the listings in the Stamp Act show – paper mills were manufacturing an immense range of weights, dimensions, and qualities in their products. Although the problem has received hardly any attention in the histories of early accounting practice, the supply of paper for the keeping of accounts was no easy matter – especially if the tradesman was to follow some of the grandiose schemes proposed by many contemporary accountancy advice books.

From modest beginnings at the turn of the seventeenth century, British home production of paper increased from some 2,000 tons in 1700 to about 15,000 tons per annum in 1800. In 1700 nearly 200 paper mills, scattered across Scotland and England, were supplying regional stationers and feeding an increasing demand for paper for wrapping, writing, and printing.[41] In 1738 278 paper mills were recorded in the excise returns for England and Wales, three-quarters of which manufactured coarse papers only. In 1785 381 licences were issued to paper makers in England and Wales. By 1800 the number of licences issued had risen to 417.[42] Throughout the century, the greatest concentration of paper mills remained in south Buckinghamshire, Hertfordshire, and Middlesex, with a further large scattering of mills throughout Kent.

Changes in the types of paper made for printing were particularly marked. Many new patents for the manufacture of white papers were granted in late Stuart Britain. White paper production, together with that of blue paper and millboard, used (among other things) for binding, attracted much comment at the turn of the century. In Scotland, where twelve mills had been established before 1700, there was a massive increase in output from an annual production of board and paper of some 100,000 lbs in 1750 to over 2 million lbs by 1800.[43] Production, however, was still by manual labour. All early papers were laid papers made by hand from a pulp of linen rags with a wire screen mould and strengthening frame. A paper mill driven by a Boulton and Watt steam engine was set up at Wilmington near Hull in 1786, but it was a short-lived experiment. The first successful paper-making machines were established by Henry and Sealy Fourdrinier at Two Waters, Hemel Hempstead, and by John Gamble at St Neots in 1803. The machines were adapted from the invention of Nicolas Louis Robert at the Essonne Mill near Paris in 1798. They introduced a continuous process of paper manufacture from a belt of wire mesh over which the pulp flowed to felt rollers and steam-heated drying drums.[44] Before the Fourdrinier machine (capable of making 1,000 lbs of paper a day) the maximum daily output from a paper mill was 100 lbs. By 1810, however, only a handful of paper mills had adopted power-driven machinery. In the same year, the Fourdriniers were also declared bankrupt.

One of the most common complaints of the local stationer throughout the century continued to be over shortages of paper. Paper selling was a common staple of the local general storekeeper – even though it is now difficult to retrace the supply of paper from mill to wholesaler and to retail stationer and bookseller. Many bales of paper were sent along newly opened trading routes, and many of the suppliers of paper were local. In Kirkby Stephen in the 1740s, the storekeeper, Abraham Dent, was stocked by the main paper suppliers of Kendal, Thomas and James Ashburner.[45] Large numbers of regional mills were established before mid-century and local dealers like the Ashburners flourished in most nearby large towns within a few years of the founding of each mill. In order to ensure a sufficient and constant supply of paper, however, it was often necessary for the regional stationer to open commercial negotiations with a London wholesaler rather than with a local manufacturer. Henry Crossgrove in Norwich and Samuel Farley and Joseph Bliss, the publishers of two early Exeter newspapers, for example, relied upon a London wholesale stationer.[46] By the 1790s Soulby, in remote Ulverston, was selling fifteen types of writing paper and eight types of drawing paper.[47] In London, where the manufacture of paper had moved largely to the surrounding villages even by 1700, stationers developed a complex system of paper warehousing and distribution to the regions.

After the imposition of the stamp duty in 1712, the importance of supply from the metropolis was increased.[48] Subsequently, the only legal source of supply for newspaper stamped paper was the warehouse of the Commissioners of Stamps in Serle Court, Lincoln's Inn, to where unsold papers also had to be returned in order to claim a rebate. Other duties were also applicable. In Dent's area, John Moore supplied the paper for legal instruments that by 1770 bore a stamp duty of two shillings and sixpence in every sheet used in an indenture, lease, bond, or deed without a separate rate.[49]

In addition to stamped and unstamped paper, the stationer also entered into a number of agreements with manufacturers of quills, wafers, slates, sand, and other stationery items sold to both business and private customers. In the towns demand was heavy. From the 1750s the Edinburgh bookseller-stationers Alexander Kincaid and Alexander Donaldson were ordering quills from their supplier in batches of fifteen hundred at a time.[50] At the same period, local administrations were putting in large orders for their own paper, "skins" and "texts" (sheets and blank forms of vellum for legal documents), standishes, and ink. Civic and business accounts of the period reveal a diverse array of other stationery requirements, such as the cords and large cardboard labels extensively used in filing incoming bills and receipts.[51] In one full surviving record of the sales of such items by a bookseller – the ledgers of John Clay of Daventry – what is most striking is the great distances Clay was prepared to order from in order to maintain an adequate stock. His main supplier of pens, pencases, ink, inkpots, and sealing wax was Heatley Noble of Birmingham. Clay bought his quills from Robert Taylor of Nantwich and Laxton of Peterborough. He ordered blank books from suppliers in Bristol and Louth. He obtained paper from mills in Worcestershire, Gloucestershire, Oxfordshire, and Northamptonshire. Clay's chief paper supplier was Robert Allen of Boughton mill outside Northampton, but wrapping paper came from John Jones of North Newington mill near Banbury.[52]

Most of the unprinted paper sold by the stationer for business purposes was almost certainly used for account books and ledgers. As financial and commercial practice became more complex, printer-stationers offered more sophisticated services. The supply of specialized ledgers and record books was an indispensable feature of new banking and credit facilities. In the City simple creditors' and debtors' ledgers could not cope with the complexities of new forms of financial and trading transactions. New types of business organization required specific stationery tailored to individual operations. Inevitably, however, the history of the production and sale of account books is very difficult to recover. Even where bound business ledgers survive they share with their owners a marked reluctance to reveal much about their origins. In an age when paper was such a scarce and valuable commodity it was also the fate of much of it to be reused until worthless.

Nevertheless, the production of durable ledgers was one of the most heavily advertised skills of the wholesaling and local stationer. Neither Collins nor Bliss was made wealthy by the sale of reading books alone. An important and expanding part of their business was supplying local tradesmen with day and waste books and other business ledgers. The surviving stationers' inventories reveal substantial stocks of account books, but most orders were made up to the individual requirements of the customer whether he was merchant, shopkeeper, farmer, householder, alderman, or magistrate. A whole ledger could contain two or three hundred pages and charges could be high. In 1757 Alexander Smiton, bookseller of Edinburgh, charged one customer eight shillings for eighty-two sheets of foolscap, four shillings for binding these in two books, two shillings and fourpence for ruling six lines on each page, and eight pence for a six-sheet index.[53] In Kirkby Stephen Abraham Dent was selling a variety of paper at between threepence and one shilling a quire, and shop books of five quires bound and ruled for six shillings. Smaller ready-made shop books were sold for about four shillings and memorandum or waste books for one shilling and sixpence. Stationers also catered for specialist needs according to the locality. At Portsmouth from the 1670s Robert Hartford manufactured ledgers for shipping accounts and for copying bills of lading.[54] Lockett in Dorchester, in his rhyming advertisements, offered for sale

> Red Books too, which partly shew,
> How it is our Millions go.
> Books full bound, or only half
> In Morrocco, Sheep or Calf
> Marble Paper'd green or blue,
> Neatly gilt and letter'd too.[55]

Many stationers, including Lockett and William Craighton, offered to bind their books, usually employing a contracted bookbinder. The binder could also be engaged independently by the purchaser of papers or unbound books. If we are to judge by newspaper advertisements, many booksellers were anxious to secure experienced binders. For example, in April 1780 "an eminent bookseller in the country" was searching, through the mediation of John Bell the London publisher, for a "steady, sober" journeyman bookbinder "to engage by the year."[56] In the 1790s Soulby offered his Ulverston customers "pocket books – morocco and black leather, with straps, locks or clasps, made to any pattern."[57]

Craft bookbinding received little recognition even in the eighteenth century. Today most scholarly attention is reserved for the skilled binding and leatherwork that adorns special collections of printed books.[58] In the eighteenth century bookbinding was described by one youth's guide to trades as having "no great Ingenuity in it, and requires few Talents ... a moderate Share of Strength is requisite, which is chiefly employed in beating the Books with a heavy Hammer." According to the guide, a bookbinder seldom earned more than ten shillings a week and was unemployed for half the year.[59] Surviving wills and inventories confirm bookbinders as men of small means, and not in the same league as bookseller-publishers or the larger stationers.[60] Sanguine of the Strand was one of a select group of binders serving the City, and one who also featured regularly in the *Daily Advertiser* in the final third of the century.[61] Rarely was bookbinding the sole occupation of the binder, however. Sanguine, for example, also advertised as a maker of combs and purveyor of strops and razors. In Scotland parchment-making and bookbinding were traditionally combined with window glazing. Robert Morison of Perth, a successful bookseller, stationer, and binder to the town's governing officers, was also postmaster and glazier. Lesser bookbinders practised as saddlers, glovers, and other leather-workers, but were also dyers, cutlers, and even coopers.

By the end of the century booksellers were advertising an extensive choice of business bindings. William Smart, owner of "a genteel shop adjoining the Town Hall" at Worcester, begged leave "to inform the Merchant and Tradesman, that he being some Time Stationer to the principal Bank in Bristol has it in his Power of supplying them with all the different Sorts of Books made use of in the Compting House, ruled to any Pattern and bound in any kind of Binding, neat and firm, on the lowest terms."[62] During the century red morocco binding became the recognized packaging for small account books. London, Edinburgh, and Dublin newspapers are full of binders' notices with numerous advertisements for exclusive morocco work. Late in his career Sanguine was to specialize in morocco binding and in tambour silk for ladies' pocketbooks. The insuring and hiring man made notorious by the literature against the state lottery was known as the "morocco man" after the ledger he carried with him. The largest account books, however, were still covered in vellum (or indeed made up from vellum), with leather and calf reserved only for special orders.[63]

There is also evidence of new tensions between binders and booksellers at mid-century as demand and competition grew. It was still usual for printed books to be offered to the public unbound, leaving the customer free to choose his own binder. Increasingly, however, binding was also offered by the bookseller. In Ipswich, William Craighton II engaged in a very public dispute with one of his former employees, Page, in the columns of his own newspaper.[64] Part of the cause, it would seem, concerned not only printed books, but also the general increase in demand for the binding of blank volumes, notably business ledgers.

Much of the earliest regional printing originated from the demands of municipal government rather than from commissions from local traders. Certain country jobbing printing apparently even predated the lapse of the licensing laws in 1695. The Licensing Act of 1662 actually included special mention of books of blank bills, subjecting these to the same provisions affecting other printed works.[65] Large orders for regional printing were however still sent to metropolitan printers and to the licensed centres.

In 1682 the town clerk of Norwich had ordered printing from Cambridge (exempt from the 1662 restrictions) for the articles used by parish officers to certify their aldermen.[66] Within twenty years production was more local. Darker was printing apprenticeship indentures for the Exeter council before 1700.[67] In Newcastle-under-Lyme, Samuel Parsons, who set up as a stationer and bookseller in the town in 1704, was printing official handbills and borough notices on his own press. In 1732 his business was taken over by John Hewitt and the services to the council continued.[68] Stephen Bryan, founder of one of the earliest provincial newspapers, was printer to the Corporation of Worcester from at least 1718 until 1730.[69] In 1711 John White, the printer of Newcastle, advertised through his newspaper the printing of subpoenas, books of blanks, watch warrants, penances, and certificates for burying in woollen.[70] Roger and Orion Adams of Manchester were advertising similar printing services in their *Newsletter* in the 1720s. In 1728 John Collyer of Nottingham printed tickets and programs for the Corporation. In the 1730s William Chase of Norwich was earning on average £25 for jobbing for the Norwich Corporation, including printing abstracts of Acts of Parliament, combination papers, and assizes of bread and ale. In this, Henry Crossgrove proved a keen competitor.[71] John Garnett, established as the first printer of books in Sheffield by 1736, and his successor, Revill Homfray, were printing at least a dozen different types of documents and forms for the town trustees during the second third of the century. The disbursements of dozens of surviving borough treasurers' records record similar orders for local printing in almost every large town in Britain.[72] There survives at least one separately stitched town accounts book relating specifically to the orders for stationery and printing despatched (in this case) by the town clerk.[73]

Many of the official orders for printing that served local commerce derived from the judicial and administrative work of the justices of the peace. Responsibilities varied greatly between towns, something that further complicates the inconclusive debate about the relationship between local economic growth and municipal regulation.[74] Depending upon the locality, clerks of markets, mayors, aldermen, or the local magistracy officiated in assizes of bread, fixing rates according to the local price for corn and requiring town bakers to sell bread at the authorized price. Various orders for "quires of the weight of bread" were sent to the local press as well as orders for posters relating to the administration of this and other types of assize.[75] Printed notices, for example, announced assessments of charges for land or water carriage from London to the town. Various other orders specified how and where notices were to be circulated and displayed.[76] Magistrates' printing orders even include canal and turnpike administration.[77] Local courts engaged printers to print warrants and bills, blanks for recognizances, summons for juries, items to serve the local militia, and even calendars of prisoners.[78] Rare examples of the jobbing of the Collins family include a pair of commitment blanks for stealing wood (after 1775) and a warning against damaging trees (1796).[79] Surviving quarter sessions records for Hampshire show in great detail the stationery and printing orders given to local stationers such as John Measey and John Wilkes in the 1770s.[80] Procedural books of blanks were manufactured for furthering local administration from the poor law to the window tax.[81] William Dicey used his *Northampton Mercury* in the 1750s to give notice each week that he supplied "all Sorts of Blank Warrants and Summons's, Orders of Removal, Poors Warrants, Window, Highway, and Land-Tax Warrants &c." In the 1770s Barnabas Thorn, bookseller of Exeter was selling "warrants of all sorts viz land tax, window tax and highway &c."[82] At Worcester, in an example that will stand for almost any large town during the second half of the century, R. Lewis was printing "Public Accompts" for the local hospital, lists of subscribers to local charities, orders to be observed on the town's byways and in the local workhouse, and numerous notices to serve locally regulated trades from butchers to alehouse-keepers.[83] Poll books for elections were another staple of local printing. In Scotland in particular, stationers and booksellers working outside the town were encouraged to set up business within the walls. In several towns such immigrants were created free burgesses.

Even at mid-century however, most regional jobbing work was ordered directly by local business and was largely concerned with agrarian products. Printing orders from local financial and business concerns followed in the wake of new transport and postal routes. In Chester Peter Joynson, having been an apprentice of William Cooke, printer of the *Weekly Journal*, set up in the 1740s as a specialist jobbing printer serving the local businesses of ironmongers, drapers, salt merchants, and joiners. John Read, another apprentice of Cooke, began work as a specialist stationer within the town. In Edinburgh Patrick Neill, printer to the publishers Gavin Hamilton and John Balfour, took on much jobbing work for local shopkeepers and craftsmen.[84] Cheney's ledger in the 1790s shows how important the jobbing printing was to local commerce in the district of Banbury by the end of the century.[85] Cheney's jobbing printing in the 1790s earned him about £100 a year, double that of his takings in 1767, his first year of operations. His orders remained primarily related to agriculture.

At the ports the supply of printed bills of lading was increasingly necessary to the efficient identification and disposal of cargoes. From their first year the Collins brothers were advertising their services to print not only releases, warrants of attorney, and blank bonds, but also ship bills and bills of lading. Such bills were usually ordered by the shipping company or masters of the local ports. Bills were always blanks with spaces left for the names of the ship and its master, the points of departure and arrival, the witness and signature on receipt of goods, and a very large space – varying according to the type of cargo or vessel – for itemizing the offloadings. Some lading bills also had stubs for copies. All had sophisticated numbering for copying and reference in storage and indexing. Similar administrative coupons served inland waterways and roads. The manufacture of books of tickets was often a staple of local jobbing printing and vital to the expansion of many services and much retail enterprise. Tickets and posters were printed for new navigation and turnpike projects as well as for a variety of concerns for leisure and entertainment. Quires of paper bound for the turnpike were sold by Dent at one shilling and threepence each. Cheney printed the tickets for the Oxford canal. John Lawton and Mrs Elizabeth Adams printed "coal tickets" for the tolls on the canals, river, and docks under the control of the Corporation of Chester.[86] Municipal meetings about turnpikes were also regularly advertised in public broadsides.[87] Certain local managers continued to employ London printers. Strahan, for example, was commissioned by Henry Davidson of the Clyde Navigation to print bills, supporting statements, and "1,110 cards" (presumably tickets) in 1767 for which Strahan charged £96.4s.[88] By 1790 many large London printers were undertaking massive orders for business requirements – including in one instance the printing of a complete run of 5,000 books each of 350 disposable chits.

Country jobbing work increased further with the expansion of local banking facilities. Although printed prospectuses and advertisements survive from the 1690s, country banking came of age only after the mid-eighteenth century. There are examples from the late 1750s of collectors of excise accepting notes from country banks as valid currency.[89] The blanks, notes, and stamped papers were often distributed with the newspapers from central printer to local agents, although there is a frustrating dearth of actual banking records relating to local commissions.[90] Several newspaper advertisements boast that stationers have previous experience in supplying banks or mercantile companies.[91] With parliamentary sanction, Liverpool issued municipal printed notes in 1793 up to the value of £200,000. In 1803–4 Samuel Oldknow, muslin manufacturer of Stockport, was issuing notes for denominations as low as one shilling and threepence. His early experiments of the 1790s were based on handwritten notes, but from July 1793 Oldknow issued printed notes as orders upon the counting house for cash.[92] Nationwide use of notes, however, was problematic even at the end of this period. Bank of England notes were treated with suspicion outside the metropolis, and paper currency found general favour only in the decades after the American war. It is certainly important to qualify earlier emphasis upon the Irish and Scottish initiatives in the issue of banknotes, by stressing the limited avenues of note circulation. In the linen industry of northern Ireland, for example, cash transactions predominated and banknotes were unseen throughout the eighteenth century. The contrast between different parts of the country could still be great, however. In 1760 a linen merchant from County Donegal wrote that "ever since I knew business bank notes have been but of little use in this part of the kingdom where the linen trade is carried on, as nothing will carry that branch but ready money."[93] At the same period, a tourist to Munster noted that "though we have no national bank bills yet in Dublin 'tis seldom that £50 is paid in cash, bankers' notes have general currency." Crude blanks or simple scripted notes were also common in Munster, although their effect could be destabilizing as well as beneficial:

> in country fairs and markets the common people buy upon credit and give a promissory note for a cow or a horse or piece of cloth etc. payable in three months ... The non payment of these small promissory notes (which to extend credit are generally made assignable and payable to order) is the occasion of the great number of suits by civil bills which are tried upon the circuit. We heard upon the Munster circuit 2,300 civil bills.[94]

The fundamental importance of jobbing printing is that it helped overcome obstacles and limits to growth that were crucial aspects of the history of the early and the Enlightenment book trade – but aspects all too often overlooked in otherwise triumphalist accounts, including by the pioneering study of the history of the book by Lucien Lefebvre and Henri-Jean Martin.[95] Central to any analysis of these early modern bookselling careers are the constraints imposed by broader resource limitations upon business expansion – and certainly upon technological advance. Across all trades, most fixed capital was invested in ways that produced only indirect gain. The property of the shop and dwelling house, where almost all booksellers were tenants (and many were subtenants) offered no long-term investment (even though the paucity of legal or customary restraints allowed most tenants to repair, rebuild, or extend their buildings with ease). Circulating capital – that is, raw materials and goods (with books themselves as primary objects of exchange) – made up whatever long-term business investment there. By modern standards the overall result allowed a very low productivity rate, with high labour-intensity, and a vast reservoir of underemployed labour. This created very little inducement for cost-reducing innovations in all trades and industries. The book trades were clearly no exception to this, and, in the requirement to have so much capital tied up in a specific item of production – an edition – before any part of this could be sold to realize returns, the publishing sector was especially handicapped.

The economics of the early modern and eighteenth-century printing house turned in part upon the reuse of type, inevitably influencing the design of books and other printed productions, but also helping to determine the division of labour and the design and layout of the confined space of the printing house. For all printers, booksellers, and stationers, the difficulties in raising and managing credit heightened the importance of cash flow and steady turnover. This was why jobbing printing was so crucial. In speculative publication, strength of sales obviously remained the primary determinant of further trade development, while speculation on the market was of its nature fraught with peril. Until an edition was completely printed, it could not, of course, be sold; and with a new book, the publisher could never be certain of how many copies would be sold. All publishers faced high, upfront, and one-off investment coupled with potentially very slow returns. The liquidity predicament heightened the importance of sure-fire, calculable undertakings, notably the classes of patented titles, successfully reprinted time and time again, but also a much broader, more varied, and more voluminous jobbing work.

In *Histoire des choses banales*, Daniel Roche ventured one comment on the printer's role in the wider economy, although he did not expand upon upon it: "on n'en a pas encore totalement mesuré la portée et l'impact dans la vie économique française, qui bénéficie moins qu'en Angleterre du support d'un enseignement spécial, animé par les besoins du milieu des négociants avides de manuels techniques."[96] Roche kindly attributed this point to my early work,[97] and perhaps a comparison between English and French business manuals of the eighteenth century does suggest greater productivity in London than in Paris, but the broader point is again missed – that jobbing work, not book work, sustained so many printers and sustained so many contributions to economic growth, in country as well as in town. Printers made business in "l'expérience de l'urbanité," but also "au-delà de la métropole."

NOTES

1 My first full-length discussion of jobbing printing appeared in Raven (1986), currently being revised for publication; see also Raven (1996b).
2 Maslen (1993, 139); Greg (1932).
3 Maslen (1993, 152).
4 Cipolla (1973); and especially reissued volume, Cipolla (1993)
5 For further implications, see Raven (2007).
6 British Library (hereafter BL) MS 1A.53; Maslen (1993, 140).
7 J. Anderson (1940, 2); Maslen (1993, 140).
8 Needham (1986).
9 Dahl (1952, 22); Watt (1991); both cited by Stallybrass (2007).
10 As Peter Stallybrass has commented, English losses are nothing compared to those of the great printing houses of continental Europe: see Needham (1986, 31) regarding more than 130,000 indulgences ordered from printing houses in 1500 by the Bishop of Cefalù in the province of Palermo, on the northern coast of Sicily, but none of these indulgences is known to survive, not even in a fragment; notarial accounts remain the sole source for the existence of 36,000 Spanish indulgences printed by Jacopo Cromberger between 1514 and 1516; see Griffin (1988, 51).
11 Gaskell (1972).
12 Orders of 4 Dec. 1587, and of 16 Nov. 1635 (*State Papers Domestic*, CI 301: 103, 105), reproduced in Greg (1967, 43, 94–5).
13 See Raven (2007, chapter 3).
14 Maslen and Lancaster (1991); see also Maslen (1993).
15 Of these four survivals, two sets of records are relatively short: the ledger kept by Ackers from 1732 to 1748 already mentioned (and requiring new study from the perspective of jobbing printing), and some extremely brief extracts from a ledger of Henry Woodfall I, apparently running from 1734 to 1747, and reproduced in print in 1855 (P.T.P., "Pope and Woodfall" and "Woodfall's ledger, 1734–1747," *Notes & Queries* 11: 377–8, 418–20), but since lost. The fourth and much more substantial collection of surviving printing house ledgers, that of William Strahan and his successors from 1738 until the early nineteenth century, has been partly edited for the early years only by Patricia Hernlund.
16 See for instance Joan Shelly Rubin's profile of the nineteenth-century American editor and publisher George Bragdon, who relied on job work to help sustain the newspapers he produced (chapter 5) and Robert Hall's discussion of Ashton-under-Lyne bookseller John Williamson, who relied on jobbing to support his bookshop and private circulating library during the 1830s and 1840s (chapter 8).

17 Testimony of Cooke, 6 May 1726, National Archives, Kew (hereafter NA), Chester Exchequer Pleadings (Paper), 16/123 (2).
18 D. Nuttall (1969).
19 Wiles (1965, 117–18); Cranfield (1962, 198).
20 Maxted (1982, 37–76).
21 Sterenberg (1983, 28–42).
22 According to one historian of print there were very few towns in Britain in which Adams had not worked as a printer or journeyman (D. Nuttall 1969).
23 Cheney, Cheney, and Cheney (1936, 4–5).
24 Scottish Record Office, Edinburgh, Register of deeds, 171: 350–2.
25 Nichols (1966, 6: 438); Marston (1901, 85–6); Wallis (1974, 14); Granger (n.d. 6: 3135) cited in Belanger (1977: 39).
26 Further details are given in Raven (1996a, chapter 2).
27 Register of Burials, St Chad's Shrewsbury, 1678–1719, Shropshire Record Office. Shrewsbury (hereafter ShRO), 1048/30 (10 Jan. 1704).
28 Mayor's Account Book, ShRO, 3365/664, 1708.
29 Inventory of William Cook, Cheshire Archives and Local Studies (hereafter CALS, formerly Cheshire Record Office, Chester), WS 1740.
30 Will of Linden, Hampshire Record Office, Winchester (hereafter HRO), A.1829.
31 Will of Lockett, 1795, Dorset Record Office, Dorchester (hereafter DRO), W.1795 D.A. 17; attested copy of will of Collins, 1778, DRO, D660/3.
32 Hutton and Hutton (1816, 177–96).
33 An eclectic but rich assortment of such pieces can be found in the John Johnson Collection, Bodleian Library, described generally in Shackleton and Turner (1971).
34 East Suffolk Record Office, Ipswich (hereafter ESRO), FE1/15/96. All existing accounts of "William Craighton" confuse his contribution with that of his more productive son.
35 Cit. Ferdinand (1983, 81).
36 Durston advertisement, ShRO, Lloyd MSS 2118/294.
37 Newspaper files, Dorset County Museum, Dorchester.
38 Knott (1973–4, 7).
39 Twyman and Rollinson (1966).
40 Of many examples, account of John Measey stationer (with enclosure), HRO, Q.T.10: 10.
41 Coleman (1958).
42 Shorter (1966, 10).
43 Thomson (1974, 74).
44 Further details are given in Coleman (1958, 180–90).

45 Willan (1970).
46 Crossgrove to the Rev. John Strype, 27 June 1715, British Library, Add. MSS 5853 (Cole Collection, vol. 52): 108; Maxted (1982, 46).
47 Twyman and Rollinson (1966, 18).
48 After the first Act to impose an excise tax on home-produced paper (1711), some 26 further acts were passed in the next 150 years.
49 Dowell (1965, 3: 290).
50 Edinburgh University Library (hereafter EUL), Special Collections, La II: 508.
51 Of many examples from this period, Chamberlaine's Accounts, 1729–44, Staffordshire Record Office, Stafford (hereafter StRO); Chamberlaine's Accompt Book, 1732–64, Herefordshire Record Office, Hereford (now the Herefordshire Archive Service) (e.g., f.408, order of 23 August 1756).
52 Details from Feather (1985, 202–6). His general argument is qualified by Fergus and Portner (1987, 147–63).
53 Account of George Wallace, EUL, Special Collections, La II: 694.
54 HRO, QR. Misc. I. 34: 34–43.
55 *Lockett's Address to his Friends*, broadside handbill, [1788].
56 *London Evening Post* 11 April 1780.
57 Trade advertisement, reproduced in Twyman and Rollinson (1966, 18).
58 Exceptions include B. Middleton (1963).
59 Campbell (1747, 135).
60 John Bewell, d. 1705, bookbinder of Ipswich, was worth at death £11.6s.8d, ESRO, FE1/5/121.
61 Recurrent monthly advertisements include the *Public Advertiser*, 5, 19 & 26 Jan. 1780, 3, 4 & 27 April 1780, 11 May & 21 June 1780.
62 Smart advertisement, 28 July 1774, Palfrey Collection, Hereford and Worcester Record Office, Worcester (now renamed as the Worcestershire Archive and Archeology Service and hereafter WAAS), Palfrey Collection, Foley Scrapbook, b.899: 31/8a, iii.
63 *A General Description of all Trades* (1747).
64 *Ipswich Journal*, 24 Nov., 1 & 8 Dec. 1750. This is also noted in Oldham (1958).
65 14 Car. II c. 33.
66 Stoker (1977, 95).
67 Feather (1985,104).
68 StRO, Chamberlaine's Accounts, 1729–44, 1745–65.
69 WAAS, Quarter Sessions Order Book, II (1714–31): 84a, 219a, 255a.
70 *Newcastle Courant*, 4 August 1711.
71 Stoker (1977, 106); Norfolk Record Office, Norwich, Chamberlain's Accounts and Misc. Chamberlain's Vouchers, 21b (3).

72 The survival of records is variable however, ranging from the splendid Treasurers' Accompt Books of Hereford and Norwich to the bundles of virtually illegible vouchers and receipts (from which an original but now lost main ledger was compiled) at Shrewsbury and at Reading.
73 ShRO, Mr. Loxdale's Accounts, 3365/664.
74 For one strongly argued view of this, see Corfield (1982).
75 CALS (now incorporating Chester City Record Office), Treasurer's Account Books of the City of Chester, 1759–73, TAB/7 (and corresponding Treasurer's Day Books for 1756–64, TAY/1–4) provide several examples. A remarkable series of 70 printed forms, 1759–80, for "Prices of grain meal and flour as sold in the corn market in Kingston-upon-Hull ... the day of" etc., are held at the Goldsmiths' Library.
76 ShRO, Quarter Sessions Records, Orders and Minutes of J.P.s, 1755–67 "Misc" 3365/2446, and Orders, 1767–78 3365/2447.
77 Notable surviving examples include CALS, Quarter Sessions, enrolment, registration, and deposited plans.
78 Bedford Record Office, Quarter Sessions Records, 1775–95, and considered further in Pickford (1982). Also ESRO, HRO, Leeds City Archives and West Suffolk Record Office, Bury St Edmunds, quarter sessions and municipal records.
79 Salisbury Museum, 104/1964; 197/1945 – I am grateful to Christine Ferdinand for these references.
80 HRO, Q.T.1, General Accounts, 1715–1760; Q.T.10, County Hall Yearly Accounts, 1769–1806, e.g., 8–12.
81 Of various surviving evidence, DRO, D367/E56, printing accounts, 1740; or for Southampton, NA, E.181–84.
82 *Exeter Journal*, 12 June 1772.
83 WAAS, Palfrey Collection, Foley Scrapbook, b899: 31/8a, iii.
84 NLS Ledgers of Patrick and Adam Neill, 1764–73.
85 Cheney, Cheney, and Cheney (1936, 1–20).
86 CALS, Treasurer's Accounts 1759–73, TAB/7: 80^{v} (including a payment of £1.14s for 20 quire of coal tickets "and binding the same in 4 books," Dec. 1766).
87 CALS, Treasurer's Accounts, 1768, TAB/7: 92.
88 BL, Add. MSS 48,803a: 86^{v}, Strahan Ledger.
89 Pressnell (1956, 61).
90 Nottingham Central Library copies of the *Leicester and Nottingham Journal* from the 1760s have various MS marginalia relating to the sale of blanks by the newsmen.
91 Smart of Worcester, for example, in the *Worcester Journal*, 28 July 1774.
92 Unwin (1924, 182–3, 185, 190).

93 Abercorn MSS, T.2541/IA1/6A/14, Nathaniel Nisbitt to the Earl of Abercorn, 17 February 1760, cit., Crawford and Trainor (1969, 25).
94 Willes MSS T.2368, tour of Edward Willes, cit., Crawford and Trainor (1969, 26).
95 LeFebvre and Martin (1976).
96 "We have not yet entirely measured the scope and impact [of the printer's work] in French economic life, which was supported less than was the case in England by special instruction inspired by the the business community's enthusiasm for technical manuals"(Roche 1997, 63).
97 Roche (1997, 282n45) cit. Raven (1996b).

2 "I have hitherto been entirely upon the borrowing hand": The Acquisition and Circulation of Books in Early Eighteenth-Century Dissenting Academies

KYLE ROBERTS

In early 1722, dissenting academy student Philip Doddridge found himself in the unusual position of having a guinea to spend on books. The number of people he consulted on what title he should purchase attests to the uncommonness of the opportunity. Over the course of several weeks he queried his benefactor (a fellow classmate), his tutor, his former tutor, a recently graduated classmate, and his sister about what he should buy. That guinea enabled him to participate in the marketplace, to acquire a desirable consumer good, at a time when books remained expensive and scarce. But Doddridge's dilemma was not in deciding which title he most wanted for himself, but in which promised to do the most for his academic community. "I have hitherto been entirely upon the borrowing hand," he explained to his former tutor, "and I should have been glad to have some book of such note, as that I might, in my turn, oblige my fellow pupils with its perusal."[1] For Doddridge, access to books meant the opportunity to fully participate in the rituals of sociability built around books that structured the eighteenth-century dissenting community. Gratification came not from possession, but participation.

As England grew in the early eighteenth century, so, too, did literacy, the availability of texts, and the love of reading. The nation's population expanded rapidly during this period, by just over a million people between 1696 and 1756, a 17 per cent increase.[2] Remarkable economic development accompanied this dramatic demographic growth, as did a 50 per cent increase in rates of literacy. Some areas, such as Northampton in the English Midlands, a stronghold of dissent and Doddridge's eventual home, enjoyed even higher rates of literacy.[3] According to James Raven, a major transformation in the market for books began in the 1690s and accelerated after the 1740s. Where the consumption of books had once been largely the domain of the elite, an eighteenth-century commercial revolution in the book was fostered by the demand of middling and propertied classes. "[B]ooks, magazines and prints themselves became prominent exemplars of the new decencies and conveniences gracing the homes of the middling sort," Raven explains. Cartelization of the book trade meant that new books remained "grossly overpriced," yet over the course of the century, the elite no longer stood as the primary consumers of printed books.[4] A profusion of commercial and subscription lending libraries put books into the hands of enthusiastic English readers from a range of class backgrounds. More than just the desire for respectability drove this development. A genuine love of reading, argues David Allan, emerged during this period from a variety of wellsprings. "[T]he potent combination of pleasure-seeking and profound moral earnestness, of the highest idealism and the most instrumental and pragmatic functionalism," he explains, "contributed simultaneously to the contemporary love affair with reading."[5] Doddridge shared this love.

Young Doddridge's dilemma reminds us that social practices, networks, and institutions proved just as, if not more, important than market forces in driving the circulation of texts in early Georgian England. As the introduction to this volume along with the essays by Christine Pawley, Robert Hall, and Ronald and Mary Zboray remind us, informal dissemination turned out to be just as, if not more, important than the marketplace and formal institutions for the acquisition of reading material in communities beyond the metropolis. London remained the centre of book production during this time, but the vast majority of the English population resided outside of urbanized market towns and cities and depended upon other means for access to books.[6] Doddridge was born in London, the descendant of urban English dissenting and German Protestant ministers. He traded the London of his birth for the rural villages and market towns of the Midlands, traditional strongholds of dissent, in adulthood.[7] His voluminous correspondence, notebooks, and papers from his time as a student and later a tutor at Independent Dissenting academies, and the seven hundred books from his library now at Dr Williams's Library, London, document his active participation in this burgeoning world of print. Physical distance from London's printers, booksellers, and formal libraries did not impede Doddridge's access to books. Instead London stood as one node in a broad web of networks – primarily, but not exclusively, of fellow dissenters – that stretched across the nation on which Doddridge depended. Given Doddridge's extensive surviving record and his prominence within the Dissenting community, his experience challenges us to think carefully about the acquisition and circulation of books, and the forces that drove them, beyond the marketplace and formal institutions of the metropolis in the first half of the eighteenth century.

This essay explores the circulation of texts and the social practices of print during two early phases of Philip Doddridge's life in the English Midlands. It begins with his arrival at John Jennings's Academy in Kibworth Harcourt, Leicestershire, in October 1719 at the tender age of seventeen.[8] By the end of his life, Doddridge had emerged as one of the eighteenth century's most important dissenting authors, ministers, and educators. But at Jenning's Academy, he was like scores of other young men from dissenting families sent to receive ministerial and professional training. Every reader is, of course, different, although Doddridge's reading experiences and habits over the next four years mirrored those of his contemporaries. A decade later, Doddridge made a less common move when he opened his own academy in Market Harborough, Northamptonshire, and soon after moved it to Northampton. Graduates of dissenting academies more often became local ministers than tutors. A new academy needed a library, and Doddridge's efforts to build one are the focus of the second half of this essay. Once again he relied upon the social practices, networks, and institutions of the broad community of dissent to provide him with books. In the end, Doddridge's example reminds us of the limitations of our models of circulation and reception that privilege the market and formal institutions over more informal means.

An Academy Education

"You have now an opportunity for treasuring up valuable knowledge under the conduct of a very worthy tutor," Samuel Clark wrote to Philip Doddridge in the spring of his first year at John Jennings's Academy in rural Kibworth Harcourt. "[A]s I doubt not but that you improve that advantage to the utmost, so I am desirous it may be continued to you as long as possible: for I would have you furnished, not with a bare superficial taste of literature, but with so rich a stock of solid knowledge as may abundantly qualify you for whatever service God may call you to in his church."[9] As Doddridge soon discovered, that "stock of solid knowledge" came in a variety of textual forms. Jennings's expansive pedagogy exposed Doddridge to a large number of texts. He acquired access to physical copies of these texts by an even more diverse range of means. Outright purchase tended to be his least common mode of acquisition, and even when he had the means for it, others typically mediated his purchases. Gifting, borrowing, and even producing manuscript copies proved more customary. Doddridge embraced them all.

Dissenting academies provided Protestant students dissenting from the Church of England with a higher education similar to that available in the English universities. The restoration of Charles II in 1660 was founded upon the exclusive establishment of the Church of England. The Act of Uniformity (1662) required all clergy, teachers, lecturers, and university fellows to submit to the Anglican Church or lose their livelihoods.[10] Though dissenters were not technically excluded from the English universities, a combination of legislation, need for subscription to particular doctrinal codes, and the customs and practices of the universities themselves made it difficult for dissenters to obtain a conventional university education. Dissenting academies developed into an alternative system for training Presbyterian, Congregational, and Baptist ministers, as well as providing a university-level education to the sons of wealthy dissenters destined for careers in trade and commerce. Many of the earliest academies were run on a small scale, with a handful of students studying under the supervision of an established minister, often in his home. In the eighteenth century, several academies emerged as more robust institutions, with purpose-built academy structures, multiple tutors, and a greater number of ministerial and lay students. Jennings's Academy resembled the former more than the latter.[11]

That Doddridge would end up at Jennings's Academy – or any dissenting academy for that matter – was far from a foregone conclusion given his financial position. The passing of Doddridge's parents in his adolescence and the mismanagement of his inheritance made the possibility of a professional education uncertain. The only way a bright young man in his circumstances might hope to gain an education was through the kindness of others. His uncle Philip had served as a steward to the Duke of Bedford and when the Duchess of Bedford learned of Doddridge's "circumstances, character, and strong inclination to study," she offered to pay for his education so long as he agreed to conform. Doddridge came from long lines of dissenters and graciously, but firmly, refused her terms.[12] As one door closed, another opened. Doddridge considered a career in law, until Samuel Clark of St Albans made a counter-offer. Clark had known Doddridge since his removal to St Albans for grammar school, around the time of his father's death. So long as Doddridge chose "the *Ministry* on Christian Principles," Clark, and his friends, would fund his education. For Doddridge, this invitation appeared nothing less than providential. The young student moved into Clark's, house where the distinguished dissenting minister furnished him with "proper" books, directed him in his studies, and laboured to convince him to continue "to cherish religious Dispositions and Views in his heart."[13]

In October 1719, Doddridge entered Jennings's Academy in Kibworth Harcourt, a small village of 150 families in Leicestershire.[14] Evidence of the educational experience within early eighteenth-century dissenting academies is notoriously slight, although we know more about Jennings's Academy, largely because of Doddridge. Jennings began his academy as early as 1715 and later relocated to Hinckley, also in Leicestershire, in July 1722. Doddridge initially appreciated this move. Writing to an older female friend, he noted Hinckley was "one of the largest market towns in the country; and there I will meet with some pretty girls, that, if I am not prepossessed, may do me a mischief."[15] Hinckley also promised more ready access to books. Within two months of arrival, however, Doddridge grew tired of the locale, telling the same correspondent that "Hinckley is more like Egypt than Canaan."[16] Fortunately for Doddridge, his time there did not last long: he passed his final examination in late January 1723 and received a call to the pulpit of the church back in Kibworth Harcourt in April.[17] Doddridge's correspondence provides a wealth of information about his experience and the workings of the academy, as does a long letter he wrote in 1728 recounting "Mr Jennings's Method."[18] The survival of several student notebooks and textbooks produced or published by Jennings provides additional information about the world of books within the academy.

The course of study at Jennings's ran for four years, two terms (what Jennings referred to as "half-years") a year. Jennings expected entering students to have proficiency in Greek and Latin, although the extent of their knowledge varied considerably. The first two years focused heavily on an academic course similar to what students received at other academies and the English universities. It included classical studies (which included a variety of Greek and Latin poets and prose authors) and mathematics and natural philosophy (beginning with arithmetic and algebra and continuing through geometry, mechanics, hydrostatics, physics, astronomy, and the use of globes). In the first year, students also mastered Hebrew grammar, French authors, and geography. Instruction in logic, civil history, and drama continued over the first two years. In the second half of the second year, students shifted from the academic course to the theological course, focusing primarily on pneumatology (what we might today call moral philosophy), ethics, and divinity. During these half-years, they also had lectures in chronology, Jewish and Christian antiquities, ecclesiastical history, biblical criticism, the history of controversies, and preaching and pastoral care.[19] Jennings grounded his mode of instruction in lectures (in Latin) six days a week, although students also had the opportunity to participate in disputations, deliver discourses, and even perform the play *Tamerlane.*[20]

Jennings's coursework demanded a range of titles in a variety of textual forms. A surviving syllabus written in Jennings's hand sometime after 1721 lists forty-eight titles arranged in four categories that students needed to complete their course of instruction.[21] The first category – "Libri emptu prorsus necessarii" – laid out seventeen books he deemed absolutely necessary for students to purchase. These books primarily pertained to the academic course and included standard textbooks for geography;[22] geometry;[23] physics;[24] history;[25] and Hebrew, French, Greek, and Latin training.[26] For some subjects, Jennings appears to have either disliked the texts available, desired texts not easily procured, or, as often seemed to be the case, wanted texts that drew from multiple printed sources. To that end, the second category – "Libri transcribendi" – lists manuscript texts compiled by Jennings for students to copy out. Five of the seven volumes relate to the theological course, suggesting Jennings's willingness to teach the academic course with standard published texts.[27] Students came to the academy from a range of financial backgrounds, so Jennings included a third category – "Libri quos in cursu habere expromis haud parum juvabit si suppetat pecunia" – books that would be very useful to purchase if the student had the money. These eight titles supplemented the first category and functioned as useful reference titles for students' work in French literature,[28] English and European history,[29] the history of the primitive church,[30] and civil and natural law.[31] A final category – "Libri quos si quis ex proprio iam habet adferre opertet" – referred to books that students should bring to the academy if they already owned them. These fifteen titles included works students likely would have acquired for their previous grammar school education. The preponderance of works by Latin poets and prose writers[32] and Greek poets[33] reflects the extent to which grammar school curriculum focused on classical studies. Bythner's *Lyra prophetica*, Burgersdijck's *Logic*, and the Assembly's *Larger Catechism* also functioned as standard works.[34] The fortunate student who possessed all forty-eight titles had the foundation of a useful classical and theological library.[35]

Jennings's syllabus needs to be understood as the basic foundation, not the limit, of the titles to which he exposed students in his coursework. In fact, he asked them to acquaint themselves with a far larger number of texts. Intensive reading of the scriptures and extensive reading in doctrinal, controversial, and practical literature characterized his system. "I have almost finished Mr. Jennings's system of divinity; and the better I am acquainted with it, the more I admire it," Doddridge shared with his brother-in-law John Nettleton in the spring of his third year. He went on to explain Jennings's rationale and method:

> He always inculcates it upon our attention, that the scriptures are the only standard of orthodoxy, and encourages the utmost freedom of inquiry. He furnishes us with all kinds of authors upon every subject, without advising us to skip over the heretical passages for fear of infection. It is evidently his main care to inspire us with sentiments of CATHOLICISM, and to arm us against that zeal, which is not according to knowledge.[36]

Doddridge's surviving transcription of Jennings's *Theologia* (one of the seven titles listed in the syllabus) contains, at the end, a "Syllabus Librorum" to be consulted. References to specific passages in these titles would have been given out in class as illustrations of the subject at hand, with the expectation that students might copy them out and give an account of their substance at the next lecture.[37] The syllabus lists an extensive number of titles – 174 – written primarily by English and Continental authors. The quantity and length of references varied. Regardless, this represented an impressive expectation of extensive reading.

To what extent could an individual student successfully complete such a system? Again, Doddridge's notebook is suggestive. Almost every work has a mark next to it. He appears to have turned the dash ("–") next to each title into a plus mark ("+") after reading the work. This notational system suggests that Doddridge read at least 60 per cent of the works.[38] Why the other works remained unread might be a question of access (although it seems unlikely that Jennings would assign books for which students could not secure copies), a reflection of coordinated group work among academy students, or the result of simple exhaustion.[39] Doddridge, at first, did not like such a laborious system, but his admiration grew over time.[40]

In down times during the term and over breaks, books continued to hold Doddridge's interest. Reflecting on the first half of his third year, Doddridge remembered how divinity studies consumed many of his waking hours. "[H]owever, I generally find about an hour and a half in a day for the study of the Scriptures," he wrote to his mentor Clark. "The New Testament I read in the original without any commentator, but more of my time is spent in the Old, for I would willingly finish Patrick's Commentary before it is taken from Kibworth, which will be in a few months."

The urgency with which Doddridge felt the need to preserve his study of the scripture was compounded by the terms of his access to books, to which I will return later. Time spent on one set of works, he knew, was time taken away from others. "I do not entirely neglect the classics," he continued, "though I have but little time for them."[41] Doddridge's correspondence reveals the breadth of his scholarly and leisurely interests, mentioning scores of titles ranging from history to ethics, practical divinity to literature. Even at a serious, orthodox dissenting academy, reading could be as much for enjoyment as for edification. A volume of Dryden during a long coach ride or "the classics, the *Spectator*, essays, poems, and travels serve for the entertainment of our idle hours."[42]

Not only does Doddridge's correspondence document the breadth of his reading during his time in Jennings's Academy, but it also reveals the variety of strategies he employed to gain access to texts. London throughout this period stood as the centre of the English book trade, a centralizing and dominating force unrivalled in other regions of the Atlantic world. Hundreds of printers across Greater London turned out hundreds of thousands of sheets a year that were bound by local binders and distributed to market towns across England and around the world.[43] Some, perhaps many, of these books would have been available in Hinckley and nearby Leicester.[44] Doddridge made occasional trips to London during his summer break, but for much of the year he depended upon a web of local and national booksellers and dissenters to supply his needs.[45] Occasionally he had the means to purchase new or used books, but more often he relied upon gifts or loans. He might even make a manuscript copy. All of these strategies reveal the interconnectedness of the metropolis and the hinterland in the circulation of early eighteenth-century texts.

Throughout the school year, Doddridge had the occasional opportunity to acquire new books through arrangements made by Jennings with a London bookseller, but his limited funds as a scholarship student made this mode of acquisition uncommon. Each January, Doddridge forwarded the bill from the previous half-year to his mentor and sponsor Samuel Clark. Board and tuition made up, by far, the greatest expense (£8 10s), but also listed were books and the occasional article of clothing.[46] "The books are such as we read in our course," Doddridge explained about the expense, "and which Mr Jennings thought proper to provide for us himself."[47] To that end, Jennings had ordered a handful of texts for all his students from the London bookseller John Clark.[48] This way London imprints of Peter King's *An Enquiry into the constitution, discipline, unity and worship of the primitive church*[49] and an *Appendix to Logic*[50] entered

Doddridge's possession in the fall of his third year,[51] while in his fourth, he acquired a Dutch imprint of Spanheim's *Elenchus*[52] and a London edition of the English translation of Du Pin's *Ecclesiastical History*.[53] Doddridge also took advantage of Jennings's London connection to acquire two additional texts for his personal use: a Hebrew Bible, to replace one "in a very scurvy condition," and an interleaved New Testament in which he could make "observations on texts of scripture that might probably be of use" on clean sheets rather than in the cramped margin.[54] Fearful of being perceived as abusing Clark's generosity, or perhaps anticipating criticism for the additional expense, Doddridge assured him that every expense was necessary. "I have always endeavored to avoid every thing that looks like extravagance," he pleaded, "and you may depend upon it shall continue so."[55]

The windfall of a guinea to purchase books after Christmas in 1721 reveals in rich detail the careful consideration Doddridge gave to acquiring books of his own. The money came from his classmate, Jonathan Cope, "a gentleman of considerable estate," to whom Doddridge seems not to have been very close.[56] But that did not stop him from accepting the gift.[57] "I must be obliged to lay out this in books," Doddridge explained to Clark of Cope's stipulation, "for he intimated that he gave it me for that purpose."[58] What would he purchase? He turned to his academy classmates and to far-flung relations and friends for advice. To one, he related his initial inclination to make a practical purchase, such as Prideaux's *Connection*, that would benefit his studies.[59] Cope, however, hoped that he "would furnish [himself] with some books that are not in the house already."[60] Doddridge's thoughts turned to the remaining volumes of a title he had been reading for his own enjoyment. A month previous, close friend and former classmate Obadiah Hughes had sent him the first volume of John Scott's *Christian Life*, a popular devotional guide.[61] But before Doddridge committed, he sought approval. Jennings found the idea a fine one and promised "to complete the set the next time he goes to London" and to "endeavor to get it as cheaply as possible."[62] Cope shared his initial intention to present Doddridge with the title instead of the money, but had been unable to secure it at Derby.[63] Even the recommendation of leading Anglican historian and theologian Gilbert Burnet, albeit in his published opinion in *Pastoral Care*, received credit as having "inclined me to fix upon it."[64] The purchase seemed nothing short of providentially determined.[65]

Doddridge's expectation that owning Scott's *Christian Life* meant he no longer had to be "entirely upon the borrowing hand" reminds us of a second, and even more widespread, mode of book circulation. Accounts of and requests for loans pervade Doddridge's correspondence. When he could not afford to purchase a book, he turned to family, friends, classmates, and the broader dissenting community. Appreciating how fundamental borrowing was to the academic community, in particular, and the dissenting community, in general, helps us appreciate how the simple acquisition of Scott's *Christian Life* meant as much for the status it afforded Doddridge when he shared the text with others as for his own access to it. Borrowing was a privilege Doddridge had long enjoyed, but had seldom been able to reciprocate.

Family members and friends frequently found themselves called upon to supply books from their households. "I desire you would send me, besides the books I mentioned at Hampstead, the discourse on Free-thinking, Clark's Annotations on the New Testament, and the odd volumes of Hall's Contemplations," Doddridge asked his sister Elizabeth in the summer before his final year at the academy.[66] A year later, he wrote her again asking to borrow – "till I can better afford to buy one" – his brother-in-law's concordance. "Locke upon the Epistles would be very useful to me, if he could well spare it"; he continued, "but I would not put him to any inconvenience."[67] Samuel Clark similarly loaned his young protégé books as need arose.

Libraries – public, private, or academic – played a crucial role in sustaining students. Jennings's pedagogical style required access to a far larger number of books than students could purchase or borrow from family and friends, so he assembled a library. Here students found the texts they needed to complete the references they received in lecture each week and discovered new ones that challenged and, sometimes, perplexed them. "We have some of Godwin's books in the library, and some of the great Dr Owen's," Doddridge shared with his brother-in-law, half-jokingly continuing, "but you know I am not very fond of mysterious men."[68] At the end of his third year, Doddridge related to Clark that he might just stay at the academy over the summer break, "for here are a great many books, that I am afraid I shall never find time to read." Despite this, Doddridge went to London anyway.[69]

Little remains of the library that Jennings built. No catalogue of the collection has survived to show the types of books that Jennings deemed worthy or necessary to acquire for his studies. The best description of Jennings's library comes from a long letter describing the course of education, reading, and daily life at the academy written by Doddridge five years after it ceased to be.[70] Students had "free Use of all his Books," which could be found in two libraries. All students could access the first library, which consisted of classics, poetry, history, travels, and practical divinity.

Jennings believed these works "might be entertaining and useful in any Part of our Course." The second library, however, he restricted to those who had reached the theological course, which began in the fourth half-year, or the second term of the second year. These works consisted of critics, philosophy, ecclesiastical history, church fathers, and polemical divinity. Had these works been "meddled with" too soon, it would have only "confounded us, and have hinder'd us in the Studies which were our immediate Business." Schoolboys did not always treat these books as well as they should, he confessed, but he felt that the generosity of students and others in making gifts to the library more than outweighed any damage inflicted.[71] During Jennings's life, the academy library provided Doddridge with access to a broad range of texts. After his death, some of its titles became part of Doddridge's own academy library.[72] The second section of Jennings's Syllabus – Libri Transcribendi – reminds us of the ongoing importance in the eighteenth century of manuscript publication. Scholars have often assumed that the rise of the printed word hastened the decline of manuscript publication, but the real cost of books continued to be high during this period and print runs comparatively small.[73] Every student in the academy engaged in the work of making at least seven books, according to the syllabus. As D.F. McKenzie reminds us, every translation involves the production of new meaning.[74] While intended as transcriptions, each of these works became a new text through the choices – major and minor – students made during production. In addition to copying Jennings's works, students often had their own notes from classes bound for future preservation. The survival of so many notebooks from dissenting academies today is evidence of the value students and their descendants placed upon them. In fact, they might have valued them even more than printed books. Manuscript publications required significantly more effort, contained far less readily replaceable material, and bore the personal mark of their creator in a way that printed books did not.

Many of the works the students copied were authored by Jennings. Over his short career, Jennings produced multiple texts – manuscript and printed – for the use of his students, likely out of dissatisfaction with the commercially produced texts available to him. This act of production should not be seen as piracy, as a means of skirting copyright, but as an effort to produce a new text focused on what his students actually needed. Students were certainly aware of the origins of the material they read. For the class on biblical critics, Doddridge noted that the manuscript textbook was "an abridgement from a considerable book by Mr Jones, which treats of such subjects as the antiquity of the Hebrew language, its points, the

Massora, Talmud, and Cabala," itself likely another manuscript publication.[75] Jennings also paid printers in Northampton to print two textbooks for him, a *Logica* and a *Miscellanea*. The *Logica* represents Jennings's personal synthesis of the topic, built largely upon Locke's *Essay on Human Understanding*, but packed with references to twenty other texts.[76] The *Miscellanea* is, as the name suggests, a collection of material on topics as diverse as psalm singing, oratory, algebra, romances, heraldry, metaphysics, mechanics, and chronology.[77]

Like other dissenting academy tutors before him, John Jennings made his rural dissenting academy an active site for the production and circulation of manuscript and print publications. Far from the publishing metropolis, Jennings's Academy instilled in the young Doddridge a range of strategies for acquiring texts that he would use for the remainder of his life. Outright purchases proved uncommon. Instead, Doddridge relied upon the social rituals, networks, and institutions of dissent to supply the texts he needed for his studies and recreation.

An Academy of His Own

"Lady Russell has given me a very good pair of globes," Doddridge wrote to friend and in-law Ebenezer Hankins in May 1731 about his efforts to furnish his new academy in Northampton. "I should be obliged to you," he continued, "if you would please to speak to Dr Beard about a microscope, which he told me he would be so good as to buy for me when he went to London." Globes and microscopes allowed Doddridge to be on the forward edge of contemporary pedagogical practice, but it was books that he needed more than anything for his academy to run. A few weeks before, Hankins had sent him a copy of *Reliquiæ Baxterianæ*, the posthumously published autobiography of leading seventeenth-century Nonconformist minister Richard Baxter. Upon receiving this classic dissenting text, Doddridge carefully inscribed its title page "In Usum Academiae Ex Dono Dom: Hankins 1731" in recognition of his friend's generosity and placed it in his academy's library.[78] "You do very well to remember my library, to which I hope we shall *both* be annual benefactors," Doddridge concluded.[79]

As a student, Doddridge depended upon the generosity of others for access to the books he needed; as an academy tutor, he relied upon others to furnish the books his students needed. Over his years after graduation as a minister in Kibworth Harcourt and Market Harborough, Doddridge began to acquire pertinent volumes, but his pedagogical intentions, modelled on those of Jennings, required significantly more works than his ministerial wallet could afford. "I would not go to any great price," he wrote to Hankins in anticipation of an inquiry into how much he would be willing to pay for a microscope; "nay, if I were to choose for myself, I would not go to any price at all!"[80] A manuscript "Catalogue of Books given to the Academical Library with the Names of the Donors" (c.1730–3) attests to Doddridge's success in convincing others to support his endeavours. While some dissenting academies built their libraries through the acquisition of significant ministerial collections, Doddridge's library grew piecemeal through his purchases and donations from a range of individuals.[81] Over the academy's first three years, Doddridge secured 104 titles (totaling 162 volumes) from 61 donors. The "Catalogue" reveals much about the availability and circulation of texts in the Midlands in the second quarter of the eighteenth century and the motivations of donors, male and female, clerical and lay, local and metropolitan.[82]

Despite protests of indifference and lack of preparation, Doddridge assumed the role of tutor in July 1729. Following overtures from local dissenting clergy the previous year, he had sounded out his mentor, Samuel Clark, about the wisdom of such a move. "They urge, that it may be an advantage for me to go over Mr Jennings's course again in such a manner," Doddridge wrote at the time, although he remained adamant that "I should not afterwards pursue the business of a tutor."[83] Torn between his faith in Jennings's method and insecurity about his own abilities, Doddridge eventually reconciled the two.[84] The proposal of his fellow minister David Some at a general meeting of local Noncomformist ministers in April 1729 to establish a dissenting academy at Market Harborough met with their unanimous support. They "engaged to render every encouragement and assistance in their power."[85] He did not face much competition, as the primary dissenting academies of the time were located either in London or at Findern near Derby. The twenty-seven-year-old minister began prudently, taking on only a handful of students put forward by his acquaintances.[86]

Within six months, Doddridge relocated his pastorate and academy to Northampton, the most important market town in the county.[87] Doddridge's reputation as a moderate Calvinist preacher and his focus on cultivating personal devotion among his congregants partially explains his appeal to Northampton's Castle Hill Congregational Church, whose members also valued his work as a tutor and sought to accommodate his move. "They could have a house fit for your academy on easy terms," Samuel Clark wrote him in October, "and [...] they would furnish some of the rooms for you at their own expense." They even offered to reimburse his former tutor's widow, Mrs Jennings, in whose house Doddridge ran the academy in Market Harborough, for the loss of revenue from boarding if she chose not to move to Northampton. In sum, Clark relayed, "the people were so set upon having you upon any terms, that they would do any thing for you in their power."[88] For Doddridge, though, the decision proved far from easy. Responsibility for a larger congregation and the students he had already begun to train weighed heavily on his mind, but in time he believed Providence called him to the new position.[89] On 13 January 1730, Doddridge noted in his diary that he began housekeeping in Northampton and "took possession of that chamber in which I hope to spend most of the remaining studious hours of my life."[90]

Having made his commitment to the dual life of pastor and tutor, Doddridge spent the next few years developing his academy, which included providing books for the use of his growing number of students.[91] He continued to purchase a few titles with his own money, as he had done over the previous decade.[92] His means certainly had increased as a result of his move, as he related in a detailed letter to Mrs Owen, his future wife's aunt. "You know, madam, that though under no necessity of doing it, yet I chose to spend the first years of my life with a little congregation in the country, where my income was but just enough to maintain me, and to furnish me with a few books," Doddridge wrote in August 1730. He continued:

> I am now indeed settled much to my satisfaction, with a large and flourishing congregation, though few of them make any great figure in the world. Their stated subscription is above seventy pounds a year, and the perquisites will, so far as I can guess by what I have already received, make it above eighty. I have about thirty pounds a year coming in by my pupils.

But Doddridge's desire for books outpaced his funds, especially after he married and began a family. He turned to his local Noncomformist ministerial colleagues, who had pledged "every encouragement and assistance in their power," and that of the broader dissenting community, to share the burden of building a library for his academy.

The information recorded in the "Catalogue of Books Given to the Academical Library" provides valuable insights into Doddridge's strategies for acquiring texts in his new role as tutor. Of the 104 titles listed in the "Catalogue," ninety-two can be identified by title and edition. Another eight can be identified by title but not edition. Three cannot be identified by title or edition and one listing represents, in fact, seven volumes of "miscellaneous tracts."[93] Many titles in the "Catalogue" correlate with

2.1 Doddridges's inscriptions of Hankin's gift *Reliquiae Baxterianae* (1696) in 1731

listings in four catalogues from academies that inherited Doddridge's library after his death in 1751. Two of these catalogues (1838 and 1977) have been entered in Dissenting Academies Online: Virtual Library System (vls.english.qmul.ac.uk), demonstrating the usefulness of online databases of circulation in doing this kind of work, as seen in the essays in this volume by Julieanne Lamond on the Australian Common Reader and Frank Felsenstein, Joel Shrock, and Lynne Tatlock on What Middletown Read.[94] If an edition of a work listed in the 1730s catalogue is found in a later catalogue, and if the publication date of that edition predates the presumed date of donation (c. 1730–2), then I have assumed it is most likely the same physical copy. Approximately 83 per cent of the works listed in the 1730s catalogue are present a century later in the 1838 catalogue.[95] Surviving books from Doddridge's Library in the collection of Dr Williams's Library, London, allow for confirmation of this approach. Doddridge often wrote the name and year of donation on the title page of works given to the academy library (see, for example, fig. 2.1). In all, more than a third of the titles in the 1730s catalogue survive at Dr Williams's Library today.[96]

Works donated to Doddridge's Academy library range from a 1570 edition of Calvin's *Commentary on Isaiah* to a 1730 edition of L'Enfant's *History of the Council of Constance*, but the majority had been published in the half-century before donation (see fig. 2.2 for a distribution of the titles).[97] No hard-and-fast definition exists of what qualifies as a "new" title in the second quarter of the eighteenth century, but given the length of time that booksellers kept books in stock, it is not unreasonable to consider works published in the previous decade as recent titles. Thus over a quarter of the titles given to the academy may be considered recent. More than half had been published in Doddridge's lifetime and

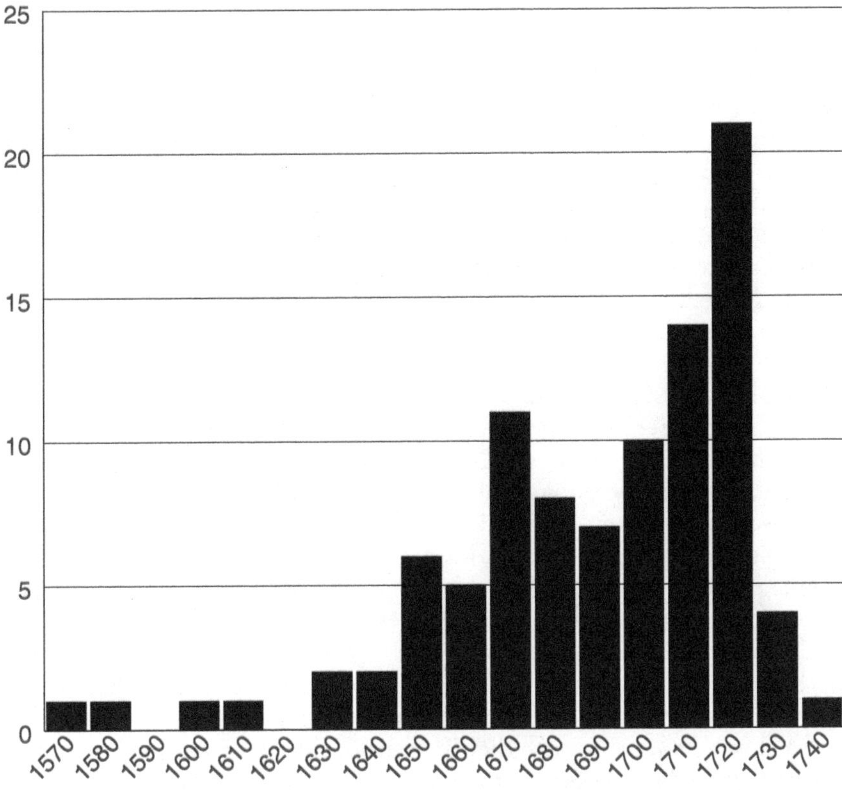

2.2 Donated Titles by Decade of Publication (n = 95)

the bulk of the remainder had been published in the second half of the seventeenth century. The handful published before 1650 represented classic texts – commentaries by Calvin and Willett, Hebraist studies by Fuller and Weemes, and harmonies by Lightfoot and Chemnitz, Leyser, and Gerhard – used in theological training.

Donors contributed both new and used books to Doddridge's Academy. London bookseller Richard Hett's gift of L'Enfant's *History of the Council of Constance* likely came from the shelves of his shop at the Bible and Crown in the Poultry, drawn from the allotment he received as one of the subscribers to the new edition.[98] Doddridge would have been accustomed to receiving works from Hett, who served as the London publisher for his and many other dissenting authors' work.[99] Charlton Palmer, a student at Doddridge's

Academy, and his mother also contributed books they had close at hand, but these were used books, having belonged to their deceased father and spouse. The copy of Spanheim's *Dissertationes de praestantia et usu numismatum antiquorum* (1671)[100] given by Palmer bore his father's 1687 ownership inscription while the Greek New Testament (1707) presented by his mother bore an effusive inscription from Doddridge.[101] Other surviving books bear evidence of prior ownership. Such is not surprising given the range of publication dates in the books donated and the importance of the second-hand book trade to the circulation of texts at this time.

The "Catalogue" testifies to London's dominance of the eighteenth-century English publishing trade, but the seventeenth-century titles on the list suggest that donors were consuming books from a more varied range of printers. More than 80 per cent of the donated titles published in the eighteenth century came from London presses, compared to slightly more than half of the titles published before that period.[102] One in four seventeenth-century books donated to the academy came from Dutch presses in Amsterdam, Leiden, Utrecht, and Gouda. There is also a strong showing by printers in Cambridge, Oxford, Geneva, and Paris. These trends speak to the availability of texts on the one hand and the specialized nature of Doddridge's project on the other. Given that the majority of donors came from hamlets and market towns outside of London, it is perhaps less surprising that their access to books was circumscribed by the control of distribution by metropolitan booksellers. Yet dissenters long had a close relationship with their Dutch cousins and consumed imported books that spoke to common theological concerns.

The books donated, perhaps not surprisingly, reflected the primary academic interests of Doddridge. Works of divinity, history, science, philosophy, and law constitute a majority of the titles. Theological works make up more than 40 per cent of the listed titles.[103] They include scholarly commentaries by Continental and English Protestant scholars, a handful of sermon collections from dissenting and Anglican divines, and a few devotional works.[104] Doctrinal literature, works intended to establish the truth of specific doctrines and evidences, made up the bulk of the donated theological materials.[105] This included works by popular dissenting theologians Edward Reynolds, John Owen, and William Bates as well as Continental scholars Witsius, Limborch, and Stegmann. History titles, which make up almost a quarter of the overall number, vary as much as divinity titles in their scope.[106] Histories cover the span of recorded time, from Millar's *The history of the Church under the Old Testament* (1730) through Schlater's *An original draught of the primitive church* (1717) and Fuller's take on the Crusades in *The historie of the holy warre* (1651); Shuckford's more comprehensive *The sacred and prophane history of the world connected* (1728) took a longer approach. The history of England could be understood historically, through Daniel's *The collection of the history of England* (unclear edition) and Fuller's *The church-history of Britain* (1655 or 1656), and contemporaneously, from opposing viewpoints, through the *Reliquiæ Baxterianæ* (1696) and Burnet's *History of his own Time* (1724–34). The same interest that had led Doddridge to pursue the donation of globes and a microscope made him receptive to scientific works by such leading scholars as William Whiston, Robert Boyle, Isaac Newton, William Cheselden, and Marcello Malphigi.[107] Classic works by jurists Selden, Pufendorf, and Grotius laid the foundation for the study of civil and natural law.[108] Topping it off were works of philosophy and logic by Watts, Oldfield, and Scheibler.[109]

Just as intriguing are the works not found among the donations. For some of the subjects at the core of Doddridge's curriculum – classical languages and literature, geography, mathematics, and belles-lettres – precious few works were donated.[110] Perhaps he had already built up a sufficient collection of such titles in the years since he finished his schooling. More likely, instruction in these works was limited to a small number of textbooks that Doddridge expected students to either purchase or copy. For some genres, such as fiction, students at Doddridge's Academy looked elsewhere for books, as Jan Fergus has shown for a slightly later period.[111] The categories that I employ in no way delimit Doddridge's use of these works for teaching purposes. Many could do double and triple duty. Works of history would have been brought into theological discussions, and many of the scientific works sought to reconcile natural and divine law.

Little explicit discussion survives explaining the rationale for what was given and why, but we can infer some basic parameters from the surviving record. In all likelihood, Doddridge played a guiding hand in directing the donations. None of the works are out of line with the types of texts found in eighteenth-century dissenting academies. Donors did not saddle Doddridge with books for which they no longer had use. Instead, what we see is Doddridge building up a library that would work with the pedagogical method of giving references, which he inherited from Jennings. The posthumous publication of his course of divinity lectures reveals the extent of this system. A "Catalogue" at the end of the 1763 volume lists 376 titles "drawn up from the Author's library," but analysis of the works referenced within the volume reveals a number almost three times that.[112] Doddridge's teaching required access to a sizable number of works; his academy's library would be a primary source for finding them.

Doddridge's ability to acquire works depended upon his connection to rural and metropolitan networks of dissent and the personal relationships that he cultivated within them. Analysis of the background and circumstances of sixty-one donors to the academy library between 1730 and 1733 reveals their membership in a number of overlapping and intersecting networks. Geography, station, education, patronage, and friendship are just a few of formal and informal factors that bound these men (and handful of women) together. As donors to a library, they found their access to print culture, in turn, shaped by these networks. As tutor, pastor, colleague, kinsman, and friend, Doddridge assiduously cultivated these relationships. While some donors elude identification today, few of the donations appear to be random. For all, dissent proved common cause. From the wealthy patron to the consort of his wife, from the venerable pastor to the youngest ministerial student, the investment in Noncomformity was personal; it extended far beyond donations to an upstart academy.

Mapping reveals that the academy's base of support came from two traditional strongholds of dissent: the Midlands and London (see Map 2.1).[113] Both regions had been hotbeds of Puritanism under James I. Many retained their sympathies through the Restoration of Charles II, and refused to conform under the 1662 Act of Uniformity. Sixty ministers in Northamptonshire, for example, found themselves ejected by the Act.[114] Seventy years later, few of this courageous generation survived, but their descendants held firm to their support of dissent. Of the fifty-six donors whose residence is known, 45 per cent came from the Midlands and another 27 per cent came from metropolitan London. Perhaps surprising is the absence of support from the southwest, the other traditional stronghold of Noncomformity. In the academy's twenty-one-year existence, more students came from the southwest than anywhere else, but in the early years, the majority of the students came either from the Midlands or London. Not all giving, of course, was altruistic. Donors often gave based on the expectation of what they would receive, whether it was the education of their sons or a new crop of ministers for their churches.[115]

Analysing donors on the basis of their station in society reveals interesting trends among Doddridge's supporters and the types of works that they gave. The "Catalogue" demonstrates the presence of donors from four different stations – nobles, ministers, laypeople, and students – within the dissenting community. Analysing the genre and average age of the titles that each gave offers some provisional insights into their intentionality. No donor explicitly recorded why she or he gave the books she or he did. While it is easy to overgeneralize, we can read motivation in the patterns that emerge among the choices made by each group.

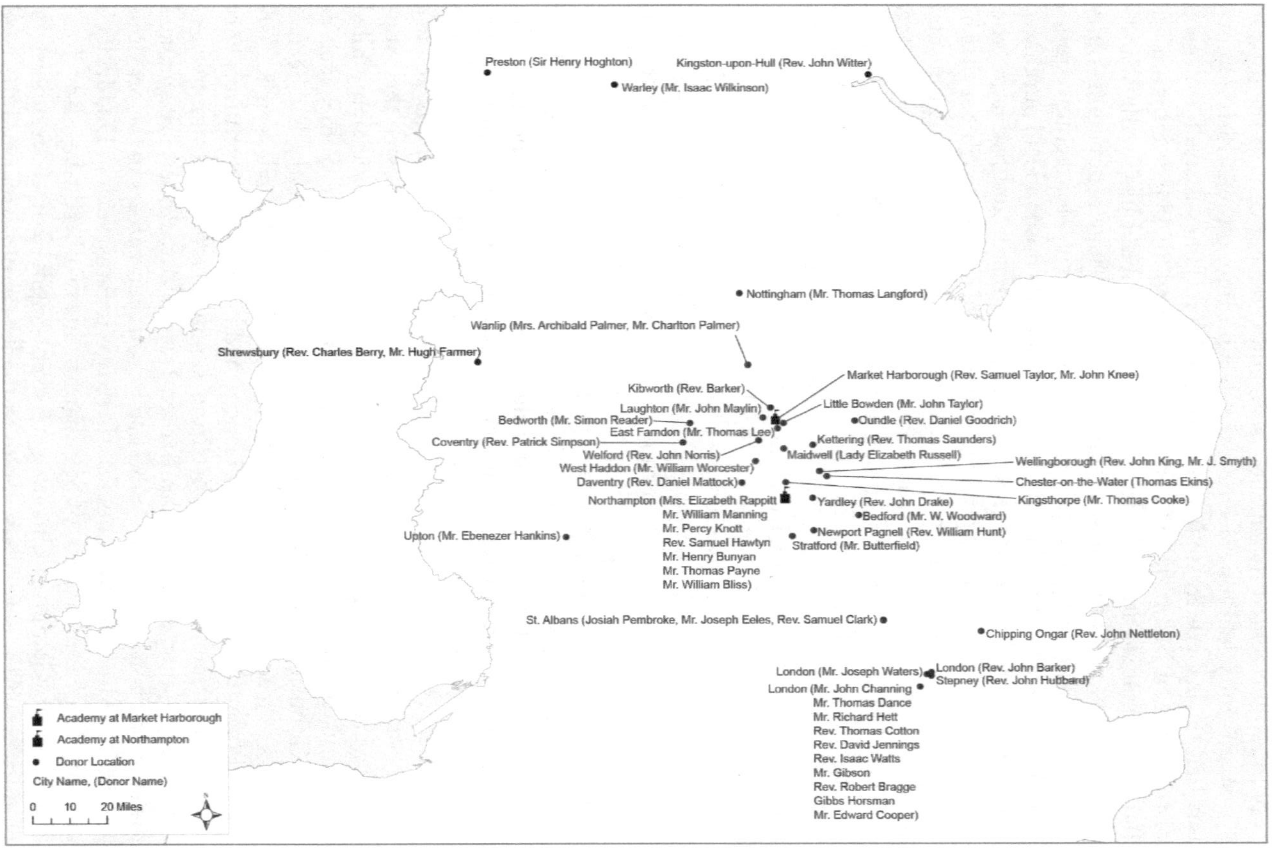

2.1 Primary Residence of Donors Listed in the "Catalogue" at Time of Donation

Nobles represented the smallest segment, three per cent of the total.[116] Nonconformity had long been on the decline among the British nobility, but Lady Elizabeth Russell, widow of the Hon. James Russell, sixth son of the Duke of Bedford, and her second husband Sir Harry Hogton, 5th Baronet, remained steadfast. In contrast to the wife of her first husband's eldest brother, Lady Russell supported Doddridge's noncomformity instead of encouraging him to conform. She also had a local connection, a Northamptonshire estate in Maidwell that her first husband had purchased with her dowry.[117] Doddridge was its frequent visitor and her active correspondent during this period. It may well have been through her that he met Sir Harry, who stood in Parliament for Preston during this time and who helped found Presbyterian chapels all over Lancashire. His nephew and heir Henry would later attend the academy.[118] While Lady Russell donated a copy of Edward Harley's recent *An Abstract of the Historical Part of the Old Testament* (1730),[119] Broughton, instead, gave an early edition of an important work by Gilbert Burnet.[120] The works of the Anglican Burnet particularly appealed to Doddridge; more works by Burnet than any other author have survived from the library.[121] For Lady Russell and Sir Harry, donating books demonstrated and confirmed the generosity and the obligations of their rank as well as their commitment to supporting dissenting education. For Doddridge, their donations were valued as much for their content as for the patronage to which they attested.

Dissenting ministers made up over a third of the donors to the academy library during this period.[122] Doddridge later struck up friendships with Anglican ministers, but at this early point, he appears to have support primarily within his own faith community. Fellow ministers, many of them Independents, in neighbouring Midlands towns, in the metropolis, and in a handful of other towns – St Albans, Shrewsbury, Hull – showed their support for his endeavour by donating a range of works. Young clergy filled the pulpits of churches in the Midlands during this time. Some, such as Daniel Goodrich of Oundle and Daniel Mattock of Daventry, had been at Jennings's Academy with Doddridge, while Thomas Saunders of Kettering and John Drake of Yardley Hastings had been at Bedworth Academy around the same time.[123] Support from London came from more venerable clergy – men such as John Barker, Isaac Watts, Robert Bragge, and the elderly Thomas Cotton – who had begun their careers in the previous generation. Ministers from outside these two regions, such as Doddridge's mentor, Rev. Samuel Clark of St Albans or his brother-in-law, Rev. John Nettleton of Chipping Ongar, were evenly split. For older ministers, Doddridge's Academy likely spoke to the legacy of dissent and the need for future propagation; for younger ministers, it was about the creation of a centre for dissenting learning that would sustain them in their isolated communities far from the metropolis.[124]

Ministers tended to donate older works of divinity or history, although some gave small collections of more specialized texts. The average publication date of a book given by a local minister was 1687 and for a London minister 1686. Rev. John Drake of nearby Yardley Hastings gave two classic works of law by John Selden[125] while Rev. Samuel Hawtyn, who often filled in for Doddridge in his absence and later opened his own academy, gave two works of science, a 1729 edition of Isaac Newton's *Principia*, and a 1726 edition of William Cheselden's *Anatomy of the Human Body*.[126] Rev. Samuel Clark gave eight titles, the largest donation by a single individual. Works given by Clark were, on average, two decades older than those given by Midlands or London ministers. The titles suggest he carefully selected works that fulfilled a cross section of what Doddridge taught. These included a combination of English and Continental works such as a commentary on Daniel by Willett;[127] histories by Godwin and Fuller;[128] a philosophical lexicon and essays by Micraelius, Oldfield, and Schriebler.[129] Whether ministers procured these works from second-hand book dealers or pulled them off their own library shelves requires further inquiry. The answer is probably a combination of both. Many ministerial donors were noted authors, but they tended not to donate their own works. For example, Isaac Watts, whose works were well represented in the collection, donated not something of his own but the first English translation of the Swiss theologian Samuel Werenfels's *A Discourse of Logomachys* (1711).

Laypeople made up an even greater percentage of the donors than ministers and tended to donate newer titles. Nearly 40 per cent of the identifiable donors sat in the pews rather than stood in the pulpit each Sabbath.[130] Among the London laity, the average publication date was 1717. The average among the Midlands laity was older at 1697, but dropping the one work significantly older than the others – a 1586 edition of Augustine's *Works* given by schoolteacher Thomas Lee of East Farndon[131] – the average date of publication rises to 1706. In both regions, gifts from the laity proved to be significantly more recent than gifts by their community's clergy. While the clergy stocked the library with classic seventeenth-century scholarly texts, the laity made sure students had access to more recent work.

The titles given by the laity were just as scholarly as those given by the ministry. In fact, one of the hallmarks of the dissenting community was its members' stomach for strong meat. Mrs Elizabeth Rappit of Northampton, companion of Doddridge's wife Mercy, gave a recent edition of Bishop Ussher's classic *Body of Divinity* while Mr Thomas Dance of London donated John Owen's *Two Discourses Concerning the Holy Spirit*.[132] Works of doctrinal and controversial divinity dominate, but the laity seemed somewhat more inclined to give works of practical divinity, such as the collected sermons of popular noncomforming and conforming clergy William Harris, Edward Reynolds, and Isaac Watts.[133] A few even donated important works that spoke to their involvement in some of the leading intellectual currents of the day. John Taylor, from the hamlet of Little Bowden in Northamptonshire, gave two recent works on astronomy by Isaac Newton's successor at Cambridge, English theologian and mathematician William Whiston.[134] The apothecary and pioneering Arabist John Channing of London presented to the library the works of Walter Moyle, the British politician, political writer, and advocate of classical republicanism.[135]

Laypeople's decisions to give newer works say as much about their access to books as to their motivations for making a donation. The laity certainly had older works in their personal collections according to Doddridge's first biographer. "He hath mentioned it as an Advantage to him," Job Orton recounted of Doddridge's time in Kibworth Harcourt after his schooling and before opening the academy, "that having but few Books of his own, he borrowed of his Congregation what Books they had in their Houses, which were chiefly the practical Works of the earlier Divines of the last Century. By reading these he was led into a serious, experimental and useful Way of Preaching."[136] Orton does not explain whether the laity held onto these classic works because they preferred them or because they could not afford or did not have access to more recent works. The laity went out of their way to present Doddridge's Academy library with *new* works.

Students and their parents made up the final segment of donors. While the "catalogue" is chronological by year of donation over its first four pages (101–4), the final page is primarily gifts by students.[137] The donations of eight students, out of the twenty-two that enrolled between 1729 and 1732, are listed, as well as the gifts of the parents of two students.[138] The group represented 16 per cent of the listed donors.[139] The practice of student donations to the library had been established early on. "Each Student at his Admission contributed a small Sum towards enlarging the Collection," a former student remembered; "The Student's Name was inserted in the Book or Books purchased with his Contribution, and it was considered as his Gift."[140] A set of "Rules relating to ye Library" drawn up in 1743 specified that students on the four-year track should pay a guinea for books at the start of their second year (or a half-guinea at the start of the second term). Dates inscribed in extant books bear out this practice, with some exceptions.[141] Students not listed as having made donations might have had sponsors who had already made donations. Doddridge acknowledged as much in a spring 1736 letter to his old friend, the minister John Barker of Hackney, although he did not discourage Barker from giving future gifts.[142]

Students might have had their names inscribed in the volumes, although it is less clear what role they had in selecting the work(s) acquired. Donations attributed to students tend, on average, to be over a generation old (1694), although some, such as the *Commentaries* (1570–83) by John Calvin given by John Maylin, were significantly older. The subjects of these works cover the major genres represented overall, suggesting that Doddridge might have told them what would have been an appropriate title to purchase, or even taken their money and purchased it on their behalf, as Jennings had done when Doddridge was a student. Even more intriguing is the suggestion in a letter from Rev. John Barker, dated 2 July 1737, about a contribution for another student that he sponsored. "I believe you have heard, by Mr. Hett [the London bookseller with whom Doddridge worked], that I have paid 10*l*. for Mr. Steffe, and promised four guineas to him, to be expended for a book, which I think may be useful in your library," Barker wrote. Working with a London bookseller as an intermediary made a great deal of sense given Hett's easier access to the books that Doddridge desired.[143] We can only speculate as to how many more students' donations might have been acquired in a similar way.

Conclusion

Philip Doddridge's experience, first as a student and later as a tutor, acquiring books in the English Midlands reminds us of the importance of print networks in the circulation of texts and the limitations of our models for understanding this process. There is a danger in placing too much emphasis on market forces in undergirding this process, especially in areas beyond the metropolis. Robert Darnton's iconic "communications circuit," for example, is predicated on economic transactions, between authors, publishers, printers, shippers, booksellers, and finally the buying public.[144] Thomas Adams and Nicolas Barker's alternative to Darnton's model, which shifts the focus from human agents to events in the life of bibliographical texts, offers an improvement by thinking more broadly in terms of distribution, reception, and survival. Yet even this model continues to privilege economic factors over social ones in the circulation of texts.[145] Like the farm families of Iowa in Pawley's essay or the home and battlefront denizens during the American Civil War in the Zborays' essay, Doddridge relied upon a variety of informal means – gifting, loaning, arranging purchases, and creating manuscript publications in order to access texts. All occurred not simply as a result of market forces within a national economy but rather because they reinforced bonds of friendship and fostered understandings of the obligation of reciprocity within the dissenting community. Networks wove together dissenters in certain places – the Midlands, London – that became nodes for dissent in a web that stretched to include those scattered across the kingdom.

Whether inquiring of friends and family what book to purchase with the windfall of a gifted guinea or how to build a library for his new academy, Philip Doddridge knew that the acquisition of texts could rarely be reduced to a simple market transaction, and instead depended upon the coordination of a complex range of social practices, networks, and institutions. While some might have found all these negotiations daunting, Doddridge appears to have relished the challenge. And his efforts paid off. By his death in 1751, he had amassed a library of a few thousand volumes, a significant achievement for the time, all the more so given his distance from the metropolis and the manner in which the collection grew. Perhaps the greatest measure of success for Doddridge was that he was no longer "entirely upon the borrowing hand," but could provide that for others.

NOTES

The author wishes to thank Isabel Rivers, Tessa Whitehouse, and David Wykes for sharing their extensive knowledge of Doddridge and his academy.

1 Philip Doddridge to Samuel Clark, [March] 1721/2, in Humphreys (1829, 67).
2 The English population increased from 5.118 million in 1696 to 6.149 million in 1756. Suarez (2009a, 3).
3 Doddridge's Northampton, the historian Lawrence Stone estimates, had a rate of male literacy comparable to Oxford at 74%. Suarez (2009a, 11).
4 Raven (2009a, 86).
5 Allan (2008, 2).
6 Suarez (2009a, 5) notes that 17% of all English residents lived in towns with 5,000 or more inhabitants; by 1750, that number had grown to 21%.
7 For more on Doddridge's background, see Isabel Rivers, "Doddridge, Philip (1702–1751)," *Oxford Dictionary of National Biography*, Oxford University

Press, 2004; online edn, Oct 2009 [http://www.oxforddnb.com/view/article/7746, accessed 9 Feb. 2013] and Deacon (1980).

8 Orton (1766, 14).

9 Samuel Clark to Philip Doddridge, 28 March 1720, 1:32–4.

10 "Protestant Dissent," Dr Williams's Centre for Dissenting Studies [http://www.english.qmul.ac.uk/drwilliams/academies/protestant.html. accessed 6 August 2014).]

11 I. Parker (1914); McLachlan (1931); Rivers and Wykes (forthcoming).

12 Orton (1766, 12–13).

13 Orton (1766, 14). G. Nuttall (1979, x).

14 Lee and McKinley (1964).

15 Doddridge to Mrs Farrington, March 1721/2, 1:76.

16 Doddridge to "Mamma" Farrington, 27 August 1722, 1:147.

17 G. Nuttall (1979, xi); and Doddridge to Clark, 6 April 1723, 1:215–18.

18 "Dissenting Education and the Legacy of John Jennings, c.1720 – c.1729," ed. Tessa Whitehouse, Dr Williams's Centre for Dissenting Studies (second edition, revised 2011), http://www.english.qmul.ac.uk/drwilliams/pubs/jennings%20legacy.html.

19 Whitehouse 2011 includes several sources for reconstructing the academic course, such as "Introduction to John Jennings's Academy" (c.1719–21), "John Jennings's Academy Timetable" (c.1720s), and Philip Doddridge's "Account of Mr Jennings's Method" (1728) in "Dissenting Education and the Legacy of John Jennings, c.1720–c.1729."

20 This is the *Tamerlane* (1702) of Nicholas Rowe not Christopher Marlowe. G. Nuttall (1979, xi). See Doddridge to "Mr Whittingham," 17 April 1722, 1:112–15.

21 John Jennings, "Notebook" (unpublished manuscript, c.1730–3), New College Library Collection (hereafter NCL), MS L.185, Dr Williams's Library, London (hereafter DWL), 18–20.

22 Patrick Gordon, *Geography anatomiz'd: or, the geographical grammar* (eight editions between 1693 and 1719).

23 Euclid, *Euclide's Elements; the whole fifteen books compendiously illustrated by Mr Isaac Barrow* (ten editions between 1655 and 1714).

24 Jean Le Clerc, *Joannis Clerici Physica, sive de rebus corporeis libri quinque* (seven editions between 1696 and 1708).

25 Thomas Goodwin, *Moses and Aaron* (fourteen editions between 1625 and 1685); Peter, Lord King, *An enquiry into the constitution, discipline, unity & worship of the primitive church* (seven editions between 1691 and 1719); Louis Ellies Du Pin, *A new ecclesiastical history* (multiple editions); and Friedrich Spanheim, *Selectiorum de religione controversiarum, etiam cum Graecis et Orientalibus, et cum Judaeis* (multiple editions).

26 Includes Bythner's *Hebrew Grammar*, a Hebrew Bible, a French New Testament, a Latin dictionary, and a Greek Testament.

27 Works clearly related to the academic course included the *Arithmetica* and the *Miscellaneorum Pars secunda*, while works for the theological course included *Anatomia*, *Antiquitates Hebraeorum*, *Lectiones Criticae*, *Pneumatologia & Ethica*, and *Theologia*.

28 French grammar, dictionary, and François Fénelon's *Les aventures de Télémaque* (originally published 1699), which students read in their first year.

29 Samuel Pufendorf, *An introduction to the history of the principal kingdoms and states of Europe* (eight editions between 1695 and 1719); J. Crull, *A supplement to Mr. Samuel Puffendorf's Introduction to the history of Europe* (two editions); and possibly, Laurence Echard, *The history of England* (three editions between 1707 and 1720).

30 William Sclater, *An original draught of the primitive church* (London, 1717).

31 Hugo Grotius, *De Jure Belli ac Pacis Libri Tres* (first published in Amsterdam in 1625) and Samuel Pufendorf, *Of the law of nature and nations* (three English editions between 1681 and 1717).

32 Texts by classical authors would have been broadly available, so it's difficult to pinpoint specific editions. Latin authors included Caeser (*Commentaries*), Salust, Terence, Cicero (*Orations* and *de Oratore*), Horace, Ovid, Juvenal, Virgil, and Lucan.

33 Greek authors included Homer and *Poetæ minores Græci* (Cambridge and later London, 1712 – and nine previous editions).

34 The most recent editions of each were Victorinus Bythner, *Lyra prophetica Davidis Regis; sive Analysis critico-practica Psalmorum* (Londini, [1679]); Franco Burgersdijck, *Institutionum logicarum libri duo* (Cantabrigiæ, [1680]); and *The confession of faith, and the larger and shorter catechisms first agreed upon by the Assembly of Divines at Westminster* (Edinburgh, 1697).

35 For the main categories of religious books in the eighteenth century, see Rivers (2009).

36 Philip Doddridge to John Nettleton, 27 February 1722/3, 1:198–9.

37 For more on Jennings's pedagogy, see Rivers (2003, especially 9–10).

38 108/174 of the books have positive marks. 24% of the titles listed are clearly negatives (41/174) while the remaining titles have no marking at all. See Doddridge, "THEOLOGIA. sive Pneumatologiae & Ethica Pars IIa" (unpublished manuscript, c.1718–21), NCL, MS 28.117, DWL.

39 "the references are generally long, and consequently that, though we have no evening lecture, still we have less time for our private studies than we ever had in any of our former half years." Doddridge to Clark, 3 January 1721/2, 1:35.

40 Compare Doddridge to Clark, 13 December 1721, 1:41–2 with Doddridge to Clark, [March] 1722, 1:68.
41 Doddridge to Clark, 3 January 1721/2, 1:35, 36.
42 Doddridge to Clark, 1 December 1722, 1:175.
43 Raven (2009b, 294); Suarez (2009b, 39–65).
44 On the provincial book trade, see Feather (1985) and Bell and Hinks (2009, 335–51).
45 Doddridge to Elizabeth Nettleton, 30 July 1722, 1:139–43.
46 Doddridge to Clark, 28 January 1722/3, 1:189, mentions a gown for £1 14s 2p. This was apparently a clerical gown that Doddridge needed following his ordination.
47 Doddridge to Clark, 28 January 1722/3, 1:189.
48 Samuel Clark would have known John Clark well, as the latter published a volume for him in 1720. See Samuel Clark, *A Collection of the Promises of Scripture under their Proper Heads* (London, 1720).
49 King, *An Enquiry into the constitution, discipline, unity and worship, of the primitive church* (London, 1713). Doddridge's copy (with manuscript notes) survives in NCL, 3005.F.16, DWL.
50 Unclear what this text is.
51 Doddridge to Clark, 3 January 1721/2, 1:34–5.
52 Spanheim, *Selectiorum de religione controversiarum* (four editions between 1697 and 1719).
53 Du Pin, *A new ecclesiastical history.* Multiple editions of each volume were published between 1695 and 1703. It is unclear which ones Doddridge owned.
54 Doddridge to Clark, 3 January 1721/2, 1:35.
55 Doddridge to Clark, 28 January 1722/3, 1:189.
56 Dissenting Academies Online: Database and Encyclopedia, Dr Williams's Centre for Dissenting Studies, http://dissacad.english.qmul.ac.uk/ ID no. 644, accessed 19 January 2013.
57 "Mr. Cope left us this morning, and I think there were no tears shed on our side. If however his masterly sense and ready wit had been softened by a little more humanity and good nature, he would have been beloved as much as he is admired," Doddridge wrote David Some Jr on 24 December 1722, 1:208.
58 John Scott, *The Christian life, from its beginning, to its consummation in glory* (London, 1681). Doddridge to Clark, [March] 1721/2, 1:60.
59 Humphrey Prideaux, *The Old and New Testament connected in the history of the Jews and neighbouring nations* (London, [1716–18]).
60 Doddridge to Clark, [March] 1721/2, 1:67.
61 Doddridge to Hughes, [21 December] 1721, 1:59.
62 Doddridge to Clark, [March] 1721/2, 1:60.

63 Doddridge to Clark, [March] 1721/2, 1:67.
64 Doddridge to Clark, [March] 1721/2, 1:67.
65 He also promised to read from it to his sister next time he was at Hampstead. Doddridge to Elizabeth Nettleton, [February] 1721/2, 1:47.
66 Doddridge to Nettleton, 30 July 1722, 1:142–3.
67 Doddridge to Nettleton, 4 June 1723, 1:241.
68 Doddridge to John Nettleton [February 1721/2], 1:44. Doddridge grew to respect (and understand) the works of schoolmaster Thomas Godwin (1586/7–1642) and leading Independent minister John Owne (1616–83). He included both in the academy's curriculum and library.
69 Doddridge to Clark [March 1721/2], 1:70.
70 To whom Doddridge wrote the letter is a matter of some dispute. See Tessa Whitehouse, "An Introduction to Philip Doddridge's 'Account of Mr Jennings's Method'," in "Dissenting Education and the Legacy of John Jennings, c.1720 – c.1729," ed. Tessa Whitehouse, Dr Williams's Centre for Dissenting Studies (second edition, revised 2011), http://www.english.qmul.ac.uk/drwilliams/pubs/jennings%20legacy.html.
71 "Philip Doddridge's 'An Account of Mr Jennings's Method'," in "Dissenting Education and the Legacy of John Jennings, c.1720 – c.1729," ed. Tessa Whitehouse, Dr Williams's Centre for Dissenting Studies (second edition, revised 2011), http://www.english.qmul.ac.uk/drwilliams/pubs/jennings%20legacy.html, 31.
72 Surviving examples at DWL include a Greek Bible published at Frankfurt in 1597, Sprat's *History of the Royal-Society* (1667); Polydore Vergil's *De inventoribus rerum libri vii* (Amsterdam, 1671), "another Latin work on Hebrew antiquities," and William Whiston's *Primitive Christianity Revived* (1711). See G. Nuttall (1977, 34).
73 Allan (2008, 212). The standard texts on manuscript publication in this period include Beal (1998) and Love (1993).
74 McKenzie (1986, 20). Quoted in Chartier (1994, 5).
75 Doddridge to Clark, 13 December 1721, 1:41. This would have been an abridgment of a work by Samuel Jones, Tutor at the Tewksbury Academy. Mark Burden, *A Biographical Dictionary of Tutors at the Dissenters' Private Academies, 1660–1729* (Dr Williams's Centre for Dissenting Studies, 2013), 320–9.
76 Jennings, *Logica In Usum Juventutis Academicae* (Northampton, 1721). See Doddridge to Clark, 13 December 1721, 1:40 for his discussion of the texts within. Doddridge's copy survives in NCL, 3005.D.16(a), DWL.
77 *Miscellanea in Usum Juventutis Academicae* Part I (Northampton, 1721). Doddridge's copy also survives in NCL, 3005.D.18, DWL.
78 NCL, 3003.A.13, DWL.

79 Doddridge to Hankins, 10 May 1731, 3:79.

80 Ibid.

81 The library of Mile End Academy (1754–69), for example, grew from the donations of ministerial collections assembled by Richard Rawlin, John Guyse, and Thomas Hall. See K. Roberts (forthcoming).

82 Philip Doddridge, "A Catalogue of Books given to the Academical Library with the Names of the Donors," in John Jennings, "Notebook" (unpublished manuscript, c.1730–3), NCL, MS L.185, DWL.

83 Doddridge to Samuel Clark, April 1728, 2:449–50. See also Doddridge to Lady Russell, 9 April 1728, 2:453.

84 "I am sensible of my deficiency in every branch of learning, which makes me the readier to enter on a scheme which may probably be for my own improvement," he wrote to Samuel Clark, "and I think Mr Jenning's lectures and method so good, that I cannot but hope it will be an advantage to my companion to go over them, though it be with the assistance of so poor a guide." Doddridge to Clark, April 1728, 2:449–50.

85 Doddridge to Samuel Clark, 7 August 1729, 2:487 mentions that he has had the students five weeks.

86 Humphreys (1829, 2:483). See also Rivers (2003, 12). Job Orton recorded four students in Doddridge's first class. See 5:547–552 for a list of all of Doddridge's students.

87 Greenall (1979, chapter 8).

88 Clark to Doddridge, 21 November 1729, 2:494–5.

89 On opposition to Doddridge's relocation, see Orton (1766, 55–9); G. Nuttall (1979, xii).

90 Humphreys (1829, 3:2–5).

91 I am grateful to David Wykes (2002) for sharing his work on Doddridge's students.

92 Many surviving books at DWL bear his inscription, date of purchase, and price paid, attesting to his ongoing acquisition of works.

93 These bound volumes have not yet systematically analysed or included in my calculations. At least three survive today in the New College Library Collection at Dr Williams's Library, London. Each is inscribed with the name of the donor, Josiah Pembroke, Esq., and the year of donation, 1731. 3007.F.22 contains 6 tracts dating from 1712 to 1716; 3007.F.9 contains 8 tracts; 3007.E.15 contains 8 tracts all from 1710.

94 The catalogues in the VLS are the 1838 Shelf List from Coward College (1833–50), NCL, MS L82, DWL and the 1977 shelfmark catalogue for the Doddridge books in New College, London (1850–1977). Catalogues not in the VLS are the c.1800? author catalogue from John Horsey's Academy, Northampton (1789–98), NCL,

MS L89, DWL, and the c.1822 author catalogue and shelflist from Wymondley College (1799–1833), NCL, MS L73, DWL.

95 86 out of 104 titles.

96 40 out of 104 titles.

97 Dissenting Academies Online: Virtual Library System, ed. R. Dixon and K. Roberts (http://vls.english.qmul.ac.uk/cgi-bin/koha/opac-detail.pl?biblionumber=24024, accessed on 23 December 2012) and Dissenting Academies Online: Virtual Library System, ed. R. Dixon and K. Roberts (http://vls.english.qmul.ac.uk/cgi-bin/koha/opac-detail.pl?biblionumber=6355, accessed on 23 December 2012).

98 Jacques L'Enfant, *The History of the Council of Constance* (London, [1730]).

99 The ESTC lists nineteen different printings undertaken by Hett (170?–66) of Doddridge's work. See G. Nuttall (1979, 74, 87, 93, 95, 125, 189, and 392). Clark and Hett were at the Bible and Three Crowns from 1726 to 1737. See *London Topographical Record* (1907, 4:66). See brief biography at http://thesaurus.cerl.org/record/cnp00027853.

100 Dissenting Academies Online: Virtual Library System, ed. R. Dixon and K. Roberts (http://vls.english.qmul.ac.uk/cgi-bin/koha/opac-detail.pl?biblionumber=7439, accessed on 23 December 2012).

101 Dissenting Academies Online: Virtual Library System, ed. R. Dixon and K. Roberts (http://vls.english.qmul.ac.uk/cgi-bin/koha/opac-detail.pl?biblionumber=4046, accessed on 23 December 2012). See NCL, 3003.C.8, DWL.

102 44 out of 54 eighteenth-century titles came from London presses, compared to 25 out of 45 seventeenth-century titles.

103 43 out of 104 titles.

104 Commentaries – (Harley), Willet, Roberts, Lightfoot, Calvin, Pareus, Fowler; Devotional works – Drelincourt on Death, Pascal's thoughts, Bates's *Spiritual Perfection*, Beveredge's *Private Thoughts*; and sermons – Gastrell, Watts, Goodwin, Harris, Boyse.

105 Rivers (1982, 127).

106 24 out of 104 titles.

107 15 out of 104 titles.

108 5 out of 104 titles.

109 6 out of 104 titles.

110 Two classical works (Suetonious and Juvenal) and a Latin lexicon; Montfaucon's *Travels* (1712); and Rapin's *Works* (1706).

111 Fergus (2006, 189–93).

112 The editor goes on to note that "many of the books referred to were wanting, or the editions different," but he hoped the reader would be able

to find the passage anyway. See "A Catalogue of the Authors mentioned in this Work, where the Pages only are referred to; with the Editions to which the References are made, and the Number of Pages in the Volume," in Philip Doddridge, *A course of lectures on the principal subjects in pneumatology, ethics, and divinity: with references to the most considerable authors on each subject* (London, [1763]), [597–602]. I am grateful to Robert Strivens for sharing his painstaking work reconstructing the references in the text with me.

113 By the Midlands, I mean students from Northamptonshire, Leicestershire, and Warwickshire.

114 Coleman (1853, Introduction).

115 Wykes (2002, 5–6).

116 2 out of 61 donors.

117 Cruickshanks, Handley, and Hayton (2002, 5:322).

118 Stanford (1881, 27–2)8. On Houghton, see http://www.historyofparliamentonline.org/volume/1715-1754/member/hoghton-sir-henry-1679-1768. Nephew Henry enrolled in 1746. See http://dissacad.english.qmul.ac.uk/new_dissacad/phpfiles/sample1.php?parameter=personretrieve&alpha=3546.

119 Edward Harley, *An abstract of the historical part of the Old Testament* (London, [1730]).

120 Gilbert Burnet, *History of the reformation of the Church of England …* (London, [1681]).

121 Geoffrey Nuttall counted 11 surviving works by Gilbert Burnet from Doddridge's library, the most of any author. See G. Nuttall (1977, 34).

122 21 out of 61 donors.

123 See Dissenting Academies Online: Database and Encyclopedia (http://dissacad.english.qmul.ac.uk/new_dissacad/phpfiles/) and *The Surman Index Online* (http://surman.english.qmul.ac.uk/) for more information on their education.

124 There is also evidence of the borrowing of books by local dissenting ministers.

125 John Selden, *V. cl. Joannis Seldeni De synedriis & praefecturis juridicis veterum Ebraeorum libri tres* (Amstelaedami, 1679) and John Selden, *Joannis Seldeni De jure naturali et gentium* (Argentorati, [1665]). For more on Drake, see *Surman Index Online* 7842.

126 William Cheselden, *The anatomy of the human body* (London, [1726]) and Isaac Newton, *The mathematical principles of natural philosophy …* In two volumes. (London, [1729]). For more on Hawtyn, see *Surman Index Online* 13712.

127 Andrew Willet, *Hexapla in Danielem* ([Cambridge], 1610).

128 Thomas Fuller, *The historie of the holy warre* ([Cambridge], 1651) and Thomas Goodwin, *Romanæ historiæ anthologia recognita et aucta* (London, 1658).

129 Johann Micraelius, *Lexicon philosophicum terminorum philosophis usitatorum* (edition unclear); Joshua Oldfield, *An essay towards the improvement of reason; in the pursuit of learning, and conduct of life* (London, [1707]); and Christoph Scheibler, *Philosophia compendiosa* (Oxoniæ, 1671).
130 24 out of 61 donors.
131 Augustine, *Opera* (Paris, 1586). Lee gave two out of the original ten volumes from this work.
132 James Ussher, *A body of divinity: or, the sum and substance of Christian religion* (London, 1702) and John Owen, *Two discourses concerning the Holy Spirit, and His work* (London, 1693).
133 A Mr Butterfield of Old Stratford, Northamptonshire, donated William Harris's *Practical discourses on the principal representations of the Messiah throughout the Old Testament* (London, [1724]); Gilbert Horseman, a leading London lawyer, gave *The works of the Right Reverend Father in God, Edward Reynolds, D.D.* ([London] either 1678 or 1679); and Henry Bunyan, a deacon of Doddridge's Castle Hill Church, gave Isaac Watts's three-volume *Sermons on various subjects* (London, 1729).
134 William Whiston, *Prælectiones astronomicæ Cantabrigiæ in Scholis publicis habitæ* (Cantabrigiæ, 1707) and *Astronomical principles of religion, natural and reveal'd* (London, 1725).
135 Walter Moyle, *The works of Walter Moyle Esq; none of which were ever before publish'd* (London, [1726]) and Anthony Hammond, *The whole works of Walter Moyle, Esq; that were published by himself* (London, [1727]). For more on Channing, see Savage-Smith (1988, 63–80).
136 Orton (1766, 26–7).
137 Determined by matching inscriptions in surviving books with the list. They might have been recorded separately or entered at a later time, as this is the only place where the chronology breaks down. Donated works from Simon Reader, which are dated 1733 in Doddridge's inscription, are listed before donated works from Hugo Farmer, which are dated 1731.
138 For a complete list of the 201 students who enrolled at Doddridge's Academy between 1729 and 1750, see Humphreys (1829, 5:546552).
139 10 out of 61 donors.
140 Orton (1766, 98–9).
141 Surviving books given by Hugh Farmer are dated 1731, the year he entered the academy, rather than his second year in 1732. See NCL, 3007.A.11 and 3007.E.1, DWL.
142 "Your generous present shall excuse this gentleman from any contribution to the library, which I might otherwise have expected," Doddridge wrote; "but if, some time hence, he think fit to take a course of lectures

in experimental philosophy, I question not but that you would be willing that he should contribute at least half a guinea towards the expense of the apparatus, to which all, but those on the funds, give a guinea each." Doddridge to John Barker (c.1736), 3:206–7.

143 John Barker to Doddridge, 2 July 1737, 3:250.

144 Darnton (1982).

145 Adams and Barker (1993, 5–43). For Darnton's reflections on Adams and Barker's model, see Darnton (2007).

3 The Eighteenth- and Early Nineteenth-Century Evolution of Indian Print Culture and Knowledge Networks in Calcutta and Madras

KENNETH R. HALL

Today academic discourse uses the term "Orientalism" to refer to patronizing Western colonial and post-colonial attitudes towards Middle Eastern, Asian, and North African societies. Edward Said's 1970s critique argued that Western imperialists from the eighteenth century validated their implementation of authority over Asian populations by viewing them as static and undeveloped. Apologists for colonial rule, Said claimed, believed that Oriental cultures could be studied and depicted, with the intention of reproducing and/or upgrading them in the Western image. Implicit in this self-justified fabrication was the idea that Western societies were more developed, rational, flexible, and ultimately superior to those of the non-West.[1] In Said's view purposeful colonial and post-colonial-era Western scholarship and literary and artistic representations provided a necessary transition between knowledge and power that emphasized the superiority of Western knowledge over non-Western, which sustained Western hegemony.[2]

Western and non-Western scholars inspired by Said have assessed early British governmental publication initiatives in India, particularly those emanating from the three initial regional centres of colonial authority: Calcutta, Madras, and Bombay.[3] The most recent have re-evaluated colonial-era Western scholars' previous approaches to corporate levels of Indian literacy, which were often based in the foundational preconception that British imperial authority in India had been marked by progressive innovation.[4] By the late nineteenth century, colonial-era Western scholars shared the preconception that deficiencies in contemporary Indian literacy resulted from India's traditional cultural insularity. By contrast, earlier scholarship debated whether this was the case, notably when English scholars demonstrated that India's Sanskrit linguistic heritage was comparable to that of the Western classical languages (e.g., Greek, Latin, and Persian) and embraced Indian scholars as their equals. This study distinguishes between the earliest era of East India Company authority in India, in contrast to direct British colonial rule following the 1857 Sepoy Mutiny, with focus on the significant print culture consequences of the early East India Company mandate that newly arrived Company administrators had to achieve fluency in India's regional languages prior to assuming their postings.

Company colleges in its coastal Calcutta, Madras, and Bombay urban centres initially trained newly landed British administrators in the Hindi and Urdu languages, which they regarded as the legacies of prior Mughal-era Islamic authority in North India. The English conceived of themselves as the heirs to the Mughal throne, which dictated that they pursue the development of an India-based print culture to sustain the Company's imperial administration and its language training needs. When it soon became clear that Hindi was exclusively a North Indian language and Urdu was substantially spoken by the former Mughal Muslim elite, the Company transitioned their language study programs to provide their English colonial administrators with functional fluency in a variety of critical regional languages, which allowed them to more effectively assess and govern Indian society in partnership with their regional civil service Indian subordinates. This also dictated that the Company administration finance publications of regional language and culture textbooks that were produced by Indian print shops. Increasing popular regional language literacy under British rule created a marketplace for a rapidly expansive Indian book industry in the late eighteenth and early nineteenth centuries. This newly inclusive print culture not only sustained English rule, but was foundational to societal integration. But the secular book trade reinforced regional rather than national identities, with long-term implications. That the era of British Company rule was ultimately foundational to English hegemony in India but was also the grounding for the assimilation of South Asians into regional rather than a national consensus complicates retrospective application of the Orientalist critique.

This study finds that Warren Hastings's post-1773 implementation of English colonial authority, notably his indigenous language and publication initiatives that sustained an India-based hybrid print culture, was more complex and subtle than a straightforward application of British imperial authority. Hastings did not demand absolute Indian submission to English administration, exclusive English language use in governmental transactions, or maximum taxation payments from the Company's South Asian subjects.[5] This more authoritarian approach emerged only following the then British government's direct takeover of India from the Company following the 1857 Sepoy uprising. The implementation of new, more direct, and exclusionist colonial policies and administration after that event (which was reflected in the transitional print culture of that time) was in part consistent with recent Orientalist scholastic characterizations relative to an emerging indigenous Indian "urban" Westernized elite. In contrast, recent revisionist scholars have countered by documenting the surge in popular regional language literary publications consequent to the implementation of British Company colonial authority in the late eighteenth century. Regional vernacular press publications retained long-standing regional characterizations consistent with public literary recitations, dramatic and dance performances, and religious rituals and festivals that countered broadly based societal Westernization.

Recent revisionist scholarship has redefined traditional South Asian literacy as being more than the transmission of knowledge in print, and instead embraces the notion that knowledge of the written word in traditional religious and secular texts did not necessarily translate into readership, but that knowledge transfers based in traditional textual transmission in oral recitations or in dramatic and dance rituals allowed illiterate and semi-literate audiences to share written texts in communal reading sessions, in religious ceremonies, and in dramatic and musical performances. Thus scholars now see regional print cultures in India emerging from rich pre-print literary traditions, written and also oral. Long-standing oral renditions of texts continued in both formal and informal settings, as the initial printed texts were widely sung, read, and performed, adding to the written text bodily languages, musical traditions, and popular practices that connected printed and the pre-printed literary forms. Against the Western notion that literary consumption was done through private reading, in India there is still a range of performing arenas from households to wider public spaces that connect performance and textual matter in ways that allow variable consumption of printed texts. Thus this continuity of the oral and pre-print traditions prevents the printed text from being fixed, as multiple reading and consumptive practices encourage personal appropriations that still shape India's popular print marketplace.[6]

In sum, this is a comparative study of the distinctive characteristics of the Calcutta and Madras Schools of Orientalism, as these regional scholastic institutions of mixed Indian and British membership related to and were embedded in the development of regional Indian print culture. The publication of books, training manuals, and other materials served as a vital arena of intercultural exchange in early English colonial India. Documentation of India's emergent "national" and "regional" print cultures provides a vantage point from which to view the evolving relationships between colonized and colonizer, focused on the transitional dynamics of the relationship between the British and Indian populations centred in the expansive cosmopolitan cities of Calcutta and Madras in the late eighteenth and early nineteenth centuries. At the time, both urban centres were modest-sized colonial outposts rather than the metropolitan settings they are today. The differences and similarities of English East India Company policies in northeast and southern India resulted in distinctive regional print culture agencies and knowledge networks that remain a factor in contemporary India.

The hybrid print culture that took shape in India during the period of Company authority underscores a key point of this volume: colonial and other supposedly peripheral settings were sites of locally initiated creativity, inclusive of modifications of existing textual communities, and not just of passive reception. Other essays contained here, most notably Lara Putnam's analysis of early twentieth-century Caribbean print circuits, emphasize the ways in which local residents of seemingly subordinate places subject to metropolitan authority nonetheless played active roles in the creation of meaning and knowledge. That was clearly the case in early colonial India, where the collaborative character of publishing provided opportunity for indigenous populations and their pre-existing communal literary expressions to shape an emerging print culture in a manner that belies simplistic formulations of Orientalism.

I. Early English East India Company Era Print Culture

The founding head of the English East India Company authority in 1773, Warren Hastings, implemented company policies sympathetic to local languages and cultures. Resulting Company-sponsored language studies, dictionaries, text translations, and historical scholarship were the end products of functional partnerships between English and South Asians. In 1776, Hastings published the *Code of Gentoo Laws* in India, which he solicited from the English philologist Nathaniel Brassey Halhed (1751–1830), a Company employee who was based in India. Halhed was asked to translate into English the Hindu legal code, so that the English Company authorities could better understand native laws. The work served to correct Western misinterpretations of Hindu law, and to show that it was fully adequate as the most appropriate legal system for local application, as opposed to Western-style laws, in the multicultural and diversely religious region of Bengal. In preparation, Halhed sought advice from experienced native lawyers, who provided verifications of both the Persian and Urdu versions and their Sanskrit originals, and the services of the local *pundit* (traditional religious scholar) Panchanana Karmakara, also a blacksmith and descendant of a long line of Indian calligraphers and metallurgists, who crafted and supervised the necessary English and Indian script print typefaces.[7] Accompanied by the translator's preface and a glossary, this extensive code remains of relevance to scholars of Indian law and history to this day.

Hastings solicited and published other early Company-printed works in both English and vernacular languages to negate the necessity of direct (and expensive) English colonial rule in India. Hastings reasoned that though English laws and governmental policies were more sophisticated and efficient than India's native laws and practices, English laws and government that derived from English history and culture were not applicable to India. Instead, in agreement with Hastings that a society's foundational sense of its own history was vital, early Company-sponsored colonial scholars found that Indian vernacular sources provided a solid base from which English and Indian historians could mutually discern India's historical past, with the intent of confirming rather than demeaning India's own notable history. In turn, Hastings and other early English East Indian Company administrators did not view India as a savage state, but determined that Indian laws, whether in written or oral documentation, were frequently more appropriate to regional enforcements and adjudications, fearing that to do otherwise would alienate Indians with significant and long-term negative consequences.[8]

Printing in India had its origin in the sixteenth century, soon after the arrival of Portuguese trade ships. The locations of the earliest printing presses coincided with that era's prominent ports of trade, the initial Portuguese and Dutch trade bases at the west coast ports of Goa and Cochin (Kochi) that were also the centres of early Christian missionary activities. The earliest recorded missionary press was at Cochin (1579), following designation by Pope Paul IV as the centre of the Catholic diocese of Cochin in 1557.

Subsequent transition to English East India Company rule in the late eighteenth century brought the transformation of India's print culture from the initial Western evangelist Indian language translations of Bibles and worship materials at the early mission presses. New Company, college, and private presses published textbooks, English-language translations of classical Indian texts, and regional language grammars and dictionaries

Early Indian Print Culture

- -1579 Printing at Cochin
- -1712 The Tranquebor Press
- -1751 Tranquebor Printing & Publishing House, Madras
- -1761 Vepery SPCK Press
- -1795 Serampore Missionaries
- -1809 Punjabi Press, Ludhiana
- -1817 American Mission Press, Bombay
- -1820 Native School and School and School Book Committee, Bombay
- -1820 Bihar Lithography, Patna
- -1822 Printing of 'Pamcopa Khyana' in Marathi at Courier Press, Bombay
- -1825-26 Printing in Gujarathi, Industani Parsi
- -1829 Fr. Benjamin Bailey's first printing press at Kottayam
- -1830 Captain George Jervis Lithographic Press at Poona
- -1830 Greenway family press at Kanpur (Lithographic Hindi Work)
- -1830 Lithography Press, Madreas Presidency
- -1831 Fort. St. George Press and College, Madras
- -1799-1833 Sarafoji Maharaja Press in Tanjore
- -1838 Gurumukhi Grammar printed at Punjabi Press
- -1841 Bahu Mahajan Litho Press to print "Prabhakar" a Marathi Weekly
- -1843 "Upadesha Chandrika" monthly, edited by Pandit Movabhat Dandekar, printed at Mahajan Press
- -1844-48 The Delhi Oordoo Ukbar, Delhi
- -1849 Benaras Ukbar Press, Benaras-Benaras Ukbar printed in Nagari script
- -1850 "Dhumaketu" Weekly at Mahajan Press
- -1851 English-Punjabi Dictionary printed at Punjabi Press
- -1861 Times of India press, Bombay

BIBLICAL AND CHURCH PUBLICATIONS

CIVIL ADMINISTRATION, EDUCATIONAL, AND LEGAL PUBLICATIONS

DICTIONARIES/GRAMMARS
TRANSLATIONS OF FOLKLORE AND INDIAN TEXTS
DHARMASASTRA, QURANIC, AND OTHER CODES OF LAW
NOVELS
NEWSPAPERS

3.1 Early Indian Print Culture

authored by English and Indian scholars to train newly arrived English civil servants at the Company's rapidly developing Calcutta, Madras, and Bombay urban centres. Foundational and secondary Orientalist publications on Indian history, culture, religion, language, law, government administration, and the Indian natural realm resulted from tripartite partnerships among missionaries, English and Indian College instructors, and Company-supported Asiatic Societies that subsidized the scholarship of their multilingual European and Indian members (see fig. 3.1).

II. The Initiation of Calcutta-Centred Print Culture

The victory of the English East India Company troops under Robert Clive against the French and their Indian allies at Plassey in 1757 generated a critical point of transition in the history of printing in India.

After 1773, with Parliamentary backing, Warren Hastings, the newly appointed Governor-General of Bengal (1773–85), implemented East India Company authority over India based in three coastal urban centres: Calcutta, Madras, and Bombay. In doing so he sustained administrative British elite competent in Indian languages who could work within traditional Indian institutions and traditions, a mix of direct rule and "princely states." As previously noted, Hastings intended from the beginning to create foundational social and intellectual exchanges between English administrators and locals based in a functional British-Indian bipartisanship. Under the Regulating Act of 1773 that authorized parliamentary control over the East Indian Company's administration of India, Hastings built a new governmental system upon the Company's previous contacts and partnerships with Mughal rulers and their subordinates in North India. As the old political networking had been based on the use of the Persian and the North Indian Persian-derivative Hindustani (Urdu) languages, Hastings dictated that these be the critical initial vernacular of Company diplomacy, administration, and courts of law (rather than English) in its bilingual contacts with South Asians. But he also determined that his most immediate need was to secure translations of the variety of Hindu and Muslim laws into English as critical references for new English administrators, and the translation of English regulations into local languages to make them accessible to long-standing literate South Asians as the foundation for future English-Indian partnerships.[9]

Hastings's initiatives were initially centred in the Company's administrative core at Calcutta, Bengal, where newly arriving Company administrators were expected to learn Persian and Urdu. But it became immediately clear to Calcutta-based Company administrators that the northeast regional Bengali language was more commonly spoken than North Indian Persian and Urdu (the favoured languages of Mughal rule), and, with significant consequence, that contemporary Bengali derived from the classical Indian Sanskrit language rather than Persian. Soon Company administrators were initially trained in classical Sanskrit, which served as the language base for their subsequent instruction in Bengali and other critical North Indian regional languages.

As previously noted, in 1776 the East India Company employee Nathaniel Halhed (1751–1830) published *A Code of Gentoo Laws*, based on a Persian-language version of an enduring Sanskrit original text, which was printed on the first Bengal press that he had set up in Hugli (Hooghly) north of Calcutta, formerly the centre of Portuguese and Dutch trade in the lower Ganges Delta region. While this Indian press edition was initially provided to India-based administrators, a private luxury edition was subsequently printed in London for East India Company promotional distribution there. Halhed followed in 1778 with a *Grammar of Bengali Language* text that he printed in partnership with the Bengali S. K. De. This book was dedicated to extracting the "pure" language from previous Muslim and Portuguese influences, and thus initiated what would become known historically as "British Orientalism" and the "Bengal Renaissance," which anticipated a renewal rather than a Westernization of pre-Muslim Indian civilization.[10] Halhed's book was also notable for its assertion that Sanskrit was philologically connected with Persian, Arabic, Greek, and Latin, thus elevating "original" Indian society and culture to the ranks of a Western "classical civilization" prior to the overlay of regional "Western" Muslim authority in India. The *London Critical Review* characterized the book in its September 1777 publication:

> This is a most sublime performance ... we are persuaded that even this enlightened quarter of the globe cannot boast anything which soars so completely above the narrow, vulgar sphere of prejudice and priestcraft. The most amiable part of modern philosophy is hardly upon a level with the extensive charity, the comprehensive benevolence, of a few rude untutored Hindoo Bramins ... Mr. Halhed has rendered more real service to this country, to the world in general, by this performance, than ever flowed from all the wealth of all the nabobs by whom the country of these poor people has been plundered ... Wealth is not the only, nor the most valuable commodity, which Britain might import from India.[11]

Following Hastings's lead, subsequent Company heads commissioned new documents of government in Oriental script necessary to support Company rule, which required the services of a new print industry headquarterd in the Company's administrative centre at Calcutta. Charles Wilkins, a nephew of the English printer Robert B. Wray, assumed the task, and introduced a set of Bengali language types in 1778. Nathaniel Halhed's *Grammar* was the first printed book in an Indian vernacular (Bengali) using the Bengali types designed and produced by Wilkins and Bengali Panchanan Karmakar at James Augustus Hicky's privately owned press – which would subsequently become the Honourable Company Press. In 1780, the former debtor's prison inmate Hicky published the first English-language newspaper in India, the weekly *Hicky's Bengal Gazette*, which inspired Indians to publish newspapers of their own (fig. 3.2). Hicky's paper survived until the 1830s, when it was displaced by *The Englishman*,

HICKY'S
BENGAL GAZETTE;
OR THE ORIGINAL
Calcutta General Advertiser.

3.2 *Hicky's Bengal Gazette*

published in Calcutta from 1811 to 1818, which is today known as *The Statesman*. Each of these publications served an emerging Calcutta-based Indian middle class, in contrast to the regional vernacular Indian publications that served the wider traditionalist Indian literate public.

Hicky's paper introduced the early news style of Indian newspapers, filled with dramatic portrayals of scandal, rumour, and slander, that were consistent with traditional popular drama, but also offering a voice against corruption, which contributed to the previously noted removal of Warren Hastings from office in 1785. In 1799, when England was at war with France, Company administrator Arthur Wellesley (the future Duke of Wellington) outlawed freedom of the South Asian press, which remained in force until 1835. In 1823, the foremost Indian Orientalist writer of that era, Rammohan Roy, and other Indian press owners, with the support of *The Englishman*'s editor James Silk Buckingham, protested in a failed joint legal case titled "*Areopigitica* of the Indian Press," taking the name of John Milton's anti-censorship essay. This unsuccessful legal appeal to the Company Privy Council was consistent with that era's pattern of heavy censorship and surveillance in England, due to fears that the French Revolution might encourage popular uprising. Rammohan Roy's Persian-language paper *Mirat ul Akhbar* (1822) was an important forerunner of Indian middle-class print culture of a highly educated, cosmopolitan Persian-speaking (as a legacy of Mughal rule) and mostly Hindu traditional elite, against numerous popular vernacular presses that served a broader literate audience. Buckingham's *Calcutta Journal* appealed to the more upscale liberal-minded English residents of Calcutta.

Of parallel significance, Company authorities were instrumental in the founding of the Asiatic Society of Bengal (1784), which was a purposeful attempt to create an inclusive forum for a dialogue between Company authorities and the emerging Indian middle class (see fig. 3.3). William Jones (1746–94) was a key figure in the development of the Asiatic Society of Bengal, which became the foremost civil voice of Indian and English scholarship on India and the development of English/British Orientalism. Jones received a judicial appointment to the Supreme Court of Bengal in 1783, and was subsequently the author of numerous influential books on Indian law, music, literature, botany, and geography, and made several of the first English-language translations of Indian literature. He was the initial European to observe that Sanskrit resembled classical Greek and Latin, as this led to the noted corrective that North Indian languages derived from Sanskrit rather than Persian. In *The Sanskrit Language* (1786) Jones went further in proposing that all the base classical-era languages of the West had a common root. This was consistent with a study by the French Jesuit Gaston-Laurent Coeurdoux in a memoir sent to the French Academy of Sciences in 1767, which included German and Russian in the Indo-European linguistic mix. Jones was also the first scholar to propose a racial division of India involving an early Aryan (Indo-European) invasion, but in his time there was insufficient literary or archaeological evidence to support it.[12] Speaking to the Asiatic Society in Bengal in 1786, Jones proposed that

> The Sanskrit language, whatever be its antiquity, is of a wonderful structure; more perfect than the Greek, more copious than the Latin, and more exquisitely refined than either, yet bearing to both of them a stronger affinity, both in the roots of verbs and in the forms of grammar, than could possibly have been produced by accident; so strong, indeed, that no philologer could examine them all three, without believing them to have sprung from some common source, which, perhaps, no longer exists.[13]

3.3 Asiatic Society of Bengal

When Warren Hastings initiated the Asiatic Society of Bengal in 1784, he intended it to offer scholarly support for members of his acculturated British service elite, such as Jones. These men were conscious that their public and professional responsibilities required understanding and benevolent dedication to the wider Indian population. Above all, Jones and Hastings agreed that Company civil servants needed to communicate with Indians by learning their languages, and as the basis of functional Indian partnerships. To this end, Hastings linked the Asiatic Society to the new English College of Fort William, where incoming British civil servants were trained in Indian languages. He also entered into a publication agreement with the neighbouring Serampore (Danish) Baptist Mission, which had the best Sanskrit press in the world, and a core of Hindu scholars who were capable translators, Indian typescript fabricators, and printers.[14] Thus the foundational tripartite partnership was formed among the Asiatic Society, the Fort William College, and the Serampore Mission. William Carey, the clerical founder of the Serampore Mission in 1800, became a professor at Fort William, and used this base to lead the variety of Indian-language initiatives that followed, including the substantive employment of Indian scholars as

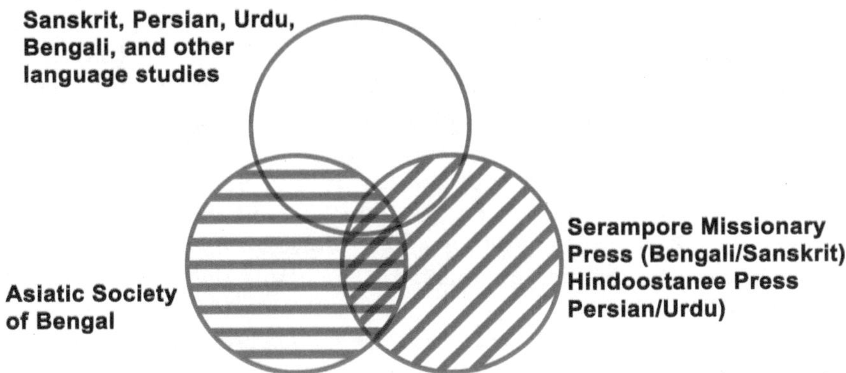

3.4 Calcutta-centred Orientalism

Indian-language instructors, and as the talented translators and craftsmen in the expanding Mission Press (see fig. 3.4).

III. The Serampore Mission Press

Serampore was well prepared to serve as the base for the study of India's popular cultures and languages, as the mission's substantial record of early nineteenth-century printed editions of biblical texts into local vernaculars attests. The Serampore Mission Press had the costly type fonts for the irregular and neglected languages of India;[15] from 1805 the Press printed works in regional Bengali, Urdu, Oriya, Tamil, Telegu, Kanarese, and Marathi scripts. The Mission gained financial sustenance, recognition, and social mobility within the European community, which ultimately provided potential for mass evangelization. The Mission staff prepared grammars and dictionaries of Indian languages for the College of Fort William and their own students' use, as this also led to publication of the Bible in various regional Indian languages to promote the conversion of the Hindu masses.[16]

The Mission had been founded in 1800 by William Carey, a former indigo planter and Indian labour supervisor, when its staff consisted of Carey's family and two missionaries who had English criminal records for their public support of the French Revolution. The missionaries collectively worked on the basis of a Morovian model of pooled earnings for the common good and renunciation of private gain. Carey was the treasurer, John Fountain the librarian, and William Ward, a trained printer, assumed control of a wooden printing press that he bought in Calcutta at a cost of £40. Ward set the first types, and built the Serampore publishing house for books written in the vernacular languages of India. Joshua Marshman (the son of a weaver and subsequently a seamen) and his wife coincidentally opened two Serampore English-style boarding schools for boys and girls of European and Eurasian parentage. These became the basis of the Serampore College and the Calcutta School Society, both of which provided educational opportunities to Bengalis. Marshman's *Hints Relative to Native Schools, Together with the Outline of an Institution for Their Extension and Management* (Serampore Press, 1816) became the manual for the Calcutta School Society.

The year 1800 was critical for Bengal, as the Danish government sided with the French during the era of global warfare between the British and Napoleonic France. Consequently, English troops occupied Serampore in May 1801, and power over the Mission and its press passed into English hands. The linguistic ability of Carey and the printing ability of Ward were vital to the success of the College of Fort William. Company payments for Serampore's printing covered missionary expenses, and allowed them to evangelize Indians rather than being constrained in Serampore. Their mission was awarded the first such Company charter granting them the right to conduct Christian missionary activity in India. Carey summarized these rapid transitions in a 1804 correspondence:

> The Society is expanding ... We have purchased 13 ½ *bighas* of land in Serampore for 10,000 Rupees and so the Society now has two of the Best Houses in Serampore ... The Press is humming ... My *Bengali Grammar and Colloquies* and *Bashoo's History* ... these are sold off. The Government took 100 copies of each for the College. We are printing the *Hiopodesha* from Sanscrit into Bengali and the *Mahabharat*.[17]

In another letter dated 10 December 1805, Carey reports:

> The College and the Asiatic Society have agreed to allow us three hundred Rupees a Month to translate and publish the Sanskrit Writings of the Hindoos, the profits of the Sale to be ours. Sir J. Anstruther has very kindly addressed a Letter to learned Bodies [in India] to recommend the Work. He told me last Friday that he would also address the Court of Directors on the same subject.[18]

The Serampore Press, under contract to do College of Fort William printing, was spending 37,966 rupees per year at that time for printing expenses.[19] In January 1806, Carey wrote that "My whole time is now occupied in translating and preparing copy for the press";[20] in the following month he reported that "the translation of the *Ramayana* occupies all the time I can spare; it is esteemed the first poem that ever was written by the Hindoos."[21] On 14 March: "I hope our translations of the *Ramayana* will serve the Mission for it respects temporal supplies. We have 300 Rupees a month for it besides the profits issued from the sale ... The translation so occupies my time that I have little leisure for writing."[22] By 1807 the Press had moved into "more commodious premises" and was managing at least three presses producing "seven major and current Indian languages."[23]

The Mission Press was at that time the chief instrument for college publications, though other local printing firms under Indian ownership developed, also with college support. But the new presses could not match Ward's inventiveness, as in 1807 he had four fonts of Indian type: Devanagari, Bengali, Oriya, and Marathi.[24] By 1810 the Press was printing the scriptures in six languages, and developing translations to six others.[25] By 1812, when a fire destroyed Ward's printing shop, fourteen fonts in Eastern languages and manuscripts were destroyed.[26]

In 1801 Carey had supervised the editing of the first textbook reader for Bengali students, the *Kathopakathan* (Dialogues), which was a social document depicting the various castes and classes of eighteenth-century rural Bengal based on the analysis of local speech patterns. This was the first book by a European that was not focal on Hindu high culture. Carey's compilation dignified the manners, customs, and language of merchants, fishermen, women, beggars, day labourers, and other commoners. The *Dialogues* was also the first European publication to show sensitivity to the special qualities of Indian regional culture, and especially to the diversity of Bengali tradition. Carey did this through sequential studies of speech patterns. Carey's *A Grammar of the Bengalee Language* (Serampore Mission Press, 1801) demonstrated degrees of regional linguistic sophistication and cultural refinement according to social status rather than by economic well-being. Brahmins, respected for their knowledge and superior language skills, lived differently from rural people in villages. This publication became a valuable basis for future studies of regional change, as Calcutta developed into a major British colonial urban hub with substantive integrative regional cultural impact.

IV. Competing Early Presses

Among the Mission Press's Calcutta competitors was the Hindoostanee Press. It came into existence ultimately in response to Warren Hastings's charge to prepare Persian-language translations, for which the Fort William College Persian Department, consisting of both Indian and British instructors, developed texts on Persian grammar. The College staff also created a superior Persian typography in 1805. John Gilchrist, a specialist in Urdu, with fellow instructor William Hunter supervised the writing of textbooks subsidized by the College Council to "develop a complete system of Hindoostance Philology."[27] Gilchrist acquired his own printing press, which he named the Hindoostanee Press, subsidized by an annual guarantee of College purchases for the Urdu program, and the right "to sell such works wherever I please and to enjoy every right and privilege as an author in the utmost acceptation of that term." The Hindoostanee Press did well. In 1803 Gilchrist completed the translation of *Aesop's Fables*, *Oriental Fabulist*, which he paired in a book with other ancient "fabulists" in Urdu, Persian, Arabic, Sanskrit, Bengali, and English, and the Persian *Gulistan*. He introduced the European principles of punctuation, word separation, and "joining the letters of each vocable as much as possible."[28] In his estimate, "the Hindoostanee will ascend as high on the Indian scale ... as the English has done in a similar predicament in our own country."[29] By 1803 the Press had published forty-four books, mostly translations of Persian and Arabic classics and a small number of original compositions. Shortly thereafter Gilchrist returned to England, leaving the management of the Press to Hunter, who won the contract to publish the College/Asiatic Society's *Asiatick Researches* journal in 1808.

Against the Persian-Urdu group, College instructor H.T. Colebrook became the champion of Sanskrit studies, its derivative vernaculars, and Hinduism. He promoted a program to define the cultures of India, and made the important case that Hindi predated the Persian language and Persianized Urdu. Colbrooke's 1804 books published by the Serampore Mission Press, using a perfected Devanagari script syllabary, included several works on Sanskrit: the *Sanskrit Dictionary*; the *Hitopadesha*; and a popular lexicographical work, the *Amara Kosha*, which was a thesaurus of Sanskrit written by the Jain or Buddhist scholar Amarasimha during the late Gupta era (c. seventh century). Colebrook's books maintained the essence of the original but provided marginal notes to make his publications more comprehensible to his students. In 1810 Colebrook's *The Translation of Two Treatises on the Hindu Law of Inheritance*, which became mandatory reading and reference for Company judicial officials, demonstrated how Europeans were intellectually able to pull together what the early British administrators characterized as a chaotic and contradictory Hindu legal system. Colebrook' major conclusion was that there was not a single judicial law of inheritance in India, but of greater importance this work on legal diversity opened discussions of wider cultural differences in the Indian regions, and how European intellect differed from that of Indians.[30]

An enterprising Indian formerly employed by the Serampore Press, Ganga Kishore, was the first South Asian to establish an independent press publishing books in Bengali, first in Calcutta and then from a village outside the city. He had agents in towns and villages who sold his books.[31] Indian booksellers also were beneficiaries of the new book trade. Initially booksellers received partial College subsidies, to counter students reselling College library books at high rates to the public. In 1811 the College contracted several legitimate Indian booksellers in Calcutta to handle its surplus publications.

V. The Madras School of Orientalism

The Fort William/Asiatic Society of Calcutta intellectual alliance was the model for similar developments in Madras. The Madras centre came into existence following the Mysore Wars of 1799, as English troops consolidated their hold over South India. Subsequently the College of Fort St George in Madras became the training centre for arriving junior civil service officers assigned to the region. Coincidentally, the Madras Literary Society was founded by the College's head Indian linguist, F.W. Ellis, a member of the Asiatic Society of Calcutta. Ellis produced a body of knowledge about South Indian languages and their history, which provided the first studies that distinguished southern Indian culture from that of the north, and invited others to conduct their own explorations of Indian regional variations. Much of this initial research on South Indian society and culture was based on studies of a substantial amount of materials and reports collected by Surveyor General Colin Mackenzie (1754–1821) during his late eighteenth-century travels through the newly annexed Indian south on the English East India Company's behalf. Similar to the successful pattern previously developed in Calcutta, Madras-based English and Indian scholars initially partnered in their studies of Indian languages, culture, and law. In doing so they challenged the Calcutta Society's inclusive view of India that ignored regional differences. The most notable outcome was

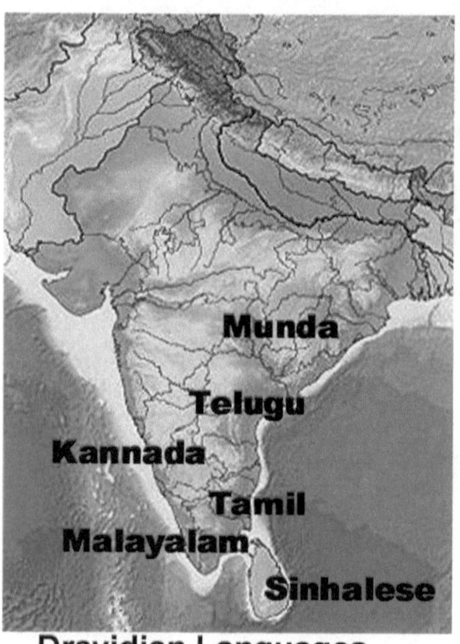

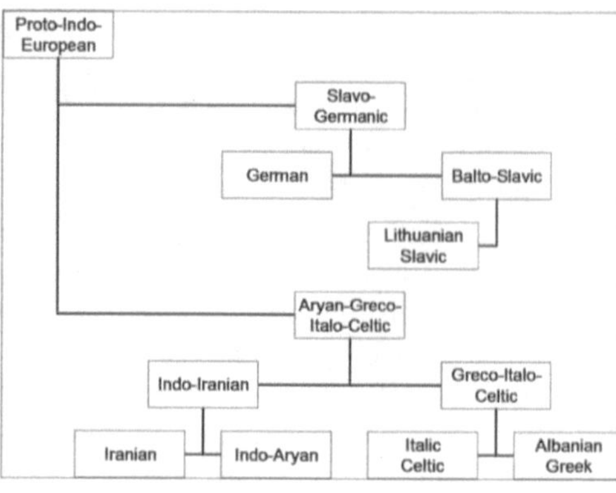

3.5 Family Tree of Indo-European Languages/Distribution of Dravidian Languages

the Madras School's proof that South Indian languages were not derived from Sanskrit, but were linked to a separate historical linguistic evolution (see fig. 3.5). Similarly, these Madras School scholars demonstrated that wider South Indian culture, its languages, history, literature, religion, and law, differed from that of North India. Their intention was not to displace Calcutta as British India's foremost intellectual centre, or to create a dichotomy between the Calcutta and Madras Orientalist schools, but to challenge prior assumptions and to amend initial errors related to Indian civilization.[32]

The point of both the Calcutta and Madras Orientalist traditions was to synthesize indigenous knowledge through productive scholarly interactions between British civil servants and their Indian assistants and Indian scholars and place it within European traditions of scholarship. As previously noted, in traditional India the highest level transformation of information to knowledge was based in "knowledge making" in religious institutions and royal courts for "publication" in ritual canon and handwritten texts, and the subsequent circulation of knowledge through memory culture and manuscripts that were often the substance for oral performances. In contrast, the new Orientalist knowledge "information order" was based upon government and university support of scholarship, published in printed editions that circulated cheaply and in large numbers through wider markets. The key difference between the nineteenth-century Indian and Western intellectual traditions and those of the past was that in the previous Indian order selected scholars and clerics working within the courts and religious centres read, drafted, and assessed letters and written and oral documents. The new India Orientalists, working within the secular world, conducted grammar-grounded scholarship centered on written texts, inscriptions, and transcripts of oral tradition supplied by English and Indian colonial administrators and by college-based European and Indian researchers and translators, headmasters, teachers, and Brahmin and non-Brahmin students.[33]

One result of this new secular, scholarly approach was a shift in the prevailing English conception of pre-colonial and colonial India. The Calcutta School of Orientalism's (Asiatic Society) initial leaders, William Jones, Henry Thomas Colebrooke, Horace Hayman Wilson, and James Prinseps, had developed a North India–centred view of the Indo-European language family that was proposed to be foundational to India-wide patterns. In law this was based on the Sanskrit *Dharmasastra* texts, as these portrayed the fundamental beliefs of Indian populations; in history, the weak historical sense of ancient India prevalent in eighteenth-century India was based on Mauryan-era Asokan inscriptions, and an inscription-based historiography of India's ancient past; and in religion, Indian diversity was demonstrated in the variety of the Hindu sects. The Calcutta School depicted the North Indian *zamindari* system of property holding, which was thought to be based in delegated assignments of property rights by Oriental despots and their subordinates, as similar to that of feudal Europe's seigneurial network of assigned fiefs.

The Madras School's study of South Indian Dravidian languages offered corrective alternatives, with substantive implications. Madras-based scholars documented that Indian law was most commonly variable customary law rather than uniform law. They reconfigured the region's past from the detailed accounts of impressive numbers of South Indian inscriptions that allowed reconstruction of chronological grids and more detailed historical analysis than was possible in underdocumented North India. Revisionist studies of religions based on new archaeological, text, and epigraphic sources factored the corrective importance of Jainism and Buddhism into the development of Indian religious tradition. In property holding, the local alternatives of *ryotwari* (cultivator landholding rights) and *mirasi* (a variety of hereditary landholding transfers, use, and income rights) forced the restructuring of the Company's taxation. Of wider significance, the essay "The Dravidian Proof," published by F.W. Ellis in 1815, demonstrated that the two most prominent languages of South India (Tamil and Telagu, among the eighty-five South Asian languages then argued to be indigenous) were historically related to one another, and most significantly were not derived from Sanskrit. This negated H.T. Colebrooke's previously cited 1801 publication, which had incorrectly concluded that all the modern languages of India were derived from Sanskrit, and William Carey's 1814 *Telagu Grammar*, which concurred in linking the South Indian Telagu language to Sanskrit. Colebrooke's and Carey's studies were at that time widely considered the most significant outcomes of the Calcutta School of Orientalism.[34]

Ellis and the Fort William College staff convinced the government of Madras to end the initial Calcutta School policy (derived from previous Mughal-era English contacts) of universally giving Hindustani- (Urdu) and Persian-language training priority. They argued their need to emphasize Tamil and Telugu studies instead, as these regional languages better prepared civil servants for South India postings. New company arrivals at Madras would still learn Sanskrit first, but would follow with Tamil- and Telugu-language studies to sustain their regional assignments. In contrast, the Company colonial army posted in the south and elsewhere continued to favour Urdu- and Persian-language training, as the legacy of the Mughal/Muslim era continued and numbers of hereditary Mughal Muslim Sepoy troops remained the core of the Company infantry. Consequently, newly arrived administrators posted in Calcutta increasingly trained in regional languages (e.g., Bengali) rather than Persian and Urdu.

In South India the Nawab of Arcot, who retained regional princely powers over southeast India under Company rule, continued to patronize Islamic scholarship and Urdu and Persian linguistics into the mid-nineteenth century (see fig. 3.6).[35] After he relocated his residency to Madras in the nineteenth century, Islamic scholarship based at his court served as the third South India regional intellectual hub, but secondary to the College and the Madras Oriental Society, which focused on Tamil and Telagu studies.[36] In common with the scholarship at the College of Fort William, the College Press (subsequently the Fort St George Press) and the Madras-based Christian Knowledge Society's Press at the Vepery Mission published numerous works by Indian Muslim authors.

3.6 Stringer Lawrence, who established the Madras Army, with Muhammed Ali Khan Wallajah, the Nawab of Carnatic. This painting has had recent prominence in post-colonial debate for its purposeful portrayal of the friendship and administrative partnership between Stinger, the then-commander of English East India Company forces based in Madras/Fort St George, and the Indian lord of southeastern India. See Morris (1973).

VI. Missions, Missionaries, and Entrepreneurs

As detailed above, there was an evolution from the initial portraits of "heathendom" to more complex ethnography. This transition paired with the shift of the agency of Indian publications from the initial European missionary presses to a secular mix of Company, Company-licensed, and private European- and Indian-owned presses. The East India Company's publication patronage was self-serving but with wider consequence, in that it provided materials and the means by which its administrative staff received quality foundational instruction in regional languages and cultures from English and Indian instructors. This local language-based training empowered the arriving Company administrators to better understand the nuances of their local assignments, and thus (in theory if not in practice) to better manage their Indian subjects. The acceptance of Sanskrit as a foundational "Western" language and root of contemporary North Indian languages, and subsequent appreciation of the Tamil-based South Indian language tradition, lay the groundwork for East India Company arrivals and Indian employees to think of South Asians as partners rather than English subjects.[37] This attitude of "embracing" the locals as partners would later change for various domestic, cultural, and religious reasons.

Under Company rule, Madras eventually became the foremost seat of printing among the colonial urban centres. The London-based Anglican Society for Promoting Christian Knowledge (SPCK) established a mission base at Vepery (then situated just outside Madras) in 1726, as an extension of the more southern Coromandel coast Danish Lutheran Tranquebar Mission (established in the seventeenth century), and was subject to the authority of the French port of trade at Pondicherry that lay between the two. The SPCK, initially barred from India by Dutch East India Company merchants, gained its foothold when it responded to a 1712 appeal from the Danish mission by supplying a printing press with type, paper, ink, and a printer to facilitate their publications. A letter dated 1713 from Bartholomäus Ziegenbalg (1682–1719), the then head of the Tranquebar Danish Mission, to an Anglican missionary at Madras celebrated this collaboration:

> We may remember on this Occasion, how much the Art of Printing contributed to the Manifestation of divine Truths, and the spreading of Books for that End, at the Time of the happy Reformation, which we read of in History, with Thanksgiving to Almighty God.[38]

Thereafter the Tranquebar Mission printing press, enabled with locally designed Tamil and Telegu typefaces, began printing small publications such as *A General Description Of Malabar Heathendom*, *Four Gospels And Acts*, and *Accursed Heathendom*, which were usually antagonistic to Hindu beliefs and principles (see fig. 3.7).

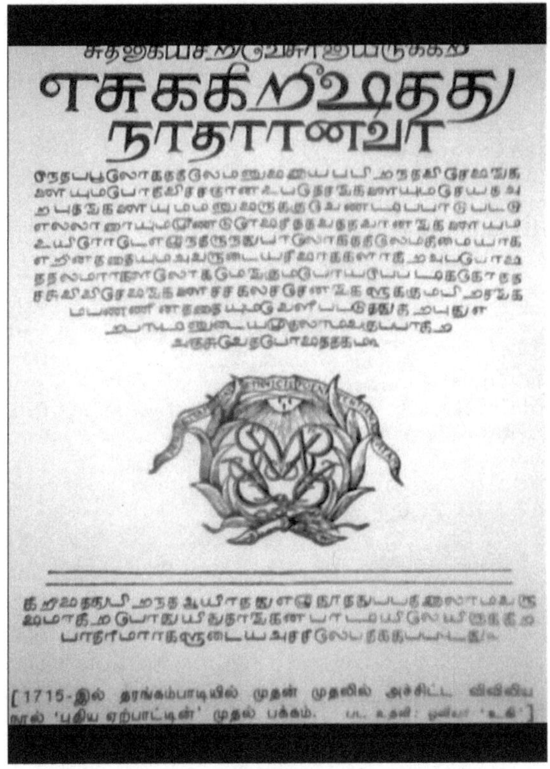

3.7 Published Tamil-language translation of the Bible, 1715

The new Vepery Mission (1726) was initially supported by the English monarchy, which supplied a printing press at its start to allow it to provide printed materials to sustain the Mission's activities. When the Company army annexed the French Pondicherry colony in 1761, they appropriated the Tranquebar Mission printing press, its prized typefaces, and its printer, and transferred their press operations to the Vepery Mission at the initiative of the Tamil scholar and SPCK German missionary Johann Phillip Fabricius (1711–91). In return the Mission agreed that the printing demands of Fort St George would be given priority. Initially Fabricius had problems importing paper adequate for his press's needs from Europe, but this was locally resolved when Indian entrepreneurs in Madras started to manufacture their own paper. In 1762 the SPCK press published a calendar

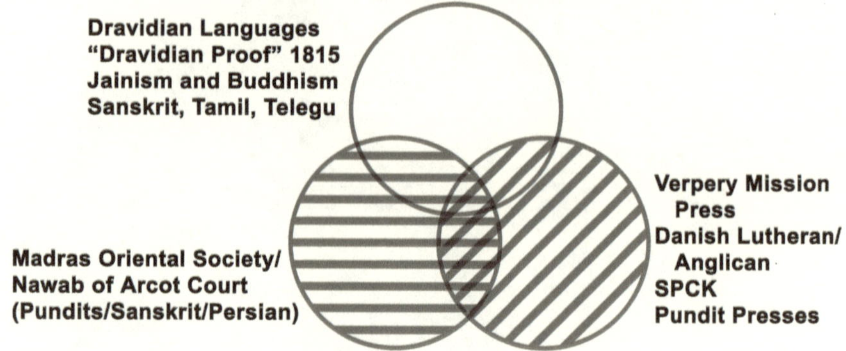

3.8 Madras School of Orientalism

and several Tamil-language books, pre-dating books printed in Calcutta by a decade (see fig. 3.8).[39] By that time the Mission was the base for a network of linked South Indian missions and schools, notable for their education of European and Tamil students.[40]

In 1766, when Vepery purchased new publishing equipment confiscated by the Company from Pondicherry, its productive centre shifted to Fort St George, and it subsequently became the Government Press on Mount Road. The Vepery Press, renamed the SPCK Press under Fabricius's management (1740–91), composed and printed a Tamil book on catechism (1766) with typefaces cut in Germany. By the next decade the SPCK Press itself crafted new South Indian–language typecases, allowing the publication of Fabricius's [Tamil] *Translation of the New Testament* (1766/1772); and his still widely used *Dictionary of Tamil and English* (1779), published under the title *A Malabar and English dictionary, wherein the words and phrases of the Tamilian Language, commonly called by Europeans the Malabar Language.* Fabricius's dictionary built on the SPCK missionary Bartholomaus Ziegenbalg's previous *Malabar* [Tamil] *English Dictionary* (1715), and the Goa-based Portuguese scholar Antao da Proenca's *Tamil-Portuguese Dictionary* (1679). In 1793 Fabricius published his Tamil-language translation of John Bunyan's *Pilgrims Progress*, which marked the beginning of a new age of Indian publications of Western and Indian novels. In the mid-nineteenth century this press was eventually sold to the American Board of Commissioners for Foreign Missions (The American Board of Missions, or ABM) in Citadaripet (today incorporated into modern Chennai); when the ABM left India in 1886 the SPCK-Diocesan committee reaquired the press and renamed it the Diocesan Press, which still exists today.[41]

Fabricius's contemporary, Jean-Antoine Dubois (1765–1848), was a French Catholic missionary who factored as a major figure in early nineteenth-century print culture. When he arrived in India in 1792, Dubois was initially attached to the French Pondicherry mission. In the aftermath of 1799 regional warfare he went to Mysore to reorganize the Christian community that had been shattered by the South Indian ruler Tipu Sultan. Subsequently Dubois became the director of the Catholic Seminary of the Foreign Missions, and a member of the Literary Society of Madras. His notable achievement was his book *Hindu Manners, Customs and Ceremonies* (1816),[42] which was followed by a revised and expanded French-language edition, *Moeurs, institutions, et ceremonies des peuples de l'Inde* (Paris, 2 vols., 1825), and *Expose de quelque-uns des principaux articles de la théogonie des Brahmes* (Paris, 1825).[43] His books were not so much drawn from the Hindu sacred books as from his own careful observations (which remain meaningful), as he is often thought of as India's first Western ethnographer. He made notable general observations of late eighteenth- and early nineteenth-century Indian society, and especially recorded his impressions of the functional caste system; commentaries on "Brahminical life"; and records of religious feasts, temples, and objects of worship.

In 1807 Lord William Bentinck purchased his original French manuscript for the East India Company Press paying eight thousand rupees, leading to its 1816 London publication in English translation. Dubois's other major work was *Letters on the State of Christianity in India*, in which he asserted his opinion that, under existing circumstances, there was no possibility of "overcoming the invincible barrier of Brahmanical prejudice" to allow the conversion of Hindus to Christianity. He acknowledged that lower castes and outcastes might be converted in large numbers, but among the higher castes,

> Should the intercourse between individuals of both nations, by becoming more intimate and more friendly, produce a change in the religion and usages of the country, it will not be to turn Christians that they will forsake their own religion, but rather ... to become mere atheists.[44]

His opinions were attacked in England, where two Anglican ministers, James Hough and H. Townley, published rebuttals in *A Reply to the Letters of the Abbe Dubois* (London, 1824) and *An Answer to the Abbe Dubois* (London, 1824).[45]

Parallel to eighteenth-century printing efforts by the Protestant missionaries at Tranquebar, Jesuit Constantine Joseph Beschi (1680–1747) was an equally significant contributor to the development of regional nineteenth-century Tamil print and literature.[46] Differences in Christian beliefs and opinions of Indian religion were expressed in theological debates in printed books and pamphlets published by the Lutherans. Beschi's initial impact was limited by the lack of a Jesuit-owned printing press in his era, though the Jesuits had initially introduced printing in Tamil at Goa, as noted above. His early publications were usually dictionaries and grammars, but he was the first to focus his writings on influential pieces of literature. His publications' eventual popularity in the early nineteenth century followed from his compromise with, rather than his critique of, local customs. In contrast to the restraint of the missionaries, Beschi was known to regularly dress in Indian court fashion, including expensive jewellery, and regularly socialize with local rulers. Despite his aristocratic image, Beschi was also popularly known as a magical Indian "poet-saint" with supernatural literary skills and powers of persuasion and prowess. Literary histories attribute Beschi's written works as constituting the substructure of modern Tamil literature. Beschi's *Parramarta Kuruvin Kattai* or *Guru Simpleton* was the first printed book of traditional Tamil folktales, which was published in London in 1822, sold in India in 1824, and was subsequently printed in India in 1845.

Beschi's *Guru Simpleton* achieved wide popular status in India, as it blended popular oral tradition with Tamil folklore in a European story form. In brief, the story is a social critique, initially focused on a self-centred husband who sends an ignorant and self-promotional holy man (*sadhu*) to his home to perform a spiritually cleansing *puja* ritual. The clever wife, angry with her husband for sending the *sadhu* and expecting her to entertain him until her husband's return, presents a rice-beater as the false ritual instrument of choice. When she reports that her family's ritual tradition dictates that the ritualist must take rice-beater beatings on the family's behalf, the *sadhu*, who had expected a reasonable payment for his services, quickly flees. When the husband returns he is dumbfounded by the *sadhu*'s failure to perform such a basic household cleansing ritual, as his wife does not reveal the truthful reason. Although Beschi claimed that the sole purpose of the book was to disseminate amusement and humour among both locals and missionaries, his recent biographer asserts that he was ultimately seeking a publication patron to underwrite his serious scholarship and folktales, as "print was a more reliable contemporary medium to demonstrate correct spelling than local scribes and copyists." His book's success encouraged other anthologies of Tamil-language tales and folklore. Today's scholars estimate that in 1700 there were 266 Tamil language books in print, but by 1800 there were 1,000 published each year.[47]

VII. Nineteenth-Century Pundit Presses in South India

In response to the new publishing houses that resulted from the College and Missionary enterprises, numerous Tamil and Telugu *pundit* presses began printing Sanskrit, Tamil, and Telugu literary works during and after 1830. These texts had previously been recited by pundits at regional courts and the residencies of major landholder (*zamindar*) patrons. Among the notable Tamil presses were Kalvi Viakkam (1834), the Sarasvati Press (1835), and Kalivi Kalanchiyam (1839). Vivilla Press, initially Hindu Bhasha Sanjeevini (1854), the dominant Telugu press, was run by numbers of former Hindu pundits and the newly educated graduates from the College of Fort St George. The major pundit presses depended on the text-making, printing skills, and linguistic training their staff had learned from College and English missionary instructors, and rewrote old books to conform to newly standardized Tamil- and Telugu-language instruction. Collectively the pundit presses benefitted from new urban literacy and prosperity, and were welcomed as representative voices of the traditional Hindu community against the Christian missionaries, British rule, and assertive urbanism in general.

In traditional South India, court-based Brahmin pundits ("gurus") and lower caste *karanams* ("commoners") used their language mastery and political, administrative, advisory, and instructional skills to secure patronage, whether as court residents or itinerants.[48] Pundits were above all skilled in Sanskrit, which was the basis of their focal scholarship on classical Sanskrit texts and poetry compositions in Sanskrit, Telugu, and Tamil. *Karanams* were notable for their skills in everyday affairs, as masters of sale deeds, village accounting, penmanship, and local histories, and were also the narrators of secular stories, proverbs, and verses, and most had multiple language versatility in political, administrative, and secular affairs. A mid-nineteenth-century Telugu poem on *karanam* reflected on their new role:

They now read proofs at print shops
Just to stay alive,
or teach Telugu to the white Huns,
expounding religion in the houses
of those grocers who give them credit.
Phenomenal scholars have been humbled.
Times have changed.[49]

While some *karanams* successfully transitioned into new occupations (including government administration), and others into the composition of new literature for the Madras and other new urban-centred popular presses, most pundits did not embrace modern scholarship, or transform literary languages into modern languages through print, but focused instead on the grammar of classical literature to sustain traditional culture. This was especially the case among the Telugu-language scholastic community, as pundits responded to the need for language instructors at Fort St George, with long-term consequences. A pundit Telugu-language instructional core at the College produced editions of Telugu literary texts, and assisted in the development of a new Telugu-English dictionary that was necessary for English-speaking Company employees to pass required appointment tests.[50] Under the direction of Chinnaya Suri (1806–62), headmaster of Telugu and the senior Telugu pundit at the College of Fort St George (subsequently Madras University), the Telugu-language instructor pundits reinforced a traditional literary model based in classical Telugu and Sanskrit that authorized words and grammar.

The *Bala-vyakaranamu* (1858) grammar and the prose *Pancatantramu* (1853) were the foundational standards taught at the College and Madras Presidency schools. Nearly every Telugu teacher in the schools and the editors of major publishing houses were patrons of the traditionalist Chinnaya Suri system. Students studied the classical poet Nannaya's Telugu version of the Sanskrit *Mahabharata* epic poem as the basis of their passing the standardized exams that were required to secure job placement certificates. A scholarly commitment to secular spoken Telugu was thus denied Madras Presidency scholars, but scholastic Telugu had no use in everyday life. Telugu grammatical accuracy and standardization based in archaic language forms took precedence over the popular use or transmission of new knowledge via "modern" Telugu.

A dichotomy of Telugu-language publications resulted. Madras Telugu presses as elsewhere (usually owned by local *zamindars*) were controlled by College-trained pundits who published books consistent with Chinnaya

Suri's language rules, in contrast to popular presses that sold books that were disapproved of by the pundits to literate but not "scholarly" elite readers who were used to listening to oral narratives in contemporary popular poetic recitations or song, and to lower castes who bought less expensive books printed on cheap paper that were consistent with their popular oral practices.[51] Newspapers and popular journals were published in modern Telugu, but this "new" Telugu literature was rejected by academic institutions until the 1970s. Many educated and upwardly mobile native Telugu speakers subsequently embraced English as their preferred language of culture and prestige, as traditional Telugu became the language of backwardness (literary debate consisted of regressive classical discourse on the grammatical acceptability of selected words) and their secondary language. George Norton, President of the College of Fort William board, in his 1842 Annual Report of the University, critically addressed this language instruction problem:

> [Telugu language instruction is] ... chiefly related to the legends and factions ... as they are fanciful. Such morality and practical maxims as are taught, are not such as are likely to meet the appropriation of European minds, at least – nor indeed of the better portions of the Natives themselves, neither is it to be denied that much is to be found in these works which no other than a deprived intellect could tolerate.[52]

In contrast, Vicakaperuman Aiyer, Head of the Madras University High School and Professor of Tamil at the College, offered this contemporary evaluation (as instruction in Tamil language at the College, as previously noted, was "progressive" rather than "regressive"):

> The English who rule this country, and other Empires, have dispensed with teaching literature, grammar, geography, astronomy, and so forth through verse form; now they teach their children in clear prose. For that reason, the children of Europe are able to read many books quickly, to discover so much and be capable of doing so much ... In order that the children of our nation do not waste away their lives we must quickly produce books in clear prose ... for use in schools so that they can ... gain the knowledge necessary for all sorts of employment.[53]

VIII. Agencies of Knowledge Production in Eighteenth- and Early Nineteenth-Century India

This study has ultimately addressed the importance of a developing India printing industry and print culture centred on Bengal in northeast India and the Coromandel and Malabar coastlines of southern India. This emerging, initially European, and subsequently indigenous print industry was critical to durable knowledge production by a variety of human agencies. Transition to English East India Company rule in the late eighteenth century shifted the primary agency of print culture to the Company's colleges at Calcutta and Madras. This enabled the joint ventures of English and Indians in the studies, instruction, and linked scholarship of language, at first by the missionaries and Indian scholars who jointly taught regional languages to newly arrived English Company administrators. The initial mission presses profited from their publication runs of serviceable books for students that subsidized their printing of the missionaries' scholarly works on Indian languages, beliefs, and conduct that were foundational to future studies of Indian civilization by both European and Indian scholars. Shortly thereafter an emergent Indian popular press published literature more consistent with traditional standards. The early missionaries and English and Indian scholars in turn expanded into wider Orientalist knowledge networks that were sustained by the new Asiatic Societies in Calcutta and Madras, which became the third cosmopolitan hubs in the tripartite alliances among the Company colleges, the Christian missions, and the learned Societies. This foundational era of English sovereignty was notable for the collaborations between European and Indian urban-based academics in their attempts to reimagine Indian tradition, reinforced by the Company's encouragement and the French Revolution era's notions of human equality. This era of collaboration and its results are represented in figure 3.9.

The Orientalist advantage depended on highly educated missionaries and Orientalists who drew from the secular and Enlightenment character of their research (over prior narrow missionary interests and traditional Indian scholarship), and especially their greater openness towards India and Indian religions, sustained by a wealth and newly available documentation collected by English officials. This perspective negated the prior missionaries' and Indian clerics' fears of committing doctrinal incorrectness and their pre-emptive censorship of Indian sources.[54] Orientalists had the advantage of manpower and money, supplied by Company officials, in contrast to the earlier Christian missionaries, who were constantly appealing for resources and adapted their mission initiatives to avoid alienating their benefactors. While the missionary scholarship had previously ended in unpublished manuscripts, the Company sustained their publications by the guarantee of College textbook sales revenues that subsidized specialized books. Wider book sales benefitted from greater demand for advanced

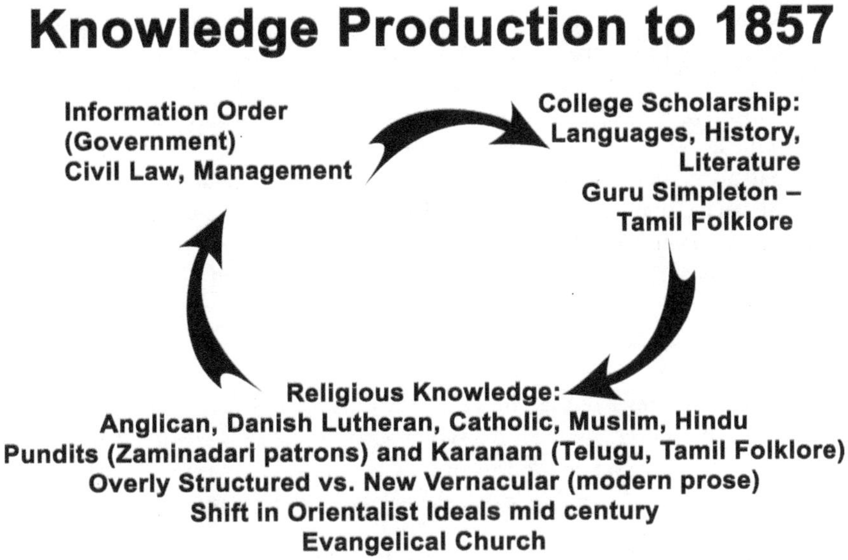

Knowledge Production to 1857

Information Order (Government) Civil Law, Management

College Scholarship: Languages, History, Literature Guru Simpleton – Tamil Folklore

Religious Knowledge: Anglican, Danish Lutheran, Catholic, Muslim, Hindu Pundits (Zaminadari patrons) and Karanam (Telugu, Tamil Folklore) Overly Structured vs. New Vernacular (modern prose) Shift in Orientalist Ideals mid century Evangelical Church

3.9 Knowledge Production to 1857

scholarship among a wider public readership that initially resulted from College textbook requirements in upper division courses. As popular literacy increased there was an expanded readership for college texts and other scholarly works among Indian college graduates who were not employed by the Company but who frequently became schoolteachers for a rapidly urbanizing, better-paid, and increasingly literate workforce. An emergent Indian mercantile, professional, and administrative middle class also provided an expanded readership for these texts, as also demand for a variety of popular publications provided by new secular presses.

Christian missions had previously lacked direct and prolonged access to Indian scholars due to their anti-Enlightenment theology and limited institutional resources. In contrast, Orientalist research projects depended on Indians in the development of language0studies materials, in support for other research projects, and in the publishing industry. Western scholars had Indian partners and assistants, and Asiatic Societies were integrating agencies that welcomed both Western and Indian members. Knowledge production resulted from these alliances. Western scholars learned from Indians and the Indians were directly exposed to elite Western society and culture. Mutual Sanskrit studies were the initial common linkage as

Indians and Westerners found themselves sharing Aryan languages and heritage (including Sanskrit literary proof of Noah's flood), which made Hinduism "safe" for English Anglicans. The initial Deist roots of Company employees made them less critical of the Hindu religion and caste hierarchies. New printing press technology also had wider impact, as regional popular presses targeted the increasingly literate public in their sales of vernacular and literary works that retained the characterizations of regional oral traditions.

All Westerners were not in agreement on the potential of Indians and their traditional society, as represented in John Leyden's c. 1819 challenge to the moral and racial character of Hindus:

> The moral character of the Hindus – "the blameless, mild, patient, innocent children of nature," as they are ridiculously termed by gossiping ignoramuses, who never set eyes on them ... is as utterly worthless and devoid of probity, as their religion is wicked, shameless, impudent, and obscene.[55]

This contrasts with the Orientalist William Erskine's characterization of an ideal Orientalist, but also raises the question of whether Indian society was in equity with that of the English:

> [The Orientalist scholar F.W. Ellis] was remarkable for the proficiency he had made in the various languages of Southern India, and for his thorough acquaintance with the manners, customs and literatures of the Hindus. He is said to have written the Tamil with great elegance, and was a poet in that tongue ... He was eager to improve the conditions of the natives, but had perhaps too high an opinion of their literature and acquirements ... He lived much among the natives and had a perfect knowledge of their habits and thinking.[56]

Herein, traditional literary forms were judged to be problematic as they were traditionalist or overly structured. This was especially the case among contemporary Telugu-language publications printed at the South India pundit presses, as discussed above. In the mind of the Orientalist, literary modernity needed to move away from traditional Indian compositions that were mired in a literary past, to a New Vernacular in the form of modern literary prose that was original and ethical, as this was being initially achieved in the Madras-centred elite South Indian Tamil- and Calcutta-centred North Indian Bengali-language presses. Mid-nineteenth-century Orientalist idealists projected that social reform and education could effectively graft onto Indian learning traditions to bring about needed reforms and modernizations, as this had been their hope by initially empowering the Telugu pundits, with regressive consequences. Among mid-nineteenth-century Orientalists the most critical issue was whether Hinduism was the principle obstacle to this achievement of secular modernity. Coincidentally, they found themselves having to neutralize the increasing pressure of mid-nineteenth-century Evangelical Christianity that advocated Christian conversions over religious tolerance. While the Orientalists' preference was unforced Westernization, as this would result in a productive synthesis of Indian and Western knowledge traditions, the opposite occurred after the 1857 Sepoy Revolt, when the then British government took direct control and implemented forced changes consistent with Western utilitarian values, which judged Indian knowledge traditions to be inferior to those of the West.

NOTES

1 Said (1978) became the basis for Post-Colonial Studies.

2 This approach was rooted in Antonio Gramsci's concepts of hegemony and Michel Foucault's sense of theories of discourse. See Gill (1993); Foucault (1972; 1973); Ghosh (2008); Trivedi (2008).

3 Berry (2007); Ghosh (2008).

4 Fraser (2008).

5 Ironically, Hastings was recalled from India in 1785 and impeached for corruption in England in 1788, largely due to revelations in the emerging Calcutta English-language press, which were local initiatives resulting from Hastings's patronage of the first English translations of classical Indian texts, including the spiritual Hindu *Bhagavad Gita* (1784) that is also notable for Hastings's Preface. Fraser (2008, 4).

6 Ghosh (2008). Ghosh makes the case that the traditional Indian ritualized context of reading transforms the book or written text into a ritualized and sacred object. Against Western myths of limited literacy in pre-colonial India, the act of reading was traditionally "invested with considerable ritualistic, symbolic and social significance ... (that) fragmented readers into separate parallel domains." The written word was not just available to literate audiences, "nor was the dissemination of the written text limited by the personalized interpretations of a few privileged individuals. It was accessible to even wider illiterate groups through communitarian ceremonial reading sessions and local performative traditions"(39). "It was the adaptability of the printed book that ensured its commercial survival in an environment where oral entertainment ruled" (51).

7 Fraser (2008, 3–15).
8 Brockington (1989, 91–108). Consistent with this study's view of the surviving evidence, Brockington concludes that Hastings was more sympathetic to English-Indian partnerships and knowledge exchanges than subsequent nineteenth-century British colonial administrators.
9 Kopf (1969); Cohn (1996).
10 Rocher (1983); Fraser (2008, 10–14) discusses the importance of what some scholars have called this "Halhed moment" of transition from previous regional Indian communication by speech, ritual, gestures, and script to printed texts as a significant mark of Indian cultural passage – at that moment the Ages of Speech and Script were then superseded by the Age of Print, with substantive consequences. Fraser summarizes this scholarship, which followed anthropologist Benedict Anderson's discussions of "print capitalism" impact on non-Western societies in the colonial age (Anderson, 1992).
11 *Critical Review*, London, Sept. 1777; W. Dalrymple (2004, 40)
12 Trautmann (1997).
13 Sir William Jones, *Discourses delivered before the Asiatic Society: and miscellaneous papers, on the religion, poetry, literature, etc., of the nations of India*. Printed for C.S. Arnold, 1824.
14 Fraser (2008, 2–16), "The Problematics of Print."
15 Fraser (2005, 14–18).
16 Dieh (1964) provides a detailed annotated bibliography of the Press's annual publications, as that of its contemporary competitors.
17 Carey to Fuller, 27 February 1804, in Carey Letters Box 3; Kopf (1969, 76).
18 Carey to Fuller, 10 December 1805, Carey Letters, Box 3, cited in ibid.
19 William (1892, 17).
20 William Carey to the Baptist Mission Society, 1794–1830, Carey Letters, PA III, 222.
21 Carey to Morris, 7 February 1806, Carey Letters, PA III, 161.
22 Carey to Fuller, 14 March 1806, Carey Letters, not numbered. Kopf (1969, 78).
23 Khan (1961, 240, 231); see also Wenger (1961, 1–11).
24 Khan (1961, 252).
25 Marshman (1867, I:421–2).
26 Carey to Sutcliffe, 24 July 1812. Carey Letters.
27 Kopf (1969, 81); 12 January 1802.
28 *Oriental Fabulist, or Polyglot Translations of Ancient Fables from the English into Hindoostanee, Persian, Arabic, and Sanscrit by Various Hands Under J. Gilchrist.* Calcutta: Hinoostanee Press Harkaru Office, Calcutta, 1803, 82.
29 *Oriental Fabulist* (1803, 83).
30 Trautmann, passim.

31 Kopf (1969, 120–1).
32 The referential "Madras School of Orientalism" derives from Trautmann (2009) rather than in earlier references. See also Venkatachalapathy (2012).
33 Cohn (1996); Trautmann (1997); Ghosh (2008); Venkatachalapathy (2012)
34 Trautmann (2006).
35 This painting of Stringer Lawrence and the Nawab has had recent prominence in post-colonial debate for its purposeful portrayal of the friendship and administrative regional partnership between Stringer, the then commander of British East India Company forces based in Madras/Fort St George, and the Indian lord of southeastern India. See Morris (1973, 134).
36 More (2004).
37 This early approach to South Asians in Company India is especially notable as it contrasts with contemporary portrayals of Southeast Asians as "heathens" and other negative declarations against non-Indian Asians in the records of the English East India Company's initial failed attempts to establish permanent trading bases in the Indonesian archipelago and South China Sea. Consequent to the English East India Company's generally positive experiences in South Asia, Indians were portrayed as civilized and logical English commercial partners, against other Asians, including the Chinese maritime diaspora active in the region. See Gilbert (2011).
38 Sweetman (2004, 24 [inclusively 12–38]); App (2010, 77–132).
39 Frykenberg (2008).
40 Westcott (1897).
41 Blackburn (2006, 59–72).
42 *Description of the Character, Manners and Customs of the People of India, and of their Institutions, Religious and Civil.* London: Longman, Hurst, Rees, Orme and Brown, 1816. Derived, as Murr (1977) shows from G.-L. Coeurdoux's original manuscript, *Moeurs et coutumes des Indiens*, now lost. See also De Smet (1990).
43 *Letters on the state of Christianity in India, in Which The Conversion On The Hindoos Is Considered As Impracticable. To which is added a vindication of the Hindus, male and female, in answer to a severe attack made upon both by the Reverend*. London: Longman, Hurst, Rees, Orme, Brown and Green, 1823.
44 Trautmann (1997, 37).
45 James Hough, *A Reply to the Letters of the Abbé Dubois on the State of Christianity in India*. London: L.B. Seeley & Son, 1824; H. Townley, *An Answer to the Abbé Dubois in which the various wrong principles, misrepresentations and contradictions, contained in his work, entitled "Letters on the State of Christianity in India" are pointed out; and the Evangelization of India is, both on sound principle and on solid fact, demonstrated to be practicable*. London, 1824; see also "Refutation of the Letters of Abbe Dubois" (1825).

46 Blackburn (2006, 59–72).

47 Blackburn (2006, 72).

48 Rao, Shulman, and Subrahmanyam (2001, 93–139) for discussion of *karanams*.

49 Shulman and Rao (1998, 47).

50 Schmitthenner (2001).

51 Rao (2004, 161 and 165 [detailed listing]).

52 "Native Education in India, A Review of its State and Progress in the Presidency of Madras," 1848, cited in Blackburn (2004, 134). Norton's report, which in overview is a pro-Indian voice, also states his opinion that "the bulk of Native writings (which are poetical) contain little else than legendary and superstitious nonsense."

53 Cited in Blackburn (2004, 135).

54 Trautmann (2009, 239).

55 John Leyden, cited in Morrow (1819, lxv) as cited in Trautmann (2009, 244).

56 National Library of Scotland, Erskine Papers, Mss 35.1.5. f.21, as cited in Trautmann, loc. cit., 246.

4 Beyond the Market and the City: The Informal Dissemination of Reading Material during the American Civil War

RONALD J. ZBORAY AND MARY SARACINO ZBORAY

On 4 January 1863 Anne Loomis North wrote from Washoe City, Nevada, to her brother back home in Syracuse, New York, as she waited for news he had doubtless already read: "We have had great hope, from the Emancipation proclamation. I hope we may hear tonight, that it has been issued."[1] The Presidential order declaring slaves free in the rebelling states had been transmitted via telegraph on the evening of January 1, and most people near Northern metropolitan centres were able to read it in the newspapers within a day or two.[2] By the time Anne was writing, it had already reached out-of-the-way Soldier, Kansas.[3] It was probably the most widely read public document of the Civil War, but it was late in coming to Washoe. Anne was hardly surprised by this, as she explained to her brother, "Our news is rather slow, nowadays. High winds frequently blow down the telegraph wires." The Morse-coded Proclamation relayed at the speed of electricity to printing offices would have to await calmer weather. Even without the wind, "our telegrams are ... sometimes three or four days old." She keenly felt deprived of news in her isolated quarter of the country. "We receive Brown's paper,"[4] she noted, referring to a local sheet, "and the St. Paul Press,[5] but no other Eastern papers." The mails that carried these were "still quite regular" but hardly timely, as letters "came through in a little over three weeks." This discussion followed upon one about no "Pacific Rail-road being built, till after the close of the war." Trains would link Washoe only in 1872 to what geographer Allen Pred has called emergent national "city-systems," with their "information flows" of newspapers and other print.[6]

Compare Ann's experience in Washoe to that of Horatio Nelson Taft, a denizen of Washington, DC. Just nine days after she corresponded with her brother, Horatio scribbled in his diary:

> The first thing that I hear in the morning is the *cry* of the News Boys, "*Baltimore Sun* & *Clipper*," "*Morning Chronicle*," "*Northern Battle*."

> At 3 o"clock the "Star." about 4 o'ck it is "*Star 2nd Edition*," "*Northern Union Victory*." after the N[ew] York mail gets in which is about 6 o'clock, the boys run through the Streets crying "*N[ew] York Herald, Tribune, and Times*." The Baltimore papers and the Washington papers are sold at three cents, the NY at 5 cts, which are about three times the size of the "*Sun*" or *Star*. The old "Intel[l]igencer" is distributed without any *Noise*. It stands on its *dignity*.[7]

Horatio, like others living in metropolitan areas, was swimming and sometimes drowning in newsprint morning, noon, and night. Two papers brought by car from nearby Baltimore, the *Sun* and the *Clipper*, were already hitting the streets along with the local morning daily as Horatio was rising from bed. Two editions of the major evening daily in Washington, DC, the *Star*, came out before the clerk called it a day at the U.S. patent office.[8] Three New York dailies arrived by train after sunset, and sometime during the day the locally published *Intelligencer* appeared. Little wonder that Horatio did not have to wait like Anne for a text of the Presidential order. He recorded on the very day it was signed, "The expected Proclamation is 'out' tonight in the 'Star.'"[9]

Two news readers, one far beyond the metropolis and one deep inside it, experienced the extreme ends of the spectrum from scarcity to abundance of print.[10] But scarcity, as we will see, could be mitigated by the efforts people undertook to use informal means, outside of market-oriented distribution (e.g., subscribing to national magazines) and institutional dissemination (e.g., borrowing from social libraries), to make their reading life full. Traditionally, scholars have gauged the commercial or institutional availability of print in rural or small-town America by investigating local bookstores,[11] presses,[12] book ownership patterns,[13] or social libraries.[14] Alternatively, some map availability by tracing transportation routes from the cities to the hinterlands.[15] A wide range of sources have been called upon in these studies, including probate inventories,[16] library charges,[17] bookstore advertisements,[18] libraries' records,[19] and literary societies' annual reports.[20] However, by their nature, such sources cannot easily capture dissemination beyond the point of sale or institutional contact.[21]

Personal letters and diaries are particularly revealing of the non-commercial and extra-institutional ways that people circulated print matter.[22] We combed over 5,583 Civil War–era letters and diaries and recorded every encounter with print culture reported in them by 1,106 individuals, at least 10 from each state or territory, soldiers as well as civilians. Because less than 20 per cent of all Americans lived in urban areas at the time[23] and because most soldiers were deployed for combat in and around Southern towns, or in the wilderness, the vast majority of these people were operating, like Anne Loomis North, well beyond the metropolis and thus beyond the easy reach of formal urban print distribution. We discovered that it was through friends' and family members' informal loans and gifts – not commercial venues or lending institutions – that these readers most frequently acquired reading materials. The war's destruction of presses, dislocation of businesses, and derangement of transportation routes made these readers more dependent than ever on informal dissemination.[24]

Here we can only sketch some of the instances of how this type of informal dissemination operated in both the Union and Confederacy, and in areas contested by the two.[25] We intend to show that readers beyond the metropolis managed to avail themselves, through informal dissemination, of a wide array of print matter that helped them counterbalance commercial and institutional print scarcity. But this kind of circulation did not simply supplement formal distribution, for it fostered an entirely different communications environment than that which characterized commercial and institutional dissemination. Printed items disseminated through informal channels lost some of their impersonality as market-distributed commodities because the channels through which they flowed were, by their very nature, heavily mediated by interpersonal and group interactions. A book, magazine, or newspaper travelling through such personal networks became enriched with specific social meanings.[26]

That enrichment has implications for Civil War historiography. For many historians, the Civil War represents a turning point in terms of economic consolidation, bureaucratization, and allegiance to the nation.[27] Literary specialists, too, point to these factors as instrumental to the production of "patriotic gore," the nationalistic literary output of the era.[28] Yet, as Alice Fahs argues, "[i]n the realm of literary culture, however, the war was often interpreted as personal experience in such a way as to complicate emergent understandings of an organized or centralized nationhood." Printed material itself, including newspapers laden with patriotic verse and stories, could appeal to intimate sentiments, social sensibilities, and local identities.[29] When print – even the most hard-core news item – was disseminated informally, it often became imbued with additional patriotic signification or a patriotism mediated by local communities. That informal dissemination underwrote the enduring strength of local connections touches on a question of concern to many historians: why soldiers fought in a war with such high casualty rates.[30] After all, what soldiers read informed the sense of duty and obligation that some historians point to as their motivation. "Cause" – in its varied iterations – as a motivation for fighting was being constructed, we would argue, not so much through an individual soldier's direct encounters with the patriotic printed word,[31] as through reading mediated by networks of informal print dissemination that reoriented the reader back to family and community. Because reading material sent through social channels tied soldiers closer to loved ones, it probably did more to shore up morale than newspapers or other items impersonally purchased in camp and its environs from sutlers or vendors.[32]

Because most informally distributed items were sent from afar, they were dependent upon the postal service, express companies, and personal couriers to reach recipients. We begin below with these long-distance relationships and then move to face-to-face interactions. Newspapers sent in the mail by families and friends, not publishers, were the most common print matter informally entering communities beyond the metropolis. As an alternative to sending such transient papers, which could easily go astray, people enclosed newsclips in envelopes, and transcribed extracts and quotations from periodicals and sometimes other printed sources in their letters. Also coming from a distance were books, gifts that were often tucked into express packages, or mailed separately at rates higher than those accorded newspapers. Of course, printed materials continued to be given as gifts in person and lent that way as well. But the war provided novel situations of face-to-face exchange and other forms of immediate acquisition. One of these was confiscating items lost on the battlefield, discarded on army routes, abandoned at plantations, and pilfered from personal libraries; these often entered into the social life of the scavengers, who sent them home as relics. Another was swapping newspapers by military personnel with the enemy across picket lines; these forged temporary bonds of truce and trust. As we will see, there was a dual purpose at work in this kind of dissemination: providing people beyond the metropolis with materials they would not have otherwise had, and conveying to them the "social imprint"[33] – an intangible personal impress or material marking in the form of marginalia or inscription – the books, magazines, and newspapers acquired as they moved from hand to hand far from any original point of sale.

Transient Papers

Sending newspapers via the postal system was the most cost-effective way that private citizens could communicate with one another over long distances.

The lowest rate for sending letters virtually anywhere within the Union was at least three times more before 1863; the lowest letter rate in the Confederacy throughout the war was 2.5 times more.[34] Not surprisingly, then, transient newspapers served as a surrogate for writing, a way of keeping lines of communication flowing.[35] However, demand for newspapers surged during the war and so transient papers' textual content itself was valued along with the social handshake they represented. Recipients of transient papers could acquire for free a wider array of titles than would be feasible by paying for subscriptions. In this way, the New York *Herald* could reach into even the smallest Midwestern town and a town's local newspaper could wind up being read in the far West or in an Eastern metropolis.[36]

To send a transient paper, someone had to write the recipient's name and address (and nothing more) on it or on an open-ended wrapper into which it was placed, put stamps on it, and then go to a post office to mail it. When postal rates changed, as they did in July 1863, eager recipients were sure to remind senders. One Ohioan deployed to Big Black River, Mississippi, implored his wife on the first day of that month to send him copies of the *Holmes County Republican* and the *Holmes County Farmer*: "I do wish you would put up one of each every week, put two 'one cent' Stamps on the Bundle and send them to me."[37] Because senders were prohibited from writing anything else, even their own name, on penalty of paying letter-rate, it was hard for recipients to know sometimes exactly who mailed them a paper. "Some kind friend, I don't know who, has sent me 'Frank Leslie's Illustrated Newspaper' for three weeks for which I am very thankful," a twenty-one-year-old Piqua, Ohio, schoolteacher mused in March 1862; "it may be Mr. Jeffrey, It looks like his handwriting."[38] To avoid confusion, people alerted recipients in letters that they would be getting a transient paper and that they should acknowledge receipt, so correspondence became a regulating mechanism for the flood of papers. One Sumner, Kansas, carpenter serving as a Union sergeant in Tennessee informed his wife in May 1863, "I have sent you several papers have you got them I will send you 2 with this letter let me know in your next if you git them."[39] Because letters and transient newspapers often travelled together, people mentioned them in the same breath. "Will send my letter & some *papers* to the post office by the first opportunity," a tailor's wife in Waynesboro, Virginia, promised her Confederate husband away at the front.[40] A transient paper's journey did not always end with addressees, for they could be but one link in a chain-letter effect of further dissemination. "*Send me some papers*," a rural Virginia minister's daughter requested of her father in the army in June 1862, and explained, "if you only knew how one paper was caught at and sent all over the county."[41] Transient news was contagious.

In northern metropolitan areas papers could, increasingly throughout the war, arrive at one's doorstep through official carriers. But most rural areas in the Union and the Confederate states were not yet provided with this service. So people there improvised modes of direct delivery. Passing steamboats could pitch papers to addressees, as in one instance on Stones River in Murfreesboro, Tennessee, as noted by a local planter's daughter in May 1861: "The 'Hope' passed up earlier than usual, threw off a paper to Bro. Wilson."[42] Unofficial couriers could be recruited to do the job. "There is a soldier who carries & brings letters & papers from the [Virginia] 55th [Infantry] once a week," one woman told her father in that regiment.[43]

Soldiers constantly requested papers from home.[44] Some did this because they could not get news in their remote location. A sergeant in Sugar Creek, Kansas, in January 1862, beseeched his wife, "I would like you to send me some late papers for we hear nothing heare."[45] Being on the march made it particularly hard to get the news. "Please send me a newspaper if you have an opportunity to do so," a Virginia private in the Chesapeake Artillery wrote to his aunt in October 1862. "I have [not] seen one since I left Gordonsville," where a battle took place the previous July.[46] Sometimes not just any paper would do; it had to be published in the home town. "I have not seen a Paper from Holmes County since the 28th of December," a Mississippi-based Ohio colonel from there complained to his wife in July 1863, after six months of deprivation; "I would like to read the local news."[47] The news desired did not have to be of events of great import. "Send me a San Antonio newspaper with social news," a Mexican-American captain serving in a Texas regiment in Louisiana requested of his brother-in-law back home; he explained on another occasion, "Anything that comes from San Antonio makes my heart glad."[48] Such local news was considerably more relevant than metropolitan dailies to dislocated military personnel and civilians craving news of home.

People back home welcomed the chance to send papers to the front. One motivation was humanitarian. After packing "two letters and two papers for Rob," her brother, a young women in Scipio, Ohio, in October 1861 remarked that she "Felt sorry for the [poor] boys that lay in camp and have to endure so many hardships and are cheated out of what they ought to have." One more reason was to share the reading of a particular item with the soldiers. "Charlie, have you read Carl Schurz's speech upon 'Restoring the Union by extinguishing Slavery?' It is a magnificent address," another Ohioan asked her soldier fiancé in March 1862. "In it he says – but stop I will send you the paper that contains it and you can read it for yourself."[49] Sending transient papers could thus open spaces in letters for writing about other matters. Conversely, newspapers could substitute for stationery, albeit in defiance of the law prohibiting such markings. The penalty for writing anything on newspapers except the name and address of the recipient was a higher, letter-rate postage payment.[50] "Having received a *Journal* from you this morning endorsed with a wish to hear from me, I take this opportunity ... for sending a few words," an Irish-American officer serving in Tunstall's Station, Virginia, wrote to his wife in May 1862, referring to the contraband lines she scratched in the transient paper.[51] The need to communicate was so great, it was worth the risk of personalizing the print media.

Not all papers commuted from home to battlefield, for the direction of flow was commonly reversed. Sometimes rural soldiers were deployed to metropolitan areas where they could supply folks back home with big-city newspapers and enjoy a night out on the town too. "I was to the Theater last night and saw M[a]cBeth performed it is one of Shakespeers best plays, it was played pretty well," a Kansas sergeant told his wife, who was staying with relatives in Lafayette, Indiana, in April 1863; "I will send you the Nashvill Union it is one [of] the best union papers printed in the south[.] I have sent 2 or 3 to Father has he got them I will send you papers often."[52] Even if soldiers were not within walking distance of a city, some still could take advantage of metropolitan papers' wide distribution to send transient news home. Stationed in Maryland Heights near Harpers Ferry, one soldier had enough access to Baltimore dailies to keep up with national news and to mail papers to his wife in New Cumberland, West Virginia. "I send you a Baltimore American with the President's decision in, on the disaster at Winchester," he wrote, in November 1863, regarding Abraham Lincoln's refusal to court-martial an incompetent Union general.[53] Local small-town papers that soldiers came across in their out-of-the-way sojourns could be as valued as their urban counterparts. "I thank you for the Fort Smith Union ... which you had the kindness to send me," one Swiss immigrant in Winesburg, Ohio, wrote to her husband in Arkansas.[54] No paper was too insignificant to send home.

The worth of transient papers, whether sent from camp or home, was often gauged by their social meaning. The woman just mentioned, for example, added, "I always feel quite proud of such things from [you] and I take care of them as I would of a sacred memento."[55] Thus papers could become tokens of social exchange over long distances. Anne North in Washoe, Nevada, whom we met at the outset, after complaining about her lack of news from the East, subsequently was deluged with periodicals in response. Her parents in Syracuse, New York, sent her *Ballou's Dollar Monthly* (Boston), *Godey's Lady's Book* (Philadelphia), *M'me Demorest's Quarterly Mirror of Fashions* (New York), and the *Onondaga Standard* (Syracuse), among other unnamed items.[56] She reciprocated with her own local sheet, the *Washoe Times*. "We receive the Standard now regularly, for which we are *greatly obliged* to you," she wrote in April 1863; "It is a real treat to us all. I hope you enjoy our little paper as much."[57] Sending newspapers could serve a parenting purpose for families separated by the war. A Florida railroad magnate in Gainesville sent to his wife in Fernandina a "batch of newspapers," including "some New York papers ..., [and] a Richmond paper containing a letter from the Rev Mr Palmer which will repay your perusal. It is a very interesting & high toned production." He then turned his attention to his son, with specific directions: "Tell Wick I will be obliged to him if he will read it with attention – but *not at night*, for the print is very fine & bad." The paper was but a prelude to a future reunion, a temporary surrogate for face-to-face instruction: "I will discuss it with you when we meet."[58] Papers were instrumental to maintaining social ties in a time of turmoil.

However crucial to social relationships transient papers were, they often failed to arrive at their intended destinations. Carriers were tempted to steal them, and people who received misdirected papers held on to them because of their use value as reading matter. "You say you send me a paper every day," a Union adjutant in camp near Stafford, Virginia, just before the Battle of Fredericksburg in December 1862, complained to his father in Pittsburgh; "I have had about one or two a week (on average)."[59] His father soon responded with a new tactic: hiding newsprint in sealed letters. "I have just cut from the [Pittsburgh] Chronicle Major Moody's description of the battle of Fredericksburg ... and as most of the newspapers I send you do not reach you[,] I will enclose this."[60] Thereafter, the adjutant's father stopped sending newspapers and opted to mail newsclips at the more expensive letter rate.

Print in Envelopes

The Pittsburgher was not alone in choosing correspondence as a more secure form of delivery than transient papers. Out in Nininger, Minnesota, a schoolteacher's wife explained in a letter to her husband, a corporal in Little Rock, that "I did not send the papers that I was going to but I have cut the pieces out that I wished you to see. Will send them in this as you will be more likely to get them."[61] Inside the folds of many letters could be found short clippings from newspapers and other periodicals. These solved a problem other than the losing of newspapers in the mail system. Many transient newspaper senders, as we have seen, intended the recipient to read a specific item in the paper, but post office regulations prohibited marking these passages by pen or pencil. So, why not cut out the column of interest and stuff it in an envelope? Alternatively, senders copied down extracts from printed materials – a means of delivering the printed word without scissoring the page. That these are important ways of disseminating print beyond the metropolis is often overlooked because focus has fallen on intact books or periodicals as intellectual units read in their entirety. The very fact that clips and extracts bore abundant physical traces of the sender – e.g., selection, careful cutting, marginalia, painstaking transcription – gave them power. The social imprint on clips and extracts, after all, is more obvious than upon transient papers, which could only bear the mark of the sender's hand in inscribing the destination to which the paper was sent. Papers travelled alone, while clips and extracts sojourned with correspondence. Furthermore, the enclosures and extracts invited an intertextuality between them and the content of the accompanying letter.

While many of the short pieces clipped from papers were literary (especially verses), some highlighted specific political and economic issues – especially after mid-1863, when readers began to weary of daily reading and writing about war news in their diaries and letters.[62] It follows that they figured in opinion-sharing and sometimes in opinion-making. A farmwoman in Spring Hill, Texas, enclosed a clip, in January 1864, to her husband, a cavalry lieutenant in Marksville, Louisiana, about measures in the Lone Star State to counter currency depreciation and chart its own course within the Confederacy. "I send you Gov. Murrah's message. I do not know that you have seen it. Whether or not, I believe you will appreciate my motive,"[63] which apparently was to soften the hardened stance he had expressed against the governor.[64] Clips could concisely convey new political positions. "A move has been on foot during the last week, to Substitute Greenbacks for our present hard currency," a Reno prospector announced to his brother in Dutch Flat, California, in May 1864, about a "mass meeting" on the topic at which he spoke. "A paragraph, from one of our daily papers, which I enclose will Show you how I Stood."[65] Since newsclips said it for them, senders were spared from inscribing in their own handwriting their sometimes controversial opinions.

Sending clips could also relieve correspondents of the burden of reporting details of the death of loved ones. Obituary notices said it all. After rumours of a July 1862 accident on board a Union vessel on which her brother served, one cotton factor's wife in Madison Springs, Georgia, put out a call to her family members to find out his fate. "Yesterday came a few soiled hurried lines in pencil from Willie [her husband, a cavalry officer] dated June 29th enclosing a piece from a Philadelphia Newspaper confirming the loss of the Mound City & death of my brother John. God grant we may meet in that delightsome Land, 'ere many years have passed away!'"[66] Sometimes a social visitor could bear grim tidings in an envelope. "After dinner Mr. Cabell brought us a letter enclosing an extract from the *Lynchburg Republican* saying that Cary was mortally wounded on the 25th,"[67] a Virginia planter's daughter wrote about her brother in May 1864. Clippings on their own without supporting evidence, however, could give a false impression in a time of conflicting news and unreliable published death lists. This report, like many, proved inaccurate.[68]

Senders could enclose multiple clips in their envelopes. In this way, they became akin to news aggregators, pulling together diverse choice pieces. In October 1862 a Confederate private stationed in Camp Forney near Mobile collected telegraphic reports for his wife back home in Cushing, Alabama, in order to give her hope for their side's eventual victory in the war. "I send you some dispatches giving an account of [Gen Braxton] Bragg's fighting in Kentucky," he noted, warning her that "They are rather conflicting" – typical of journalism at the time – "But there is no doubt but he gained a great victory."[69] People on the home front provided the valuable service for loved ones in the army away from news outlets. To do so, civilians, especially women left behind,[70] had to scan the latest news with a discerning eye, given the often unreliable reportage, the chaotic deployment of troops on uncertain battlefields, and quickly shifting tactical manoeuvres. This was particularly true during the early stages of the war. After reading the news shortly before fighting broke out in northern Virginia in July 1861, a tailor's wife in rural Staunton clipped some items she deemed trustworthy for her husband, a private on the march, about a build-up of forces that could signal a clash of arms near Camp Garnett where his brother was stationed. She knew from reading these pieces that they contained indispensable information of which he might not have been aware; soldiers on the march seldom had access to the latest newspapers. But rather than taking up valuable space on the sheet writing out the details, she took scissors in hand, and inserted the clips into an envelope with her letter filled with family business. "I send you some pieces from the last '*Spectator*,'" she wrote him of a local paper. One was a published letter "from Camp Garnett (from Col. [Jonathan M.] Heck) stating that his command was getting along finely, & were eager & ready for a fight."[71] Another was a "letter asking for assistance for the Hospital at Beverly," on the road from camp. She pieced together the Heck letter with the hospital information to conclude, correctly, that a battle was nigh – the July 11 Battle of Rich Mountain – and that the brother's unit would be engaged. Senders feared that the accumulated pile of clips carried in correspondence might overwhelm recipients, but usually it was welcomed. "You speak of '*troubling*' me with 'these scraps,'" a mother in Marion, Ohio, replied in July 1863 to her son in the Union diplomatic corps. She assured him, "Don't think so; everything that affects you in any way interests me." Any intelligence relayed from the world her son inhabited was worthwhile: "Read the copies of enclosed dispatches with much interest."[72] It drew her closer to him by helping her imagine his consular life in Hamburg, Germany.

Extracts performed much of the same social work of clippings.[73] They differed in that they allowed the sender to retain the original copy, but because they were handwritten, the social imprint was highly tangible. These pieces of lovingly rendered script further narrowed the distance between dislocated friends and family. A young woman in the isolated North Carolina uplands copied a published poem for her cousin in Okolona, Mississippi, in February 1863: "I send you some verses which I think you will read with interest both for their intrinsic merit and on account of their *Southern* origin." Written by a major in the First North Carolina Regiment, they reflected the cousins' ancestral ties to the area. "The author formerly lived in Watauga County," the sender explained. "He was killed in one of the battles around Richmond. Do you not think them beautiful?"[74] That kind of question soliciting a response to extracts was not uncommon and cemented further the social bonds of correspondents. This was especially true when senders personalized the extracted material by adding their own improvisations upon it. A Confederate private at Dog River Factory, Alabama, took the liberty of abridging "The Widowed Heart," by British poet Charlotte Elliott, for his wife in June 1862. "I have picked out two verses which I think is applicable to your case. And pay particular attention to the last vers[e]," he enjoined his spouse, who was lonely and constantly worried about her husband and two brothers in the army. The extract began with the line "Poor desolated heart!" and ended with Heaven's "balm for hearts bereft and riven" that "Illume[s] the eternal words."[75] She replied that it "was beautiful poetry you sent me and suited my case very well. I receive a portion of that balm evry day. I feel like a pore desolate heart but I have a friend that sticketh closter [closer] than a brother that watches over me and you." The extract not only fortified her, but inspired a flourish of extracting and paraphrasing: "Iff you meet with troubbles / and trials on the way / Cast your care on Jesus / and don't forget to pray."[76] She continued to alter published poets' words. In October of that year, as her brother was dying in Knoxville, she sighed, "Oh! that this unholy war would cease." She summoned lines from Oliver Goldsmith's "The Hermit," and, in identifying with the poem's hero, Edwin – a broken-hearted, cloistered lover – substituted her own name "Linny" for his in one of the lines she extracted: "No, never from that hour to part / we'd live and love so true / The sigh that rends thy constant heart / Should break thy Linny,s too."[77] Some extractors refrained from adding their own words, but took comfort in simply writing those of others as a meditative act of sharing. "My dearest Love I felt happy in God this morning and was singing to myself when presently I took up your Hymn Book and oppened it by guess and the first Hymn that presented itself to my eyes was this," a Kansas wife visiting Missouri informed her soldier husband in April 1863. "I will copy for it done my soul good and expressed exactly my feelings and therefore I think it will do you good also."[78] The labour of extracting gave these scribblers a semblance of personal agency under the stress of war: they could do something good for someone in need, emotionally and literarily.

Gifting and Lending

We have seen how transient newspapers and short pieces circulated informally through the mails created opportunities for getting reading material that would otherwise have been out of reach. Under conditions of scarcity beyond the metropolis, gift giving and lending could also augment the local stores of available printed matter, especially books and magazines. True, sending transient papers, clips, and extracts was a type of gift giving; after all, few people asked for them back. Yet these differed from traditionally conceived gifts insofar as they lacked significant monetary value and they often were resent by the recipient – the aforementioned chain-letter effect. Books and monthlies, the most common literary gifts, tended to cost more and were meant to be kept and appreciated by recipients. These were often given face to face, or sent through express companies, in addition to the mails.

Most literary gifts were occasional and conferred upon children or young adults, but those who were in need could receive them from more metropolitan areas any time of the year. In May 1863, for example, Anne North in Nevada was grateful to her parents in Syracuse for bestowing books upon her children: "The children *all* would thank you for the books you sent – they are greatly pleased with them." Even the youngest "Georgie looked at his once or twice with evident pleasure at being remembered, but cannot think of confining his attention to one thing long enough to *read a book*."[79] For a sixteen-year-old Mexican American on a remote California ranch an unexpected gift of the novel *The Count of Monte Cristo* "brought me ... from town to day" by a local judge from Los Angeles, so excited her that she "Commenced reading it to night."[80] Even adults continued to solicit literary gifts from parents. A recent immigrant in Esther, Minnesota, in November 1862 hinted at some gift ideas to her father in Norway explaining that in the American books available to her, "the print is poor, by no means as good as the print in the Norwegian books." She added, "Speaking of Norwegian books, there are none to be had for miles and miles."[81] Her father apparently promised to send her the gifts, for she reminded him in a later letter, "It would be wonderful to get the books. Whenever you have the opportunity, send them."[82] The parental function of book giving was transferred to army ranks, where reading matter of any sort was craved. "This morning Col. Andrews made me a present of a volume of Shakespeare," a Minnesota corporal in Arkansas told his wife in December 1863. "The colonel is a dear friend to me; but estimates me far above my real worth."[83] He may have read this Christmas gift as a signal of his aspirations for promotion, for officers often displayed bound volumes in their tents for visitors, as a mark of their status.

Naturally, officers' quarters became something of a lending library for subordinates. The case of Christian A. Fleetwood, an African American sergeant major in the Fourth Regiment United States Coloured Troops, serving in Virginia in 1864, is instructive. With a voracious appetite for reading, he supplied himself well throughout the year 1864 by borrowing from white officers around him – his captain, lieutenant, major, even the chaplain. Among "papers & books" he mentions acquiring in this way were a Beadle dime novel, a historical romance by British novelist G.P.R James, a novel about a young man making his way in the world, and *The Count of Monte-Christo*, as well as the *Atlantic Monthly, Harper's Monthly*, and a "glee book."[84] Because none of his officers were black he had to subscribe to African American periodicals like the *Christian Recorder* and the *Anglo African*.[85] Exchange among peers created an exclusive social reading circle. Having "not seen a newspaper in three days," in his camp at Mine Run, Virginia, in January 1864, an Irish American lieutenant from Ohio sought out something to read during a visit to a captain's quarters: "Was over to see [Billy] O'Shea to-night. Borrowed a philosophical work from him."[86] The tug of sociable book borrowing among bunkmates can sometimes be felt even as an officer penned a letter home – in this instance, he was interrupted for the pragmatic purpose of lending a volume for military instruction. "I am lying flat on my bed with my writing *consarns* before me," a Minnesota corporal scribbled to his wife in October 1861. "Hold on a minute. Cressy wants my tactics, and Dr. Pride is pulling my coattail for something."[87] The printed word played no small role in camaraderie. Sometimes friendships between civilians and officers on the march, however evanescent, were forged over a borrowed volume. One captain posted near the plantation home of a young woman in Bayou Boeuf, Louisiana, in August 1864, returned to his tent with an armful of literature and promises to "call again to return the books ... loaned him."[88]

For book-starved Southerners whose new purchases dwindled down to almost nothing because of the Union blockade, the collapse of publishing houses, shortages of paper, and massive inflation, a well-stocked home library, often brimming with classics and other older works, became a haven. Borrowing from it allowed literary sensibilities to continue; single books that might not otherwise have been used passed through several hands. The aforementioned Louisianan, for example, raided her cousin's stash of volumes from his nearby plantation mansion in October 1863: "Returned home late in the evening, brought with me several large books that cousin Bob wished me to read." As she rode home in a cart with her precious commodities, "the mules got frightened and tried to run." Although advised by the driver to "jump out," she, not wanting to injure her takings, instead "stepped out carefully and held on to [her] package of books," which included William H. Prescott's 1837 *Ferdinand and Isabella* and Thomas Moore's poems published around 1806.[89] Shortages that necessitated borrowing induced readers to turn to titles they would have cast aside in better times. "I have been reading several old English plays from a large volume Uncle John lent me, and have enjoyed them very much," a West Virginia woman told her diary in January 1862. "Home's old play of 'Douglass' is [a] delight, and Howe's 'Fair Penitent' and 'Jane Shore' are very pretty and some comedies have amused me no little especially 'The Devil to Pay.'"[90] Some readers no doubt discovered for the first time that musty books from another decade could be entertaining. These venerable imprints often spent time on the road during the war. When citizens of the Confederacy closed up their homes due to regimental mobilization in their towns or enemy occupation of their state, they often packed up their home libraries and sent them to safer places where they would not be confiscated or destroyed – much to the benefit of their new guardians. One maimed veteran, who moved in with his brother-in-law in Lenoir, North Carolina, after being discharged, had sent his library there before joining the family. His niece wrote in February 1862 of her father and the newcomer: "He and Uncle Walter spend most of their time reading. They have Uncle Walter's library here, and I think they bid fair to read the whole of it through." For her father, the library helped stabilize his life: "Pa thinks so much about the War that I believe it would affect his health seriously if he did not do something to divert his mind."[91] As the Confederacy crumbled around them, the home library that retreated in the face of the enemy remained standing.

Print Acquisition in Enemy Confrontations

Home libraries left behind did not fare as well. Conquering enemy soldiers often ransacked them or stole their contents sometimes to send back home, as war relics – another way print circulated beyond the metropolis. When Yankee cavalry came to formerly Confederate-controlled Upperville, Virginia, in December 1864, they descended upon one farm home with a vengeance. "They would not wait for me to unlock any drawers, but with their heavy boots kicked and broke open my handsome furniture," wrote a farmwife whose husband was off fighting. "In the Library they broke open the oak book case, threw everything out of it over the floor, took the books, paper, etc.[,] ... and took some of the handsome books from the table."[92] Sometimes Confederate officers who anticipated Union occupation sequestered away libraries of prominent citizens, but often to no avail. This happened in Winchester in 1862 to the local collection of Senator James Murray Mason, away in England on a diplomatic mission, as Nathaniel Banks's Union army approached the town. Within a year Union forces had ferreted out the books' scattered hiding places. Writing home to his wife, a West Virginian sergeant explained, "These books were taken out of Mason's house by the rebels, about two weeks before Bank's army first came in here, and given to the citizens, to keep the Yankees from getting them." The holdings proved to be a bonanza for him and his comrades: "I have now selected the 'Congressional Globe' of the 35th Congress, both sessions, and one other session of another congress. I do not remember the No. I have also maps off in sections of the states and territory's." He got greedier still: "If I can, I am going to look over another pile tomorrow morning, and if I find anything interesting I will send it." Obviously, such a large "box of books" could not be easily mailed at a low cost, so he ventured approaching a private company for "sending them home by express if we can find no other way."[93] The volumes taken captive would find a place on a new bookshelf in enemy territory.

The war rendered some books momentarily homeless, however, until someone found them lying on the ground and adopted them. Soldiers dropped books on the march, lost them in the heat of battle, or threw them out train windows for scavengers to hunt. These were yet other means by which print was scattered about through informal dissemination. The young Louisianan, who so highly regarded her borrowed books from her cousin's plantation library, could not bear to see a novel go to waste that was discarded by a passing Union soldier who may have helped himself to some produce from her garden in March 1864. "Rose early this morning, dressed and went in the yard and hoed around a few of my flowers before breakfast," she recorded; apparently having found an orphaned volume in the dirt, she "came in and read a few pages in a very good novel left here by the yankees." She stretched out her reading of the book for a week before she revealed the title: "Finished my novel – 'Redman O'Neil or the Substance and the Shadow' today – very good and highly interesting."[94] Published in 1859, the tale at least was a little fresher than that reading matter available in her relatives' libraries. A book found on the ground was sometimes the only trace left by a missing combatant, giving a clue about his last whereabouts. The day after the Battle of Brandy Station (9 June 1862) in Virginia, the largest cavalry engagement in the nation's annals, a participant inscribed the grim news of finding a victim's abandoned volumes: "I ... took five men with me to collect the dead and wounded," he scrawled. "We could not find Charles' body – we found his Bible and blank book."[95] While these items were recovered by a comrade, soldiers were painfully aware that books they took into battle might fall into the wrong hands. After tearing up a letter from his wife for "risk of having it read for the amusement of the Yankies," a Confederate captain facing the enemy in Virginia wrote to her in August 1861 that "It is almost as bad as loosing [*sic*] – my Bible would be."[96] Not all literary objects found on the ground fell there by accident, nor were they all so precious. For servicemen encamped outside of regular newspaper distribution channels, deliberately discarded news was like manna from Heaven. "Not a day passes but that we receive the daily Louisville papers which passengers on the trains are kind enough to throw down to us," a Minnesotan surrounded by guerrilla fighters and bivouaced ten feet away from a railroad bridge in Camp Rough and Ready (Hardin, Kentucky) told his wife in January 1862. Found papers could be put to emancipatory purposes, too. One slave, who joined in an exodus of contrabands into federally controlled Stafford County, Virginia, took advantage of papers left behind by Fredericksburg Confederates in advance of the first Yankee occupation of the city in April 1862. Union "Soldiers off duty, gathered around us and asked all kinds of questions in reference to the Whereabouts of the 'Rebels,'" he remembered. "I had stuffed My pockets full of Rebel Newspapers and, I distributed them around as far as they would go greatly to the delight of the Men, and by this act Won their good opinions right away."[97] No matter what the circumstances of their orphaning, such printed items soon found ready step-parents.

One of the most remarkable practices that developed during the war, probably starting in 1862, was newspaper exchanges across enemy lines by pickets. They sometimes stood at the very flashpoint where opposing armies met and so were within shooting range of one another. Instead of taking fire, the soldiers facing off came somehow to recognize their mutual needs for printed news and conspired together to call a truce to swap papers. The implications of this – fraternization with the enemy – alarmed the high command so that it became formally forbidden and could lead to court-martial proceedings.[98] "They say the Yankee pickets on the other side offer ours sometimes to exchange papers," an army wife at Camp Nickajack, Georgia, informed her sister in Mississippi in August 1863, "but our men are not allowed to have anything to do with them."[99] Still, soldiers persisted and some commanding officers turned their backs, so great was the need and the social impulse to share news. One Confederate adjutant in Hamilton, Virginia, in May 1863, described how it was done:

> We had some fun a few days ago down on the River with the Yankee pickets. we have been in the habit of exchanging papers with them, by meeting each other in the middle of the River, both sides are very friendly on picket. One of our men (Smith) met one half way and exchanged with him, as they approached each other, the Yankee said hallo, old pard have you any Tabacco for me, O, yes a small piece; thank you sir. and he started back after receiving his paper and Tabacco. another Yankee seeing his friend meet with such good success, started and swam across.[100]

Needless to say, when done across rivers, the practice mostly took place in seasons before the water turned icy cold. One ingenious solution to the problem of frigid waterways separating pickets was to devise small boats for shipping papers and other goods across to the enemy. A Catholic priest with the Fourteenth Louisiana depicted it in April 1863: "At various places along [the picket] line our boys were amusing themselves by sending across the river their little schooner, laden with tabacco and other commodities to the Yankee pickets who lined the banks of the Rappahannock, receiving in exchange Yankee papers, coffee etc." It took not a little coordination and abundant trust to pull off exchanges.[101] The momentary exchange of papers could lead to sustained sociabilities. "A number of the rebels have come over to this side and talked to our men for hours, some of our boys have also gone over and talked to them, and exchanged papers," a West Virginia Unionist lieutenant on the Potomac noted in July 1863, shortly after the Battle of Gettysburg. "They make an agreement before either party ventures to cross that they will not harm or detain each other."[102] Soldiers recognized the odd "time-out" effect of newspaper exchange. A Georgia dirt farmer "on picket on the banks of the Rappahannock" in June 1863 watched in amazement as "2 of the 2nd Vermont regt swam over to us [t]o day, and exchanged papers." He reflected that "pickets acts [*sic*] quite different now from what the[y] did last year for then we were shooting at each other every sight of each other." He was nevertheless well aware of the tenuousness of the peaceful social relations paper exchange fostered: "But when we meet in Battle we are quite changed."[103] Still, for a brief moment, this Confederate was able to engage some friendly conversation and get hold of "a late New York Herald" he could never have imagined seeing on his farm in Worth County, Georgia.[104] As unlikely as it may have seemed, via enemy confrontation, print matter was informally disseminated throughout the war-torn American landscape.

Conclusion

The war had changed the face of dissemination in that it made informal ways of circulating print more important than ever before. A dramatic increase in postal activity during the war[105] signalled that more and different print materials were reaching a wide variety of places beyond the metropolis. Certainly periodical subscriptions accounted for only some of this activity; much of the remainder was due to transient papers, other mailable print items, and correspondence bearing newsclips and extracts. Alongside government-sponsored shipments, private express companies that cheaply carried bundles filled with food and clothing, with a book or two thrown in, thrived during the war.[106] One of these packages reached the Union-occupied Sea Islands in South Carolina, where Charlotte Forten, an African American schoolteacher from the North, was helping to bring literacy to the freedpeople. "In Miss T.[owne's] box came my parcel – so long looked for – containing ... a 'Liberator,' the first that I have seen since leaving home" on 22 October 1862. Back in Salem, Massachusetts, she had been a devoted reader of William Lloyd Garrison's abolitionist sheet, which circulated widely throughout the North from its Boston publication office, but had long been banned in the South. "How great a pleasure it is to see it. It is familiar and delightful to look upon as the face of an old friend," she wrote after Thanksgiving. "It is of an old date – October 31st – but it is not the less welcome for that." It must have seemed strange for her to open its pages under her new circumstances. "And what a significant fact it is that one may now sit here in safety – here in the rebellious little Palmetto State and read the 'Liberator,' and display it to one's friends, rejoicing over it in the fulness of one's heart as a very great treasure."[107] The paper was a "treasure" because it was not to be had in the South, because it came packaged with letters from loved ones back home, and because the "old friend" could finally be openly "displayed" to the new friends she grew to love on the Islands – the freed people who called her their teacher. Her act of sharing the paper – she probably lent it or read it aloud – was but one of the millions of face-to-face transmissions of printed material that occurred during the war in locations far from urban presses.

All of this activity, this informal dissemination, can be easily overlooked in the search for print beyond the metropolis. While studies of the rural bookstore, social or public library, publishing house, tract society, subscription agent, or newspaper press contribute greatly to an understanding of how people in the outskirts of urban areas received print, there is yet much more to be done on informal types of dissemination. In this volume, we see evidence of book sharing by dissenting ministers in eighteenth-century England (chapter 2); of the informal circulation of black newspapers in the interwar Caribbean (chapter 7); and of the sharing and oral reading of newspapers among English millworkers (chapter 8). Here we have concentrated on print materials circulating, but volumes could be written on the same print materials as they were used in everyday life. Although we touched upon some of these ways, the same sources we consulted – personal letters and diaries – yield insights into reception practices like reading aloud (itself a form of dissemination), the deployment of quotes from one's reading, the selectivity exercised in scrapbooking, and the recounting of discussions informed by reading printed news.

Considering dissemination and reception in this larger context is part of a worldwide movement among third-wave audience scholars seeking the meaning of reading as intrinsic to cultural, social, and political life.

Their goal is to "grasp ... 'media culture' particularly as it can be seen in the role of media in everyday life."[108] As we progress with our research, we are beginning to understand the "media culture" of the Civil War as a new environment for amateur production, informal dissemination, and common folk's reception practices. Clippings, for example, are but a sign of a news obsession that took hold after the first shots were fired. Transient newspapers provided vital information – such as troop movements, soldier correspondence, and death notices – that allowed readers to trace people tossed about by the war. Reading volumes of fiction, belles-lettres, histories, and biography faded before this intensive perusing of news columns. This is evidenced in the dramatic slowdown in occasional literary gift giving among adults. More reading and study was done in seclusion; but at the same time the need to maintain social ties through shared print grew as the war was shattering relationships due to the dislocation and, often the death, of loved ones. Those needs were perhaps more urgent in small towns and rural areas, where people had greater dependence upon fewer nearby neighbours and kin, and where, because of more limited access to formally distributed print, they hung on to every word that came to them. As we have seen, they often took it into their own hands to get supplies of printed matter. In this way, readers beyond the metropolis remained connected – to one another and to the unfolding national drama.

NOTES

The research on which this essay is based has been funded by a twelve-month National Endowment for the Humanities Fellowship (2012) awarded to Ronald J. Zboray. It draws from a book in progress, tentatively titled *The Bullet in the Book: Life, Death, and Reading during the Civil War*. Related research was previewed in "The Bullet in the Book: Reading Cultures during the Civil War," the 2010 Edward G. Holley Memorial Lecture delivered at the plenary session of the Library History Round Table at the American Library Association annual convention.

1 For this and the other quotes from her throughout the rest of this paragraph, see Anne Hendrix Loomis North, Washoe City, Nev., to George Lewis, 4 Jan. 1863, John Wesley North Papers, Huntington Library, San Marino, Calif. (hereafter, "JWNP-HL"). Stonehouse (1965). All quotations in this essay are as written; grammar, spelling, and punctuation are original and have not been corrected.

2 Zboray and Zboray (2011); Holzer (2012, 129–31); and Klingaman (2001, 229).

3 Samuel J. Reader, Soldier, Kan., to Ferdinand J. Wendell, 4 Jan. 1863, Samuel James Reader Letters, Kansas Historical Society, Topeka, Kans.

4 This is probably the *Morning Transcript*, published in Nevada City by Nathaniel P. Brown, who, like North, was a migrant from the Northeast and a devoted Republican. See "Nathaniel P. Brown," in *A Memorial and Biographical History of Northern California* (Chicago: Lewis Publishing Co., 1891), 327–9.

5 *The Saint Paul (Minn.) Daily Press* (1861–4).

6 *Virginia and Truckee Railroad: Queen of the Shortlines*, www.virginiatruckee.com (accessed 1 Feb. 2013); (Pred 1973; 1980, 2–4).

7 Horatio Nelson Taft, Washington, D.C., 13 Jan. 1863, Diary, Horatio Nelson Taft Diary, Library of Congress, Washington, D.C. (hereafter, "HNTD-LC").

8 Stepp and Hill (1961).

9 Taft, 1 Jan. 1863, Diary, HNTD-LC.

10 R. Brown (1989) traces the move from colonial scarcity to antebellum abundance of print.

11 Lindell (2004).

12 Stern (1956).

13 M. Harris (1971).

14 Stiffler (2011).

15 Zboray (1989).

16 Gilmore (1989); Kett and McClung (1984).

17 Zboray (1991); Pawley (2001).

18 D. Stewart (1978).

19 Wiegand (2011); Pawley (2010).

20 Hevel (2011); Hovde and Fritch (2005).

21 Some of the essays in this volume address circulation outside institutions in the formal marketplace. Our own study shows how earlier informal circulation patterns persisted into the mid-nineteenth century. For the prior century, see Kyle Roberts, "'I have hitherto been entirely upon the borrowing hand': The Acquisition and Circulation of Books in Early Eighteenth-Century Dissenting Academies," which describes the "rituals of sociability built around books" (1) loaned and borrowed in John Jenning's Academy in Kibworth Harcourt, a village in Leicestershire, England. The role of British mid-nineteenth-century local, non-commercial institutions in disseminating reading material under conditions of limited access is analysed in Robert Hall's essay "At the Dawn of the Information Age: Reading and the Working Classes in Ashton-under-Lyne, 1830–1850." A similar expansion to ours of the scope of print culture inquiry beyond authors, publishers, retailers, and readers, can be found in James Raven's recovery of job work printing in chapter 1, "Non-Metropolitan Printing and Business in Britain and Ireland between the Sixteenth and Eighteenth Centuries: Some Thoughts."

22 Diaries, of course, can be effectively used to study more formal and institutional circulation outside of the metropolis, as can be seen in Christine Pawley's "Organized Print: Clara Steen and Institutional Sites of Reading and Writing in the American Midwest, 1895-1920," and Lydia Wevers's, "Uneasy Occupancy: Sarah Grand, *The Beth Book*, and a Colonial Reader," both essays for this volume.

23 Traditionally, since 1930, the population threshold for judging a place as urban is a very low figure of 2,500 residents. Based on this, the exact figure for the 1860 urban population is 19.77 per cent. However, if a higher threshold of 100,000 residents is used as a yardstick of metropolitanization, then the percentage drops to 8.39 per cent. Figures calculated from Wilkie (1976); "United States Urban and Rural Population: 1790 to 1990," www.census.gov/population/censusdata/table-4.pdf (accessed 2 Feb. 2013).

24 On some of the practices related to reading during the Civil War, see Zboray and Zboray (2002). See also Kaser (1984). There are scattered references to soldiers' reading in Wiley (1952, 153–7). See also McPherson (1998).

25 The literature by journalism historians on the Civil War is vast, but very little of it deals with issues of distribution or reader reception. See, for example: Andrews (1955; 1970); Coopersmith (2004); B. Harris (1999); Dicken-Garcia and Dell'Orto (2008); and Van Tuyll (2000). Other journalism history sources on the war include Bulla and Borchard (2010); Sachsman, Rushing, and Morris (2008); Sachsman, Rushing, and Van Tuyll (2000); Van Tuyll, (2005); Risely (2001); J. Brown (2002); W. Thompson (1961); and Tucher (2006).

26 On literary commodification and the social, see Zboray and Zboray (1996a; 2005). Essays in this volume by Kyle Roberts (chapter 2) and Robert Hall (chapter 8) also emphasize the ways that sociability imbues texts with particular meanings.

27 Faust (1988). Bensel (1991); G.M. Fredrickson (1965); and Nevins (1959–71).

28 Aaron (1973); Wilson (1966).

29 Fahs (2001, 11).

30 McPherson (1997); Jimerson (1988); Hess (1988); and Gallagher (1997; 2011).

31 McPherson (1997, 92–3).

32 On the role of newspapers in morale building, see McPherson (1998).

33 Zboray and Zboray (2006, 221–42).

34 According to an Act of 3 March 1851, the postage on prepaid domestic letters, one half ounce or less, was from 5 cents to 3 cents within 3,000 miles (if not prepaid, the price remained five cents); Cullinan (1968, 63). As of 30 Aug. 1853, sending printed matter, like transient papers, under three ounces, cost one cent (Bissell and Kirby 1879, 446). As of 30 June 1863, the postage on print matter rose to two cents for four ounces and for letters to three cents for each

half ounce (each additional half ounce cost another three cents) United States, Post Office Department (1863a, 9, 11 [Sec. 23, p. 705]). In the Confederacy beginning with its formation in 1861, sending transient newspapers under three ounces published in the self-declared new nation cost two cents (and two cents for each additional ounce), whereas mailing one-half-ounce letters cost five cents within five hundred miles and ten cents beyond (and five cents for each additional ounce); Confederate States of America, Post Office Department (1861, 9). Kielbowicz (1989, 91–2).

35 Zboray (1993, 119–21); and Henkin (2006, 43–50).

36 For example, see Sarah E. Andrews, Hudson, Wisconsin, to James A. Andrews, 20 Nov. 1864 (Miller 1955, 30); Anne Hendrix Loomis North, Washoe City, Nev., to George S. Loomis and Mary Anne Lewis Loomis, 12 Apr. 1863, JWNP-HL; Wilder Dwight, Camp near Berryville, Va., to [William Dwight and Elizabeth Amelia Dwight], Brookline, Mass., 12 Mar. 1862 (Dwight and Dwight 1891, 206).

37 Marcus M. Spiegel, Big Black River, Miss., to Caroline Frances Hamlin Spiegel, 1 July 1863 (Byrne and Soman 1985, 298).

38 Estelle Morrow, Piqua, Ohio, 2 Mar. 1862, Diary, Estelle Morrow Diary, Indiana Historical Society, Indianapolis.

39 David Baker, Nashville, Tenn., to Rebecca Baker, 2 May 1863 (Petree 1994, 60).

40 Martha S. White Read, Waynesboro, Va., to Thomas Griffin Read, 16 Feb. 1862, Read Family Correspondence, Special Collections, University of Notre Dame, South Bend, Ind. (hereafter, "RFC-UND").

41 Mary Virginia Ward, Tappahannock, Va., to William Norvell Ward, 9 June 1862, Ward Family Papers, Library of Congress, Washington, D.C. (hereafter "WFP-LC").

42 Catherine Sills Carney Poindexter, Murfreesboro, Tenn., 21 May 1861, Diary, Kate S. Carney Diary, Southern Historical Collection, Wilson Library, University of North Carolina, Chapel Hill, N.C.

43 Mary Virginia Ward, Tappahannock, Va., to William Norvell Ward, 10 June 1862, WFP-LC.

44 Zboray and Zboray (2012).

45 David Baker, Sugar Creek, Kans., to Rebecca Baker, 12 Jan. 1862 (Petree 1994, 15).

46 John Hooff, Winchester, Va., to Mary Blincoe Ward, 2 Oct. 1862, WFP-LC.

47 Marcus M. Spiegel, Big Black River, Miss., to Caroline Frances Hamlin Spiegel, 1 July 1863 (Byrne and Soman 1985, 298).

48 Joseph Rafael Calistro de la Garza, Alexandria, La., to Bartholomew Joseph de Witt, 9 Sept. 1863, and Joseph Rafael Calistro de la Garza, Camp Holmes, Little Rock, Ark., to Elena de la Garza Yturri, 20 Aug. 1862 (J. Thompson 2011, 19 and 9).

49 Rachel Ann Stewart [*sic*] Cline, Scipio, Ohio, 12 Oct. 1861, Diary, Annie R. Stuart Diary, Center for Archival Collections, Bowling Green State University, Bowling Green, Ohio. Adelaide Eliza Case, Mecca, Ohio, to Charles N. Tenney, 23 Mar. 1862, Correspondence of Charles Tenney with Adelaide Case, University of Virginia, Charlottesville, Va. She probably refers to "The Suicide of Slavery: Speech of Carl Schurz Delivered at the Cooper Institute, New York, March 6, 1862," reprinted throughout the Union (e.g., *Washington Reporter*, 20 Mar. 1862).
50 United States, Post Office Department (1863a, 705; 1863b, 39); Confederate States of America, Post Office Department (1861, 5–6).
51 Patrick Robert Guiney, Tunstall's Station, Va., to Jeannette Margaret Doyle Guiney, 20 May 1862 (Samito, 1998, 101–2).
52 David Baker, Nashville, Tenn., to Rebecca Baker, 17 Apr. 1863, (Petree 1994, 56–7 and 199).
53 Milton Byron Campbell, Maryland Heights, Md., to Mary Campbell, 1 Nov. 1863 (Fluharty 2004, 81). "The Case of General Milroy," *The Daily Age*, 31 Oct. 1863.
54 Marie Elise Dubach Isley, Winesboro, Ohio, to Christian H. Isley, 18 Oct. 1863, Isely Family Papers, Wichita State University, Wichita, Kans. (hereafter, "IFP-WSU). *Fort Smith Union* (1863).
55 Marie Elise Dubach Isley to Christian H. Isley, 18 Oct. 1863, IFP-WSU.
56 Anne Hendrix Loomis North, Washoe City, Nev., to George S. Loomis and Mary Ann Lewis Loomis, 1 Mar. and 12 Apr. 1863, JWNP-HL. See also, in the same collection, her letters to them of 1 and 15 Feb., and 12 Oct. 1863.
57 Anne Hendrix Loomis North, Washoe City, Nev., to George S. Loomis and Mary Ann Lewis Loomis, 12 Apr. 1863, JWNP-HL.
58 David Levy Yulee, Gainesville, Fla., to Nannie C. Wickliffe Yulee, 5 Mar. 1863, David Levy Yulee Papers, University of Florida, Gainesville, Fla.
59 Albert Metcalf Harper, Stafford, Va., to John Harper and Lydia Electa Metcalf Harper, 2 Dec. 1862, Harper Family Papers, Library and Archives Division, Senator John Heinz History Center, Pittsburgh (hereafter HFP-HHC).
60 John Harper, Pittsburgh, to Albert Metcalf Harper, 27 Dec. 1862, HFP-HHC.
61 Elizabeth Caleff Bowler, Nininger, Minn., to James Madison Bowler, 14 Oct. 1864 (Foroughi 2008, 259).
62 We received this impression from reviewing our entire corpus of research; around July 1863 peak periods of written news discussion replace the relatively constant stream.
63 Harriet Eliza Person Perry, Spring Hill, Tx., to Theophilus Perry, 29 Jan. 1864 (Johansson 2000, 206).
64 Theophilus Perry, Trenton, La., to Harriet Eliza Person Perry, 17 July 1863 (Johansson 2000, 150).

65 George Washington Cassidy, American City, Nev., to Christopher Columbus Cassidy, 30 May 1864, Papers of George W. Cassidy Collection, University of Nevada, Reno, Reno, Nev.
66 Eleanor Kinzie Gordon, Savannah, Ga., 6 July 1862, Diary (Robertson 1986, 506). John H. Kinzie, Jr, appears in "List of Casualties on Board the U.S.S. Mound City" (C. Stewart, 1910, 180–1).
67 Lucy Gilmer Breckinridge, Grove Hill, Va., 30 May 1864, Diary (Robertson 1994, 189).
68 Lucy Gilmer Breckinridge, Grove Hill, Va., 2 June 1864, Diary (Robertson 1994, 190).
69 Grant Taylor, Camp Forney, Mobile, Ala., to Malinda J. Slaughter Taylor, 18 Oct. 1862 (Blomquist and Taylor 2000, 110).
70 On women constructing a political consciousness from their newspaper reading, see Zboray and Zboray (2010); and Zboray and Zboray (1996b).
71 Martha S. White Read, Waynesboro, Va., to Thomas Griffin Read, 10 July in letter dated 9 July 1861, RFC-UND. John Henry Read, Camp Garnett, Rich Mountain, Va., to Martha S. White Read, 23 June, 1861, RFC-UND.
72 Martha S. White Read, Waynesboro, Va., to Thomas Griffin Read, 10 July in letter dated 9 July 1861, RFC-UND. Nancy Dunlevy Anderson, Marion, Ohio, to James House Anderson, 5 July 1863 (Anderson 1904, 290). Scrapbooks were one way of controlling the profusion of clips. See Garvey (2012).
73 Extracting as a form of circulation outside the traceable market operates in much the same way as the citation. See, for example, Brad Evans's discussion of the "movement of shared points of reference through [*bibelots*] magazines," in his essay for this volume, "What Travels? The Limits of Late 19c Print Circulation; or, From Paris to Muncie, With Love."
74 Laura Lenoir Norwood, Lenoir, N.C., to Ellen Howe Richardson, 11 Feb. 1863, Chiliab Smith Howe Papers, Southern Historical Collection, Wilson Library, University of North Carolina, Chapel Hill, N.C. (hereafter, "CSHP-UNC")
75 Grant Taylor, Dog River, Ala., to Malinda Taylor, 8 June 1862 (Blomquist and Taylor 2000, 34–5).
76 Malinda J. Slaughter Taylor, Cushing, Ala., to Grant Taylor, 19 June 1862 (Blomquist and Taylor 2000, 43–4). The lines are paraphrased from William Walker's song "Faithful Soldier."
77 Malinda J. Slaughter Taylor, Pickens County, Ala., to Grant Taylor, 22 Oct. in letter dated 21 Oct. 1862 (Blomquist and Taylor 2000, 113).
78 Marie Elise Dubach Isley, St Joseph, Mo., to Christian H. Isley, 12 April, 1863, IFP-WSU. The hymn was William Cowper's "Welcome Cross."
79 Anne Hendrix Loomis North, Washoe City, Nev., to George S. Loomis and Mary Ann Lewis Loomis, 31 May 1863, JWNP-HU.

80 Mary Refugio Carpenter Pleasants, Los Nietos, Calif., 8 May 1862, Diary, Pleasants Family Papers, University of California at Irvine, Irvine, Calif.
81 Gro Nilsdatter Svendsen Skrattegaard, Esther, Minn., to Nils Knudsen Gudmundsrud, Nov. 1862 (Farseth and Blegen 1950, 30).
82 Gro Nilsdatter Svendsen Skrattegaard, Esther, Minn., to Nils Knudsen Gudmundsrud, 25 Mar. 1863 (Farseth and Blegen 1950, 35).
83 James Madison Bowler, Little Rock, Ark., to Elizabeth Caleff Bowler, 23 Dec. 1863 (Foroughi 2008, 221).
84 Christian A. Fleetwood, 7, 9, 23, 24, 30, and 31 Jan., 2 Feb., 15 Mar., 19 and 21 May, 4 June, and 9 Sept. 1864, Diary, Christian A. Fleetwood Papers, Library of Congress, Washington, D.C. (hereafter, "CAFP-LC"); Arthur Townley, *Hates and Loves; or, The Lesson of Four Lives* (New York: Beadle, 1863); George Payne Rainsford James, *The Woodman: An Historical Romance* (London and New York: G. Rutledge [*sic*], c. 1849); Edith J. May, *Bertram Noel: A Story for Youth* (New York: D. Appleton, 1859); Alexandre Dumas, *The Count of Monte-Christo* (London: G. Routledge, 1854).
85 Fleetwood, 31 Jan., 31 July, and 7 Sept. 1864, Diary, CAFP-LC.
86 Thomas Francis Galwey, Mine Run, Va., 4 Jan. 1864, Diary, Thomas Francis Galwey Diaries, Library of Congress, Washington, D.C.
87 James Madison Bowler, Fort Snelling, Minn., to Elizabeth Caleff Bowler, 19 Oct. 1861 (Foroughi 2008, 35).
88 Teresa Rebecca Milburn, Bayou Boeuf, La., 14 Aug. 1864, Diary, Teresa Milburn Diary, Historic New Orleans Collection, New Orleans (hereafter HNOC).
89 Teresa Rebecca Milburn, Bayou Boeuf, La., 16 and 18 Oct. 1863, Diary, HNOC.
90 Mary Eliza Ida Powell Dulany, Oakley, Upperville, Va., 6 Jan. 1862, Diary (Mackall, Meserve, and Sasscer 2009, 60). *The London Stage: A Collection of the Most Reputed Tragedies, Comedies, Operas, Melo-Dramas, Far ces, and Interludes...* (London: Lackington, Allen, 1804–27) contains "The Fair Penitent" and "Jane Shore" by Nicholas Rowe and "Devil to Pay" by C. Coffey. "Douglas" by John Home may have been bound into a different edition.
91 Laura Lenoir Norwood, Lenoir, N.C., to Ellen Howe Richardson, 11 Feb. 1863, CHSP-UNC; (Barney 2008).
92 Mary Eliza Ida Powell Dulany, Oakley, Upperville, Va., 26 Dec. 1864, Diary (Mackall, Meserve, and Sasscer 2009, 190).
93 Milton Byron Campbell, Winchester, Va., to Mary Campbell, 8 Mar. 1863 (Fluharty 2004, 31).
94 Teresa Rebecca Milburn, Bayou Boeuf, La., 31 Mar. and 6 and 7 Apr. 1864, Diary, HNOC (J. Smith 1859).

95 Joseph Warner Lewis, Culpepper, Va., to William Norvell Ward, 10 June 1863, WFP-LC.

96 John W. Bratton, Germantown, Va., to Elizabeth Porcher Dubose Bratton, 25 Aug. 1861 (Bratton 1942, 31).

97 James Madison Bowler, Hardin Ky., to Elizabeth Caleff Bowler, 10 Jan. 1862 (Foroughi, 2008, 45). John Washington, Fredericksburg, Va., reminiscence, Apr. 1862 (Shifflett, 2008, 48).

98 "Capt. Albert S. Cloke" (obituary), *New York Times*, 6 Mar. 1890.

99 Laura Caroline Howe Williams, Camp Nickajack, Ga., to Ellen Howe Richardson, 14 Aug. 1863, CSHP-UNC.

100 James West Pegram Ward, Hamilton, Va., to Mary Virginia Ward, 26 May 1863, WFP-LC.

101 James B. Sheeran, Winchester, Va., 26 Apr. 1863, Diary (J. Durkin 1960, 41).

102 Milton Byron Campbell, Sharpsburg, Md., to Mary Campbell, 21 July 1863 (Fluharty 2004, 53).

103 George Washington Hall, Camp Barton, Fredericksburg, Va., 10 June 1863, Diary, George Washington Hall Diary and Memoir, Library of Congress, Washington, D.C. (hereafter GWHD-LC).

104 George Washington Hall, Staunton, Va., 4 June 1863, Diary, GWHD-LC.

105 Leech and Nicholson, 1879, 51–2.

106 Nevin (1974).

107 Charlotte Forten, St Helena, S.C., 27 Nov. 1862, Diary (B. Stevenson, 1988, 406–7); on Forten's time in Salem and her reading of and writing for the *Liberator*, see Zboray and Zboray (2005, 43–57, 173–4).

108 Alasuutari (1999, 6).

5 Cosmopolitan Ideals, Local Loyalties, and Print Culture: The Career of George Chandler Bragdon in Upstate New York

JOAN SHELLEY RUBIN

At the conclusion of Sherwood Anderson's novel *Winesburg, Ohio* (1919), George Willard, who has been working as a reporter for the Winesburg *Eagle*, signifies his coming of age by climbing aboard a train that will carry him to the city, leaving behind as a mere backdrop to his "manhood" the site of his youth. Anderson's final scene embodies a sharp separation between the provincial and the cosmopolitan, the rural and the urban. An entire American pastoral tradition undergirds that dichotomy, with cities the supposed repositories of both excitement and vice and the countryside the site of virtuous serenity or stultifying boredom, depending on one's point of view. Yet even as Anderson contributed to the polarization captured in the phrase "the revolt from the village," he also moderated the depiction of the metropolitan milieu as entirely distinct from less populated locales; *Winesburg, Ohio* suggests that George's boyhood has prepared him for his new habitat insofar as it has endowed him with "the sadness of sophistication." Interestingly, among the agents of that sophistication (apart from his raging hormones) are two aspects of print culture: his work as a reporter, in which he learns lessons about the human condition from the residents of Winesburg who open up to him, and his encounters with books. "I've been reading books and I've been thinking," George tells Helen White just before leaving town. "I'm going to try to amount to something in life."[1]

Anderson's novel thus points the way to an interrogation of the concept of "print culture beyond the metropolis" by prompting these questions about the lived experience of individuals: To what extent did the production, dissemination, and consumption of print shorten or eradicate the distance between the metropolis – considered as a sensibility rather than simply as a place – and the non-metropolitan United States? In what respects did institutions and practices that preserved local distinctiveness coexist with elements of print culture that drew active readers and writers into urban-based national networks and cosmopolitan ways of thinking? To what degree is the relationship between the small town or city and the metropolitan centre misrepresented by the phrase "beyond the metropolis," given that for individuals such as George Willard, the metropolis, in tension with the ethos of the small town, was inescapably present?

To pose these questions is not in the least to minimize the importance of regional publishing houses, differential access to print, or the large numbers of readers who did not share urbane tastes and values. (Carl Kaestle and Janice Radway have pointed out the existence of diverse local cultures of print within the city itself.)[2] It is merely to assert that we may be better served by adopting the sort of dynamic model of culture that has been the gift of the history of the book to historical study, wherein scholars have envisioned fluid boundaries between such constructs as the oral and the written, the elite and the popular, the high and the low, the national and the global.[3] We may want to add the rural and the metropolitan, the provincial and the cosmopolitan, to that list.

Furthermore, I employ those categories with the understanding that what counts as freedom from entrenched preconceptions, a determination to dissolve local allegiances in favour of the universal, and openness to new and discomfiting ideas – a working definition of cosmopolitanism – varies with time and place, just as the city itself grows and changes.[4] To transcend one's local situation and embrace a larger entity like the nation can be seen as a move in the direction of cosmopolitan behaviour, yet when the breadth denominated by a national perspective hardens into nationalism it becomes the opposite of a cosmopolitan outlook. (Hence the efforts of recent literary scholars and philosophers to counterpose nationalism and cosmopolitanism.)[5] In fact, perhaps the most difficult challenge facing historians exploring the relationships between the metropolis and the countryside is to find a language that does justice to the subject. Several contributors to this volume, most notably Frank Felsenstein and Lynne Tatlock, wrestle with this issue. "Provincial" sounds pejorative, and "cosmopolitan," with its suggestion of laudable refinement, was appropriated in the late nineteenth century for magazine titles and club names even when the contents of such publications and the activities of such groups were not especially broad-minded or intellectually advanced. Similarly, everyone knows the cliché that New York City residents are the most provincial Americans. For want of better choices, however, I have retained those terms provisionally in order to lay out a case study – the life and career of the nineteenth-century newspaperman George Chandler Bragdon (1832–1910) – that may help at least to clarify the problem of language, if not its solution.

Bragdon was a small-town newspaper editor and publisher in upstate New York, ending his days in the "emerging metropolis" of Rochester. He was also a published poet, essayist, and historian. His most enduring legacy was as the father of the moderately famous Claude Bragdon, an architect and theatre designer during the Progressive era who was responsible, among other things, for the "Song and Light" events held at Central Park in the 1910s and who, imbued with theosophy and spiritualist ideals, promoted the concept of the fourth dimension. His father's fame was limited to a wide circle of acquaintances and to the members of the New York Press Association, an organization of country editors. Furthermore, given George Bragdon's own interests, especially as he grew older, in Eastern religion and the occult, he cannot be labelled a typical reader. Nevertheless, his life compellingly demonstrates how various modes of participation in print culture beyond the metropolis – reading, editing and publishing, engaging in forms of literary sociability, writing – were conduits to a national and even an international orientation, while they simultaneously involved the operation of print-centred institutions of more limited reach.

Bragdon's career can be reconstructed from his sporadic letters and his voluminous journals. Bragdon kept a journal from the age of twenty-two; forty-six years later, in 1890, he recopied and condensed his old journals in new notebooks. That action suggests a man devoted to order, as well as a figure reckoning the accomplishments of his life. (Bragdon also made scrapbooks of newspaper clippings by covering over every bit of the surface of the discarded periodicals he tore up and used for backing – another sign that "compulsive" might not be too strong a word to describe his record-keeping habits.) But the journals are notably devoid of comments on Bragdon's emotions. Furthermore, like many of his contemporaries, Bragdon created commonplace books – reading notes consisting of passages copied out from his favourite authors. As Anthony Grafton has pointed out, the act of assembling such volumes signals the compilers' declarations to posterity, as well as to themselves, that they belong to the fellowship of well-read individuals.[6] In this respect Bragdon resembled John Vaughn Miller, the Brancepeth, New Zealand, sheep station clerk whose marginalia are described by Lydia Wevers in chapter 9 of this volume. But beyond Bragdon's obvious pride and pleasure in reading, he left no traces in these pages – no annotations or marginal comments of the sort favoured by Miller – to indicate any responses to his reading beyond his desire to maintain a handy collection of excerpts he could consult and reread. This reticence is consistent with Bragdon's son Claude's remark that there was "something stony about the Bragdons,"[7] although one might question whether Bragdon was any colder than other middle-class Victorian men who adhered to the period's ideals of manly self-restraint. Given the frustrations of the documentary record, Bragdon is somewhat elusive as a personality, but this much (gleaned primarily from what others said about him) can be asserted at the outset: he was earnest, amiable, "droll,"[8] "gentle,"[9] loyal to principles and to friends.[10] Those qualities helped to shape a life that was suffused with print.

The Restless Reader

George Chandler Bragdon was born on a farm at Chestnut Hill in Richland, Oswego County, New York. Until he was almost eighteen, he was instructed at home and in the district school; subsequently he continued his education at Falley Seminary in Fulton, where his uncle was principal. Thus equipped, he taught school for a couple of years, interspersing that enterprise with farming. The intertwining of the rural and the urban, as well as manual and intellectual labour, stands out in a retrospective preface Bragdon wrote for his journals: in the space of a paragraph he mentioned that he read Shakespeare for the first time – "all his plays and poems" – at the end of his second winter term as a teacher; travelled to the metropolis (in this instance, Chicago), where he worked in an uncle's glazier shop; found employment on a farm eighteen miles west of the city; but spent most of his time working in a grocery store. He simultaneously exhibited a Franklinesque hunger for self-improvement by joining a debating club consisting predominantly of young lawyers. When he returned home to continue his studies in preparation for college, he attended a weekly lyceum meeting also populated by young lawyers, this time from "the village."[11] By the time he entered Union College as a junior in the fall of 1854, Bragdon had thus experienced forms of literary sociability in both urban and rural settings, established what would become a lifelong practice of attending lectures and discussions, and read extensively in both prescribed curricular materials ("surveying and logic") and on his own.[12] That same year, his brother Charles furnished an even better example of the entanglement of the provincial and the metropolitan by serving as an assistant on the *Prairie Farmer*, an agricultural newspaper issued in Chicago; a few years later he became editor of *Moore's Rural New Yorker*, based in Manhattan.

Following his graduation from Union, George Bragdon taught school in Pulaski, New York, and apprenticed in a law office for a brief time. He also underwent a period of religious struggle, in which he grappled with the issue of whether he was a suitable candidate for the ministry. The struggle is visible in the letters he wrote to his future wife, Katherine (Katie) Shipherd, the daughter of a Presbyterian clergyman. (The Shipherds had moved from upstate New York to join Charles Finney at Oberlin College; Bragdon himself travelled to Oberlin for one term in the fall of 1857.) At issue was the doctrine of "perfection" that Rev. Shipherd and Finney were promulgating (apparently along somewhat different lines). "A God of *rigid justice* would assuredly destroy me for each of the thousand things that I have said and done and thought since I hoped I was converted," he explained in the spring of 1858. "It is my *consciousness* of this, dear Katie, that *compels* me either to reject your father's interpretation ... or to give up my hope in Christ or rather, give up the belief that I *have* a hope in him. Clinging to the last, I must reject the first."[13]

Reading played a double role in this crisis – as both a source of and an anodyne for doubt. What stands out in the letters Bragdon wrote to Shipherd, and to her mother, is the way in which he turned almost naturally to print to resolve matters one way or another. After his teaching stint in the winter of 1857, Bragdon had taken time off to live on the farm and engage in self-education, a move that, he averred in retrospect, "though it left my purse in a poor condition," produced an "overcompensating effect" in knowledge.[14] But at the time the price of never having read "as much in one year before" seemed high.[15] In June, he confessed to Mrs Shipherd that he had prayed, sobbed, and in his "heart" accepted himself as a Christian in spite of "a few undefined doubts that infidel books had given me."[16] His relief, it turned out, was only temporary. A few months later he reported that he had found in the *Life* of the popular Congregationalist preacher Edward Payson the necessary reassurance that other Christians had experienced similar bouts of uncertainty; remarking to Katie that he had been "anxious" for her to read Payson herself, he declared, "It makes me feel stronger."[17] At the same time, he commended John Locke's *An Essay Concerning Human Understanding* as the work that had been "of more direct service to my *intellect* than almost any other book."[18] Whether Locke increased Bragdon's deistic tendencies or whether he bolstered Christian orthodoxy for him is impossible to say; what is clear is that Bragdon had, by his twenties, already developed an interest in the nature of the human mind, and a propensity for intellectual inquiry generally, that he would evince as a reader throughout his life.

Over the next several months, the balance between faith and uncertainty shifted in the latter direction: "I have schooled myself in doubt," he wrote Katie, "and it is very hard indeed for an habitually doubtful mind to exercise strong faith."[19] In the fall of 1858 Bragdon declared, "My religious experience seems to me to be as changeable as the wind. More and more I am convinced that if the Christian is the *perfect* man *I* am *not* a Christian."[20] A few weeks later he gave up the idea of a religious vocation entirely, concluding instead to return to teaching. Bragdon implicated his encounters with print in the decision: "My past education," he told Shipherd, "has not been at all calculated to fit me for the ministry."[21] Interestingly, Shipherd's response to this news was to urge Bragdon to go back to books, i.e., to reread Payson, which Bragdon undertook to do. But the charm had worn off: "My brain is crammed with theological theories," Bragdon commented, "which are night and day perplexing me."[22] Although he continued the practices of Bible memorization and church attendance, as well as some further doctrinal study, the upshot of this immersion in reading and reflection was a questioning of clerical authority and an open-mindedness that might be characterized as a predisposition to cosmopolitanism.

In the same period, Bragdon leavened his explorations of doctrine with classics, poetry, and fiction.[23] In his letters recording his experiences with the works of Harriet Beecher Stowe, the writer he mentions most frequently, one glimpses the depth of feeling that reading produced in Bragdon, as well as the emotional weight the exchange of books bore in Bragdon and Shipherd's relationship. "My love," he wrote Katie in the spring of 1858, "I have been reading the first story in your [copy of Stowe's] famous 'May Flower' this afternoon. It is a gem, and has made me very anxious to read the book through ... [Stowe's] delineations of the characters of 'James Barton' and 'Uncle Phil' gave me more pleasant, tingling excitement than any thing that I have lately read. Some of Grace Griswold's ways made me think of you. From my heart I thank you for leaving the 'May Flower' with me. It must have been a self sacrifice to you."[24] Bragdon's adoption of a critical stance in his implicit demand for skilful character portrayal as well as his movement from the page to life ("made me think of you") were among the practices that contributed to his engagement as a reader.

His quotation in his letters to Shipherd of lines from Emerson, Pope, and Montaigne, as well as a reference to Henry James as a rising star, are further testimony to the breadth of knowledge with which reading had endowed Bragdon by his late twenties. In 1860 Bragdon undertook one last teaching assignment, this time in the railroad town of Centralia, Illinois (population 5000), that seems to have thrown into relief his standing as a man who had gained entrée into the world of learned culture. Bragdon had travelled to Chicago to attend a national fair of some sort and had decided to seek work in the region. But the Centralia position proved disastrous because the children in his charge were of "the class of people here that they call 'Suckers,'" whom Bragdon described as "very ignorant and very obstinate."[25] One remark at this time suggests the extent to which, thanks to print, he had come to see himself (in contrast to the "Suckers") as part of a network of educated individuals widening out from New England: he determined to continue his subscription to the *Atlantic Monthly*, because "I know not how to do without it."[26]

After about 1860, it becomes harder to track with chronological precision Bragdon's propensities as a reader, but his undated commonplace books and the comments about him at his death suggest the broad outlines of his interests. He became, above all, a disciple of Emerson, in whom, one obituary writer suggested, "he discerned, indeed, a kindred spirit."[27] Over the course of his life, he read extensively in English poetry as well, copying lines from Arnold, Tennyson, Browning, Shelley, and Wordsworth, among others. In a notebook he gave to his son Claude on Claude's fifteenth birthday in 1881, he mustered "sayings of some of the wise and good, to think about," including epigrams from Carlyle, Thoreau, Victor Hugo, and, again, Emerson.[28]

These relatively conventional Victorian figures nevertheless coexisted in Bragdon's reading repertoire with others who reflected his growing fascination with unorthodox religion. That interest, a consequence of his prior struggles and a reflection of his cosmopolitan inclinations, developed in tandem with Bragdon's career as a journalist in New York's small cities and villages.

The Country Editor

At the end of his unhappy interlude in Illinois, and following his marriage to Katie in April 1860, Bragdon re-experienced the pull of his local loyalties, returning to the area near the eastern shore of Lake Ontario where he had been born. Through the intervention of a friend who was a lawyer and a publisher, he secured a job in the small city of Watertown that made him a producer as well as a reader of print: he became editor of the Watertown *Daily News*. This venture inaugurated a period of almost twenty years during which Bragdon moved from one local newspaper to the next as editor or publisher, so it is worth pausing to recall the nature of the small-town press at this time. The number of so-called country papers was on the rise, increasing from around four thousand in 1870 to more than twelve thousand by 1890.[29] Those figures conceal considerable variation: whether a paper was a daily or a weekly and hence how much it strove to report national and international news in a timely fashion; whether it included the prefabricated inside pages (called "readyprint" or "patent insides") that became available after 1861; how many pages it contained; where the bulk of the advertising came from. In general, though, like their big-city cousins, which had not yet embraced the ideal of "objectivity," these newspapers were (at least at the start of Bragdon's career) often partisan affairs; in John Tebbel's words, "Almost every village as large as a thousand inhabitants had at least two papers, usually representing opposite political faiths." When towns grew above ten thousand they were likely to have a daily.[30]

As Frank Luther Mott explained, it was easy enough to scrape together enough capital to start a weekly: the expenses for the publisher typically consisted of acquiring "an ancient Washington hand-press, or a newer hand-cranked cylinder press, with a few cases of type, an imposing stone, and perhaps a small foot-power press for job-work." Credit was available for printers' supplies, and "readyprint" houses supplied paper to their customers. But once a newspaper was started, sustaining it often proved more difficult. Thus the phenomenon of the itinerant editor or publisher who bought and sold a local paper as if participating in a real estate transaction – making a purchase, staying a year or two, selling his interest in the publication, and moving on to the next small community to do the same thing all over again. Writing in 1884, S.N.D. North called such a journalist the "*ignis fatuus*" of the press.[31] And that is exactly what Bragdon became: although his son Claude, in his autobiography, described his father as a bad businessman (and although that may have been the case), he was a recognizable type, and no greater a failure than countless other newsmen of his era.

Bragdon's "peripatetic" pattern, to use Mott's word, took only a few months to set in.[32] Under his editorial direction, circulation on the Watertown *Daily News* rose initially from eight hundred in mid-March to twenty-two hundred by August 1861.[33] (The total population of Watertown in 1860 was just over seventy-five hundred.) But then in January of 1862, A.H. Hall, the paper's publisher, sold it to the proprietors of the Watertown *Reformer*, another daily with which it had been in direct competition. There followed a period of uncertainty in which rival Watertown papers, including the *Reformer*, made overtures to Bragdon. Then he went off to Alexandria, Virginia, to take charge of an abandoned "rebel paper" that Hall had acquired, agreeing to stay around three weeks. Although in the end he declined to buy the paper from Hall, the readiness with which Bragdon signed on for the Alexandria assignment is notable, suggesting that for all his upstate New York ties (he left Katie behind), he was of a mind to explore new enterprises regardless of geography. In any case, the Alexandria job enabled him to broaden his horizons by travelling to Washington, where he saw the actor Edwin Forrest perform at Ford's Athenaeum and visited the Smithsonian Institution.[34] He then returned to Watertown to contemplate his next move. At the beginning of September 1862 he took a position as news editor (he soon became city editor) on the Utica, New York *Morning Herald*, where he remained until early 1865. He next relocated to the small Jefferson County, New York, town of Adams, where he published a weekly, the *Adams Visitor*, for three years.

It would be a mistake, however, to think of Bragdon's life at this time as a parochial one punctuated by forays into more populated settings like Washington: a kind of fixed point with outward projections. Rather, Bragdon's experience, even in the role of editor "beyond the metropolis," continued to integrate the local and the cosmopolitan, in which some aspects of print culture provided opportunities for intellectual breadth and connection to metropolitan centres while others were more provincial in character.

In particular, the political affiliations Bragdon sustained as a journalist contributed to the double presence of small-town and metropolitan interests. Bragdon was a Republican, and the papers on which he worked were largely Republican papers, embroiled in the factionalized party battles of the second half of the nineteenth century. In Bragdon's case, politics meant, on the one hand, an intensification of county and state ties. Country editors were also often job printers who depended on the largesse of politicians in their attempt to secure government contracts. (Job work remained a vital source of revenue in this era, much as it had been for the early modern and eighteenth-century English printers and booksellers described by James Raven in chapter 1.) Bragdon lobbied assiduously for such work. While in Adams, he noted in his journal, "Am trying to secure the printing of the session laws from the Supervisors, and therefore go to Watertown often these days. Am told that my prospects are good. George Bagley is engineering my interests."[35] A few weeks later he learned by telegram that the *Visitor* (as well as the Watertown *Reformer*) had been "selected by the [R]epublican caucus" of the county legislature for the job. Subsequently, he set his sights on printing the "State canvass."[36]

On the other hand, politics was a means by which Bragdon transcended the local to the extent that it connected him to nationally visible figures and issues – in particular, to the controversial Republican Party boss Roscoe Conkling. Conkling represented Oneida County in Congress from 1859 to 1863 and served again from 1865 to 1867, when he was elected to the Senate. (He remained in office until 1881.) A lawyer by training, Conkling was handsome, flamboyant, arrogant, and a brilliant orator; his biographer David M. Jordan describes him as "angry, haughty, and larger than life."[37] Conkling built his reputation on legal victories in the upstate region; once elected to Congress, Jordan writes, he was "physically present in Utica from time to time," but after 1859 "the nation would hear his voice, and would feel the impact of his personality." By 1870, Conkling had secured control over the most important patronage vehicle in the country – the New York Custom House – and was the undisputed head of the Republican Party in New York. At the same time, Conkling exerted a spellbinding effect over President Ulysses S. Grant. Those roles pitted him against both the notorious Democratic Tweed Ring that ran New York City and the Liberal Republicans who championed civil service reform. As divisions within the Republican Party hardened, Conkling became an even more powerful and polarizing figure, emerging as the leader of the so-called Stalwart faction, which placed New York Custom House Collector Chester A. Arthur on the Republican ticket, as vice-presidential nominee, in the election of 1880.[38]

Bragdon met Conkling in Utica and the two men became friends. (For a time while Bragdon was working on the *Morning Herald*, they lived in the same boarding house.) As the Civil War raged, Bragdon was a frequent witness to Conkling's speeches before rallies on behalf of the Union and at Republican mass meetings.[39] When Bragdon was getting the Adams newspaper venture off the ground, Conkling offered to help him in any way he could.[40] "Received advertisement of U.S. loan," Bragdon recorded in his journal, "... for which I suppose I am indebted to Conkling."[41] When his son was born in 1866, Katie proposed naming him Roscoe.[42] The relationship continued into the 1880s.

Bragdon's friendship with Conkling, although built on their common roots in upstate New York, allowed the editor a glimpse of and a link to the highest level of American government. "Conkling returned from New York," Bragdon had written in March of 1864, "and told me he found a great deal of president-making going on."[43] A few months later the politician entertained the editor in his room with stories of "some of his Congressional experiences."[44] Entrée to this realm of cigar smoke and spoils was not a ticket to cosmopolitanism if the term is equated with broad-mindedness and intellectual refinement, yet Conkling was a "more cultivated and cosmopolitan" individual than many of his Congressional cronies – well educated, more comfortable in big cities than in Utica, and a ladies' man to boot.[45] In any event, the Conkling connection arguably gave Bragdon a sense of vicarious participation in the wider world (specifically the metropolises of Washington and New York City), as well as the feeling of being a political insider that, one imagines, shaped his voice as an editorial writer.

Another kind of combination of small-town and metropolitan elements appears in the actual contents of the newspapers with which Bragdon was affiliated in these first stages of his career, and in the institutions that shaped those contents. Stories and notices originated in part from the system known as the exchange. In place since the early nineteenth-century, the exchange enabled newspapers "in the absence of strict copyright enforcement and with a prevalent laissez-faire attitude among editors about reprinting material," as Charles Johanningsmeier has written, to clip and publish articles from other newspapers and magazines, sometimes crediting the source – and sometimes not.[46] The exchange involved the swapping of all sorts of information, with datelines from neighbouring counties as well as from New York or Paris; and yet, by permitting the country press to surpass as well as to serve local interests, it was a practice that could foster greater identification with a national and even international outlook.

The Watertown *News* has not survived, but the point can be cemented with respect to Bragdon by examining the Adams *Visitor*, the weekly that Bragdon started in 1868. This was a true country newspaper, consisting of four pages, but the motto on its masthead, "Keeping Step With Progress," suggested the editor's ambition to counter the image of the town (population 3,848 in 1870) as a rural backwater. Still, the last two pages of the paper had a decidedly provincial flavor: they were solely dedicated to serving the local function of providing space for the publication of legal notices, together with advertisements for patent medicines, dress goods, hardware, and other products. Likewise, the two left-hand columns of the first page carried local advertising. The second page listed railway timetables and recorded county legislation. Nevertheless, the *Visitor*'s news and editorial material, enriched by the exchange system, was more of a hodgepodge of local and non-local items than the phrase "country newspaper" might imply. As a weekly, the *Visitor* made no pretense of offering up-to-the-minute news coverage; instead, Bragdon assembled the paper's front page with an eye to stories of human interest: a death from hydrophobia in Syracuse, an article on the bridge across the Mississippi recently constructed in St Louis, a tantalizing tale of "A Young Pastor's Indiscretion."[47] Some of those articles verged on the sensationalism that would come to characterize the metropolitan press by the turn of the twentieth century; others strike the modern reader as merely quaint. Even if not what today we would call "hard news," however, many of the features on the front page gave the paper something of a cosmopolitan, or at least an international, element. One story on poisonous air in crowded halls contained quotations from the Paris correspondent for the *New York Times*; another in the same issue described a large stable in New York City.[48] In addition, a column on page one headed "Variety" consisted of squibs gleaned from the exchange, including a note from *Scientific American* and a report from a Madrid paper about the altitude of the Pyrenees. News briefs on the second page were divided into "Miscellaneous," "Personal," and "Foreign" items, the latter further removing the *Visitor* from the category of strictly local journalism.[49] The editorials on the same page likewise addressed national issues, such as the impeachment of President Andrew Johnson.

Moreover, like papers large and small all over the country, the Adams *Visitor* advised its readers about the choice of books and, implicitly, the path to becoming a more cultured person. Book reviews imported from other papers carried the imprimatur of the metropolis: the 23 January 1868 edition ran notices for two volumes of the Diamond Dickens (a set published by Ticknor and Fields), one from the Boston *Commonwealth*, the other from the New York *Christian Advocate*. The same issue included the recommendation (written as a separate item on the editorial page) that readers subscribe to the magazine (founded three years earlier) that epitomized the educated American's cosmopolitan aspirations in the mid-nineteenth century, *The Nation*: "It is the ablest and best political and literary weekly in the country."[50] Thus even this paper from the smallest community in which Bragdon worked as editor went well beyond local interests.

Literary Sociability

If the pages of the newspapers he edited indicate some of the ways in which Bragdon straddled the smaller locality and the metropolitan area in the 1860s, so do the accounts in his journals of the relationships he forged in Watertown and Utica. During this period, Bragdon enjoyed the tutelage of Dr William Van Vranken Rosa, whom today we would call a mentor. Rosa, "a student and admirer of Swedenborg" and a believer in ghosts, brought the stereotype of the village radical to life.[51] Rosa was Bragdon's frequent companion at dinner and on walks; more than that, he advised him about reading and business decisions. "Dr. Rosa told me not to fail to read Monte Christo," Bragdon recorded in February 1862. But Rosa's primary intellectual influence seems to have been in the direction of philosophy and free thought. The next month, Bragdon read Felix Eberty's *The Stars and the Earth* (1849; 1861), subtitled *Thoughts Upon Space, Time, and Eternity*, on Rosa's recommendation; his receptivity to Rosa's suggestion shows how far his drift away from Christian perfectionism had proceeded since the late 1850s.[52] The friendship – and the reading advice – continued after Bragdon left Watertown. In 1863, when Bragdon, having relocated to Utica, contemplated returning to Watertown and purchasing an interest in the *Reformer* from its new owner, Rosa cautioned him to steer clear of the deal.[53] But for all his practicality, Rosa simultaneously remained a guide not just to Swedenborgianism but to other alternatives to Christian morality and theology: he lent Bragdon George Sand's *Consuelo* and Bulwer-Lytton's *Zanoni*, the former from the pen of a writer notorious for her extramarital affairs, the latter an exploration of Rosicrucian and occult themes.[54] In addition, he pointed Bragdon to a free-thought tract entitled *Ecce Homo* (1866).[55] The two had a long discussion about the recently founded utopian agricultural community in Vineland, New Jersey, where several Watertown families were moving.[56] Bragdon's relationship with his mentor strengthened his ties to Watertown; it was a part of the local context in which he operated. Yet Dr Rosa can also be credited with pushing Bragdon beyond provincial attachments. Tellingly, Rosa confided in Bragdon that, were it not for his father's presence in Watertown, he would move to New York.[57] Bragdon developed a similar relationship with one of the editors of the Utica *Herald*, identified only as Mr Davis, with whom he read Browning and Wordsworth aloud; this individual, too, wished to leave Upstate New York for the big city.

While Bragdon forged locally grounded literary friendships with men who dreamed of escaping the provinces for the metropolis, in other respects Bragdon's sensibility was shaped by the way in which the metropolis came to the provinces. Following the practice he had established in his youth, Bragdon was, in the 1860s, an avid lecture-goer, as well as a devotee of concerts and other entertainments. In Utica during the spring of 1863, for example, Bragdon heard Henry Ward Beecher speak on New England and viewed General Tom Thumb and his wife.[58] In the space of three weeks in November, he attended three concerts: one by a

Scotch balladist, another by "Father Kemp's Old Folks," and a third featuring the composer and pianist Louis Moreau Gottschalk, then on tour in the North. At Mechanics Hall, he listened to "Miss Susannah Evans, the Welsh girl orator." In the same period, he also went to a lecture by the abolitionist and suffragist Anna E. Dickinson, who "made a decided sensation." Notwithstanding his relationship with Conkling, Bragdon made the acquaintance of the civil service reformer and editor George William Curtis when Curtis came to town to lecture on "The Way of Peace."[59] The next month brought an Italian opera troupe, a Boston minister, and a speaker from the nearby town of Amsterdam, as well as addresses on "The National Heart" and "Destiny and Duty" by figures who appear to have been local clergymen.[60] Bragdon's notations in his journals about these events document the rich cultural life available "beyond the metropolis" to individuals intent, as Bragdon was, on the acquisition of knowledge and aesthetic pleasure. Moreover, the eclectic character of Bragdon's interests, which ranged from popular sensations (Tom Thumb) to serious intellectuals (Curtis), speaks to the porousness of the boundary between "high" and "low" culture in the lives of educated individuals. But equally striking is the fact that Bragdon's location in Utica allowed him access to a network of thinkers and artists who enjoyed national prominence, enabling him to engage in an American cultural life that formed a common bond between the residents of metropolitan centres and less populated areas.

Bragdon's habit of lecture and performance attendance persisted when he himself travelled to New York City, creating a continuum between his life upstate and the metropolitan milieu. His decision to set up a weekly country paper in Adams necessitated the purchase of a press and other "printing material," some of which Bragdon arranged to secure by visiting New York.[61] On the trip he went to Barnum's Museum, saw a play entitled "Bosom Friends," and heard Beecher preach at Plymouth Church on "disciplining the mind to habitual happiness."[62] The following year he was in the city again; he saw Edwin Booth in *Hamlet* and made another stop at Barnum's. These activities sound like those of a typical tourist, but for the high level of comfort with the New York environment that Bragdon's journals exude: in between the museum and the theatre he spent his days making the rounds of newspaper offices to meet and hobnob with editors (some friends, some new acquaintances).[63] Thanks to his professional ties and his already developed sophistication, Bragdon moved as easily in this world as he did upstate.

It is nonetheless true that, once settled in Adams, Bragdon had to content himself with slimmer pickings culturally than Utica had afforded.

In this context he relied on a local institution of the sort that existed in small towns all over the country: the literary society. His intellectual vitality (and presumably his desire for sociability) led him to the Adams Literary and Scientific Association, an organization that met approximately twice a month to hear papers by members (all of whom seem to have been men). The participants included several reverends, a professor, and a theological or medical doctor. The subjects under discussion reflect Bragdon's continuing involvement in religious speculation and debate: he heard presentations on "The Immortality of the Soul"; "Divine Providence"; and the controversial topic of "Geology and the Bible." This group of men also pondered psychology and "The Use of Reason." Darwin, whose *Origin of Species* Bragdon "looked a little into," seems to have loomed in the background of these conversations.[64] Such activity cannot easily be classified as cosmopolitan or provincial, especially without further evidence of the erudition – or lack thereof – that these solid citizens brought to their meetings. But for Bragdon it is clear that the literary society in Adams further nurtured the tendency towards broad-mindedness and unconventional belief that his encounters with Dr Rosa were simultaneously fuelling: in 1867 he read his own paper on "Free Thought" to the group, which occasioned questions from one minister and a request for the manuscript from another.[65]

Bragdon's venture in Adams ended in the spring of 1868 when he sold his paper for $1600 to A.B. DeLong and George H. Babcock.[66] A period of uncertainty ensued, but by the fall he had decided on a course of action: he relocated to Ithaca (eventually moving Katie and his children there) to publish a weekly entitled the *Ithacan*. The setting was promising as a site for recruiting readers, Cornell University having been founded three years earlier, and Bragdon excitedly reported a flurry of interest in the new publication.[67]

Sites of Cosmopolitanism and Sociability in the Late 1860s and 1870s

Bragdon's account of his Ithaca period adds another item to the list of factors that (in this instance temporarily) shaped his participation in a world of print characterized by elements of both small-town and cosmopolitan culture: his proximity to a university with aspirations to international stature. The *Ithacan* was a country paper, to be sure. In an early number Bragdon (or his associate, H.D. Cunningham) contrasted his purpose with that of a metropolitan newspaper. "The New York papers are local for the nation," the *Ithacan* explained. "New York has as little part in them as Philadelphia, Chicago or Omaha. They are the medium of communication between one section of the land and another."[68] On the other hand, his foremost aim, as an advertisement for the *Ithacan* announced, was "to give a full and accurate Record of Village and County Matters" so as to be "A Local Family Paper of the First Class."[69] For that reason, evidently, Bragdon saw no threat to his business in running an ad for the New York *Weekly Tribune*, which touted in large type that it was "published in New York City" and proclaimed: "No other New York paper furnishes so Large and Valuable a Variety of Reading."[70] The *Ithacan* carried courthouse proceedings, the Erie Railroad timetable, obituaries, notices of Tompkins County Temperance Society meetings, and a column headed "Rural and Domestic" that featured tips for farmers and homemakers, many borrowed from other newspapers.

Yet the *Ithacan* was decidedly different from the Adams *Visitor* because its local news included reporting on the eminent (as well as the less heralded) figures who, as visiting lecturers or permanent faculty members, passed through Cornell's halls. What is more, the potential readership of the paper was unusually highly educated: "The population of the place is about 9000, Yankee, cultivated," Bragdon wrote Katie.[71] With that audience in view, Bragdon decided to offer wide coverage of books and the arts. Faculty scholarship also provided opportunities for job printing. Furthermore, instead of needing to rely on the Literary Society of Adams or even the Utica cultural scene, Bragdon had the activities of the university from which to glean edification and entertainment.

Thus Bragdon reported on several lectures by Goldwin Smith, including two on "Oxford" and one on "Relations Between England and America."[72] Smith, who was British by birth and a former Regius Professor of Modern History at Oxford, and who spent 1868–72 as Professor of English and Constitutional History at Cornell, was a symbol of transatlantic liberal culture; he personified Victorian cosmopolitanism. (The bench that he bequeathed to the Cornell campus upon his departure for Toronto is inscribed "Above all nations is humanity.") Smith asked Bragdon to publish two thousand copies of "Relations between England and America" in pamphlet form; the result was that Smith was "much in the [Ithacan] office" for several days correcting proofs and demonstrating in conversation that "his knowledge is very extensive in many directions."[73] Similarly, Bragdon reported for the *Ithacan* on lectures about English literature by George William Curtis and the poet James Russell Lowell; as in the example of Smith, both their subject matter and their transatlantic standing as Victorian intellectuals meant that Bragdon had before him (and placed before his newspaper's subscribers) two additional models of a cosmopolitan sensibility. Excerpts from Emerson and from Curtis's reportage, as well as an account of a lecture by the naturalist Louis Agassiz, set the tone of the *Ithacan*'s first issue.

The literary columns of the paper were likewise pitched at the level of well-schooled, avid readers. Although it is impossible to say with certainty that Bragdon wrote them (they were unsigned), they contained thoughtful reflections on new works that were consistent with Bragdon's style and mentality. The first number of the paper, for example, included a review of *Passages from the American Notebooks of Nathaniel Hawthorne*, which had previously been serialized in the *Atlantic Monthly*.[74] Other columns noticed fiction such as Mayne Reid's *The Child Wife* and Marion Harland's *Ruby's Husband*.[75] In addition, the *Ithacan* surveyed magazines that carried literary content and made recommendations about whether a given issue was worth obtaining: not only the *Atlantic* (where Lowell, "the most trenchant and most entertaining of American critics,"[76] held forth) but also *Putnam's*, *Lippincott's*, the *Galaxy*, *Packard's Monthly*, and, for children, *Nursery* and *Our Young Folks*. That feature, which noted the cities from which most of the magazines emanated, presumed that readers of the *Ithacan* participated in the networks created by the wide circulation of the periodicals, and drew them more fully into those networks. Similarly, an early issue of Bragdon's paper carried book advice by Bronson Alcott, transmitted by a New York *Tribune* correspondent;[77] an artefact of canon formation, the Alcott essay implicated residents of Ithaca in a national literary culture, the standards for which emanated from the metropolises of Boston and New York City. Each number also printed at least one poem, usually by a contemporary British poet, underscoring the transatlantic nature of Victorian intellectual life.

Beyond the pages of the newspaper, Cornell University as an institution enabled Bragdon to forge relationships that transcended the local, connecting him to the realm of national politics in the same way that his friendship with Conkling operated. Ezra Cornell was a Republican member of the New York State Senate and Assembly and had used his legislative position to secure funds for the university under the Morrill Land Grant Act. His son, Alonzo B. Cornell, whom Bragdon met in Ithaca, was one of Conkling's chief lieutenants, and eventual governor of New York. But more important to Bragdon's day-to-day survival was that the university furnished him with business. "Ezra Cornell called at the office," he noted shortly after starting the paper. "[He] gave me the names of 12 persons in various parts of the world to send the *Ithacan* to, and told me to send the bill for their subscriptions [for] one year to the college office, and it would be paid."[78] Commencement in 1869 produced demand for three hundred extra copies, with a total sale of twelve hundred. Cornell anniversaries and traditions such as glee club concerts provided Bragdon both diversion and copy.

Bragdon seems to have been in his element during his Ithaca sojourn, but it appears that the paper was a victim of its own success: by the summer of 1869 an investor who had initially lacked the funds to become Bragdon's partner on the *Ithacan* had joined with another journalist to buy him out and transform the paper into a daily.[79] The fall found Bragdon casting about for his next enterprise; by the following spring, he had decided to return to Watertown to start a new paper, the Watertown *Post*. The first number appeared on 14 July 1870, and the last under Bragdon's editorship just a little over a year later, in October 1871, when Bragdon sold out to another publisher.

Leaving his family in Watertown, Bragdon then staked his fortunes on another new journalistic undertaking: this time in New York City. The paper, a sixteen-page weekly in which he had a one-third interest, was called the *Financier*, and seems to have offered news of markets and investment opportunities, with much space devoted to the issues of tariffs and free trade that were then the subject of intense debate.[80] The *Financier* did not meet its expenses, and Bragdon left it in February of 1873 when his partners (in another indication of the volatility of the newspaper business in this period) decided to start an illustrated daily. The *Financier* itself survived until 1875.

Of greater interest, however, is the effortless quality of Bragdon's relocation to New York, as if he did so not with reluctance or discomfort but in the same spirit of readiness to embrace metropolitan opportunities that he had exhibited as a traveller to the city. His attendance at regular meetings of the Liberal Club exposed him to the thought of the day on such subjects as phrenology; on one occasion, he heard Horace Greeley talk on "Protection," with a rejoinder from Henry Demarest Lloyd, then secretary of the Free Trade League.[81] Most striking is his participation in two groups, the Cosmopolitan Association and the Cosmopolitan Conference. At meetings of the former, Bragdon heard a lecture by Frances Willard, the temperance leader, as well as a talk on Malthus's ideas of population. The Cosmopolitan Conference, founded in January 1871, was dedicated to the discussion of "plans by which remunerative work can, at all times, be found by both sexes, provided if necessary by the state";[82] the organization was also the site of dialogue on graduated taxation and reached out to trade unions in envisioning the formation of a political party dedicated to its goals. The names of the groups suggest the readiness of Bragdon's contemporaries to treat the label "cosmopolitan" as a synonym for "progressive" and "forward-thinking." Bragdon's involvement makes it likely that he thought of himself in the same terms.

But if Bragdon slid easily into the cultural life of the metropolis, he just as easily slid out again when the *Financier*'s fortunes did not improve – first back to Watertown in the summer of 1872, then (after a brief return to the *Financier* on salary) to Dansville, New York, home of the Jackson Sanitorium, famous for its water-cure regimen. Originally drawn to Dansville to recuperate from his own illness, Bragdon stayed on to work for the Dansville *Advertiser*, published by A.O. Bunnell. He remained for a year. In December of 1874 he shuttled back to Watertown, taking up a position as city editor and editorial writer on the Watertown *Times*, where he stayed until Bunnell lured him back to Dansville in 1877 with a guaranteed income of $1000 a year for five years.[83]

Although Bragdon managed to fulfil only two years of his agreement, his Dansville connection was an important one for the rest of his life, because of Bragdon's long-standing practice of seeking literary sociability wherever he found himself: he became a charter member (along with Bunnell and several members of the Bunnell family) of a reading group known as the Coterie, which met in members' homes. Bragdon served as the initial president of the club, which first convened on 17 November 1873; in 1898 he was present for the Coterie's "Silver Anniversary" celebration. "There were good readings, sharp criticisms and animated discussions," a participant later recalled of the early meetings. The aim of the group was to produce "clear, bright grains of wisdom," which, as one member put it on the Coterie's twenty-fifth anniversary, could not be obtained through "study" alone, but instead required "the wind of talk" to "winnow" knowledge and "blow away the chaff."[84] That observation highlights the expectation of sympathetic social exchange the Coterie entailed, which, as in any book club, depended on local ties. Bunnell and Bragdon in particular shared a prior friendship and a common identity as country editors. Yet the curricula of the Coterie seem to have been designed according to a model of the cultured person as an individual acquainted with a broad range of Western and non-Western historical and literary subjects. That aspect of the undertaking connected members to ideals of liberal education and self-culture emanating from American colleges and embodied by similar reading clubs well beyond Dansville. The group devoted every other year (at least in the organization's first twenty-five years) to the exploration of

Shakespeare. To judge from a surviving detailed brochure describing the 1899–1900 season (when Bragdon was still listed on the club's planning committee), eclecticism and international scope were the hallmarks of the Coterie's courses of study in alternate years. Themes included "Egypt," "Ancient Religions," and "Modern Authors." Earlier seasons had been dedicated to readings in German literature, the exegesis of Milton, or the examination of other specific historical eras.[85]

The Coterie of course was not unique even in Bragdon's experience, but it differed from the literary society to which he had belonged in Adams in several ways: it included women as well as men; it was thematically coherent and highly structured; and it was unusually long-lived. It was also dead serious, predicated as it was on the assumption that the social interaction it fostered was a means to the improvement of both taste and ethics, as well as a "monument" to the "culture and refinement" of the community. This is not to say that the meetings were cold or humourless: one former Dansville resident remembered George (and Katy) Bragdon as "especially clever in the work of the club; witty, cheery and entertaining." Moreover, the designation "Coterie" suggests some attempt to convey exclusivity and sophistication (the group was known initially merely as a Reading Club), so there were social benefits to be gained by membership that went beyond the elevation of aesthetic standards. Nevertheless, at the time of the Silver Anniversary, Bragdon (the poet of the occasion) linked the "moral and intellectual blessing" of the Coterie with twenty-five years of American technological and intellectual progress; through the agency of "the numerous Coterieans of investigating mind" who had "favored this fair valley, and the country and mankind," the village of Dansville took its place beside Chicago and New York City in a modern world of marvels.[86]

The New York Press Association

Bunnell also figured in an additional print-centred institution that reflected provincial and cosmopolitan values simultaneously, and in which Bragdon was an eager participant: the New York Press Association. This organization, a trade association for country editors, was founded in 1853 as the Western New York Typographical Association, but gradually broadened its purview to the entire state. Its early goals were to protect members from competition and loss of revenue by undertaking to fix subscription and advertising rates, and to make it "a duty of each member to report swindling advertisers to the secretary." (Bunnell served in that position for thirty-six years beginning in 1868.) After the Civil War, the group evolved into an effective lobbying group for the country press on other matters such as libel laws. Furthermore, the Press Association's annual four- to five-day conventions provided opportunities for the editors to solidify their professional identity and to acquire practical knowledge by attending programs on such matters as the responsibilities of journalism, equal compensation for "females in the composing room," and "Soul Life of Man and its Proper Development." For decades conventions also included the recitation of a poem composed for the occasion.[87]

Equally important, the meetings of the Press Association enabled those present to deepen friendships among themselves: they permitted what Bunnell, in the *New York Press Association Authorized History for Fifty Years, 1853–1903*, called the "harmonizing and congenializing" of the members' "feelings," as they drew "closer together both in sympathies and purposes." (The conventions particularly strengthened Bunnell's relationship with Bragdon, who ultimately assisted him in preparing the Association's history; in the preface to the book, Bunnell acknowledged Bragdon as "my faithful friend of many years.") Bragdon, who began attending conventions in 1867, often ran into acquaintances en route to the convention site on the train (railroad and steamship companies underwrote the editors' travel expenses). At the meetings themselves, activities such as musicales, excursions by boat, dances, and banquets allowed the conventions to nurture "charming camaraderie."[88]

Nothing sounds more provincial than a bunch of country editors from the towns and villages of upstate New York gathering to talk in Penn Yan or Saratoga or Elmira about how to further their own interests. One pictures the newspapermen posing for the ritual photograph each year, fresh from a steamboat ride on Cayuga Lake or around the Thousand Islands, filled with "genial good fellowship and hearty cordiality"[89] and personifying the evasive banality that Jackson Lears has attributed to middle-class American life in the late nineteenth century. Certainly to the extent that the New York Press Association differentiated its mission and interests from those of metropolitan journalism it helped to inculcate a provincial outlook among its members. And yet that is not the whole story of the group's impact. In 1872, for example, Bragdon attended the convention at Watertown at which "a large company of Southern editors," chiefly from Virginia, Maryland, and North Carolina, joined the New Yorkers in an effort to foster the reunification of the nation. "Before the feast was ended," Bunnell explained in his history, "the editors knew no North and no South, no East and no West."[90] The speakers and invited dignitaries members encountered at the convention also reflected the group's desire to be part of a national culture of letters. In 1873, meeting in Poughkeepsie, the Press Association imported Henry Ward Beecher from New York City to give the annual address, which Bragdon heard; in 1874 at Lockport, Bunnell noted for the record that Henry Wadsworth Longfellow, William Dean Howells, Oliver Wendell Holmes, and other literary lights had regretted their inability to attend. Speaking in Troy in 1880 was the ubiquitous George William Curtis, who commented, predictably, that "the servility to party spirit is the abdication of the moral leadership of opinion which is the great function of the political press."[91]

Those elements of the Press Association's activities testify to its members' aspirations for recognition as figures who wielded influence and authority beyond their small-town locality. On several occasions, moreover, the Press Association actively fostered interaction between rural and urban settings by moving the venue for the convention to the metropolis itself. For its thirtieth anniversary in 1883 the group met in New York, where the politician Chauncey Depew, speaking at a public meeting in Madison Square theatre, gave an oration on "The Liberty of the Press." Beginning by assuring his audience that "the country press lives and thrives notwithstanding the overshadowing influence of the great metropolitan journals," he went on to blur the distinction between the two forms of journalism, equating them as agents of progress and sources of enlightenment.[92] Similarly, the next year, before an excursion to Montreal from Plattsburgh, members of the Press Association heard a Syracuse editor speak on "A Century of Journalism." These orations, together with the physical presence of the audience in the city, enabled the editors to identify with their metropolitan counterparts and made it possible to imagine themselves as citizens of the nation as a whole. As if to underscore that point, the New York Press Association's 1886 convention met in Washington, D.C. President Cleveland staged a reception for the members, who mingled as well with congressional delegates and other dignitaries, including "the oldest and best known of the Washington newspaper correspondents."[93] The next year the group met in Boston.

Bragdon was thoroughly ensconced in the fraternity of newspapermen that the Press Association represented, frequently referring in his journals to encounters with former colleagues (several of whom wound up on New York City newspapers) whenever he travelled. Yet in 1879 he suspended his career as a journalist (extricating himself from his contract with Bunnell) for the more lucrative (and still print-based) opportunity to write patent medicine advertising for an entrepreneur in Rochester. This arrangement was short-lived. There followed another unsettled period in Bragdon's life when he returned to the Dansville *Advertiser* (and to the Coterie) on a temporary basis, and then moved back to Oswego to take charge of the editorial work on the *Times*. For three years, he achieved some stability, exercising once again his propensity for literary sociability by organizing a club of twenty-six members known as "The Round Table." (Its first meeting was devoted to reading from Longfellow's "Evangeline"; subsequently the group read Shakespeare and Tennyson.)[94] Again, however, the national impinged on the local: When the *Times* became an opponent of the Arthur administration, Bragdon declined to stay on as editorialist.[95] Then an Oswego paper for which he briefly worked failed because it could not secure "expected city printing."[96] At this point Bragdon sought out Conkling's help in obtaining a post office appointment[97]; when that did not come through, he took up another print-related job, canvassing for the *American Cyclopaedia*.

Cosmopolitan Opportunities and Local Allegiances in the Emerging Metropolis

In January 1884, Bragdon relocated to Rochester and assumed a position on another newspaper, the *Union*. "I am to do the work of the literary department, assist on the editorial page and select the miscellany," he explained.[98] At the end of November, he was out of work again, although his family remained in Rochester, which then became Bragdon's permanent home. Over the next few years he was variously the editor of an unprofitable illustrated trade paper in Syracuse, a writer for the Oswego *Palladium*, an employee of the American Loan Association, and a compiler of statistics for Appleton & Company, while augmenting his income selling encyclopedias. (He also sold an article to *Cosmopolitan* magazine entitled "Carnegie's Triumphant Democracy.")[99] In 1891 he began editing a "Home and Farm" department for the Rochester *Post Express*, the most high-toned of the city's dailies; how long he continued is unclear. In this period, the same paper also published at least a dozen articles by Bragdon ranging from reminiscences of Conkling, to "Aphorisms from Emerson," to an essay on "Ignorance and Belief," as well as occasional book reviews. In 1899 he returned to Dansville to assist Bunnell on the *Advertiser*, but by this time Bragdon – now in his late sixties – seems to have stopped looking for full-time employment and to have concentrated on free-lance writing. Except for an editorial job in 1904 on the *Farm Stock Journal* (the weekly organ of the *Post Express*) and a position as exchange editor in the fall of 1906, Bragdon's career as *ignis fatuus* of the press was in abeyance during the latter decades of his life.[100]

But not his activities as an individual who relied on local print-based institutions to cultivate cosmopolitan tendencies. At the end of the nineteenth century, Rochester was what the historian Blake McKelvey characterized as an "emerging metropolis"[101] – a setting that afforded Bragdon numerous opportunities to perpetuate the patterns of literary sociability he had established earlier. Among the groups to which he belonged was one in which his son Claude was also active: the Vagabond Club. The group often prefaced its meetings with lunch, adjourning to the back room of a used bookstore known as Humphrey's. Members gathered at Humphrey's again before dinner, "attracted," Claude Bragdon wrote in his autobiography, "solely by the pleasure of one another's company."[102] While the purpose of the group was to foster witty entertainment and predominantly male fellowship (women were not official members although they often joined the proceedings), the bookstore venue suggests that the Vagabonds had a vested interest in seeing themselves as well-read sophisticates. As Claude Bragdon wrote in an essay published in the *Book-lover* in 1904, the "conjunction" of members always eventuated in "good talk," all the participants being "men of the world."[103] Elsewhere he pronounced the Vagabond Club "representative of urban Bohemia of the Mauve Decade."[104] (The name of the club echoes Bliss Carmen and Richard Hovey's *Songs of Vagabondia*, a paean to the bohemian life published in 1894.) Among the figures of national reputation who visited the Vagabonds at Humphrey's were the comedian Francis Wilson, the actor E.S. Willard, and the popular lecturer DeWitt Miller – a cast of characters whose presence accentuated the worldly tenor of the gatherings.

Beginning in 1897, Bragdon was active in another club with a name that conveyed the same receptivity to the offbeat and the artistic: the Bohemians. (Again, the label may have been a nod to another, more prominent group of contemporaries, the journalists, artists, and businessmen of San Francisco who populated the Bohemian Club there.) In practice, the Rochester Bohemians were more conventional than their name suggests: membership, which was by invitation, consisted of faculty members from the University of Rochester, at least one local minister, and other pillars of the community. Joseph O'Connor of the *Post Express*, the city's most erudite newspaperman, often presided at the club's fortnightly meetings. The Bohemians resembled the Dansville Coterie (which Bragdon continued to attend when in the village) in including both men and women, and in the seriousness with which participants presented papers on such subjects as the later plays of Shakespeare, "Emerson as a Poet," and the popular novel *David Harum*. The club served as well as a forum for social exchange (it met in members' homes) and for discussion of historical topics and current events.[105]

In the 1880s and 1890s, Bragdon likewise found ample opportunity to pursue his literary and cosmopolitan interests outside the boundaries of formally organized club life. He met the scholar and writer Irene Sargent on a trip to Utica, heard her lecture on Dante, received a set of manuscripts from her to "look over," and was possibly responsible for the publication of one of her papers in the *Post Express*.[106] He went to "a striking lecture" on the Ten Commandments by the Ethical Culture movement founder Felix Adler.[107] He listened to poems of Tennyson and Owen Meredith read aloud.[108] Especially noteworthy is the number of friends or acquaintances who asked him for comments on poetry and prose in manuscript.[109] Although he continued to attend services at a Presbyterian church, Bragdon was active in theosophical circles and sought out encounters – in person or in print – that furthered his spiritual explorations. When the theosophist Annie Besant came to Rochester to lecture on reincarnation, karma, and human brotherhood, he attended a small gathering in her honour and was impressed by her knowledge and poise.[110] A month later he recorded his positive response to a "fine looking Hindoo" who was slated to give several presentations in town.[111] He sent to the *Century* magazine a manuscript of some interpretations of the *Gulistan*, the work by the Persian poet Sa'di that had inspired Emerson; subsequently he published some of Sa'di's sayings in the *Post Express*. In 1900, as a member of still another print-based social group, a men's literary club connected with Plymouth church, he presented a paper on "Metempsychosis."[112]

Thus the "emerging metropolis" of Rochester allowed Bragdon to exercise his eclectic taste in reading, expand his spiritual horizons, and engage in broadening intellectual exchange: now, having given up his status as country editor, he was more fully the cosmopolitan. (In 1899, when he went back to Dansville temporarily to work again on Bunnell's *Advertiser*, he wrote in his journal, "I notice how narrowing prolonged village life is.")[113] In these later years Bragdon likewise continued to display a sense of ease in the thoroughly metropolitan milieu of New York City. On one trip in the fall of 1895, he stayed at the Players Club, where, on three successive evenings, he conversed with "a number of men of note," including the actor and dramatic critic John Malone, the writer James Clarence Harvey, and the artists C.S. Reinhart, Childe Hassam, and W.T. Smedley. Print became the currency in these transactions, because Bragdon cemented his newfound friendships by sending several of the men copies of his recently published book of poetry.[114]

Yet the metropolis ("emerging" and otherwise) remained commingled for Bragdon with the rural and small-town locale, as had been the case earlier in his life. For one thing, he periodically spent time at the "Hill," his boyhood home, haying, milking cows, and doing other chores, so that the farm never entirely disappeared from his consciousness.[115] More to the point, small towns were instrumental to Bragdon's relationship with print culture even after he relocated to Rochester. From the 1890s until his death in 1910, Bragdon was repeatedly involved in writing projects that arose from (and did not usually succeed in transcending) small-town connections. His acquaintance with Conkling seems to have furnished material for a novel that he wrote and revised multiple times. Bragdon tried – and failed – to place it with national publishers: Scribner's, Lippincott, D. Appleton, Henry Holt. (He also submitted shorter pieces in the *Youth's Companion* and the *Saturday Evening Post*, which were apparently rejected.) He had more success with the locally oriented compendium entitled *Notable Men of Rochester and Vicinity*, published by the firm of Stoddard and Seward of Buffalo (1901). Of particular interest is the fact that the aforementioned book of poetry, *Undergrowth* (1895), depended for its existence on a regional publisher, R.J. Oliphant of Oswego; Bragdon delivered the manuscript by hand and personally "supervised" its appearance.[116] Bragdon also found a niche as a local historian. Bunnell commissioned him to write a history of Dansville in 1901. Three years later – the same year that his history of the New York Press Association appeared – he produced a booklet about Rainbow Lake in the Adirondacks, as well as a history of Livingston County. A history of Orange County followed in 1908. There were exceptions to this pattern: through the practice of newspaper reprinting, in 1898 one of Bragdon's poems appeared first in the San Francisco *Call* and then in the New York *Times*. Notwithstanding his ambitions to tap into the national networks for the circulation of print that served him as a reader and as a journalist, however, in his role as a poet and freelance writer Bragdon was defined by his lingering provincial affiliations. These affiliations even coloured an event that took place in the midst of the metropolis itself: in 1906 Bragdon read a poem at the banquet of the Society of the Genesee at New York's Waldorf Astoria hotel, where a group of transplanted upstate New Yorkers assembled to celebrate their Rochester-area roots.[117]

In a famous passage from *Winesburg, Ohio*, Anderson reminds his readers of the "vast change" that has occurred during the fifty years preceding the appearance of his novel in 1919. "Books ... are in every household, magazines circulate by the millions of copies, newspapers are everywhere.

In our day a farmer standing by the stove in the store in his village has his mind filled to overflowing with the words of other men. The newspapers and the magazines have pumped him full ... The farmer by the stove is brother to the men of the cities, and if you listen you will find him talking as glibly and as senselessly as the best city man of us all."[118] Anderson was not wrong about the transformations wrought by the outpouring of cheap print in the late nineteenth century, yet, again, his depiction of the separation of urban and rural America in the post–Civil War era seems overdrawn at least in the case of individuals who, like Bragdon, relied for their livelihood as well as their edification on the printed word. Even in the years between 1865 and 1884, Bragdon was "brother to the men of the cities."

Still, at his death in 1910 several obituary writers characterized him as a journalist "of the old school," a figure who belonged to an earlier era when the writer's "personality," "character," and penchant for fine style counted more than it did in the early twentieth century.[119] Soon "American moderns," as Christine Stansell has called them, would swell the population of Greenwich Village, promulgating a cosmopolitan sensibility compounded of sexual freedom, radical politics, artistic experimentation, feminism – and disdain for small-town America. Claude Bragdon, who had educated himself by reading his father's books,[120] and whose immersion in the occult built on his father's openness to alternative spiritualities, travelled in Europe as a young man (something George Chandler Bragdon never did) and pursued his architectural and theatrical interests in Boston, Chicago, and New York. In 1924 he moved permanently from Rochester to Manhattan, later admitting that in his former location he "was never without the sense of somehow being an alien" and revelling in the chance to be "in the centre of great events" that New York City afforded.[121]

By contrast, George Chandler Bragdon's was a "bookish"[122] cosmopolitanism, achieved in part through his sojourns in larger cities but also acquired in (and limited by) the home library, the country newspaper office and the state press association, the upstate New York lecture hall and the literary club. To look "beyond the metropolis" in the late nineteenth century is thus to understand that cosmopolitan mentalities are multifaceted and variable over time, that they can exist in tension with local ties, and that print culture can simultaneously support both sets of ideals and loyalties. It is also to become familiar with residents of America's rural areas and small towns for whom the metropolis, however geographically distant, was always there.

NOTES

1 S. Anderson (1976, 234, 236).
2 Kaestle and Radway (2009, 25).
3 Amory and Hall (2000, 10–11).
4 Hollinger (1985, 59).
5 The pre-eminent theorist of cosmopolitanism is Appiah (2006). Other perspectives are represented in *The Cosmopolitan Reader* (Brown and Held 2010). For a sensitive discussion of the "dynamic tension" between nationalism and cosmopolitanism with reference to a particular American institution, see Ray (2013).
6 Grafton (2012, 4–5, 8).
7 Claude Bragdon (2006, 4).
8 Unidentified obituary, box 11, folder 2 (newspaper clippings), Bragdon Family Papers Addition, Rare Books and Special Collections, Rush Rhees Library, University of Rochester. The collection is hereafter cited as BFP.
9 S. H. L., "A Gentle Philosopher," letter to the editor of unidentified newspaper, 13 August 1910, box 11, folder 2, BFP Addition.
10 "George C. Bragdon, Poet-Editor, Dead," *Rochester Democrat and Chronicle*, nd, box 11, folder 2, BFP Addition.
11 George Chandler Bragdon (hereafter GCB), preface to journal, 1832–1883, box 82, folder 6, BFP.
12 GCB, March 21, 1854, journal, 1832–83.
13 GCB to Katherine Shipherd, 31 May 1858, box 81, folder 2, BFP.
14 GCB to Katherine Shipherd, 11 October 1858, box 81, folder 3, BFP.
15 Ibid.
16 GCB to Catherine Schermerhorn Shipherd, 25 June 1857, box 81, folder 1, BFP.
17 GCB to Katherine Shipherd, 23 Oct. 1857, box 81, folder 1, BFP.
18 GCB to Katherine Shipherd, 23 Oct. 1857, box 81, folder 1, BFP.
19 GCB to Katherine Shipherd, 30 July 1858, box 81, folder 2, BFP.
20 GCB to Katherine Shipherd, 8 Sept. 1858, box 81, folder 3, BFP.
21 GCB to Katherine Shipherd, 22 Sept. 1858, box 81, folder 3, BFP.
22 GCB to Katherine Shipherd, 8 Oct. 1858, box 81, folder 3, BFP.
23 GCB to Katherine Shipherd, 5 Nov. 1858, box 81, folder 3, BFP; GCB to Katherine Shipherd, 3 Dec. 1859, box 81, folder 5, BFP.
24 GCB to Katherine Shipherd, 12 May 1858, box 81, folder 2, BFP.
25 GCB to Katherine Shipherd, 13 Oct. 1859, box 81, folder 4, BFP.
26 GCB to Katherine Shipherd, 10 Nov. 1859, box 81, folder 5, BFP.
27 Unidentified obituary (probably from a Theosophical publication), box 11, folder 2, BFP Addition.

28 The Emerson notebook is in box 10, folder 4, BFP Addition. The notebook given to Claude Bragdon is in Box 10, folder 1, BFP Addition.
29 Mott (1941, 478).
30 Tebbel (1969, 250); Mott (1941, 478).
31 Mott (1941, 478–9). North is cited in Mott (1941, 478–9).
32 Mott (1941, 478–9).
33 GCB, entry labeled Watertown, 1861, journal 1832–83.
34 GCB, April 4, 1862, journal 1832–83.
35 GCB, Nov. 11, 1865, journal 1832–83.
36 GCB, 24 Nov 1865 and 5 Dec. 1865, journal 1832–83.
37 D. Jordan (1971, 1).
38 D. Jordan (1971, 20, 127).
39 GCB, 18 Aug. 1862, 25 May 1864, journal 1832–83.
40 GCB, 15 Sept. 1865, journal 1832–83.
41 GCB, 8 May 1865, journal 1832–83.
42 GCB to Katherine Shipherd, 6 and 7 Aug. 1866, box 6, folder 1 BFP Addition. See also GCB's article on Conkling, "Brave and True," *Rochester Post Express*, 18 June 1892.
43 GCB, 11 April 1864, journal 1832–83.
44 GCB, 11 June 1864, journal 1832–83.
45 D. Jordan (1971, 145, 213).
46 Johanningsmeier (1997, 39).
47 Adams *Visitor*, 23 Jan. 1868.
48 Adams *Visitor*, 16 Jan. 1868.
49 Adams *Visitor*, 16 Jan. 1868.
50 Adams *Visitor*, 23 Jan. 1868. Within a few years the *Nation* would also stake out a position in favour of civil service reform and in opposition to Conkling, but tensions within the Republican Party had not yet grown to the point where Bragdon's endorsement of the *Nation* jeopardized his relationship with the politician.
51 GCB, 20 Jan. 1862, 18 April 1867, journal 1832–83.
52 GCB, 10 Feb. 1862, 7 March 1862.
53 GCB, 24 Sept. 1863, journal 1832–83.
54 GCB, 10 Aug. 1866, journal 1832–83.
55 GCB, 5 Jan. 1867, journal 1832–83.
56 GCB to Katherine Shipherd, 4 Oct. 1868, box 81, folder 10, BFP.
57 GCB, 24 Sept. 1863, journal 1832–83.
58 GCB, 23 Mar 1863, 20 April 1863, journal 1832–83.
59 GCB, 7, 10, 19, 20, 25 Nov. 1863, journal 1832–83.
60 GCB, 7, 9, 16, 22 Dec. 1863, journal 1832–83.

61 GCB, 1 May 1865, journal 1832–83.
62 GCB, 30 April 1865, journal 1832–83.
63 GCB, 2, 20 May 1865, journal 1832–83.
64 GCB, 11 Nov., 1865, 9 Jan. 1866, 28 Jan. 1868, 21 Jan. 1867, journal 1832–83.
65 GCB, 27 Feb. 1867, journal 1832–83.
66 GCB, 28 April 1868, journal 1832–83.
67 GCB, 5 Dec. 1868, journal 1832–83.
68 "Taking Newspapers," *Ithacan*, 19 Dec. 1868.
69 Advertisement, *Ithacan*, 5 Dec. 1868.
70 Advertisement, *Ithacan*, 12 Dec. 1868.
71 GCB to Katherine Shipherd, 17 Oct. 1868, box 81, folder 10, BFP.
72 GCB, 19 May 1869, journal 1832–83.
73 GCB, 26 May 1869, 2 June 1869, journal 1832–83.
74 "New Books," *Ithacan*, 28 Nov. 1868.
75 "New Books," *Ithacan*, 25 Dec. 1868.
76 "Magazines," *Ithacan*, 19 Dec. 1868.
77 "Miscellaneous Items," *Ithacan*, 5 Dec. 1868.
78 GCB, 20 March 1869, journal 1832–183.
79 GCB, 21 July 1869, journal 1832–83.
80 GCB, 4 Feb. 1872, journal 1832–83.
81 GCB, 10 March 1872, 28 Jan. 1871, journal 1832–83.
82 "New-York," *New York Times*, 2 Jan. 1871.
83 GCB, 6 June 1877, journal 1832–83.
84 "The Coterie" [pamphlet], (1899?: Dansville: New York), BFP.
85 *Celebrating the Silver Anniversary of the Coterie* (1898, 7, 12).
86 *Celebrating the Silver Anniversary of the Coterie* (1898, 16, 20, 24).
87 Bunnell (1903, 11, 14, 24).
88 Bunnell (1903, 4, 5, 55).
89 Bunnell (1903, 15).
90 Bunnell (1903, 18).
91 Bunnell (1903, 34).
92 Bunnell (1903, 38).
93 Bunnell (1903, 46).
94 GCB, 5 May 1882, 13 Oct. 1882, journal 1832–83.
95 GCB, 10 Nov. 1882, journal 1832–83.
96 GCB, 2 Apr. 1883, journal 1832–83.
97 GCB, 22 May 1883, journal 1832–83.
98 GCB, 4 Jan. 1884, journal 1883–98, box 10, folder 2, BFP Addition.
99 GCB, "Carnegie's Triumphant Democracy," *Cosmopolitan* 2:39 (1886–7).

100 GCB, 10 Sept. 1906, journal 1883–98.
101 McKelvey (1961).
102 Bragdon (2006, 247).
103 Bragdon (1904).
104 Bragdon (2006, 247).
105 GCB, 15 May 1897, 31 March 1898 journal 1883–98; GCB 24 Feb. 1899, 3 March 1900, 17 March 1900, journal 1898–1906, box 82, folder 7, BFP.
106 GCB, 11, 14, 20 May 1894, 30 June 1894, journal 1883–98.
107 GCB, 18 Feb. 1884, journal 1883–98.
108 GCB, 20 Nov. 1886, journal 1883–98.
109 GCB, 4 April 1892, journal 1883–98.
110 GCB, 28 Aug. 28, 1897, journal 1883–98.
111 GCB, 15 Sept. 1897, journal 1883–98.
112 GCB, 21 Nov. 1900, journal 1898–1906.
113 GCB, 4 July 1899, journal 1898–1906.
114 GCB, 11,14 Nov. 1895, journal 1883–98.
115 GCB, 20 May 1900, 10 July 1900, journal 1898–1906.
116 GCB, 3, 10, 24 Aug. 1895, journal 1883–98.
117 GCB, 5 Nov. 1895, journal 1883–98.
118 S. Anderson (1976, 70–1).
119 "George Chandler Bragdon," *Rochester Herald*, 8 Aug. 1910.
120 Bragdon (2006, 51).
121 Bragdon (2006, 93).
122 GCB is described as "bookish" in an unidentified obituary, box 11, folder 2, BFP Addition.

6 What Travels? The Movement of Movements; or, Ephemeral Bibelots from Paris to Lansing, with Love

BRAD EVANS

As Pascale Casanova has observed, much of the literary world in the late nineteenth century was looking to Paris as the "capital" of "the universal republic of letters" – "a republic having neither borders nor boundaries, a universal homeland exempt from all professions of patriotism ... a transnational realm whose sole imperatives are those of art and literature." However, at least one avant-garde German magazine was looking instead to North America.[1] *Pan*, a renegade little magazine later known for having helped the spread of art nouveau throughout Europe, had picked up on a growing movement for what it winningly referred to as the "goblin literature" being published in the United States by a class of small magazines, not unlike itself, "fight[ing] a fresh and joyous fight against the *fin-de-siècle* attitude of complacent weariness":

> For about three years cheap small-sized bi-monthly magazines, in which young writers and artists endeavor to put up a new tune, have been published in the larger cities of North America. To take note of this phenomenon is worth it already for the simple reason that the American variety of modernity functions as a peculiar correlate to the common definition of "new" and "young." Given their tendency, one could define these pocket magazines as "periodicals of protest" – as one of them, *The Philistine*, calls itself – because the best of them are guided by the deep wish to counteract thoughtless and vulgar sensationalism thanks to criticism and autonomous artistic contributions.[2]

What is both pleasantly surprising and problematic about the recognition in Germany of these "pocket magazines" in the United States – where hundreds of them had begun to spring up starting in 1894 – is that, on the whole, the fad in the United States was taking its cues from Paris, where

6.1 *Pan*, published out of Berlin from 1895 to 1900, joined *Jugend* (started in 1896) and *Simplicissimus* (also started in 1896) in bringing the little magazine movement and the spirit of Montmartre to Germany. *Pan* also had its eye on the "periodicals of protest" coming out of North America

a similarly oppositional vogue for avant-garde magazines had taken shape in the previous decade. Moreover, similar small fads for this new form of little magazines, which were known in America as "freak magazines," "fadazines," or "ephemeral bibelots," seem to have been popping up all over the world at this time – in England, Germany, Austria, Russia, Japan, India, South America. Apparently, most of these also had the oppositional aesthetics of Parisian nightlife largely in view as an ideal of the "new" in art and life.[3] *Pan* may have been right that the "American variety of modernity" was playing a somewhat different tune than European versions of the same; and yet, what is perhaps even more interesting is not the difference but the fact that the phenomena of these little magazines devoted to the "new" was, itself, spreading in many disparate places, from cosmopolitan centres to the provinces. The fad in the United States was largely over by 1898, but not until after exemplars of the journal had flared up across the country, from *The Lark* in San Francisco and *M'lle New York* in New York, to *The Philosopher* of Wasau, Wisconsin, and *The Clack Book* of Lansing, Michigan (figs. 6.1 to 6.6).[4]

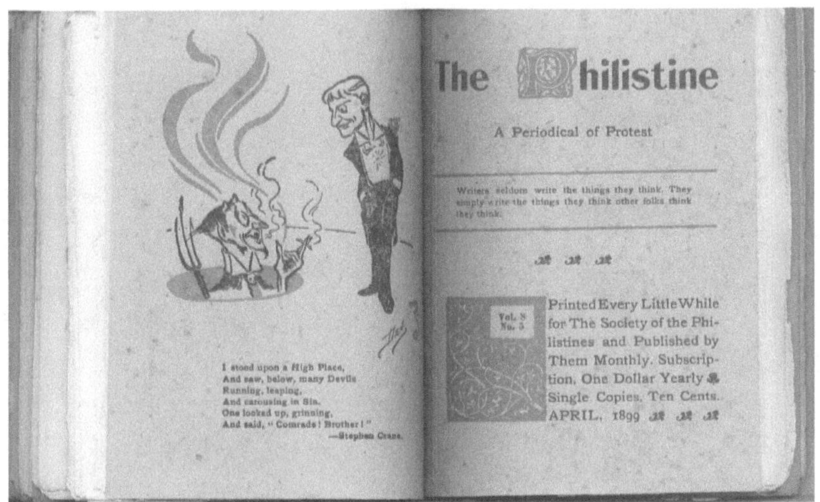

6.2 *The Philistine* in 1899 featured a poem by Stephen Crane and image by W.W. Denslow, whose illustrations for *The Wonderful Wizard* would be published the following year.

6.3 *The Lark*, showing the primary editor, Gelett Burgess, at work amid the detritus of other ephemeral bibelots, including *The Philistine*, *The Echo*, *The Chap-Book*, *Le Petit Journal des Refusées*, and *The Bibelot*.

6.4 *M'lle New York*, with "les chats noirs" on the cover.

6.5 *The Philosopher*, cover, February 1899, published out of Wasau, Wisconsin. Little Magazines. Rare Book Division, Department of Rare Books and Special Collections, Princeton University Library.

6.6 *The Clack Book* "lays an egg" on its cover for April 1896, a self-deprecating pun on sister magazines *The Lark* and *The Chap-Book*. Little Magazines. Rare Book Division, Department of Rare Books and Special Collections, Princeton University Library.

The question of interest to this chapter does not concern the circulation of these little magazines taken individually, but rather the circulation of the fad for them as a whole. How does a movement move? How does a vogue, like this one for these avant-garde little magazines, catch its wave? And, assuming that it was drawing on a style and sensibility that got its start in the acknowledged capital of modernity, what was left of Paris by the time the vogue had made its way to the smaller towns and villages of middle America? When a taste for a particular kind of publication spreads, what spreads with it – and is it still the same taste? The interest of my chapter is not in cosmopolitanism per se, although one might say that a sentiment of the cosmopolitan (as described in this volume in various ways by Rubin, Felsenstein, Pawley, and Tatlock) was to some extent a result. Rather, the interest for me is in understanding the significance of circulation in the production of avant-garde movements, which actually demands holding at bay the more finished notion of cosmopolitanism, which was the end product of the circulation I mean to describe.

The notion of circulation I want to develop, then, is different from the one Casanova outlines in *The World Republic of Letters*, even though much of her analysis describes the Francophilia of the bibelots movement quite well. Casanova's argument concerns literary value and transnational canon formation, whereas what interests me here is how circulation establishes the groundwork for the innovation of art movements. When Casanova set up her Paris-centric thesis on "the republic of letters," she expanded a sociological model of value familiar from Pierre Bourdieu in which literary reputations are established by a work's circulation in a world literary system. Her now familiar argument suggests that works achieve value when they are taken up by the "sanctioning authorities" of universal judgment – consecrated by translations, critical studies, tributes, judgments, prizes, and verdicts. When this happens, literary works are in effect transmuted into a different category of being. They cross over a metaphorical border, undergoing an "almost magical metamorphosis of an ordinary material into 'gold,' into absolute literary value"; they are annexed into the autonomous literary sphere of the universal.[5] This kind of model works particularly well for describing the good fortunes of individual authors, and her readings of Kafka and Faulkner, for example, have been singled out for praise. It is, moreover, almost certainly the case that many of the American bibelotists involved in the vogue for little magazines evoked Paris for precisely the reasons suggested by Casanova. They saw it as a symbol of the autonomy of art and the restorative ethos of universality, a counterpoint to the stultifying conservatism and consumerism dominating the American publishing industry.

If Casanova's model works well for understanding the fortunes of individual authors and books, it seems less adept at accounting for the ebb and flow of artistic movements, for which we will need to pick up on a different part of Bourdieu. As other critics of Casanova's work have pointed out, there are other kinds of world literary systems at work than those fashioning literary canonicity.[6] The canonization of individual authors, or even individual styles, is not the apropos thing here, but rather processes of imitation and dissemination. Or rather, two different kinds of processes are present: imitation of Parisian models or ideas about Parisian culture; and processes of in-group formation through circulation. It is not really a matter of gaining acceptance with the existing in-group, but rather of trading on the capital the in-group has among a separate, and smaller, circle in a process of collective identity formation. The American bibelots recognized themselves and each other as part of a movement because they recognized their shared circulation of Parisian materials.

The bibelots are as far from canonical as one might imagine, so much so that they have not, for the most part, even come up for Google digitization; and yet one finds in them explicit examples of the kind of aesthetics of revolt – deeply ironic, anti-establishment, depersonalizing, post-impressionist, abstractionist, proto-Dadaist – that came to represent the more well-known twentieth-century modernist little magazines like *Blast*, *Poetry*, *The Blind-Man*, *Rhythm*, and *The Egoist*. I want to suggest that the 1890s bibelots played their part by establishing the idea of extensive and intensive circulation within a tight network of publications as, itself, a kind of artistic formalism, a style around which the social project of artistic modernism could take shape. By turning circulation into a kind of art, of the sort we have commonly referred to via the historical discourse of "art for art," they in effect redefined the aesthetic public sphere. Readers may recognize in this thesis a reformulation of one of the old stories about modernism, that one of its defining characteristics was the fascination with art about art. But I want to direct attention to the fact that this idea about artistic reflexivity implies movement within a networked system, the circulation of attention as it links one art object to the next. In the pages that follow, I try to elucidate what it actually means to think of print circulation in these terms, first as circulation within an evolving network, and second as the circulation of a movement.

I. Structural Holes and Parallel Planes

The "fresh and joyous fight" propelling the fad for little magazines like *Pan* and *The Philistine* was a print-circulation phenomenon with the peculiar characteristic of being conceptually global and practically local. While drawing on the ideal of Paris, much of what *The Philistine* was protesting was the national publishing industry in the United States represented by the period's major publishing houses and their illustrated monthly magazines, *Harper's*, *The Century Illustrated*, *The Atlantic Monthly*, and *Scribner's*, as well as by the newly emergent mass-market magazines like *The Ladies' Home Journal*, *Munsey's*, and *McClure's*. In opposition to the gentility and conservatism of American realism espoused by the influential editor and novelist William Dean Howells, and the distressing commercialization of the arts perceived to be taking place in the mass-market monthlies, the vogue for these ephemeral journals took up the politically oppositional stance of the genre of small-format, limited-circulation, avant-garde publications that had emerged in the Parisian artistic cabarets of the preceding decades. In the opening number of one of the most important American bibelots, *M'lle New York*, its editors devoted themselves in Rabelaisian fashion to the Bacchanalia of the mob, the "joyously vulgar mob," "that glorious clientage of Shakespeare," which in its avowed ignorance and with its force of instinct made the crusades, the Reformation, the modern drama, the French language, not to mention wit, learning, and art. In more recent times, the editors continued, the mob had been emasculated under the influence of "the male blue-stocking, William Dean Howells" and "female blue-stocking, Richard Harding Davis," who helped transform it into a mere magazine reading "public" and the poet into "lickspittle," and thus "M'lle New York is not concerned with the public." It will be for the mob, "the aristrocracies of birth, wit, learning and art and the joyously vulgar mob."[7]

Had Casanova known about American ephemeral bibelots, she might have seen them largely confirming her suggestion that Paris was adopted as the symbol of an "autonomous literary space": "Thanks to its promotion of the law of universality in the world of letters against the ordinary political laws of nations, France became an alternative model for writers from every part of the literary world who aspired to autonomy."[8] But the situation is rather more interesting when staged with less austerity. What the American bibelotists drew from Paris was a sentiment about the evolving structure of the aesthetic public sphere, which was tied to the particular counterculture of the artistic avant-garde that had been developing there in the *petites revues* since the 1870s. The journal the American bibelots looked to more than any other was surely *Le Chat Noir*, a publication of the cabaret of the same name that played host to the poets, performers, painters, and prostitutes congregating there under the shadow of decadence and the bohemian fin de siècle (fig. 6.7). In one recent account, Daniel Tiffany has described how artists drew on the underground culture of *Le Chat Noir* and its sister cabarets in aligning the clandestine appeal of Parisian nightlife historically and conceptually with modernist lyric poetry. Like the cabaret, poetry at the end of the century could be described as "an impossible event yielding unmappable places in language and queer combinations of social being."[9] On the ground, this involved the development of arts stressing movement in the moment and, as a result, the modernity of the ephemeral. The cabarets were known in particular for their shadow theatres, obscurantist prose poetry, serpentine

LE
CHAT NOIR

Organe des intérêts de Montmartre

MONTMARTRE

LA LUNE

Paraissant toutes les Nouvelles Lunes

LES LUNATIQUES

6.7 *Le Chat Noir*, the magazine started in 1882 by Rodolph Salis for his cabaret of the same name, with its cover design by Henry Pille, became a model for the American ephemeral bibelots.

6.8 *La Lune*, October 1865, was the first in a series of parodic art magazines, featuring the work and editorship of André Gill. Censored by the French government, the magazine was subsequently rechristened under three new names, *L'Eclipse* in 1868, *La Lune Rousse* in 1876, and *La Petite Lune* in 1878.

dances, and off-colour ballads, all of which were tinged with an off-colour parodic form, known as *le fumisme*, bent on sending the strictures of bourgeois society "up in smoke." This sensibility had been coming of age in the print form of little magazines since the 1870s in countercultural art-movement journals associated with groups like the *Hydropathes* and *Les Arts Incohérents*. One sees the American ephemeral bibelots taking up many of the same oppositional attitudes of journals like *La Lune*, *La Petite Lune*, *L'Eclipse*, *L'Hydropathe*, and *Le Mirliton* (figs. 6.8 to 6.13); the poetic formulations of symbolists like Verlaine and Mallarmé; and the *Japonisme*-inspired post-Impressionism of the poster art of Jules Cheret and Henri de Toulouse-Lautrec.

LA LUNE ROUSSE

JOURNAL SATIRIQUE, LITTÉRAIRE ET ILLUSTRÉ

POURQUOI J'AI FONDÉ la "LUNE ROUSSE"

BONIMENT

6.9 *La Petite Lune.* 14 June 1878.

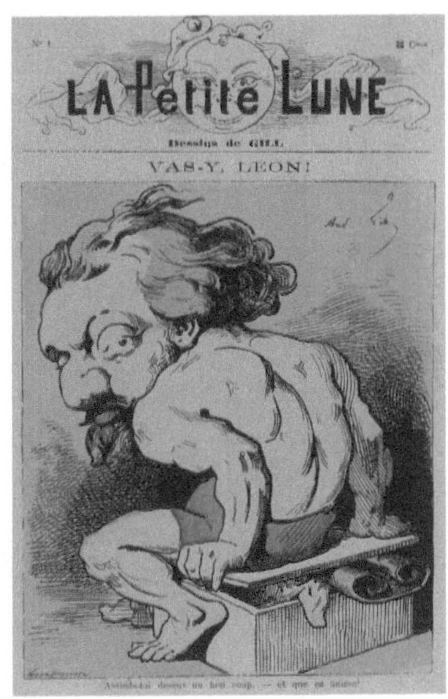
LA Petite LUNE

Dessins de GILL

VAS-Y, LEON!

6.10 *L'Eclipse*, 2 July 1876.

1re ANNÉE – No 6. Prix : 10 centimes. Le 5 Avril 1879

LES HYDROPATHES

JOURNAL LITTÉRAIRE ILLUSTRÉ

Rédacteur en chef : Émile GOUDEAU

Directeur-Administrateur : Paul VIVIEN	ABONNEMENTS :	Secrétaire de la Rédaction : J. JOUY
BUREAUX	Paris. — Province. — Étranger	BUREAUX DE VENTE
50, Rue des Écoles, 50	Un an : 8 francs	13, Rue Monge, 13.

L'hydropathe SARAH BERNHARDT

6.11 *Les Hydropathes* (occasionally written simply *L'Hydropathe*), published from 1879 to 1880 by Emile Goudeau, whose name initiated the pun for the title of the magazine (*goût d'eau*) and the eclectic coterie of artists organized under the umbrella of the term. Goudeau went on to edit *Le Chat Noir*.

Le Mirliton

ARISTIDE BRUANT

LE MERLE BLANC

6.12 Jean Caillou (pseudonym of Théophile Steinlen, Swiss, 1859–1923), *Le Merle Blanc*, cover of *Le Mirliton*, October 1885. Stencil-coloured photorelief. Collection Zimmerli Art Museum at Rutgers University, Acquired with the Herbert D. and Ruth Schimmel Museum Library Fund. 1990.0736.001. Photo by Peter Jacobs.

6.13 Théophile Steinlen (Swiss 1859–1923), *Le Mirliton*, 9 June 1893. Note the reproduction of Toulouse-Lautrec's famous poster of Aristide Bruant. Stencil coloured photorelief. Collection Zimmerli Art Museum at Rutgers University, Acquired with the Herbert D. and Ruth Schimmel Museum Library Fund. 1990.0736.002. Photo by Jack Abraham.

And yet, the fact remains that there was, on the whole, very little actual circulation between the Paris journals and those drawing upon them, especially not if, when talking about circulation, we are talking as we normally do about the movement of print objects. For magazines, this means dealing with certain bibliographical records like periodicity (weekly, monthly, or quarterly circulation), price, subscription lists, publication history, editors, and publishers. These are all the statistics, for example, that Frank Luther Mott collected in his magisterial *A History of American Magazines* (5 vols., 1938–68), and they have continued to be used as a major criterion in judging the historical and artistic significance of given journals, where influence is judged by longevity and circulation numbers. For Casanova, the primary currency of literary prestige was translation, which means another print-dependent form of circulation, since what gets translated in a straightforward sense are works of poetry, fiction, or prose – that is to say, things that must be written down, printed.[10] By either of these criteria, the fleeting craze for freak magazines noted by *Pan* was truly ephemeral. Even the most successful of the American bibelots, titles like *The Lark* and *M'lle New York*, had circulation numbers in the low thousands and a longevity of only two years. There is scant bibliographical evidence from the French library archives that the American bibelots ever made it to France, and there is no evidence that any of them were ever translated in their entirety. As I will discuss momentarily, neither did (nor were) the French *petites revues* in the United States.

What happens, then, if instead of considering circulation per se, we turn the problem on its head and consider blockages to circulation? How does looking at non-circulation change our conception of the movement of this countercultural vogue from Paris to other locales? There clearly was some kind of network situation developing around the global bibelot craze, with a shared style and mood and sense of moment. However, it was a situation characterized by what, borrowing loosely from network vocabulary developed in sociology, we might think of as the arcane bridging of "structural holes" and the extension of separate network domains alongside each other in non-intersecting parallel planes.[11] The bibelot movement was defined by the largely autonomous emergence of tight clusters of magazines, and each cluster was seemingly cut off from the others like galaxies of stars separated by the darkness of empty cultural space.[12] At times, this space could be defined geographically, with networked clusters taking shape in particular national and linguistic regions, with seemingly very little if anything bridging the spaces between them. At other times, the magazines were geographically right on top of each other, publishing not only at the same time but in the same city, but they still remained unlinked, as if extending on parallel planes, as we will see with the case of an American magazine published in Paris called *The Quartier Latin*. But on occasion, there were bridges over the blockages, like the article in *Pan* that made linkages apparent and unavoidable. I would suggest that it was the creative energy linked to the construction of these bridges – bridges that were often assembled from the most ephemeral of *ficelles*, the most extenuating and outrageous of links – that came to be understood as constituting the artistic and intellectual innovation of the avant-garde. Instances of bridging across the structural holes and between planes, stray links running between otherwise unconnected clusters of magazines and coteries of artists, produced the effect of non-complacency and revolt for which the ephemeral bibelots were known. More often than not, what made them "new" and "modern" was not aesthetic innovation in anything like the pure sense, but rather their creative brokerage of blockages, accomplished through their reiteration and repurposing of material linked from elsewhere.[13]

Blockages to the creation of network links take many forms, but there is perhaps no greater barrier to circulation than the entwined hydra of nation and language. Even within national borders, the American bibelots had hardly any circulation at all, and there is almost no evidence of their actual physical circulation across national borders, either on a subscription basis or in any other formal manner. The same holds for the French *petites revues*. As was the case with their American counterparts, the French journals only very rarely published as many as a thousand copies. In 1900 Remy de Gourmont compiled a bibliography of 130 French *petites revues* in which he wrote, comically but in all truth, that many were so *petite* that their titles had already become enigmas.[14] According to the *Union List of Serials in Libraries in the United States and Canada* (3rd ed.), the most important of the French magazines, *Le Chat Noir*, was held by only 4 of the 956 American libraries it catalogued (UCLA, Harvard, Yale, and the New York Public). By way of comparison, *The Clack Book* and *M'lle New York* were both held by 12 American libraries, *The Lark* by 46, *The Chap-Book* by 60, and *Harper's Monthly* by upwards of 500. French libraries have only very limited holdings of the American bibelots, a couple of copies of *The Lark* and *The Chap-Book* and none of the others, and it is difficult to know when they acquired them.[15]

If nation and language is the biggest blockage, a far more surprising one comes when we recognize the dimensional aspect of the problem. Even those magazines most poised to have an international audience appear to have carried on very much parallel, but unconnected, existences – as if disseminating along parallel, non-intersecting planes. A most interesting case of this comes with *The Quartier Latin*, a bibelot brought out in English by the American expatriate community in Paris, which was published simultaneously in Paris, London, and New York from 1896 to 1899 (figs. 6.14 and 6.15). Despite its international points of origin, *The Quartier Latin* positioned itself from the start in relation to the American, and to a lesser extent the British, art journal movement, not in relation to the French. In the announcement of the first edition, the magazine took leave to introduce itself by way of a nod to one of the forerunning American bibelots, *M'lle New York*, presenting its readers to "Mlle. Quartier Latin, a young *débutante*, who, after the manner of most *demoiselles (Américaines)*, will have lots to say for herself, and try, in an ingenuous sort of way, to amuse

6.14 and 6.15 *The Quartier Latin*, a journal edited by young American artists living in Paris and published simultaneously in Paris, London, and New York between 1896 and 1899. Rare Book Division, Department of Rare Books and Special Collections, Princeton University Library

you" (1:1, 1). Its editor, Trist Wood, makes it immediately clear that she is not a Montmartre girl. He explicitly draws a link between "M'lle Quartier Latin" and her "sisters," *The Chap-Book*, *The Lotus*, *The Philistine*, *The Bibelot*, and *The Lark*, offering them "a warm greeting":

> [M'lle Quartier Latin] hopes that the fact that she was born away off in Paris will not cause them to entertain towards herself any distant feeling … [T]hough she gets her dresses in Paris – and where in the world is there better material for beautiful attire, or more cunning hands to fashion it? – she has no inclination on that account to put on airs or appear vain.

Like many of the ephemeral bibelots, *The Quartier Latin* made a habit of publishing blurbs about itself from other magazines, and its citation index is impressive for its lack of notices by French journals. Instead, it included the *Chicago Inter-Ocean*, the *Philadelphia Inquirer*, the New Orleans *Times-Democrat* and New Orleans *Picayune*, as well as the *East Anglican Times* and the Sheffield *Independent*. In each case, the reviews evoke comparisons to other English-language journals. *The Westminster Budget* wrote, for example, that "*The Quartier Latin* reminds one of the *Yellow Book*, but for our part we greatly prefer both the art and letterpress of the former." The circulation of American and British little magazines seems to have run largely on a parallel plane with the French *petites revues* – two planes expanding simultaneously but not interconnecting.

I will move on shortly to consider what actually does circulate between those two planes, what kind of material actually does bridge the structural holes separating network clusters. But before doing so, it is worth noting that while national and language barriers play a large role in structuring this situation, that is hardly the end of the story. What is most immediately surprising about *The Quartier Latin* is this fact that despite being "compiled in Paris," and regardless of the extent to which it was embedded in the Paris art scene, it maintains its Anglo-Saxon identity and distribution network. It sets itself up as being both within and outside the main run of French art and culture, inside to the extent that its art is just as good, outside to the extent that its American and British sense of moral decorum is not compromised, just decoratively adorned at the edges.

Surprisingly, the vogue for these little magazines also ran very much on parallel planes to the mainstream literary press in the United States; that is to say, one needs also to account for structural holes between the little magazines, the literary monthlies, and the mass-market press. We can get a feel for this situation by considering the number of times the magazines cited each other, their citational networks.[16] While a survey of 50 of the most prominent American bibelots shows that they cited the mainstream magazines with some regularity, such citations were entirely unidirectional and, compared to their citation of other bibelots, quite thin. *The Century Illustrated*, for instance, registered as a fairly significant node, being cited by 8 different bibelots, but they each only cited it once. By contrast, *The Lark* was cited by 7 different bibelots, but it was cited 20 times. *The Philistine* was cited by 11 different bibelots, and it was cited 21 times. *The Chap-Book* was cited by 10 different bibelots, and it was cited 30 times. And it is absolutely striking how silent the major monthlies were about the bibelot vogue. *Harper's Monthly*, *The Century Illustrated*, *Scribner's Monthly*, and *The Atlantic Monthly*, together, cited *The Chap-Book* only once, ever, in a fleeting mention in an 1897 *Harper's* article about book illustration.[17] I have found not a single other instance of the citation of any of the freak magazines on the pages of their mainstream brethren, which is a remarkable fact given the number of bibelots being published and the significance of the authors publishing in them, including most notably Henry James, Kate Chopin, and Stephen Crane.

It is, of course, difficult to conjecture on the source of a silence. Were we following Bruno Latour's ideas about the nature of network associations to the letter (were we good "ants," as Latour's "actor network theorists" like to call themselves), we might simply work around this blockage. Since there was no link, there could be no transformation, according to Latour, and I take to heart his admonition to move on to a description of the links that do exist, and thus make a difference, as opposed to an explanation of ones that do not.[18] But there can also be useful speculation about silences. A few things seem clear – and they help to describe the shape of the network assembled by the ephemeral bibelots, for which the blockage served as a kind of accelerant. There are, of course, all of the ethical objections the monthlies may have had about the bibelots, that they were, say, untoward, perfervid, unserious, or foreign. In what might have been a typical reaction, had there been any other reaction, the American naturalist author Frank Norris complained that *The Lark* was "delightful fooling, but there's a graver note and more vital to be sounded."[19] Just as interesting, though, is the fact that the major monthlies rarely cited any other magazines. It is not simply that they are not citing the bibelots. Rather, the kind of aesthetic they practised was one in which citation did not play the same role that it did for the bibelots. The monthlies reviewed literary and artistic works, whereas, as we shall see, the bibelots, in effect, reviewed each other, linking together a shared aesthetic public by situating works within the field of publication they and their brethren were creating and defining (as *Pan* did when noting the goblin literature in the American bibelots). Art for the monthlies would stand on its own merits and meet the test of time, whereas for the bibelots art emerged as a product of circulation within a reflexive field of citation. Moreover, the monthlies sought an institutional permanence, where significance was demarcated by circulation numbers and the authority of the editorial presences. The bibelots, by contrast, were programmatically small and ephemeral, devoted not to permanence but to the fleeting traces of the contemporary moment.

The point to retain is that these instances of non-circulation, whatever their cause, make visible what I take to be the characteristic element of both the ephemeral bibelot movement and the new aesthetic public sphere, namely, its intense aesthetic investment in a particular kind of circulation, which I will now describe. In order to see this investment, it has been necessary to mark out the negative space. As we will see, disassociated from (if not independent of) the genteel monthlies and the emerging mass-market magazines, the ephemeral bibelots delimited their field of circulation in order to turn circulation, itself, into an object of artistic play. Unlike the other publications, which always imagined their audiences in the broadest and most open terms, the bibelots moved along much more precisely defined routes, with so few links across structural holes and between parallel plains that they are recognizable as a different class of publication. They moved along exceptionally tight and improbably self-reflexive networks, making it difficult for those from the outside world to connect with them, which is to say that just because there might have been flights linking the goblin literature in America's ephemeral bibelots to the avant-garde in both Germany and Paris, it does not follow you could catch a connection from any of those points to other destinations. Access was limited.

II. Links and Bridges

What, then, does circulate? If not print matter, what contributes to the acute sense that the ephemeral bibelots, together, constituted a movement, a fad, a phenomenon, a protest, the new? How are we to understand the bibelot movement as such, when, as a movement, the bibelots did not themselves move? I am going to suggest that the best way to think about this problem is in terms of an expanded definition of citational practice.

To go back to Tiffany's description of Parisian nightlife, the clandestine space he elaborates is also one of sociability, and for all the sense of disorientation and loss that comes with entering into it, so too does the desire for connection. To the extent that this historical situation coincides with the artistic forms emerging from it, as manifest in the ephemeral bibelots, what one sees is a kind of mad grasping after associations, an artistic fascination with the trace of linkages. The blockage of circulation is only one half of a dialectic, the other being the development of intense citational networks within the clusters.[20] The little magazines often read like elaborate in-jokes, several-layer-deep parodies and elusively biting commentaries about the movement itself. This is another version of print circulation, not the movement of print matter through the market but the movement of shared points of reference among the magazines. Circulation is not only about physical objects moving in geographical space, but also about what moves in the citational space between the bibelots. Movement in this expanded sense could usefully be imagined as happening in the links (also called edges) between nodes within clusters, as well as in the bridges spanning the structural holes and jumping between parallel planes.

The point is that the network, itself, implies a modality of non-print circulation, circulation without the movement of paper. And yet the situation is complicated by the fact that any kind of thing can be a link, and any kind of thing can be an edge, as we will see below. The broader question of how the movement moved is tied to the variety of these modes of citation. As we will see, our sense of the movement's movement was not tied to any one of these particular modalities, but rather to a kind of scintillation effect, when a spark made the jump from one plane to the next and was reflected and refracted in a variety of ways in a new network cluster.

a. Authors and Artists

Perhaps the most obvious links between magazines are the people who published in them. Authors and artists are circulated by magazines in the sense of the magazine being a vehicle for the dissemination of their work to the public, and we might then intuit their social interaction, and its influence on the shape of artistic movements, based on the venues in which they published.[21] A no less active social interaction occurs, however, when these same individuals become entities mentioned by the magazines. Indeed, citation becomes at least as important as publication when we are interested in the question of how networked publics take shape. To think of citations, and in turn of the citation of citations, as links and bridges – as solutions to the blockage of circulation within and between magazine clusters – requires a rather different way of conceptualizing their circulation, one in which a network edge is equated with the activity of tracing circuits between magazines. Authors and artists in this sense not only gain a larger audience by being circulated by individual magazines, but they also become points of reference holding magazines together as a movement.[22]

Some interesting things happen when thinking of artistic production in this way. For instance, the publication of a story, poem, review, or illustration becomes the functional equivalent of any other form of citation. Authors and artists do not have to actually have their work published in the magazines to serve as a link. Their names merely need to be bandied about between them. They can, moreover, index movement between magazines regardless of the valuation placed upon them. A negative review can in some circumstances count the same as a positive one, just as a universally panned poem can play the same role as a good one. William Dean Howells never published in the American ephemeral bibelots, but he was cited by at least thirteen of them, almost always negatively. Robert Louis Stevenson was cited by more than twenty of the bibelots in universally positive terms. And Stephen Crane was not only reviewed widely both positively and critically by them, but he was also published in them regularly. Much of his poetry, for example, appeared at some point in *The Philistine*. The citation of all three of them – the shared negative comments about Howells, the positive valuation of Stevenson, and the mixed publication and reception of Crane – work to assemble the network in much the same way. When shared as a point of reference by more than a single magazine, authors and artists become citational indices indicating movement within a networked cluster.

b. Translations

The gold standard in Casanova's version of the world literary system is translation, and it is obviously an important process for moving authors out into citational space. Surprisingly, it was infrequently practised among the bibelots. Among American magazines, the two most prominent for translations were surely *The Chap-Book* and *The Quartier Latin*. Curiously, *The Chap-Book* was more prone to publish its French authors in French than to translate them, as it did with two pieces by Mallarmé; it also published the untranslated French versions of both a multi-page review of the poetry of Arthur Rimbaud and an original poem, "Les Loisirs de la Poste."[23] *The Quartier Latin* was more ambitious in terms of actual translations, publishing more of them than any of the other American bibelots. For example, they ran a racy story by Joris-Karl Huysman, the quintessential French decadent novelist, about an artist falling in love with his studio model who turns out to have been a society woman posing for him on a dare. And yet even in *The Quartier Latin*, translation was exceptionally rare, coming less frequently than one might expect.

A related anecdote about the limits of translation concerns the poet Stuart Merrill, who is almost certainly the most important fin-de-siècle American writer who remains almost entirely unknown to American literary historians. At one time an acolyte of William Dean Howells, he moved to Paris as a young man and became a member of Mallarmé's circle of symbolist poets, a regular fixture in the French *petites revues*, and the author of five well-received volumes of poetry. But he was never translated. He introduced Walt Whitman and Oscar Wilde to the French little magazines, and translated many of the French symbolists in one of the earliest English-language editions of their poetry, *Pastels in Prose* (1890).

In many ways, he was a bridge between the two national language clusters. But he also marks the limits of translation as a bridge, the very high bar it set. An untranslated American writing in French, Merrill was and has remained a marginal figure to both national literary traditions.

c. Genres (Blurbs and Stories-without-Words)

Genres can serve a citational role in much the same way as people. Genres of particular importance to the bibelots included several with particular histories in France at this time, including caricature and the prose poem. One might also say that the shared format of the bibelots – beautifully illustrated, deckle-edged, oddly shaped – constituted a genre in and of itself, and thus was inherently a citational practice. I want to detail two other genres, the blurb and the story-without-words, which seem to have developed particularly in the bibelots, and which are interesting because of the specificity of their treatment of citation.

The most straightforward opportunity for citation comes with critical reviews, and a particular version of this practice rose to the level of a new art form in the bibelots, which began republishing extravagantly punning, comical excerpts about themselves from other magazines and newspapers. These were similar to what we know today as "blurbs," which is the word I will use to describe them here (even though the meaning today is no longer quite the same) because it was coined in 1907 by America's leading bibelot editor, Gelett Burgess. He first used the term on the advertising dust jacket for his book of essays entitled *Are You a Brom* where he included a picture of "Miss Belinda Blurb … in the act of Blurbing" – "All the Other Publishers commit them. Why Shouldn't We?" (fig. 6.16) The self-mockery of Belinda's blurb was the culmination of a form developed in the bibelots in the previous decade, in which editors culled short quips about their publications from other magazines and strung them together in long lists. It was a genre of auto-blurbing, of self-puffing.[24] So, for example, in the fifth number of *The Lark*, Burgess blurbed his own magazine by publishing the following self-send-up, in French:

> C'EST un assez modeste Créature que THE LARK; elle ne se melle pas de Personnalités; étant un Oiseau matineux, elle s'occupe du Ver. Elle ne pousse cependant pas l'Insouciance jusqu'à ne pas écouter les Notes louangeuses des Cages d'en-bas habitées par les Autres. THE LARK n'est pas ingrate, et elle remercie le CRITIC* des Renseignments sur sa Circulation; le BOSTON JOURNAL† qui la trouve un peu sauvage; le CHAP BOOK‡ qui l'appelle

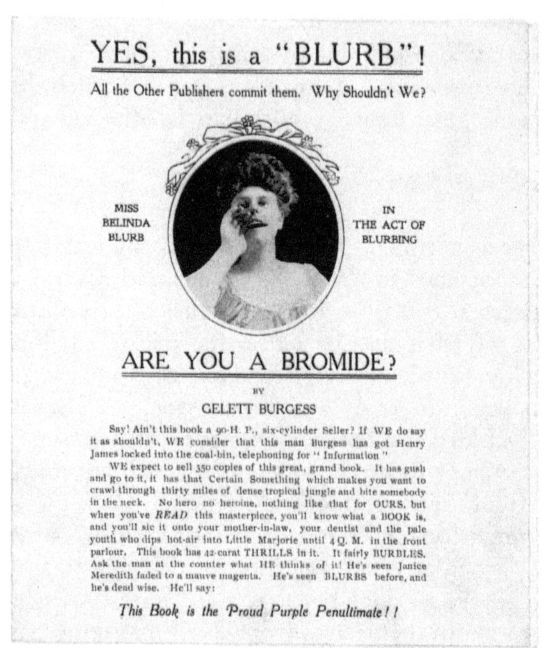

6.16 Gellet Burgess, editor in the late 1890s of *The Lark*, *Le Petit Journal des Refusées*, *The Milkmaid*, and *L'Enfant Terrible*, coined the word "blurb" in 1907 to announce the publication of his collection of humorous essays, *Are You a Bromide?*

intime; le NEW YORK TIMES** qui voit en elle une Menace à la Modernité chicagoenne, et le NEW YORK TRIBUNE †† gentil Savant de la LARKE-OLOGIE, qui la nomme L'OIE, sans doute à cause de ses Oeufs d'Or.[25]

* "–One bookseller tells me that he has sold 100 copies." (!)

† In an editorial comment, remarkable only for its length and the fact that it calls *The Lark* an "ornithological specimen," and its opening article an "epiologue."

‡ "It is an assertion of the right of the artist to be wayward, and indulge in innocent drollery. Its friends will be appreciative, but there will not be many of them."

** "Incredibly, even impossibly, 1895; written by *les jeunes*, and delightfully young they are."

†† "One more hysterical magazine – from a realm remote from the moorings of intelligence."

6.17 *Oskolki*, a Russian "skinny magazine," which published something like a "blurb" from a young Chekhov in 1883. Houghton Library, Harvard University, p RB8.A100.881o.

While not so witty, in general, as this one, a remarkable number of the bibelots published pages of auto-blurbs of this kind for themselves with each issue, often in the form of short comments or notes reviewing what was happening in other little magazines. Thus even more directly than when citing authors and artists, the blurbs establish explicit citational links between the bibelots themselves.

Another blurb example comes in the Russian bibelots – one that admittedly raises a number of questions about how far we want to trace these connections. Very early in his career, Anton Chekhov wrote ephemeral pieces for a number of journals known to Russian literary historians as "skinny magazines" – among them *Sverchok* (*The Cricket*), *Budil'nik* (*Alarm Clock*), and especially *Oskolki* (Fragments, or sometimes Splinters) – the more serious literary monthlies being known there as "fat magazines."[26] It is perhaps less surprising than it might have been, therefore, to see that

Chekhov had produced something very close to Burgess's long-form auto-blurb for an article for *Oskolki* in 1883:

> Don't read the *Ufa Province News*: you won't find any information about Ufa province in it.
>
> The Russian press has many sources of light at its disposal. It has *The Komarovo Light*, *The Rainbow*, *Light and Shade*, *The Ray*, *The Little Light*, *Dawn*, etcetera. So why is it still so dark then?
>
> It has *The Observer*, *The Invalid* and *Siberia*.
>
> The press has *Entertainment* and *Little Toy*, but it does not follow that it has much fun …
>
> It has *The Voice* and its own *Echo* … Yes?
>
> Whatever is ephemeral cannot boast about its *Century* …
>
> *Rus* has little in common with Moscow.
>
> *Russian Thought* is sent … in a strong envelope.
>
> Then there is *Health* and *The Doctor*, but meanwhile, how many graves there are![27]

We know that Chekhov had worked with at least a few of the papers he blurbs here, his brother having noted his association with *Light and Shade*,[28] and at the very least his grouping of them together suggests their coherence as a class of magazines, a Russian bibelot vogue. It seems very clear that Burgess did not read Russian and knew nothing about *Oskolki*, which, at any rate, predated his own bibelots by a decade. The point would be for us to hear the echo between Chekhov's version and Burgess's, linked via the elaboration of the genre of the blurb in the French bibelots. I come back to this problem in the conclusion.

One other shared genre prominent in the little magazines was the pictorial narrative, or story-without-words, undertaken in an infantile manner and often telling a macabre story. The genre was initiated in *Le Chat Noir* by artists like Théophile-Alexandre Steinlen, Willette, and Caran d'Ache, and one sees it carried over with great regularity in the American bibelots. For example, Crotin's "Comment On Devient Anarchiste" in *Le Chat Noir* clearly resembles Burgess's "Elliptical Wheels on a Cart" from *The Lark*, sequential line drawings coupled with a droll sense of knowingness (figs. 6.18 and 6.19). The use by both magazines of this genre is not directly citational in the way of the blurb, but as with reviews, they establish the trace movement between magazines, such that one expects that a "linked in" reader of *The Lark* would sense that Burgess was indexing Paris with his elliptical wheels image, much as if he had commented

6.18 and 6.19 E. Cottin's "Comment on devient anarchiste," published in *Le Chat Noir,* 2 July 1892, and Gelett Burgess's "Elliptical Wheels on a Cart," published in *The Lark*, no. 8, December 1895.

on, say, Mallarmé. Genre citation, that is to say, works as a link in much the same way as author citation. It can be judgment-neutral, sharing the same form without necessarily sharing the same meaning, the magazines' judgment being irrelevant to their ability to help construct and reiterate the network.

d. Style (Le Fumisme)

In the examples I have given up to now, I have avoided suggesting anything so ambiguous as "style" as an example of a citational practice. Style seems to be what develops along the citational lines themselves, a more subjective feeling or mood emanating from the sense of connection. There is, to be sure, a shared sensibility with both blurbs and stories-without-words, though as I have tried to point out with all of the examples up to now, there is also a way in which a citational force offers the trace of movement regardless of whether it shares a meaning. In this last example, I want to show the citational effect of a shared style that operates independently of the genre in which it is enacted. More than the others, it emanates from the connection itself, and is dependent upon readers capturing the trace of movement.

Parody is one of the oldest citational practices, and it has had, of course, a special place in French letters since the time of Molière. In the late nineteenth century it developed into a pointed, oppositional style known as *le fumisme*, described by Georges Fragerolle as having the goal of "cutting open the smug sky under which we live."[29] Daniel Grojnowski has argued that *fumisme* bequeathed to modernism its "sneer and renunciation of the ideal": "The *fumiste* avoids discussions of ideas, he does not set up a specific target, he adopts a posture of withdrawal that makes all distinctions hazy, and he internalizes Universal Stupidity by postulating the illusory nature of values and of the Beautiful, whence his denial of the established order and of official hierarchies."[30] The significant point about the *fumiste* style coming out of these journals is that one cannot help but understand it as part of what Mary Shaw has identified as a "group phenomenon," in which elements of parody functioned not only to signify breaks with literary and artistic traditions, but also to form links "for initiated readers with a network of other contemporary, subversive, avant-garde texts." As she goes on to point out, "when this work is rediscovered ... it is less because our attention is captured by the particular merits of a certain writer's work than because of the work's manifestation of a given writer's inextricable involvement with the general spirit of these avant-garde groups."[31] The references in *fumisme* are so many times removed that they were often imperceptible to the uninitiated, and often continue to be so to this day. But for those within the group, the links were strong and exceptionally generative.

The *fumisterie* most visible in the American bibelots took shape around certain iconic images, like the black cat made famous on the pages of *Le Chat Noir*. Parodic iterations of that image appeared all over the bibelots, on the head of a *Vogue* cover girl and in the margins of an absurdist prose poem in *Le Petit Journal des Refusées*. Always the same cat, but with some parodic refunctioning, the ubiquitous *chat noir* indexed Paris and also the group of readers linked into the network who would recognize the play on that image (figs. 6.20 and 6.21; see also figs. 6.4 and 6.7).

6.20 "Le Chat Noir" on the cover of *Vogue*, 31 January 1895. At the time, *Vogue* was very much in the mould of the bibelots, publishing wicked short stories by Kate Chopin and Parisian-inspired line drawings by Louis J. Rhead.

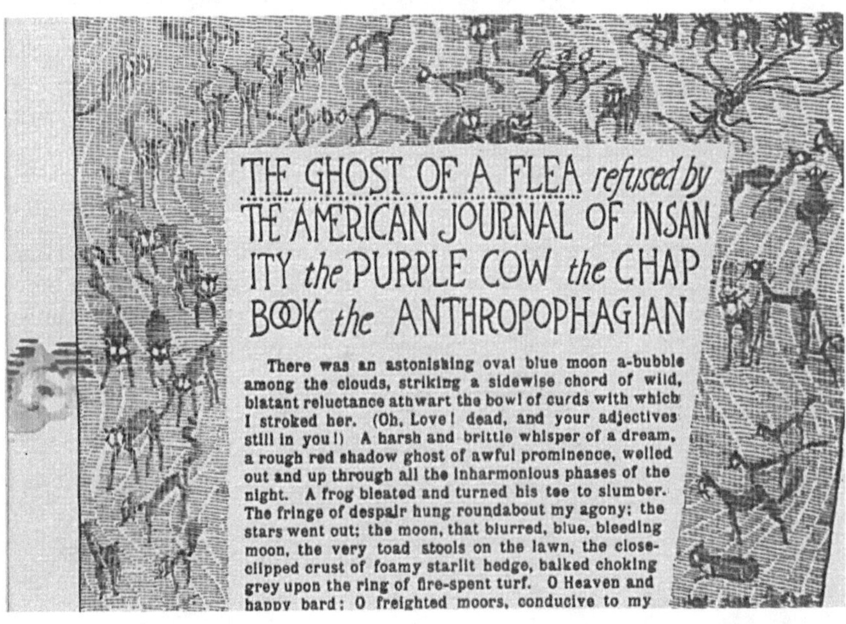

THE GHOST OF A FLEA *refused by* THE AMERICAN JOURNAL OF INSANITY *the* PURPLE COW *the* CHAP BOOK *the* ANTHROPOPHAGIAN

There was an astonishing oval blue moon a-bubble among the clouds, striking a sidewise chord of wild, blatant reluctance athwart the bowl of curds with which I stroked her. (Oh, Love! dead, and your adjectives still in you!) A harsh and brittle whisper of a dream, a rough red shadow ghost of awful prominence, welled out and up through all the inharmonious phases of the night. A frog bleated and turned his toe to slumber. The fringe of despair hung roundabout my agony; the stars went out; the moon, that blurred, blue, bleeding moon, the very toad stools on the lawn, the close-clipped crust of foamy starlit hedge, balked choking grey upon the ring of fire-spent turf. O Heaven and happy bard; O freighted moors, conducive to my

6.21 Detail of the border design for Burgess's "The Ghost of a Flea" in *Le Petit Journal des Refusées*, 1896.

6.22 Burgess's *The Purple Cow*, published in the first number of *The Lark* in 1895

Another example comes with a "purple cow" that Burgess made famous in one of the early numbers of *The Lark* (fig. 6.22):

I never saw a purple cow,
I never hope to see one.
But I can tell you anyhow,
I'd rather see than be one.

"The Purple Cow" went on to achieve a kind of epigrammatic fame, with a variety of punning retakes quickly showing up in competing bibelots. For instance, *The Lotus*, from Kansas City, only half-facetiously recommended Burgess for a laureate position as our national bard before offering Arthur Grissom's parody of the lines:

"I never saw a purple cow,"
A bardlet wrote to get a laugh;
If he had used a looking-glass,
He might have noticed a green calf.[32]

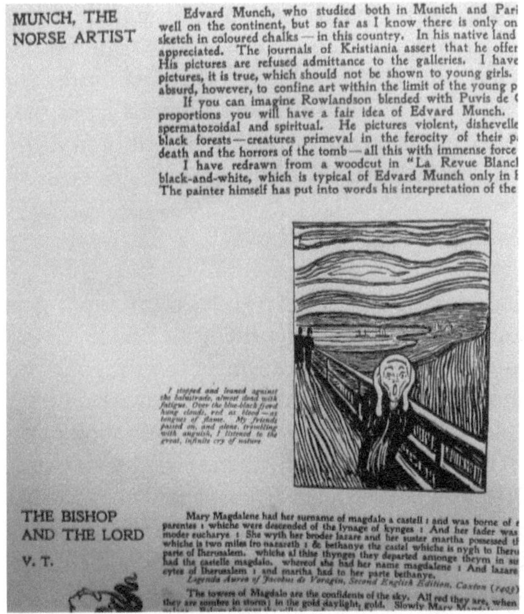

MUNCH, THE NORSE ARTIST

Edvard Munch, who studied both in Munich and Pari
well on the continent, but so far as I know there is only on
sketch in coloured chalks — in this country. In his native land
appreciated. The journals of Kristiania assert that he offer
His pictures are refused admittance to the galleries. I have
pictures, it is true, which should not be shown to young girls.
absurd, however, to confine art within the limit of the young p
If you can imagine Rowlandson blended with Puvis de
proportions you will have a fair idea of Edvard Munch.
spermatozoidal and spiritual. He pictures violent, dishevelle
black forests — creatures primeval in the ferocity of their p
death and the horrors of the tomb — all this with immense force
I have redrawn from a woodcut in "La Revue Blanc
black-and-white, which is typical of Edvard Munch only in
The painter himself has put into words his interpretation of the

I stopped and leaned against the balustrade, almost dead with fatigue. Over the blue-black fjord hung clouds, red as blood — as tongues of flame. My friends passed on, and alone, trembling with anguish, I listened to the great, infinite cry of nature

THE BISHOP AND THE LORD

V. T.

Mary Magdalene had her surname of magdalo a castell : and was borne of
parentes : whiche were descended of the lynage of kynges : And her fader was
moder eucharye : She wyth her broder lazare and her suster martha possessed th
whiche is two miles fro nazareth : & bethanye the castel whiche is nygh to Iheru
parte of Iherusalem. whiche al thise thynges they departed amonge theym in su
had the castelle magdalo. whereof she had her name magdalene : And lazare
cytes of Iherusalem : and martha had to her parte bethanye.
Legenda Aurea of Jacobus de Voragin, Second English Edition, Caxton (1493)

The towers of Magdalo are the confidents of the sky. All red they are, when
they are sombre in storm] in the gold daylight, gold. Slowly Mary Magd

6.23 *The Scream*, a "whimsical black-and-white, which is typical of Edvard Munch only in his whimsical mood," redrawn for *M'lle[] New York* 1:10 (January 1896) from a woodcut in *La Revue Blanche*

James Huneker had a much darker take on the "Purple Cow" in *M'lle New York*, where he published a horrific dream tale about a purple turtle, "The Ghost of a Turtle: A Fable for Naughty Nurses."[33] It starts with an invitation in the margins, "Why should an etiolated Lark alone be naif? Let us all be naif. Let us be Humperdincked and rejoice with childish laughter at Purple Cows and Chortling Turtles." The story then paints an age-warped scene in which a five-year-old boy named Goo-Goo, dressed in a brown velvet Fauntleroy suit, smokes cigarettes and drinks brandy while torturing a "very, very old lady," who sits trapped in a high chair playing toy blocks. He threatens to bring in his "purple turtle" if she doesn't tell him the name "of the animal that gives us milk." The story culminates after a page with Goo-Goo "annoyed" that the nurse has died of fright, but giving a "delirious dance of joy": "Why, Maddy, do you know that you are dead? How jolly! Maddy will soon be a Skellack! Maddy, you look like a Skellack." The boy, we are told, grows up to be a great actor, "a marvelous portrayer in Ibsen's sorrowful dramas." The story is so dark as to take away just a bit of the surprise we experience upon finding in *M'lle New York*, just four numbers later, a reproduction of Munch's quintessential expressionist image, *The Scream* (fig. 6.23). We have moved quite far from Burgess's purple cow, which was already at some distance from the black cat; and yet, particularly given the historical development of *fumisterie* as an avant-garde style, it seems clear that the citational index to both of them remains.

III. From Paris to Lansing, with Love

All of these citational modalities – people, translation, genre, and style – establish indexical relations among ephemeral bibelots, *petites revues*, and skinny magazines. The bibelot movement in effect moves through these links. We might summarize with three quick remarks. First, the movement moves in little pieces. The issue is not the dissemination of the entire class of magazines, but rather the assemblage of the class by way of individual links. Second, the sense we have of the movement as such, as a coherent phenomenon and not merely random coincidences, comes by way of the swarming multiplication of these minor links. The feel for individual magazines as being part of a movement is not dependent on any kind of direct association between their editors, or any statistical characteristics of their actual circulation in the literary marketplace. Rather, the sense of the movement moving comes by way of the linking of links, and so what we are really talking about is an expanding assemblage of connections. These connections, moreover, do not circulate evenly or randomly, like a drop of dye in a glass of water, but rather they are distributed through unevenly weighted hubs; and they constantly change, the arrival of nodes and links continually altering the topology of the network.[34] As suggested in the article in *Pan* with which we began, the network circulated through hubs like *The Chap-Book* and *The Lark* to an exponentially higher degree than through the smaller magazines; and yet their presence allowed the smaller magazines to link in to the circulation of the movement as a whole. Finally, the movement moves without geographical centres, happening as easily in small towns in America as in Paris, given that all you need to establish a relation is to pick up a book. Just because the American bibelots were looking to Paris does not mean that the circulation of black cats between them had anything to do with the geographical space of Paris. The "world republic of letters" was a citational point of reference for the bibelots, not a geographical one.

What would it really mean, however, to say that the movement circulated to the small towns of, say, the American Midwest? The freak magazines of the 1890s may have been ephemeral, and they may have been broadly dispersed; however, the tightly clustered network configuration assembled by way of these modalities of citation helps us better understand what it means to talk about the modernist refashioning of the aesthetic public sphere. It is the space of a different kind of artistic circulation, and small towns were well represented. We cannot tell much of this story from currently available resources on the history of reading. For example, the What Middletown Read database, which several of this volume's contributors employ to track the reading habits of public library patrons in Muncie, Indiana, during the height of the bibelot vogue, from 1891 to 1902, does not record any of the ephemeral bibelots having made it to the public library.[35] The *Union List of Serials*is not much more helpful, not listing any holdings of them in the Midwest, but it is spotty on regional coverage. What can be said is that magazines of this kind appeared in many American cities and small towns across the entire country, for example, *The Optimist* (Boone, Iowa, 1900–1); *Pot-Pouri* (Fremont, Ohio, 1898–9); *The Ishmaelite* (Indianapolis, Indiana, 1897–9); *The White Rabbit* (Oberlin, Ohio, 1897); and *The Kiote* (Lincoln, Nebraska, 1898–1901). As with *The Chap-Book*, which was started at Harvard before relocating to Chicago, many of these were coming out of university towns. What allowed these magazines to jump the track, as it were, assembling the traces of links across structural holes and non-intersecting dimensional planes, was the expanding assemblage of this avant-garde public sphere.

So let us conclude in two small towns with *The Clack Book* from Lansing, Michigan, and *The Philosopher* from Wasau, Wisconsin. What is so striking about both of these magazines is the number of citational links circulating between them in their very first numbers. *The Clack Book* came out first, starting in 1896, and it is evident from the *fumisterie* of its first cover – a fairly self-evident mash-up of *The Lark* and *The Chap Book* suggesting idiomatically that one or the other of them had "laid an egg" – that it means to enter directly into the fray of the American goblin literature (see fig. 6.6). Perhaps just a bit further afield, it would even seem to index *Le Mirliton*, a French *petit revue* started by Aristide Bruant on the tails of the success of *Le Chat Noir* – *Le Mirliton* being the name of the new cabaret that Bruant started in the building that *Le Chat Noir* occupied before moving to a bigger space (fig. 6.13). To the extent that it is an Americanization of the French, the origin of its title points us towards "*claque*," the organized group of hired applauders that became a regular part of opera performances in the 1830s. *The Clack Book* is full of such applause in a self-satirical mode, making regular citations in the early going to authors and artists central to the bibelot network, and to other freak magazines, including *The Echo*, Percival Pollard, *The Lotus*, Stephen

Crane, *The Philistine*, Aubrey Beardsley, Will Bradley, *Bradley, His Book*, Yone Noguchi, and Gelett Burgess; and it demonstrates the citational circulation of the movement by linking to *The Iconoclast* from Waco, Texas, and *The Optimist* of Detroit. Two months after the arrival of *The Philosopher* on the scene, *The Clack Book* gives it a blurb: "There is a new Philosopher among us – a new exploiter of the world's very old philosophy ... It is not a very hot Philosopher as yet, this new arrival upon the arena, but since in the same breath it lauds the legacy and damns the Gilder family, to say nothing of omitting periods in punctuation, something may come of it."[36] The next month, *The Clack Book* would lament the passing of *The Lark*, which had ceased publication after two years, with a stylistically similar blurb anthropomorphizing the bibelot's title: "The poor Lark! did she soar too high or did she sing to deaf ears?"[37]

What is significant for understanding how the bibelot movement moved is that *The Philosopher*'s opening numbers make so many of the same moves, eliciting so many of the same citations (see fig. 6.5). *The Philosopher* typifies not only an American bibelot, but also the movement of the bibelot movement, by the swarming multiplication of links one finds in it. As noted by *The Clack Book*, Ellis sets out the project of his "booklet" in contradistinction to "the Gilder family," who "have hamstrung the literature of our land enough, what with their Century Magazine, and their Critic, and the cheapjohn receptions, and all the flapdoodle in which they delight."[38] (Recall that *M'lle New York* had started in the very same way, sharing the negative citation through Gilder.) *The Philosopher*, too, notes the passing of *The Lark*, and cites Yone Noguchi and *The Philistine*; in the same section of notes; it even sends out a blurb to *The Clack Book*, "Michigan being the state where good celery comes from, and celery being an excellent sedative."[39] The point of all of which was to ensconce the magazine in the ethos and the aura of the bibelot movement, which in effect meant assembling its citational credentials, circulating a shared set of references. It joins itself to the assemblage, and in multiplying the links accelerates the movement's movement.

Moving, then, out from Wasau and Lansing, what one sees happening with the repetition of this citational mode is its reformulation as an aesthetic form in its own right. The bibelot vogue is moving, and also assembling an aesthetics of movement. The links and bridges, figured as such, are not merely the traces of a literary-social network; rather, they are, themselves, developing into the subject of aesthetic elaboration. They become new genres and encourage new styles. It has been typical to say of modernist texts that their engagement with other works of art signals their exclusion of (or retreat from) material and political concerns that had preoccupied both sentimental and realist fiction. While it may well be that the bibelots are no less hermetic in their insistent reflexivity than the works of modernist art they in many ways anticipated, they nonetheless circulate dramatically, worldwide, in tightly clustered networks. The notion of structural holes and non-intersecting planes structuring this new aesthetic public sphere should help us reconsider their relation to the public at large. Not just a production of Paris, London, and New York, the bibelot vogue took shape from the surging citational waves being actively assembled in the proverbial Lansings and Wasaus (and St Petersburgs) of the world. *Pan*, in the end, may have been exactly right to be looking in such places for the "fresh and joyous fight against the fin-de-siècle attitude of complacent weariness.

NOTES

1 Casanova (2004, 29).

2 A. Warburg, "Amerikanische Chap-Books," *Pan* 2:4 (October 1896), 345–8, 345. My thanks to Ariane Mühlethale for bringing *Pan* to my attention and for providing the translation.

3 For overviews of these publications in America, see K. MacLeod (2008); and B. Evans (2012). On Spanish-American reviews, see Hanneken (2010); Franco (2006); and Aching (1997). On Japan, see "The Extensions of Literary Activity." (1896). On India, see Alam and Chakravarty (2011); Radice (1991). On Russia, see A. Durkin (1997).

4 Had he been born forty years later, one can only guess that the small-town newspaper editor George Chandler Bragdon (1832–1910), described in this volume by Joan Shelley Rubin, would have been publishing an ephemeral bibelot instead of a country paper; and one can also assume that neither he nor the publishers of the bibelots would have been much interested in the books coming out of Germany that are the subject of Lynne Tatlock's essay. While both Parisian and German texts circulated in rural America, they signified quite different things.

5 Casanova (2004, 126).

6 These critiques tend to focus on Casanova's investment in the symbolic economy of aesthetic value instead of the political economy of hegemony, and on Paris instead of the world elsewhere. Representative discussions include Prendergast (2004); Damrosch (2003); McGann (2008); Ferguson (2008); and Hanneken (2010).

7 *M'lle New York* 1:1 (August 1895), n.p.

8 Casanova (2004, 87).

9 Tiffany (2009). See also Cate and Shaw (1996).

10 There are obviously more complex ways to theorize translation, and I discuss some of them below; the most influential of recent works on the subject has surely been that of Emily Apter (2005). Casanova's argument is interested in the more straightforward version of translation.

11 On structural holes, see in particular the publications of Burt (1992), starting with *Structural Holes: The Social Structure of Competition*. The emphasis for Burt is not on the hole so much as the bridge; he has shown in empirical studies that actors who span structural holes often accrue certain advantages, arbitrage opportunities, for instance, and the development of reputations (sometimes earned) for innovation. Burt's model is one of several developed by network sociology to describe a similar diffusion phenomenon. See, for contrasting examples, Granovetter (1973) and Watts (2002). There is not space here to review recent literature on the influential return of sociology, generally, as a field of interest in literary study. I will only note that that even though the most obvious bridge has been Bruno Latour, and especially *Reassembling the Social: An Introduction to Actor-Network Theory* (Latour 2005), Latour is largely absent from the citations of major American sociologists and mathematicians engaged in what has been called the "new science of networks." See Watts (2004), doi: 10.1146/annurev.soc.30.020404.104342. For an application of network theory in literary study having both a useful overview of the state of the field and topical relevance to my work on the ephemeral bibelots, see So and Long (2013), as well as the website for their digital humanities project at the University of Chicago, https://lucian.uchicago.edu/blogs/literarynetworks/research/ (accessed 4 July 2013).

12 Coincidentally, at the same time as the worldwide cascade of interest in ephemeral bibelots, there was a growing interest in what the anthropologist Franz Boas (1887, 485–6) called "The Occurrence of Similar Inventions in Areas Widely Apart." The topic there was "primitive" folk art, but the curiosity about diffusion or parallel invention was alive and well for the avant-garde too. For a discussion, see B. Evans (2005).

13 A similar idea is developed by Burt (2004, 349) when he suggests that "[b]rokerage across the structural holes between groups provides a vision of options otherwise unseen, which is the mechanism by which brokerage becomes social capital." I would thus argue that the bridging of structural holes distinguishes the innovation of the avant-garde from what Pawley (this volume) describes as the sentiment of racial commonality and mutual sociability developed in the farm journals in which Clara Steen Skott published. The farm journals exhibit a much more evenly distributed network structure.

14 Gourmont (1900, 2). Gourmont's bibliography has an American counterpart, Frederick Faxon's (1903) *Ephemeral Bibelots.*

15 In a recent history of *The Chap-Book*, Giles Bergel (2012, 168) cites anecdotal evidence from a letter to the magazine's publishers to the effect that it was "impossible to get *The Chap-Book* in Paris."

16 Note that the theoretical point, here, is a bit different from one that might be inferred by Joan Shelly Rubin's account (in this volume) of the life of the small-town newspaper editor, George Chandler Bragdon (1832–1910). My point is not about readership, but about the networks the magazines established for themselves through their citation practices. Bragdon was dearly attached to his subscription to the *Atlantic Monthly*; in his sixties, he was also a member of two clubs in upstate New York that would very much have been aware of the bibelot movement, the Vagabond Club (which shared its name with a volume published by the editor of the *Chap-Book*, Bliss Carmen), and the Bohemians. We can assume that Bragdon might have read both the *Atlantic Monthly* and the *Chap-Book* in the 1890s, but that does not obviate the fact of the gap between the two magazines' citation networks.

17 Laurence Hutton, "Literary Notes," *Harper's Monthly* 94:564 (1897), 1.

18 *Reassembling the Social*, 147.

19 Frank Norris (1986, 1113), '"An Opening for Novelists,' Novels and Essays." The essay was originally printed in the *Wave* (22 May 1897), which while not exactly a bibelot was not at all part of the genteel class of monthly magazines.

20 There is a massive sociological literature on citation networks. For a sample of foundational works, see D. Price (1965); Kessler (1963); and Crane (1972).

21 So and Long (2013), for example, have taken precisely this approach in their work on modernist literary networks. See citation above, n11.

22 The idea here is similar to what Lucy Delap and Maria DiCenzo (2008) have called "periodical communities."

23 Stephane Mallarmé, "Arthur Rimbaud," *The Chap-Book* 5 (1896) 8–17; and Mallarmé, "Les Loisirs de la Poste," *The Chap-Book* 2:3 (1894), pp. 111–15.

24 The form I am describing is part of the late nineteenth-century economy of "puffing," described by Laurel Brake (2012, 424), "whereby a network of friends assures that their books are noticed, in prominent places, and largely favourably, by an exchange of favours."

25 My translation: She is quite a modest creature, *The Lark*; she does not bother herself with personalities; being a morning bird, she busies herself with worms [a play on "verse"]. Nonetheless, she does not go so far as to feign indifference to the laudatory Notes from the cages down below where other birds live. *The Lark* is not ungrateful, and she thanks *The Critic* for the information about her circulation; *The Boston Journal*, which finds her

a bit wild; *The Chap-Book*, which called her risqué [being a play on *un journal intime*, a diary]; *The New York Times*, which saw in her a menace to the "modernité chicagoenne" (i.e., to *The Chap-Book*), and *The New York Tribune*, kind professor of larkeology, which names it a goose, undoubtedly because of her golden eggs.

26 Anton Chekhov's brother, Mikhail, whose memoir was translated into English and republished last year, confirms that *Sverchok* (The cricket) had been "modeled on the French magazines of the day" by its editors Evgeny and Mikhail Verner, who had lived abroad for a long time. They also published *Around the World*, which introduced the Russian reading public to the writings of Louis Henri Boussenard, Robert Louis Stevenson, and Henry Rider Haggard, all of whom were frequently cited by the American bibelots. See Chekhov (2010, 6–17, 83).

27 Published in *Oskolki* in January 1883. The excerpt is translated in Bartlett (2004, 133).

28 Chekhov (2010, 79),

29 Georges Fragerolle, "coupe[r] le ciel de prud'homie sous lequel nous vivons," quoted in Cate and Shaw (1996, 23).

30 Grojnowski (1996, 104).

31 M. Shaw (1996, 128, 130).

32 Walter Blackburne Harte, "Comment," *The Lotus* 1:5 (1 February 1896), 135.

33 James Huneker, "The Ghost of a Turtle," *M'lle New York* 1:7 (November 1895), n.p.

34 In fact, they exhibit many of the characteristics of "scale-free" networks described by Barabasi (2009, 412–13).

35 See What Middletown Read: http://www.bsu.edu/libraries/wmr/index.php (accessed 4 July 2013).

36 *The Clack Book* 2:5 (March 1897), 183.

37 *The Clack Book* 3:1 (April 1897), n.p.

38 *The Philosopher* 1:1 (January 1897), 31.

39 *The Philosopher* 1:3 (April 1897), n.p.

7 Circum-Atlantic Print Circuits and Internationalism from the Peripheries in the Interwar Era

LARA PUTNAM

In the decades after the First World War, European and Euro-American dominion reached maximum geographic spread – and scientific racism reached maximum stridency in efforts to justify it. Yet the legitimacy of global white supremacy was also challenged as never before. Not only in New York and Paris but in port towns from southern Africa to eastern Panama, colonized peoples envisioned international collectives, some proclaiming unity based in race or ancestry, others stressing the common circumstances of non-white peoples worldwide. This chapter suggests that the circulation of newspapers published by people of colour at the tropical peripheries of the British and American empires in the 1920s and 1930s helped make those expansive collective identities possible.[1]

I begin by exploring the factors that drove the growth of newspaper publishing and readership among colonized people throughout the anglophone Atlantic in the 1920s and 1930s, drawing examples from southern Africa in particular. I then examine in detail the functioning of one regional print circuit within the British Empire: black-run papers of the circum-Caribbean. Practices of circulation and reader participation here knit together both face-to-face and imagined communities. The latter included both race-specific and cosmopolitan versions. That is, while some stressed belonging to the "Negro Race," others saw themselves as part of a totality of peoples of colour confronted by white supremacy. Finally, I trace the strategies of glossed citation that allowed peripheral authors of colour to make evident the limits of white sympathy and to assert themselves as coeval peers to metropolitan debate about the non-white world – as subjects rather than objects of inquiry.

Overall, I argue that specific practices of circulation, citation, and commentary within the interwar peripheral press encouraged readers and writers of colour to understand their own struggles as part of a larger whole.

The Rising Tide of Colour: Colonized Peoples and Internationalist Visions in the Interwar World

Challenges to the political structures, labour systems, and cultural claims that secured European domination over non-European peoples surged at far-distant sites in the interwar era. Indian nationalists – Mohandas Gandhi most prominent among them – organized against the British Raj. Afro-Americans mounted newly forceful challenges to Jim Crow and its Northern variants; participants dubbed this the emergence of a "New Negro," who refused to live in fear. Jamaica-born Marcus Garvey's Universal Negro Improvement Association (UNIA) grew explosively, encompassing hundreds of thousands of members worldwide within a few years of its 1918 founding. In southern Africa multiple groups struggled against efforts to strip economic and electoral rights from non-whites. In sum, at sites across the anglophone greater Atlantic and the British Empire – and in the French colonial world and East Asia as well, though they will not be my focus here – the 1920s and 1930s saw new challenges to the intellectual claims and political and economic structures of white supremacy.[2]

In fact, one of the more detailed global accounts of this movement was penned by the very author who gave us the term "white supremacy": white supremacist Lothrop Stoddard, in his 1920 jeremiad *The Rising Tide of Colour and the End of World White Supremacy*. Modern readers rarely look past Stoddard's frank racism: he was, unapologetically, rooting for white supremacy to survive. But if we attend to Stoddard's descriptions rather than his prescriptions, we find a quite interesting set of assertions about an emerging global anti-racist alliance. Stoddard pointed to the spread of race-based immigration bans that barred non-whites from the growing economies created by settler colonialism, including the United States, Canada, and Australia. As a result, in Stoddard's words, "the rising tide of color finds itself walled in by white dikes debarring it from many a promised land which it would fain deluge with its dusky waves."[3]

Stoddard's tidal metaphor and macrostructural/demographic focus emphasized the social depth and diffuse synchrony of the emerging challenges to white supremacy. In this they offer a useful complement to recent scholarly research on this era, which has tended to focus on the few rather than the many, albeit with fascinating and illuminating results. Over the past decade, new research on interwar internationalisms has revealed interconnections among a range of activists and intellectuals of colour who had previously been slotted into separate histories as "black nationalists," Socialists, Communists, bourgeois reformists, assimilationists, Garveyites.

These rediscoveries have helped build a more accurate picture of the overlapping strands of what we now often call "black internationalism."[4] Further research has revealed, too, connections and parallels between these activists and intellectuals and the ones who spearheaded the simultaneous flowering of Asian and other anti-colonial internationalisms.[5]

Yet the pieces of this story that took place in the well-studied metropoles of New York, London, and Paris are just part of the picture. Even the activists and intellectuals of colonial birth who travelled to the metropoles and then on to other colonies, knitting together webs of connection as they did so, are only part of the story.[6] Intellectual challenges to white supremacy came from within the margins as well. Pan-Africanism, pan-Asianism, pan-Arabism, and other internationalisms emerged as multiple voices within multiple societies spoke out at once.

In the understanding of human collectives embraced by many at the time, such synchronic "awakenings" seemed natural. Stadial thinking held that each "race" or "people" developed through stages over time, and as a unit. In contrast, scholars today understand collective identities as social constructs – ideas, grounded in practices shaped by structures of power – rather than mystical commonalities borne in the blood and waiting to be awaked. Why then did this particular moment see so many awakenings?

Benedict Anderson famously argued that the nineteenth-century newspaper spurred the growth of nationalism by making possible the imagination of community on a new scale.[7] This essay suggests a pattern compatible with that analysis, but more wide-ranging in its coordinates and outcomes. The colonial press in the early twentieth century fed new internationalisms as well as new nationalisms. Local papers went to battle within local struggles, and foregrounded colony-wide critiques. Yet at the same time, because of particular characteristics of their circulation and coverage, they gave readers and writers the opportunity to locate themselves within much broader collectives.

While some of those collective identities echoed lines of race or ancestry, others did not. Identifications that superseded race were being generated from and for the peripheries as well. Historian Nico Slate has advanced the term "colored cosmopolitanism" to denote an anti-racist vision "that transcended traditional racial distinctions, positioning Indians and African Americans together at the vanguard of the 'darker races.' … Advocates of coloured cosmopolitanism fought for the freedom of the 'colored world,' even while calling into question the meanings of both colour and freedom."[8] While Slate focuses on Indians and African Americans – the latter as the self-declared vanguard of global change – we will see that voices from the colonized peripheries likewise spoke of the shared position of "colored races" struggling in tandem against a white supremacist world order.

Part of what fostered race-specific internationalisms and colour-conscious cosmopolitanism in the interwar era were the practices of reading, writing, and circulation of the peripheral press.

Editors across Empire: Writers and Reading Publics of Colour

In the wake of the Great War, Lothrop Stoddard wrote, "Chinese scholars, Japanese professors, Hindu pundits, Turkish journalists, and Afro-American editors, one and all voiced drastic criticisms of white civilization."[9] He was right as far as he went, but his laundry list of bogeymen fell short. The scope of participation in this international, contestatory republic of letters spread further outside of the Northern Hemisphere than he wanted to recognize. "Afro-American editors" were numerous and prolific in this era, but they were not alone.

To be sure, the *Chicago Defender* and *Pittsburgh Courier* developed impressive international subscriberships and offered sustained international coverage.[10] Larger still was worldwide circulation of the UNIA's *Negro World*, which reached between seventeen thousand and sixty thousand in the early 1920s, distributed through newsagents and local chapters where governments permitted its entry and surreptitiously in the hands of black seamen where they did not. Published in New York by a series of mainly British Caribbean-born editors, the *Negro World* included pages in Spanish and French and carried reports from correspondents from Capetown to Santiago de Cuba. The paper was fundamental to the way Garveyism, in the words of Michael West and William Martin, "gave black internationalism, for the first time, a return address."[11]

Paris and London saw innovative black-run periodicals in this era as well, and these too circulated overseas.[12] But the interwar surge of periodicals by and for publics of colour did not merely radiate outward from North Atlantic capitals. Research on African newspapers, print culture, and public spheres, for instance, has debunked any false assumption that "New African" modernity "derived from" New Negro modernity.[13] As we shall see, international networks certainly shaped both the trajectories of the men who founded papers in interwar Africa and the provenance of the news items that graced the papers' pages. But these connections were not unidirectional, and they included dense lateral branching as well as circuits linking metropole to colony.

In West Africa, Accra was home to the *Gold Coast Leader*, *Gold Coast Nation*, *West African News*, and *African Morning Post*, among others.[14] Such papers generated, Stephanie Newell argues, a "particular new public: a trans-colonial reading public, politically articulated, joined by their shared identity as members of the British Empire" even when separated by ideology, class, and locale.[15] The optic of the West African press went beyond the borders of the continent and even the British Empire, with critique of European hegemony forming a connective line. Thus in the pages of their local papers, "readers in Accra or Freetown or Lagos could access information about Home Rule campaigns in India and Ireland, the activities of the Ku Klux Klan in North America, Japan's economic transformation and the emergence of racial segregation in South Africa. Throughout empire, readers were thus articulated – connected together, spoken for and speaking for themselves – in new ways by their English-language newspapers."[16]

The contents and impact of southern African papers seem to have been similar, especially by the late 1920s, suggesting how the circulation of papers between regions tended to align their scope of vision and dialogue. John Tengo Jabavu founded *Imvo Zabantsundu*, the first black-owned paper in southern Africa, in 1884. The paper combined English- and Xhosa-language pages, and in its first decades focused largely on local events and the struggles of the Cape Colony's non-white bourgeoisie against ever-deepening discrimination. After Jabavu's death in 1921, his son Alexander Macaulay Jabavu assumed the editorship. *Imvo* in the 1920s continued to protest the crescendo of race-based restrictions on political and land rights, and grew increasingly supportive of more radical challenges in the form of the South African Native National Congress (SANNC), the Bantu Union, and the Industrial and Commercial Union (ICU) trade union. *Imvo*'s pages also carried news of DuBois and Garvey and other Afro-descended organizers of Americas, whose strategies and whose declarations regarding Africa were hotly debated in the paper's Xhosa-language pages.[17]

Colonial capitals had long been home to newspapers published by white elites or expats, and read by a small subset of the wider populace. This was something different. If we track developments across the British circum-Atlantic (and perhaps beyond as well), we see the impact of mobility in setting the conditions for a multiplying non-elite press. The interwar years found new people in new places with new things to protest. In Africa, the economy of twentieth-century empire depended on the mass mobilization of labour within or between British-ruled territories: to mine gold, diamonds, or copper; to harvest cocoa or palm kernels. Coercive recruitment and taxation kept wages low and profits high. In the Caribbean in the same years, mines and export agriculture (driven by U.S. investment in Spanish American republics) similarly drew British colonial labourers far from home. Labor migration created both reasons for protest and new settings – crowded and heterogeneous ports, especially – where protest might spread. The travels of potential writers, the migration of potential readers, and the growth of oppositional organizing came together to spur the founding of periodicals by men who were not white and not elite, and who knew they were not alone.

Let's take two African examples. Mission-educated clerk and interpreter Solomon Plaatje (1876–1932) was among the founders of the South African Native National Congress, and travelled to London as part of SANNC delegations in 1913 and 1919 to seek imperial action against new laws that stripped land and rights from non-white Southern Africans. From London Plaatje travelled on to the United States, reaching out to W.E.B. DuBois and speaking to mass meetings alongside Marcus Garvey in New York and Toronto in 1921. These personal connections, made possible by initial print-borne contact, laid the groundwork for sustained exchange of and through the periodicals Plaatje and these Afro-Caribbean and Afro-American allies published from distant edges of the Atlantic. Over his four decades of activism Plaatje would found or edit newspapers including the *Bechuana Friend* and *Friend of the People* in Kimberley and the *Bechuana Gazette* in Mafeking.

Born twenty years after Plaatje, in Nyassaland, present-day Malawi, Clements Kadalie (1896–1951) followed the steps of many from his community to Johannesburg, and then kept going. In Cape Town in 1919, he founded the Industrial and Commercial Union and led a dockworkers' strike. Fellow leaders included men from Cape Town's several-hundred-strong British West Indian community, among them passionate Garveyites who sped circulation of the *Negro World* and formation of UNIA chapters. In 1920 Kadalie co-founded the Cape Town *Black Man*, a newspaper that supported both the UNIA and ICU, and in 1923 he founded the ICU's *Workers' Herald*. Although Kadalie's class origins and labour focus were quite different from Plaatje, his newspapers located themselves within the same international dialogue, one that offered a wide range of strategies towards the common goal of Negro advance: Kadalie reprinted articles from Garvey's *Negro World*, DuBois's *Crisis*, and the black Socialist-run *Messenger* alike.[18]

Shifting our optic from British colonies in Africa to British colonies in the Americas, we see a similar tale. There was a surge of newspaper publishing by British West Indians in the first decades of the twentieth century, driven by fundamentally parallel dynamics. Far-travelling editors, migratory readerships, and race-conscious organizing (of varying ideological stripes) went hand in hand. One example of this has already been mentioned multiple times: the founding of the UNIA's *Negro World* by Jamaican immigrant Marcus Garvey in New York in 1919, in the midst of the mass migration then transforming Harlem, where by the mid-1920s one-quarter of residents were British West Indies–born. But Harlem was only the latest of a string of migratory destinations, and the same dynamic held elsewhere. Jamaicans, Barbadians, and others had travelled by the tens of thousands to opportunities in Panama, Venezuela, and Trinidad in the late nineteenth century, then in still larger numbers to Panama for canal construction after 1903, to United Fruit plantations and ports, and to Cuba after the Great War for sugar's "Dance of the Millions." By 1930, multigenerational British Caribbean communities in the Spanish-speaking Greater Caribbean totalled more than 150,000 souls, and 130,000 more British Caribbean immigrants and their children resided in the United States, in Harlem and Brooklyn most of all.[19]

Literacy in the British West Indies was relatively high and, reflecting the self-selection of long-distance migrants, literacy among British West Indians abroad was higher still. Thus in the Panama Canal Zone in 1920, nine out of ten British West Indian residents were literate. Among British West Indians in Costa Rica in the 1920s, the figure was eight out of ten. In each case, this meant that black immigrants were not only more literate than the island-born peers they left behind, but markedly more literate than the Spanish-speaking citizens who surrounded them.[20] The circum-Caribbean migratory sphere, then, was home to a savvy, literate, highly mobile working class, connected by ties of kinship, communication, and associational life to multiple far-flung sites.[21]

The same years that saw British West Indian migrants stretch their networks of support from Port of Spain to Panama to Brooklyn witnessed a flowering of the anglophone circum-Caribbean press, led by a new generation of men from outside elite circles. There were newspapers owned, edited, and read by British colonials of colour in St George's, Grenada; Bridgetown, Barbados; Port of Spain, Trinidad; Georgetown, British Guiana; Kingston, Jamaica; Panama City, Panama; Port Limón, Costa Rica; Bluefields, Nicaragua; and beyond.[22] Some of the interwar surge in publishing by men of colour in the British Caribbean was driven by the impact of the Great War itself, as men who had served in the British West Indies Regiment returned home with intensified awareness of the metropolitan radical press (including the *Negro World*) and new commitment to struggle for equal rights in their societies of origin.[23] Upon returning from service in Palestine, for instance, Barbadian Clennell Wickham became first columnist, then editor of the *Barbados Weekly Herald*, his editorials calling out racist injustice on the island, across the empire, and around the globe.[24]

A similar vision drove the editorial creations of men whose travels carried them less far, yet whose experience of white racism likewise came with built-in awareness of its geopolitical context. Jamaica-born Sidney Young moved with his parents to Panama at the height of U.S. canal construction, attended school in Jamaica, then returned to the isthmus as a young adult. A few months spent as a messenger for U.S. administrators convinced him never to work in the Canal Zone again. After several years as a cable editor on isthmian papers, Young convinced the Yankee editor of the *Panama American* to allow him to create a "West Indian" page within the paper, which soon became a centrepiece of community life and debate. Forced out in 1927, Young founded his own *Panama Tribune*, the mouthpiece and meeting place of British West Indian Panama for the next half century.[25] Circulation reached six to eight thousand, with subscribers at each nodal point of the British Caribbean diaspora: Limón, Costa Rica; Bluefields, Nicaragua; Harlem, NYC; Barbados; Jamaica.[26]

Whether published within British colonies or at migratory destinations, the newspapers of colonials of colour were rarely anti-colonial in any simple sense. (The newspapers edited by Harlem-based Caribbean radicals like Hubert Harrison were in this sense the exception rather than the rule.)[27] Rather, they denounced injustice and abuse and insisted that the rights of loyal subjects of the king be respected, whatever their colour. Between the hair-trigger defensiveness of local white elites and Great Britain's plaintiff-friendly libel laws, this made lawsuits an ever-present threat. Libel action shuttered the London-based *African Telegraph* in 1919, after it republished an exposé from the *Gold Coast Leader* on the flogging of women in Nigeria.[28] A libel suit forced Clennell Wickham out and bankrupted the *Barbados Weekly Herald* in 1930.[29] Ben Azikiwe's *African Morning Post* was shut down by a similar action six years later.

More broadly, Seditious Publications Ordinances – hurriedly drafted by Whitehall officials and enacted by panicked local elites as Garveyism and labour strife blossomed in the wake of the First World War – were used to bar the entry of publications that preached "Bolshevism" or "race-hatred."[30] "In a community like ours, where there are many people not well instructed and not well informed," explained the governor of Trinidad in 1920, "publications calculated to upset and make them disloyal and work up their minds any idea of a racial war or a class war" are particularly dangerous.[31] To the contrary, though: it was the fact that colonial publics were becoming well-informed that was dangerous to imperial rule.

Viewing the interwar British Atlantic as a whole, then, the broad outlines of a multisited and multidimensional process are clear. A crucial handful of intellectuals and activists travelled along the sinews of empire in the first decades of the twentieth century. A far greater number of working-class migrants set themselves in motion seeking wages and advancement, from Jamaica to Cuba, Bridgetown to Harlem, Botswana to Johannesburg (and Alabama to Chicago). An even greater number of men and women stayed and laboured closer to home. The first category was over-represented among the founders of periodicals, and the second over-represented among their readers. But the public sphere the periodicals created was open to all three – even to men and women who were not themselves literate, but took part in debates at beer stands or butcher shops that drew ideas from the text that some neighbours could read.[32] With reason Olver and Meyer have described the public sphere as the space where "the routed" and "the rooted" connect.[33]

In sum, international mobility and connections – actively initiated from multiple sites, it bears repeating, rather than diffused downward from Harlem or Paris – shaped the interwar surge of publishing by editors of colour for readerships of colour. We now turn from the international ties that shaped the papers' founding to the international dimensions that shaped their impact. We will explore first the practices of readership and circulation, and then the editorial content, that undergirded global awareness and overlapping identifications. We will do so focusing on a subset of the worldwide press of colour: the circum-Caribbean circuit described above.

Looking Outward from the British Caribbean: Overlapping Collectives Made Real

Visiting the Isthmus of Panama in 1912, British traveller Winifred James described the "negro settlement" just outside the canal's Caribbean terminus in Colón:

> The houses, large, wooden, two-storey dwellings, with verandahs and balconies and galvanized iron roofs, are ranged up along the left side of the railway line. In these houses scores of families live together, and on the verandahs and balconies everything happens. From the windows of the carriage one sees the

> life of the encampment going on. In a corner of the verandah a naked little brown thing is splashing delightedly in his bath and evading furiously the mother, who is waiting her chance to take him out. Near by a woman treadles industriously away at her sewing-machine, and a big placid nigger man reads his paper and smokes his pipe, regardless of the dogs and the children and the chickens that are swarming under his feet and over his head and everywhere round about him.[34]

An Australian feminist and freethinker, James was imbued with the class and race prejudices of her day but was also a careful observer, in particular of domestic spaces other travellers overlooked. What she captures for us here is newspaper readership's embeddedness in working-class life in the Greater Caribbean. On the islands' rural villages, where among the older generation literacy was uncommon, we hear of newspapers read aloud by a lettered few – the shopkeeper, the tailor – and then debated with "indignation," anxiety, and "the unlettered man's respect for the written word" by those clustered round.[35] But in migratory destinations like Colón, with their broadly literate working-class populations, first-hand readership was widespread. The communicative space it generated knit together face-to-face communities while linking them to distant destinations, just as did the reading practices outlined in Robert Hall's account of nineteenth-century English mill workers elsewhere in this volume (see chapter 8).

George Westerman, who began his career as sports editor for Sidney Young's *Panama Tribune* in 1928 and rose to be associate editor and eventual owner, described that paper's circulation within British West Indian Panama: "It has accurately been determined that each copy of the paper is read by at least five persons, passing from hand to hand over the entire week until the next issue is off the press ... In barber-shops and hair-dressing parlors, professional offices (medicos, dentists, lawyers) the TRIBUNE is always handy to while away the time of waiting."[36] A testimonial in the Limón, Costa Rica, *Searchlight* in 1927 records the same person-to-person circulation taking place on a region-wide scale: "It is my habit, <<good or bad>>, to send a weekly copy of your Invaluable Weekly to Trinidad, so that my relatives may see what is what in Limon. Again, I send a weekly copy to Colon to a girl friend, who passes it around to her girlfriends, and comment about the doings of Limon. Now and then I would send a copy to Jamaica, to my school friends. And I also keep a weekly copy for my further reference."[37]

Even as the Limón *Searchlight* was read in Panama, the *Panama Tribune* was read in Limón: by the *Searchlight* editors, who quoted from it and commented on it, and by local subscribers, who likewise felt empowered to write in response. The same pseudonymous Firefly whose circulatory habits "<<good or bad>>" are described above regularly sent updates on Limón's civic uplift to the *Panama Tribune*. A typical 1931 letter listed by name all attendees at a banquet hosted by three newly founded young people's social clubs (250 miles away in Costa Rica), which the Firefly presented as promising signs of a new era in which "our Negro community" would be "dragged out of the armour of slovenness, and bask in a soothing sunshine of racial love and unity."[38] Because readership of multiple prints overlapped, and overlapped with face-to-face ties, and letters from readers bridged them all, distinct papers fused into a participatory space within which the lived and the printed realms formed a continuum rather than a categoric break. Thus the busy Firefly could use the Letters section of the *Searchlight* to call out a young man of Limón for fostering gossip, adducing as supporting evidence the fact that the same fellow had been "well-scolded through the *Panama Tribune*" the previous week (well scolded by the Firefly him/herself, perhaps, though this our Firefly neglects to say).[39]

The Firefly was not alone in using the local press as an extension of personal and civic life. In the *Panama Tribune*, a typical page of "Happenings in the Zone Towns" included news of a dozen individuals' visits to friends, travels home to Jamaica, and hospital stays; upcoming events of the Alliance Literary and Debating Society and the Nightengale Sporting and Social Club; Kitchener's Domino Club's "crushing defeat" of the Gold Coast Domino Club; the St Teresa Church's "box suppers" and the La Boca Athenaeum's mock trial (starring "Clarence Darrow" for the defence); the Gatun Silver Club Football Team's challenge to all comers; and, posted as news from the Canal Zone town of Red Tank, the death in New York City of "old Isthmian resident" Aaron Brathwaite, who had left Panama fifteen years before: "He leaves to mourn their loss a wife, five children, a brother and sister in New York; his mother, two brothers, two sisters and other relatives in Barbados; a brother in Havana, Cuba, and a brother and daughter who reside in Chorillo [Panama]."[40] Brathwaite had been gone for a decade and a half, but his brother Moses in Red Tank did not doubt that Aaron's friends on the isthmus needed to hear of his passing; and surely they did. The convergence of communications technology, popular literacy, and mass labour migration had created a periodical press uniquely suited to maintaining transnational ties to kith and kin, whether between neighbouring ports like Limón and Colón or across the 2,000-plus miles from Chorillo to Harlem or Brooklyn to Barbados.

How did the members of these communities define themselves? Within which imagined collectives did they locate themselves? When they spoke of "we" and "our people," who did they mean? And how was this connected to the discursive positioning of the papers they read? Layers of identification both overlapped and evolved over time. Consistently, editors like Sidney Young pushed for loyalties larger than their readers' instinctive frames, at least to judge by the amount of ink spent haranguing readers to look beyond island "chauvinisms" and embrace two causes: West Indies–wide solidarity and the uplift of the Negro people worldwide. West Indies–wide federation remained a driving dream for a handful of educated activists and journalists in New York and a few island capitals, but never captured popular hearts and minds with the same intensity.[41] The embrace of Negro peoplehood, in contrast, was deep, broad, and growing. Popular black internationalism in the British Caribbean diaspora both sped the expansion of the UNIA and was massively reinforced by it.[42] The Firefly's framing of a local club event as a step towards "racial love and unity" would not have been out of place in the Limón press two decades before; by 1932 it was utterly commonplace.[43]

The periodical press was not just a medium for the communication of race-based identification: the black press itself became both banner and bond, a source of pride and a space for connection. Among the statistics published by Sidney Young's "West Indian Page" in 1926 as evidence of the "Amazing Progress of Negroes in U.S." was the fact that while in 1863 only two "negro newspapers" existed, today there were 412 "periodicals published by or for colored people" in the nation to the north.[44] "Only through the Negro Press are the deeds of black men accurately portrayed," explained a letter to the editor in the inaugural issue of Young's *Panama Tribune*.[45] Readers schooled each other on appropriate epistolary conduct under these circumstances. As one correspondent explained in 1930, "Environments have caused the Negroes to be long deprived of privileges, and now having the privilege to our own paper, we should endeavour always to write Articles that are educative, for the people are being educated through the Press."[46] Racial pride required a particular print etiquette: "Frivolities and scandals cannot help to nationhood, but will retard progress and destroy the morals of many, then we should write intelligently for all eyes are watching us. Anyone who realizes what is race consciousness, cannot expose, disgrace and scandalize their people before the nations of the world."[47]

Thus readers' writing as well as editors' editing powered the black internationalism of these papers. It is impossible to gauge the role of editors in winnowing readers' letters, of course. Yet repeatedly letter writers in Panama and Costa Rica staked out positions far more "race conscious" than the editors' editorial stance. Young himself, for instance, adopted a sympathetic but critical line on the organizational moves of Marcus Garvey. Yet fervent reader-written paeans to Garvey's accomplishments filled Young's papers' pages well into the 1950s. Throughout the 1920s and 1930s black internationalism was a constant tonic. Readers hailed each other in the *Tribune*'s and *Searchlight*'s pages week after week, in poetic apostrophe and in concluding perorations: "Awake Negroes!" "Negroes, awake!" "Sons of Ethiopia, rise!"[48] Doing so they made this printed space their own, and defined their own in terms of race.

British West Indian readers' notion of the proper mission of a race-conscious press drew on multiple models, the Afro-American press most prominently. Here too the existence of local newspaperswas key, because the infrastructure they created made it possible for readers to access foreign papers far more readily than would otherwise have been the case. Newsagents at every major port managed sales for popular foreign papers, whether from nearby islands or distant metropoles, and they advertised these offerings in the local press. As early as 1904, Trinidad's Port of Spain *Daily Mirror* carried advertisements for subscriptions to such periodicals as "The Coloured American Magazine," promised to fulfil all hopes of "what a magazine should be such as the needs of the Afro-American people require."[49] (This was the *Coloured American Magazine* edited by Pauline Hopkins in Boston from 1900 to 1904, years when, it should be noted, hundreds of people from the British Caribbean were settling in Boston and Cambridge every year.)[50] By the 1920s the *Chicago Defender* and *Pittsburgh Courier* were not merely present in the Caribbean in the form of republished articles but had their own subscribers across in the region, in Panama, Jamaica, and Costa Rica in particular.

And here again, readers wrote back. The active engagement woven by the Firefly, Moses Brathwaite, and their fellow "Negro people" of Panama, Colón, and Limón was replicated, albeit with less density and continuity, on a hemispheric scale. A single "Questions and Answers" column in the pages of the *Pittsburgh Courier* in 1936 carried inquiries from H. Samuels in Pedro Miguel, Canal Zone, about where he might study dentistry (answer: contact Howard University); from Port Limón, Costa Rica, about where one might obtain "a history, including pictures, of the colored boxers?"; another from Port Limón, asking where to purchase "a history of Ethiopia"; and a letter from a man in Tela, Honduras, seeking news of his brother and two uncles in New York or Boston. The return addresses of these letters sketched out precisely the geographic contours of the western edge of the British Caribbean migratory system. The content of the letters sketched out the breadth of topics that had come to be seen in a black internationalist frame.

When these correspondents perused the *Courier*'s advice column for answers to their queries, they would have found their letters published amidst one from Wichita, Kansas, about where to find material on "fascism, communism, socialism and their effect on the American Negro"; another from Gary, Indiana, about how to raise funds for Ethiopia; and another from Mrs A.H. in New Iberia, Louisiana, to whose queries "When will my other boy be free from the pen? Will I ever be happy in life?" the *Courier* could offer no answer at all.[51] But perhaps what mattered was that the question was heard by men and women far away, who reconfirmed through these pages just how much they shared.

Black Internationalists and Coloured Cosmopolitans ... Sometimes One and the Same

Two thousand three hundred miles southeast of New Iberia, Louisiana, sits the island of Grenada, population ca. 1915 around sixty-six thousand. T.A. Marryshow founded *The West Indian* in Grenada in that year, and for the next four decades used it as pulpit in his quest for political rights and West Indian unity. In its earliest years, the already crusading *West Indian* spoke from a carefully race-neutral subject position on behalf of equal rights within the empire. However, Marryshow's editorial positioning would evolve over the course of the 1920s, in ways that suggest, as did the evolution of Mac Jabavu's *Imvo*, the impact of the expanding black press. By 1930 Marryshow's editorial subject position was explicitly one of colour. (Port of Spain's *Labour Leader* followed exactly the same trajectory in the same years.) Arguments for race-blind rights and political reform continued to fill its pages, but the panorama it offered readers was no longer centred on island and empire. Rather, the broader landscape of black struggle worldwide had come to the fore. The *West Indian* embraced the same interlocutors as did the Limón *Searchlight* and the *Panama Tribune* and the South African papers edited by Plaatje and Kadalie: Garvey's *Negro World*, DuBois's *Crisis*; the Chicago *Defender* and Pittsburgh *Courier*; the short-lived *Revue du Monde Noir* and *Dépêche africaine*.

International in its dialogues, the *West Indian* was also international in its destinations. Circulation reached sixteen hundred in 1922, then shrank as economic crisis tightened, but these copies travelled far.[52] By 1930 Marryshow published a bimonthly Overseas Edition "which," he assured readers, "circulates throughout the West Indies, Central America, among West Indians in the United States, United Kingdom and farther afield."[53] The importance of labour migration in driving the circulation of this as other Caribbean papers is underlined by the prominent advertisements that each week urged readers to "Give Friends Abroad the Overseas" and promised pages "Crammed tight with interesting facts that will be a boon to Grenadians absent from the homeland."[54]

Meanwhile, the range of international news covered for those readers was coterminous with the *West Indian*'s contemporaries in West Africa as profiled at the start of this essay and the *Panama Tribune* and Limón *Searchlight* discussed above. A typical issue of the *West Indian* in 1930 covered "the fight being waged against the Colour Bar in London"; racist declarations by South African General Smuts in New York; news of local politics, regional cricket, and international boxing; and an inspiring global summary quoted from W.E.B. DuBois's *Crisis*, used to frame a discussion of recent successes by reform activists in Barbados:

> The bell has struck. India has declared for independence.
>
> China is determined to try all residents in China in her own courts.
>
> Egypt has elected a Parliament of Nationalists, and Ethiopia has sent a Minister to England.
>
> The myth of the divine overlordship of Europe over the coloured world is beginning to fade.[55]

Which people were "our people" within this "coloured world"? Marryshow never abandoned his early insistence that for the peoples of the region, West Indian must be the paramount political identity. Not for nothing is he known today as the "Father of Federation." But in the *West Indian* of the 1930s Marryshow's commitment to a West Indies–wide cultural and political allegiance sat alongside a black internationalism that foregrounded the "Negro Race" as worldwide collective, which in turn nested within a vision of the "coloured world" struggling in synchrony against white domination.

Even more than Marryshow's *West Indian*, Sidney Young's *Panama Tribune* placed race-based solidarity front and centre in the 1930s. Importantly, too, Young emphasized parallels among the distinct "colored races." In this his editorial line echoed that of DuBois and Marryshow – for whom India, China, Egypt, and Ethiopia served together as evidence that the "myth of the divine overlordship of Europe over the coloured world" was collapsing – and differed from Garvey, who at times adopted a more exclusionary vision of "racial struggle" in which "asiatics," say, were seen as competitors rather than possible kin.[56] Young offered readers an anti-essentialist anti-racism – something close to Slate's "colored cosmopolitanism."

As with Marryshow, Young wrote from a position shaped by nested and mutually reinforcing internationalisms. An editorial on the League of Nations' takeover of Liberian finances in 1932, for instance, began by describing this as a "severe blow to the national aspirations and racial pride of Negro people throughout the world" – placing the race-based collective front and centre. But Young then shifted to a broader frame. Summoning evidence from across history and across the colonized world, he pointed to the brutalities of Belgians in Africa, the "historic crimes" of "Spaniards in Peru and Mexico who destroyed a glorious people," the slaveholding U.S. South, the "Boers in South Africa, and the British in India." He used this global analysis to undercut the racist claim that Liberia's troubles proved "Negroes are unable to rule themselves." "To pretend that the atrocities committed by Liberians against the original natives make the Liberian government unworthy to maintain its independence is to forget the facts of history," wrote Young: "No greater atrocities have ever been committed against innocent people than by the white nations in their colonial expansion."[57]

Young routinely described all "colored races" as suffering from the "domination of the white nations" and the "theory of Nordic supremacy" that sought to naturalize it.[58] Doing so amplified both the breadth of historical evidence that could be marshaled, and the weight of history still to come. "The black man is not temperamentally a revolutionist," Young averred, describing his people's patience and religiosity in tones momentarily essentialist. In the very next sentence, though, he pointed across continental space to establish a relation of parallels between races: "but the yellow race is in arms and the black 'worm' might turn."[59] Young then invoked the widest international collectives – "the darker races" (united by colour) and "the subject races" (united by imperial subjugation) – and declared them ready to wreak justice. "If the supremacy of the Nordic, white supremacy cannot be maintained, cannot compete against the darker races except by right of conquest made possible by force of arms, or by repression through might and power, it will not be long before the subject races learn from their masters and some terrible holocaust wreck the structure of civilization."[60] The tide of colour was rising.

Glossing: Engaging White Metropolitan Coverage of the Non-white World

In addition to drawing heavily on articles from the U.S. black press, circum-Caribbean newspapers published by and for British Caribbean people of colour also drew on many publications not by people of colour at all. These included daily papers from New York and London and a plethora of journals covering global developments that were written by progressive activists or professional experts or both. All these periodicals pronounced upon the "problem of color," but they did so from without rather than within, and it mattered. Exhortations to coloured advance or critiques of coloured leaders' failings had an entirely different valence when penned by white authors for a white readership. Even declarations of sympathy and support carried a paternalistic charge. The editors and readers of the circum-Caribbean black press relied upon these periodicals for news of the distant struggles that fired the internationalist imagination. Yet they were unwilling to leave their hierarchies and exclusions unchallenged. Thus in the pages of the *Panama Tribune*, Limón *Searchlight*, *West Indian*, and others, editors and letter writers regularly offered extended riffs on articles from elsewhere and how they should be read.

In August 1930, for instance, the editors of the Limón *Searchlight* prefaced a lengthy excerpt about caste division within India with the following introduction:

> There has been so many opinions relative to the similarity of treatments handed out to the Negro race as compared to the Indian problem now in discussion, that we are tempted to reproduce the following article from the pen of the famous American author Miss Katherine Mayo; so that our readers may get an inside glimpse of some of the real causes prompting <<Ghandi's call for civil disobedience>>, and see in how far they coincide with some treatments to the Negro of a couple decades ago.[61]

The author being quoted was U.S. feminist and anti-immigrant nativist Katherine Mayo, whose 1927 denunciation of the treatment of women and girls within India, *Mother India*, written at the encouragement of British authorities, had inspired outrage among Indian nationalists.[62] While Gandhi and others denounced Mayo for her very partial reading of the Indian present, the *Searchlight* editors instead offered a very partial reading of Mayo's work itself, glossing Mayo's descriptions of poor conditions as revealing the "real causes" behind Gandhi's protests. A tome read at the time (and since) as imperial apologia was thus transformed into a brief against imperial rule.

Moreover, whereas metropolitan commentators – the "so many opinions" the *Searchlight* editors referenced – were content to debate "similarity of treatments" of Indians under British rule and "the Negro race," the *Searchlight* went beyond description to stress lessons for action. The prefatory sentence, its length an index of the extent of reframing required, continued:

> as well as to see how intrigues by Religion, and other diplomatic propaganda, are brought to divide the thoughts of solidarity of any subjected races, and rendering the tasks of leaders to higher thoughts of freedom so onerous, and almost impossible to attain the success achievable only by unification of ideas and actions, because how can any cause, <<be it ever so inspired>> succeed in the uplift of a Race, when propaganda of class against Mass keeps the group divided and antagonistic to themselves.

The editors had begun by reminding readers that Mayo was famous and American, borrowing her prestige while ignoring her agenda. The lessons they instead instructed readers to see – the need for internal solidarity in the fight for "the uplift of a Race" – are the lessons these same pages pounded home in Garveyite poems and civic notes week after week.

Readers too read widely, and commented on what they read. A few months before the excerpting of Mayo, for instance, a letter from "Africanus" to the *Searchlight* had detailed debates within India and Gandhi's demands as laid out in "the columns of his newspaper 'The Young India.'" Africanus concluded his or her letter by comparing Gandhi to "the great Negro leader Marcus Garvey ... who like Gandhi is not afraid of imprisonments, in a cause which he feels is righteous as he feels his body is at the disposal of those in authority but the righteousness of his soul in the cause of the freedom of thought for his Race is from God."[63] For Africanus, Indian nationalist and black internationalist struggles paralleled each other even in their religious dimensions: Hindu and Christian visions of anti-racist struggle here become one and the same.

The circum-Caribbean papers covered U.S. imperialism in the Caribbean almost as closely as British imperialism in India and Africa, and here too readers brought their outside reading to bear for their fellow readers. A 1930 letter to the *Searchlight* from "A French Negroid" reported at length on "a recent article written by John H. Allen in *The Current History* of May," among other things quoting Allen quoting William Jennings Bryan's bemused response to Allen's report on the island that

Bryan and his government had invaded: "Dear me, think of it, *Niggers speaking French*."[64] The self-identified "French Negroid" (the pseudonym itself an ironic comment on North American racializations) built a lengthy commentary around Bryan's travesty, with a breadth of reference that showcased the sophisticated knowledge "French Negroid" possessed of U.S. politics, geopolitics, and world cultures while underscoring Bryan's ignorance of the same. The consequences of such wilful ignorance in a world order marked by white supremacy, "French Negroid" concluded, were predictable and tragic: "How unlogical is it to think that people of the type of Mr Bryan, should be entrusted with the welfare of the very people who, with anticipation they belittled and begrudged. May we ask then, Is it a strange thing that the American intervention? in Haiti or anywhere else serves only to sow hatred for themselves and their country"?[65] He ended by praising "Mr Allen as a writer" for "do[ing] justice to his conscience" and placing the truth above loyalty to flag. Allen had revealed the hypocrisy of anti-Haitian propaganda by "proving that foreigners especially Americans have contributed prominently in fomenting revolutions among the natives in Haiti and are the chief factors in bringing about the condition of chaos which existed in the country and which these foreigners exploit to their advantage and to the detriment of the natives."[66]

Well-placed metropolitan authors could offer reports from inside the halls of congress (as in Allen's interview with Bryan) or corporate boardrooms (provided by Allen as "former Manager of the Banque Nationale de la Republique de Haiti"). These were invaluable to colonial readers and writers who sought to craft oppositional analyses of the interwar interventions, from Liberia to Haiti, which imperialist ideologues offered as proof of white virtue and black inability to self-rule. Yet even white sympathizers wrote their accounts of colonial resistance from a vantage of implicit privilege: they claimed the right to judge. Caribbean commentators begged to disagree. More precisely, they refused to beg at all.

A July 1930 letter to the *Searchlight* on "Manhata Ghandi and his Revolution without violence" offered a detailed account of Gandhi's life and formative experiences with racism in Natal, as well as the key events that built Indian resistance to colonial rule, including the 1919 "atrocity" in Amritsar, which the author framed as confirmation of racial character: General Dyer could have avoided violence, "But it is the old policy of the Anglo-Saxon race whether in Europe or in America, whether in dealing with individuals or communities, to emphasize torture and dread and to avoid entertaining or meeting other races on a platform of equal rights."[67] The letter writer drew at length on the analysis of W.H. Roberts in a 1923

Political Science Quarterly article, noting in conclusion Roberts's judgment that (in our author's paraphrase) Gandhi should "realize that only as India becomes economically stable and sound and intellectually emancipated, and united through long cooperation in common practical tasks, can they deserve freedom or use it rightly."[68] Here the author, who signed him- or herself "ANTI-IMPERIALIST," lived up to that name:

> And although Prof Roberts concedes to acknowledge [Gandhi] as <<great>> we cannot agree with his well founded Imperialistic philosophy when he uses the word <<deserve>> in the above statement. If the East Indians are not prepared to rule their own country that does not follow that they do not <<deserve>> freedom, and we believe that Ghandi is well aware of the unpreparedness of his people on account of the complexity in its traditions and customs, but it is a fact that Ghandi <<deserves>> to keep the fire of NATIONALISM in the hearts of his people so that imperialism will not smother it into perpetual servitude and servility.[69]

This author, and those above, refused to concede discursive authority to the metropolitan voices on whose reporting their knowledge of the world of colour continued in part to rely. Editors and letter writers used frames and glosses to build a critical optic, ensuring that white authors' own positioning was not allowed to remain an unmarked category. When an author (like "Mr Allen" on Haiti) transcended the ideological blinders of his or her racial position, it was remarked, and when an author (as "Prof Roberts" on India) failed to do so, that was remarked too.

Let us look back to the report on South African General Smuts's speech in New York that appeared in Marryshow's *West Indian* in 1930. The article was credited to an author identified only as "The West Indian's New York Correspondent." Throughout, the unnamed author interspersed his or her eyewitness reporting with commentary juxtaposing Smuts's comments to the reality of South African blacks' experiences, thus demystifying the edifice of scientific racism on which Smuts sought to build. "Smuts says that, besides coming over here to boost the League of Nations, which is saying in other words" – our correspondent here decodes – "that besides coming here to invite America to join hands with European nations in an orderly and uninterrupted system of mass exploitation of undefended countries as inhabited by 'subject-peoples,'" Smuts also claimed a desire "to 'study' the American Negro in order to find out the latent capacity in his brother black of Africa."[70] This Smut had declared after first laying out a brief for excluding all Africans within Africa from the vote, education, and free economic advance, all in the disinterested service of preserving their "natural" state.

At this point our correspondent's ironically annotated narration of Smuts's speech breaks out into straight declamation:

> Within the past twenty-five years the Negro of this country has been over-studied by European and other outsiders. He has been weighted, measured, and examined, investigated, vivisected, analysed, as has no other specimen in creation. He is something new that was not calculated upon and there seems to be nervousness due to the thought that hundreds of millions of black people are likely to become just as new also. The Rising Tide of Colour of the present means that uneasy lies the head that wears the crown – of domination.[71]

Once again, we see an author observing the observers, and enacting his or her right to comment critically upon them. Not only does the correspondent critique scientific racism and its role in the self-interested politics of men like Smuts "The Slaughterer." Our correspondent also signals with understated ease the cosmopolitan coordinates of the print culture within which he or she writes. "Uneasy lies the head that wears the crown – of domination," writes our author, adding to the ringing conclusion of Henry IV's soliloquy from Shakespeare's 1597 play two words – "of domination" – that shift the focus from the burdens of rule to the burden of being ruled. What drives the unease of the rulers is "The Rising Tide of Colour" – a phrase intentionally echoing Lothrop Stoddard's (then) decade-old screed, and here used to encompass both the newness of "the Negro of this country" and the simultaneous transformations underway among "hundreds of millions of black people" worldwide.

The examples I have given were commonplace. Newspapers printed by editors of colour in St George's, Grenada, and Port Limón, Costa Rica, and Panama City, Panama, and Bridgetown, Barbados, in the interwar era brimmed not only with international commentary but also with commentary on international commentators. The authors injected themselves and their readers into an international dialogue about race and justice in the modern world. If empire could not adapt to their awareness, they argued, a conflagration was coming. "Those who sow the wind," wrote Sidney Young in 1930, "verily reap the whirlwind."[72]

Conclusion

The interwar years saw subjugated minorities and oppressed majorities mount new challenges to political exclusion. The era generated, too, a varied but resonant range of race-conscious internationalisms and colour-conscious cosmopolitanisms. Crucial in that process was the growth of a non-metropolitan press written and read by men and women of colour, and the particular practices of circulation and republication that came to characterize it. In the pages above we have explored one peripheral press circuit, suggesting some of the ways in which readers' habits, editors' choices, and strategies of critical citation all linked it to places far distant.

This regional story suggests that the periodical press played a role in the worldwide interwar surge of oppositional internationalisms. Local papers enmeshed in international print circuits offered colonials of colour a panoramic view of the evolving geopolitics of white supremacy – and a transnational public sphere in which to debate their response. Despite the force of arms, despite repressive might, the bell of resistance struck in the interwar era again and again. The tide of colour rose as people chose to identify their struggles as part of a rising tide, and chose to identify their communities as part of a larger whole. The sufferings of the "natives of Haiti" at the hands of invaders amazed that "*niggers*" could *speak French*; "the fire of NATIONALISM in the hearts of" Gandhi's people: these were read into the record as pieces of a single, global struggle.

The breadth of reader participation that we have seen in British Caribbean papers published in Panama, Costa Rica, and Grenada suggests that, at least for one historical moment, supralocal identifications – both race-based internationalism and colour-conscious cosmopolitanism – resonated with more than a small elite or militant vanguard. Awareness of the complex participatory world of these peripheral press circuits thus should raise new questions about the intellectual closures of the era that followed, as decolonization in a Cold War context created national institutions and curtailed other possible futures. At the same time, awareness of the publishers and publics profiled above should further amplify calls for scholars to explore print culture beyond the metropoles. The Firefly, Moses Brathwaite, Africanus, A French Negroid, and their fellow readers did not think they were alone, and most likely they were not.[73]

NOTES

1 In researching this article, the *Barbados Weekly Herald*, *Limon Searchlight*, *West Indian*, *Panama American*, and *Panama Tribune* were consulted on microfilm at the National Library of Barbados, Biblioteca Nacional de

Costa Rica, British Library Newspaper Reading Room, and via inter-library loan, respectively; the Port of Spain *Weekly Guardian*, *Daily Mirror*, *Argos*, and *Labour Leader* were read in print originals at the National Archives of Trinidad and Tobago; and the *Pittsburgh Courier* was accessed through the ProQuest Historical Newspapers database.

2 For incisive overviews of this moment focused on Afro-diasporic thinkers and activists, see West and Martin (2009); Baldwin (2013).

3 Stoddard (1920, 9). See also Runstedtler (2013, 106–7).

4 E.g., Winston James (1998); B. Edwards (2003); Pennybacker (2009); Polsgrove (2009); Makalani (2011).

5 E.g., Duara (2001); Stolte and Fischer-Tiné (2012); Goswami (2012). On the connections between black and Asian internationalisms, see especially Prashad (2002) and Slate (2012).

6 E.g., Boittin (2005); Prais (2008); Ewing (2011); and James (2015).

7 B. Anderson (1991).

8 Slate (2012, 2). For a relevant but distinct exploration (centred on cosmopolitanism as openness to cultural borrowing, rather than cosmopolitanism as a non-culture-bound theory of political rights), see Newell (2011b).

9 Stoddard, (1920, 13).

10 Von Eschen (1997); Turner and Turner (2005); Putnam (2013b).

11 West and Martin (2009, 10). Martin (1976, 4, 106, 16); R. Hill (1991, 997–1000), along with other volumes in the same invaluable series.

12 E.g., Macdonald (1992); B. Edwards (2003).

13 Olver and Meyer (2004, quote 8).

14 Newell (2009, 1–15, esp. 1–3); more broadly on colonial newspapers and anti-colonial protest Betts (1985, 162–4).

15 Newell (2011a, quote 27).

16 Newell (2011a, 28). See also Barber (2006); Prais (2008).

17 Switzer (1990, 87–109, esp. 105–6).

18 Hill (1991, 212; 2006, cxxxviii); Vinson (2009); Bonner, Hyslop, and Van der Walt (2007); Van der Walt (2007).

19 Putnam (2013b, ch. 1). See figures and map in Putnam (2014).

20 Putnam (2013b, 128–9).

21 Putnam (2009); Putnam (2013a).

22 Putnam (2013b, ch. 4); Lent (1977). On A.R.F. Webber's British Guiana *Daily Chronicle* (1919–25) and *New Daily Chronicle* (1925–30) see Cudjoe (2009).

23 Winston James (1998, 52–65); Howe (2002); Goldthree (2013).

24 E.g., Clennell Wickham, "The Colour Bar: An Incident and Some Thoughts," *Barbados Weekly Herald*, 24 Feb. 1925, 4; Hunte (2001).

25 Putnam (forthcoming); Corinealdi (2011, 27–9); Gately (2013).

26 Schomburg Center for Research in Black Culture, New York Public Library, George Westerman Collection, 32/3: "Panama Tribune: Its Origins, Purposes, Accomplishments and Impact" (undated ms. by George Westerman); George S. Schuyler, "Schuyler: America's Canal Zone Policy Is a 'Disgrace'," *Pittsburgh Courier*, 31 July 1948, 1.
27 Perry (2001); Parascandola (2005).
28 Elkins (1972, 57–8).
29 Hunte (2001, 133–48).
30 See, e.g., "Legislative Council Debate," *Trinidad Weekly Guardian*, 27 Mar. 1920, 7–9; "The Sedition Bill: Thirty One Citizens Protest," ibid., 9; "Why The Sedition Bill is Necessary," ibid., 11.
31 Trinidad and Tobago, *Debates in the Legislative Council of Trinidad and Tobago* [Hansards], *Jan.-Dec. 1920* (Port-of-Spain: Government Printing Office, 1921): Debate of 5 March 1920; Second debate 19 March 1920.
32 E.g., de Lisser (1971, 8, 17); Lamming (1991, 92, 101).
33 Olver and Meyer (2004, 8).
34 Winifred James (1913, 232–3).
35 Lamming (1991, 92).
36 Westerman, "Panama Tribune," unpaged.
37 "The Firefly Responds," *Limón Searchlight*, 12 Sept. 1931, 3. Such evidence suggests the practices of informal sharing and distribution described by Ronald and Mary Zboray in chapter 4 extended well beyond the Civil-War-era United States. The work of Kyle Roberts and Robert Hall (chapters 2 and 8) also offer evidence of this kind of hidden circulation.
38 "Jottings from Port Limon," *Panama Tribune*, 19 July 1931, 11.
39 Letter to editor, *Limón Searchlight*, 5 Sept. 1931, 6.
40 "Happenings in the Zone Town," *Panama Tribune*, 29 May 1932, 12.
41 Duke (2009); J. Parker (2004).
42 R. Hill (2011); Putnam (2013b); D. Dalrymple (2008); Sullivan (2012).
43 E.g., Putnam (2009, 111).
44 "Amazing Progress of Negroes in U.S.," *Panama American*, West Indian section, 14 Feb. 1926, compiling statistics from the "Negro Year Book for 1925–26."
45 Letter to the editor, "A Few Cheery Words," *Panama Tribune*, 11 Nov. 1928, 8.
46 "Anonymous Letters," *Limón Searchlight*, 1 March 1930, 4.
47 Ibid.
48 E.g., among many, S.H. Johnson, "Sons of Ethiopia," *Panama Tribune*, 11 Nov. 1928, 8.
49 "The Coloured American Magazine," *Port of Spain Daily Mirror*, 13 Oct. 1904, 9; "Review: The Coloured American Magazine," ibid., 11 Aug. 1904, 13.

50 By 1910 Massachusetts was home to 2,120 immigrants born in the "Other West Indies" (that is, the Caribbean outside Cuba or Puerto Rico). United States (1913–14, ch. 10, 840).
51 P.L. Prattis, "Questions and Answers," *Pittsburgh Courier*, 28 Nov. 1936, 14.
52 Grenada (1922, 132); and subsequent.
53 Masthead, *West Indian*, 11 Feb. 1930, 1.
54 "Give Friends Abroad the Overseas," *West Indian*, 11 Feb. 1930, 5.
55 "The Bell Has Struck in Barbados," *West Indian*, 9 Feb. 1930, 4.
56 See Putnam (2013b, ch. 4, ch. 6).
57 "Liberia and the League," *Panama Tribune*, 29 May 1932, 8.
58 "Walls of Hatred," *Panama Tribune*, 17 Feb. [?] 1932, 8.
59 Ibid.
60 "The Color Bar in South Africa," *Panama American*, 6 Feb. 1926.
61 "The Indian Problem as Compared to the Negro Question," *Limón Searchlight*, 23 Aug. 1930, 1.
62 Sinha (2000); Teed (2003).
63 "Demands of Mahatma Gandhi in Bombay," *Limón Searchlight*, 1 Mar. 1930, 2.
64 Letter to the editor, "What William Jennings Bryan thought of the Haitians Niggers," *Limón Searchlight*, 14 June 1930, 2. The article referenced must be John H. Allen, "An Inside View of Revolutions in Haiti," *Current History* 32 (May 1930): 325–9. See discussion in Kazin (2006, 230 and 352n44).
65 "What William Jennings Bryan thought of the Haitians Niggers," *Limón Searchlight*, 14 June 1930, 2.
66 Ibid.
67 "Manhata Ghandi and his Revolution without violence," *Limón Searchlight*, 5 July 1930, 3. The article cited is W.H. Roberts, "A Review of the Gandhi Movement in India," *Political Science Quarterly* 38, no. 2 (June 1923): 227–48.
68 "Manhata Ghandi and his Revolution without violence," *Limón Searchlight*, 5 July 1930, 3–4.
69 Ibid., 4.
70 "General Smuts Likens Negro to the Ass," *West Indian*, 9 Feb. 1930, 4.
71 Ibid.
72 "Reaping the Whirlwind," *Panama Tribune*, 18 May 18, 1930, 8.
73 Despite obvious differences, we might draw a parallel to the experiences of Clara Steen as described by Christine Pawley in chapter 14. Though a rural, white, farm American, she, too, found through active participation in print culture a sense of connection to a regional, racialized public. In both rural Iowa and the Caribbean a specialized press built a distinctive, imagined identity.

PART TWO

Place

8 At the Dawn of the Information Age: Reading and the Working Classes in Ashton-under-Lyne, 1830–1850

ROBERT G. HALL

Over the course of human history, the age of information has dawned many times. At different times and in different places, sharp accelerations "in the amount of information that people had access to" have taken place.[1] One such acceleration occurred in Britain with the advent of what James Secord has called "the industrial revolution in communication." In the first half of the nineteenth century, the number of published books in Britain increased from somewhere around two thousand titles per annum to slightly over seven thousand titles; in a similar fashion, the production and sale of newspapers, periodicals, tracts, and printed matter of all kinds took off.[2] Looking back to his childhood and teenage years during the 1830s and 1840s, W.E. Adams identified this dramatic surge of publications "in all branches of human knowledge" as one of the defining features of his lifetime.[3] Literary scholars and historians have examined, in some detail, this outpouring of print and its impact on the landed and middle classes, but they have only begun to explore a closely related question: how did working-class readers, like Adams, experience the age of information?

One way to answer this question is to examine reading sites or spaces available to working men and women in the 1830s and 1840s; in this context, a reading site is simply a place, the physical setting, in which readers come into contact with printed texts.[4] In many cases, reading spaces also helped to provide the working classes with something that was very rare – "well-lit, decently furnished, warm and comfortable" places to read.[5] They were not, however, simply the physical spaces in which readers encountered texts; the nature and practices of a reading site, together with contact with other readers, shaped the reading experience and meaning itself. Reading sites, like libraries, "are places that are greater than the sum of their books."[6] This study of reading spaces, like the essays of Lydia Wevers and Joan Rubin, explores this last issue and considers the significance of *where* reading experiences take place.[7]

In his autobiography, William Lovett nicely summed up how the lack of reading sites affected working-class readers in the small towns and villages of his youth. Though fond of reading, he encountered in his search for "instructive books" some serious difficulties. "There was," he was careful to note, "no bookshop in the town – scarcely a newspaper taken in, unless among a few gentry ... With the exception of Bibles and Prayer Books, spelling-books, and a few religious works, the only books in circulation for the masses were a few story books and romances, filled with absurdities about giants, spirits, goblins, and supernatural horrors. The price of these, however, precluded me from purchasing any."[8] In some places, like the small cotton town of Crompton, just north of Oldham, reading sites were still few and far between in the 1840s. "There was," Samuel Bamford observed, "no mechanics' institute – no public library – no reading room, except for one supported by chartists – nor any bookseller's or stationer's shop."[9] Members of the working classes who lived in these "obscure" or "rustic" places "seldom see a periodical of any kind but such as first passes through the hands of the *laird*, the minister, or the merchant."[10] In the case of Manchester, a major provincial city, Martin Hewitt has identified for this period, however, a multiplicity of reading sites: news agencies and bookshops; Conservative, Reform, and Chartist newsrooms and meeting places; Mechanics' Institutions and lyceums; circulating libraries; friendly society and trade union lodges; and various parish and congregational libraries.[11]

In terms of its size and the density and variety of its reading sites, Ashton-under-Lyne was somewhere in between the extremes of Crompton and Manchester (see table 8.1). Built on the banks of the Tame River, "a stream rising in the Yorkshire moors," it was a small industrial city, with a population of about twenty-three thousand in 1841; the working classes made up at least 75 to 80 per cent of the total population. Ashton did not have the diversified occupational structure of Manchester or its large commercial and financial sectors. The local economy relied heavily on a single industry, the cotton industry.[12] It also lacked Manchester's cultural and intellectual network of musical societies and scientific, literary, and professional organizations and clubs; it certainly never developed anything equivalent to the famous Literary and Philosophical Society of Manchester.[13] There were in Ashton only a limited number of places that offered working men and women the opportunity to read newspapers or books; in the 1840s, these reading sites included: bookstores and news agencies, circulating libraries, church and Sunday school libraries, the Mechanics' Institution, the Dukinfield Village Library, and Chartist association rooms. Of these, only the Chartist reading sites managed to reach a mass audience of adult working-class readers. Well aware that many of "the people" were not fully literate and often lacked the means to purchase books or newspapers, Chartist leaders and activists adopted in Ashton a variety of reading strategies, from the provision of cheap publications to the promotion of oral readings and discussion classes, to promote democratic reform and to break "the exclusive privileges of the titled and the great" to science, politics, literature, and other branches of knowledge.[14]

I.

Between 1830 and 1850 the low literacy rates of working men and women and the high prices of books and periodicals placed very real limitations on access to the printed word and shaped how the working classes in Ashton experienced the coming of the age of information. In the first half of the nineteenth century, literacy was crucial to gaining access to the ever-expanding world of news and information; however, there were at this time different ways of defining literacy (and illiteracy). For many contemporaries, as well as later historians, writing, even something as simple as signing one's name, was a reliable indication of literacy. "It must be taken as a general rule," noted Frederic Hill, "that where an individual is unable to *write at all*, he is not able to read with sufficient fluency to enjoy the occupation."[15] This "general rule" suggested that many of the working classes in Ashton were unable to read with any real degree of ease or fluency. "Out of 990 couples, or 1980 persons, that were married in the parish church of Ashton-under-Lyne, between June 30th, 1838, and June 30th, 1843," observed John Ross Coulthart, "only 192 wrote their names, the remaining 1788 having made marks, and declared, in the presence of the clergyman or clerk in attendance, that they were incapable of writing. If writing, therefore, is to be considered a criterion of the education of a people, verily the inhabitants of this town are in a pitiable condition."[16]

The overall situation in Ashton was not, however, quite as dismal as these figures might suggest. Literacy, or in this context, the ability to sign one's name, varied from generation to generation. The couples who were married at the parish church between 1838 and 1843 certainly represented, in terms of literacy, Ashton's lost generation; in 1843, only about 11 per cent of males and 7 per cent of females signed the marriage register. The recollections of

William Aitken, who was about the same age as these men and women, lend support to Coulthart's findings. "When I was a little boy," he recalled about the 1820s, "such a thing as a child reading was almost unknown, and boys who could work the rule-of-three were considered wonders."[17] But for the grandparents and parents of this lost generation, the ability to sign was much more widespread, especially for men (61 per cent male, 18 per cent female in 1803; male, 68 per cent, female, 28 per cent in 1823).[18]

The emphasis that Sunday schools and dame schools placed on reading, at the expense of writing and other skills, meant, moreover, that in the cotton district these figures on the ability to sign clearly underestimated the size of the reading public. A survey by the Manchester Statistical Society in the mid-1830s highlighted some of the problems with the practice of relying on signature rates as the basic test of literacy. The agent, or agents, who carried out this house-to-house survey discovered that among the working classes of Ashton, the number of persons "who can read only" (4334) almost equalled the number of persons "who can read and write" (4723).[19] Many often read, however, at a very basic level and lacked what Samuel Smiles called the "means and opportunities" to practise their reading skills on a regular basis; in fact, many members of the working classes eventually lost altogether "the art of reading in their adult years."[20] For many of those who did not completely fall out of the habit, reading was often an unpleasant and laborious task. "There are," observed James Heywood about one working-class neighbourhood, "very few of the heads of family ... who have formed the habit of reading, or are capable of understanding or enjoying a book."[21]

In the 1820s and 1830s several developments converged to create this state of things in Ashton. The population of Ashton and its neighbour Stalybridge underwent an "immense increase" as a result of the migration of "people coming from the surrounding parts of Cheshire, Derbyshire, Yorkshire, and from the poorest hand-loom weaving districts of this county."[22] Between 1821 and 1841, Ashton grew dramatically, more than doubling in size during these two decades (see table 8.1). In 1851 only about 42 per cent of Ashton's powerloom weavers and 43 per cent of its mule spinners were natives of the town; however, the vast majority of migrants came from towns and hamlets within a twenty-mile radius of Ashton.[23] This surge of migrants into Ashton, together with the influx of children and young adults into the cotton mills and "the frequent removals of the labouring classes, in order to obtain work," disrupted what Bamford called the daily "fire-side education" of children by their parents.[24] This approach to teaching reading and writing was once common

Table 8.1 Ashton Population Growth, 1801–61

1801	1811	1821	1831	1841	1851	1861
6391	7959	9222	14,035	22, 678	29,791	34, 886

Proportional Change in Decennial Population, 1801–61

1801–11	1811–21	1821–31	1831–41	1841–51	1851–61
1.245	1.158	1.521	1.615	1.313	1.171

Sources: *Parliamentary Papers* (Commons) 1852–3 [1631] LXXXV: cxxvi; *Parliamentary Papers* (Commons) 1852–3 [1632] LXXXVI: 78; *Parliamentary Papers* (Commons) 1862 [3056] L: 59, 541; *Parliamentary Papers* (Commons) 1872 [c. 676] LXVI, pt.1: 34, 187. Ashton has been defined as the municipality.

among handloom weavers in Ashton and elsewhere in the cotton district. "My work," recalled Joseph Greenwood about his early days as a bobbin winder for his parents, "was at the loom side and when not winding my father taught me reading, writing, and arithmetic."[25]

At the same time, migration and rapid population growth overwhelmed the very basic system of formal education that existed in Ashton.[26] "As regards day-schools for the children of the working classes," observed the factory inspector Leonard Horner, "no part of the manufacturing districts has been allowed to remain in a more destitute state than that embracing the towns of Ashton-under-Lyne, Dukinfield, and Staleybridge."[27] There were in fact only about a dozen or so day schools in Ashton in Pigot's 1841 directory; however, this certainly was not a complete list.[28] Although William Aitken's school did not appear in Pigot's directory, it was a thriving school at the time, with 160 day and evening pupils, and it provided Aitken with a comfortable income of about £3 a week; most of his students came from working-class families. High-minded and conscientious, he tried to instil "into their minds the rudiments of a thoroughly good education" and to educate them "in the true principles of democracy, and without religious sectarian compulsion of any kind."[29] Most of the day schools in Ashton did not live up to these high ideals; moreover, only about eleven hundred young scholars, or about 12 per cent of all working-class children in Ashton, attended a day school in the mid-1830s.[30] For the most part, working men and women sent their children to day schools only briefly, if at all, and instead relied on dame schools and Sunday schools. Usually kept by women or sometimes by old men, the former taught reading and perhaps some domestic skills, for a few pennies a week. At the latter, education was one of a distinctly religious character, with an emphasis on reading. "The pupils are first taught," noted Angus Reach about Manchester Sunday schools, "to read; then scriptural extracts, or the Scriptures themselves, are put into their hands; and instructions in psalmody are diversified by familiar moral and doctrinal addresses and examinations into the contents of the chapter or passage last studied." The teaching of writing, or indeed of any "secular" subject, was something that many Sunday schools were careful to avoid.[31]

To their credit, Anglican and dissenter Sunday schools in Ashton parish taught, free of charge, around 4370 scholars, or about 46 per cent of the children and teenagers in Ashton in the mid-1830s. The quality of the education that these scholars received was very modest, or as one critic put it, "so superficial that it cannot be properly termed education."[32] Indeed, William F. Lloyd, secretary to the Sunday School Union, frankly acknowledged the limited accomplishments of most Sunday school scholars. If students regularly attended for three years, they "can read their Bibles plainly; other books they would be more puzzled with, as being less familiar with them." Writing was, however, another matter altogether. To acquire "a common plain hand," sufficient for a working man, students would also need to attend a writing school for several evenings a week for three years.[33] This sort of regular attendance was, however, impossible for many children. The working classes were not, as Aitken put it, an "entirely stationary people." Families moved in search of employment; children often began work in the mills as early as the age of seven and after a long week of labour wanted "their liberty" on Sunday.[34]

What also limited access to the age of information was the expense of newspapers, books, and pamphlets. This was, as Kyle Roberts has pointed out, an issue for the studious Philip Doddridge in the eighteenth century, and it was still a problem a century later.[35] The high prices of books and periodicals, Lovett and Collins argued in 1840, placed them "beyond the means" of working men and women.[36] "Many of the noblest productions of our best writers," William Linton added, "are sealed books to the People: their scarcity or high prices is an effectual bar to their general appreciation."[37] This state of things was not simply a product of the law of supply and demand. In this period, the government used the taxes on knowledge, especially the stamp duty on newspapers and the excise duty on paper, to keep up prices and to restrict access to the world of print. Even with the reduction in 1836 of the tax on newspapers from 4d to 1d, most weekly provincial newspapers still sold at around 4d to 4½d, a prohibitive amount for most working-class readers; a daily newspaper was for a working man "an unattainable luxury."[38] In the case of publishers who specialized in cheap literature, the tax on paper represented a serious expense, but the high prices of new books also reflected the pricing and market strategies of the traditional book trades of this period. Many publishers and booksellers viewed the profitability of "cheap publications" with a deep sense of scepticism and preferred to target "an exclusive market, whether of individual customers or circulating libraries."[39] In practical terms, this meant that one of Sir Walter Scott's novels sold at £1 15s, or about twice the weekly wage of a female powerloom weaver. The effect of this pricing system, a *Northern Star* editorial argued, was to grant "exclusive privileges in the use of books to the wealthy."[40]

II.

The lack of a public library (until the early 1880s) in Ashton and the high prices of books and periodicals meant that working men and women relied on a variety of free or inexpensive reading sites to gain access to the age of information.[41] In the 1830s and 1840s the reading sites available to members of the working classes in Ashton represented a range of religious, social, and political interests and varied considerably in physical nature and in the texts that they provided. At one end of this spectrum of interests was the relatively expensive Mechanics' Institution (with an annual subscription of 10s.) and its middle-class sponsors, who hoped to uplift the moral character of the working classes and to instruct them in the principles of "science and mechanical philosophy."[42] In a similar fashion, two newspaper reading rooms in the town, the "Reform News-room" and the "Conservative News-room," were careful to ensure that readers were exposed only to the correct political principles; both of these reading rooms relied on the support and patronage of gentlemen and manufacturers and carried only newspapers that advocated the politics of their party.[43] At the other end were Chartist reading spaces, with their emphasis on free and open access to knowledge of all kinds. Somewhere in between were the more commercially oriented reading sites of booksellers and newsagents.

In this period, bookstores that sold only new books were extremely rare. Most booksellers dealt in a range of goods, from stationery and account books to violin strings and copybooks, and often carried out framing and "every kind of letter press printing."[44] In a variety of ways, they also acted as reading sites. Booksellers, especially those with an eye to working-class customers, allowed readers to browse and even to do serious reading and used their shop windows to create what Charles Manby Smith called a "university" for "the moneyless million"; in fact, the shop window represented, in this period, a crucial source of information and reading matter

Table 8.2 The Ashton Books Trades, 1832–61

	1832	1841	1851	1861
Booksellers, Printers, And Stationers	3	6	17	29
Population	14, 035	22,678	29, 791	34, 886
Per Person	1 per 4678	1 per 3780	1 per 1752	1 per 1203

Sources: *Pigot's Directory*, 1832 and 1841; *Slater's Manchester and Salford Directory*, 1851; *Slater's Manchester Directory*, 1861.

for the working classes.[45] To attract customers, booksellers tried to create a "commotion at the window" through the display of handbills and advertisements, newspapers, tracts, and even poems as well as "numerous songs, ballads, tales, and other publications."[46] Several Ashton booksellers, like John Williamson, also ran circulating libraries; these loaned books by subscription or for a modest fee and typically specialized in "novels and the lighter literature of the day."[47] Circulating libraries did carry, though, more serious fare – not only Matthew Lewis's lurid Gothic novel *The Monk* but also the works of William Shakespeare, John Milton, Samuel Johnson, and Laurence Sterne.[48]

Between 1832 and 1861, a dramatic increase in the number of commercial reading sites took place (see table 8.2). These figures for the Ashton book trades under-report, however, the total number of those who made a living from the buying and selling of books, newspapers, pamphlets, and broadsides; in general, bill stickers, ballad sellers, street hawkers, and small-time or occasional newsagents did not appear in the directories of the period.[49] And yet, despite these limitations, these figures clearly demonstrate that during this period, the growth in the number of booksellers actually outpaced population growth. This increase also suggests a growing demand for the printed word among the working classes. Very few, if any, of these booksellers were able to rely strictly on the wealthy middle classes; they typically did their shopping elsewhere. It was in Manchester, as one of the pastors of Albion Independent chapel pointed out, that the well-to-do members of his congregation "made most of their valuable purchases."[50]

In the early 1850s the middle and working classes of Ashton (especially the former) supported more than two dozen places of worship; the libraries of these churches and chapels represented, in theory at least, potential reading sites for the working classes. The reading room and library of Albion Independent chapel provided a range of papers and serials, like the *Examiner and Times* and *Family Treasury*, and contained around five hundred volumes; however, in the late 1860s, the total number of readers came to only about fifty.[51] In many ways, this lack of readers was hardly surprising. Although church libraries sometimes included a number of "religious and controversial novels," they specialized in sermons, biblical commentaries, prayer books, and theological and devotional works of "a serious character"; moreover, the truly devout took a dim view of reading any kind of "secular" titles, even the improving *Chambers's Edinburgh Journal*, on the Sabbath, the one day of leisure for working men and women.[52] For the most part, these libraries were also of an "exclusive" nature and made their collections available only to clergymen or to members of the congregation who were in good standing. The latter were relatively uncommon among the working classes of Ashton. The 1851 religious census revealed that on March 30th only about 25 per cent of the inhabitants of the town and environs attended a worship service; the majority who stayed away on that Sunday were working men and women.[53]

The lending libraries of Sunday schools were able to reach a wider reading audience. Although they too consisted largely of "religious books" or "periodicals that blend religious and useful information," Sunday school libraries also provided young and teenage readers with "historical and biographical works, voyages, travels &c." as well as *Robinson Crusoe* and *Pilgrim's Progress*.[54] If nothing else, they helped to instil in at least some of their students a love of reading. "My regular attendance at Sunday School," recalled Lorenzo Quelch, "created a desire to read any books I could get hold of, beside the study of the bible, and I read practically the whole of the books provided by the Sunday School library which of course had a religious bias."[55] Some Sunday school readers even discovered excitement and adventure in the most unlikely of these publications. The young John Taylor derived "the greatest pleasure" from the monthly magazine of the London Missionary Society, with its stories of "the missionary John Williams, and his graphic descriptions of the South Sea Islands and their savage inhabitants."[56] Pious and godly in their intent, these stories were still ripping good yarns.

Just as the middle classes tended to dominate Anglican and dissenter places of worship, so they established early on their control over the Ashton and Dukinfield Mechanics' Institution. Founded in 1825, the goal of its middle-class patrons was "to bring within the reach of all, but more particularly the working classes, the acquisition of useful knowledge – to diffuse the correct principles of science and mechanical philosophy."[57] The gentlemen and manufacturers who created the Mechanics' Institution originally made provisions to include working men on its governing committee, but

Table 8.3 Membership, Ashton and Dukinfield Mechanics' Institution

	1836	1844	1851
Merchants and Manufacturers	44	35	30
Professionals	4	10	14
Shopkeepers	22	29	57
Clerks	25	13	40
Mechanics and Millwrights	16	8	16
Building and Other Trades	50	5	30
Factory Workers	65	13	90
Youths and Apprentices	33	14	25
Women	–	5	7
Others	–	2	2
	259	134	311

Sources: Tameside Local Studies Library, MI 1/1/1, Ashton and Dukinfield Mechanics' Institution, Annual Reports, 1836 and 1844; MI 1/1/2, Annual Report, 1851.

they eventually dropped the rule that two-thirds of the committee's members "be taken from the operative classes."[58] Over time a small group of regularly re-elected officers, most notably the mill owners Charles Hindley, Hugh Mason, and Samuel Robinson, came to dominate the institution. This lack of democratic governance, together with the unease of workers who faced the prospect of sitting "in the same room with the better clad, and possibly better mannered, shop assistants and clerks," put off many potential subscribers; the lingering bad feelings from the 1830-1strike and the rise of Chartism intensified these issues. As a consequence, working men made up for most of the 1830s and 1840s a minority of the members of the institution; at the lowest point, in the mid-1840s, only about a dozen factory workers, about 10 per cent of the total, were members of the institution (see table 8.3).[59]

The high cost of an annual membership (10s p.a.) also acted as a deterrent for many working men. This represented around half a week's wages for a mule spinner or an overlooker in the weaving shed. The method of payment, in annual or quarterly instalments, was an obstacle for many working men, who typically preferred to make small weekly contributions of a penny or two. Those who were willing and able to pay the hefty annual subscription did enjoy some very real benefits – they could take out books from the library, attend lectures and classes, and consult periodicals in the reading room .[60] And yet, despite the advantages of membership, the 10s annual subscription remained a contentious issue, one that never really went away. In 1844 members of the committee of the Mechanics' Institution formally considered "the propriety of reducing the rate of admission" and ultimately decided to create a new class of members. For 13 pence a quarter, "library members" were entitled to "the benefits of the Library only." This concession did not lead, however, to a dramatic increase in the membership roll; for most working men, any kind of charge was, as Smiles pointed out, "an obstacle."[61]

For a price, then, the Mechanics' Institution made available to members its library and reading room. The annual expenditure on "new books, periodicals, and stationary" was actually quite modest, only about 16 per cent of the total budget for 1843–4. The reading room regularly supplied eleven weekly and monthly periodicals, like *Chambers's Edinburgh Journal* and the *Mechanics' Magazine*, but for over two decades, it took in no newspapers. Eventually, in the late 1840s, the Mechanics' Institution did introduce newspapers into the reading room. A few years later readers could choose from among eight titles; these included the *Times*, several Manchester newspapers, and the *Liverpool Mercury*.[62] In terms of book purchases, the committee of the Mechanics' Institution typically avoided "expensive works, whatever may have been their merit" but always welcomed the donation of titles by well-wishers and patrons. Over the course of 1843–4, the library added 45 volumes, 31 by purchase and 14 by donation.[63] The latter was a common practice among the Mechanics' Institutions of the day. "Many of the books," observed George Dawson about their libraries, "are gift books, turned out of people's shelves, and are never used, and old magazines of different kinds, so that, out of 1,000 volumes, perhaps there may be only 400 or 500 useful ones. The rest are, many of them, only annual registers and old religious magazines that are never taken down from the shelves."[64] Too often, Samuel Robinson conceded, library shelves consisted largely of "works which are old and out of date." A new member "is attracted by the promise of a Library: he comes and finds, that from the expense few new and really valuable books can be admitted, and retires disappointed."[65]

In spite of these shortcomings, the committee of the Ashton and Dukinfield Mechanics' Institution took great pride in its mission to introduce members to "works of a high scientific character" and thus "to elevate and refine" their character and reading habits.[66] The way in which its members used its collections was, however, a different matter altogether. There was, as Julieanne Lamond observed about the situation in Australia, a "tension between the intentions of middle-class patrons and the actual desires and reading habits" of working-class members.[67] Those who frequented the library generally preferred the novels of Charles Dickens and Frederick Marryat and other forms of light reading; "abstruse and learned works, requiring close application," the committee observed, "lie upon the shelves quite neglected – the members have neither time nor taste to read them."[68] This was still true in the late 1850s, when fiction "issues" represented, by far, the largest single category (at about 26 per cent of the total issues in 1858–9). History and Biography and Miscellaneous Prose were also popular categories (at 19 per cent and 18 per cent, respectively); however, Arts and Sciences made up only about 7 per cent of the total number of issues.[69]

Although the Mechanics' Institution eventually introduced newspapers into the reading room and tried to create a more comfortable and inviting setting for readers, it made up no effort to accommodate or certainly to encourage a popular form of reading among the working classes – oral and collective reading and discussion. This tendency of the Mechanics' Institution to promote the silent and solitary approach to reading limited its appeal to the working classes. Oral readings, Bamford emphasized, had been crucial to the popularity of the Mechanics' Institution in nearby Middleton in its early days. "We read," he recalled, "striking passages from history, biography, navigation or travels, explaining, in our humble way, such parts as required it; questions were asked, answers were given, discussions would sometimes take place ... As our attendants at the readings increased, subscribers to our library did the same."[70] Under pressure from a wealthy patron, Bamford and his friends reluctantly agreed, however, to drop these weekly public readings and to give the patron "the power of removing any book to which he objected." Reflecting on this incident years later, Bamford acknowledged that these concessions led to a sharp decline in "the vitality" of the Mechanics' Institution. "Although we were more comfortably situated," he noted, "we were also more dull, and as we plainly perceived, less useful in the matter of book circulation."[71]

Although the Dukinfield Village Library intended, like the Mechanics' Institution, "to raise the character, refine the habits, and improve the condition" of the working classes, it was less expensive and more welcoming and open in its approach to governance and reading.[72] Founded in 1833, it was, Hugh Mason acknowledged, the main rival to the Mechanics' Institution, "charging a much smaller sum for the use of books" (1d per week).[73] This relatively inexpensive subscription meant that in the early 1840s it had around 158 members, "chiefly of the operative class." Members in good standing were able to take out and read books in their own homes and to make recommendations for future purchases; membership also gave them the right to vote in annual elections for members of the committee.[74] Well aware of the demand for newspapers, the Village Library committee decided early on to add the *Times* and several Manchester papers to the reading room and to focus on the acquisition of books "particularly adapted to the Amusements and the Wants" of the working classes.[75] "The number of volumes in the library," noted Edwin Harrop in 1844, "was 1,218, and those most read were travels and works of light reading."[76] Indeed, Samuel Robinson, who served as president of the Village Library for a number of years, took a relatively positive view of light reading and even novels. "If we can entice any individual from bad company or the beer-shop," he declared, "to turn over the pages of a Walter Scott, a Defoe, or a Goldsmith – to dwell for instance on the simple but sublime heroism of a Jenny Deans – the patience and energy of a Robinson Crusoe – or the Christian and domestic virtues of a Vicar of Wakefield – something surely has been gained to the cause of morality."[77] Robinson also believed that fiction was a way of appealing to those who "have never been accustomed to read."[78]

And yet, despite its efforts to attract this important group, the Village Library enjoyed at best a very limited success among the working classes. This was also the case with most of the other middle-class sponsored reading sites. Fees, overbearing patrons, a limited selection of titles – all of these alienated potential readers. Working men also were put off by efforts to control and regulate their reading and by the need to tidy "themselves up to associate with better-off people."[79] Sometimes it was a matter of limited and inconvenient hours. Manchester's famous Chetham's Library, though a free library for all to use, was in the early 1850s "open six hours out of the twenty-four, but these hours fall precisely within that part of the day in which people who have to work for bread are cooped up at their occupations."[80]

When "the most intelligent portion" of the working classes, like the Owenite Socialists, or the Ancient Shepherds, or the earnest autodidacts of the Ashton Mutual Improvement Society, set up libraries and reading sites, they generally avoided these kinds of issues. These societies were "self-supporting and self-governing" institutions, ones that took pride in their working-class membership and in their freedom from "meddling patrons." Their reading rooms and libraries were "unsectarian" and imposed on readers "no religious or political test." The library of the Ashton Mutual Improvement Society, its historian was careful to emphasize, contained almost six hundred volumes in which writers of "all shades of opinion are fairly represented":

> On History: Rollin, Josephus, Gibbon, Hume, Smollet, Robertson, D'Aubigne, Allison, Lamartine, Guizot, &c. On Science: Humboldt, Herschel, Combe, Fowler, Lawrence, Mackintosh, &c. On Biography: Plutarch,

> Bamford, Johnson, Barker, Lord Brougham, &c. On Theology: Paley, J.G. Rogers (of Albion-street Chapel), Theodore Parker, J.J. Holyoake, the Koran of Mahomet, &c. On Politics: Smith, Carpenter, Paine, Dale Owen, Robert Owen, Goodwin, Cobbett &c. On Belle Lettres: Shakespeare, Milton, Shelley, Byron, Burns, Mackay, Scott, Chesterfield, Channing, Bulwer Lytton, Dickens, William Howitt, Chambers's, &c., &c.[81]

For a variety of reasons, however, these societies all failed to reach a mass audience of working-class readers. In some cases, like the Ashton Mutual Improvement Society, the small size and limited funds of the organization were serious obstacles; in addition to these problems, the Owenite Socialists had also earned a certain notoriety for their attacks on organized religion and for their views on private property and family and marriage.[82] In other cases, like the friendly societies, the lack of members and scarce resources were not the issues. In Ashton and environs, the membership of the Loyal Order of Ancient Shepherds was in the early 1850s over two thousand; at this time, the Independent Order of Odd Fellows had about nine hundred members.[83] Although these local friendly societies certainly took an interest in "the moral and intellectual welfare" of their members and often advocated the founding of libraries "in connection with our Lodges," they devoted most of their efforts (and funds) to the provision of sickness and funeral benefits and to sociability, not to education or to libraries.[84]

Determined to put into practice their beliefs about democracy and the power of knowledge, the Chartists took a different approach; they invested considerable time and energy in the creation of reading sites for "the people." In the late 1830s, the most high profile of these reading spaces in the Ashton area were the bookshops and news agencies of John Deegan, Edward Hobson, and John Williamson. Along with labour and free-thought publications, they sold a wide variety of radical papers and titles, like Colonel Francis Maceroni's *A New System of Defensive Instructions for the People*, and made an easy penny, as one critic put it, "by vending ballads and pamphlets."[85] Their bread-and-butter was, however, the *Northern Star.* In early 1839, when political feelings were running high, Hobson ordered around 1330 copies for the Ashton area alone. This translated into a readership in the tens of thousands. (Patricia Hollis has estimated for the somewhat cheaper unstamped newspapers of the 1830s a ratio of twenty readers to every copy that was sold.)[86] On a regular basis, Chartist booksellers and newsagents turned their shop windows into reading spaces; they filled them with "Chartist and other radical pamphlets, etc.," placards, and bills and advertisements of all kinds and displayed manifestoes and addresses "pasted on a board" next to their doors.[87] They also ventured into publishing and turned to, as James Raven has noted for an earlier period, jobbing printing as a way of making money.[88] John Williamson sold stationery, newspapers, and books at his Stamford Street shop and carried out as well all kinds of printing work: tickets for Chartist dinners and tea parties, election placards, friendly society publications, and the weekly newspaper *McDouall's Chartist and Republican Journal.* Over the course of the 1840s, Williamson published a collection of Chartist and labour songs by the local poet John Stafford and William Aitken's *Journey Up the Mississippi*, an account of Aitken's flight to the United States after the collapse of the 1842 general strike; in 1847 he brought out (for the price of 1d) the first local newspaper, *The Ashtonian*, a monthly miscellany of poetry and local news.[89]

If Chartist readers lacked the ready cash to purchase reading materials at a bookstore, they could simply visit the local Chartist association. In the early 1840s there were at least five Chartist localities within a four-mile radius of the Ashton marketplace.[90] They typically provided, free of charge, the *Northern Star* and a variety of other newspapers, like the *London Telegraph* and the *Liverpool Mercury*, as well as a welcoming fire and good conversation and made available to "the people" small libraries of really "useful" works on politics, history, and literature.[91] In many cases, these libraries were, at least originally, very modest in size and scope. "At that time," remarked William Hill about the early days of the Chartist Institute in Stalybridge, "a little box, about 16 in. square and 12 in. deep, contained our library, and then held all the slates and copybooks belonging to the scholars of the institution, as well as a few numbers of *Chambers' Information for the People*, which latter constituted our class books, and altogether forming our library stock."[92] In other cases, the Chartist association libraries took a more ambitious form. At nearby Royton, the library of the Chartist reading room was an eclectic mixture of fiction, poetry, Chartist and free-thought texts, abolitionist writings, and travel books. "Their books, or the principal part of them," a visitor noted in 1850, "were Joyce's Scientific Dialogues, the Vicar of Wakefield, Volney's Ruins, the Elements of Drawing, Hunt's Trial at York; the Labourer (O'Connor's); Small Farms, by the same; Byron's Beauties, Douglas's Narrative of Slavery, Howitt's History of Priestcraft, Sillet on Spade Husbandry, Paine's Rights of Man, the Orators of France, Travels in America, and the Scottish Chiefs."[93] On important occasions in the history of "the people," like the anniversary of the Peterloo massacre or Henry Hunt's birthday, local associations also organized and sponsored democratic dinners at which members recited Robert Emmet's famous speech at his treason trial and gave dramatic readings from Constantin Francois Volney's *Ruins of Empire* and other well-known radical and Enlightenment texts.[94]

Although these Chartist reading sites made provisions for silent and solitary reading, they also made possible a rather different approach to reading, one that was oral and collective. This kind of informal circulation of texts, as Ronald and Mary Zboray have pointed out, was common among readers in the nineteenth century.[95] It was a way of dealing with the scarcity and high prices of newspapers and indeed of publications of all kinds. For many Chartists, even though the *Northern Star* retailed for only 4 1/2 d, it was beyond their limited means; consequently, friends and neighbours often clubbed together to buy a shared copy. Every week, on Saturday, recalled Benjamin Grime about his youthful days in Oldham, he walked from "North Moor, across Tommyfield to Owd Knight's, for a copy of the *Northern Star*, which was the joint property of his father and a few of the neighbors. The paper would then be read in some retired place, on the grass if in summer, or it would be read over the 'tot of whoambrew' at some of the hush shops which could then be found in every street within a few yards of each other."[96] This approach was also a way of reaching out to and including those who were not fully literate. "Often enough," Samuel Shaw emphasized, "some of those who subscribed could not read a line. My parents lived in Platt Street, Hyde, and my father and his friends would gather in our kitchen, where my mother, who was a good reader, would read aloud from the *Northern Star*."[97] Sympathetic master artisans or publicans and tavern keepers, like James Duke of the Bush Inn, often kept copies of Chartist publications on their premises and encouraged oral readings and discussions of the *Northern Star*.[98]

This weekly newspaper, easily the most widely circulated paper in Ashton, also served as a way for working men and women to come into contact with the age of information. Through its narrow columns, readers were able to follow national and international events and business (and sometimes even scientific) news and to scrutinize detailed accounts of Chartist activities and lectures in hundreds of associations and localities all across the nation. The *Northern Star* also carried a weekly letter from the foremost national leader of the movement, Feargus O'Connor, and published book reviews, fiction, poetry, and an endless stream of letters from loyal (but often critical) readers.[99] The reviews and extracts that appeared in the *Star* exposed its readers to a variety of literary and political texts, some new, some classic, from Shakespeare and "Beauties of Byron" to Mary

Wollstonecraft's *A Vindication of the Rights of Woman*.[100] Advertisements for Chartist booksellers and publishers also gave readers glimpses into the richness and variety of the world of print beyond the *Northern Star* itself. In his advertisements in the *Star*, John Cleave offered for sale "To the Reading Chartists" inexpensive editions of Robert Southey's *Wat Tyler*, Byron's *Vision of Judgment*, John Milton's *A Speech for the Liberty of Unlicensed Publishing*, weekly numbers of James Fenimore Cooper's novels and of Tobias Smollett's *Peregrine Pickle*, and a variety of works by Robert Owen and Thomas Paine.[101]

III.

In their efforts to create open and democratic reading spaces for "the people," the Chartists broke with many of the practices of middle-class sponsored reading sites in Ashton and challenged the ways in which class shaped access to the age of information. "Towns and cities," Richard Rodger has observed, "were the information highways of the nineteenth century." Overlapping networks of coffee houses, taverns, public houses, clubs, literary and scientific societies, and associations of all kinds acted as forums for the exchange of the latest news and gossip about business, politics, the arts, and society.[102] But admission to this new world of information and news was not freely available to all. Too often poverty and class distinctions excluded, as Bamford put it, "a person in humble life, however meritorious."[103] Through "class legislation" and the taxes on knowledge, the government, the Chartists argued, intensified these problems and helped to make books and newspapers privileges that only the wealthy could enjoy.[104]

To right these wrongs, the Chartists tried to spread news and information "in every direction on the easiest terms."[105] They did not pursue, however, this worthy goal purely out of altruism or an idealistic commitment to democracy. Through their efforts to create democratic reading spaces, they hoped to draw working men and women into the movement and to instruct and unify "the people." On many occasions they also failed to live up to their own high ideals; they did not hesitate to promote the publications and newspapers of their political "friends" and used their influence to prevent "the circulation of any paper they do not approve of."[106] In other words, the Chartists, like all the groups that created reading sites in Ashton, self-consciously tried to influence working-class readers and to shape their views on politics and society. Sunday schools, Mechanics' Institutions, Chartist associations – they all had agendas. This basic fact of life points to the highly politicized nature of reading sites in this period; access to the age of information was for most working men and women through organizations with partisan political and ideological allegiances. Even booksellers, who were in the business of making money, were also men of well-known political opinions. In terms of party politics in Ashton, Luke Swallow and George Orme had ties to the Conservative Party; William Micklewaite printed and published the monthly Liberal paper *Ashton Times and Oldham Visitor*.[107] Other booksellers, like Edward Hobson and John Williamson, were Chartists and freethinkers; the blind ex-powerloom weaver Henry Hindle was an Owenite Socialist.[108]

Throughout this period, class and politics suffused and shaped reading sites and reading experiences in this small industrial city and placed some very real restrictions on access to the age of information. And yet, despite all of these obstacles, members of Ashton's working classes were able to enter the ever-expanding world of print; however, variations in levels of literacy and education certainly affected the nature and degree of their exposure and led them to adopt different strategies in their pursuit of knowledge. For William Aitken, Chartist and passionate autodidact, reading was "a habit as necessary to an educated man's comfort as warmth and clothing." Determined to take advantage of every spare moment, he read in the spinning room "amidst the whirl of machinery and in his solitary chamber after the day's prolonged toil."[109] Well-read in literature, history, and science, he regularly quoted "the writings of our best poets" in his speeches and lectures and recommended to all "the pursuit of Scientific Knowledge" as the most "pleasing" of all occupations.[110] A man of far-ranging interests and intellectual curiosity, Aitken regularly lectured on the Chartist circuit and published in the 1840s *Journey Up the Mississippi* as well as popular science articles on hydrostatics and Archimedes and a number of poems.[111] His fellow poet John Stafford, who "never had the opportunity of learning either to read or write," followed a different path.[112] On special occasions, like Chartist dinners to commemorate the Peterloo massacre, he contributed to the evening's proceedings by singing, to a popular tune of the day, "Peterloo" or one of his other compositions; with the help of the printer and bookseller John Williamson, he crossed over in 1840 into the world of print with the publication of a collection of his songs. This slim volume demonstrated that through his involvement in Chartist culture, with its emphasis on oral reading and discussion, Stafford was familiar with the history and key texts of the movement and knew something of the world beyond Ashton. In these songs, he mentioned Manchester, Plymouth, and London and made references to slavery and convict ships bound for Australia; in his song "Miners," he reminded his audience of the example of the French Revolution.[113]

In spite of success stories, like John Stafford, there was, as the Chartists themselves admitted, a "vast substratum in society which is, generally speaking, beyond the reach of our public meetings, lectures, and even newspapers."[114] Relatively untouched by advances in education, Mechanics' Institutions, and "the onward march of knowledge," these working men and women knew little of the outside world or of national and international events. "Millions of men and women," recalled J.R. Clynes about his childhood in the cotton district, "died in their own towns and villages without ever having travelled five miles from the spot where they were born. To them the rest of the world was a shadowy place merging into the boundaries of unreality."[115] To understand the mysteries of life, they turned, not to science, but to astrology, fortune telling, and magic. [116] Belief in "fairies and boggarts" and even in dragons lived on in the "vales and nooks" and isolated villages of the cotton district.[117] People there continued to consult "cunning men and wise women" about lost property (and persons), money matters, and love affairs.[118] For these members of the working classes, the arrival of the age of information was still decades away.

NOTES

1 Headrick (2000, 7–8).
2 Secord (2000, 2, 24–6, 30–1). See also Fyfe (2012, 1–11).
3 W. Adams (1969, 42). Born in 1832, Adams was a Chartist in his youth; he later served as the editor of the radical *Newcastle Weekly Chronicle*. For an influential study of reading and the working classes in his period, see Rose (2001).
4 Reuveni (2002, 274); King and Plunkett (2005, 237–9); Chartier (1994, 8–9); Colclough (2011, 3:99–114); Hobbs (2011, 2:121–38).
5 Ginswick (1983, 3:58).
6 Black, Pepper and Bagshaw (2009, 1).
7 See chapters 9 and 5.
8 Lovett (1967, 17). Born in 1800, Lovett was active in radical and later Chartist politics in the 1820s and 1830s.
9 Bamford (1972, 36). Born in 1788, in Middleton, near Manchester, Bamford was in his youth a handloom weaver and a radical. He published several volumes of poetry and later in life a two-volume autobiography.
10 Lovett and Collins (1969, 49). *Chartist Circular*, "Preface," v.
11 Hewitt (2000, 64–6).

12 Ginswick (1983, 1:86). In 1841 the cotton industry employed over 43 per cent of adult males and around 25 per cent of adult females. See R. Hall (2007, 160, 163); *Parliamentary Papers* (Commons) 1844 [587] XXVII: 68–96.

13 Hewitt (1996, 29–35, 46–7, 66–91); Kargon (1977, 1–33).

14 William Aitken, *A Journey Up the Mississippi River From Its Mouth to Nauvoo, the City of the Latter Day Saints* (Ashton: John Williamson [1845]), 25. Between 1838 and 1848 Chartism was a mass movement for democratic reform. It derived its name from the Six Points of the People's Charter: annual parliaments, universal (male) suffrage, equal electoral districts, abolition of property qualifications for Members of Parliament, voting by ballot, and payment for Members of Parliament.

15 Frederic Hill, *National Education; Its Present State and Prospects*, two volumes (London: C. Knight, 1836), 1:251. For two recent perspectives on the significance of signature for the study of literacy in the nineteenth century, see Vincent (2000, 8–19); Crone (2010, 3–6, 20–2).

16 John Ross Coulthart, *A Report on the Sanatory Condition of the Town of Ashton-under-Lyne* (Ashton: Luke Swallow, 1844), 42. For other estimates of literacy for the Ashton and Stalybridge area, see Stephens (1987, 94–5); Harrop (1983, 37–53).

17 *Parliamentary Papers* (Commons) 1867–8 [402] XIV: 383. Coulthart (1844, 42–3). Born around 1814, Aitken married Mary Taylor in 1835. See Hall and Roberts (2000, 10:3–6). The rule of three was a mathematical rule for solving proportions.

18 Coulthart, *A Report on the Sanatory Condition*, 42–3. Most of the young men and women who married during this five-year period were born between 1815 and 1825.

19 *Report of A Committee of the Manchester Statistical Society on the Condition of the Working Classes, in an Extensive District in 1834, 1835, and 1836* (Manchester, 1838), xii. Ginswick, ed., *Labour and the Poor*, 1:68; Hill, *National Education*, 1:17, 104; Hewitt (2000, 64–5).

20 *Parliamentary Papers* (Commons) 1849 [548] XVII: 125, 179, 129. "Report of a Committee of the Manchester Statistical Society, on the State of Education in the Township of Pendleton, 1838," *Journal of the Statistical Society of London* 2 (March 1839): 67–8.

21 James Heywood, "Report of an Enquiry, Conducted from House to House, into the State of 176 Families in Miles Platting, within the Borough of Manchester in 1837," *Journal of the Statistical Society of London* 1 (May 1838): 35.

22 *Parliamentary Papers* (Commons) 1835 [500] XXXV, Appendix C: 216.

23 R. Hall (1991, 279).

24 Samuel Bamford, *Early Days* (London: Simpkin, Marshall, & Co., 1849), 41–2. *Parliamentary Papers* (Commons) 1834 [572] IX: 20.

25 *Co-Partnership*, September 1909: 131.

26 There was in England no universal system of elementary education until after the passage of W.E. Forster's Education Act (1870). In the 1830s and 1840s, the means of education available to working-class children typically included day schools, dame schools, and Sunday schools. See *Report of a Committee of the Manchester Statistical Society on the State of Education in the Borough of Manchester in 1834* (London: James Ridgway and Son, 1835), 7–20.

27 *Parliamentary Papers* (Commons) 1842 [410] XXII: 5.

28 *Pigot's Directory* (1841).

29 National Archives, Home Office 20/10, Interview with William Aitken; *Ashton Reporter*, 2 October 1869; *Northern Star*, 9 December 1843. For an overview of Aitken's career as a Chartist and labour leader, see R. Hall (2007, 140–58).

30 *Report on the Condition of the Working Classes, in an Extensive District*, xii.

31 Ginswick (1983, 1:68). *Report of a Committee of the Manchester Statistical Society on the State of Education in the Borough of Manchester in 1834*, 7–20; Samuel Robinson, *Address to the Dukinfield Sunday School* (1840), 16.

32 *Report on the Condition of the Working Classes, in an Extensive District*, xii. See also, Edward Baines, Jr, *The Social, Educational, and Religious State of the Manufacturing Districts*, fourth ed. (London: Simpkin, Marshall and Co., 1844), Table 2, Sunday Schools and Day Schools. For a critical view of Sunday schools, see Edwin Butterworth, *An Historical Account of the Towns of Ashton-under-Lyne, Stalybridge, and Dukinfield* (Ashton: T.A. Philips, 1842), 104.

33 *Parliamentary Papers* (Commons) 1834 [572] IX: 97.

34 *Parliamentary Papers* (Commons) 1867–8 [402] XIV: 383; *Parliamentary Papers* (Commons) 1831–2 [706] XV: 448–54; *Parliamentary Papers* (Lords) 1819 [24] CX: 38–40.

35 See chapter 2.

36 Lovett and Collins (1969, 49).

37 *National* (1839): 3.

38 St Clair (2004, 309–10); Wiener (1969, 1–5, 12–14); Read (1961, 66–7); *Northern Star*, 4 January 1851. In the 1830s the taxes on knowledge consisted of the following: a stamp duty on newspapers, a levy on advertisements, the excise duty on paper, and assessments on almanacs and pamphlets. See Wiener (1969, 1–2).

39 Knight (1927, 262–3, 280–1). See also Wiener (1969, 12–14); Fyfe (2012, 1–2, 18–21).

40 *Northern Star*, 29 August 1840. For wages in the cotton industry, see R. Hall (2007, 165).

41 Greenwood (1894, 92–3); Lock (1981).

42 Charles Hindley, *An Address Delivered at the Establishment of the Mechanics' Institution, Ashton-under-Lyne, June 22, 1825* (Ashton, 1825), 3–4, 11; Tylecote (1957, 247–8).

43 *Manchester Guardian*, 16 July 1845; *Manchester and Salford Advertiser*, 19 July 1845.
44 For a revealing advertisement for Edward Hobson's shop, see *Ashton Chronicle*, 19 May 1849. Colclough (2009, 255); St Clair (2004, 189–91); Fyfe (2012, 97–8, 136).
45 C. Smith (1857, 9).
46 Lindsay (1898, 9–11); Dunning (1977, 140); Plummer (1860, xxi); Bamford, *Early Days*, 90.
47 *Slater's Manchester and Salford Directory* (1851); *A Manual for Mechanics' Institutions* (London: Longman, Orme, Brown, Green, and Longman, 1839), 53–5; Allan (2008, 148–9, 153–4); Colclough (2000, 26–7).
48 Christopher Thomson, *The Autobiography of An Artisan* (Nottingham: J. Shaw and Sons, 1847), 65–7.
49 Kellett (1968, 211); Tillott (1972, 84–5).
50 J. Rogers (1903, 107–8). Rogers spent fourteen years in Ashton as the pastor of Albion Independent chapel.
51 R. Hall (2007, 166). *Half A Century of Independency* (1867, 75).
52 Ginswick (1983, 1:73); Axon (1877, 38, 144). J.K. (1858, 3). Hoare (2011, 227–8).
53 R. Hall (2007, 88, 166); *A Manual for Mechanics' Institutions*, 53–5.
54 *Parliamentary Papers* (Commons) 1834 [572] IX: 95, 98, 176; C. Shaw (1977, 218–19); Bezer (1977, 166–7).
55 Quelch (1992, 4). Born in 1862 in rural Berkshire, Quelch attended a Congregational Sunday school until the age of twenty-one.
56 John Taylor, *Poems, Chiefly on Themes of Scottish Interest* (Edinburgh: Andrew Stevenson, 1875), 8–9.
57 Hindley, *An Address Delivered at the Establishment of the Mechanics' Institution*, 3.
58 *Rules and Orders of the Ashton-under-Lyne and Dukinfield Mechanics' Institution for the Promotion of Useful Knowledge among the Working Classes* (Ashton, 1825).
59 Tylecote (1957, 249–54); Farish (1996, 46). For the 1830–1 strike, see R. Hall (1991, 101–12); Steinberg (1999, 206–26).
60 *Rules and Orders of the Ashton-under-Lyne and Dukinfield Mechanics' Institution*; Frank Curzon, "Some Statistics of the Huddersfield Mechanics' Institution," *Transactions of the National Association for the Promotion of Social Science* (1859): 345–6; *Manchester Guardian*, 24 October 1838.
61 *Manchester Guardian*, 5 October 1844. Tameside Local Studies Library, MI 1/1/1 Ashton and Dukinfield Mechanics' Institution, Annual Report (1844): 3. *Parliamentary Papers* (Commons) 1849 [548] XVII: 127.
62 Tameside, MI 1/1/1, Annual Report (1844): 2–3; *Manchester Guardian*, 14 November 1849; MI 1/1/2, Annual Report (1851): 6–7.

63 Tameside, MI 1/1/1, Annual Report (1844): 2–3.
64 *Parliamentary Papers* (Commons) 1849 [548] XVII: 79.
65 Samuel Robinson, *To the President, Committee, and Members of the Dukinfield Village Library, This Farewell Address* (Ashton, 1843), 8, 12.
66 Tameside, MI 1/1/1, Annual Report (1844): 2.
67 See chapter 13.
68 Tameside, MI 1/1/1, Annual Report (1844): 2; *Manchester Guardian*, 5 October 1844.
69 Tameside, MI 1/1/2, Annual Report (1859): 3.
70 Hewitt and Poole (2000, 181).
71 Ibid., pp. 181–2.
72 Robinson, *Farewell Address* (1843), 16.
73 *Manchester Guardian*, 5 October 1844.
74 Butterworth, *Historical Acccount*, 175. Samuel Robinson, *An Address to the Subscribers to the Dukinfield Village Library* (Ashton, 1835), 12–13.
75 *Fourth Annual Report of the Dukinfield Village Library Reading Room* (Dukinfield, 1837), 1–2; Robinson, *Farewell Address*, 8.
76 *Manchester Guardian*, 5 October 1844.
77 Robinson, *Farewell Address*, 19.
78 Robinson, *Address to the Subscribers*, 20.
79 Elliott (1861, 677).
80 Waugh (1892, 47). *Parliamentary Papers* (Commons) 1849 [548] XVII: 81–2.
81 J.K. (1858, 12–13). *New Moral World*, 20 April 1839; *Northern Star*, 3 June 1848.
82 *New Moral World*, 20 April 1839. At this point, the local Owenite association had 58 members and candidates. In 1853 15 members of the Ashton Mutual Improvement Society attended its Christmas dinner. See J.K (1858, 3–4, 8).
83 *Loyal Ancient Shepherds' Quarterly Magazine* (October and April 1853); *Parliamentary Papers* (Commons) 1854 [412] VII: 64.
84 *Loyal Ancient Shepherds' Quarterly Magazine* (July 1853 and April 1855); Gosden (1961, 138–54). Cordery (2003, 12–41).
85 *Manchester Times*, 9 June 1838; *Northern Star*, 23 February 1839; NA, HO 40/37, copy of Francis Maceroni's *A New System*. See also Hobson's obituary in *Ashton Reporter*, 17 August 1867.
86 *Northern Star*, 23 February 1839. Hollis (1970, 119).
87 Dunning (1977, 140). *Northern Star*, 27 August 1842.
88 See chapter 1.
89 Williams and Williams (1991); Tameside, L322, William Aitken, "To the Non-Electors and Electors of the Borough of Ashton-under-Lyne" (Ashton: J Williamson, 1841); *Loyal Ancient Shepherds' Quarterly Magazine* (July 1845): 32; *McDouall's Republican and Chartist Journal*, 3 April 1841; John Stafford,

Songs, Comic and Sentimental (Ashton: J. Williamson, 1840); Aitken, *Journey Up the Mississippi.*

90 There were Chartist localities in Ashton, Stalybridge, Dukinfield, Mossley, and Hooley Hill. See *Northern Star*, 10 October 1840; 11 December 1841; 1 and 15 January 1842; 18 June 1842.

91 Ibid., 24 February 1838 (Mossley); 3 February 1844 (Hyde); 29 October 1842 and 23 December 1848 (Ashton).

92 *Ashton Reporter*, 2 October 1858.

93 *Manchester Guardian*, 5 January 1850.

94 *Northern Star*, 15 November 1845 and 17 November 1838.

95 See chapter 4.

96 Grime (1887, 26). See also Epstein (1976, 72–4).

97 T. Middleton (1932, 122–4).

98 Epstein (1982, 68–9); *Northern Star*, 17 March 1838.

99 Epstein (1982, 60–84); Roberts (1995, 55–70).

100 Chase (2007, 118–19); Sanders (2009, 77–8); *Northern Star*, 9 October 1841.

101 *Northern Star*, 12 January 1839; 4 July and 19 December 1840; 16 January 1841.

102 Rodger (2000, 235).

103 Hewitt and Poole (2000, 91).

104 *Northern Star*, 29 August 1840 and 30 August 1851.

105 Ibid., 27 June 1840.

106 See the letter to the editor from "A Nantwich News-Agent" in the *Northern Star*, 27 May 1848.

107 Williams and Williams (1991) See also, *Ashton Reporter*, 14 November 1874 (Orme's obituary).

108 *Ashton Reporter*, 17 August 1867 (Hobson's obituary); *Northern Star*, 21 October 1843; *Reasoner*, 30 September 1857. In the 1851 census, Hindle's address was 252 Stamford Street. See NA, HO 107/ 2233; *New Moral World*, 12 March and 19 November 1842.

109 *Loyal Ancient Shepherds' Quarterly Magazine* (July 1847): 288; *Oddfellows' Magazine* (July 1857): 129–30.

110 *Ashton News*, 2 October 1869; *McDouall's Chartist and Republican Journal*, 10 April 1841.

111 *Northern Star*, 23 January 1841; 23 April 1842; 17 October 1846; 8 January 1848; *McDouall's Chartist and Republican Journal*, 10 April–28 August 1841. For a selection of his poetry, see Hall and Roberts (1996, 46–54).

112 *Northern Star*, 16 November 1839.

113 R. Hall (1999, 244–5); Stafford, *Songs, Comic and Sentimental.*

114 *Northern Star*, 17 May 1851.

115 Clynes (1937, 1:33). Axon (1870, 4–5).
116 Axon (1870, 4–5); *Ashton Reporter*, 26 September 1857; Waugh (1855, 213–14).
117 Waugh (1855, 213–14); Axon (1870, 4–5). For dragons, see S. Evans (1915, 338–40, 343); *Glossop Chronicle*, 24 January 1902.
118 Axon (1870, 4–5); Waugh (1855, 213–14); Bamford (1972, 205–10). See also Davies (2003).

9 Uneasy Occupancy: Sarah Grand, *The Beth Book*, and a Colonial Reader

LYDIA WEVERS

In 1898 John Vaughan Miller, an office or "station" clerk working on Brancepeth, a large sheep station in New Zealand, destroyed Sarah Grand's *The Beth Book*, and wrote an article for the local newspaper declaring it a work of "original depravity" and its author a woman of "horrible nastiness and blasphemy." Miller's opinion of the novel was briefly recorded amidst his more usual work of noting stock tallies, supplies, orders, invoices, and receipts, daily tasks that were part of his job as the sheep station's clerk. The complex farm business that Miller administered was recorded in invoice books, ledgers, letter books, and a large folio annual diary, in which Miller mixed farm business with his own more personal record of daily life, interpellating gossip, quarrels, love affairs, visitors, and his opinions about many things, including, from time to time, what he was reading. These records are still extant, and kept, as they would have been in Miller's day, in the farm office, a small wooden building at the back of the grand homestead where the station owners lived. (The building is now unoccupied.)

In April 1898 Miller noted in the station diary the publication of one his anonymous leader articles in the local paper, the *Wairarapa Daily Times*. (He published more than one hundred articles over his thirteen years in the job.) Entitled "Originals and Copies," it is a reflection on readers and reading and opens with the contention that there is no "Laureate worthy of the name in prose fiction as well as in poetry" in the present day. "Originals and Copies" is Miller's portrait of himself as a reader. It reveals the assumptions that lie behind his own practice and beliefs and that set up his attack on Sarah Grand, her novel, and its readers. He excoriates not only Sarah Grand and *The Beth Book* but also George Moore's *Mike Fletcher* and *A Mummer's Wife* as works that are "unclean," objecting to their "original realism" and decrying the novelists as never having "risen superior to the vilest characteristics ... of the ancestral monkey."[1] Miller's vituperative heat raises a number of questions. What was driving it, and why did these novels arouse so much feeling in him? How does the location of the reader and his lived experience, not only colonial, not only provincial, but living in a remote rural community, affect his responses? To redeploy a question Joan Rubin raises elsewhere in this volume, to what extent did the consumption of popular British fiction, expressing the sensibility as well as the place of the metropolis, activate anxieties about cosmopolitan ways of thinking, or distance from them? What role did reading and print culture more generally play in the construction of colonial life? Did it accentuate the sensibility of the reader as peripheral or did it, as Christine Pawley suggests in chapter 14 of this book, illustrate the indispensability of organized print in the mediation of provincial life and personal circumstances?

John Vaughan Miller's life trajectory followed the arc described by many nineteenth-century British colonists: away from metropolitan society to a place in the bush on the other side of the world. In this respect he was unlike George Chandler Bragdon or Clara Steen, the American readers and participants in print culture described by Rubin and Pawley, whose literary sociabilities were conducted in settings where "provincial" was clearly delineated from an accessible, though distant, metropolis. Once Miller had emigrated to New Zealand he never returned to anything resembling a metropolis, but he did his best to continue his literary and intellectual interests for the rest of his life. The son of an Anglican clergyman, Miller was born in Kent in 1839 and educated at a grammar school; he may have spent some time at theological college. He worked as a clerk in the Admiralty before emigrating to New Zealand with his wife and nine children in 1880. He had a small mixed farm at Motueka in the South Island but apparently failed to make it sufficiently productive. In 1893 a notice of his bankruptcy appeared in the local newspaper, and at the end of that year he arrived, on foot, to start his job as station clerk at Brancepeth, a farm at least eighty miles and a sea crossing away from Motueka, where his wife and family remained. For the thirteen years that he worked on the station (1894–January 1908) he saw them only once a year, though he sent regular remittances and exchanged letters with his wife every week. His physical separation from his family was partly a consequence of the 1890s economic depression, which hit New Zealand and Australia very hard and drove many men away from their families in pursuit of scarce jobs. Miller recorded large numbers of these men, known as "swaggers" because they carried their belongings in a "swag" (tied up in a blanket), arriving at the sheep station in search of work. But the distance between Miller and his family may also be related to an entanglement of bankruptcy and alcoholism. A notice appeared in the paper at the time of his bankruptcy prohibiting Miller from entering licensed premises in the Motueka region. It seems very likely that these circumstances burdened Miller's cultural self-identification, his class consciousness, and his behaviour, making him deeply conscious of his shifting social position and the vulnerability of his familial and economic networks. His social and cultural contexts were abraded, and reading was a form of mitigation.[2]

Brancepeth, like a number of other large sheep stations in New Zealand (seventy-six thousand acres at the time Miller worked there) retained a library onsite for the use of its three hundred employees and their employers, Hugh and Ruth Beetham. There were in fact two libraries. One was the family's personal library and contained books brought from England in 1856: Homer and Virgil in Latin text, improving works of scholarship, useful manuals, Shakespeare and Milton. Like many colonists the Beetham family took seriously the New Zealand Company's 1844 propaganda that a "well-conducted colonist is of necessity a reading man."[3] In the 1890s the family library was also the smoking room, furnished with leather chairs and mounted antlers. A subscription library was added in the 1880s that grew to contain two thousand books, mostly in cheap colonial editions. The physical distinctions between these two library collections and their contents suggest divides of status, value, and behaviour that inflect Victorian attitudes to reading, and play into separations between a discomfiting new cosmopolitanism and conservative cultural traditions. The family books are mostly non-fiction, cherished objects and not much used; station library books are overwhelmingly fiction in mass-produced editions, battered, dirty, and broken. They visibly evoke different reading behaviour and motivations, different classes of readers, and differential values ascribed to books.

Miller became the secretary of the Brancepeth Library Committee in January 1894, the month he started his job. He was its principal and most visible user and driving force until he left the station as a result of ill health in 1908. There were about twenty regular users who subscribed annually for many years, and more than that again who subscribed for periods of time; generally the latter were seasonal workers like shearers and carpenters. It was also used by the sheep station owners, Hugh and Ruth Beetham, their family and guests, and the governess who educated their daughters Thyra and Weva. The collection was housed in a building that had the station office at one end and the library, with a separate entrance, at the other, making it part of Miller's physical domain. The library was where the newspapers were held – several local papers as well as British and Scottish papers – and a large supply of periodicals, including the *Illustrated London News, Sporting & Dramatic, The Graphic, Review of Reviews, Westminster Magazine*, and the *Leisure Hour*; in the printed catalogue of 1895 a list of rules was set out that included the injunction that no reader was to hold a newspaper or periodical for more than fifteen minutes, suggesting the importance of organized print culture, specifically periodical and newspaper publication, in nineteenth-century reading practices. Christine Pawley has described the Steen family's "newspaper room" and noted that writing for newspapers was one of the few expressive outlets for women. Miller similarly used the local newspaper as an expressive outlet for comment and reflection. And it seems – from the repeated references in the Brancepeth station diary to the newspaper supply and to his own articles – that newspapers provided not only a vital link to a world outside the farm and the colony but a means of participating in it, a form of dialogic sociability.

Miller was not the librarian (a role filled by the carpenter, who was paid a small annual honorarium), but he was clearly the person in charge of the collection, ordering the books, cataloguing them, helping the librarian to cover them with a cloth he described as "red linenette," and selecting books for acquisition. Subscribers could make use of a Suggestions Book (sadly disappeared from the records), but in 1896 Miller established a Committee of Taste, which consisted of himself, library committee President Hugh Beetham, his wife, Ruth, and the governess, to oversee selection. It seems that the Committee made an effort to keep current, as is suggested by Miller's denunciation of *The Beth Book* the year after it was published, lending support to Kate Flint's argument that the attraction of popular fiction was a means of asserting a claim to be modern, "in the know."[4] This may have been particularly important to far-off colonial readers, though participation in print culture as a means of maintaining modernity and currency despite distance and delay brought its own set of problems and obstacles.

Miller's reaction to *The Beth Book*, though perhaps singular in its extremity, was not unique. Many critics disliked it; it is likely Miller had seen reviews in the periodicals or newspapers held by the library. The New Zealand papers reprinted British reviews and added mixed comment of their own: the *Auckland Star* declared *The Beth Book* "tedious, prosy and irrelevant beyond words" while the *Wanganui Herald* found it "deserves to be widely read, pathos and humour being happily blended" and praised its "graphic force in delineation." A similar reception occurred in Australia: the *Town and Country Journal* of New South Wales declared *The Beth Book* of the type doctors recognize as "pathological," its five hundred-oddpages "tedious and dreary beyond expression." Sarah Grand and her novel received considerable and various coverage in colonial papers, from announcements that the book was in stock even in tiny country towns to reviews and biographical articles about Grand. One particularly newsworthy anecdote focused on Grand's reaction to an unfavourable review in the *Daily Telegraph*. The *Star*, a New Zealand paper published in Canterbury, featured a gossip column entitled "Miss Colonia in London," which opined that "It is surprising to find a clever capable woman like Sarah Grand following in the footsteps of Miss Marie Corelli and assailing the reviewers who do not happen to like her books in hysterical Billingsgate."[5]

So where does Miller's especially heated response come from? It appears to derive from several factors. One of them is the importance of reading in his assertion of his social identity, particularly as an arbiter of taste. Generally, Miller's comments reflect what Sarah Wadsworth has called a "near-obsession" about the cultural status of books and reading, especially fiction, in the nineteenth century. There was already a good deal of comment in colonial newspapers about the deleterious shift to reading fiction. Dulcie Gillespie-Needham has concluded that by the 1890s most New Zealand libraries issued more than 80 per cent fiction, and in some cases it may have been closer to 90 per cent. In the Auckland *Herald* for 16 September 1899, "Britannicus" argued that the amount of fiction turned out of the printing press each year is "truly appalling," and a lecture by a Mr McGregor reported in Miller's local paper, the *Wairarapa Daily Times*, in 1906, claimed that the borrowing rate for fiction in the public library was six times that for non-fiction. None of this is news, but it does describe the context in which Miller's diatribes about *The Beth Book* occurred.[6]

The Beth Book (1897) was the fourth of Grand's novels to be acquired by the Brancepeth Library. The first was *The Heavenly Twins*, followed by *Ideala*, *Our Manifold Nature*, and finally, after the ruckus about *The Beth Book* (which is perhaps a little surprising), *Babs the Impossible*. Based on the library copies' physical appearance today, Grand's novels were among the most heavily used of the holdings in New Woman novels. This is particularly true of *The Heavenly Twins* (1894). And while heavy use does not mean that readers liked them – indeed, it may mean the reverse – it does indicate that there was considerable traffic. All four have annotations by Miller that reveal his presence as a reader in Grand's fiction before and after *The Beth Book*: he has glossed and edited twice in *The Heavenly Twins*; *Ideala* and *Our Manifold Nature* both contain glosses and corrections in Miller's hand; *Babs the Impossible* has a trace in his hand that suggests he read it. *The Heavenly Twins* stayed in circulation after the destruction of *The Beth Book*, despite its gruelling description of Edith Beale, a bishop's daughter married off to a syphilitic army Major, who gives birth to a deformed baby before dying herself.[7]

It is not hard to imagine what Miller objected to in *The Beth Book*. Grand's description of Beth McClure's brutal manipulative husband and the suffering of her marriage is protracted but disturbing, and Beth's husband works at a lock hospital treating prostitutes and is also a vivisectionist. As Penny Boumelha has said, writing of Thomas Hardy, "This is the period in which sexuality moves decisively from the area of moral discourse to that of scientific discourse."[8] Miller's article references X-rays and the "ancestral monkey" and hints, I think, at his reaction and resistance to this discursive turn, which he saw as degrading and contaminating. He expostulated that *The Beth Book*'s author, along with George Moore, were

> Original only in the sense of being aboriginals of the literary world, who have never risen superior to the vilest characteristics, habits, customs and passion of the ancestral monkey ... "The Beth Book" (which bears the most originally stupid title ever given to a book) turns the "X rays" on to original depravity; but the only original thing about the book is the horrible nastiness and blasphemy of the woman who wrote it, and still calls herself a woman. As for the women who *read* it! ... a woman's soul may pass pure, if such be her terrible fate, through *fact*, but not through *fiction*.[9]

It is likely also that the politics of Grand's New Woman heroine sparked his fire as much as medical naturalism and what novelist Grant Allen, at this time, called terrifying frankness about sex. Elizabeth McClure leaves her husband and becomes an activist and public speaker, exemplifying her destiny, declared in Grand's subtitle, as a "Woman of Genius." Penny Boumelha, tracing the derivation of the phrase "Woman of Genius," concludes that claiming this status for their heroines was a risky strategy for New Woman novelists, as the creativity and intellectualism of a genius was thought to be only a step away from idiocy and criminality in contemporary pathology.[10]

In "Originals and Copies," Miller makes a pre-emptive claim to textual authority before denouncing *The Beth Book*:

> When a man has been for many years a student, and has read, and re-read, all the best things said by the best men in the best possible way, his mind becomes saturated with the thoughts of these men, and the recorded expression of those thoughts is inseparable from his own ideas. He cannot, even if he would, shake himself free from them, or divest himself of their influence. This is especially the case if his memory is retentive of what he reads, and if he has books on hand to enable him to verify his quotations.[11]

Borrowing Carlyle's famous phrase, the Heroes of Literature, Miller argues that the reader whose mind has been shaped and moulded by these influences since infancy can have nothing new to say. Instead, Miller writes, "He may confer great pleasure and benefit on many by his tasteful and reverent re-setting of some of the gems which the old masters of their craft mined and dived for."

Miller here claims his place among "great and wise readers" who, like him, can recognize the "imperishable words of the Immortals" as they are reproduced in literature. For a column and a half, in a dazzling display of his own retentive memory and capacity to reset old gems, he identifies trails of what he calls kidnapping or plagiarism – Bacon out of Solomon, Tennyson from Shakespeare from Tibullus, Ben Jonson from Philostratus – trails that delineate the patriarchies of literature and scholarship and demonstrate Miller's conviction that newness, or "originality," is not the point of literature. New Women novelists, and specifically *The Beth Book,* he argues both obliquely and directly, are depraved deviations from the great traditions of literature, though of course the object of his attack is Grand's content rather than the "literariness" of her novels. (Like other New Women novelists, Grand wrote in a consciously literary style.) As a whole Miller denies the existence of women of genius, as writers or as readers. The tenor of "Originals and Copies" suggests that "Woman of Genius" is a category he is sufficiently provoked by to resist it substantively as well as rhetorically.

Later that same year (1898), Miller wrote a satirical letter to the editor of the local paper purporting to be a female journalist looking for work. The letter mocks precisely the kind of figure Grand presents in Elizabeth McClure:

A MODEST REQUEST

To the Editor
Sir, – I shall be obliged by your placing me on your staff as a leader writer. I am settled in the neighbourhood, and have leisure time in the evenings while my husband does the housework and attends to the boots. You will perceive from this specimen leader that I enclose that I can turn out a finished article and that I am no literary hack. You will observe that I step off rather showily at starting, but soon settle down in a lively trot of twelve slips an hour. – I am, etc

JOCOSA MORDAX
December 12th, 1898.[12]

Miller's reactions to the New Woman are of course not unusual among male English readers in the 1890s, but there is also a specific colonial context. In the 1890s New Zealand was a relatively progressive place, passing the Matrimonial Property Act in 1894, universal suffrage (which included indigenous Māori women) in 1893, and the Divorce Act in 1898. The pace of social change must have added energy and anxiety to the gender debate generally, already at a high pitch because of the advent of suffragism and New Women. *The Beth Book* was not the only novel to suffer Miller's censorship. In 1902 he persuaded Hugh Beetham to suppress circulation of Lucas Malet's *The History of Sir Richard Calmady*. He wrote in the station diary entry for 20 April 1902:

> The "History of Sir Richard Calmady" by Lucas Malet is not only a fearfully wearisome story; it is as blasphemous and lascivious a book as ever was written – some parts are worthy of the very worst French sensualists – The way in which Lady Calverley in 618 pages inspects her moral secretions is as tiresome as it is odious – she looks at them thro' a telescope, a microscope, a magnifying glass, a monocle, a camera obscura, a horse collar, the Röntgen Rays, a stereoscope, the electric light, and a candle with the extinguisher on. The whole motive of the book is vile and revolting in the extreme. No girl could ever be a modest girl after reading it – the book is intentionally morbid, filthy and wicked. It is sure therefore to have a large sale. It is the story of Titania and Bottom turned into monstrous lechery.

The History of Sir Richard Calmady was one of six of Lucas Malet's novels held in the collection. Miller's extended metaphor links to the figures of speech he used to denigrate *The Beth Book* and is revealing about what disgusted him. Malet's novel included sexually explicit material and featured a "feminist socialist activist" as its heroine. Talia Schaffer has called it groundbreaking for its psychological development and complex discourse: these are the features that Miller's list of optical illuminations attacks.[13] Lucas Malet was the pen name of Mary St Leger Harrison, the daughter of Charles Kingsley, a writer and thinker Miller deeply admired. In 1899 he declared Kingsley's *Life and Letters* to be the best book he had read for years and ordered a copy for his wife; before being so affronted by Richard Calmady, Miller had read Malet's earlier novels attentively. Indeed, New Woman novels as a category of the Brancepeth library show many signs of Miller's reading: marked passages, marginal comments, and glosses. Gender roles were a burning issue for him, as they were for other readers whose marginalia survives. And gender is the most common category of comment and annotation in the collection, reflecting a deep reservoir of assumptions and stereotypes unremarkable to many nineteenth-century readers, assumptions and stereotypes which operated as a matter of course in daily life, though freshly mobilized and energized by reactions to feminism.

Like Australia, New Zealand in the nineteenth century was a society of pronounced gender imbalance, especially in rural areas. At Brancepeth, a workforce of about three hundred included just a tiny number of female house servants. None of them were library subscribers, though it is reasonable to suppose that the wives and daughters of the few men who worked and lived on the station with their families – only a handful – would have shared their library books. The principal female readers were Ruth Beetham, her daughters, and the various governesses. Ruth Beetham's annotations of books held in the station library iterate the same spectrum of conservative gender and class attitudes as Miller's. She heavily annotated Marie Corelli's novel *Boy* (1900) and asserted on the facing title page that there were "thousands of Mrs Darcy-Muirs in England + NZ." The novel depicts Mrs Darcy-Muir as a negligent wife and mother, having "let herself go" after marriage and not taken proper care of her child.

Miller's attitudes are, of course, widely asserted in nineteenth-century literature as a whole and lie behind the fierce uproar generated by New Woman novelists and feminism more generally. He embodies and advocates for the idea of "book-love" as *Fraser's Magazine* extolled it in 1847, the "good angel" uplifting the working man who, full of noble aspirations, reads from great works to his uncomprehending but approving wife, sewing by the fireside.[14] Such a picture is implicitly and explicitly avowed in most of Miller's writing. Indeed, if the whole of Miller's writing – his articles, diary entries, and marginalia – composes a self-portrait of a reader, it is clear that for him reading is a gendered form of work in which the reader proves himself worthy of his material, and in which his ongoing labour of judgment and discrimination proves him not to be the "flimsy, desultory reader" denounced by Carlyle, a reader who flies "from foolish book to foolish book, and get[s] good of none, and mischief of all."[15]

Reaction to the New Woman is, however, only one manifestation of Miller's responsive reading. The range and scale of his reading reveals a far more complicated set of motivations and behaviours and illustrates not just what might be at stake in the act and description of reading but how these intellectual, social, and emotional investments might take on greater weight and edge in a small, rural, colonial community. Miller's articles in the local newspaper were always a demonstration of his reading and scholarship; he wrote as if he was the representative of a cosmopolitan intellectualism in the provinces and continuously bears witness to the indispensability of print. But he also displayed his learning in ways visible to much smaller and semi-private publics, or only to himself: in his annotations of books held in the library and in his comments and learned asides in the station diary. Owing perhaps to the circumstances of his life, including his education and tastes, reading was the scaffold supporting Miller's self respect. He embodied Thomas Augst's description of reading as "a habit one wears in public," devoting a lot of ink and energy, around the edges of what was a time-consuming and demanding job, to the production of a steady stream of articles, poems, parodies, and letters in the local paper.[16] These were a mix of textual performance and admonition, most revealing in their representation of what he thought of himself, but also a gauge of his engagement with topical issues: the Boer War, education, the Church of England, the Indian Mint – a catholic mix of British, colonial, and local concerns. In his newspaper articles he drew widely on the English canon, referencing or quoting Milton, Shakespeare, Jonson, Bacon, Macaulay, Tennyson, Browning, Carlyle; classical authors such as Terence, Seneca, Augustine, Horace, and Virgil, and European scholars like Giordano Bruno, Pascal, and Goethe. He made liberal use of Latin and Greek, often using phrases in Greek in his articles, and peppered his diary entries with phrases or comments in French, German, Italian, Latin, Greek, and (once) Hebrew. In the library books he glossed words derived from Greek or Latin and included marginal scholia in both languages with references. His instructive marginalia in the Brancepeth library books are also a display of pedantry – there is no grammatical mistake that escapes his red pen. The quantum of his published and unpublished commentary reveals a man who is seriously over-educated for the job he finds himself in, and whose anxiety about his own class status finds expressive outlet across the range of his private, semi-private, and public annotations and commentaries as a reader. The primary field in which he asserted his class and status, or at least the primary field that is visible to history, was in his public and private performance as a reader and scholar, metonyms of class.

If reading facilitates literary sociability, as Joan Rubin argues, Miller's behaviour as a reader is both an expression of such sociability, in that he participates in the organization of the library and its facilities and shares reading preferences with other members of the farm community, and a manifestation of unsociable practices. Some of his reading behaviours implicitly exhibit a passive-aggressive characterization of other readers, implyingthat they need his assistance to identify quotations or gloss classical references. These attitudes are consistent with the way Miller writes about his fellow workers in the station diary, which is threaded with narratives of feuds and quarrels. He makes scornful remarks on the table manners, hygiene, and behaviour of his fellow employees, and refers to other people's interactions with his employer: these notations constitute a kind of policing of the social layers of the farm community. Miller recorded every visitor, how long they stayed, where they slept, and where they ate. His discrimination of hierarchies of authors and texts are mirrored in his inscription of the social world he inhabited, suggesting the multiple ways in which reading tastes and behaviours are one expression among many of habitus. There were gradations of eating places that ranged from the men's cookhouse to the saloon, used only by Miller and other senior staff, to the family dining room, He noted every occasion on which he dined with the family and also when other guests or staff were invited, advising a visiting surveyor that dinner jackets were required. The station diary was a public record and it is likely that it was read by a number of others, from nosy passersby to Miller's employer, Hugh Beetham. Some of Miller's non-English entries, particularly his transliterated Greek, were designed to defeat prying eyes, but the palimpsest of languages was also making the point that not all readers are equally equipped. They show off cultural capital, something that was always at issue in his uneasy occupancy of his colonial life.

In the station diary he frequently notes book orders he makes for himself or his family and books lent or borrowed, usually between the governess Miss Liddle, Ruth Beetham, and himself, though sometimes he recommends books to other family members. The books noted in the diary are non-fiction devotional verse and essays, prayer books, Apirana

Ngata's *Maori Grammar*, a Greek lexicon, C.S. Calverley's poems, Kingsley's letters, and an edition of Shakespeare. His articles are likewise carefully judged in their presentation of Miller as a well-read man: they refer to Tennyson, Carlyle, George Eliot, Gissing, Froude, Hardy, Austen, Dickens, and Trollope. With just a few exceptions, they mention popular Victorian authors or what he referred to as "Fashionable Novels" only to disparage them. But the library books tell a different story. Miller was unable to prevent himself from reacting to any textual or physical error: a misbind, a grammatical mistake, a typo or misspelling. He glossed Greek and Latin wherever it occurred, and if he spotted an allusion he asterisked a note at the bottom of the page. He noted plot and other errors, such as Thackeray's description in *Pelham* of a garden flaming with crocuses and sunflowers, plants which flower in different seasons. In this form he was an active and interactive presence across a big range of the library's popular fiction holdings. Marie Corelli, R.L. Stevenson, H. Rider Haggard, Adeline Sergeant, E.P. Roe, Mary Cholmondeley, M.E. Braddon, Mrs Henry Wood, S. Baring Gould, Henry Merriman, Zola, Grant Allen, Rita, Joseph Hocking, Iota, Israel Zangwill, Ellen Thorneycroft Fowler, and Walter Besant all reveal Miller's hand, a hand which is often critical but whose tracks illuminate reading choices that are in some senses outside the self-projection he offered to the public in the newspaper and in his interactions with other members of the Brancepeth library committee.

Alongside his compulsively editorial and reactive marginalia runs another stream of annotation by Miller that is less obviously marked and seems to be driven by a different motivation. Many books, including a number of Lucas Malet's earlier novels, have page numbers jotted by Miller inside the back cover. It is often possible to guess what might have caught his eye. For example, in Sarah Grand's *Babs the Impossible*, on the page he noted there is a couplet that evokes some of Miller's diary entries:

> Work without hope drops nectar in a sieve
> And hope without an object cannot live.

Miller frequently expressed his dislike of his job and once described himself as a white slave. Every so often there is a more overt textual flag. The page number reveals a line or a paragraph that has been marked with a careful and unobtrusively pencilled dot. Two examples strike me. One is from Frank Frankfort Moore's *Phyllis of Philistia* (1895), a courtship and marriage novel. The pencilled dot is placed next to this sentence on page 352: "He had heard the wife who had deserted her husband in favour of the teetotal platform, cry out for another chance when her husband had died far away from her." Miller's working life at Brancepeth, precipitated by bankruptcy and alcohol, took him away from his wife for fourteen years, during which his health declined. Does the placement of this dot evoke a more complex reading of the events and the relationship that led to his alienation and exile from his wife and family? Miller's most opaque reading traces may offer a glimpse, I think, of how personal and fictional narratives entangle in the reader's mind. His emotional biography perhaps even more poignantly shadows the text in this dotted passage on page 222 of Lucas Malet's novel *Mrs Lorimer* (1886):

> It struck Mr Mainwaring that his own life, looking back on it, was very like the history of that day. A cheery start in the morning sunshine; a capital horse under him; hope for the coming hours; plenty of friends; a splendid burst for a few hours over the grass, when the pace was hot and his blood tingled with healthy excitement. The pottering about the dreary woodlands, in the chill mist, drawing and drawing for the fox that could never be found; and, at last, the long lonely ride home in the cold and growing darkness. The day dying, the sport all over, only the weariness and want of success left. Dirty, bespattered, old – that was what it all came to in the end. Alas! For the pity of it!

Miller was not an unobtrusive man. His many interventions in the library books and his records of station life illustrate an opinionated and angular textual and physical presence. But some things were kept from view during his time at Brancepeth. It is likely his employer knew of his bankruptcy, and possibly of his drinking problem, but neither event is ever mentioned in the station diary or alluded to in any of Miller's writing. Yet he must have been plagued by guilt and humiliation and suffered the loss of his family acutely. Personal feelings are almost never mentioned by Miller. When his twenty-one-year-old son Tony died in 1901 and he was unable to get to the funeral, he allowed himself only one oblique expression of grief, much later in the station diary.

But everyone on the Brancepeth station would have known Miller's handwriting, which appeared on their bills, contracts, and public notices, so his marginalia can be said to anticipate a knowing readership, and one to whom he was demonstrating an important dimension of his public and private persona. Likewise his newspaper articles, though published pseudonymously, seem to have been recognized: he mentions people commenting on them. But the dots with which he marked passages draw little attention to themselves and are perhaps only visible to someone like me, scouring each page for signs of a reader's passing. What seems always to be the case is that they mark passages of reflection and feeling that are not hard to connect to his biography, situation, and imagined state of mind and make up the most discrete and submerged level of his layered history of response with its many registers and multiple pseudonyms. It is ironic, but also fitting, that among the most affecting of the passages he marked are those from the pen of a New Woman novelist whose fiction also attracted some of his most searing commentary.

What then does John Vaughan Miller illuminate in the "elusive" history of reading? In no sense is John Vaughan Miller a professional reader or writer. He was only discoverable as a named reader by working backwards from the evidence of his reading tracks in the library books to the script that filled the station diaries. Many things about his life are still unknown, and despite a large family of descendants, there are no surviving family records, saved letters, or memory of him, with the exception of one photograph recovered from England. His pseudonymous newspaper articles were similarly only discoverable because he noted both when he wrote them and the date of publication in the station diary. Although he is in some senses, then, anonymous and private, he declares himself as no ordinary reader at every turn and behaves as if he has a stake in a literary profession, is a man of textual authority and a citizen of the world republic of letters. All of which raises questions. Who was Miller writing for? Many of his scholia, it seems, deliberately exceeded the capacity and education of the other library subscribers, which was probably part of the point he was making, but was Miller also in some sense writing for history, waiting to be found by an archival researcher like me? H.J. Jackson has described marginalia as a "letter in a bottle" for this reason, but she also cautions against reading marginalia as offering direct access to the reader's mind, noting that readers who write in books are subject to conventions, expectations, and complexities of motivation and historical circumstance like anyone else.[17] The range and spectrum of Miller's forms of engagement as a reader and writer amply evidence this point. And yet what does it mean? Does he reveal nothing but the conflicts, misfortunes, and passions of a personal history, like and unlike so many others who spent their lives consuming books? Or does he illuminate something beyond himself? The answer I think lies somewhere in between. The role reading could play in Miller's life was intensified by his colonial location. Colonial readers did not only set out, as Miller did, to entertain themselves and maintain their cultural knowledge by reading; reading was also a portable and demonstrable form of credential. By demonstrating textual and literary skills, even remotely, such as by carrying a volume of Tennyson in a swag, the colonial reader could articulate a set of distinctions that endorsed his or her claim on social status. The characteristics I have suggested Miller displays above – education, pride, competition, anxiety, shame, pedantry, knowledge – were intensified by Miller's colonial location but also illustrate the multiple utilities of reading in negotiating life circumstances. Reading is the passport to cultural standing.

Robert Darnton has famously challenged book historians to pay more attention to the where of reading.[18] It seems to me that book historians should also, and congruently, pay more attention to the what, and how it sets itself against, or in synchrony with, the where. Miller in some respects was a very conventional reader. He operated within what I call the "orbit of intention" – his responses to what he read were fully textually engaged and conformed to the book's intentionality. But thinking about the what as well as the where of his reading is suggestive and evocative of how reading interacted with multiple dimensions of his social world, and particularly with his peripheral, colonial position. These books and the accompanying archive of newspaper articles and diary entries articulate their reader's relation to place in ways that open many layers of interpretation, traversing the dialogic interactions of provincial and metropolitan, personal and cosmopolitan, reader motivation and status, and the psychology and performance of reading within big discourses such as class and gender.

NOTES

1 John Vaughn Miller, "Originals and Copies," *Wairarapa Daily Times*, 6 April 1898; Grand (1897).

2 For more detail on Miller (and the Brancepeth Sheep Station), see Wevers (2010).

3 "Review," *New Zealand Journal*, 6 July 1844, cited in Traue (2007).

4 Flint (2001, 31).

5 *Auckland Star*, 15 January 1898; *Wanganui Herald*, 16 March 1898; *Town and Country Journal*, 15 October 1898; *Auckland Star*, 22 January, 1898.

6 Wadsworth (2006, 98); Gillespie-Needham (1971, 417); *Auckland Herald*, 16 September 1899; *Wairarapa Daily Times*, 18 May 1906.

7 Annotations are from extant copies in the Brancepeth Sheep Station Library, Brancepeth, Wainuioru, Wellington, New Zealand.

8 Boumelha (1982, 13).

9 Miller, "Original and Copies."

10 Boumelha (1997, 172–3).

11 Miller, "Original and Copies."
12 "A Modest Request," *Wairarapa Daily Times*, 12 December 1898.
13 Schaffer (2002).
14 "Book-Love," *Fraser's Magazine* 36 (1847): 199, cited in Flint (1995).
15 Thomas Carlyle, "Letter to an Unidentified Correspondent," The Carlyle Letters Online: The Collected Letters Vol. 16 (http://carlyleletters.dukejournals.org/cgi/content/full/16/1/lt-18430313-TC-UC-01, accessed 15 November 2013).
16 Augst (2007, 11).
17 Jackson (2001, 99).
18 Darnton (1990).

10 Alger, Fosdick, and Stratemeyer in the Heartland: Crossover Reading in Muncie, Indiana, 1891–1902

JOEL D. SHROCK

The Burt family read voraciously and from all appearances had a deep and abiding love of reading. The Muncie Public Library served as the central institution in the lives of the Burt family through which they developed a family reading culture. Carrie Burt raised three sons in Muncie, Indiana, after the 1889 death of her husband Theophilus, a drugstore clerk. The eldest child, Frank, was born in 1877, soon followed by George (1879), and then Robert (1883). All of the Burt boys devoured books at a prodigious rate, taking their cue from their mother, Carrie. She had joined the Muncie Public Library under her maiden name, Carrie Andrews, as a single nineteen-year-old young woman in 1875, the year before she married Theophilus.

We know that reading played a vital part in the lives of this family because of the information in the fully searchable database What Middletown Read, which holds the information from the old circulation ledgers of the Muncie Public Library from 5 November 1891 through 3 December 1902, though circulation records are missing from May 1892 through November 1894.[1] These records permit us to follow with some certainty the reading patterns of Carrie Burt and her sons over a twelve-year period, during which she checked out 188 books and performed 220 separate transactions at the Muncie Public Library. This amounted to a rate of more than 1.8 books per month for twelve years and does not account for any reading that she did in the library.[2] The middle son, George, signed up for his own card on 23 January 1892 and immediately began reading consistently at the rate of 2.4 books per month and checking out material from the library 2.8 times per month until July 1902. Frank signed up for his own card in 1892, but his name does not appear in the registers until February 1895. From that date until November 1902 the eldest Burt boy checked out 173 books, an average of 2.4 books per month. Robert did not manage to join until 28 January 1896. The youngest brother still managed to check out 110 books for an average of 2.2 books per month over more than a five-year period.[3] Over the 104 months the Muncie Public Library was open from November 1891 to December 1902, these four family members checked out 678 books, an average of 6.5 books per month even though two of the boys were only active part of the time. The Burt family visited the library more than twice per month and the four often visited on different days!

The What Middletown Read database and the Burt family's experiences demonstrate the importance of the public library as an institution in Muncie, the elevated status of reading, and the different audiences who read juvenile boys' books in the late nineteenth century. Indeed, the central focus of this project is to explore the crossover readers of juvenile boys' books and magazines in the What Middletown Read database. By crossover reading, I mean in this instance the tendency of girls to read material that was marketed to boys. Though the mass popularity of juvenile writers like Horatio Alger and Oliver Optic is well known, surprisingly these writers and others like them dominated the circulation figures for all books checked out by Muncie Public Library patrons. All four members of the Burt family checked out significant numbers of books by authors like Alger, Edward Ellis, and G.A. Henty. What kinds of boys were reading these books? Were the readers of Horatio Alger and Oliver Optic young men in the lower middle class or working-class boys looking to rise into genteel respectability like the literary example of Ragged Dick?[4] Did adults cross over into boys' territory and read books by the likes of G.A. Henty, Edward Ellis, and Harry Castlemon? Were girls involved in this kind of crossover reading during these heavily sex-segregated decades? Would a young lady dare read Frank Stockton's tales of swashbuckling pirates? Many scholars have contended that from the mid-nineteenth century until the 1910s there was significant crossover readership, with boys and girls reading adult literature and women and men reading juvenile literature.[5] What Middletown Read firmly establishes that the answer to all of these questions is a resounding yes; neither age nor sex kept Muncie library patrons from reading books geared towards a specific group. Crossover reading occurred consistently among all groups, and the What Middletown Read database provides clear data that girls and adults were in fact consistent and important parts of the boys' juvenile literature readership just as boys read adult- and girl-oriented fiction.

Before turning to the analysis of readership patterns it is worth noting that databases such as What Middletown Read allow us to investigate in new ways the borrowing choices (and by inference the reading behaviour) of ordinary library patrons. This chapter represents one of several investigations of the data provided by the What Middletown Read database that are included in this volume. Contributions by Lynne Tatlock and Frank Felsenstein also use What Middletown Read data to explore print culture. Elsewhere in the volume, Julieanne Lamond exploits the Australian Common Reader, a resource similar to the What Middletown Read database, to examine borrowing patterns among patrons of the Lambton (New South Wales, Australia) Mechanics' and Miners' Institute during the early twentieth century, and Kyle Roberts employs catalogue and circulation data contained in Dissenting Academies Online to investigate reading behaviour and print culture among a distinct religious group in the English Midlands during the eighteenth century. Though separated by time and distance, each of these tools permits us to see and understand in new ways the centrality of books and reading in the daily lives of ordinary people across the modern world.

The Burt family certainly demonstrated a commitment to reading that transcended any purely didactic motivation. What the lives of Carrie, Frank, George, and Robert Burt bring into sharp focus was the importance of reading built into the routine of their lives. July 1896 provides a stark view of the role the library played in their lives. On Wednesday, 8 July, Carrie, Frank, and Robert all checked out books. The following Saturday, 11 July, Carrie, George, and Frank visited the library and checked out books but not Robert. A week later on 18 July Carrie returned with Frank and Robert for new reading material, and just three days later this trio all checked out more books on Tuesday, 21 July. George joined the other three for a trip to the library on Saturday, 25 July, and all four Burts checked out books. They did not stop by the Muncie Public Library haphazardly or episodically, but guided by Carrie Burt the family routinely and purposefully visited monthly, seeking out books to provide entertainment and edification.

This type of reading culture was only possible because of the changes to the production and publication of all kinds of literature. Reading material availability exploded after the Civil War and like other consumer goods became an increasingly important part of people's everyday lives. Scarcity of reading material characterized the first half of the nineteenth century, and the growing demand for literature after the Civil War from a white population that boasted literacy rates over 90 per cent spurred the massive growth of new printed materials. Unlike Civil War soldiers described by Ronald and Mary Zboray in "Beyond the Market and the City: The Informal Dissemination of Reading Materials during the American Civil War" who had to create informal networks so they could get reading material, the reading public after the 1870s lived through a veritable explosion of print media. The publication of new books grew by 300 per cent between 1880 and 1900, newspapers experienced a 700 per cent increase in circulation between 1870 and 1900, and magazine circulation had expanded to 65 million by 1900. New and larger distribution networks created by railroads, postal subscription, and mail order catalogues brought newspapers, magazines, and books into almost every conceivable part of the country. Printed material was the first mass media, providing both information and leisure to Americans. People avidly consumed printed material, which transformed the nation just as dramatically as the introduction of radio or television would in the twentieth century.[6]

If is often difficult for modern Americans to understand the place reading had in the lives of Americans like Frank, George, and Robert Burt before the advent of movies and radio. Henry Seidel Canby, literary critic and editor of the *Saturday Review*, candidly described the centrality of reading for middle-class Americans of the 1890s in his memoir, *The Age of Confidence*:

> And hence my reading memories are of absorption in a book, earless, eyeless, motionless for hours, a life between covers more real than outer experience, such an obsession in reading as I believe does not exist now ... It [reading] was an extension without break or casualty of our own lives, and flowed back freely to become a part of our mentality.

As Canby suggested, and many current historians have noted, reading held a special place for middle-class Americans in the Gilded Age that it would not have after the 1920s and the emergence of new mass media. For people like Canby reading illustrated the gentility and refinement of the reader, serving as a class marker that differentiated respectable folk from rough. Reading was the main form of home entertainment, created self-improvement, and fostered a common literary heritage that united middle-class readers in a cosmopolitan culture.[7]

All kinds of new reading publics were emerging, however, well beyond the control of Northeastern cultural elites like that to which Canby belonged. This pattern trend is illustrated elsewhere in this volume, such as in Brad Evans's account of the spread of styles associated with ephemeral bibelots and in Christine Pawley's depiction of a thriving farm press that helped define a rural American print culture. Horatio Alger illustrated the massive expansion of a type of reading that received almost universal opprobrium from the high literary establishment. Even though Alger emerged from the genteel classes of the Northeast and attended Harvard University, this author certainly was not celebrated as one of the greats of New England literature, but was instead often derided as the purveyor of sensationalized drivel.[8] What these critics feared and understood all too well was the growing adventure genre aimed at boys that was rapidly expanding into massive popularity. Literary entrepreneurs with their finger on the pulse of American culture began to pour out juvenile literature directed specifically towards boys that self-consciously tamed the action and violence of dime novels and adapted them to middle-class values.[9] Middle-class Victorians denounced sensationalism and violence in dime novels in the 1850s and 1860s, but many parents tolerated these elements in books and magazines for their own children by the 1880s and 1890s.[10] Horatio Alger and his mentor William Taylor Adams (Oliver Optic) between them wrote hundreds of novels published from 1861 to 1899 that concentrated on success stories spiced with adventure. They were joined by British writers like R.M. Ballantyne, who focused on adventures in exotic locales. Soon a new group emerged that included Charles Fosdick (Harry Castlemon), Edward Ellis, William O. Stoddard, Kirk Munroe, and G.A. Henty, all of whom were part of the deluge of adventure books for boys.[11]

From the moment they were able to get their library cards the Burt brothers dove into boys' adventure books. Alger, Optic, Ellis, Castlemon, and Henty were common favourites, providing almost endless adventure. These brothers found that a library card in Muncie allowed them to escape into history, adventure, and even romance. George has the longest-running record and offers the best example. On 23 January 1892, he joined the Muncie Public Library, getting his own card and number, patron 2957. It turns out that like many twelve-year-old lads in 1892, George loved a ripping tale of adventure. On the very first day he had his new library card George checked out Richard Meade Bache's *The Young Wrecker of the Florida Reef, or, The Trials and Adventures of Fred Ransom* – he liked it so much that a little over three months later he checked it out again. Tearing through this exciting tale of sailing and exploration in Florida, George returned to the library three days later and checked out the library's most popular author, Horatio Alger, to follow young Tom's many adventures across America's Great Plains in *The Young Adventurer*. Four days passed and he was back, checking out *Miles Standish: The Puritan Captain*. Horatio Alger must have struck a chord with young George because within a week he was back for *The Young Miner*, and two days later *Mark, the Match Boy*. By May 1892 (the point at which the What Middletown Read records are interrupted) George Burt had checked out fourteen books in only four months: ten boys' adventure novels (eight by Alger), a few histories, and a book on agricultural chemistry.[12] As Julieanne Lamond notes in her discussion of the Lambton (Australia) Mechanics' and Miners' Institute (chapter 13 of this volume), readers such as George Burt could enter a "zone of connection" created by the common print culture they experienced and perhaps by a shared interest in ideas or values in those books. George entered this widespread community when he read the ever so popular Horatio Alger.

Derided by critics and almost universally loathed by librarian organizations for decades, this type of boys' literature preferred by the young Burt brothers clearly played a very prominent role in boys' reading from the nineteenth century into the twentieth. Critics were even more outraged when a new hardback juvenile novel industry emerged at the turn of the century. Entrepreneur Edward Stratemeyer blended the working-class dime-novel tradition with the Alger- and Optic-style middle-class success novels to produce a new middle-class adventure fiction for boys. From the dime-novel trade Stratemeyer adopted the use of staff writers who wrote under pseudonyms, humour, and non-stop action, which he mixed with the late nineteenth-century middle-class morality he found in the Alger books to create a new genre of series books. After writing on his own for a few years, the Stratemeyer Syndicate was fully formed by 1906. An entrepreneur sensitive to emerging markets, Stratemeyer targeted middle-class boys still living at home "dreaming of independence and adventure free of parental restrictions."[13] Stratemeyer's Rover Boys and Tom Swift series appeared respectively in 1899 and 1910 and quickly dominated the juvenile market, followed by Stratemeyer's even more popular Hardy Boys series beginning in the 1920s.[14]

Individual stories like the Burt family can only take the analysis so far, and aggregate circulation statistics offer another compelling element to the story of the crossover reading habits of the people of Muncie in the 1890s. Astonishingly, the three most circulated authors in the entire library were in order Horatio Alger, Oliver Optic, and Harry Castlemon. Five other writers of boys' adventure stories cracked the top 20: Edward Ellis (5th), G.A. Henty (11th), Charles King (12th), Kirk Munroe (16th), and John T. Trowbridge (19th).[15] Studies of library circulation data have yielded surprising results. Particularly surprising is the fact that Horatio Alger was the undisputed king of the Muncie Public Library.[16] The people of Muncie borrowed Alger's books 9,230 times, 1,500 times more than the second-place author and 4,000 more than the third. Even Louisa May Alcott's books paled in comparison, circulating only 2,120 times. By themselves the eight boys' writers who cracked the top twenty in circulation accounted for 30,846 out of 175,178 total transactions in the library, or 17.6 per cent of all books and magazines checked out. If other prominent boys' writers like R.M. Ballantyne, Edward Stratemeyer, Frank Stockton, James Otis, Everett Tomlinson, and William Drysdale (this is by no means an exhaustive list from the library) are added to the circulation numbers of juvenile magazines and the two most popular writers of girls' literature, Martha Finley and Louisa May Alcott, they account for more than 25 per cent of the entire library's circulation transactions. Ironically, with the exception of perhaps Stockton and Alcott, these were exactly the kinds of books young people were encouraged not to read by many educators and professional librarians. They were not "socially desirable" and rarely appear in surveys of what children were reading in this period or what they should have been reading.[17] Yet, just as Julieanne Lamond has found, similar types of "light," "genre" fiction writers had massive circulation numbers in the late nineteenth century and dominated transactions in the Lambton Mechanics' and Miners' Institute just as they did in the Muncie Public Library. In spite of opposition from educators and librarians this type of fiction was immensely popular. Clearly, juvenile literature played a key role in the Muncie Public Library and was part of at least one out of every four transactions.[18] One of the primary reasons that these books were so readily available in the Muncie Public Library was that, like the majority of such institutions, it did not have a professional librarian concerned with promoting the "right" kind of reading before 1902.

Circulation statistics can also be examined by sex, age, and occupation classification. Whenever these categories are sorted in these ways the overall number of searchable transactions are necessarily narrowed because of incomplete demographic information for all patrons. Broken down by sex, the transaction total number with identifiable information is 166,192 transactions – 45 per cent by men and 55 per cent by women of all ages. When exploring the data for the occupational category, the total number of transactions with such data is 132,500 transactions. The database sorts occupation classification into five categories and the percentages are out of the total transactions: total blue collar 38 per cent, unskilled 8 per cent, semi-skilled 10 per cent, skilled 20 per cent, total white collar 62 per cent, low white collar 36 per cent, and high white collar 26 per cent. White-collar patrons generally dominated the sheer number of transactions, particularly the low-white-collar category. Using almost any search parameter, the lower-white-collar category usually accounts for the most transactions out of the unskilled, semi-skilled, skilled, and high-white-collar subcategories.[19]

Since this study is focused on crossover reading, the ability to control for age in sorting the data is essential, but doing so created some interesting twists in the data. Controlling for age and still searching all transactions is more difficult because of the twelve-year range – readers who were nineteen in 1891 would be thirty-one in 1902. Even so, using the baseline of a birthdate in 1872, so as to capture all teen and young adult readers for the era, the database shows that just over 62 per cent of all transactions were performed by patrons under the age of thirty-one. Boys and young men accounted for 52 per cent and girls and young women were 48 per cent of all readers under thirty-one years of age. Looking at the occupational category breakdown within the age breakdown also yielded surprising results that varied from the overall statistics and provided a caution about taking the domination of lower-white-collar patrons at face value without further analysis of the data. The class differentiation in transactions softened for the younger patrons (under the age of thirty-one) with blue-collar youth claiming 43 per cent of transactions and white-collar 57 per cent – a 5 per cent difference from the overall averages. Young women and girls went the opposite way, with white-collar patrons checking out 64 per cent of all items and blue-collar only 36 per cent. Young men and boys completely went against the grain of the dominant statistical trends; blue-collar patrons performed just over 50 per cent of all transactions and white-collar just under 50 per cent. The low-white-collar group was still the largest of the five occupational subgroups, but a narrow focus on this trend hides the fact that among younger men and boys blue-collar readers checked out as many books and magazines as their white-collar counterparts.

Sorting the data into more discrete parts by examining individual authors yielded even more surprising and telling results that are evident in table 10.1. The great problem with using this database is the massive amount of data that is generated. It is easy to get lost in minutiae, chasing down patron after patron. Only by condensing the data do patterns emerge. The first definitive result was that crossover reading by adults played an important role throughout the twelve-year period. Again, I divided older and younger readers by searching based on birthdates for those born after 1871 and before 1872. For none of the top boys' authors did adult readership fall below 15 per cent of total transactions. Horatio Alger, Oliver Optic, Edward Ellis, John Trowbridge, James Otis,

R.M. Ballantyne, and Thomas Knox all had greater than 20 per cent adult readership. Standouts for adult readership were clearly Frank Stockton with almost 42 per cent and Charles King with just over 37 per cent (table 10.1 and fig. 10.1). These statistics are born out by the Reading What Middletown Read search tool at Washington University, which is employed by Lynne Tatlock in chapter 11 of this volume. It sorts data according to age much more precisely than is possible by using the raw data from the database, but it cuts out about a third of the total transactions for various reasons.[20] King's crossover popularity with older patrons makes sense since he was a former general in the U.S. Army and wrote histories of battles and wars that could attract a mature audience. John Roy Musick and Paul Ford demonstrate that crossover reading also worked in the reverse. These men both wrote popular histories not explicitly directed towards a juvenile market, and yet their readership was primarily under the age of thirty-one.

The second definitive result was that girls and women also constituted a significant readership of these overtly male-oriented authors even though in most of their books girls and women play decidedly secondary roles; and boys also constituted a significant minority of readers of titles by girls' writers like Martha Finley.[21] Female readership ranged between 11 and 53 per cent for every writer of boys' literature in the sample for an average of almost 19 per cent for all juvenile writers, Alger through King (table 10.1, fig. 10.3). Horatio Alger was clearly the most popular with girls and young women of the eight writers of boys' literature who were among the top twenty in library circulation totals (Castlemon, Optic, Ellis, Henty, King, Munroe, Trowbridge). Alger's overall popularity in the Muncie Public Library is the most likely reason for this because the qualitative differences between Alger's and Optic's novels are minute.[22] Conversely, boys constituted 16 per cent of Martha Finley's readers and more than 35 per cent of Louisa May Alcott's audience (table 10.1). It might appear strange that girls and young women constituted such a large part of the audience for these books if one simply looked at cultural commentators like Theodore Roosevelt, who subscribed to the idea of clear separate spheres for men and women, particularly given that these novels often presented a more strenuous image of masculininity.[23] The reality of reading habits was vastly more complicated than Roosevelt's stark gender division. It is in reality not surprising at all that girls and young women constituted a large minority of the readership of these boys' novels. It makes sense given what we know about the highly eclectic reading tastes of boys and girls in this era. Theodore Roosevelt could

Table 10.1. Juvenile Reading: Age Distribution

Author	> 31 years old (Born pre-1871)	< 31 years old (Born post-1871)	< 31 years old Female	< 31 years old Male	< 31 years old Blue Collar	< 31 years old White Collar
All books	38.75	61.24	48.2	51.79	43.48	56.46
Horatio Alger*	20.1	79.91	23.66	76.33	51.37	48.62
Harry Castlemon*	15	80.04	13.5	86.87	52.62	47.37
Oliver Optic*	23.88	76.11	12.84	37.71	47.98	52.01
Edward Ellis*	23.8	76.19	12.04	87.95	55.14	44.85
G.A. Henty*	25.42	74.57	14.82	85.17	48.97	51.02
William O. Stoddard*	19.08	80.91	10.94	89.05	49.22	50.77
John T. Trowbridge*	24.76	75.73	17.51	82.48	50.79	49.20
James Otis*	20.95	79.04	15.77	84.22	53.37	47.62
Frank Stockton*	41.97	58.02	52.73	47.26	45.51	54.48
Kirk Munroe*	16.35	83.64	10.45	89.54	56	43.99
R.M. Ballantyne*	27.61	72.38	16.07	83.92	52.2	47.79
Edward Stratemeyer*	18.77	81.22	11.55	88.44	48.46	51.53
Everett Tomlinson*	16.85	83.14	11.26	88.73	56.99	43
William Drysdale*	17.97	82.02	18.25	81.74	48.9	48.1
Thomas Knox*	25.21	74.78	13.95	86.04	59.72	40.27
Randolph Hill*	24.44	77.55	13.15	86.84	47.91	52.08
Charles King*	37.35	62.66	47.89	52.1	46.3	53.69
St. Nicholas Magazine	31.27	68.72	35.5	64.49	53.7	46.29
Harper's Young People Magazine	25.81	74.18	26.7	73.29	46.71	53.28
John Roy Musick	32.24	67.75	17.24	82.7	51.09	48.9
Paul Ford	42.17	57.82	70.9	29.8	24.32	75.67
Martha Finley	29.18	70.81	83.67	16.32	57.87	42.12
Louisa May Alcott	31.44	68.42	69.46	30.53	54.66	45.33

*All authors who explicitly wrote for a juvenile boy audience are listed in order of circulation popularity. The magazines, Musick, Ford, Finley, and Alcott are included for comparison.

urge gender differentiation all he liked, but the data show that boys and girls often crossed over and read books aimed towards a specific gender (table 10.1).

The final area that yielded significant data was the blue-collar/white-collar split among boys and young male readers. Out of the 17 authors I examined, 12 had a blue-collar/white-collar split in readership that was within 3 percentage points, and blue-collar readers were the majority for Alger, Castlemon, Ellis, Trowbridge, Otis, Munroe, Ballantyne, Tomlinson, and Knox. Ellis, Munroe, Tomlinson, and Knox were all more than

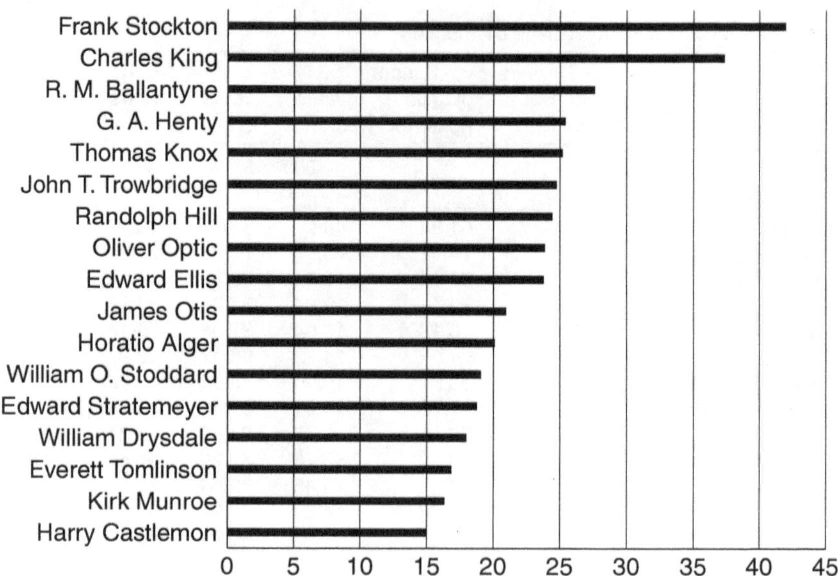

10.1 Readers > 31 Years Old

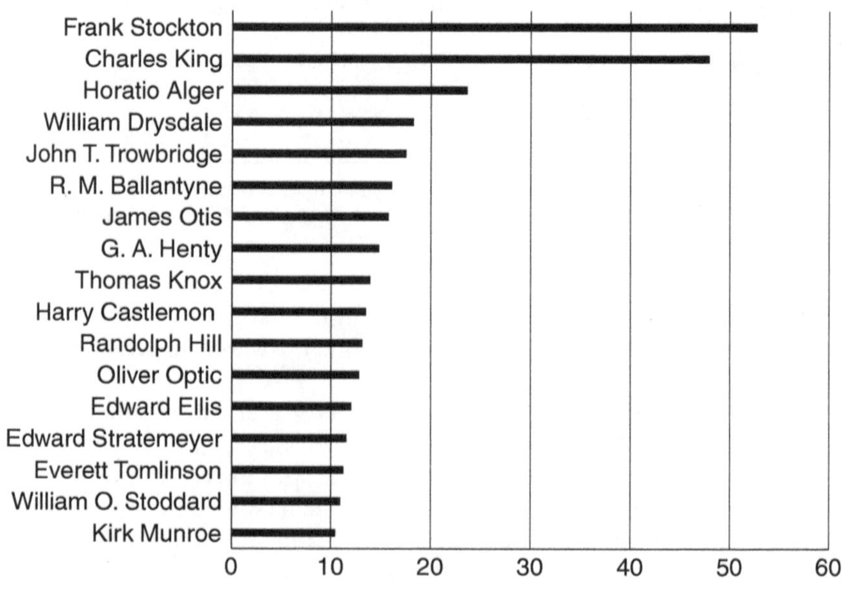

10.2 Female Readers < 31

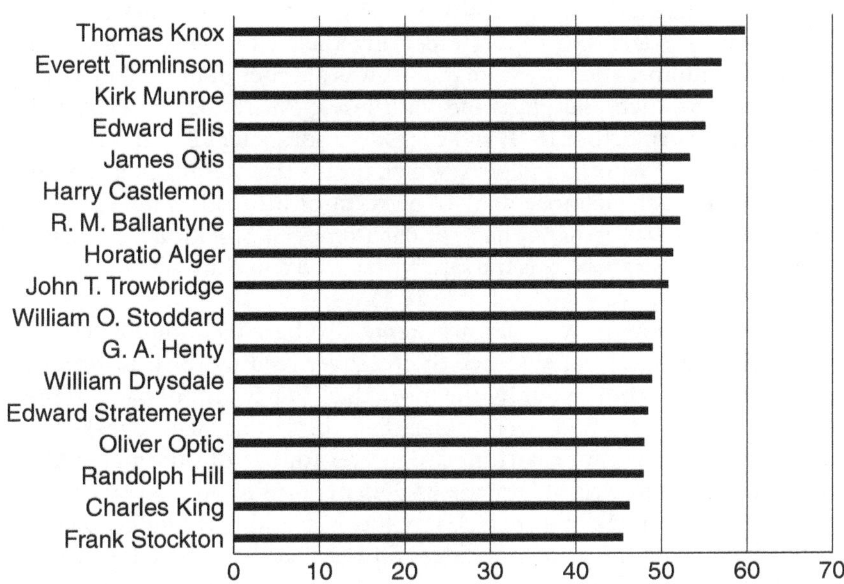

10.3 Blue Collar Readers < 31

seven percentage points higher among blue-collar readers. Figure. 10.3 shows the high percentage of blue-collar readers for all of these authors and the narrow range, 59.7to 45.5 per cent. Young females (fig. 10.2) and readers over the age of thirty-one (fig. 10.1) were attracted to only certain authors, such as Frank Stockton, and not others, such as Kirk Munroe. In short, boys and young men of all backgrounds borrowed all of these writers, whereas girls, young women, and all readers over thirty-one years old were far more selective in which authors they chose to read.

Among the individual authors a few had such distinctive results that they deserve to be discussed separately. Frank Stockton's numbers illustrate the fact that while he was a popular children's writer for part of his career, starting in the 1880s he began to write primarily for adult audiences and he at times had strong female characters. His novel *Rudder Grange* is an excellent example of both aforementioned elements and was a popular book in the Muncie Public Library.[24] Stockton was a good boys' fiction writer and was hired by Mary Mapes Dodge as her assistant editor at *St. Nicholas Magazine* from 1873 to 1877 specifically to bring more boys' adventure literature into what was, and still is, considered the best children's magazine of the era.[25] His stories are sharp, energetic, and normally of better quality than those by Alger and Optic, especially their later work.[26] Stockton's circulation numbers demonstrate that he was a writer popular with adults, with young women and girls, and with boys. Nearly 42 per cent of his readers were born before 1871, and of readers born after 1871 almost 53 per cent were young women and girls, which means that young men and boys made up only a shade more than 47 per cent of his readership. Only one other author, Charles King, had similar numbers. Stockton's circulation numbers demonstrate he was the rare writer who could attract wide readership from almost every group (table 10.1).

The results from *St. Nicholas Magazine* also bear mentioning. Scholars have provided anecdotal evidence of crossover reading for this magazine and this finding is borne out by the more than 31 per cent of patrons born before 1871, all of whom were older than thirty-one, who checked out the magazine. Even more startling are figures for patrons born after 1871. Young women and girls only made up 35.5 per cent of young readers! The long-time editor of *St. Nicholas Magazine*, Mary Mapes Dodge, believed that girls made up the primary readership and that they needed to work to attract more boys.[27] Clearly, either Dodge's assumption was incorrect, or Muncie had strange readership patterns, or Dodge did a remarkable job in attracting boys to the magazine in the 1870s and 1880s.

By examining the data in aggregate, however, certain lending tendencies are obscured. The data on older patrons checking out juvenile books and magazines seemed particularly susceptible to misinterpretation (fig. 10.1). Using the raw data from table 10.1 and the Reading What Middletown Read search engine we can easily find that at least 20 per cent of Alger readers were over the age of twenty.[28] Reading What Middletown Read even provides a breakdown by exact age. The problem with these statistics, however, is that they cannot account for who actually read these books. Were adults checking out these books for themselves or for children? Carrie Burt is a great example. From January 1892 to June 1896, Carrie checked out exactly five books by Horatio Alger, three by Castlemon, one by Oliver Optic, and one by Edward Ellis. It is a reasonable assumption that she was checking these novels out not for herself but for one of her three sons. At this time only George was actively using his card. While it was common for patrons to allow other people to use their cards, the Burt family never used each other's cards. Not one time in hundreds of transactions did Carrie loan her patron number to her children nor did the children use another brother's card. We know this because each transaction in the ledgers included the card number and the name of the person using it. But Carrie could have checked out books in her own name for the boys. Her reading choices ran to writers such as Charlotte Brontë and Oliver Wendell Holmes, and numerous historical romances. Still, it is impossible to discount that she did read some of these novels, perhaps to vet them for her boys or for simple enjoyment. Lizzie Burson Claypool, the wife of a local stock dealer, checked out only one boys' book, Alger's *Luke Larkin's Luck*. She was born in 1854 and checked out exactly 100 books during the twelve-year circulation ledger run. Claypool had no pattern of checking out books for children and she had no children that appear in library records. Again, it seems likely that she checked this book out for herself, though it is possible the novel was for a visiting relative or friend's child. While Burt and Claypool's reading habits are open for debate, another older reader, James Nelson, checked out boys' literature almost exclusively for the entire twelve-year period, when he was thirty-seven to forty-nine years old, and he was single. Given the overall statistics and the sheer number of older patrons checking out juvenile literature, it seems that, while the percentages must be treated cautiously, adult crossover readership did occur in relatively substantial numbers.

It is feasible to try to control for adults checking out books for children as much as possible when examining the transactions for a single author. Instead of looking at all nine thousand transactions for an author like Alger, I chose a writer with a smaller number of books and transactions, but one who would expand into tremendous popularity by the first decades of the twentieth century, Edward Stratemeyer. By looking at all of the patrons of a single author one can identify patrons' exact ages instead of relying upon the larger age range. Eight of Stratemeyer's early books are in the collection, including five histories on the Spanish-American War and three career stories, which circulated 545 times to 216 patrons.[29] I examined each patron who checked out one of his books. This can only be accomplished by clicking on each individual person and determining the exact age of the patron by locating their recorded birthdate and the date of the transaction. Of these 216 patrons, 102, or 47 per cent, were ages 10–19 with an average age of 14.5. It is difficult to tell if the remaining adult patrons checked out these books for themselves or for their children, but at least 28 adults over the age of 20 with no apparent children checked out Stratemeyer books. Including the adults in the calculations provides an average Stratemeyer reader age of 17, and in all likelihood, given the cautious manner in which I counted possible adult readers, the average age was higher. When establishing which adults checked out the books for themselves I chose to count only single adults and adults who had been married less than six years with no identifiable children. Of these 28 adults, 20 were in their twenties, 4 in their thirties, 3 in their forties, and 1 in his fifties for an average age of 27.4 years. Even this very conservative count shows that 13 per cent of Stratemeyer readers were adults over the age of 19. This finding is very consistent with the more general analysis of Stratemeyer readership from the Reading What Middletown Read data which provides unfiltered data that demonstrate 28 per cent of Stratemeyer readers were 20 and older as well as the raw data from table 10.1, which shows that almost 19 per cent of Alger readers were over the age of 31.[30] These data strongly suggest that the average age of Stratemeyer readers in 1900 could have been as high as the late teens or early twenties. All of the evidence indicates a strong pattern of adult crossover reading.

Given these very strong trends of adult crossover reading in Muncie it is amazing that adult reading of juvenile literature declined markedly within just a few decades after 1902. Stratemeyer also provides insight into the end of crossover reading in the early twentieth century as literature became more age specialized and sexual themes appeared commonly in adult literature and feature films. Juvenile reading of adult literature became increasingly problematic as sexual themes that were inappropriate for young audiences blossomed in the 1920s. While adult literature quickly adapted to the looser morality and public sexuality of the 1920s, juvenile fiction remained tied to a stricter moral code for obvious reasons.[31] At the same time that these moral changes were transforming adult literature, a new kind of juvenile book started to dominate the market. After Stratemeyer created his successful syndicate by 1906, he began developing series novels that would quickly climb to dominate juvenile reading – particularly the Rover Boys (1899) and Tom Swift (1910). While literally hundreds of series were published for young people in the early twentieth century, the Rover Boys and Tom Swift novels were the two top-selling series, respectively selling 5 million and 6.5 million copies, until the advent of the Hardy Boys series in the 1920s and the Nancy Drew juggernaut in the 1930s.[32] These books were so popular that a famous 1925 survey of more than 36,000 students' reading habits found that the Tom Swift series books were the most mentioned, 98 per cent of students read series books, and Stratemeyer Syndicate books dominated the preferences of fifth through eighth graders.[33] In a 1929 Knoxville survey of junior high school reading habits, Tom Swift books were second only to the Bible as the most read single book over one week, and the Tom Swift and Rover Boys books came in first and third as the most read books by boys over the current school year. Similar results appeared in a 1930 Pittsburgh survey of junior high school reading.[34]

The fact that adults and children began to stop crossover reading was illustrated by the decline in the average age of Stratemeyer readers. What Middletown Read demonstrates that the average reader age for Stratemeyer from 1891 to 1902 was at least 17 and probably higher. The 1925 Winnetka, 1929 Knoxville, and 1930 Pittsburgh surveys clearly demonstrate that series books dominated boys' reading between the ages of 10 and 14, which indicates that the average age of Stratemeyer readers was declining. Indeed, the 1925 Winnetka Survey found that the average Tom Swift reader's age was 12.3 years old, which was more than two years younger than the average teenage Stratemeyer reader in the Muncie Public Library 23 years earlier. By the 1960s Stratemeyer publishers targeted 10 to 14 year olds and 20 years later in the 1980s focused on eight to 10 year olds.[35] As crossover reading declined the average age of readers for popular boys' literature fell. Changes in the quality did not drive this age shift, since the Stratemeyer novels are of very similar quality to what was produced by Optic and Alger. Boys had always been the primary audience of boys' novels, and it is clear from the reading patterns of Frank, George, and Robert Burt that their preference for the juvenile writers faded as they grew older and the likes of Castlemon and Henty appear far less frequently in their transactions as the Burts aged.

Part of the decline of crossover reading is almost certainly a factor of reading level. Reading What Middletown Read also provides an analysis of reading level of the most popular books in the Muncie Public Library. Unsurprisingly, Alger's books are uniformly in the lowest difficulty half of the spectrum, which might explain his popularity. But then again so is Mark Twain's *Huckleberry Finn*. More surprising is that other juvenile writers score in the top half of reading difficulty, including Castlemon, Munroe, Ellis, and Ballantyne.[36] Even so, as the school year expanded, attendance became mandatory in the Progressive Era, and high schools rapidly grew by the 1920s, there is little doubt that the reading level of all Americans increased. By the 1920s younger boys were reading more of these types of books than their predecessors had been during the 1890s. Young men of the next generation stopped reading juveniles even earlier. What the falling readership age of Stratemeyer's series fiction starkly illustrated was the decline of crossover readership that had defined American reading patterns before the 1920s.

The Muncie Public Library clearly played a central role for the citizens of Muncie. The library circulation records run through the 1890s, which was a decade of tremendous growth for the city. Muncie began 1890 with a population of 11,345 and ended the decade with 20,942 residents.[37] Of these 20,942 residents, 4008, 19 per cent, had a library card for the Muncie Public Library. How the books the people of Muncie read influenced them is a far more difficult question to answer, but one answer is Frank Burt's story, which sounds like it is straight from the Horatio Alger novels he read as a child. Starting as an office boy with the Ball Brothers Glass Company, he worked his way up over the next fifty-five years to clerk, bookkeeper, salesman, plant manager, and finally to sales manager of the consumer products division before his retirement in 1950. Almost immediately after retirement Frank enrolled in Ball State Teachers College as a full-time student and earned his degree in 1954. He served as an Elder in Muncie's First Presbyterian Church and was an important leader in Muncie's Masons.[38] Frank Burt was a native son who exemplified what the founders of the library hoped it would provide: a commitment to a broader intellectual culture and refinement that would lead to intellectual refinement, success, and respectability. Carrie Burt and her three sons were emblematic of the dedication that the people of Muncie had to their library as a central institution in the city and to the importance of reading in their daily lives, which connected them to a much broader culture, if in somewhat surprising ways.

NOTES

1 What Middletown Read, http://www.bsu.edu/libraries/wmr/. All statistical data in this project is generated from this database.
2 The library was open for 92 months in this 12-year time span.
3 From when George began his card, January 1892, to his last transaction, July 1902, minus the 29 months the library was closed leaves a total of 86 months George was actively borrowing. Frank's active transactions were over a 72-month period and Robert's transactions over a 50-month period.
4 Questions of readership have been exceptionally difficult to answer and most solid data have come from surveys of reading habits. For two of the best explorations of readership, see Nackenoff (1994, 181–203) and Denning (1987, 27–46).
5 D. Macleod (1998, 129–31); Mintz (2004, 186); A. MacLeod (1994, 117–20); Howells (1900, 940); Lears (1981, 103–6); Nelson (1989); Gannon (2004).
6 Sicherman (2002, 140–1); Schneirov (1994, 5, 60).
7 Canby (1934, 208); Sicherman, (2002, 141–9); L. Stevenson (1991, 33–4).

8 Nackenoff (1994, 250–60); Garrison (1971, 327–34; 1979, 207–17); Carrier (1965, 179–233, 267–71, 344–53); Carrier (1985, 219–94); Alice Jordan (1948, 32).

9 There was certainly adventure literature in the eighteenth and nineteenth centuries that contained the elements of violence and domination that strongly appealed to young people, particularly books by Sir Walter Scott, James Fenimore Cooper, Alexandre Dumas, and Jules Verne. These books, however, were primarily written for adult audiences and became part of the children's library over the course of decades.

10 For scathing attacks upon dime novels, see Denning (1987, 9–13, 27–61); Carrier (1965, 1985); Garrison (1979, 211–13); Nackenoff (1994, 50–60); Gannon and Thompson (1992, 119).

11 Nye (1970, 61–87); Rodgers (1974, 125–52); Nackenoff (1994); Scharnhorst and Bales (1985); Scharnhorst (1980); Billman (1986); Johnson (1993).

12 What Middletown Read, http://www.bsu.edu/libraries/wmr/.

13 M. Connelly (2008, 27–31); See Billman (1986, 1–45); Johnson (1982, xiii–xxxiii, 1–17; 1993, 18–63, 162); Nye (1970, 76–87).

14 Nye (1970, 61–87); Billman (1986, 1–54); Johnson (1993, 162).

15 I refer to William T. Adams as "Oliver Optic" and Charles A. Fosdick as "Harry Castlemon" because these writers are listed by their pseudonyms in the library registers.

16 Horatio Alger was one of the first authors who mass produced juvenile adventure novels with distinctive middle-class values. Individual sales of Alger's books did not make him such a cultural phenomenon – though *Ragged Dick* was a bestseller and *Tattered Tom* and *Fame and Fortune* came close to the mark – but the overall sales of his nearly one hundred juveniles clearly did. Alger himself estimated his sales at around 800,000 copies during his lifetime. Ironically, in the twenty years after Alger's death, cheap reprints of his books fuelled a remarkable resurgence in Alger's popularity, selling an estimated 17 to 20 million copies, though in the 1920s his popularity waned quickly. Scharnhorst (1980, 140–1).

17 Arthur Jordan (1921, 1). I would encourage anyone interested in understanding reading preferences to use this source. The entire first chapter explores several different surveys on reading preferences from the 1897 to 1920 before he executes his own survey.

18 What Middletown Read, http://www.bsu.edu/libraries/wmr/. These overall circulation statistics can be found by clicking the "User Guide" tab at the bottom of the home page then by clicking the "Data Summaries" tab.

19 The occupational categories employed in the What Middletown Read database are unskilled (blue collar), semiskilled (blue collar), skilled (blue collar), low white collar, and high white collar. These occupational groupings

are taken from a long-established and commonly employed system devised by Alba M. Edwards (1933). Children and other non-working patrons were categorized according to the occupation of the head of their household. See also Thernstrom (1999, 289–302).

20 Reading What Middletown Read, http://talus.artsci.wustl.edu/ballStatePresentation041812/. This search tool makes examining data much quicker and provides statistics that are very close the raw data statistics.

21 Nackenoff (1994, 221); Billman (1986).

22 Rodgers (1974, 125–52).

23 Roosevelt (1900, 573) urged boys to adopt the same "strenuous life" values and behaviors that he had proposed for men just a few months earlier; Kimmel (1996, 127, 139, 141–55); Lears (1981, 104–39).

24 Frank Stockton, *Rudder Grange* (New York: Scribners, 1879); "Frank Richard Stockton," *Dictionary of American Biography* (New York: Charles Scribner's Sons, 1936). Gale Biography in Context. Web. 9 Feb. 2013.

25 Fuller (1984, 20); Kelly (1974, 24); "What 'St. Nicholas' Has Done for Girls and Boys" (1890).

26 "Jack-in-the-Pulpit," *St. Nicholas* 2 (August 1875): 648–9; Fuller (1984, 28); Gannon and Thompson (1992, 16, 19); Frank Stockton, "Buccaneers of Our Coast," *St. Nicholas* 25 (November, February, May 1898): 4–14, 279–87, 549–58.

27 "Jack-in-the-Pulpit," *St. Nicholas* 2 (August, 1875): 648–49; Fuller (1984, 28); Gannon and Thompson (1992, 19).

28 Reading What Middletown Read, http://talus.artsci.wustl.edu/censusQuery/queryDemographicByReading.php.

29 What Middletown Read Project, http://www.bsu.edu/libraries/wmr/.

30 Reading What Middletown Read, http://talus.artsci.wustl.edu/censusQuery/queryDemographicByReading.php.

31 White (1992, 16–56); Breu (2005, 1–22); Madden (1968); Wilkinson (1984); Sklar (1992); Mellen (1977, 27–138); Haskell (1973, 91); May (1980, 59, 98–9, 237–41).

32 Billman (1986, 17–26, 37); M. Connelly (2008, 5–46); Johnson (1982, xiii–xxxiii, 1–17); Johnson (1993, 162).

33 Ross (2009, 640).

34 Jennings (1929, 339, 344); Rinehart (1931, 31–3); Washburne and Vogel (1927a, 1927b).

35 Ross (2009, 640); Jennings (1929, 339, 344); Rinehart (1931, 31–3) Washburne and Vogel, (1927a, 1927b); Billman (1986, 95).

36 Reading What Middletown Read, http://talus.artsci.wustl.edu/muncie132WebContent/readingScores.html.

37 "Population of Places Having at Least 2,500 Inhabitants in 1900 and 1890," Table 91, 138 (Abstract of the Twelfth Census of the United States, 1902).

38 Minnetrista Heritage Archives, Frank E. Burt, 20 June 1947. This is a tribute book to Burt for his service to the Masons. In the back of the book is a program for a Mason's "Dad Burt Night" from 13 April 1963, and most of the information here comes from the tribute letters, particularly one from Edmund F. Ball, President of the Ball Brothers Company.

11 Romance in the Province: Reading German Novels in Middletown, USA

LYNNE TATLOCK

What does it mean for popular literature to migrate across national boundaries via translation, marketing, and publication? To what extent, furthermore, does reading such literature constitute cosmopolitan reading if that literature has become homogenized as a result of its circulation, that is, less recognizable as an Other to be consciously embraced and instead perceived as always already native fare? In his study of canon formation in nineteenth-century Germany and America, Hugh Ridley begins to address the second question when he observes that popular literature tends in fact to participate in and emanate from supranational taste formations and therefore may never belong to any particular culture to begin with: "[U]nder a certain level," he maintains, "popular literature loses any element of national reference and shows itself to be not only international in conception and production, but also both at home in and foreign to every culture within which it is read."[1]

Even literature that at some point may have been felt as national in its home context will be perceived differently abroad, perhaps received in terms of pre-existing ideas about its original context but most certainly in terms of the concerns of the receiving culture. In other words, a novel originally written in the German language in a European context is not necessarily read in North America as markedly foreign or particular to any one historical place once it has been translated, repackaged, sold, and circulated in a new context where it, as a translation, is in effect a native product. Furthermore, such an international novel may be enjoyed and sought after in different national contexts simply because it resembles other favourite books and not because readers understand it to paint a picture of German life "as it really is." Nevertheless, the very fact of its being one among many such "German" books, in a form of branding, can promise the kind of reading experience that readers seek while encouraging associations of certain ideas, feelings, plots, and mores with a place called Germany. Interest in translated popular literature may therefore have more to do with plot, genre, motif, and values than specific national origins, even if national origin is one way of identifying books that offer pleasurable reading and even if information about another culture is a secondary effect of reading.

Such perception of sameness in supposing shared norms and values certainly could fuel a universalist sensibility. It does not, however, necessarily come about via the "recognition of difference" and thus probably does not constitute the acceptance of difference and embrace of those different communities as equals, which Ulrich Beck and Edgar Grande assert as the sine qua non of cosmopolitanism. This question of cosmopolitanism constitutes a central concern of this volume to which we will return below.[2]

As we shall see in what follows, in the late nineteenth century a set of German novels written in the wake of *Jane Eyre*, novels that pleasure readers with adventure and happy endings within domestic parameters and that portray spunky heroines who attain their heart's desire, occupied significant space in the reading of certain demographic groups in Muncie, Indiana. While we cannot know for certain what these historical readers took away from their reading, we can reasonably speculate, along with Ridley, that these texts did exert authority over the imagination of their readers and that this fiction therefore once constituted "a force to be reckoned with."[3] These German novels represent a world in which virtue prevails, sentiment and emotion matter, redemption and happiness are possible, and marriage is their reliable guarantor. In these novels, especially those characters living in the so-called home towns in the German regions distant from modern urban life, achieve this happiness founded in intimate heterosexual bonding and its accompanying social renewal.

Patterns of library transactions in Muncie suggest that especially female readers bought these scenarios and these ideas and returned to them repeatedly in their selection of books to read, particularly in their teens and twenties. Borrowers sometimes read these German novels serially – apparently identifying them by author, translator, and/or branded series – and sometimes simply read them in the context of the English-language novels they somewhat resembled.

I have told the story of many of these books and their American publishers and translators at length in *German Writing, American Reading: Women and the Import of Fiction (1866–1917)*. This essay takes a closer and renewed look at the historical reading of these books. Transaction data from the What Middletown Read database, which I could not consider in any sustained way in that first project, make visible patterns of reading by ordinary readers, suggesting why these Americans read these German novels in the province.[4] Let us now turn to the texts, the books, and their readers.

I. Crossing the Atlantic

Following the American Civil War and into the new century, in the absence of an enforceable international copyright law and in the interest of profit, American publishers and translators rendered German books into American English and marketed and sold them to American readers, thus making them widely available to the largest national reading audience that had ever existed.[5] An important subset of these German books in American translation was composed of entertaining domestic fiction of various stripes, fiction largely by women that usually had made its first appearance in the German-speaking territories in serialized form in such periodical publications as the *Gartenlaube* and the *Deutsche Roman-Zeitung*. The authors of these novels had written them largely for venues that emphatically announced their Germanness and, in the case of the *Gartenlaube*, pursued a program of promoting identifiably German production – from fiction to illustration.[6] As Henry Pochmann's tallies confirm, three of the approximately twenty authors whose works belong to this subset of novels number among the most translated German authors of any kind in nineteenth-century America. Moreover, in Pochmann's rankings under the rubric "lesser fiction and prose writers" translated from German into English, three authors of domestic romance – E. Werner (pseud. of Elisabeth Bürstenbinder), E. Marlitt (pseud. of Eugenie John), and Wilhelmine Heimburg (pseud. of Berta Behrens) – occupy three of the five top spots.[7]

In many cases of the approximately one hundred original novels by approximately twenty authors that constituted this vogue of German fiction, more than one translation circulated in the United States – Werner's *Flammenzeichen*, for example, in as many as six.[8] From 1868 to 1917, the approximately two hundred translations of these many novels proliferated in multiple editions and reprint editions that amounted to hundreds of thousands of books. One of the first of these novels to be translated, Marlitt's *Old Mam'selle's Secret*, circulated in at least 108 issues over sixty years. As the translations, editions, and issues accumulated, the vogue crested around 1900.

Sometimes the title pages of these novels signalled that they were translated from the German; sometimes they did not. One important subset of this group, published by J.B. Lippincott, to which we will return repeatedly, did, however, visibly circulate with a "German" label: while marketed, sold, and purchased individually as well, this group of novels began appearing in the 1870s in advertisements as a series labelled "Popular Works from the German, Translated by Mrs. A.L. Wister." Over the course of four decades, the name Annis Lee Wister, supported by Lippincott's marketing, came to be associated with good reads from Germany. In this vein the *New York Times* noted in 1907 on the occasion of Wister's last translation from the German: "We have known novel readers to make a complete list of her translations, with the intent to read them all, with anticipations of pleasure."[9]

Wister's translations had in fact quickly become popular American reading. When in 1876, 39 American publishers participated in a contest with *Publishers' Weekly* to select the most saleable novels in the United States,[10] eight of Wister's first nine translations of German fiction made the list of the 204 most saleable novels: Marlitt's *Old Mam'selle's Secret* placed mumber 23, followed by four more novels by Marlitt – in position 27, *The Second Wife*; position 50, *Gold Elsie*; 95, *The Little Moorland Princess*; and 114, *Countess Gisela* – and in position 119, Ernst Wichert's *The Green Gate*; 180, Wilhelmine von Hillern's *Only a Girl*; and 185, Fanny Lewald's *Hulda*. The only other German novel on this list was Auerbach's *On the Heights*. Otherwise the list comprises 182 English-language novels, nine French novels, *Don Quixote*, and Hans Christian Andersen's *The Improvisatore*. The French novels (works by Victor Hugo, Alexandre Dumas père, Eugène Sue, Jules Verne, George Sand, Madame de Staël, Alain-René Lesage) offer entertainment different from the domestic romance that characterizes the German group.

The 1876 list, headed by Miss Mulock's *John Halifax Gentleman* in first place and Charlotte Brontë's *Jane Eyre* in second, offers a view of the literary landscape in which this German domestic fiction circulated: recent and older fiction, romance, domestic fiction, historical novels, and some outliers. *Jane Eyre* looms particularly large as both a novel popular in the nineteenth century and one that would, unlike many other works on this list, endure as classic reading.

The resemblance of the German novels, especially Marlitt's, to *Jane Eyre* merits a closer look. Both textual analysis of Marlitt's novels in particular and preliminary experiments with topic modelling reveal that, in their support of domesticity and marriage within romance plots, Wister's selections bear an affinity to *Jane Eyre* and thus also to many other English-language novels on the list that share common elements with Brontë's novel.[11] Indeed, the German novels belonged to a long-enduring international taste formation visible in 1876 in the liking for *Jane Eyre*. As I outline below, the choices of Muncie library patrons betray a preference for romance plots in provincial domestic settings, be these German or otherwise, that exhibit a resemblance to *Jane Eyre*, even as library users actually checked out Brontë's novel much less often than its German avatars.

II. German *Jane Eyres*

The tenth-most-read author in the Muncie Public Library, Marlitt, experienced from 1868 into the 1920s by far the greatest proliferation of American editions and issues among the novels that I here label "German domestic romance novels," that is, fiction built around love stories that conclude in marriage or restored marriages and that evince clear allegiance to family and home as "the site of identity formation, conflict, culture, and politics, indeed, as the place where history is made."[12] The origins, popularity, and circulation of Marlitt's novels and novellas most forcefully address the questions raised by Ridley's sense that popular literature may be at home nowhere and everywhere, for although Marlitt wrote in a national context for an emergent national public, a groundbreaking and internationally beloved British novel profoundly influenced her work.

All of Marlitt's fiction first appeared in the national liberal family magazine *Die Gartenlaube* and, as has often been pointed out, contributed substantially to increasing its circulation during the years 1865–87).[13] As Todd Kontje has shown, Marlitt's novels and novellas evince rich evidence of a particular historical epoch in a particular geographic place.[14] Indeed, Marlitt's evocation of her home region, Thüringen; her inclusion of references to historical events, certain turns of phrase, and material objects from her historical moment; and her incorporation of German high-cultural elements nicely fulfilled the express goals of the founder and editor of *Die Gartenlaube*, Ernst Keil, to create a "thoroughly German magazine" that projected German political unification.[15] Nevertheless, Marlitt's fiction almost immediately became an international phenomenon. Translated in its own time into at least ten languages (including both British and American English), it soon belonged to world reading.

German author though she was, from the start Marlitt did not write in a context devoid of reading material from abroad; indeed, in the nineteenth century favourite German reading, as Albert Martino's study of nineteenth-century German lending libraries has shown, was international in origin.

In addition to popular German-language authors including Marlitt, Germans avidly read Hugo, Sue, Verne, G. Sand, Oliphant, Thackeray, Marryat, Scott, Bulwer-Lytton, and H.C. Anderson – to name some favourites – in the period 1849–1914.[16] Marlitt, who served as companion and reader to Princess Mathilde von Schwarzburg-Sondershausen for ten years (1853–63) before she tried her own hand at fiction, surely had become well versed in the international world of novels and novel reading by the time she herself began writing. Her fiction especially evidences the influence of Charlotte Brontë's *Jane Eyre* (1847; first German translation 1848), which had circulated widely in Germany in English, in several German translations, and as a popular and often-performed play (1853) during the decade and a half before her first work appeared in print.[17]

Before we turn our attention to the historical reading of Marlitt in the United States alongside *Jane Eyre* and other English-language novels, a brief look at her novels and novellas as German avatars of *Jane Eyre* will highlight her literary debt to this important English work and provide a first indication of a long-enduring taste formation. First, the resemblance of Marlitt's fiction to *Jane Eyre* is by no means subtle or hidden. In an early review, the German literary pundit Rudolf von Gottschall indicated similarities in Marlitt's first full-length novel, *Goldelse*, to Brontë's novel and years later again pointed out in passing in his history of German literature that the English Jane, who herself belonged to a tradition already familiar in Germany, was the prototype for Marlitt's female protagonists.[18] In 1870, when he first noted that Goldelse was a "milder Jane Eyre" and that the object of her affection recalled Brontë's Rochester, Gottschall in any case recognized what any other experienced reader could have consciously recognized or at least instinctively felt.[19]

Of what do these resonances consist? First and foremost, we should not overlook the obvious, namely, that all of these works conclude happily after many trials. Characters overcome, with a marriage or a restored marriage, what Pamela Regis has termed "ritual death," a point in the narrative in which the hoped-for union of the hero and heroine and the happy resolution of the plot seem impossible.[20] Brontë and Marlitt both wrote novels in which domestic bliss is desirable and possible, though granted to few; these novels enrapture readers with the difficult journey necessary to reach that happy ending. Such endings of course define the romance genre more generally; Marlitt's affinity for *Jane Eyre* is closer still. While I cannot explore the similarities in detail here, the following brief review documents some of the striking similarities testifying to the enduring presence of *Jane Eyre* in Marlitt's oeuvre.

Marlitt locates her plots exclusively in regional settings and generally in a town or country mansion harbouring a secret that must be brought to the surface and put right to resolve conflict and restore social harmony. Her characters, like Mr Rochester and Jane, are well educated, sometimes bourgeois and sometimes lower nobility; the heroine is usually fifteen to twenty years younger than the hero. These matches may involve inequality of social status and experience, but they depend on the intelligence and courage of both parties. Often the woman, although in all but one of Marlitt's novels not officially a governess like Jane, displays a pedagogical bent, as does the eponymous Goldelse, who has just taught a music lesson when the novel opens. Family, in all its joys and horrors, is central to the plot, and a happy marriage (or projection thereof) in the concluding chapters holds out the hope that women (and men) will find contentment within domesticity.

More particularly, the following plots evidence similarities with *Jane Eyre*. Marlitt's *Goldelse* involves a backstory of a gypsy in effect held captive by a husband who worships her. The discovery of her hidden coffin enshrined in the castle in which the protagonist's family has settled provides not only a titillating plot element but raises central questions of freedom, ancestry, and inheritance. An insane woman named Bertha (recalling Brontë's Bertha Mason) meanwhile menaces the heroine. As Norbert Bachleitner points out, in *Amtmanns Magd* (The Bailiff's Maid) a governess must lead a double life while she straightens out family circumstances.[21] In *Das Heideprinzeßchen* (The Little Moorland Princess), the central character recounts her own story in the first person, as in *Jane Eyre*, concluding in the present moment of writing surrounded by husband and family. The hero suffers from compromised vision that ultimately heals; the heroine, diminutive like Jane, must uncover the mystery of secret apartments in the house, banish the horror of her profligate aunt who lurks just beyond the garden walls, and learn whom to trust. In *Das Geheimnis der alten Mamsell* (The Old Mam'selle's Secret) the orphaned Felicitas develops a crucial relationship with the maiden aunt whom the family has unjustly banished to a secret mansard apartment and ultimately marries the older son of the house. Like Jane, Felicitas is raised in an adoptive family as one of their own until the benevolent father dies, at which point her fortunes change for the worse. *Die zweite Frau* (The Second Wife) features a hidden woman of colonial origin who lies comatose as a result of a brutal attack by one of the novel's villains, somewhat recalling Brontë's Bertha Mason.[22] Moreover, Liana, the second wife, must contend with the vestiges of her husband Raoul's past: the misbehaved child from his first marriage, his first wife whose perfume still permeates the private spaces of the home, and the love who once abandoned him who is now free to marry him. Raoul has married Liana in search of a governess for his son without intending to consummate the marriage.

Blaubart (Blue Beard, translated as *Over Yonder*), furthermore, overtly gives voice to the affinity of Marlitt's plots to *Jane Eyre*, which, as Heta Pryrhönen argues, is a "Bluebeard" tale, in its reliance on the heroine's "[hysterical] quest for knowledge" that depends on "relating material spaces to mental states" and in its featuring of the captive or hidden woman, a plot element that recurs in *Goldelse*, *Geheimnis*, *Die zweite Frau*, and *Die Frau mit den Karfunkelsteinen* (The Lady with the Rubies) too.[23] In *Blaubart*, however, Marlitt, akin to another English novelist, Jane Austen in *Northanger Abby*, fashions a text that takes a mildly ironic stance towards the central heroine's overactive imagination: the woman who appears to be held captive in her neighbour's home is actually the male protagonist's sister who suffers from a disfiguring disease and has withdrawn from society of her own volition.

Curious heroines abound in Marlitt's texts, but they often misread the intentions of the hero (just as Jane almost wilfully misreads Rochester), even as they are also irresistibly drawn to him. Typically they cannot give voice (or indeed even consciously recognize) the love and sexual attraction they feel without first being coaxed into confession of their "true" feelings (as Rochester coaxes Jane). The fencing between the hero and heroine that structures sections of *Jane Eyre* also shapes Marlitt's plots. While the hero may appear to have the upper hand and while the heroines make mistakes in judgment, the novels also tend to conclude with the heroine exercising considerable control within the limited sphere of the household, just as Jane does, since after all Rochester has lost his left hand and is nearly blind. In plots of delayed gratification in which the German equivalent of Jane's "Reader, I married him" is all the more joyful because long in coming, Marlitt knew how to satisfy the taste for domestically inflected romance, as had Brontë with *Jane Eyre*.

While she did write additional novels, Brontë never offered her readers a second *Jane Eyre*. Marlitt, by contrast, penned ten novels and three novellas over twenty-three years, works of fiction that strongly resemble one another and also *Jane Eyre*. Marlitt's critics have frequently sniffed at the formulaic quality of her writing, yet her international success suggests that precisely this aspect played a crucial role in her popularity. It supported serial reading, giving publishers and readers multiple and repeated opportunity for profit and pleasure.

II. Historical Reading of German Novels in Translation

Abundant evidence exists for the enduring popularity in the United States of translated German domestic romance fiction well into the new century. Late nineteenth- and early twentieth-century library catalogues from libraries across the nation testify to the wide availability of German domestic fiction in translation, in some cases, as many as thirty or forty years after they were first published in America.[24] The multiple American translations of Marlitt's novels in particular were regularly reprinted and sold individually and in series targeting various audiences. Publishers appealed both to readers interested in "classic reading" and those interested in romance. Late-century packaging and advertising within the books suggest that the publishers especially sought adolescent readers and that these readers might, on the one hand, have been propelled to read by their own preferences for romance and, on the other, by adults' preference for them to read "classics." The floral cover designs and cover images of young women and girls in late nineteenth-century and early twentieth-century editions of Marlitt's novels appear to target especially female readers.[25]

Even as they provide evidence for publishers' cultivation of purchasers and librarians' sense of the preferences and needs of their patrons, the publishers' survey of 1876, library catalogues, book covers, and series bearing witness to the circulation of German novels in translation cannot tell us who actually read them and how they figured in historical readers' choices of leisure reading in general. For data that brings us closer to these readers, we turn now to two sources: (1) exemplars of books with dedications and signatures; and (2) circulation records from the Public Library of Muncie, Indiana.

Physical examination of books belonging to this set of German novels in translation yields evidence especially of women's reading and ownership of these novels.[26] Among these, ten Wister translations once owned by Amanda A. Durff testify, furthermore, to the way in which matched covers encouraged collection. Featuring a uniform embossed design consisting of Wister's signature and a cherubic cupid perched on a flowering branch, each book cover is of a different colour, making the individual volumes easy to spot on the shelf. Each spine displays the title, the publisher, and the designation "After the German by Mrs. A.L. Wister."[27]

Amanda acquired these novels over a time span of eight years (1884–92). She recorded in pencil the month and year of the acquisition of each and placed inside the front cover a bookplate with her printed name and a picture of a young woman in eighteenth-century dress. In Amanda's collecting of them these objects took on a life of their own. Their embellished covers both signal their membership in a set and lend them value for home decoration; they may have lined bookcases in her home as part of the interior decor and served as a sign of her preferences and imaginative life. The meticulous care she accorded them suggests that she understood them to have an inherent value as collectible items.

An exemplar of Nathaly von Eschstruth's *The Erl Queen* exhibits similar long-term cherishing of a book translated from the German, cherishing that extended from maidenhood into married life. In 1900 "Miss Nellie Rank" presented the book to "Miss Ethel Roby." Ethel apparently took it with her into her marriage, placing a bookplate in it and later representing herself in the same exemplar as "Mrs. Percy H. Bell."[28]

Ethel's copy of *The Erl Queen* and many, many additional exemplars bear witness to a culture of gifting in which books bound giver and receiver; in the case of these German books that culture is highly feminized. Of eighty-one exemplars from this group of German novels that contain the names of the owner (dedicatee) or gift giver, sixty-four owner/dedicatee names can be identified as unambiguously female; "Jessie," "Billy," and "Willie" may also have been female. In four cases, as the exception that proves the rule, the name of the recipient/owner is unambiguously male, but in two of these exemplars, the name of the gift giver is unambiguously female, again suggesting the way in which these books may have figured in women and girls' lives, that is, the reading culture of the female *gift givers.*

As their dedications indicate, these gift books bound the recipient to the giver across generations (mother, children, grandmother, uncle, adult friend, teacher), occasionally across genders, and through friendship. The dedications give tantalizing indications of relationships sealed by a meaningful choice of book. Buck and Annie presented *The Second Wife* to "Mama" on her birthday in 1899; Paulina S. Schwarz received a copy of *A Brave Woman* from her teacher, Miss Florence J. Pepin, in 1896; in 1903 Mr J. Barnes presented a copy of *The Princess of the Moor* to Miss Bertha Hamilton in a stiff, childish handwriting.[29] A dedication in a copy of *The Old Mam'selle's Secret* "For Julia from Grandma," dated 1922 and thus written after American interest in nineteenth-century German domestic fiction had waned, evidences belated reading. Julia's grandmother may have selected the book recalling her own adolescent reading.[30]

III. Reading in Muncie

To what extent, then, do these signed exemplars represent a larger American readership of German domestic fiction in translation and in particular, in keeping with the theme of this volume, as it was configured in provincial settings? Let us turn now to Muncie, Indiana, and the reading of German novels in translation there and thus move from book purchasers and owners to book borrowers.

The digitized circulation records of the Muncie Public Library (5 November 1891–3 December 1902, with a year and a half hiatus, 28 May 1892–5 November 1894) offer a rich resource for tracing the reception of these German novels in translation by historical readers. Furthermore, given the policy of the library that allowed patrons to check out only one book for two weeks at a time, the patterns in the transaction data speak with considerable force to reader preferences, that is, we may reasonably assume that some care went into the choices the patrons made and that a borrowed book was likely to be read. What is more, as recognized in the Middletown studies of the 1920s, Muncie, in its very ordinariness, offers a creditable test case of late-century American provincial reading. The sociologists Robert S. Lynd and Helen Merrell Lynd deemed Muncie "representative ... of contemporary life" on account of its climate, size, patterns of growth, growing and diverse industrial base, local artistic life, and "absence of any outstanding peculiarities or acute local problems which would mark it off from the mid-channel sort of American community." As they noted, it was located in the Midwest, where "two stream of colonists met in the middle region of the United States."[31]

Circulation data from this modest popular library holding ca. 11,356 volumes (ca. 6,048 titles) indicate strong preferences for the novels of E. Marlitt and interest in related German novels, all of which end happily in marriage or spousal reconciliation. In the aggregate, German domestic romance tallies 3,264 transactions, that is, 28 works (42 books) accounted for 1.8 per cent of the 175,262 transactions occurring during those years. These 28 novels (42 books) constituted .46 per cent of the total titles (ca. 6,048) and almost .37 per cent of the total volumes (ca. 11,356) held in the library – volumes include each issue of a magazine and each volume of multi-volume works such as encyclopedias. Given that magazines were checked out most often of all available publications, figuring the German share in terms of volumes rather than titles gives a more accurate picture of circulation: a comparison of .37 per cent of the holdings with 1.8 per cent of the total transactions makes clear the relative popularity of these books.

Present in the form of 23 books (11 works), Marlitt ranks tenth of all authors checked out from the library. Her five top-circulating novels – *Gold Elsie*, *The Old Mam'selle's Secret*, *The Second Wife*, *The Lady with the Rubies*, and *The Little Moorland Princess* – in their various translations together log 998 transactions (on average, 117 per year); 79 per cent (757 of 962) of the transactions (in which the gender of the borrower can be determined) are tied to female borrowers. The median age of patrons associated with these transactions, male or female, whose age is known, is 22, 22, 25, 26, and 23 respectively. The age range with the most checkouts for *Gold Elsie*, *The Old Mam'selle's Secret*, *The Lady with the Rubies*, and *The Little Moorland Princess* is 15–19 followed by 20–9. In the case of *The Second Wife*, as we shall remark further below, the groups 15–19 and 20–9 borrowed the book in more or less equal numbers.

The transactions involving Wister's translations also serve as an index of the popularity of these German domestic romances. The 28 exemplars of her translations logged 2,809 transactions.[32] This number approaches the 2,976 transactions recorded for the 40 books by the seventh-most-read author in the library's holdings, Louisa May Alcott. If Wister were categorized as an author – and Lippincott encouraged book buyers to think of her in this way – she would rank ahead of Marlitt and immediately following Alcott in eighth position.[33] Wister's translations in fact surpassed Alcott's novels in average number of checkouts during these eight and a half years: Alcott's 40 books averaged 74 each; Wister's 28, 100 each. Muncie patrons who borrowed any one of Wister's translations of domestic fiction usually followed up by checking out at least one more or, as in the case of five novels by Heimburg, they borrowed another book by an author Wister had translated that was available from another translator and publisher.[34]

How then did the liking for certain translated German fiction figure in general fiction reading in Muncie? The top one hundred authors checked out of the library provide a first look at reading patterns. Readers chose largely anglophone authors; international reading is thus largely constituted by British authors whose popularity matches American authors. Of these one hundred authors, only four foreign-born authors wrote in languages other than English and first published their works outside the United States. Of these, three wrote in German – in addition to Marlitt, Heimburg (no. 42), and Ossip Schubin (no. 94) – and one, Jules Verne (no. 95), wrote in French. The best-selling Polish novelist Henryk Sienkiewicz placed no. 102.

Within this anglophone reading, the translated German romances nevertheless occupy significant space. In the aggregate, the 33 books (20 works) by the three German-language novelists (Marlitt, Heimburg, Schubin) ranking in the top 100 far outpace the transactions of the 37 books by Dickens held in the library: the former logged 2,802 transactions, the latter 691. Checked out on average 84.9 times each, these most-borrowed German novels also circulated far more widely than the 19 books (15 works) of Miss Mulock (including *John Halifax, Gentleman*), the twenty-fourth-most-read author, which were checked out 970 times, that is, on average 51 times each. Of these 33 German books furthermore, 21 are Lippincott editions, and all but one are Wister translations.

Affinity analyses of the Muncie data by book and author provide further clues as to how Marlitt's novels figured among other favourite reading in the Muncie library. The most-read authors sort into roughly three clusters according to overlap in readership as indicated by library transactions. In fig. 11.1, the choices of mostly male patrons whose taste gravitated towards (and was largely limited to) books by Horatio Alger and related authors form the dense cluster on the upper right. The cluster on the lower right comprises books by Alcott and similar authors for girls, as preferred by mostly female patrons. The much more diffuse – diffuse because it comprises more authors and less overlap – left-hand cluster includes all of Wister's translations and any additional translations of these same German authors (Marlitt is marked in solid black), as well as such authors as Brontë, Augusta Jane Evans, Mrs Alexander, Mary Jane Holmes, Caroline Hentz, Thomas Hardy, Charles Reade, F. Marion Crawford, Clara Louise Burnham, Frances Hodgson Burnett, Amelia Edith Huddleston Barr, Booth Tarkington, Henry James, and Mrs Oliphant; these borrowers are more likely female than male. The median age of those who borrowed books in each of the three clusters is 14, 14, and 24, respectively.

These median ages highlight the fact that the traffic in the Muncie Public Library reflects especially the taste of younger patrons, with over 45 per cent of the transactions of those whose age is known carried out by users under 20. Unsurprisingly, their selections indicate what gave them pleasure, even if this pleasure was sometimes also edifying: girls' stories and boys' stories.[35] But older female readers also read for pleasure: women, 20–30, in fact pursued novel reading similar to that of younger female readers. Although these older women no longer frequently checked out books for girls, such as the Elsie Dinsmore series, and although they read more broadly, many nevertheless selected German domestic romances in translation alongside other books that promise to deliver the reading pleasure of romance, adventure within domestic bounds, and even social justice. In the reading of this second, older group, Marlitt's *The Second Wife* ranks no. 20 (discounting magazines) of 2,579 titles borrowed, with four additional Wister translations in the top 50 titles. *The Second Wife* hints at reading that deals with more mature problems; it, like Hillern's *Only a Girl* (no. 25 discounting magazines), raises the

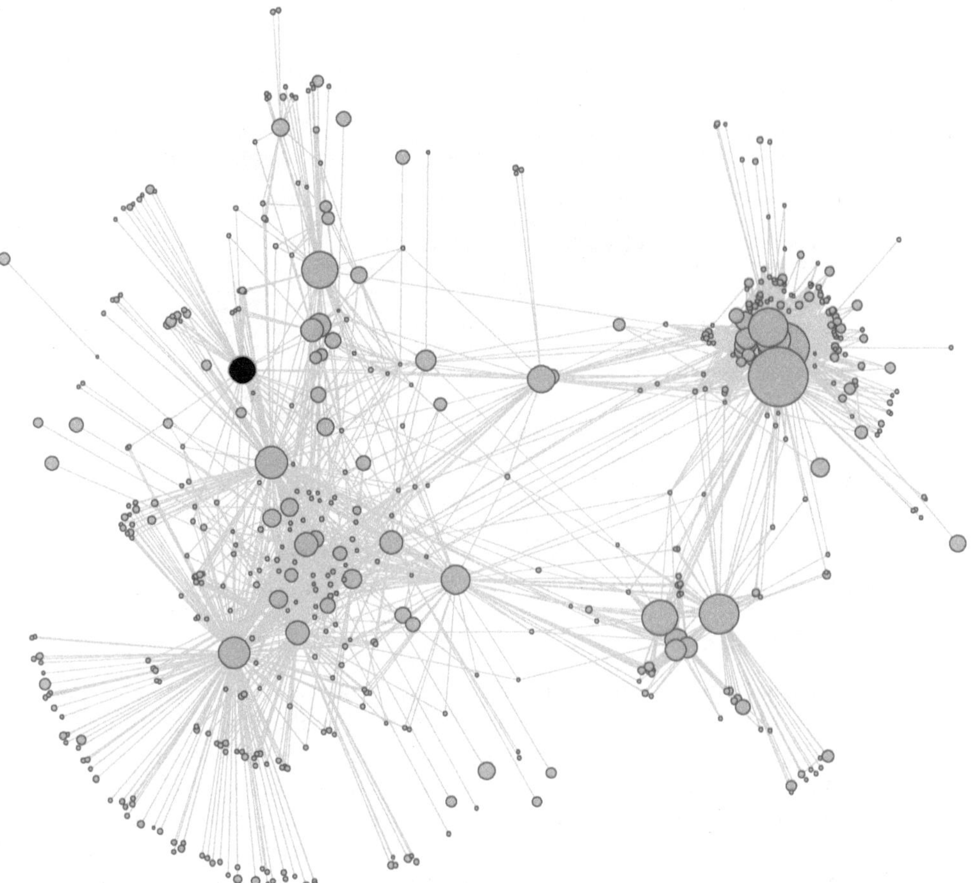

11.1 "Market Basket" analysis of reader preferences by author in Muncie, Indiana, 1891–2, 1894–1902. Nodes indicate authors that were checked out at least 20 times; their size indicates relative popularity; connecting lines (edges) indicate that at least half of all persons who checked out author A also read author B or vice versa.

possibility that marriage will not work out or that intellectual women might not be suited for marriage or find it possible to pursue anything but domestic interests within marriage, only to close with the reassurance that, in the case of these protagonists, it will, they are, and they can.

Affinity analysis further indicates that many patrons who checked out authors belonging to the third cluster likely had read at least

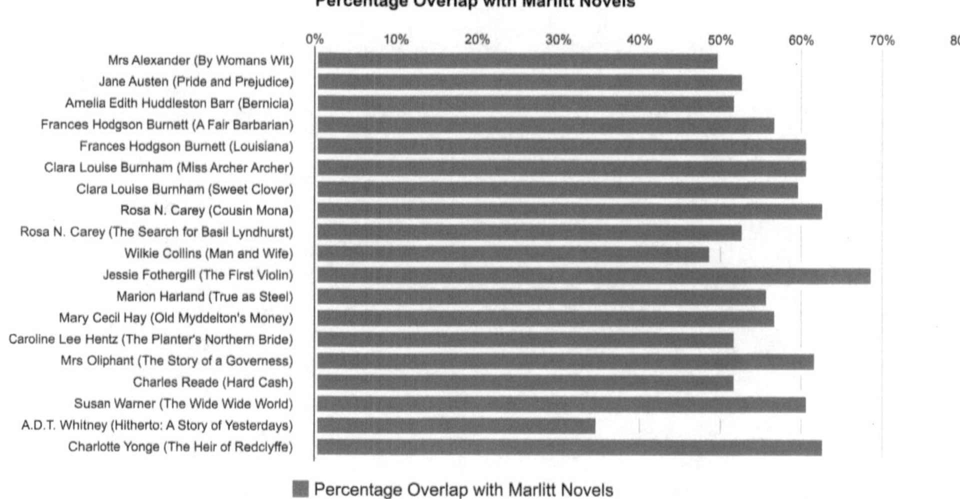

11.2 Muncie Public Library (1891–1902 [8.5 yrs]) borrowers of selected British and American women's fiction who borrowed at least one novel by E. Marlitt

one German book in translation, probably one translated by Wister. Sometimes a single patron read through significant numbers of these novels, suggesting selection by brand recognition. Mrs B.W. Alexander, for example, appeared in the Muncie records for the first time on 8 October 1901, when she checked out Schubin's *A Leafless Spring*. Thereafter fifty more transactions appear under her name as borrower over the course of a year and three days. Nine of these fifty-one transactions (18 per cent) involved translated domestic romance novels, originally written in German.[36]

Fig. 11.2 offers examples of then-popular "women's fiction" held in the Muncie library and borrowed at least ninety-three times over the course of eight and a half years. Each bar indicates the percentage of borrowers of the respective novel who also checked out at least one book by Marlitt. The 50 per cent or greater overlap in most of these examples indicates the high profile that Marlitt's translated novels occupied in the reading horizons of Muncie patrons who liked writing in this vein. It is thus not surprising that, by contrast, the 174 borrowers of Indiana author Booth Tarkington's *The Gentleman from Indiana* overlap with Marlitt's by only 34 per cent and the 110 of the classic *Robinson Crusoe*, a book with little in common with Marlitt's, by less than 10 per cent.

The eight and a half years of Muncie transaction records reveal, furthermore, that patrons who read any literary texts at all of German or Austrian origin most likely read Marlitt, Heimburg, Schubin, and others like them. Goethe by contrast is represented in the library by *Faust* alone, which sparked little interest. Only one patron checked out Schiller's *Sämtliche Werke* (Collected works), which were available only in German. No other canonical German author appears in the holdings of the library; indeed, few male German authors then thought to offer important or at least respectable reading – not even Gustav Freytag, who had been widely read in translation in America – were available in Muncie in this decade. Furthermore, *The Swiss Family Robinson*, the popular novels of Berthold Auerbach, and *Grimms' Fairy Tales*, though present in the library, attracted much less attention than German domestic romance fiction.

Muncie library users who checked out German domestic romance novels were less likely to have read other books translated from the German than other English-language fiction. Of a pool of 984 patrons who checked out (1) a book by Marlitt, (2) a book by one of these four male German authors (Goethe, Wyss, Auerbach, Grimm Brothers), or (3) both, 607 (61.69 per cent) read Marlitt only, 219 (22.26 per cent) read only the male authors, and 158 (16.06 per cent) read a book from both groups. Compare this 16.06 per cent with the 51.13 per cent overlap with Marlitt in borrowers of a single book – *Hard Cash: A Matter-of-fact Romance* – by the British author Charles Reade and the 56.07 per cent overlap with borrowers of the American Southern writer Marion Harland's *True as Steele*. The comparatively low overlap of borrowers of Marlitt and those of the male German authors suggests that the choice of books had less to do with the cultural provenance of the text in question than with its genre, brand recognition, and/or the gender and age of the borrower. These are the "zones of connection" that Julieanne Lamond encourages us to explore further in chapter 13 of this volume.

Likewise, borrowing of Marlitt does not show a particularly high correlation with borrowing other fiction originally written in a language other than English. The percentage of borrowers of at least one book by each of the following French authors who also checked out at least one book by Marlitt is consistently under 50 per cent: Verne, 20.9 per cent; Hugo, 34.65 per cent; Dumas père, 37.13 per cent; Sue, 37.25 per cent; and Sienkiewicz, 39.61 per cent. The percentages of borrowers of fiction by French women who also checked out Marlitt is, however, somewhat higher, namely, 48.78 per cent for de Staël and 54.23 per cent for Sand. Here again the gender of the reader and the genre of the book apparently matter more to selection than the national origin of the book. Indeed, a check of patrons' gender via extant census data reveals that in the case of Verne, Sienkiewicz, Sue, Hugo, and Dumas, 81 per cent, 50 per cent, 50 per cent, 45 per cent, and 41 per cent respectively of the patrons who checked out their works were male; for de Staël and Sand the percentages of transactions by male patrons amount only to 23 per cent and 35 per cent, respectively.

German, Austrian, or Swiss ethnicity, as identified by the birthplace of the patron, the patron's mother, or the patron's father, appears not to have exercised significant influence on the choice to read German literary fiction in translation in Muncie. Of the readers who had read *both* the domestic romances and the above-mentioned male German authors, not a single reader shows evidence of German, Swiss, or Austrian ethnicity.

Rosa Burmaster, whose parents hailed from Germany, presents in this respect a case in point.[37] Rosa did not check out Wyss's *The Swiss Family Robinson* from the Muncie Library, but her ten-year-old brother, Huston Burmaster, did, just like any number of boys his age; nor did she borrow *Grimms' Fairy Tales*. Instead, in August 1896, at age sixteen, following patterns similar to those of her non-ethnic-German peers, she borrowed Wister's translation of Marlitt's *At the Councillor's* in between her serial reading of Martha Finley's Elsie Dinsmore novels.[38] Over the next three months she checked out eight German domestic romance novels and thereafter two more novels by Marlitt, reproducing the "binge reading" she exhibited in her reading of Finley's series.

Such binge reading of course was not confined to adolescents. In 1895, at age thirty-nine, Carrie Andrews Burt also showed signs of a passing passion for these novels.[39] After checking out her first Wister translation, *Only a Girl*, she followed it with five additional similar German books over the next year and a half. During that same period she also read *Jane Eyre*. So did Mable Hartman in 1901, but not until after she had begun two years earlier at age fifteen to read Wister's translations (starting with *The Second Wife*) and had checked out these and related German novels 17 times over a year and 10 months (for a total of 23 borrowings of German novels over a span of two and a half years). Mable did not in fact read *Jane Eyre* until she had first checked out several of the German novels more than once (over six months apart) in apparent repeat reading and in what in the case of *The Lady with the Rubies* (1899, 1900, 1901) and *At the Councillor's* (1899, 1900, 1901) must have been an annual ritual.

As outlined above, in American publishers' sense of the market in 1876 *Jane Eyre* had set the tone. If *Jane Eyre* led American sales and embodied American readers' taste in 1876, data from the Muncie Public Library from two decades later indicate that, although Brontë's novel was still being read, its popularity had diminished over time or at least did not extend to this Midwestern library. In Muncie, however, Marlitt's *Second Wife* (first translated 1874) had retained traction: the 266 transactions recorded for this novel surpass the 116 transactions for *Jane Eyre* by 129 per cent. Moreover, the 116 checkouts of Brontë's novel do not begin to approach the 1,823 for Marlitt and the 2,809 for Wister.

Demographic data attest to similarity in readers of *Jane Eyre* on the one hand and Marlitt on the other: the median age for those who borrowed *Jane Eyre* was 24 as was that for borrowers of Marlitt's overall. Like those of Marlitt's novels, they were largely female (75 per cent Marlitt; 73 per cent *Jane Eyre*). Moreover, 56.57 per cent of the checkouts of *Jane Eyre* correlate with at least one checkout of a novel by Marlitt. At ca. 188,100 words, however, *Jane Eyre* is nearly a third longer than even the longest of Marlitt's five most-read novels, *The Little Moorland Princess* [ca. 129,800], and much longer still than the other four: *The Second Wife* [ca. 100,500], *Gold Elsie* [ca.114,220], *The Lady with the Rubies* [ca. 111,700 words], indeed, nearly twice as long as *The Old Mam'selle's Secret* [ca. 95,400 words]). The coincidence of median age and gender of the readers, the affinities of the novels in plot and motif, the difference in complexity and in length, and the far greater circulation of Marlitt's novels suggest that in Muncie the German novels had displaced *Jane Eyre* with ordinary readers as lighter reading that delivered similar gratification.

By the end of the nineteenth century *Jane Eyre* had already acquired something akin to the status of classic reading that it now enjoys and was accordingly being reprinted with a variety of publishers. Appleton, for example, published the novel in 1898 in a series entitled "World's Great Books"; the following year Grolier published it as volume 61 in its series "The World's Great Classics." Presumably the 116 Muncie readers who checked it out had some sense of that acquired status, but in the 1890s, the by then 50-year-old novel lived on in this library as favourite leisure-time reading also (perhaps more so) in its avatars, some of the most important of which were German in origin, which were borrowed much more frequently. Those seeking foreign settings, happy endings, mystery, drama, and adventure within a domestic frame wherein romance culminated in marriage could find those elements in the shorter and somewhat newer German novels.

V. How German Was It?

When Otto Heller complained in 1905 that translated German domestic fiction was creating a false impression of German womanhood and supporting "American ignorance of contemporary German literature" and especially lamented the popularity of Wister's translations, he had a point.[40] As the Muncie data indicate, Heller correctly recognized that ordinary Americans were reading Marlitt and authors like her rather than Goethe and other German male authors of pretension or important contemporary authors, such as Frank Wedekind, Hermann Sudermann, Gerhart Hauptmann, Helene Böhlau, and Gabriele Reuter, none of whom was available in Muncie to begin with.

But even as Heller objected to cultural transference via domestic fiction, since, in his view, these novels purveyed false impressions of German mores, culture, and conditions, he remained blind to, or at least unwilling to consider, the possibility that this "entertainment fiction,"[41] as he derisively labelled it, transmitted positive images of Germany and German writing that may have increased, rather than diminished, Germany's esteem in the eyes of some American readers who used the designation "after the German" to identify books they might like to read. In Marlitt's novels, Wister's translations, and other German novels in their orbit, these Americans found not images of militarism and aggression, ponderous philosophizing, or frightening modernity or urbanity, but rather pictures of Germany as a land of enduring middle-class virtues and values, one that allowed warm sentiment, domestic bliss, a modicum of female agency, and happy endings tied to social justice and social obligation; in short, a German import that brought Germany close to these Americans' wishes for their own lives.

As American reviews frequently noted, these novels are entertaining while other writing from Germany is not. An entire coterie of German novelists, the *New York Ledger* averred in 1895, had over the years furnished an "exceedingly large [American] public" with "bright and agreeable reading, even if it may be deficient in depth"; their work, the *Ledger* emphasized, had "the knack of interesting readers," a trait lacking in weightier works.[42] In part, they entertain because they are closer to American tastes to begin with. In 1873 *Lippincott's Magazine* praised newly translated German fiction as enjoying popularity in America "in part because the life which they depict has closer internal analogies to our own than to that of England or of France." These depictions appealed to both Germans and Americans, the magazine asserted, because they were "suffused with a romantic glow" that had elsewhere been supplanted by realism.[43] Lippincott's insistence on shared tastes resonated with other such assertions as that of Gostwick and Harrison, who noted in 1870 that "the literature of the American nation" has "during recent years ... more and more united itself with the literature of the German people."[44]

VI. Happiness Made in Germany

Such asseverations of cultural affinity, however, raise again the possibility that in German domestic romance fiction, American readers sought renewal of the pleasures they had always already sought in English-language fiction. One thing seems certain: the keen pleasure of happy outcomes in which wrongs were righted and the male and female protagonists were restored to one another was critical to the popularity of German domestic fiction in Muncie and elsewhere in America. Among the nearly one hundred novels in translation affiliated with Marlitt, Wister, and the other authors Wister translated, only a small handful do not end with marriage or reconciliation within marriage; those that do not, such as *Beetzen Manner*, usually did not sell and in fact are not present in the Muncie library to begin with.[45] As the reading denizens of Muncie, perhaps some of the same borrowers who had checked out *The Old Mam'selle's Secret* or *The Second Wife* two and a half decades earlier, told the sociologists Robert S. Lynd and Helen Merrell Lynd in the 1920s, they sought happy endings in their reading.[46]

Germany, in translation only dimly legible to an American anglophone public in the form of a few textual markers, becomes in these novels the land of possibility, adventure, and wish-fulfilment within the domestic sphere – that is, the land of possibility for those who already lived in "the land of unlimited opportunity" but who experienced life within narrow parameters dictated by class, age, gender, and provinciality. In the 1920s, the Lynds noted that the denizens of Muncie read magazines "for the vicarious living in fictional form they contain" with reading centring on "the idea of romance underlying the institution of marriage,"[47] namely, for similar purposes, contents, and frames as those offered by German domestic fiction. In the nineteenth century, the "German brand" of the novels that has concerned us in this essay consisted in affective elements and domestic (though foreign) settings and values that shaped romance plots that ended well. Americans could enjoy these narrative elements as pleasurably alienated versions of the norms to which they themselves were attached by virtue of their social and psychological positioning. They thus read a set of novels that delivered favourable images of Germany as a culture sharing American domestic values and generally supporting the domestic values that shaped life in the province.

Present-day research on reading and reading socialization finds, furthermore, that fiction aids readers in managing their affective lives and learning to form social bonds. Christoph Klimmt and Peter Vorderer, for example, underline the positive effects of reading novels, asserting that it can improve one's mood and help one to shut out quotidian worries. In conjuring up a pleasant situation, it helps restore the well-being of body and psyche.[48] Further, they confirm the role of reading in the expansion of affective experience and thus to the development of empathy and connections to social networks and institutions.[49] In his historical study of public libraries in America, Wayne A. Wiegand comes to similar conclusions, namely, that the main purpose of these institutions of reading, "as crafted by local leaders and users," "was to foster the kinds of social harmony that community spaces and stories, experienced and shared, provide."[50] Of the preference for novels with happy endings as favoured readings of the members of the Women's Club of Muncie, James Connolly and Frank Felsenstein observe, moreover, "The romantic elements of each narrative provided reassurance of happy endings that affirm the possibilities of social reform."[51] The attraction of these women to stories that reflected their own optimism supports Ridley's assertion, cited at the outset of this essay, that fiction exercises authority over the imagination and is therefore a force "to be reckoned with."

American reviewers who in the 1870s praised the ever-growing stock of German novels in translation for their "peculiar tinge of romance"[52] themselves support the idea that Americans read them not for their verisimilitude, but rather their emotional effects and positive outlook. Such novels, set in far-off Germany, offered American readers the pleasure of affirming their belief in virtue, romance, and the possibility of happiness in marriage while suspending the exigencies of social and psychological realism. Indeed, German novels in American translations provided new stories and reinforced old ones about the happiness that marriage could bring. While this American-created German brand reinforced nineteenth-century ideas of Germany as the land of romance and sentiment, its long-term popularity and effects likely had more to do with Americans' management of their own affective lives through reading, foreign or otherwise.

A signed copy of Marlitt's *In the Schillingscourt*, a novel that concludes with the restoration of communal harmony, restitution for the wronged, and a transatlantic marriage, testifies to precisely such functions of reading. On the front flyleaf the gift giver wrote "Emmie A. Matt June 1, 1901"; on the back flyleaf she entered lines by Robert G. Ingersoll: "Love is the only bow / on Life's dark cloud / – Love is the builder of / Every hope. With Love / Earth is heaven, and / We are God," replacing "home" with "hope."[53] This substitution, deliberate or otherwise, suggests that Marlitt's novel spoke to her wish to believe in the futurity offered by happy endings in novels such as this one. Unlike the fairy tales by the Brothers Grimm that were later adapted under the Disney brand, popular German domestic romance need only to be translated; these novels came pre-equipped with happy, hopeful endings.

Were then those who liked to read these German novels reading as cosmopolitans, given, after all, that they were reading American-produced iterations of international bestsellers that resembled other international bestsellers in genre, motif, and affect? As Joan Shelley Rubin and Frank Felsenstein point out elsewhere in this volume, there is no simple answer to this question.[54] If "cosmopolitan" suggests an attempt to become a citizen of the world through informed reading of material from many parts of the world that requires the acceptance of difference, the reading of these novels likely did not stem primarily from cosmopolitan impulses. In some respects the books simply reflected the provincial context in which they were being read in Muncie. Yet the province of this fiction lies at the centre, not at the margin implied by the term "province" itself. Lightly exotic for Americans since it is German and thus, at least superficially, foreign, the province is stripped in these texts of the tedious and mundane and transformed into a place where wishes come true against the odds. Borrowing them from the public library therefore likely indicates the pursuit of reading that affirms deeply held values, offers hope, and gratifies wishes, in short, reading that suggests that what seems impossible in everyday life is truly possible in a mythological elsewhere found in books; it probably does not constitute a conscious pursuit of foreign literature coupled with an openness to difference. On the other hand, reading German novels as affirmative of shared values does operate within the penumbra of ideas of cosmopolitanism, according to which common morality overrides difference.

The American declaration of war on the German Empire in 1917 must in any case have challenged positive associations of regional Germany with felicity within the institution of marriage and discouraged ideas of sameness across national difference or indeed impulses to bridge difference. And while we do not know precisely which books Muncie readers read thereafter when they sought to manage their affective lives through affirmation, restoration, and recreation in their reading, given the anti-German sentiment of the interwar period, we can guess that they did not turn first to nineteenth-century fiction labelled "from the German."

NOTES

This essay could not have been written without the work of Stephen M. Pentecost, Senior Digital Humanities Specialist, in the Humanities Digital Workshop at Washington University, who downloaded the Muncie data, created a census data query, undertook affinity analysis of transactions, and found ways to visualize this data. Likewise Douglas W. Knox, Assistant Director, played an invaluable role in guiding student teams. Barbara Barrow, Benjamin Davis, and especially Brooke Shafar, and Julia Wu deserve recognition for their significant help with tallying, manipulating, and visualizing the Muncie data.

1 Ridley (2007, 121).

2 Beck and Grande (2007, 13). In this volume, see especially the discussions of cosmopolitanism in essays by Frank Felsenstein (chapter 12) and Joan Shelley Rubin (chapter 5).

3 Ridley (2007, 119).

4 Tatlock (2012). The Muncie circulation data figure minimally in this account since I did not have access to the circulation records until the book was in press. While my book treats nearly exclusively the works of women writers, in considering the Muncie data in this essay, I included one novel by Adolf Streckfuss translated by Annis Lee Wister and strongly associated with those by the women novelists. I omitted the five novels held in the library by Louise Mühlbach, although I include her novels in my book, since these historical romances belong to domestic fiction only in a more expanded sense of the term.

5 Kelley (1984, 10–11).

6 Belgum (1998, 21).

7 Pochmann (1957, 346–7).

8 Tatlock (2012, 167–8).

9 Untitled notice, *New York Times* (1 June 1907): BR352.

10 The list excluded works by Bulwer-Lytton, Dickens, George Eliot, Scott, and Thackeray "since they of course stand at the head of standard novelists, and the works of these alone would easily outrun the specified number of fifty titles." "The Prize Question in Fiction," *The Publishers' Weekly*, no. 127 (20 May 1876): 633.

11 For a discussion of preliminary results of topic modelling of the 1876 list, see Lynne Tatlock (2014).
12 Tatlock (2012, 48).
13 For an account of the national mission of *Die Gartenlaube*, see Belgum (1998, 21).
14 Kontje (2004).
15 Belgum (1998, 21).
16 Martino (1990).
17 Norbert Bachleitner (2000, 188) notes that Marlitt allegedly denied familiarity with *Jane Eyre*, asserting that such a denial must be seen as outright dishonesty or a strategic diversion. For an account of the translations of *Jane Eyre*, see Hohn (1998).
18 Gottschall (1902, 346–7); Rudolf Gottschall, "Die Novellisten der 'Gartenlaube,'" Blätter für literarische Unterhaltung 19 (May 1870): 289–93 represented in *Deutschsprachige Literaturkritik 1870–1914* (2006, 1:40–8).
19 Gottschall, "Die Novellisten der 'Gartenlaube," 291.
20 Regis (2003, 31–3, 35).
21 Bachleitner (2000, 188).
22 See Joeres (1998, 241–2) and Yvonne Defant, "Le mystère du passé hante encore: l'influence de *Jane Eyre* sur *Die zweite Frau* d'Eugenie Marlitt." In Revue LISA/LISA e-journal (online), *Writers, Writings, Literary Studies* 3 (accessed 24 June 2013).
23 Pyrhönen (2010, 2). Pyrhönen appears to be unaware of Marlitt's novels and in any case does not take account of the migration of Brontë's novel to other cultures and countries. Although she concedes that "Jane Eyre has trotted the globe, leaving non-English adaptations in its wake," she discounts these, asserting that Brontë's novel serves as "a cultural myth and mnemonic symbol" first and foremost on its home turf (meaning Great Britain) and choosing to focus on a single cultural context (Pyrhönen 2010, 11–12).
24 See thirteen such catalogues listed in Appendix B in Tatlock (2012, 269).
25 See the example of Marlitt's *The Old Mam'selle's Secret* in Tatlock (2014, Fig. 9.4)
26 Most of the books examined and all the books cited can be viewed at http://talus.artsci.wustl.edu/germanromance.
27 Exemplars of ten translations by A.L. Wister published by J.P. Lippincott and once owned by Amanda A. Durff, now owned by author: Ursula Zöge von Manteuffel, *Violetta* (1886); Wilhelmine von Hillern, *Only a Girl* (1887); E. Juncker, *Margarethe or Life's Problems* (1887); Moritz von Reichenbach *The Eichhofs* (1887); Claire von Glümer, *A Noble Name or Dönninghausen* (1888); E. Werner, *The Alpine Fay* (1889); E. Werner, *Banned and Blessed*

(1890); Ossip Schubin, *Erlach Court* (1889); Ossip Schubin, *O Thou, My Austria* (1890); Ossip Schubin, *Countess Erika's Apprenticeship* (1891).

28 Nataly von Eschstruth, *The Erl Queen*, trans. Emily S. Howard, The Snug Corner Series (New York: Wm. L. Allison Company, n.d.), flyleaf and verso of the book cover. Copy owned by author.

29 E. Marlitt, *The Second Wife* (Chicago: Donohue, Henneberry, n.d.); E. Marlitt, *A Brave Woman*, trans. Margaret P. Waterman (New York: Wm L. Allison Co., n.d.), front flyleaf; E. Marlitt, *The Princess of the Moor* (New York: Federal Book Company, no date), front flyleaf. Copies owned by author.

30 E. Marlitt, *The Old Mam'selle's Secret* (New York: A.L. Burt, n.d.), front flyleaf. Copy owned by author.

31 Lynd and Lynd (1929, 7–8). The Lynds' "Middletown studies" focus on the 1920s. The 1890s, however, serve as a point of comparison throughout and thus the study provides a useful sketch of the late nineteenth century in Muncie as well.

32 The library incorrectly lists Marlitt's *Over Yonder* (also published by Lippincott) as translated by Wister. Since Muncie readers likely thought this was another of Wister's Marlitt translations, I have included it in the transaction numbers for Wister, as does the library itself. On the other hand, the Muncie database fails to link with Wister, *A Penniless Girl*, which also belonged to Wister's series of "popular German novels." Since patrons could easily have determined that this translation was by Wister, I have added the checkouts of this book to her total.

33 This tally omits one anthology that merely contains one story by Alcott. "What Middletown Read?" Muncie Public Library, Center for Middletown Studies, Ball State University Library, http://www.bsu.edu/libraries/wmr/; Census Query created by Stephen Pentecost: http://talus.artsci.wustl.edu/censusQuery/. On Wister as author, see Tatlock (2012, 225–8).

34 Automated transaction data is keyed to the "patron," the person holding the library card, and not to the borrower, the person who signed the register. Usually the patron and the borrower are identical. Given the sheer quantity of data, I take the numbers and calculations to be roughly reliable. Whether the borrower actually read the book, checked out the book for him or herself to begin with, or was the only person who read the book of course cannot be determined.

35 Demographic information on sex, age, and ethnicity does not exist for all those who borrowed books and therefore these numbers take only partial account of the transactions. See also n34. Joel Shrock, in his essay in this volume, notes that there was some debate about the literary and moral value of the books children borrowed (see chapter 10).

36 Using a similar method, Julieanne Lamond considers the sources of these affinities in chapter 13 of this volume.
37 For more information on Rosa Burmaster, see Frank Felsenstein's essay in this volume (chapter 12). Likewise, when at age nineteen Rosa checked out the German author Georg Eber's *An Egyptian Princess*, a historical romance set in Egypt, she was behaving true to gender, though a bit precocious in age: 74% of sixty-nine *borrowers* are identifiably female; the median age of the thirty-three *patrons* whose age is known is twenty-seven. Unlike Rosa, 94.44% of the 144 borrowers of this book for whom there is demographic data show no indication of German, Austrian, or Swiss ethnicity. It is, however, questionable whether American readers associated Ebers's three Egyptian novels with Germany or German culture to begin with.
38 Eight Wister translations – *Gold Elsie, Old Mam'selle's Secret, A Penniless Girl, Castle Hohenwald, Second Wife, At the Councillor's, The Alpine Fay,* and *Little Moorland Princess* – number among the top 50 books (excluding 10 magazine titles) checked out by girls and women, 14–18. Of 2,254 titles selected by this age group, 14 Wister translations appear in the top 100 selections (excluding 10 magazines), including, in addition to the above, *Lady with the Rubies, The Eichhoffs, The Owl's Nest, Countess Gisela, Only a Girl,* and *Erlach Court*. For age 16 alone, the top 25 titles (excluding four magazines) of 1,114 titles include *Old Mam'selle's Secret, Gold Elsie, Penniless Girl, Alpine Fee,* and *At the Councillor's*.
39 On the reading patterns of Carrie Andrews Burt and her family, see the essay of Joel D. Shrock in this volume (chapter 10).
40 Heller (1905, 267).
41 Heller (1905, 252).
42 "Some German Literary Women," reprinted from the *New York Ledger* in *The Galveston Daily News*, 14 December 1895: 8.
43 William Whiston, "Our Monthly Gossip. Wilhelmine von Hillern," *Lippincott's Magazine of Popular Literature and Science*, 11 no. 22 (January 1873: 115).
44 Gostwick and Harrison (1873, 581).
45 Tatlock (2012, 86).
46 Lynd and Lynd (1929, 238).
47 Lynd and Lynd (1929, 241).
48 Klimmt and Vorderer (2004, 53).
49 Klimmt and Vorderer (2004, 39, 44, 48). See also Garbe, Holle, and Jesch (2011, 16–19).
50 Wiegand (2011, 186).
51 Felsenstein and Connolly (2015, 182).

52 Rev. of *Gold Elsie*, by E. Marlitt, *The British Quarterly Review. American Edition* 57 (April 1873): 300.
53 E. Marlitt, *In the Schillingscourt*, trans. A.L. Wister (Philadelphia: J.B. Lippincott, 1898), front and back flyleaf. Copy owned by author.
54 See chapters 5 and 12 in this volume.

12 Print Culture and Cosmopolitan Trends in 1890s Muncie, Indiana

FRANK FELSENSTEIN

On Sunday, 18 May 1902, the *Muncie Morning News* ran a brief column, reporting that Miss Rosa Burmaster wrote a letter from Rome that had been read at a local women's club the previous week.[1] From other sources, we know that at the time of writing Burmaster was a twenty-one-year-old student at the East Indiana Normal Institute, and the likelihood that she had actually penned her letter from the city of Rome to distant Muncie is extremely remote. The evidence is far stronger that her club letter was written in Muncie, and, given her socio-economic circumstances, there is little probability that she had crossed the Atlantic and visited Italy on an earlier occasion.

The main evidence for stating that Rosa was present in Muncie is the record of her book borrowing from the public library, which includes fourteen transactions in 1901 and another nine in the first half of 1902. Most pertinently, the book that she borrowed a few days prior to the club meeting was an English translation by Edgar S. Shumway of Friedrich Lohr's popular *A Day in Ancient Rome* (Boston: D.C. Heath & Company, 1887) that she took out on Saturday, 3 May, less than two weeks before her presentation. Lohr's work is written in the form of a familiar epistle, in which he invites his readers "to follow me aright" by directing "your thoughts (you know they are always ready for a flying trip from the class-room) toward sunny Italy. Fancy you are visiting me here, every one of you." We, as readers, he avers, should take his pages as "a greeting which may spur you on ... to follow out."[2] Rosa Burmaster did exactly that – she followed out – and her groundwork for her presentation to the women's club may be seen as emblematic of the cosmopolitan aspiration of a young woman from a small Midwestern city to reach out to the wider world and to share that journey with her peers in the women's club.

The vehicle that she chose to aid her in this endeavour – the most accessible one available to her – was the Muncie Public Library. In this paper, I wish to consider the place of cosmopolitan discourse both in its own right and as a meaningful component in the study of print culture, with particular reference to patterns of reading in turn-of-the-century Muncie. We shall not lose sight of Rosa Burmaster, and will return to her again in the final part of this discussion.

As a very recent and useful overview reiterates, there is no clear agreement on what constitutes the cosmopolitan.[3] Yet, the adjective "cosmopolitan" and its ancillary noun "cosmopolitanism" continue to gain traction across the disciplines as a brace of outright slippery yet nonetheless voguish terms in common service by members of the academic community. At the risk of gross simplification, a short sampling of some recent attempts at definition may prove both illustrative and demonstrative. Ulrich Beck's complex employment of "cosmopolitanism" as a contribution to a chaptered book on globalization sets the trend. For Beck, a professor of sociology at the University of Munich, the primary hurdle is in endeavouring to determine whether there is "an *actually existing* cosmopolitanism" that takes account of what a cosmopolitan society "*ought* to be," and the fundamental cosmopolitan question is the distinction between belonging or not belonging. He advocates a "new critical theory" of cosmopolitanism that "investigates the *contradictions*" besetting us at the beginning of the twenty-first century, and that "draws its critical power from the tension between political self-description and the observation of the social sciences."[4]

Acknowledging his indebtedness to Beck and, more historically, to the writings of Immanuel Kant, Michael J. Fischer views cosmopolitanism as "the dialectic between cosmos and polis," which he earlier defines as global competitions and the nation state. However, where Beck's focus is primarily on future directions, Fischer describes one kind of cosmopolitanism as a nostalgia for "cities, empires, villages, and towns of mixed population" that have been destroyed and no longer exist. He cites among multiple examples of *nostalgic cosmopolitanism* our propensity to reach back to "the Ottoman empire's millet system … as a model of a multicultural, multireligious form of cosmopolitanism to which we might look for lessons in our era of renewed ethnic cleansing and religious fundamentalisms," or to the rich layers of pre-war Viennese culture, its "modernism in science, music, literature," etc., irreversibly and forever eradicated by the Nazis. He uses his examples to bolster an argument that "simple nostalgia" is insufficient, and that "critical reflexivity and contemplation of different

… social institutions and discourses" are essential prerequisites as means for the redemption and preservation of social justice. This kind of cosmopolitanism, he claims, entices an investment in the dialectical exploration of "new and old media, life histories, ethnicity formations … as well as the ways in which social theories of change and legitimation arise out of historical experiences."[5]

A third and final brief example of the use of cosmopolitanism in academic inquiry situates itself within the present day by examining how Barack Obama's election victory in 2008 owed a great deal to the "increasing levels of cosmopolitanism" in America that were an important determinant in choosing a president from a racial minority who in earlier times would have stood little or no chance. The authors of the study, psephologists Simon Jackman and Lynn Vavreck, define cosmopolitanism historically by recognizing "its roots in ancient political thought,"[6] and cite sociological studies from the 1950s that distinguish between individuals who are "cosmopolites" and those who are "locals." For them, cosmopolites as types "are more attentive to the world than locals, who tend to be oriented toward the local community." They suggest a healthy tension between these two types, with a consequence that the voters of 2008 "were challenged by the limits of their cosmopolitanism" in their choice of candidate. They also rue the fact that, despite its wide use across the disciplines, "cosmopolitanism is underelaborated theoretically, to say nothing of our dearth of understanding of its theoretical content." For Jackman and Vavreck, an important facet of cosmopolitanism is attitudinal, "an openness to experience other cultures or customs and a belief that there is something to be gained from a connection to people and places beyond the local community."[7]

In the context of this volume, we can see how each of the above examples of present-day discourse on what cosmopolitanism represents adds valuably to our understanding of the term and the multiplicity of its uses. Beck's recognition that cosmopolitan aspirations tend to bring out the differences between a person's sense of belonging and not belonging infuses the discussion of individuals such as the sheep station clerk John Vaughn Miller and the agricultural writer Clara Steen (see chapters 9 and 14), while his insistence on the distinction between cosmopolitan ideals and quotidian realities apprises Lynne Tatlock's discussion of the reading of German fiction in translation in Muncie (see chapter 11). Michael J. Fischer's insistence on a sophisticated *cosmopolitan nostalgia* informs most of the various research projects that are featured in this book. Even though the demise of institutions such as the old Muncie Public Library in Indiana or the Lambton Mechanics' and Miners' Institute in New South Wales (described by Julieanne Lamond in chapter 13) was not catastrophic as evidenced in the examples provided by Fischer, there is value in exploring the ways in which ordinary people engaged in the world through such institutions. In so doing, we may find (as suggested below) that nostalgia for a lost past can manifest itself as anti-cosmopolitanism, the simplistic conception of an innocent world that is forever lost through the intrusion of cosmopolitan values brought about primarily by technological change. Finally, Jackman and Vavreck's acknowledgment that cosmopolitanism presupposes an openness to other cultures and customs finds a counterpart in Joan Shelley Rubin's positioning of the term "as freedom from entrenched preconceptions, a determination to dissolve local allegiances in favor of the universal, and openness to new and discomfiting ideas." Equally, her masterful recognition that the idea of the metropolis should be "considered as a sensibility rather than simply as a place" ties in well with Jackman and Vavreck's belief that, instead of lending itself to precise statistical measurement, the cosmopolitan mindset should be construed as primarily attitudinal (see chapter 5). Rather than labouring the parallels, which are multiple, the point that should emerge here is that, as much as in other academic fields, historians of print culture and of libraries are contributing to a larger and ongoing discourse, and perhaps helping to advance towards a closer working definition on the nature, ambivalence, and multiple meanings of cosmopolitanism.

In this examination of print culture in Muncie, Indiana, around the turn of the twentieth century, my own employment of the term is perhaps more pragmatic than theoretical, though I share with Jackman and Vavreck the belief that cosmopolites "are more attentive to the world than locals, who tend to be oriented toward the local community." Personal experience of spending a good part of my life in countries or cultures with different (but often too not so different) imperatives, beliefs, and value systems from those with which I grew up factors into any attempt at would-be self-definition of what constitutes cosmopolitanism. Living physically, though not always mentally, outside one's natal culture continues to be an ongoing learning process as much about the values, priorities, and lifestyle of the country left behind as of the one in which one is now resident or domiciled. Beck's perception that cosmopolitan thinking has its life force in the ambivalence between belonging or not belonging is crucial here. Cosmopolitanism presupposes a mutually beneficial, though sometimes fraught, interaction between cultures, an interaction which ideally at least can be said to contribute to the common good. That notion was well expressed in the late eighteenth century by the German poet and miscellaneous writer Christoph Martin Wieland (1733–1813), who idealized cosmopolitans as citizens of the world who "regard all the peoples of the earth as so many branches of a single family."[8] Wieland's interpretation of the term has more recently provided a basis for the definition of cosmopolitanism advanced quite influentially by Princeton philosopher Kwame Anthony Appiah, who argues that "there are some values that are, and should be, universal, just as there are lots of values that are, and must be, local." For Appiah, intellectual conversation about the meaning of those values becomes a recognizable signifier or "model" for articulating his own interpretation of cosmopolitanism. It can be enriched, he adds, through "conversation between people from different ways of life."[9] Such a conversation may appear most appropriate in the context of a metropolis, but it begs the question whether such values can be replicated in a small city like Muncie, Indiana, during what could be argued as its most formative years, in the 1890s.

It is perhaps the dilemma today of a small city to find itself torn between a desire to compete with its larger urban rivals, against which it is likely (or at least risks) to be belittled, and a counter-tendency to glorify its provincial roots and endangered rural character. Arguably, the crucial invention that sustained Muncie in the years subsequent to its sudden growth in the wake of the natural gas boom of the late 1880s and the 1890s was the motor car. By 1910 the city not only built automobiles (having previously been a Mecca for carriage building) but was also – and remained through the twentieth century – a principal centre for the manufacture of gears and other automobile parts. Throughout the whole period of existence of the old Muncie Public Library (1875–1903), when the automobile was still in process of being invented, and into the first decades of the twentieth century, when it became ubiquitous, there remained a nostalgia for small-town values and a simpler lifestyle that was non-mechanized and, to a degree, anti-cosmopolitan. The mood for this far less complicated, almost bucolic, existence is captured in an occasional poem, "The Gay Nineties," published many years later, by Dr Hugh Cowing, one of Muncie's leading physicians, and himself a patron of the library:

Yes, the Nineties were gay;
Then life was geared to a trot;
There was time to laugh and play
When the honk of the Ford was not.

The clatter of horses' feet,
The rumble of wheels in the street,
Glad sounds of that other day,
Back when the Nineties were gay! ...

You wonder how could they be gay
When rouge and lip-stick were rare;
When girls wouldn't dare bob their hair –
How could the Nineties be gay?

I answer, the Nineties *were* gay;
There was time to laugh and play;
A horse to drive, and a hand to hold,
Helped make the Nineties gay.[10]

The poem acknowledges the inevitability of progress while simultaneously ruing the loss of a slower and less-developed pace that is denoted audibly by "the clatter of horses' feet" as against "the honk of the Ford." With poetical hindsight, the 1890s are made to encapsulate that transition from an era that measured itself by the gaiety associated with simple country pleasures to a more complex, and perhaps more cosmopolitan, milieu and lifestyle that lay in store with the advent of the new century. Unlike the nostalgia in Cowing's verses for an older, more leisured way of life, the more common response is one that hails technological advancement and the putative advancement of cosmopolitan values.

The progress of Muncie's public library vis-à-vis the progress of the city was often accounted for in similar terms. In 1907 Artena M. Chapin, the city's first professionally trained librarian and inaugural Carnegie librarian, describes this succinctly by maintaining that the library has become "a factor in the life of the city, keeping pace with its growth."[11] By saying this, she was recognizing the presence of the library as an important factor in measuring not only the physical growth but also the state of intellectual life of the city at any given time. It is in such terms that it was described ten years earlier by Mrs T.F. Rose, the wife of the library's then president, in an impassioned address before "four hundred energetic club women of ... [Delaware] county, who are alive to all the issues that make for intellectual and moral improvement," assembled at a gathering of Women's Clubs that took place in Muncie in 1897. "The condition of its library," affirmed Mrs Rose, "is the intellectual pulse of a community." Casting her mind back to its foundation in 1874, she recalled that, at that now seemingly distant era, "Muncie was a town of less than five thousand inhabitants with a little brick court house and a hitching post fence around it." Since then, and particularly following the discovery of natural gas, the present city has undergone what Mrs Rose calls a "booming evolution," with "the uttermost limits of the town burst[ing] their bounds." Her portrayal here led her to voice her apprehension that, without substantial additional funding, the library risked lagging behind in its mission of promoting "higher, intellectual development," while the city advanced "in material affairs." Her plea for a new building to house the more than ten thousand volumes contained in the existing rooms was backed by "the earnest solicitation of the library board," who wholeheartedly shared her belief in the need of the city to try to achieve a balance of its material and intellectual aspirations.[12]

If the library sometimes seemed to fall behind in its cosmopolitan aspirations, the fault must be ascribed primarily to shortage of money. That is one of the reasons why the financial shot in the arm given by Andrew Carnegie (it led to the building of Muncie's Carnegie Library, opened in 1904) is so important to the development of intellectual life not only in this small city but in a host of similar local conurbations across anglophone North America. The minutes of its board, which often record protracted discussion arising from the smallest costs, provide a good indication of the library's close to hand-to-mouth existence. It easily spent all that it received by way of annual subsidies from the city council, and there was no significant reserve fund upon which it could draw in the case of an emergency. Yet, in its public face, it was more than willing to uphold the belief that it was self-sustaining. An article in *The Morning News* in 1893, "A Brief Resume of Our Public Library," typifies this attitude by insisting that since it was first "put in running order" following its organization as a stock company in 1874, it has "continued to grow until the present time [when] it has almost become self supporting." The control and "good management" exercised by the library board over "the kind of literature to be purchased" and the annual contribution of $200 by the city council have been instrumental, the anonymous writer reiterates, in making the library "almost self supporting … paying the main expenses for binding, some of which was done in our own city."

The same piece extols the library as "the pride of our city" and the "chief" of "our educational aids" in support of the work being done by the public schools. In an extended defence of books and of studious reading, the author spells out the cosmopolitan ideals associated with a library and that institution's relationship with the public it serves:

> The best index to the intelligence, culture and business ability of a community may be found in the quantity and quality of books its public, private, and professional libraries contain. In the libraries may be found the best information upon which the people daily depend, and books are the best storehouses for the mind when skill is required beyond that which is possible to be acquired in the narrow gauge of experience.
>
> Books, as is well known, contain an abridgment of the best practical ideas, tabulated and of easy access, connected by the life time toil of some veteran genius or artisan, who mould our public opinion and leave in history the primary digests upon which each succeeding generation is based. Books preserve and make permanent the reason, law and philosophies of the ages, giving us historical inferences by which to construct our sciences, and elevate our nation to a higher and better civilization.
>
> A library is an emporium of arts, the only veritable paradise in the material construction of man. It may be said of him who fails to enjoy a good book occasionally, that he lives a semi-barbaric life in which reason is cruelly formed, misguiding conceptions prescribing to his happiness and deportment, thus dispelling the basis of a philanthropic life of usefulness and instituting in its stead a mind that becomes a narrow receptacle for the legendary riff-raffs and hearsays gleaned from the lower currents of the world's ideals.[13]

The high-mindedness and quasi-Jeffersonian rhetoric of these paragraphs deserve some unpacking for they serve to represent the ideals of cosmopolitanism that fall under our earlier attempts at definition. Books are seen as the key to self-improvement. The edification to be gained from reading and study is interpreted here as the primary means by which the people of America at large, and those of Muncie in particular, may be recovered from their putative "semi-barbaric" state and elevated "to a higher and better civilization." Implicit here is the belief that, through the life experiences and the accumulated knowledge and insights that are recorded in books, we come out much better equipped to lead useful and socially meaningful lives. Without that knowledge and experience, it is alleged that the pursuit of human happiness would risk becoming a disorderly and potentially retrogressive affair. As well as commending the role played by the public library, the author extends his inquiry to a brief consideration, or "Notes" (as he calls them), of "Some of Our Leading Private and Professional Libraries of Special Merit." Among these are a number of law, medical, and theological libraries – some private and some professional – that contribute to the bibliothecal ranking of Muncie as "among the best in the State, and speak well for our professional men whose business is to educate, protect, and enlighten the people of our city." The projection of the article is upbeat in its emphasis on the role of the library as a kind of guiding light or leading indicator of the cultural ethos of a community.

The memorable delineation of a library as "the only veritable paradise in the material construction of man" may strike us today as unrealistic, even highfalutin, in its idealism, but it accords well with contemporary understanding that tied cosmopolitan aspirations with the material and intellectual advancement of Eurocentric ideas of civilization. We are fortunate here in being able to draw on the historian of the fledgling city of Muncie, Dr G.W.H. Kemper, who in his *Twentieth Century History of Delaware County, Indiana* (1908) employs the word "cosmopolitan" in terms that are strikingly analogous. Discussing what may have prompted pioneer families to settle in the county, Kemper obliquely invokes the progress of "this modern age, when men are becoming more cosmopolitan in their conditions, when provincialism and the influence of state and section are less plainly impressed on individuals." Here, what is "cosmopolitan" is seen as a counter to provincialism while simultaneously being understood to represent something more than just the development of a single community: the inexorable westward drive and cultural advancement of the United States during the nineteenth century. "It will be understood" of the places in which a settler family lived before coming to Delaware County, asserts Kemper, "that these localities were intermediate points in the westward migration, to which the family made the first stage of its journey, or stopped a few years until civilization caught up with them, and then pushed on deeper into the wilderness." [14]

A few pages later, Kemper reinvokes the word "cosmopolitan," and, in doing so, leads to a second important meaning of the term:

> As elsewhere stated, the men who developed Delaware county did not own any particular section of their previous home. The settlers were perhaps as cosmopolitan as those of any county in the middle west. Here were united in society and often in family ties those whose lives had been molded by Puritan New England and those who had no influences and customs outside of Cavalier Virginia. Yankee thrift and southern liberality became valuable elements in the new social order growing up in the middle west. So far as the recognized sections of the United States have produced each a somewhat different type of people, Delaware county has received samples of each of those types, and

> has developed a thoroughly American civilization, equally removed from the dominant characteristics of the north or the south, and from the peculiarities popularly ascribed to the eastern and to the western people.[15]

What emerges here is a complementary definition of the cosmopolitan that stresses notions of commonality, and sees the inhabitants of Delaware County as representatives of an emergent nation that is made up of largely diverse elements that can be annealed into unity in the Midwest. It should be pointed out at once that Kemper is not talking about what nowadays would be deemed as multiculturalism because the origin of all the people he has in mind is European. In a recent study, Margaret Jacob defines cosmopolitanism in today's world as translating into a "meaning closer to home, a way of living in our own multiethnic towns and cities,"[16] but such a post-colonial definition is not germane to the present context. Rather, the subtext to Kemper's use of "cosmopolitan" here should be understood to refer to the American Midwest as a location or "melting pot" in which the warring factions of North and South, that had so nearly riven the United States but forty years or so before he wrote, were able to live together and harmonize more easily than in the primary battleground states of the Civil War. In that sense, the Midwest provides for Kemper, himself a Union veteran, a model of the cosmopolitan ideal and a promising blueprint of the notion of America as a country that was strengthened by healing its earlier divisions through fostering a caucus of citizens from previously divergent and separated backgrounds.

Let us try and relate this discussion more closely to the development of the city's library specifically and to the texts it held.[17] Unsurprisingly, since Muncie was never itself a publishing centre, we find that no more than half a dozen of the books in the library's collection were actually printed or published in the city.[18] The total number of books in the old Muncie Public Library for which we have a record of their place of publication stands at 11,458. Taking that figure within state, it can be calculated that the 257 books there that contain an Indianapolis imprint make up but 2.24 per cent, and those published in Muncie only about 0.04 per cent of the whole.

Inevitably, it is New York, the established centre of the American book trade, which was the place of publication for by far the largest share of the books that found their way into the library. A total of 4,611 books, translating to 40.24 per cent of those for which we have a record of their place of publication, had or included New York in their imprint. Of these, we have circulation records for 3,338, representing 72.4 per cent of the total number of MPLholdings published in New York. The number of recorded transactions of books published in New York adds up to 97,863, out of approximately 175,000 surviving borrowing records. From those figures, we can determine that approximately 56 per cent of books that circulated during the period for which we have records contained the imprint of a New York–based publisher. If anything, that percentage underrates the circulation of New York published books in Muncie since it does not (and indeed cannot without further evidence) take account of the fact that many of the 1,273 volumes published in New York for which we have no borrowing records will have been borrowed and some of them discarded prior to the surviving transaction data, which covers most of the 1890s and the first two years of the twentieth century. In addition, a few will have reached the library and been catalogued too late in 1902 to have been put into circulation before the end of our files.[19] A conservative estimate of six out of every ten books, or 60 per cent, represents a truer figure for the number of books with a New York imprint that circulated from the library. The hegemony of New York vis-à-vis the American publishing trade of the latter years of the nineteenth century can hardly be more succinctly illustrated. It is more difficult, perhaps impossible, to gauge the extent to which cosmopolitan trends and values that we may wish to associate with New York will have rubbed off on Muncie. Yet we can at least see the connective tissue in the form of printed material as evidence of a basis for a sense of cultural engagement.

We have smaller figures of the number of books in the Muncie Public Library published in such centres as Washington, DC, Boston, Philadelphia, and Chicago, and of those that were published abroad, but suffice it to say that the origins of imprints are geographically very diverse. The range of origin of so many of the books in the library could not have been brought about without an excellent transportation system. All of the promotional literature written about turn-of-the-century Muncie makes much of the city's accessibility by railroad. One such booster lists these iron links as follows:

> The Cleveland, Columbus, Cincinnati and Indianapolis (Big Four) Railroad, the Lake Erie and Western and the Ft. Wayne, Cincinnati and Louisville Railroads afford direct communication with Chicago, St. Louis, Louisville, Cincinnati, Cleveland, Detroit and the great centers of the East and West.[20]

The relative ease with which the big cities could be visited and the number of entrepreneurs from the east (the most famous being the Ball Brothers, who relocated from Buffalo, NY, in 1887) who opened factories and set up shop there helped give Muncie a sense of being an increasingly cosmopolitan place. The holdings of its library, which came from far and wide, helped to sustain that feeling.

Within the city, a lively newspaper industry may be thought of as one of the surest indications of its cosmopolitan nature, yet (as the Lynds were to report in the 1920s) the contents of its papers may also reveal an enduring insularity. More than thirty different newspapers published in Muncie before 1904 are known to have existed. A common characteristic is that most of them were short-lived. According to Dr Kemper, the newspapers of the mid- to late nineteenth century may have "reflected a more strenuous partisanship and devoted more space to political affairs" than became the norm in the new century, but that zealousness would prompt "an organization to publish a paper during campaign and then suspend."[21]

Although not recorded in the Accessions Register of the Muncie Public Library, copies of most daily and weekly local newspapers were delivered to the library and immediately made available in the reading room. A report in *The Muncie Daily Times*, dated 22 January 1895, notes that at that time, when Muncie ranked "fifth with the cities having public libraries in this state," as many as eighteen daily and weekly newspapers were being received for "the use of the public." The 1905 printed catalogue of the new Carnegie Library presents a shorter list of a dozen "NEWSPAPERS CURRENTLY RECEIVED." These included three Muncie papers (*The Muncie Herald*, *The Muncie Star*, and *The Muncie Times*), three Indianapolis papers (*Star*, *News*, and *Sentinel*), two from Chicago (*The Chicago Record-Herald* and *The Chicago Daily Tribune*), the *Commercial Tribune* out of Cincinnati, the Louisville *Courier-Journal*, *The Washington Post*, and *The New York Weekly Tribune*.[22] No record has been preserved of the number of times that individual newspapers were consulted, but the continued subscription over a period of thirty years to several well-respected titles from major cities east of the Mississippi and the Lynds' finding that "the circulation of out-of-town papers [in Muncie] ... was negligible in 1890,"[23] provide confirmation that for the people of Muncie – or, at least for those seeking such an orifice – the library was a main window on to the wider world.

As well as newspapers, the reading room of the Muncie Public Library was reasonably well stocked with up-to-date issues of contemporary magazines and journals. In most cases, these chiefly monthly publications were collected together and bound some while after the end of any given year. Unlike newspapers, the bound issues (and oftentimes single issues before they were bound) were added to the Accessions Catalogue and accorded an accession number. Also unlike the Muncie newspapers, none of these constituted local publications, so that their inclusion in the library should be seen as so many tiny portals on the outside world.

The most popular monthlies available were *The Atlantic Monthly*, published by Houghton Mifflin in Boston, *The North American Review*, originally out of Boston but later New York, *Lippincott's Monthly Magazine*, out of Philadelphia, and *The Century* and *Harper's Monthly*, both out of New York.[24] The popularity of the five main monthly magazines points to a readership that wished to keep up with the latest trends and enjoyed reading serialized fiction by contemporary authors and reviews of some of the latest books. We do not have any evidence that the library board consulted the monthly reviews prior to ordering new books. However, the library did respond to demand and, on occasion, particularly during the 1890s, extended the number of periodicals to which it subscribed. When *The Cosmopolitan* began publishing in 1886, it soon became one of the most popular of family magazines, and, in 1891, the library added it to its subscription list.[25] To cater to a demand from women readers, the *Ladies' Home Journal*, which had begun publishing in 1883, was subscribed to from 1892, though its contents were too ephemeral to attract readers once the issues became available in bound format several years after the individual issues first reached the library.[26] It was followed into the reading room by *The Woman's Home Companion*, and *McClure's Magazine*, which only later became a woman's magazine, both first taken in 1899.[27]

Among all classes, there were quite a few individuals who made a habit of borrowing both single issue and bound periodicals. The What Middletown Read (WMR) database allows us to break down the readers of these periodicals both by occupation classification and by gender. Taking as our example here the copies of *Lippincott's Monthly Magazine*, which were available for borrowing throughout the period for which we have relevant records, we find that approximately three-quarters of the borrowers for whom we know their occupation were white collar. Of these, there were almost twice as many individual female readers as males. Among them were Mary Myers, the daughter of a poultry dealer, and Zulena Wilcoxon, a musician, both of whom stand out as frequent magazine borrowers. William Snyder, Muncie's superintendent of schools and a regular patron, was one such white-collar male reader. He borrowed different issues of *Lippincott's* at least a dozen times. Between them, Burt Bradbury, a young notary public, and his wife, Jeannie, took out different volumes of the magazine on twenty-eight occasions. Recurrent blue-collar male readers of *Lippincott's* included Norwood Carnes, a local florist; George L. Kurtz, a day labourer; and Mark D. Garrett, a printer. Among blue-collar females were Mary Leonard, a laundress; Lillie Wolfram, a bartender's wife; and Ida Brown, a saleswoman. There were very few unskilled blue-collar readers of *Lippincott's*, and those that we can identify were all male.

As daily and weekly newspapers were not included in the library's borrowing records, we cannot say for certain whether they too achieved a similar broadly based socio-economic readership. However, with their free availability in the library's well-lighted reading room, the likelihood is that they would have been, if anything, even more appealing to readers from the whole social spectrum. What can be learned from the subscription lists for magazines and the transaction record of single issues and bound volumes is that, whether seeking entertainment or instruction, the Muncie public used its reading to look outwards beyond the limits of their small city. The worlds that they encountered through their reading, whether real or imagined or a combination of the two, may have helped to induce a more cosmopolitan ambience.

There is plenty of evidence from the transaction records of the library to show how well it could support the reading demands of many blue-collar and low whitecollar patrons of the sort profiled by Robert Hall and Julieanne Lamond elsewhere in this volume. By way of a few examples here: between them, Isaac B. Saxon, a railroad switchman, and his school age son were responsible for a staggering 1,116 recorded transactions.[28] Close behind them and accounting for a joint 1,084 recorded transactions were Addie Knowlton and her far younger brother, Bobbie, whose late father had made a living as a dealer in lightning rods.[29] A mother and her son, Dora and Omer Mitchell, a glass blower at Ball Brothers, are recorded as having taken out books from the library a total of 902 times.[30] What is distinctive about such library patrons is not just that their borrowing was prolific but that they all belonged to a lower-middle-class or working-class (blue collar) background. It could be argued that as patrons they gave the Muncie Public Library its primary raison d'être, though, taking readership as a whole, their clientage and extensive borrowing record were far more the exception than being in any sense typical of library usage by the city's manual workforce. The library may have trumpeted the naked fact that its borrowing privileges constituted an amenity that was freely available to all the citizens of Muncie but, in truth, the number of workingclass readers in relation to the size of the population remained disappointingly few. Where, too, in their idealism, the founders of the library saw it as an institution that would bring untold benefits and advantages to the community through the general diffusion of knowledge about the world, it would be difficult to argue that becoming a patron was at any time an automatic pathway to socio-economic advancement. Rather, the main benefits should be figured as cultural, educational, and pleasurable. For all their use of the Muncie Public Library, these readers and others like them benefited most from what (in the grandiose words of three trustees who penned a brief history) the library aspired to achieve by "supplying and creating those forces which make for better living, a higher civilization, and the development of the whole man."[31]

In our own day, and perhaps as a counter to this kind of upbeat rhetoric, Ann C. Sparanese has argued that such seemingly beneficent motives for attracting blue-collar and labour readers to the public library in the United States during the second half of the nineteenth century might be seen as a covert form of social control. "The intellectual founders of the public library," she writes, saw it as a civic institution that "would provide an antidote to the revolutionary fervor prevalent among the working classes in Europe ... [and] would not only have a democratizing effect, but ... would combat the political extremes that they believed were the result of illiteracy and ignorance."[32] If such hidden motives were present in the thinking of Muncie's movers and shakers in the late nineteenth century, they certainly did not express them openly, but exercised what Dee Garrison has described as "the elitist nature of public library leadership,"[33] and what we might wish to interpret as a kind of benevolent paternalism in endeavouring to attract a broader readership that would ideally embrace the whole social spectrum. That they failed to attract a higher proportion of blue-collar readers belies the notion of social control unless one wished to argue that there was conscious targeting of the intellectual leaders of the labour movement. In conservative Muncie, we have discovered no direct evidence for that. More compellingly, it was through individual choice that a number of blue-collar or low-white-collar readers, albeit small in relation to their total number within the city as a whole, were drawn to the library. If its shelves were largely devoid of radical writings, that did not stop such readers from patronizing the library, as we shall see in more detail from the example that follows.

Rosa Burmaster (1880–1954), a member of the high school graduating class of 1899, provides a good illustration of at least one gifted individual from a lower-class background whose intellectual life became expanded through her use of the library. Rosa was the elder child of German-born immigrant parents, who had settled some years earlier in Spencer, Owen County, Indiana, about fifty-five miles to the southwest of Indianapolis.

Her father, Frederick (1854–1923), originally a native of Hamburg, listed his line of work as a "tinner," which seems to mean a tinsmith, a skilled blue-collar occupation. Her mother, Augusta (1858–1905), who hailed from West Prussia, is listed in the 1880 U.S. Census as "Keeping House." There may have been a further relocation when Rosa was still a small child for her younger sibling, Huston, was born in the state of Illinois in 1889. In 1895, when Rosa was about fourteen, the family moved back to Indiana, settling in Muncie, where, shortly after their arrival, she enrolled on 1 June as a patron of the Muncie Public Library, calling upon a German-born local baker to stand as her guarantor.[34] During the next seven years, the WMR records for Rosa show well over two hundred transactions, averaging more than thirty books borrowed each year. Although when he was to reach the joining age of ten in July 1899, Huston also became a patron, neither of their parents joined the library. It is unknown whether lack of fluency in English was the reason for their non-membership. However, Frederick acted as guarantor for his son, as well as later for at least two other unrelated young people who signed up as library members in 1902.

Looking at Rosa Burmaster's habits of reading as represented by the WMR records throws up a number of revealing particulars. As might be anticipated from an impressionable first-generation child of Teutonic immigrants, she showed a fondness in her mid-teenage years for German authors in translation, borrowing in quick succession during the late summer and fall of 1896 such popular romances as Moritz von Reichenbach's *The Eichhofs*, Adolph Streckfuss's *Castle Hohenwald*, E. Werner's *The Alpine Fay*, Ossip Schubin's *Erlach Court* and *O Thou, My Austria*, Eugenie John's *The Old Mam'selle's Secret*, *Gold Elsie* and *The Lady with the Rubies*, and W. Heimburg's *My Heart's Darling*. Many of these had been translated into English by Annis Lee Wister (1830–1908), and had been issued by a Philadelphia publisher in a uniform edition in 1889. The popularity of these works is attested by the fact that almost all of them were borrowed well over one hundred times by the patrons of the Muncie Public Library.[35] Over the previous spring and summer of the same year, Rosa's choice of books had been Martha Finley's popular Elsie series, which she devoured religiously, even on occasion returning with a whiff of nostalgia to the works of the same author at a later date. As a more mature choice, she never tired of Louisa May Alcott, whose *An Old-Fashioned Girl* she picked up shortly after joining the library, and to whom she returned by borrowing *Little Women*, *Little Men*, and *Jo's Boys* in 1901, by which time she was in her early twenties. It deserves mentioning that those beacons of boys' reading, Horatio Alger, Oliver Optic, and Harry

Castlemon, were completely shunned by her, not one of their books ever attracting her patronage.[36] Writers like Susan Coolidge, the author of the "What Katie Did" series, and Jacob Abbott, who authored the Franconia stories, briefly invited her attention, though she does not appear to have become a devotee of either. More so too than many other children of her age, Rosa regularly borrowed bound periodicals such as Mary Maple Dodge's *St. Nicholas Magazine*, and volumes of *Wide Awake*, and *Harper's Young People*.

Many school-age patrons of the Muncie Public Library moderated or even eliminated their borrowing once they had graduated. That is far from the case with Rosa Burmaster. While still in high school as a fifteen-year-old, she became enamoured of Charles Dickens, taking out *David Copperfield*, *Dombey and Son*, and *Oliver Twist* in successive stints over a few short weeks in 1896. Her love of Dickens manifested itself again more than two years after when she borrowed in succession *Bleak House* and *A Tale of Two Cities*, returning shortly after to reread *Dombey and Son*, and other novels later on. In the interim, her fairly precocious reading included works by Nathaniel Hawthorne, George Eliot, Oliver Goldsmith, Walter Scott, James Fenimore Cooper, and Edward Bulwer-Lytton. However, the writer who appears to have intrigued her more than any other was Thomas Carlyle. Beginning with the opening volume of his seven-part *Critical and Miscellaneous Essays*, a book that had been in the library from almost its inception and only attracted three other readers within the WMR records, Rosa took out shortly after the three solid tomes of Carlyle's *History of the French Revolution*, followed by a multi-volume text of the same author's *History of Friedrich II of Prussia*, which she consumed over two months towards the beginning of 1898. She rounded off her reading of Carlyle with *Sartor Resartus*, the mock-German setting of which may have amused her, dipping back occasionally to the volumes of the same author's essays. Among Muncie readers, her preoccupation with Carlyle, by the late nineteenth century a writer whose reputation had been undergoing an inexorable decline, remains unprecedented and unrepeated. All the holdings of Carlyle's works in the library had been gifted by one T.J. Guthrie in 1875, and no further acquisitions had been made later. Rosa Burmaster's broad, if not quite comprehensive, reading of Carlyle, while still only a high-schooler, should be reason enough to describe her as exceptional in more than one sense.

Rosa was one of thirty students who graduated from Muncie High School in 1899. Of these, ten were boys and twenty were girls, an enhanced proportion of males by comparison with adjacent years. Following her high school graduation, the WMR database holds records of Rosa's continuous use of the library through to October 1900 with a subsequent gap to April 1901, and then no borrowing records later than the end of June 1902.[37] The gaps here may be explained through the likelihood that she attended college during those times. Her obituary in 1954 states that "she was a graduate of Ball State College [at that time known as the Eastern Indiana Normal Institute] and studied for two years at Columbia University."[38] It is evident that when she returned several years later to Muncie she was qualified as an educator, and her career took her from a first position in the city at Washington Elementary School to becoming a Spanish teacher at Central High School, and finally to the post of principal of the Washington School, which she held until her retirement some twenty-five years later. Her obituary adds that "she was active from the start of her teaching career in the National Educational Association" and was prominent in establishing a much-admired pension program for Indiana teachers that provided a model for many other states.

Shortly after her high school graduation, Rosa Burmaster was one of the founding members of the Tourist Club, one of a number of prominent Women's Clubs that flourished in turn-of-the-century Muncie. According to Dr Kemper, the club was inaugurated in November 1899, and was formed "for the purpose of studying the life, history and literature of peoples in other lands by means of an imaginary tour around the world." The means by which this was achieved was by individual members penning made-up letters from different parts of the world. Between its foundation and 1907, the club's weekly meetings produced a total of 425 such letters, with the occasional participation of "real world travelers, who talked informally of foreign scenes."[39] Diverging perhaps from its original objective, when Rosa Burmaster became its president in 1906–7, the club turned its attention to the study of Shakespeare. None of the fictitious letters created by club members is known to survive, so that one can only speculate on the touristic content of the pieces that they wrote. Nonetheless, an examination of Rosa's library borrowing between late 1899 and the summer of 1902 reveals an extraordinary preponderance of works of travel, a subject area that was virtually absent from her earlier reading. The initial meeting of the club had been organized to take place in the home of Mrs Rose Budd Stewart, the wife of the Delaware County assessor, on 23 November 1899, and the following day found Rosa Burmaster poring over the shelves of the Muncie Public Library to track down a fitting book for her first presentation to the club. The choice she made, which may be deemed apt for a future teacher of Spanish, was Washington

Irving's *The Alhambra*, a classic account of a rambling expedition from Seville to Grenada. There was more than enough there for a lively talk, and, when Rosa renewed the book two weeks later, it may well have been to prepare for a second presentation. Among later borrowings that were probably inspired by her involvement with the Tourist Club were James Dabney McCabe's *Our Young Folks Abroad: The Adventures of Four American Boys and Girls in a Journey through Europe to Constantinople*, Robert Mintum's *From New York to Delhi: By Way of Rio de Janeiro, Australia and China*, and Bayard Taylor's *Views A-foot: Or, Europe Seen with Knapsack and Staff*. There is little doubt that these and other books were borrowed and read with club presentations in mind. Those presentations will almost certainly have included oral readings from her chosen texts.

Another feature of the Muncie Tourist Club that deserves brief comment is that, with the exception of Mrs Stewart, who provided a venue for the first meeting, all of the other eight founding members were immediate graduates of the Muncie High School class of 1899. As well as creating a rendezvous for cultural discussion, it is evident that this club (and perhaps others too) provided an opportunity for old school friends to bond when they were no longer together in the classroom. Most of these first members of the Tourist Club were also patrons of the Muncie Public Library, and, with those who were, we can see through their borrowing records that they too were active contributors to the club's proceedings. For example, Ethel Brady, the daughter of a superintendent at the Muncie Bridge Works, took out George Raum's *A Tour Around the World* on four different occasions, and was the single borrower of *Seal and Salmon Fisheries of Alaska*, an official government publication that will have been an unusual but instructive source for discussion. Ola Courtney, who like Rosa later became a teacher in the Muncie school system, borrowed Lafayette Loomis's *Index Guide to Travel and Art-Study in Europe* within weeks of its having already been taken out by Miss Brady, and it is likely that several of the club's presentations turned out as shared readings. "Although only flights of fancy," wrote one member in reporting to Dr Kemper the purpose of the club, "our letters describing the various scenes and incidents of travel in almost every country on the globe have been very helpful and delightful ... Each week we met to hear, read and approve the letters written – very few letters were sent home behind time."[40] There is more than enough evidence to show how tenaciously the weekly meetings of the club were indebted to the library. In their endeavours to become citizens of the world, the young women may not have achieved more than a kind of armchair cosmopolitanism, but even that would not have been possible without the browsing potential that the library could offer them.

By the time Dr Kemper compiled his *Twentieth Century History of Delaware County*, the new Carnegie Library in Muncie had been functioning for at least three years, and, even in the absence of borrowing records, there is every reason to believe that Rosa Burmaster and her fellow members of the Tourist Club made good use of the new facility. With the trajectory of her career assured, there would be little else to comment on about her, except that in the 1920s a couple of would-be social scientists found their way to Muncie, and began the Middletown project that was to make them and their subject quite famous. When Robert and Helen Lynd first came to Muncie, Kemper was still alive, and was hailed by them as a historical fountain of wisdom "whose lifetime so nearly spans that of Middletown."[41] However, it was the contemporary working people of the city to whom they eagerly turned as they began to compile their narrative and the extensive statistical information that accompanied it. Many of those working people, now in their middle age, were of the same cadre of young boys and girls, who, a quarter of a century before, had first cut their teeth as library patrons. Among those that the Lynds consulted was Rosa Burmaster, whose prominent role has recently been recognized by Sarah E. Igo, in her investigation of the Middletown studies. According to Igo, Burmaster was asked by the Lynds "to comment directly on the manuscript-in-progress. She actively collaborated with the surveyors, reviewing the questionnaires that they distributed in Muncie's classrooms and correcting wordings she thought the locals might not understand." Her terse comments on the still unpublished manuscript of *Middletown* concentrated in particular on the Lynds' remarks on the city's system of education, which she confessed "were better than I [thought] they would be," but tended to obscure under a welter of statistics the human aspects of "actual teaching."[42] It is not known whether her advice extended to commenting on the Lynds' account of the city's reading habits, but Burmaster's involvement with Middletown provides one particular link between the world of the 1890s and that of the 1920s, a bridge that was often crossed in the published study. If asked her opinion, one suspects that she would have agreed with the sound belief of her intellectual hero, Thomas Carlyle, that "the true University of these days is a Collection of Books."[43] Further, if brought into this debate and asked to provide an institutional measure of what might be deemed "cosmopolitan" about the small town in which she lived her life, I have little doubt that she would have cited the library.

Writing from a metropolitan perspective, Kwame Anthony Appiah warns that "celebrations of the 'cosmopolitan' can suggest an unpleasant posture of superiority towards the putative provincial," but (as we have seen) late nineteenth-century Muncie endeavoured to project itself as a small city that near perfectly combined so many aspects of the rural and the urban. In introducing his theme, Appiah argues well for a twofold definition of cosmopolitanism that encompasses "the idea that we have obligations to others" and that, as citizens of the world, "we take seriously the value not just of human life but of particular human lives," that we reach a recognition that "people are different ... and there is much to learn from our differences."[44] In the context of the library, the board took very seriously its custodial obligations to the citizens of Muncie both in terms of the choice of books that it deemed appropriate for them to be able to read, and in encouraging them to make best use of the institution. Whether regular use of the library helped to make its patrons into "citizens of the world" is far more difficult to ascertain. Likely, many individuals benefited from the presence of the library, but for many others – those who never ventured through its doors to browse its shelves – it was an institution that played no part in their everyday lives, and the What Middletown Read database can throw no direct light on their cultural habits. However, for its users, what the Muncie Public Library provided was ready access to a range and variety of reading material that had been unavailable to prior generations. From its inception and through to its present incarnation in the twenty-first century, the Muncie Public Library has remained an open-access library in which browsing its shelves is taken as a given. It may be argued that such free and open access to books in the context of an American small city should be seen as an enduring symbol both of its democratic and its cosmopolitan aspirations. For the majority of patrons, the Muncie Public Library offered what the British book trade historian Catherine Armstrong aptly dubbed as the positioning of "the town and its readers in a global community of knowledge," and which, no less forcefully, the Lynds described as a "vicarious entry into other, imagined kinds of living."[45] In our own age of the Internet and the World Wide Web, the locating of a small city like Muncie or many other of its ilk as an active component of a global community is becoming ever more emphatic. Cosmopolitanism takes on new meanings as we grapple with such previously inaccessible universalisms.

NOTES

1 *Muncie Morning News*, 18 May 1902 (vol. 25, no. 20, p. 10).

2 Edgar S. Shumway, *A Day in Ancient Rome, Being a Revision of Lohr's "Aus Dem Alten Rom"* (Boston: D.C. Heath and Company, 1887), [5], 94.

3 McMurran (2013).
4 Beck (2007).
5 Fischer (2009, 219, 235–8).
6 A useful historical overview of the concept of cosmopolitanism as it emerged from the ancient world can be found in the on-line *Stanford Encyclopedia of Philosophy*, consultable at http://plato.stanford.edu/entries/cosmopolitanism/ (accessed 22 August 2013).
7 Jackman and Vavreck (2011).
8 Quoted by Appiah (2006, xv).
9 Appiah (2006, xxi).
10 Hugh A. Cowing, *A Meandering Hoosier* (Muncie, 1937), 22–4. The extracts given here represent but half of the poem.
11 Chapin (1907, 2).
12 The substance of Mrs Rose's speech was published with commentary in the *Muncie Daily Herald* (23 June 1897).
13 "Libraries: Brief Resume of Our Public Library" (*The Morning News*, 12 May 1893). The author of the piece is almost certainly Nathaniel F. Ethell, the longtime editor and owner of this newspaper. Ethell was an Muncie Public Library stockholder, becoming a patron on 2 July 1875. Perhaps as a result of his spirited editorial defence of the library, he was elected to its board on 10 July 1894, and later served as its treasurer (minutes of 7 March 1899).
14 Kemper (1908, I:44–5). Muncie is the county seat of Delaware County, Indiana.
15 Kemper (1908, I:50).
16 Jacob (2006, 5).
17 This essay, as well as those by Shrock and Tatlock elsewhere in this volume, rely upon the reproduction of Muncie Public Library borrowing records found in the What Middletown Read database to assess reading behavior in this small eastern Indiana city. It should be noted that although the public library was far and away the main openly accessible resource for books in Muncie during the 1890s and at the turn of the twentieth century, there were other suppliers of books and periodicals in Muncie. Among these were smaller collections allocated for borrowing in several of the local churches, and a short-lived Working Men's Library. The high school also developed its own library. No transaction records are known to have survived from any of these other city libraries. At any given time, the town was able to support at least one viable bookstore. Additionally, a small but random selection of printed material was offered for sale at or through local drugstores. Publishers sometimes advertised their latest books in the Muncie newspapers, and it was not unusual for personal readers (usually from a wealthier or more educated background) to order books by mail for direct delivery to their homes. While many townsfolk could trace

their ancestry to Continental Europe, we have found no evidence that books in foreign languages were readily accessible to them. Paradoxically, if they harboured cosmopolitan aspirations, these will have found expression almost exclusively through works in English. Plus ça change!

18 These and subsequent figures are taken from the What Middletown Read database (www.bsu.edu/libraries/wmr). It reproduces the holdings, patron register, and circulation data for the library for most of the period between 1891 and 1902.

19 The final books entered into the Accession Catalogue before the end of 1902 (30 December) were the three volumes of *The Prose Tales of Edgar Alan Poe*, published by A.C. Armstrong & Co. of New York in 1893, for none of which do we have surviving circulation records.

20 *Muncie Illustrated* (Muncie: Commercial Publishing Co., 1897), n.p.

21 Kemper (1908, I:280).

22 *Catalogue of Books in the Muncie Public Library* (Muncie, 1905), 192. In its very early years, the MPL had taken *The Cincinnati Gazette*, but soon after substituted this with a subscription to the Louisville *Courier-Journal* (8 February 1878).

23 Lynd and Lynd (1957, 471).

24 *Harper's Weekly* in book form was borrowed only a small fraction of the number of times of its monthly parent magazine.

25 Under E.D. Walker's editorship, *The Cosmopolitan* became a literary magazine from the 1890s, featuring some of the best-known authors of the day (e.g., Ambrose Bierce, Jack London, and Theodore Dreiser). It was to transform into a women's magazine in the late 1960s.

26 Carl F. Kaestle et al. (1991, 263), gives paid circulation records in 1900 of 846,000 for the *Ladies' Home Journal*, making it the American magazine most in demand at that time. Next in popularity was *Munsey's Magazine* (also subscribed to by the MPL), which had a paid circulation of 650,000. Of the top ten magazines listed by Kaestle for 1900, the only other one subscribed to by the MPL was *McClure's Magazine*, which – in tenth place – achieved a paid circulation of 369,000.

27 Ohmann (2009, 108–9) observes that magazines "provided mass urban readership for Robert Louis Stevenson, Rudyard Kipling, Thomas Hardy, Mark Twain, William Dean Howells, Hamlin Garland, and others … [The publisher] Henry Holt worried that monthly magazines would 'kill off' books, and indeed, growth in magazine readership in the 1890s far outpaced that of books, especially among the new monthlies."

28 In the 1900 Census, their surname is recorded as "Saxton." The son's first name was probably Louis.

29 Addie Knowlton (b. 1868) married James Manor, a mail carrier, in 1886. Robert Knowlton (b. 1882), still at school, was living in Muncie with his widowed mother, Catherine, in 1900.
30 Dora was born in 1855 or 1856 and her son, Omer, in 1874.
31 Stouder, Wood, and Marsh (1905, xiii).
32 Sparanese (2002, 23).
33 Garrison (2003, xiv).
34 The baker was Aug. M. Maick, who (according to the 1900 U.S. Census) had emigrated from Germany in 1876. The likelihood is that he was Rosa's uncle or cousin since her mother was née Maick.
35 See the essay in this volume by Lynne Tatlock (chapter 11), and her seminal study of nineteenth-century German authors in translation (Tatlock 2012). Tatlock also refers to Burmaster.
36 Although not an exact contrast, Horatio Alger's *Phil, the Fiddler* and *Ragged Dick* were two of the first eight books borrowed by ten-year old Huston Burmaster after he joined the library in 1899. It is always possible that Rosa borrowed these and similar items prior to the surviving WMR records.
37 The WMR borrowing records cease after the beginning of December 1902.
38 Muncie/Delaware County Digital Resource Library at http://www.munciepubliclibrary.org/resources/local-history-and-genealogy/muncie-delaware-county-digital-resource-library/ (accessed 21 August 2013).
39 Kemper (1908 I:485).
40 Kemper (1908 I:485).
41 Lynd and Lynd (1957, 10–11). Kemper died in 1927.
42 Igo (2007, 43, 50).
43 Carlyle (1993, 140).
44 Appiah (2006, xiii, xv).
45 Hinks and Armstrong (2008, vii); Lynd and Lynd (1957, 237).

13 Zones of Connection: Common Reading in a Regional Australian Library

JULIEANNE LAMOND

In Gail Jones's novel *Sorry*, two girls living in an isolated Australian town share a theory about reading in common:

> Mary had a theory that when people read the same words they were imperceptibly knitted ... there were transactions, comminglings, adjacencies of mind and of sense ... even in the world-weariness that reading sometimes induces, they absorbed irresistibly, naïvely, elements of the lives they imagined. A kind of family without limits.[1]

The novel presents Mary's theory as naive, but nonetheless it expresses an intuitive sense of commonality or imagined relationship often attached to mutual reading of the same book – especially, as happens in library borrowing, the same copy of the same book. Later in the novel reading in common is described as providing a "zone of connection" between people distant in time and space. This term is useful for describing the uncertain yet circumscribed nature of shared reading experiences. This chapter describes the extent to which we can trace the "zones of connection" enabled by reading in a small and relatively isolated Australian town in the early years of the twentieth century by examining their library borrowing.

The Lambton Mechanics' and Miners' Institute, a small library in a mining town in New South Wales, is one of seven libraries whose records (in Lambton's case, from 1903 to 1912) are collected and digitized in the Australian Common Reader database.[2] The Lambton Institute opened in 1867; it was one of some thousand such institutes established in Australian towns and cities during the nineteenth century.[3] Such workers' institutes were the primary point of access to reading material for many Australians living outside of metropolitan cities. Mechanics' Institutes continued with some success in Australia long after the movement had declined in the United Kingdom, well into the twentieth century. Their longevity was primarily due to the lack of a strong network of public libraries, especially in regional areas, at least until the late 1930s.[4]

Lambton was, to a slightly lesser extent than the readers at Brancepeth in Lydia Wevers's study, a community whose access to books centred largely upon one institution. Such situations offer opportunities to understand what Christine Pawley has called "the social meanings of print" in a particular time and place.[5] Might there exist in Lambton what Martyn Lyons, drawing on Stanley Fish, defines as communities of readers: those "with shared values and common practices"?[6] Pawley and Wevers – in their contributions to this volume, as in their previous work – point to the importance of considering the local and social contexts of acts of reading, especially the significance of local institutions in structuring opportunities both for reading and the forms of sociability it might enable. As the contributions of Felsenstein, Shrock, Tatlock, and Roberts to this volume all suggest, digitized circulation records also offer an opportunity to investigate common reading practices. Statistical approaches to library loan data offer a detailed and complex but limited understanding of the nature of common reading practices in a specific place and time. They do not reveal conscious communities of readers, but rather networks of readers: a set of relationships between books and readers that together describe not the practices but the conditions of possibility for literary sociability. The relationships between books and readers that structure this network constitute zones of connection: between local readers and global bestsellers, Australian books and British readers, and between readers themselves.

In Lambton, a mining community consisting largely of immigrants from mining regions in England and Wales, there were densely interconnected patterns of shared reading practices. These miners and shopkeepers, women and men, formed part of the mass readerships for popular fiction and periodicals that had emerged around the turn of the twentieth century. They read extensively but idiosyncratically: their reading patterns denote an intersection between global English-language mass readerships for popular fiction and local modes of literary production and reception. Reading of popular British fiction in book form closely followed serialization in Australian periodicals; fiction by expatriate Australian writers was very popular; and reading habits and choices were also influenced by patterns of migration to the area, especially from Wales.

Borrowing from the Lambton Institute may not have made its patrons into "citizens of the world" (in Felsenstein's terms) but rather reinforced and helped to sustain the coexistence of strong ties to a local community in regional New South Wales and those to the cultures from which they had travelled and which were still referred to as "home." In Lambton, the colonial and migration context alters the provincial/metropolitan dynamic examined by Felsenstein and Rubin in this volume. Colonial readers often considered themselves not so much provincial as part of a very extended metropolis. Nonetheless, the relationship between Britain and Australia was also important in creating local communal identities. Lambton was, in Alan Lester's terms, part of an "imperial network," in which places are "partly constituted through [their] relations with other places."[7] The local community was constituted, in large part, by its relationship to a variety of other places and cultures – primarily mining regions of Wales and England. It should also be noted that many of the Australian writers the patrons were borrowing at Lambton were themselves involved in discursive negotiations of the relationship between Australian and British identity – expatriate writers such as Rosa Praed and Guy Boothby, whose work ranged in its settings across England and Australia (among other places).[8] The Lambton Institute was, perhaps, a "window to the world" – the reading of periodicals and recent fiction from the United States and Britain marked its patrons' participation in global networks of print culture. It also provided a means by which patrons could engage in the complex negotiations between different homes and cultures that was part of the migrant – and colonial – experience.

Lambton was one of a number of mining towns that sprung up to service newly opened coal mines in the Newcastle region of New South Wales (NSW) in the 1860s. This had been a mining region since 1799, initially with convict labour. In the 1850s, driven by demand for coal from Sydney and Melbourne in the wake of the gold rushes, the coal trade experienced a boom which would last until the 1890s.[9] The Scottish Australian Mining Company, which founded the major colliery in Lambton in 1863, was one of several British firms operating mines in Australia. Lambton was one of seven small communities, relatively isolated from the nearest regional centre and from each other, dependent until 1915 on the mining trade. In 1903 the population of Lambton was estimated to be four thousand.

Although Lambton had been one of the most prosperous colliery towns in the Newcastle region, the period covered by the loan records (1903–12) was one of transition for these communities. While there was some degree of recovery from poverty following the depression of the 1890s, mines in the area were beginning to give out and there was a major loss of residents from Newcastle to the newly opened mining area of Cessnock. The instability of mining work led to many miners commuting around the district, on foot or by horse and cart. These were the last years in which Lambton was first and foremost a mining town. From 1915, the new steelworks opened by BHP in nearby Waratah mediated a shift from mining to industrial work for many residents of the area.

The Australian colonies' long economic boom from the 1860s to the 1880s led to increasing numbers of migrants, most of whom were from Britain.[10] This was especially true of those who came to the colonies to work as miners; these men and their families were largely from mining areas of Wales and England. Borrowers at Lambton included, in no small number, those who had come to NSW from Wales, in particular, but also Scotland and England in the preceding twenty to thirty years. Mining is the most commonly listed occupation for patrons at the Lambton Institute (33 per cent of all patrons for whom we have occupation data). Lambton's library users also included mine owners, politicians, policemen, and a considerable middle band (almost 60 per cent of those for whom we have demographic information) of skilled tradesmen, retailers, and other service occupations required in a town that was relatively isolated from the nearest major centre.

The proportion of migrant miners at Lambton makes potential comparisons with Rose and Baggs's studies of Welsh miners, for example, particularly salient.[11] It also provides an interesting context for thinking about these readers in national terms – as "Australian readers" – when they were entirely likely to have retained strong localized identities not just in terms of the Lambton area but in terms of their countries of origin. For example, Allen Raine's Welsh-themed novels were very popular at Lambton, but so were the Australian (and Australian-themed) books by Steele Rudd and Nat Gould.

The information held in the yellowed subscribers' ledgers, stock books, and loan registers from even a library as small as Lambton is large and diverse. At Lambton there are more than 25,000 loans, involving 481 patrons and somewhere in the vicinity of 2690 titles. Many of these titles constitute what one historian of the Institute describes as "a generally unrecognized mass."[12] Her bewilderment is likely to be shared by almost anyone looking at these records, even a specialist in fiction of the period, because so many of these authors and titles dwell in what Franco Moretti calls "the cellars of culture": the mass of books that have not survived to be taught or reprinted.[13] These books, as Katherine Bode has recently demonstrated in the Australian context, form a large part of the industry of publishing and distribution of books.[14] Library loan records show they formed a very large proportion of the reading lives of "ordinary" people as well.

The status of the fiction held and loaned in the Mechanics' and Miners' Institutes and Schools of Arts in Australia was contentious, and the history of such organizations is fraught with tension between the intentions of middle-class patrons and the actual desires and reading habits of a largely working-class membership. Usually established by mine owners, as Jonathan Rose puts it, "with the frank intention of making their workers sober, pious, and productive,"[15] these institutions flourished in the coal regions of Britain in the early to mid-nineteenth century. "Around 1850, nineteen out of fifty-four collieries in Northumberland and Durham had some kind of library or reading room."[16] Social historian John Benson describes these libraries as part "of a much larger entrepreneurial offensive designed to turn the workers into a reliable factor of production."[17] The Lambton Mechanics' and Miners' Institute followed this model. It was established by the Scottish Australian Mining Company with the usual aims of workers' amenity and pacification. Thomas Croudace, Lambton Mine manager and founding president of the Institute, was reported in a local paper as follows:

> He believed that most of the disturbances that occurred between the miners and the overseers were caused by that ignorance which must necessarily exist where no means of intellectual improvement existed ... the very fact of their being allowed access to journals of all shades of opinions would prevent them from taking a one-sided view of things themselves.[18]

This institute – and the educational opportunities it presented – seems to have been intended at the outset to be a form of social control of an assertive workforce. Brian Engel describes an initially "patriarchal" relationship between management and workers at the Lambton Colliery deteriorating in the 1870s, leading to "increased activity by the union movement which brought an end the close relationship between the miners and the colliery management."[19] Croudace attempted to resign as president in this period; he (and then his son, Frank) had very little involvement with the institute from the turn of the century. Lambton seems to have followed the model of many Institutes in Britain as in Australia, run by a largely middle-class committee. Mary Rabbitt notes that "of eight presidents from 1878 to 1938, only one, Edwin Hemmings, was a miner."[20] The others included clerks, a tailor, a letter carrier, and a butcher. The committee's debates in 1882 over whether to allow the Institute to open on Sundays indicate a presumption that the core (or intended) patrons of the Institute were miners and young men. This debate also reveals the different aims of the Institute as understood by its middle-class committee. Some members extolled the virtues of the Institute in moral terms: giving miners and young men "somewhere to go" other than the public house. Others stressed that "every avenue of education should be thrown open" to the Institute's patrons.[21] The committee agreed to allow the Institute to open on Sundays, despite strong resistance from religious members who were concerned about the "secular influence" of the reading table.[22]

The Lambton Institute opened in 1867 and moved into grander premises in 1894, which included a lecture room, classrooms, and a library.[23] While the primary activity of the Institute was the provision of library services, it also provided premises and equipment at various times for chess, draughts, ping-pong, billiards, and a gymnasium. A "debating and reading class" established in 1878 was short-lived.[24] Another debating club began in 1905, which seems to have focused on questions of politics and international affairs. Croudace encouraged the Institute's committee to "procure the services of some able gentleman who would give a course of lectures,"[25] and this was undertaken very sporadically over subsequent years. Quarterly membership began at 2s 6d and rose to 3s 6d in later years. Two books could be borrowed at a time, and would incur a penalty if kept for more than four weeks. The library opened, at various times, from two to six nights a week, with the reading room open all day on Sunday from 1882.

Library holdings were acquired through donations, loans from the Public Library of NSW, and local and London purchases on the decision of the committee, with suggestions from members. On at least one occasion a "proposition book" was left on the reading table for a month, with suggestions then referred to a subcommittee to revise the catalogue.[26] Croudace rightly identifies "journals of all shades of opinion" as central to the service provided by the Institute: the library held a wide range of local and overseas magazines and newspapers (see fig. 13.1). As Laurel Brake has argued, fiction serialized in newspapers and magazines formed a significant and under-analysed proportion of the reading of this period.[27] Periodical subscriptions were decided upon by the committee and changed according to the popularity of individual titles. The *British Workman* was discontinued in 1880; its alignment with middle-class aims for working-class self-improvement might account for its lack of popularity at Lambton as elsewhere. The library also cancelled its subscription to the *Argosy* (which published sensation fiction by Charles Reade and Ellen Wood); these publications were replaced by the literary monthly *The Nineteenth Century* and a range of Australian newspapers including the *Queenslander*, the *Australian*, and the *Sydney*

THE FOLLOWING

LEADING COLONIAL AND ENGLISH

Papers and Periodicals

ARE REGULARLY RECEIVED.

COLONIAL.	ENGLISH AND FOREIGN.
Australian Star	Bow Bells
Agricultural Gazette	Boys of England
Australian Journal	Chamber's Journal
Bible Echo	Cassell's Magazine
Bulletin	Family Herald
Hansard	Glasgow Weekly Mail
Newcastle Morning Herald	Graphic
Our Boys & Girls Newspaper	Harper's Monthly
Referee	Illustrated London News
Sydney Daily Telegraph	London Journal
Town & Country Journal	Newcastle-on-Tyne Chronicle
The Australian	Nineteenth Century
Wallsend & Plattsburg Sun	Reynold's Newspaper
Young Men's Echo	

Persons wishing to become members of this Institute may do so by paying the usual quarterly subscription in advance, viz :– three shillings (3s).

Reading Room opens from 8 a.m., to 10 p.m., every lawful day. Sundays from 10 a.m. till dusk.

Subscriptions received by the Secretary and Librarian :

— JAMES MORGAN.

NOTE.—Books are not allowed out of the Library more than four weeks under a penalty of sixpence for every week exceeding four weeks ; and not more than two books allowed out at one time.

Subscribers returning books are requested to hand same to the Librarian and not leave them about the room.

Subscribers are also requested to notify the Librarian of all loose leaves in books and of any damage done to same.

13.1 Lambton Mechanics' and Miners' Institute Catalogue of Books, September 1894

Daily Telegraph.[28] This might suggest something of the tastes (and politics) of Lambton readers: sensation fiction was not heavily in circulation by the early years of the nineteenth century (although it remained popular in other Australian libraries at the time), and patrons clearly wanted to participate in the emerging national trade in news – and fiction. The *Queenslander*, in particular, carried a great deal of serialized fiction, much of it British.

In Lambton, as at many Institutes in Australia and Britain, workers consistently foiled any attempt at formal education or moral uplift: they read indiscriminate amounts of light or mass-market fiction. Dolin notes that "Mass-market fiction imported from Britain, but written in Britain, the US, Canada, Australia, and other English-speaking countries, was pervasive in Australia at this time" and dominated Mechanics' Institutes and School of Arts libraries across the colonies.[29] Martyn Lyons, in his study of the NSW Railway and Tramway Institute (one of the largest such institutes in Australia) notes that "In 1921, the central library boasted 51 titles by William Le Queux, 26 Jack Londons and 26 Rider Haggards … Readers were complimented on their good taste, illustrated by the fact that their library held 'only' 13 titles by Nat Gould and nine by Charles Garvice."[30]

Lambton, from ten to twenty years previously, could boast similar holdings, with a lower degree of "taste" indicated by high readership of Gould and Garvice. The non-fiction loans at Lambton have not been entered into the database, but although Lambton held a higher proportion of non-fiction than the other libraries in the Australian Common Reader (almost a third of the holdings), it seems that the vast majority of loans were of fiction. In 1911, for example, 3,231 books were issued. Of these, 2,940 (90 per cent) were fiction: the remainder included 180 unclassified works from the Sydney Public Library, 27 works classified as biography, 23 miscellaneous, 20 history, 18 travels, 13 science and social, and 10 poetry. The committee was clearly pleased with even this level of non-fiction borrowing, noting in its report that "the Institute had maintained the standard of previous years, both from the educational and recreation standpoint."[31] Debates about the role of libraries in providing readers with access to mass-market fiction raged in the Newcastle region as across the English-speaking world around the turn of the twentieth century.[32] The regional newspaper carried a leader in 1902 accusing libraries in the area of creating a taste for literature of "mawkish sentiment, worthless sensation, and the commonest of puerilities," and despairing that the modern habit of "gobbling" books was replacing "studious and thoughtful reading."[33]

The readership of English and American bestsellers in a regional Australian town is one instance of the ways in which local circuits of value might intersect with larger or more totalizing ones. It has become a commonplace in Australian book history that we have primarily read books from elsewhere.[34] The self-consciously nationalist literary tradition that was emerging in Australia in the lead-up to Federation in 1901 emphasized realist fiction with rural settings. The nature of the readership of these works, especially in comparison to that of "Anglo-Australian" romance writers whose work was occluded from the national tradition, remains a key unanswered question in Australian literary history.[35] Tim Dolin asks, in relation to the records in the Australian Common Reader, whether it is possible "to speak meaningfully about a reading culture – an inarticulate reading culture, indifferent to the Australianness or Englishness of the fiction it reads – as a national culture?"[36] Lambton represents an instance of Australian reading culture characterized by extensive reading across national boundaries and literary genres. Reading patterns in Lambton are different from those at other Australian libraries in the period,[37] but Lambton does provide a model for thinking about reading history in Australia: as a culture of extensive reading, and one influenced not only by books from elsewhere, but also by readers from elsewhere.

The clearest example of this is Evan Treharne, the most frequent borrower at Lambton. He is a "common reader" whose life is mostly lost to the historical record: a Welsh miner who migrated to New South Wales some time before 1883. That year, he married Agnes Stewart in Lambton. The only mention he receives in the local newspaper is in reference to the local Eisteddfod (Welsh literary and cultural gathering) in 1896, at which he won the prize for "best answers to eighteen questions." The holding of an Eisteddfod in an Australian mining town might seem out of place, but it indicates the influence of Welsh culture – and its emphasis on self-education and cultural pursuits – in this regional Australian town, as in other areas of Welsh migration in Australia.[38]

Treharne exemplifies this in that he read both widely and intensively: over the 10 years of the records he made 456 loans, borrowing the works of 189 different authors. He read many authors popular with other borrowers at Lambton: historical romances of Agnes and Edgerton Castle, Imperial adventures by Rider Haggard, U.S. best-sellers including those by Archibald Clavering Gunter, the Welsh-themed novels of Allen Raine, works by Methodist ministers Joseph and Silas Hocking (very popular in Australia in this period), the ubiquitous E. Phillips Oppenheim, and others. He also read beyond the recently popular to earlier works: Braddon, Brontë, Wilkie Collins, James Fennimore Cooper, Dickens, Hugo, Scott. His reading included political and satirical works: Upton Sinclair, David Graham Phillips, Thackeray, Mark Twain, and Steele Rudd's *Dad in Politics* (1908). The latter was among several Australian titles that he borrowed: the bush adventures of Rolf Boldrewood, the "Anglo-Australian" romances of Rosa Praed, realist bush stories of Rudd and John Barry, racing adventures by Nat Gould, and the transnational romances and mysteries of Guy Boothby. He returned to some titles (e.g., by Corelli, Boldrewood, and Bulwer-Lytton) repeatedly over the years. In this respect Treharne's reading follows a pattern that was common to all frequent borrowers in the database in that it was both extensive and intensive. Patrons at Lambton followed what Pawley cites as "the library habit of reading"[39]: they read widely, across multiple authors. They also read intensively: many books were borrowed by the same patron more than once. Thirty-five patrons borrowed the same title five or more times: some books were borrowed fifteen or twenty times by the same patron, supporting Emily Todd and Christine Pawley's findings of the continued coexistence of extensive and intensive reading patterns.[40]

Evan Treharne could also be seen as an example of the autodidact Welsh miner as asserted by Baggs and Rose: both note a strong tradition of miners' libraries and self-education in the mining regions of Wales. Treharne's borrowing might be indicative of what happens when a reader from such a tradition is transplanted into the Australian context – local works are read in the context of his extensive reading. He stands, at the very least, as an example of a working-class reader reading across and beyond the "light" fiction so often decried as the usual fare at workers' libraries. The average number of loans taken out by miners at Lambton was sixty-nine. Of the seventy-one miners in the database, nine are what we might describe as frequent borrowers (with more than two hundred loans overall). Lambton demonstrates that the patterns of literary consumption in Wales noted by Baggs and Rose were not limited to the regions in which they developed: it is not only literary works, but habits of reading, that travel.

Unlike the libraries studied by Baggs and Rose, Lambton's patrons included a good proportion of women. These are the segment of Lambton readers who have perhaps the most to offer the historian of reading. Women readers are subject to a high degree of interest among literary scholars, but to an even greater extent than the generalized "common reader," evidence about significant numbers of actual readers, especially prior to the mid-twentieth century, is scant. Associations between women's reading and frivolity, immorality, and novels lacking in literary worth are long held and pervasive. Library loan records provide an opportunity to test such assumptions against historical instances of women's reading. Zboray's study of the New York Society Library, for example, challenges the idea of an emerging "women's sphere" in the Antebellum period by finding little difference between the borrowing patterns of men and women.[41] Likewise, Pawley finds that "neither adult men nor women readers in Osage made clearly gendered choices," and Joel Shrock's essay in this volume reports a similar pattern of crossover reading among children.[42]

There are 133 women listed in the Lambton database – 28 per cent of all patrons. Women were responsible for 35 per cent of the recorded loans: on average, they borrowed more frequently than men. There was an average of 66.5 loans per female borrower, compared to 47.5 loans per male borrower. This is similar to Dolin's findings at the Collie Institute: "Women were, on average, bigger readers than men … they borrowed an average of 28 books each; men borrowed 21 books each."[43] Women represent some 30 per cent of the most frequent borrowers at Lambton: both of those who borrowed two hundred or more books over the life of the data, and of the twenty borrowers who made the most loans over the period. On the very limited measure of author gender, reading choices at Lambton do not seem to have been strongly gendered. Although women were more likely to borrow books by female authors than men were, they did not show a marked preference for these works. Men were clearly reading the work of authors associated with a female readership – at Lambton more men than women, for example, borrowed novels by Ouida and by Anglo-Australian romance writer Rosa Praed. It appears that at Lambton, as in Zboray and Pawley's studies, borrowing choices were not gendered in straightforward ways.

The challenge, and opportunity, involved in studying library circulation data is that it tracks instances of reading as they occur over time. Leah Price, in reference to Stanley Fish's work, notes that a focus on reading draws our attention away from a spatial object (the text) towards a temporal one (the act of reading).[44] Library records, as Emily Todd points out, tell us more than any other kind of reading evidence about the *pace* of reading – the time it took, the order of books.[45] The list of most-often-borrowed titles at Lambton varies significantly from year to year, and new books were purchased regularly over the period of these records. The speed and extent of this change indicates this community's participation in a kind of mass culture; or, at least, in a world of proliferating books, interested in the new. A high proportion of all borrowing within the circulation data collected in the Australian Common Reader was of recent novels: this is quite different from the "belated reading" noted by Tatlock and others in this volume in Muncie just a few years earlier. This suggests that despite their isolation from the centres of publishing and literary life, regional Australian readers were avidly interested in up-to-date book culture – mass culture, in Richard Ohmann's terms – and access to a well-stocked Institute library provided some modicum of access to it.[46]

Overall lists can obscure the temporary popularity of particular writers among these library patrons. Another way of looking at the relative popularity of different authors is to look at the proportion of loans each year represented by the work of each author (see fig. 13.2). This graph indicates the continuing appeal of global English-language success stories such as E. Phillips Oppenheim, growing interest in others, such as Baroness Orczy, and declining interest in others, such as the romances of Annie Swan and Rosa Carey. Some authors, such as David Graham Phillips, receive a spike in popularity related to the publication of a particular novel (following the publication of *The Fashionable Adventures of Joshua Craig* in 1909). Phillips's novel is one of several works with political themes that were popular at Lambton, which bears further investigation given the heavy

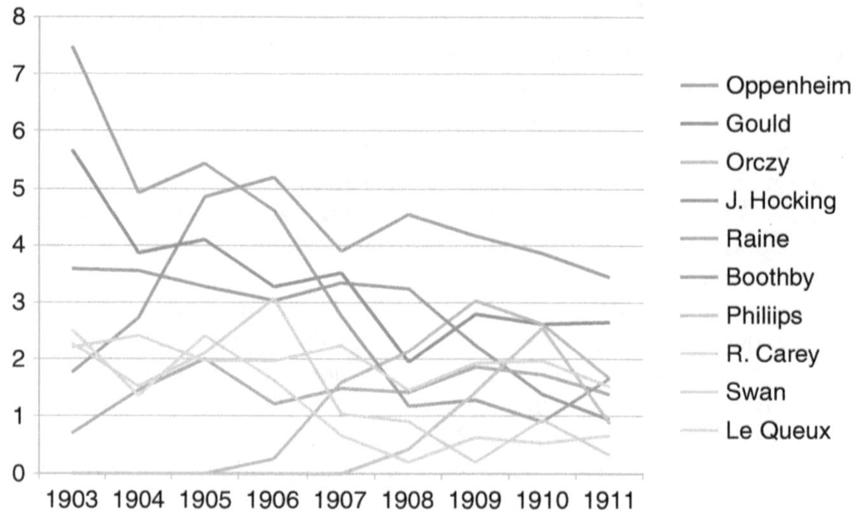

13.2 Popular authors at Lambton, by proportion of total loans each year

involvement in Labour politics among the Lambton miners. In some cases, it is clear that well-read authors at Lambton were popular throughout Australia in this period. A search of Australia's digitized newspaper database shows that Oppenheim's novels, for example, were serialized regularly in Australian newspapers and magazines throughout this decade. Oppenheim was held and borrowed at other Australian libraries but was nowhere as popular as at Lambton. Likewise, Australian expatriate Guy Boothby was much more popular at Lambton than at Collie, a Mechanics' Institute in a comparable mining town in Western Australia. Orczy also received some attention in the press over this time; Gould was ubiquitous, but Allen Raine was less consistently mentioned, suggesting perhaps that her popularity was due to a local factor (her Welsh-themed novels unsurprisingly popular with a population constituted in no small part by immigrants from Wales).[47]

One of the key questions in understanding the circulation of mass culture in this local circumstance, and the nature of common reading practices, is what proportion of borrowing was of very popular works. A large proportion of the borrowing at Lambton was of books only borrowed once, or very few times. For any given year at Lambton, at least 50 per cent of the loans were of books borrowed once to nine times. This suggests that the borrowers were not a homogenous community of readers – if anything, these patrons' reading was diverse and often extensive. This is supported by looking at individual borrowers: Treharne, for example, borrowed books by 189 different authors, Martha Charlton (wife of the local Labor MP and fifth leader of the Australian Labor Party, Matthew Charlton), 106 authors. This suggests that looking at the most frequently borrowed titles and authors ignores a great deal – at least half – of the borrowing that was taking place in these libraries.

This diversity of borrowing poses challenges for identifying and generalizing about common practices among the mass of borrowing records, especially of less popular works. One way to trace the "zones of connection" – the conditions of possibility for forms of literary sociability or common cultural capital based on these acts of reading – is to consider these readers and the books they borrowed as constituting a network. Such a network defines the relationship between objects of interest in terms of their similarity to each other. In this sense, we are considering the similarity of readers in terms of the books they have borrowed in common, and the similarity of books in terms of the readers they have shared.[48] Approaches like this have been used in computer science to analyse complex social networks such as those of Facebook and Twitter, as well as buying habits at Amazon. The Lambton Mechanics' and Miners' Institute might seem a far cry from Twitter and Amazon, but the acts of borrowing within it are also a form of network – "a pattern of interconnections among a set of things"[49] – which potentially has a social dimension. Reading in common is the basis for literary sociability: forms of social interaction enabled by or relating to reading. The network of borrowers at Lambton, unlike Facebook or Twitter users, is inarticulate: borrowers might not be aware of the other people they share books in common with. They do, nonetheless, share common practices and perhaps tastes. These are the groups of readers we can identify in databases such as the Australian Common Reader and What Middletown Read.

Once the Australian Common Reader data has been interpreted as a network of similar books or similar borrowers, we can use tools and concepts that have been developed to analyse networks to ask much more powerful questions about reader or book similarity than we could with a database alone, which in our case can help to identify common borrowing practices at Lambton. For example, there is a group of readers who have a very strong similarity to each other, discerned by querying which borrowers have 50 per cent similarity and at least ten books in common with at least one other borrower (see fig. 13.3)[50]

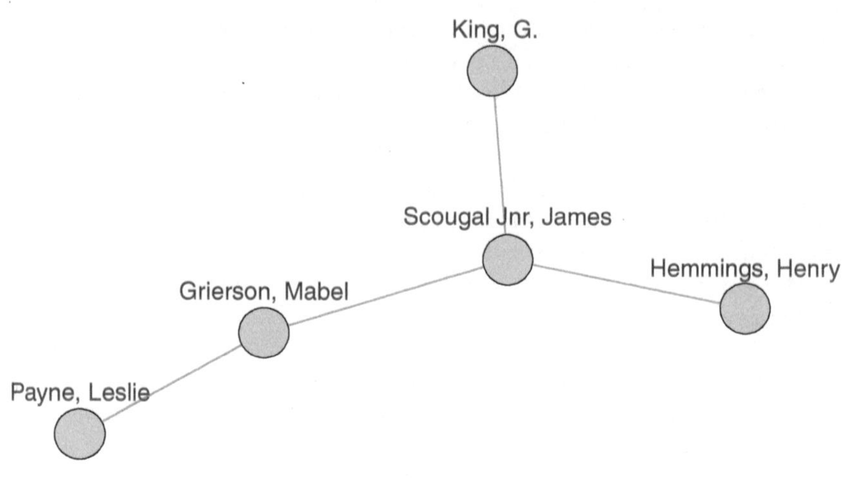

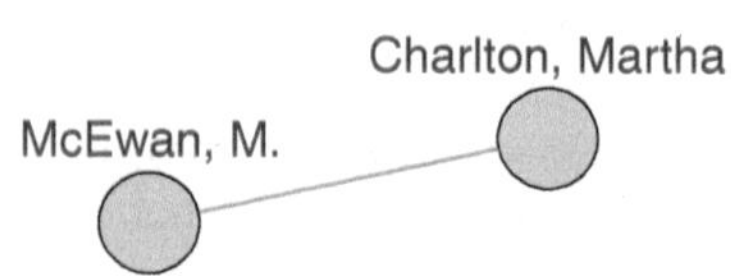

13.3 Borrowers at Lambton with at least 50 per cent similarity

This is a very high degree of similarity. For example, James Lewis Scougal, Jr (a clerk who was a member of the Lambton Institute committee and made 307 loans over 10 years) shared 183 titles across 126 authors with Henry Enoch Hemmings (wheelwright); 160 titles across 122 authors with Mabel Grierson (home duties); 147 titles across 112 authors with G. King (male, occupation unknown). Mabel Grierson also shared 146 titles across 119 authors with Leslie Payne (butcher). Martha Charlton also appears this graph: she shares 106 titles by 68 authors in common with a Miss M. McEwan. The books they borrowed included romances, spy fiction, detective stories, Australian bush comedy, sensation fiction, and others (among the "unrecognizable mass"). These are readers with a high proportion of their borrowing in common. If we relax our definition of similarity (by decreasing the percentage and/or books in common) we will be able to discern more and larger clusters of readers, and make broader generalizations about them.

Another way of exploring the relationships between books and borrowers – including all those books with few loans – is to create visualizations of the data as a network. The visualization represents each of the borrowers at Lambton as a circle. The circles are arranged so that the borrowers with the highest proportion of books borrowed in common are closest together, in a similar fashion to the affinity analysis undertaken in Tatlock's chapter. This is not a precise measure as all of the relationships between borrowers and loans need to be arranged in relation to each other, but it enables us to see, at a glance, where there are clusters of borrowers with books in common. More useful for the purposes of exploring this data is the fact that, when viewed on a computer, you can click on a circle (borrower) to see which other borrowers shared a certain proportion of books in common.

Martha Charlton, for example, shares 40 per cent similarity with two other patrons: Tryphena Jones and Miss E. Williams. The three women borrowed regularly: Charlton made 268 loans, Jones 246, and Williams 224. All three were extensive readers: Charlton borrowed works by 106 different authors, Jones 98, and Williams 126. There are 52 authors whose work these women all borrowed, and looking at their records in detail we can discern both similarities and differences in their reading patterns: Jones and Williams both read Mary Johnston and Elizabeth Gaskell; Williams read more Australian and "classic" fiction than either of the others. Jones was the most intensive of the readers, repeatedly borrowing individual works by George Griffith (4 times), Marie Corelli (5), Frank Moore (8), and Oppenheim (10 times). In addition to the query above, we can begin to see Martha Charlton as part of a network of readers with a great deal in common; in her case, the readers with whom she has the most similarity are all women.

The data visualizations help us to investigate the relationships between borrowers and books in the database, and could be a useful tool as an alternative way of exploring databases such as the Australian Common Reader and What Middletown Read. Another way to look at the broader structure of borrowing patterns in this data is cluster analysis. Cluster analysis is a form of data classification: it aims to identify underlying structure in a data set by grouping elements together according to certain similarity measures.[51] It involves representing all the data as a graph formed by a set of vertices, as mentioned above (in this case, each vertex is a book in the database), with a set of edges that are connections between pairs of vertices. Graph clustering involves trying to form groups of vertices that are strongly interconnected. Two books are connected, in this definition, if they share a borrower. These connections are dense, as you might expect: each book borrowed by Evan Treharne, for example, is connected to each other. If another reader shares one book with Treharne, each book they have read is connected to each of Traherne's, and so on.

One clear conclusion we can make from a cluster analysis of the Lambton data is that there are not discrete clusters: there are not, for example, two or more groups of readers unrelated to each other in terms of the books they borrowed as there seem to be in Muncie, as indicated by Tatlock. The most strongly connected books at Lambton are an alternative list to the most popular books – these are not the books with the most loans, but the books most likely to share a borrower with any other book in the library.

This list draws our attention to works that are frequently borrowed but not the most frequently so: works such as Charles Stewart's *The Fugitive Blacksmith*, whose use of working-class vernacular might resonate with readers of Henry Lawson's "yarns." Interestingly, half of the titles in the list are neither held nor borrowed in any of the other libraries in the Australian Common Reader database, despite overlapping time periods and, in the case of Collie, similar demographics. This suggests that Lambton was, in some respects, a distinct network of readers in the Australian context. Further research into the acquisition history of these titles might reveal some explanations for the differences. It is likely, however, given the involvement of the library committee and readers suggestion books at the Lambton Institute, that these differences are due to the tastes and interests of the readers themselves.

More interesting clusters of books with common readership are revealed by this kind of analysis if you remove the very popular books. See, for example, figure 13.4, where the books that have 206 or more connections to other books have been removed. This reveals thirty-two clusters: one, for example, linking works by Alexandre Dumas, Mark Twain, Charles Dickens, and Tolstoy; another linking Jules Verne, Elizabeth Gaskell, Marcus Clarke, and Marie Corelli; another linking Walter Besant, George Eliot, Ouida, Charles Kingsley, William Thackeray, and Thomas Reid. These are mostly works with a small readership – but such clusters give us an idea about how, and in what company, those works were read.

As with any use of digital tools for literary study or book history, these tools do not answer our questions for us. You cannot, simply by looking at them, determine the extent of similarity between readers as a whole or

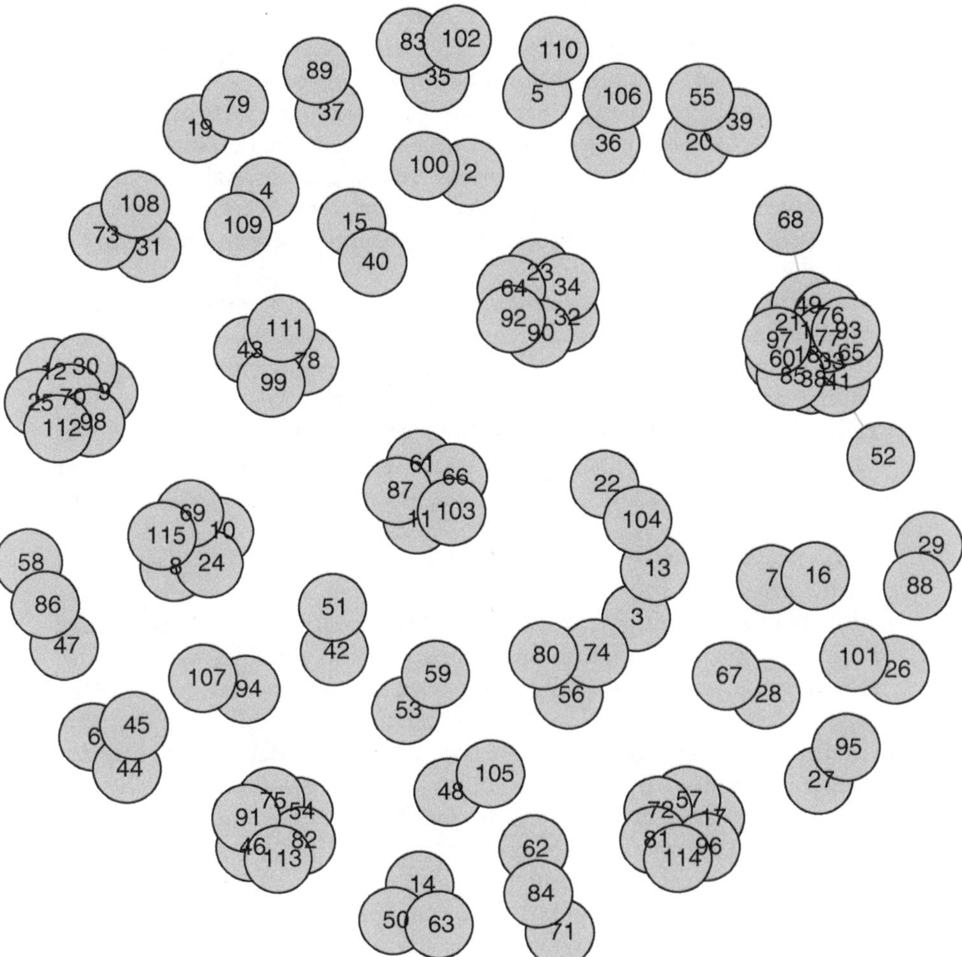

13.4 Cluster analysis of titles with books that have fewer than 206 connections to other books

within clusters. They send us back to the detail of the records, readers, and books themselves, before we can draw clear conclusions.

Treating these library loan records as large and complex data sets enables us to think about them differently: in terms of relationships between borrowers and books, and similarity between books (in terms of their borrowers) and borrowers (in terms of their loans). Most significantly for the history of reading, these techniques for exploring and classifying the data enable us to move between the general and the specific. We can attempt to make larger generalizations about the nature of borrowing in these libraries, as well as to examine in great detail the component parts of such generalizations: the borrowing habits of individual patrons or small clusters of patrons, and the readership of books that might not make it onto the top-ten lists. There is clearly a great deal more research to be undertaken on this and other libraries, especially in relation to genre and theme in the works themselves.

From this initial exploration of reading patterns at Lambton it appears that there are a number of borrowers with a great deal of what they borrowed in common. There are differences between the reading and holdings at Lambton and at other libraries in the Australian Common Reader database and borrowing was not clearly gendered, but there might be gendered networks of borrowers with books in common. It is also clear that a large proportion of the borrowing at Lambton was not of the most popular books.

Any real understanding of patterns of readership in this data is not possible without a fuller and richer sense of the literary context of the fiction that was being borrowed. Leah Price suggests that "any history of reading is also a meditation on the reading of a particular writer,"[52] but many of these writers are part of the "great unread," at least by scholars. Much of this fiction is now available online through archive.org: there are digital approaches to assessing genre through text and data mining (see, for example, work done by Matthew Jockers). There is something to be said for attempting these approaches; they might, at least, identify themes, or similarity between works. They will always be limited, however – any history of reading in this period must send us back to the work of reading and thinking about these once-popular works even if they are not of the kind usually subject to literary analysis. Looking at these library loans as data has, however, shown just how complex the networks of literary taste and habit, common practices and idiosyncrasies encompassed in these library records, and how densely interwoven but diverse the reading lives of the people of Lambton were.

NOTES

1 G. Jones (2007, 73).

2 See http://www.australiancommonreader.com/.

3 Biskup (1994, 3).
4 Lyons (1997a, 23).
5 Pawley (2009a).
6 Lyons (1997b, 10); Lamond (2012b, 27–38).
7 Lester (2001, 8).
8 Lamond (2012a, 33–46).
9 Doherty (1983, 8).
10 Eklund (2012, 11).
11 Rose (2001); Baggs (2001).
12 Rabbitt (1997, 66).
13 Cited in Parry (2010).
14 Bode (2012).
15 Rose (2001, 238). See Robert Hall's essay in this volume for another example of middle-class efforts to discipline workers through libraries, as well as working-class strategies for overcoming these efforts.
16 Rose (2001); R. Hall (this volume).
17 Benson (1980) cited in Baggs (2001, 279).
18 *Newcastle Pilot* 20 Dec 1867, cited in Rabbitt (1997, 56.)
19 Engel (2009, 119).
20 Cited in Shilling (2009, 119).
21 *Newcastle Herald and Miners' Advocate* 2 October 1882.
22 The Rev. D Young argued, as reported in the *Newcastle Herald and Miners' Advocate* 2 October 1882, that "to open the institute on the Lord's Day would have a demoralizing tendency. The papers on its table were all secular; not one of the religious publications of the day were to be found there. Their young men, therefore, would be influenced by the secular papers."
23 Newcastle Family History Society 1994.
24 Rabbitt (1997, 72).
25 *Newcastle Herald and Miners' Advocate* 29 July 1880, 4.
26 *Newcastle Herald and Miners' Advocate* 27 July 1894, 8.
27 Brake (1994).
28 *Newcastle Herald and Miners' Advocate* 29 July 1880, 4.
29 Dolin (2011, 158).
30 Lyons (1997a, 19).
31 *Newcastle Herald and Miners' Advocate* 19 July 1911, 2.
32 See for example Carrier (1965).
33 *Newcastle Herald and Miners' Advocate* 1 February 1902, 4.
34 See for example Webby (2006).
35 Eggert (2008); Dixon (2008).
36 Dolin (2011, 173).

37 For example, readership of one of the libraries' most borrowed authors, Guy Boothby, was much higher than at the Collie Institute, another miners' institute in the same period in Western Australia.
38 Jones and Jones (2003).
39 Pawley (2009a, 61).
40 Todd (2001, 199); Pawley (2009a, 100).
41 Zboray (1991).
42 Pawley (2009a, 109).
43 Dolin (2011, 164).
44 L. Price (2004, 311).
45 Todd (2001, 196).
46 Ohmann (1996).
47 In relation to Australian newspaper archives, such searches are very useful because of the existence of the national newspaper database, Trove (http://trove.nla.gov.au) and tools for searching and visualizing it such as Querypic (http://dhistory.org/querypic/). See for example a graph I created for the popular authors at Lambton here: http://dhistory.org/querypic/5p/.
48 Lamond and Reid (2009).
49 Easley and Kleinberg (2010).
50 My thanks to Mark Reid at the Research School of Computer Science, Australian National University, for his assistance in generating this and the graphs that follow.
51 Schaeffer (2007).
52 L. Price (2004, 306).

14 Organized Print: Clara Steen and Institutional Sites of Reading and Writing in the American Midwest, 1895–1920

CHRISTINE PAWLEY

In the fall of 1908, twenty-year-old Clara Steen left her family's farm near West Liberty, Iowa, and boarded the train for Ames. She was about to enter Iowa State College (later Iowa State University) as a freshman studying home economics and journalism – a combination that would stand her in good stead over the course of a long career as a farmer and rural columnist who wrote articles for agricultural and local newspapers. Clara Steen's life (she was born in 1888 and died in 1994) spanned almost the whole of the twentieth century. During that time a variety of print cultures took organizational shape, as reading and writing occurred with increasing frequency in institutional contexts. Americans in all walks of life were finding organized print more and more indispensable, and farmers were no exception.

During the period 1895 to 1920 the rural way of life was idealized in American culture, and often associated with spaciousness, health, simplicity, and virtue, as opposed to the overcrowding, sickness, crime, and sinfulness connected with life in the city. As white Americans and immigrants from Europe continued to settle on the lands expropriated earlier in the nineteenth century from Native Americans, the typical farm acreage nearly doubled, from 536 acres in 1880 to nearly a thousand in 1920. In 1910 the rural population continued to exceed that of urban areas, and farm employment reached an all-time high of 13.6 million in 1916.[1] Country life was considered the norm for Americans, and farming still looked like a good prospect for young people growing up in rural areas, as well as for immigrants. In 1908 Clara Steen no doubt imagined that she would spend the rest of her life on a farm, and planned her education accordingly.

Although the image of the individual pioneer family farm may stand in the national imagination as an icon of independence and self-reliance, the later nineteenth century saw the spread of agricultural organizations whose activities increasingly overlapped. The farm press was part of an interlocking web of agricultural institutions that featured prominently in the lives of families like the Steens – English-speaking, Protestant, and relatively prosperous. All of these institutions depended on print technology as well as on social practices of reading and writing. In part, changing farm technologies drove farmers' need for reading. In the early nineteenth century, starting with the introduction of a steel plow, new implements for plowing, sowing, reaping, binding, and threshing gradually transformed farming from a series of heavy manual tasks to a set of mechanized activities.[2] As these and other technological changes in agriculture transformed the rural landscape, farmers turned to print rather than oral tradition as a source of guidance, as they read to keep abreast of new developments, to compare prices of farm machinery, fencing, and seed, and to consult manuals on how to operate their new capital investments.[3] New machines and methods of farming were advertised and discussed in the agricultural press, and farm journals proliferated during the nineteenth century, playing an increasingly prominent part in the life of farm families.

By the early decades of the twentieth century, American farm families were increasingly enmeshed in a web of social and economic relationships that were channelled through such institutions as the farm press and farmers' clubs. Small towns like West Liberty, Iowa, serviced their surrounding agricultural areas by supplying goods and services that could not be produced on the farm, including factory products, banking and insurance, legal services, newspapers and print shops. They were also sites where farm families encountered social and cultural institutions: churches and Sunday schools, fraternal clubs like the Masons and Oddfellows, high schools and lyceums, libraries and reading rooms. As they developed from frontier-like settlements, Midwestern American towns came to resemble the East Coast communities from which many of their early settlers originated, as well as small English towns like Ashton-under-Lyne (described in this volume) that provided cultural goods to workers in the proliferating factories.[4]

By the late nineteenth century, American farmers also came into contact with official agencies, as the federal government actively encouraged farmers to turn to new methods. In 1862 the establishment of the United States Department of Agriculture (USDA) and passage of the Morrill Land-Grant Act, which set up colleges to specialize in promoting knowledge about practical subjects related to agriculture and technology, fostered a culture of research and learning among farmers. Iowa was the first state to accept the resulting grant of land to establish Iowa State College, and eventually all other states followed. The land-grant colleges gave an enormous boost to university-based research and teaching in departments of agriculture, rural sociology, agricultural journalism, and home economics.

Rural Midwestern women participated in institutions of print as both readers and writers. As contributors to rural newspaper columns, workers for the agricultural extension service, radio homemakers[5] who also published newsletters, and small-town librarians, thousands of women developed political and cultural agency through print, within their communities and beyond. These organizational sites helped structure participants' print experiences in particular ways. For example, the cultural work of print in constituting the nation employed a metaphor of domesticity – the creation of a unified "home-land" out of a multitude of disparate and contending elements – that found expression in many types of publication, including mass-market magazines, farm journals, extension bulletins, and best-selling novels. Reading and writing were also vehicles for the exercise of individual agency, as women readers and writers both challenged and reinforced these structuring forces. For Clara Steen, the institutions that enabled her agency in print included some that were still familiar as sites of reading and writing at her life's end, including the public school and university, the public library, and the local press. Other organizations that played a key part in her early reading and writing, such as the agricultural extension service and the Young Women's Christian Association (YWCA), have slipped from book historians' consciousness, at least as print culture institutions. Yet millions of American readers and writers engaged with print through these agencies.

Still, even amid the rural affluence of the early twentieth century, signs of impending decline were evident. The quality of urban life improved during the Progressive Era, and in response to perceptions that it had overtaken that of the countryside, threatening the very "civilization" that rural life depended on, in 1908 President Theodore Roosevelt appointed an investigative body, the Country Life Commission. The resulting report (published in 1911) noted that to stem the exodus from the country to the town, government and other agencies needed to address the social and physical needs of rural people. After 1914 the Smith-Lever Act established extension systems through the land-grant colleges together with the USDA, by which useful information could be passed on to farm families through practical demonstrations. An itinerant agricultural adviser in each county coordinated all areas of rural activity, whether technical, social, or economic.[6] The prime role of the agent was to educate the rural population, and the main teaching techniques were through "method" and "result" demonstration, whereby new processes for carrying out traditional tasks were irrefutably shown to produce better results.[7] Across the nation, thousands of county-based extension agents aimed "to help these rural families help themselves by applying science, whether physical or social, to the daily routines of farming, homemaking, and family and community living."[8] The extent to which individual families' lives interacted with these institutions depended on a number of factors, including geographic location and type of farming, but race and ethnicity also played an important part. In the lives of families like the Steens, agricultural institutions featured prominently. Over the next two decades these innovations became embedded in rural life as institutions with enormous reach. By the late 1940s, the Agriculture Extension Service (targeted at men) and the Home Economics Extension Service (designed for women) together claimed to be the largest rural adult education agency in the world.

Enveloped in Print Culture: The Steen Family

Clara Steen was born on a farm in Guthrie County, Iowa, the fifth of eight children. Her mother's family had moved to Iowa from Ohio; her father was a German immigrant who had left Holstein in 1872 to join family and friends in Davenport, Iowa. There he taught himself English, Clara later related, by reading the *New York Tribune*.[9] The Steens prospered as farmers, eventually joining the ranks of Iowa's affluent class. Clara's father became active in state politics, and when he was elected to the Iowa legislature, he relocated the family temporarily to Des Moines. In 1899 the Steen family moved east from Guthrie County to a better farm near the town of West Liberty, in Muscatine County.

Steen's anglophone family valued education, and at her rural school Clara was a star pupil. For the elementary grades, the children walked to their local one-room school, and then went on to high school in the nearby town.[10] In Guthrie County, the Steen farm was so far from the nearest school that Clara did not start school until she was seven, but even so, she was "promoted" to *McGuffey's Third Eclectic Reader* in her first term, as her older siblings had already taught her to read.[11] Reading and writing came easily to her, a champion speller, and from a young age she used her ingenuity to fit time for these activities into days that were filled with domestic chores. "As soon as I could keep the barrel churn going properly," she related, "[Mother] watched over this making of butter. That was one job I really liked, for I could read the Youth's Companion or other papers at the same time."[12] During a wintry period when snow prevented them from leaving the house, the ten-year-old Clara and her older sister Dora wrote a family newsletter. Later, as teenagers, the girls began to write for wider public consumption when they contributed community news to one of the West Liberty newspapers.[13] Their early participation as producers in local print culture marked their middle-class status; in Iowa as elsewhere, local cultural institutions were dominated by the more affluent residents and their families.[14]

After graduating from high school Clara herself became a teacher in local rural schools (a common practice for young women at the time) where she earned $30 dollars a month, of which two dollars a week went on room and board.[15] But by 1908 she was back at home on the family farm, getting ready to enter Iowa State College in the fall. On the first of January of that year, she started to write daily entries in a diary, a practice she maintained for many subsequent years.[16] Diary writing was a common practice among Midwestern farmers in the early decades of the twentieth century. Some diarists used simple notebooks of lined paper, but others purchased specially produced blank diaries. Publishing companies issued these in a variety of forms, a small pocket-sized book, three inches wide and six inches high, being the most popular. They provided a few lines – sometimes as few as five, but no more than twenty – on which to write.[17] What diarists recorded varied. Some commented briefly on the weather and the day's major events, and occasionally noted the title of a book or journal. Others expanded on the content of their reading, and even on the context – the time, place, and pretext – of the activity. Not uncommonly diarists might mention the cost of a subscription to a magazine, newspaper, or farm paper, and a few actually copied extracts from their reading or included clippings in their journal.[18] Adopting a terse down-to-earth style, Clara Steen recorded the events and activities that made up her daily routine, including reading and writing, first on her parents' farm in West Liberty, Iowa, then as a college student in Ames, and after she married agronomist Hans Skott, as farmer and journalist.

Social activities that revolved around reading and writing made a regular appearance in Clara's diary. Meetings of the local literary club provided a community venue for the Steen sisters to share their written work with a wider audience. In January 1908, for instance, she recorded that she had found time to write "some biographical sketches," and the following evening, at the Home Literary and Farmers' Club, the sketches appeared on the program. At the club's March meeting, the planned program proved on the short side, so Clara filled in with some ad hoc literary and musical contributions; "I spoke 'Prisoner of Chillon' and sang in girls' quartet," she told her diary. "I also helped Chas's whistling duet."[19] For Clara, Dora, and other community members, writing and reading entwined as they collaborated in the production and consumption of texts. However, most entries in Clara's diary – presumably not primarily intended for public view – reveal a life filled with practical tasks on the farm, in which time for reading and writing was short. On New Year's Day 1908, Clara wrote in her diary, "Mamma gave me a nice New Year's gift – four pullets she bought of Mr. Nauman for me." In the following days, Clara was busy "hemstitching," "baking, cleaning up," and "butchering ... we have a pig and a heifer killed."

Despite her family's relative affluence, Clara's daily life was probably little different from that of other young women living on a farm in the early years of the twentieth century. Many of the skills she needed she learned from her mother and other older women relatives, and neighbours. By the gift of four pullets, Clara's mother encouraged her to keep poultry – not only an accepted activity for women to contribute to the family table, but also one that gave them access to the market economy. Sewing her own clothes occupied much of her time, and her diary reveals that she managed to make some progress on her garments almost every day. But Clara taught herself the skill of smocking – a complex form of embroidery – from reading instructions in a mass-market magazine. Late in January, she recorded, "I learned how to smock from directions in a McCall's magazine and started it on my cream silk waist."[20] A few days later, she noted, "I worked on my waist most of the time. It is stormy and sleety outside." The following week she made herself "a purple calico apron that Dora had cut out," and the next day, "made a belt for my waist and put the finishing touches on it, then wore it to the church reception at night. We had a fine time, going to town in the sled for it."[21]

Rural Newspapers

In May 1908, a mishap occurred in the Steen family farmhouse when, Clara recorded in her diary, the shelves in the "newspaper room" collapsed, resulting in an "avalanche of papers" that was no easy job to straighten up.[22] Doubtless the incident remained in the family's memory as a tiresome accident – perhaps in retrospect even amusing. But for the historian of reading, this seemingly trivial event bears a larger significance, indicating that for the Steen family, reading carried a special value. The very existence of a dedicated "newspaper room" testifies to a family that subscribed to newspapers in large numbers, and moreover, saved them for future use.[23] Clara Steen later recalled that in 1899 to get the family's mail (in the days before free postal delivery in rural areas), her father went two miles to the nearest village twice a week, and came back "with an armful of papers – Horace Greeley's, New York Tribune ... the Christian Advocate, a weekly newspaper from the capital city, and a local paper."[24] Perhaps the Steen family subscribed to the *West Liberty Index*, or the *West Liberty Enterprise*, and possibly also to a magazine for adults or children. But for a Midwestern farm family at the turn of the twentieth century, a good number of the newspapers that they so carefully stored away would probably have consisted of farm papers.

During early decades of the twentieth century, farm families found themselves confronted with an astonishing array of newspapers aimed especially at them. In the 1880s farm journals were so widely read that four ranked among the ten top-selling national magazines.[25] Nationally, the number of farm newspapers increased from 303 in 1895 to 405 in 1920, while in the Midwest it rose from 139 to 195. Over the same time period, circulation nationwide increased from 5.5 million to over 17 million. In the early 1920s, rural sociologists reported that of nearly 450 farm families in three Iowa counties, over half took at least one local paper, one daily, one farm journal, and one general magazine. In Cedar County (just north of Muscatine County), 87 per cent of nearly four hundred farm households took farm papers, 81 per cent took daily papers, 53 per cent took other magazines, and 44 per cent subscribed to all of these categories of print.[26]

Some papers covered general aspects of farming and rural life, while others, like *Hoard's Dairyman* and the *American Horticulturalist*, concentrated on a specialized area. Some, like the *Country Gentleman,* aspired to a national audience, and others, like the *Prairie Farmer*, focused on particular states or regions. In Iowa, a leading promoter of farming periodicals was farmer and editor Henry Wallace, who in 1894 moved from editorship of the *Iowa Homestead* to *Farm and Dairy*, which he renamed *Wallace's Farmer*. Circulation of *Wallace's Farmer*, which stood at 7,500 in 1895, reached 65,200 by 1920, while another Midwestern paper, *Prairie Farmer*, rose from 25,000 to 112,128 in the same period. Farm papers hoped to reach every farm. Subscription prices were kept low, so that most farm families could afford at least one paper, and circulations were boosted by the efforts of some farmers to earn a little extra by signing on new subscribers with offers of premiums. Papers aimed some premiums, such as sewing machines, steam cookers, and a "doily stamping outfit," specifically at women. Books were another common type of premium. In 1897 *Wallace's*

Farmer offered Henry Wallace's *Letters to the Farm Boy*, while in 1913 the *Missouri Ruralist* offered *Webster's Dictionary*.[27]

From the end of the nineteenth century, Midwestern women who lived on farms or in small towns found in their local and farm newspapers a space in which to participate in the public sphere. The nineteenth-century ideology of domesticity that forbade women from speaking in public nevertheless permitted and even encouraged women to write for publication – perhaps because it was considered a less important means of communication than oral address. County newspapers tended to be written by and for men, but they often included a column written by and for women. Coverage included topics conventionally assigned to the women's sphere: in 1891, such a "World of Women" column in an Iowa newspaper listed "The Fashions – How Daughters Should be Educated – American Girls Supreme – A Notable Trousseau – Strong Women – Hints About Home."[28] But women used these columns to raise issues of suffrage, dress reform, temperance, and other political topics around which late nineteenth-century women formed voluntary associations. County newspapers also contained columns the neighbourhood "correspondents" wrote anonymously and that reported local gossip – of the benign, and sometimes not so benign, variety. It was usually women who wrote such neighbourhood columns.[29]

Advice columns to homemakers were a staple of rural newspapers and farm journals during the first half of the twentieth century. While on the one hand they helped build and maintain an imagined community of female homemakers that stretched across the United States and beyond, on the other hand they helped to highlight – and normalize – the experiences, values, and practices of some ethnic groups, while helping to erase those of others. At the same time, they represented a relationship with new technologies that both challenged and buttressed gendered identities of men as producers and women as consumers. For women especially, participation in print culture as both readers and writers played a part in maintaining distinct ethnic and national ties, as well as in the creation of a new blended identity that by the mid-twentieth century came to represent "middle America" in the popular imagination. Print networks took shape through the intertwined activities of rural columnists like Clara Steen who wrote columns for local newspapers and farm journals, and the authors of extension service publications. Rural journalists were heavily influenced by the agricultural extension service, which published its own printed information in the form of bulletins and pamphlets, distributed in huge numbers, influencing the lives of farm families – whatever their income level or ethnic background – throughout the United States. Today these reading materials are as forgotten as the readers themselves, perhaps because they are part of neither a well-recognized literary canon nor of a body of commercially produced and widely distributed popular materials like dime novels or comic books. Yet not only were these genres familiar to millions, they also provided an opportunity for the crossing of the reading/writing boundaries assumed by models such as Darnton's communications circuit.[30]

Home Economist: Reader and Writer

At Iowa State College, Clara came into contact with home economics faculty who impressed upon their students a sense of middle-class standards of diet and decor, and of the home as the sacred centre of a sacred institution – the family. "Examination Questions for Women," devised in 1915 by the home economics staff at Iowa State College's Agricultural Extension Department, posed a series of queries about homemaking for which they also provided the correct answers. So, for example, in answer to the question "Name two colors for a south room," home economics students were supposed to answer "Blue, Gray." Ten articles of equipment that "save your time and energy" might include the following: vacuum cleaner, fireless cooker, washing machine, meat grinder, mangle, bread mixer, carpet sweeper, dustless mops and duster, self-heating iron, or "necessary kitchen utensils." But the examination also asks: "Name 1 good magazine for boys, 1 for girls, 5 for the homemaker." Appropriate reading materials consisted of *St. Nicholas* and *Youth's Companion* for boys and girls, *Good Housekeeping*, *American Cookery*, *Mentor*, *Craftsman*, *House Beautiful* for homemakers.[31] Most tellingly, when asked "Why is it worthwhile for the housekeeper to study home economics?" respondents were supposed to answer along the following lines: "To renew enthusiasm, observe new methods, learn more about the science of homemaking, see homemaking in its relation to right living, realize responsibility in community life."[32]

Home economics faculty members also wrote informational pamphlets that the extension service published for use with classes on food and nutrition, decorating and furnishing the home, and health and hygiene. Although the extension movement emphasized the need for a "show-and-tell" approach to education, it also placed great faith in the printed word. Extension officials issued circulars and bulletins, and wrote articles for the farm press. The experts' approach was didactic and utilitarian, and strongly emphasized scientific values and methods. A series published in 1911 and entitled "Short Class Notes" covered such topics as bread making, cooking with vegetables, soups, and food preservation. These four-page pamphlets stressed the need for strict adherence to instructions, and clearly defined measures of quality as well as quantity. "Short Course Class Notes No. 1" included a Bread Judging Score Card for use in bread-making demonstrations, and assigned numerical values to various qualities. For a maximum of twenty points for "Flavor" out of a possible total of one hundred, for instance, the bread "should not taste of yeast and it should not taste sour or musty." For Lightness (fifteen points) it "should be equally light all through," and for Shape and Size (five points) "The loaf should rise evenly and be of uniform height in all parts."[33]

In addition to underlining the importance of measurable qualities, the publications drew on scientific knowledge, translating specialized discourse into everyday expressions that the writers assumed their audience of farm women would more readily understand. Thus, vegetables were supposed to provide "muscle-building food," "fuel food," and "mineral matter."[34] This was a language that Clara Steen absorbed in her college classes, and put into use in her own writing for publication. In an article titled "Get the Good of Grapes," she instructed her readers, "When we remember that of all the native fruits of the middle west, the grape has the largest fuel value per pound, and is classed as a food fruit rather than merely as a flavor fruit, we should try to make this valuable fruit available for use the year round. Grapes contain about fifteen percent sugar, and when very ripe, sometimes as high as thirty percent. This natural sugar, grape-sugar, gives the grape its high food and fuel value in the body."[35] At the same time, and in contrast to this modern, specialist language, the extension pamphlets provide a glimpse of housekeeping practices that a hundred years later seem primitive and even arcane. Before using a new iron pot, for instance, homemakers were advised, "Boil a double handful of hay or grass in a new iron pot before attempting to cook with it; scrub out with soap and sand; then set on full of water and let boil half an hour. After this it may be used without fear."[36] Just what dangers a new iron pot presented, the pamphlet failed to make clear. The writers set limits to the amount of knowledge they felt they needed to impart; their expertise as extension officials associated with Iowa State College, they implied, was sufficient warrant. Home economists' adoption of a rationalized, scientific approach to cooking, laundry, and other household tasks was intended to endow the homemaker with agency. Over the long run, the effect of these efforts was to buttress the institutionalization of the maker/user dichotomy in the farm press, the county newspapers, and the extension service.

The accelerating commercialization of household technology in the twentieth century depended on a typification of the homemaker as consumer. In this process, the agricultural institutions had turned out to be eager participants.

Taking her home economics professors as models, Clara Steen developed ambitions to serious writing, and made her own plans to include publishing after graduation. Along with home economics courses, she took as many journalism courses at Ames as she could, and wrote for two student newspapers. She was obviously good at it. Later her daughter recalled with pride, "For her work on *The Student*, college newspaper, and *Iowa Agriculturalist*, a monthly magazine for agriculture students, she earned the Journalism 'A' award. A 1915 newspaper clipping stated, 'For the first time, two women are in the list of those honored.' One woman received an 'A' Award the previous year."[37] Clara's progress at Iowa State College was interrupted by a period at Elmenhurst teaching in the public schools, and her diary also breaks off for a few years. While she put her academic life on hold, she thought hard about the sort of life she wanted for herself after graduating. In an article titled "To the Farm Girl at Home" that appeared in *Successful Farming* in March 1912 she plumped firmly for the rural life, seen through an idyllic, pastoral lens. "You, the young woman at home on your father's farm, you are to be envied," she lectured her readers. "If you doubt it a single instant, contrast your lot with thousands of factory girls or clerks in the cities." Such women were to be pitied, she asserted, for their "treadmill existence in some shop or factory," where the "sickening monotony of all" caused "dulled eyes and faces." By contrast, country girls "rise with the joyous notes of the orioles and robins [that call] you out to see the sun appear above the eastern hills." In this rural paradise, "daily walks are grass-carpeted and ever-changing."[38]

In another article she ruminated on the various possibilities that offered themselves to the college graduate in home economics. She wrote of a hypothetical friend who had chosen to "go back to the farm," though she had "won her degree of bachelor of science in home economics" and had a number of options open to her. She "declined to teach ... wasn't interested in extension work, nor in service as a dietitian, as were others of the class." Instead, she "deliberately chose to put her science into practice on the good old home farm." This college graduate set her sights on "a typical Iowa farm home," one of "the most prosperous type, with a big white farm house in a setting of green trees." In this idealized setting, new technologies would reduce much of the domestic burden; "I know how much the gasoline engine, the fireless cooker and vacuum cleaner can lighten the work. Feeding the hungry harvest hands is a pleasure, using the gas stove and the fireless cooker if it is too hot to have fire in the range. And selecting menus that will be of proper nutritive value – why, that's easy, with a whole garden and orchard and chicken yard and dairy to choose from." Turning her back on the kind of "endless, grinding drudgery" that Hamlin Garland portrayed "in the days of the early settlers," she would find community and companionship in "all sorts of neighborhood activities." She would teach "the kindergarten class in the country Sunday school the beautiful stories in such a way that they will always remember them," and would help "plan many social activities in the Grange, when all members of all the families around gather together for good times ... picnics, neighborhood Christmas trees, home talent plays, and so on."[39] In these publications Clara explored a metropolis/countryside dichotomy that she seemed to accept without question, coming down firmly in favour of the latter.[40] Unlike New Zealand sheep station clerk John Vaughan Miller (described in this volume by Lydia Wevers), for whom farm life failed to provide an outlet for his cultural aspirations and educational attainments, for Clara, a woman's land-grant college education was a means of improving life on the farm, not escaping it.[41] Far from occupying some imagined periphery in contrast to the implied centrality of city life, farm life was central to Clara's conception of what America as a nation was all about. She had thoroughly absorbed the ethos of the extension movement, although she still felt the need to defend rural life. For Clara, as for other country dwellers at this time, in Joan Shelley Rubin's words, "the metropolis, however geographically distant, was always there."[42]

Reading for Pleasure and Information

Despite the constant demands on her time and for her labour, occasionally Clara found an opportunity to read to herself and with friends, for pleasure and information. A couple of days after the collapse of the newspaper shelves, Clara noted that she "finished reading 'Quincy Adams Sawyer' [by C.F. Pidgin, 1900], a novel, interesting, amusing, though rather complex. It was too rainy and muddy to take my [voice] lesson this week."[43] Diary entries that described reading novels for pleasure often coincided with severe weather – both in winter and summer. In August 1909 she recorded that the days were very hot, and she found time to finish two books: Maurice Thompson's bestselling romance *Alice of Old Vincennes* (published in 1900) and Florence Kingsley's *Titus: A Comrade of the Cross.*[44] For Clara it seemed that not only did recreation always take second place to the work demands of household and farm, but that among the various pleasurable activities on offer, reading did not dominate. It was something that went on in the background of her busy life, a pastime she took for granted, and mentioned only as an aside.[45]

With her life on the farm so filled with domestic tasks, reading, writing, and church, entering college as a home economics major must have seemed a natural continuation of her existence at home – though with more reading and fewer routine chores. Clara and Dora boarded together at a house where meals were provided, giving the girls a welcome break from an endless round of cooking and cleaning at home. When not at class ("sewing lab," "Physical Culture") or working as a paid clerical assistant in the history department, Clara's life was taken up with events at the Young Women's Christian Association (YMCA), attending chapel, and a Mission Study class organized in her boarding house. Studying also occupied much of her time, and she gives the impression of having little time for reading for pleasure, although bad winter weather provided some time and space for fiction. In a February 1909 blizzard, she started to read George Eggleston's *Dorothy South*, but it took her a month to finish it – perhaps better weather intervened.[46] One evening in the middle of March, she finished *Dorothy South*, and with a friend, started John Fox's *The Little Shepherd of Kingdom Come*, a novel that sold over a million copies – perhaps the first book printed in the United States to do so.[47]

Although her taste in recreational reading was conventional, chiefly consisting of best-selling romances and other stories with a Christian theme, her writing – and presumably other reading – focused mainly on production for home and market.[48] From an early age, Clara not only sought to make money by selling her writing for publication, but also chose topics in her writing that dealt with making money or contributing in some other tangible way to the household's resources. In writing about domestic topics, Clara was participating in a self-help genre that had a long history. After graduation, while planning her marriage to Hans Skott, she continued to write short pieces for the farm press. Assigning them titles like "Threshers for Dinner" and "New Uses for Celery," Clara was writing from her own experience, not only turning a combination of her daily responsibilities on the farm and the skills learned in her college journalism classes to profitable use, but also communicating with readers of farm journals – other women like herself.[49]

Conclusion: Institutional Print Culture

To understand Clara Steen Skott's writings – both her formal publications and the entries in her diary, one has to understand the institutionalized world in which she lived – a world in which the gendered system of home economics presented some women – including farm women like herself – with unparalleled opportunities: the chance to go to college, to have a lifelong career, to earn money, and perhaps above all, to communicate with others through print. For her, domesticity provided neither a straitjacket nor a cause for resistance but, in Lora Romero's words, "an expansive logic, a meaningful vocabulary, and rich symbols through which to *think* about [her] world."[50]

Institutions occupy a useful theoretical position, in that they can mediate between the big picture – the macro: the highly general, societal level, and the micro: the level of individuals like Clara Steen. Bringing organizations or institutions into view enables the reading researcher to specify those points of interaction where individuals encounter the structuring forces of the wider society, as the interstices – the crossing points – become visible at the institutional level in a way that they are not at either a close-up or a more distant view. The organization also provides the context in which those functions separated by the economic market view of print culture exemplified by Darnton's communications circuit can truly be seen to overlap. Within organizations, the same groups of people may find themselves reading *and* writing printed texts. Writers and readers of texts may be the same individuals, but they may also be those who work closely together or share the same social space. And within organizations not only can the acts of individual readers and writers be picked out, but also the acts of individual publishers and distributors – those groups whose identity in the standard market models is shadowy, and often reduced to functionality. In this way, print producers can be both disaggregated and viewed in a detailed cultural context. Institutions are also an important source of data, especially for research into the lives of ordinary folk (those who are less likely to have left individual records).[51]

Although Clara Steen would probably have described her early life as that of a farm woman centred on her home and family, she participated in a large number of interlocking organizations that were vital to her print-culture activities. As well as belonging to informal sewing groups and a semi-formal literary association, she took part in formal but non-governmental associations that existed in many places across the nation, like the Methodist Church and the YWCA. She was an active and eager member of state and local government-sponsored organizations that encouraged or even required reading and writing, like the rural school (as teacher and as pupil), a land-grant college, the public library, and the extension movement. As a writer for and reader of the farm press (a commercial enterprise with firm ties to government) and local newspapers (also commercially constituted but with strong links to other kinds of association like political parties and business-sponsored booster groups), a network of official and semi-official organizations overlapped her life in key ways. Without these associational ties, her opportunities for reading and writing would have been much reduced. Her ability to take advantage of them derived not only from her individual desire and ability to read and write and a propensity for hard work, however, but also from an ethnic and religious identity that opened doors to these organizations and afforded her the expectation of a welcome. The popular novels published early in the twentieth century that Skott read for pleasure and relaxation as a young woman would have done little to shake acceptance of the belief that the racial and ethnic ordering of American society was anything but natural and appropriate. In this respect, the print culture fostered by state organizations like the land-grant college and the extension service meshed well with that of the commercial publishers of best-selling novels to sustain a general expectation and an ideology of white superiority.

In some ways, the story of Clara Steen Skott's life seems unremarkable in hindsight because she so closely fitted the extension service's ideal – an ideal that came to be normalized during the early and middle decades of the twentieth century. For pleasure and relaxation, Skott's own reading also followed a common path. Her favourites in the early decades of the twentieth century were books by authors of best-selling novels, like Gene Stratton Porter, Harold Bell Wright, and John Fox. Paradoxically, though, Skott's own close approximation to the extension service's norms allowed her to expand the range of her own activity both literally and figuratively through her participation in the institutionalized print culture networks of the region and the nation. Rather than write fictional stories of the type she enjoyed reading alone or with her friends and family, she chose to write in a informational genre that was to expand in the twentieth century until it threatened to eclipse – both in the popular imagination and in the narratives of professional readers like librarians and teachers – the reading of literature and stories. In so doing, she intertwined her informational writings with the experiences of her daily life and the communities in which she lived, thus counteracting the image of the institutional expert as the authoritative (white male) voice dispensing rationalized and anonymous advice. Skott's life was a seamless whole: her reading, writing, housekeeping, and farming were part of a single activity-packed existence, in which the parts were joined both logically and geographically. In her writings, Skott shifted between the impersonal scientific language she learned at college, language that assumed the existence of a gulf between author and reader, and the personal and chatty style that implied a relationship – a commonality – that assumed no barriers but bound writer and reader together in a kind of mutual sociability.

NOTES

1 Fry (2002, 26); United States, Bureau of the Census (1976, 11).
2 Bogue (1963), especially chapter 8, "How to Farm Sitting Down."
3 Throne (1951, 117–42).
4 Robert Hall, chapter 8 of this volume; as Kyle Roberts, chapter 2 of this volume, explains in "I have hitherto been entirely upon the borrowing hand": The Acquisition and Circulation of Books in Early Eighteenth-Century Dissenting Academies," in early eighteenth-century rural England reading practices were already developing in the context of informal and (increasingly) formal social groups and institutions.
5 Initially recruited by small local broadcasting stations to fill otherwise empty daytime hours in the 1920s and 30s, radio homemakers provided recipes and household tips and sometimes interacted with their children and other family members on the air. Radio homemakers were especially familiar to farm families in the Midwest up to the 1960s, or even later.
6 Brunner and Yang (1949, 13–14).
7 Brunner and Yang (1949, 114–16).
8 Eppright and Ferguson (1971, 74).
9 Clara Steen Skott, "Life in the Nineties." Undated typescript, Papers of Clara Steen Skott Box 1, Iowa Women's Archives, University of Iowa, Iowa City. Henceforth CSS.
10 Ibid.
11 Ibid.
12 Ibid.
13 Hilda Skott, "My Centenarian Mother." Unpublished typescript. CSS, Box 1, 12.
14 Pawley (2001, 14); R. Hall, this volume.
15 Hilda Skott, "My Centenarian Mother," 1–5.
16 Clara Steen Skott's diaries can be found in CSS Box 3. The final diary in this collection is dated 1990. No diaries exist for seventeen years.

17 Fry (2002, 307).
18 Fry (2002, 308).
19 Clara Steen Skott Diary, 20 March 1908. "The Prisoner of Chillon," a poem by Lord Byron, was published in 1816.
20 Ibid. 28 January 1908.
21 Ibid. 4, 5, 6, 7 February 1908.
22 Ibid. 11 May 1908.
23 Newsprint had lots of non-literary uses, of course, from wallpaper to toilet tissue.
24 Clara Steen Skott, "Life in the Nineties." Undated typescript, CSS Box 1.
25 Kaestle (1991, 279).
26 Barron (1997, 227).
27 This paragraph is based on Fry (2002, especially pages 25, 14–15, 316, 296, 43).
28 Pawley (2001, 156).
29 Pawley (2001, 219).
30 Darnton (1989, 31).
31 Iowa State College Agricultural Extension Department, "Home Economics Examination Questions for Women," 1915–16. Food and Nutrition Extension Service Publications. Box 1, RS 16/3/0/20, Iowa State University Cooperative Extension Service Archives. Henceforth ISU.
32 Iowa State College Agricultural Extension Department, "Home Economics Examination Questions for Women," 1916–17. Food and Nutrition Extension Service Publications. Box 1, RS 16/3/0/20 ISU.
33 "Short Course Class Notes No. 1" (1911), *Food and Nutrition Extension Service Publications*. Box 1, RS 16/3/0/20 ISU.
34 Ibid.
35 Clara Steen, "Get the Good of Grapes," *Successful Farming*, n.d. This article appears in CSS as an undated clipping and without full bibliographic information.
36 "Home Economics Circular no. 1," 10 June 1914, p. 14. *Official Publication of Iowa State College of Agriculture and Mechanic Arts*, Box 1, RS 16/3/0/20 ISU.
37 Skott, "My Centenarian Mother," 12.
38 Clara Steen, "To the Farm Girl at Home" (*Successful Farming*, March 1912). This article and the next (see note 38) appear as a clipping in CSS, but are not accompanied by full bibliographical information.
39 Clara Steen, "The Farm's Call to a College Girl" (*The Iowa Agriculturalist* n.d.; see note 37).
40 See Joan Shelley Rubin, chapter 5 of this volume, for an extended discussion of this dichotomy.
41 Lydia Wevers, chapter 9 of this volume.
42 Joan Shelley Rubin, chapter 5 of this volume.
43 Clara Steen Skott Diary, 13 May 1908.

44 Ibid., 15 August 1909. The Bowen-Merrill Company of Indianapolis had published Maurice Thompson's (1844–1901) novel *Alice of Old Vincennes* in 1900, but in 1908, Grosset and Dunlap of New York issued a new edition, with illustrations by F.C. Yohn. Florence Morse Kingsley's *Titus: A Comrade of the Cross: A Tale of the Christ for the Christmas Tide*, was published in 1897, but appeared in several subsequent editions.

45 Clara Steen Skott Diary, 11 May 1908, 13 May 1908.

46 Ibid., 14 February 1909. George Cary Eggleston, *Dorothy South: a Love Story of Virginia Just Before the War* (Boston: Lothrop Publishing Company, 1902).

47 Clara Steen Skott Diary, 14 March 1909. John Fox, *Little Shepherd of Kingdom Come* (New York, C. Scribner's Sons, 1903).

48 The novels that Clara and her friends enjoyed would have been familiar to the Muncie Public Library readers described in this volume by Tatlock (chapter 11) and Felsenstein (chapter 12), and the New Zealand readers described by Wevers (chapter 9). Through their reading of nationally popular fiction these rural and small-town readers thus participated in a print culture that transcended local and indeed (as in the case of Tatlock's American readers of translated German domestic fiction, and Wever's New Zealand readers of British fiction) national boundaries.

49 In July1916, Clara Steen earned $9.44 for 1259 words in an article titled "Threshers for Dinner" and in February 1917, $3.97 for 529 words for "New Uses for Celery" from the journal *Successful Farming*. Receipts for payment found in CSS, Box 1. For a detailed analysis of women readers of farm journals before 1920, see Fry (2002, especially 259–66).

50 Romero (1997, 19).

51 For an extended version of this theoretical argument, see Pawley (2009b).

Secondary Works Cited

Aaron, Daniel. 1973. *The Unwritten War: American Writers and the Civil War*. New York: Knopf.

Aching, Gerard. 1997. *The Politics of Spanish American Modernismo*. New York: Cambridge University Press.

Adams, Thomas R., and Nicolas Barker. 1993. "A New Model for the Study of the Book." In *A Potencie of Life: Books in Society*, edited by Nicolas Barker, 5–43. London: British Library.

Adams, W.E. (1903) 1969. *Memoirs of A Social Atom*. Reprint, New York: Augustus M. Kelley.

Alam, Facrul, and Radha Chakravarty. 2011. "Introduction." In *The Essential Tagore*, edited by Facrul Alam and Radha Chakravarty, 1–33. Cambridge, MA: Harvard University Press.

Alasuutari, Pertti. 1999. "Introduction: Three Faces of Reception Studies." In *Rethinking the Media Audience: The New Agenda*, edited by Pertti Alasuutari, 1–21. London: Sage Publications.

Allan, David. 2008. *A Nation of Readers: The Lending Library in Georgian England*. London: British Library.

Amory, Hugh, and David D. Hall, eds. 2000. *A History of the Book in America, Volume 1: The Colonial Book in the Atlantic World*. Cambridge: Cambridge University Press.

Anderson, Benedict. 1991. *Imagined Communities: Reflections on the Origins and Spread of Nationalism*. Rev. ed. New York: Verso.

Anderson, J.C. 1940. "Early Printing in New Zealand." In *A History of Printing in New Zealand 1830–1940*, edited by R.A. McKay, 1–32. Wellington, NZ: Club of Printing House Craftsmen.

Anderson, James House, ed. 1904. *Life and Letters of Judge Thomas J. Anderson and Wife, Including a Few Letters from Children and Others Mostly Written During the Civil War: a History*. Columbus, OH: F.J. Heer.

Anderson, Sherwood. 1976. *Winesburg, Ohio*. New York: Penguin.
Andrews, J. Cutler. 1955. *The North Reports the Civil War*. Pittsburgh: University of Pittsburgh Press.
Andrews, J. Cutler. 1970. *The South Reports the Civil War*. Princeton, NJ: Princeton University Press.
App, Urs. 2010. *The Birth of Orientalism*. Philadelphia: University of Pennsylvania Press.
Appiah, Kwame Anthony. 2006. *Cosmopolitanism: Ethics in a World of Strangers*. New York, London: W.W. Norton & Company.
Apter, Emily. 2005. *The Translation Zone*. Princeton, NJ: Princeton University Press.
Ardis, Ann L., and Patrick Collier, eds. 2008. *Transatlantic Print Culture, 1880–1940: Emerging Media, Emerging Modernisms*. London: Palgrave MacMillan.
Augst, Thomas. 2007. "Introduction." In *Institutions of Reading: The Social Life of Libraries in the United States*, edited by Thomas Augst and Kenneth Carpenter, 1–23. Amherst: University of Massachusetts Press.
Axon, William W.E. 1870. *The Black Knight of Ashton*. Manchester: John Heywood.
Axon, William W.E. 1877. *Handbook of the Public Libraries of Manchester and Salford*. Manchester: Abel Heywood and Son.
Bachleitner, Norbert. 2000. "Die deutsche Rezeption englischer Romanautorinnen des neunzehnten Jahrhunderts, insbesondere Charlotte Brontës." In *The Novel in Anglo-German Context: Cultural Cross-Currents and Affinities*, edited by Susanne Stark, 173–94. Amsterdam: Rodopi.
Baggs, Chris. 2001. "How Well Read Was My Valley?: Reading, Popular Fiction, and the Miners of South Wales, 1876–1939." *Book History* 4:277–301.
Baldwin, Davarian. 2013. "Introduction: New Negroes Forging New World." In *Escape from New York: The New Negro Renaissance Beyond Harlem*, edited by Davarian Baldwin and Minkah Makalani, 1–30. Minneapolis: University of Minnesota Press.
Bamford, Samuel. (1844) 1972. *Walks in South Lancashire and on its Borders*. Brighton: Harvester Press.
Barabasi, Albert Laszlo. 2009. "Scale-Free Networks: A Decade and Beyond." *Science* 325, no. 5939: 412–13.
Barber, Karin, ed. 2006. *Africa's Hidden Histories: Everyday Literacy and Making the Self*. Bloomington: Indiana University Press.
Barney, William L. 2008. *The Making of a Confederate: Walter Lenoir's Civil War*. New York: Oxford University Press.
Barron, Hal S. 1997. *Mixed Harvest:The Second Great Transformation in the Rural North, 1870–1930*. Chapel Hill, London: University of North Carolina Press.
Bartlett, Rosamund. 2004. *Chekhov: Scenes from a Life*. London: Free Press.

Beal, Peter. 1998. *In Praise of Scribes: Manuscripts and Their Makers in Seventeenth-Century England*. New York: Oxford University Press.

Beck, Ulrich. 2007. "Cosmopolitanism: A Critical Theory for the Twenty-first Century." In *The Blackwell Companion to Globalization*, edited by George Ritzer, 162–76. Oxford: Blackwell Publishing.

Beck, Ulrich, and Edgar Grande. 2007. *Cosmopolitan Europe*. Trans. Ciaran Cronin. Cambridge: Polity.

Belanger, Terry. 1977. "A Directory of the London Book Trade, 1766." *Publishing History* 1:7–48.

Belgum, Kirsten. 1998. *Popularizing the Nation: Audience, Representation, and the Production of Identity in Die Gartenlaube 1853–1900*. Lincoln: University of Nebraska Press.

Bell, Maureen, and John Hinks. 2009. "The English Provincial Book Trade: Evidence from the *British Book Trade Index*." In *The Cambridge History of the Book in Britain: 1695–1840*, vol. 5, edited by Michael F. Suarez, S.J., and Michael L. Turner, 335–51. Cambridge: Cambridge University Press.

Bensel, Richard Franklin. 1991. *Yankee Leviathan: The Origins of Central State Authority in America, 1859–1877*. New York: Cambridge University Press.

Benson, John. 1980. *British Coalmining in the Nineteenth Century: A Social History*. Dublin: Gill & Macmillan.

Bergel, Giles. 2012. "The Chap-Book (1894–8)." In *The Oxford Critical and Cultural History of Modernist Magazines*, vol. 2, edited by Peter Brooker and Andrew Thacker, 154–75. New York: Oxford University Press.

Berry, Joel M. 2007. "Orientalism and the Asiatic Society of Bengal." *Journal of the Oriental Society of Bangladesh* 52, no. 2. Accessed 18 February 2013. http://www.bmri.org.uk/articles/orientalism.pdf.

Betts, Raymond. 1985. *Uncertain Dimensions: Western Overseas Empires in the Twentieth Century*. Minneapolis: University of Minnesota Press.

Bezer, John James. 1977. "The Autobiography of One of the Chartist Rebels of 1848." In *Testaments of Radicalism: Memoirs of Working Class Politicians 1790—1885*, edited by David Vincent, 153–87. London: Europa Publications.

Billman, Carol. 1986. *The Secret of the Stratemeyer Syndicate: Nancy Drew, The Hardy Boys, and the Million Dollar Fiction Factory*. New York: Ungar.

Biskup, Peter. 1994. *Libraries in Australia*. Wagga Wagga: Centre for Information Studies.

Bissell, Arthur Henry, and George H. Kirby, comps. 1879. *The Postal Laws and Regulations of the United States of America*. Washington, DC: Government Printing Office.

Black, Alistair, Simon Pepper, and Kaye Bagshaw. 2009. *Books, Buildings and Social Engineering: Early Public Libraries in Britain from Past to Present*. Farnham: Ashgate.

Blackburn, Stuart. 2004. "The Burden of Authority: Printed Oral Tales in Tamil Literary History." In *India's Literary History: Essays on the Nineteenth Century*, edited by Stuart H. Blackburn and Vasudha Dalmia, 119–45. New Delhi: Permanent Black.

Blackburn, Stuart. 2006. *Printing Folklore and Nationalism in Colonial South India*. Hyderabad: Orient Blackswan.

Blomquist, Ann K., and Robert A. Taylor, eds. 2000. *This Cruel War: The Civil War Letters of Grant and Malinda Taylor, 1862–1865*. Macon, GA: Mercer University Press.

Boas, Franz. 1887. "The Occurrence of Similar Inventions in Areas Widely Apart." *Science* 9, no. 224: 485–6.

Bode, Katherine. 2012. *Reading by Numbers: Recalibrating the Literary Field*. London: Anthem Press.

Bogue, Allan G. 1963. *From Prairie to Corn Belt: Farming on the Illinois and Iowa Prairies in the Nineteenth Century*. Chicago: University of Chicago Press.

Boittin, Jennifer Anne. 2005. "In Black and White: Gender, Race Relations, and the Nardal Sisters in Interwar Paris." *French Colonial History* 6:120–35.

Bonner, Philip, Jonathan Hyslop, and Lucien Van der Walt. 2007. "Rethinking Worlds of Labour: Southern African Labour History in International Context." *African Studies* 66, nos. 2–3: 137–67.

Boumelha, Penny. 1982. *Thomas Hardy and Women: Sexual Ideology and Narrative Form*. Sussex: Harvester Press.

Boumelha, Penny. 1997. "The Woman of Genius and the Woman of Grub Street: Figures of the Woman Writer in British *Fin-de- Siècle Fiction*." *ELT Press* 40, no. 2:164–80.

Bragdon, Claude. 1904. "Among Old Books." *Book-lover* 5 (May): 585–9.

Bragdon, Claude. 2006. *More Lives Than One*. New York: Cosimo Classics.

Brake, Laurel. 1994. *Subjugated Knowledges: Journalism, Gender and Literature in the Nineteenth Century*. New York: New York University Press.

Brake, Laurel. 2001. "On Print Culture: The State We're In." *Journal of Victorian Culture* 6, no. 1: 125–36.

Brake, Laurel. 2012. "Censorship, Puffing, 'Piracy,' Reprinting: British Decadence and Transatlantic Re-Mediations of Walter Pater, 1893–1910." *Modernism/Modernity* 19, no. 3: 419–35.

Bratton, Elizabeth Porcher DuBose, ed. 1942. *Letters of John Bratton to His Wife during [the] Civil War*. McFarland, NC: privately printed.

Breu, Christopher. 2005. *Hard-Boiled Masculinities*. Minneapolis: University of Minnesota Press.

Brockington, J.L. 1989. "Warren Hastings and Orientalism." In *The Impeachment of Warren Hastings: Papers from a Bicentenary Commemoration*, edited by Geoffrey Carnall and Colin Nicholson, 91–108. Edinbugh: Edinburgh University Press.

Brown, Garrett Wallace, and David Held, eds. 2010. *The Cosmopolitan Reader*. Cambridge: Polity.

Brown, Joshua. 2002. *Beyond the Lines: Pictorial Reporting, Everyday Life and the Crisis of Gilded Age America*. Berkeley: University of California Press.

Brown, Richard D. 1989. *Knowledge Is Power: The Diffusion of Information in Early America, 1700–1865*. New York: Oxford University Press.

Brunner, Edmund de S., and E. Hsin-Pao Yang. 1949. *Rural America and the Extension Service: A History and Critique of the Cooperative Agricultural and Home Economics Extension Service*. New York: Teachers College, Columbia University.

Bulla, David W., and Gregory A. Borchard. 2010. *Journalism in the Civil War Era*. New York: Peter Lang.

Bunnell, A.O. 1903. *New York Press Association Authorized History for Fifty Years, 1853–1903*. Dansville, NY: F.A. Owen Publishing Co.

Burden, Mark. 2013. *A Biographical Dictionary of Tutors at the Dissenters' Private Academies, 1660–1720*. London: Dr Williams's Centre for Dissenting Studies.

Burke, Peter. 2009. *Cultural Hybridity*. Cambridge.: Polity Press.

Burt, Ron. 1992. *Structural Holes: The Social Structure of Competition*. Boston: Harvard.

Burt, Ron. 2004. "Structural Holes and Good Ideas." *American Journal of Sociology* 110, no. 2: 349–99.

Byrne, Frank L., and Jean Powers Soman, eds. 1985. *Your True Marcus: The Civil War Letters of a Jewish Colonel*. Kent, OH: Kent State University Press.

Campbell, R. 1747. *The London Tradesman*. London: T. Gardner.

Canby, Henry Seidel. 1934. *The Age of Confidence*. New York: Farrar & Rhinehart.

Carlyle, Thomas. (1840) 1993. *On Heroes, Hero-Worship, & the Heroic in History [1840], Lecture V*. Ed. Michael K. Goldberg. Berkeley: University of California Press.

Carrier, Esther Jane. 1965. *Fiction in Public Libraries,1876–1900*. New York: Scarecrow Press.

Carrier, Esther Jane. 1985. *Fiction in Public Libraries, 1900–1950*. Littleton, CO: Libraries Unlimited.

Casanova, Pascale. 2004. *The World Republic of Letters*. Trans. M.B. DeBevoise. Boston: Harvard University Press.

Cate, Phillip Dennis, and Mary Shaw, eds. 1996. *The Spirit of Montmartre: Cabarets, Humor, and the Avant-Garde, 1875–1905*. New Brunswick, NJ: Jane Voorheis Zimmerli Art Museum.

Celebrating the Silver Anniversary of the Coterie. 1898. Dansville, NY: The Coterie.

Chapin, Artena M. 1907. *A Sketch of the Muncie Public Library*. Muncie, IN: Privately Printed.

Chartier, Roger. 1994. *The Order of Books: Readers, Authors, and Libraries in Europe Between the Fourteenth and Eighteenth Centuries*. Stanford, CA: Stanford University Press.

Chase, Malcolm. 2007. *Chartism: A New History*. Manchester: Manchester University Press.

Cheney, C.R., John Cheney, and Walter Gardner Cheney, 1936. *John Cheney and His Descendants: Printers in Banbury since 1767*. Banbury, UK: Printed for private circulation.

Chekhov, Mikhail. 2010. *Anton Chekhov: A Brother's Memoir*. New York: Palgrave.

Cipolla, Carlo M. 1993. *Before the Industrial Revolution: European Society and Economy 1000–1700*. 3rd ed. London: Routledge.

Cipolla, Carlo M., ed. 1973. *Economic History of Europe*. 5 vols. London: Fontana.

Clynes, J.R. 1937. *Memoirs*. 2 vols. London: Hutchinson and Co.

Cohn, Bernard S. 1996. *Colonialism and Its Forms of Knowledge: The British in India*. Princeton, NJ: Princeton University Press.

Colclough, Stephen. 2000. "Procuring Books and Consuming Texts: The Reading Experience of A Sheffield Apprentice, 1798." *Book History* 3:21–44.

Colclough, Stephen. 2009. "Distribution." In *The Cambridge History of the Book in Britain, Volume VI: 1830—1914*, edited by David McKitterick, 238–80. Cambridge: Cambridge University Press.

Colclough, Stephen. 2011. "Representing Reading Spaces." In *The History of Reading, Volume 3*, edited Shafquat Towheed, W.R. Owens, Katie Halsey, and Rosalind Crone, 99–114. Houndmills: Palgrave Macmillan.

Coleman, Donald C. 1958. *The Paper Industry, 1495–1860: A Study in Industrial Growth*. Oxford: Clarendon Press.

Coleman, Thomas. 1853. *Memorials of the Independent Churches in Northamptonshire: With Biographical Notices of Their Pastors, And Some Account of the Puritan Ministers Who Laboured In the County*. London: John Snow.

Q14Condie, Victoria. 2008. "Thacker, Spink and Company: Bookselling and Publishing in Mid-Nineteenth-Century Calcutta." In *Books Without Borders, Volume 2: Perspectives from South Asia*, edited by Robert Fraser and Mary Hammond, 112–24. London: Palgrave Macmillan.

Confederate States of America, Post Office Department. 1861. *Instructions to Postmasters*. Richmond: Ritchie and Dunnavant.

Connelly, Mark. 2008. *The Hardy Boys Mysteries, 1927–1979: A Cultural and Literary History*. Jefferson, NC: McFarland.

Connolly, James J. 2008. Decentering Urban History: Peripheral Cities in the Modern World." *Journal of Urban History* 35, no. 1 (November): 3–14.

Coopersmith, Andrew S. 2004. *Fighting Words: An Illustrated History of Newspaper Accounts of the Civil War*. New York: New Press.

Cordery, Simon. 2003. *British Friendly Societies, 1750–1914*. Houndmills: Palgrave Macmillan.

Corfield, P.J. 1982. *The Impact of English Towns 1700–1800*. Oxford: Oxford University Press.

Corinealdi, Kaysha. 2011. "Redefining Home: West Indian Panamanians and Transnational Politics of Race, Citizenship, and Diaspora, 1928-1970." PhD diss., Yale University.

Costas, Benito Rial, ed. 2012. *Print Culture and Peripheries in Early Modern Europe: A Contribution the History of Printing and the Book Trade in Small European and Spanish Cities*. Leiden, The Netherlands: Brill.

Crane, Diana. 1972. *Invisible Colleges: Diffusion of Knowledge in Scientific Communities*. Chicago: University of Chicago Press.

Cranfield, C.A. 1962. *The Development of the Provincial Newspaper, 1700–60*. Oxford: Clarendon Press.

Crawford, W.H., and B. Trainor, eds. 1969. *Aspects of Irish Social History 1750–1800: Documents; With an Introduction by J.C. Beckett*. Belfast: HMSO.

Crone, Rosalind. 2010. "Reappraising Victorian Literacy through Prison Records." *Journal of Victorian Culture* 15 (April): 3–37.

Cruickshanks, Eveline, Stuart Handley, and D.W. Hayton, eds. 2002. *The History of Parliament: The House of Commons, 1690–1715*. Cambridge: Cambridge University Press.

Cudjoe, Selwyn R. 2009. *Caribbean Visionary: A.R.F. Webber and the Making of the Guyanese Nation*. Jackson: University Press of Mississippi.

Cullinan, Gerald. 1968. *The Post Office Department*. New York: Frederick A. Praeger.

Dahl, Folke. 1952. *A Bibliography of English Corantos and Periodical Newsbooks 1620–1642*. London: Bibliographical Society.

Dalrymple, Daniel. 2008. "In the Shadow of Garvey: Garveyites in New York City and the British Caribbean, 1925–1950." PhD diss., Michigan State University.

Dalrymple, William. 2004. *White Mughals: Love and Betrayal in Eighteenth Century India*. New York: Penguin Books.

Damrosch, David. 2003. *What Is World Literature?* Princeton, NJ: Princeton University Press.

Darnton, Robert. 1982. "What Is the History of Books?" *Daedalus* 111, no. (3): 65–83.

Darnton, Robert. 1989. "What Is the History of Books?" In *Reading in America: Literature and Social History*, edited by Cathy N. Davidson, 27–52. Baltimore: Johns Hopkins University Press.

Darnton, Robert. 1990. *The Kiss of Lamourette: Reflections in Cultural History*. London, New York: W.W. Norton and Company.

Darnton, Robert. 1996. *The Forbidden Best-Sellers of Pre-Revolutionary France*. New York: Norton.

Darnton, Robert. 2007. "What Is the History of Books? Revisited." *Modern Intellectual History* 4, no. 3: 495–508.

Davies, Owen. 2003. *Cunning Folk: Popular Magic in English History*. London: Hambledon and London.

Deacon, Malcolm. 1980. *Philip Doddridge of Northampton*. Northampton: Northamptonshire Libraries.

Defant, Yvonne. 2010. "Le mystère du passé hante encore: l'influence de *Jane Eyre* sur *Die zweite* Frau d'Eugenie Marlitt." *Revue LISA/LISA Writers, Writings, Literary Studies* 3. Accessed 24 June 2013. http://lisa.revues.org/3510.

Delap, Lucy, and Maria DiCenzo. 2008. "Transatlantic Print Culture: The Anglo-American Feminist Press and Emerging 'Modernities." In *Transatlantic Print Culture, 1880–1940: Emerging Media, Emerging Modernisms*, edited by Ann Ardis and Patrick Collier, 48–65. New York: Palgrave Macmillan.

de Lisser, Herbert. (Original work published 1913) 1971. *Jane's Career*. New York: Africana Publishing Corp.

De Smet, Richard. 1990. "Review of Sylvie Murr, Vol. 1: Moeurs et Coutumes des Indiens (1777): Un inédit du Père G.-L. Coeurdoux, S.J. dans la version de N.-J. Desvaulx. Vol. II: L'Indologie du Père Coeurdoux (Paris: *Ecole Francaise d'Extrême Orient, 1987)." *Indian Theological Studies* 27:371–3.

Denning, Michael. 1987. *Mechanics Accents: Dime Novels and Working-Class Culture in America*. London: Verso.

Dicken-Garcia, Hazel, and Giovanna Dell'Orto. 2008. *Hated Ideas and the American Civil War Press*. Spokane, WA: Marquette Books.

Dieh, Katharine Smith. 1964. *Early Indian Imprints*. New York: Scarecrow Press.

Dixon, Robert. 2008. "Australian Literature and the New Empiricism: A Response to Paul Eggert, 'Australian Classics and the Price of Books.'" *JASAL* Special Issue: 158–62.

Doherty, J.C. 1983. *Newcastle: The Making of an Australian City*. Sydney: Hale & Iremonger.

Dolin, Tim. 2011. "Fiction and the Australian Reading Public 1888–1914." In *A Return to the Common Reader: Print Culture and the Novel, 1850–1900*, edited by Beth Palmer and Adelene Buckland, 151–74. Farnham, VT: Ashgate.

Dowell, S. 1965. *A History of Taxation and Taxes in England*. 3rd ed. Vol. 3. London: Frank Cass.

Duara, Prasenjit. 2001. "The Discourse of Civilization and Pan-Asianism." *Journal of World History* 12:99–130.

Duke, Eric. 2009. "The Diasporic Dimensions of Caribbean Federation in the Early Twentieth Century." *New West Indian Guide* 83, nos. 3–4: 219–48.

Dunning, Thomas. 1977. "Reminiscences of Thomas Dunning." In *Testaments of Radicalism: Memoirs of Working Class Politicians 1790—1885*, edited by David Vincent, 119–46. London: Europa Publications.

Durkin, Andrew. 1997. "Chekhov and the Journals of His Time." In *Literary Journals in Imperial Russia*, edited by Deoborah A. Martisen, 228–45. New York: Cambridge University Press.

Durkin, Joseph T., ed. 1960. *Confederate Chaplain: A War Journal of Rev. James B. Sheeran, C. SS. R. 14th Louisiana, C. S. A.* Milwaukee: Bruce Publishing.

Dwight, Wilder, and Elizabeth Dwight. 1891. *Life and Letters of Wilder Dwight: Lieut.-Col. Second Mass. Inf. Vols.* Boston: Little, Brown, and Co.

Easley, David, and Jon Kleinberg. 2010. *Networks, Crowds, and Markets.* Cambridge: Cambridge University Press.

Edwards, Alba M. 1933. "A Social-Economic Grouping of the Gainful Workers of the United States," *Journal of the American Statistical Association* 28, no. 184 (Dec.): 377–87.

Edwards, Brent Hayes. 2003. *The Practice of Diaspora: Literature, Translation, and the Rise of Black Internationalism.* Cambridge, MA: Harvard University Press.

Eggert, Paul. 2008. "Australian Classics and the Price of Books: The Puzzle of the 1890s." *JASAL* Special Issue: 130–57.

Eklund, Erik. 2012. *Mining Towns: Making a Living, Making a Life.* Sydney: UNSW Press.

Elkins, W.F. 1972. "Hercules and the Society of Peoples of African Origin." *Caribbean Studies (Rio Piedras, San Juan, P.R.)* 11, no. 4: 57–8.

Elliott, Robert. 1861. "On the Working Men's Reading Rooms, as Established in 1848 at Carlisle." *Transactions of the National Association for the Promotion of Social Science*: 676–9.

Engel, Brian. 2009. "Lambton Mechanics' and Miners Institute." In *The Story of Lambton: A Suburb of Newcastle, NSW*, edited by Maree Shilling, 117–24. Newcastle, NSW: Newcastle Family History Society.

Q15Engels, Frederick. 1984. *The Condition of the Working Class in England.* London: Panther Books.

Eppright, Ercel Shipman, and Elizabeth Storm Ferguson. 1971. *A Century of Home Economics at Iowa State University:A Proud Past, a Lively Present, a Future Promise.* Ames: Iowa State University Home Economics Alumni Association.

Epstein, James. 1976. "Feargus O'Connor and the *Northern Star.*" *International Review of Social History* 21, no. 1: 51–76.

Epstein, James. 1982. *The Lion of Freedom: Feargus O'Connor and the Chartist Movement, 1832–1842.* London: Croom Helm.

Evans, Brad. 2005. *Before Cultures: The Ethnographic Imagination in American Literature, 1865–1920*. Chicago: University of Chicago Press.

Evans, Brad. 2012. "The Ephemeral Bibelots." In *The Oxford Critical and Cultural History of Modernist Magazines, Volume 2: North America*, edited by Peter Brooker and Andrew Thacker, 132–53. Oxford: Oxford University Press.

Evans, Seth. 1915. *Peakland Pickings: Historical, Anecdotal, Biographical, and Political*. No pub., no place.

Ewing, Adam. 2011. "Broadcast on the Winds: Diasporic Politics in the Age of Garvey, 1919–1940." PhD diss., Harvard University.

"The Extensions of Literary Activity." 1896. *The Dial* 21, no. 247: 177–9.

Fahs, Alice. 2001. *The Imagined Civil War: Popular Literature of the North and South, 1861–1865*. Chapel Hill: University of North Carolina Press.

Farish, William. (1889) 1996. *The Autobiography of William Farish: The Struggles of a Handloom Weaver. Reprint*. London: Caliban Books.

Farseth, Pauline, and Theodore C. Blegen, eds. 1950. *Frontier Mother: The Letters of Gro Svendsen*. Northfield, MN: Norwegian-American Historical Association.

Faust, Drew Gilpin. 1988. *The Creation of Confederate Nationalism: Ideology and Identity in the Civil War South*. Baton Rouge: Louisiana State University Press.

Faxon, Frederick. 1903. *Ephemeral Bibelots: A Bibliography of the Modern Chap-Books and Their Imitators*. Boston: The Boston Book Company.

Feather, John. 1985. *The Provincial Book Trade in Eighteenth-Century England*. Cambridge: Cambridge University Press.

Felsenstein, Frank, and James J. Connolly. 2015. *What Middletown Read: Print Culture in an American Small City*. Amherst: University of Massachusetts Press.

Ferdinand, C.Y. 1983. "Benjamin Collins: Salisbury Printer." In *Searching the Eighteenth Century: Papers Presented at the Symposium on the Eighteenth-Century Short Title Catalogue in July, 1982*, edited by M. Crump and M. Harris, 74–92. London: British Library.

Fergus, Jan S. 2006. *Provincial Readers in Eighteenth-Century England*. Oxford: Oxford University Press.

Fergus, Jan, and Ruth Portner. 1987. "Provincial Bookselling in Eighteenth-century England: The Case of John Clay Reconsidered." *Studies in Bibliography* 40:147–63.

Ferguson, Frances. 2008. "Planetary Literary History: The Place of the Text." *New Literary History* 39, no. 3: 657–84.

Finkelstein, David, and Alistair McCleery, eds. 2005. *An Introduction to Book History*. New York: Routledge.

Fischer, Michael M. 2009. *Anthropological Futures*. Durham, NC: Duke University Press.

Flint, Kate. 1995. *The Woman Reader, 1837–1914*. New York: Oxford University Press.

Flint, Kate. 2001. "The Victorian Novel and Its Readers." In *The Cambridge Companion to the Victorian Novel*, edited by Deirdre David, 17–36. Cambridge: Cambridge University Press.

Fluharty, Linda Cunningham. 2004. *Civil War Letters of Lt. Milton B. Campbell*. Baton Rouge, LA: Linda Cunningham Fluharty.

Foroughi, Andrea R., ed. 2008. *Go If You Think it Your Duty: A Minnesota Couple's Civil War Letters*. St Paul: Minnesota Historical Society Press.

Fort Smith Union. 1863. Fort Smith, AK: I.V. Green.

Foucault, Michel. 1972. *The Archaeology of Knowledge*. New York: Harper and Row.

Foucault, Michel. 1973. *The Order of Things*. New York: Vintage.

Franco, Adela Pineda. 2006. *Geopoliticas de la cultura finisecular en Buenos Aires, Paris y México: las revistas literarias y el modernism*. Pittsburgh: University of Pittsburgh.

Fraser, Robert. 2008. *Book History through Postcolonial Eyes: Rewriting the Script*. London: Routledge.

Fraser, Robert, and Mary Hammond. 2008, "Introduction," in *Books Without Borders*, Vol. 1: *The Cross National Dimension in Print Culture*, 1–12. London: Palgrave MacMillan.

Fredrickson, George M. 1965. *The Inner Civil War: Northern Intellectuals and the Crisis of the Union*. New York: Harper and Row.

Fry, John J. 2002. "Reading, Reform, and Rural Change: The Midwestern Farm Press, 1895–1920." PhD diss., University of Iowa.

Frykenberg, Robert Eric. 2008. *Christianity in India: From Beginnings to the Present*. New Delhi: Oxford University Press.

Fuller, Lawrence B. 1984. "Mary Mapes Dodge and *St. Nicholas*: The Development of a Philosophy and Practice of Publishing for Young People." Paper presented at the Annual Meeting of the National Council of Teachers of English, Detroit.

Fyfe, Aileen. 2012. *Steam-Powered Knowledge: William Chambers and the Business of Publishing, 1820–1860*. Chicago: University of Chicago Press.

Gallagher, Gary W. 1997. *The Confederate War*. Cambridge, MA: Harvard University Press.

Gallagher, Gary W. 2011. *The Union War*. Cambridge, MA: Harvard University Press.

Gannon, Susan. 2004. "Fair Ideals and Heavy Responsibilities: The Editing of *St. Nicholas* Magazine." In *St. Nicholas and Mary Mapes Dodge: The Legacy of A Children's Magazine Editor, 1873–1905*, edited by Susan Gannon, Suzanne Rahn, and Ruth Anne Thompson, 37–43. Jefferson, NC: McFarland & Company.

Gannon, Susan R., and Ruth Anne Thompson. 1992. *Mary Mapes Dodge*. New York: Twayne.

Garbe, Christine, Karl Holle, and Tatanja Jesch. 2011. *Texte lesen: Lesekompetenz–Textverstehen–Lesedidaktik–Lesesozialisation*. 2nd ed. Paderborn: Ferdinand Schöningh.

Garrison, Dee. 1971. "Cultural Custodians of the Gilded Age: The Public Librarian and Horatio Alger." *Journal of Library History (Tallahassee, Fla.)* 6:327–34.

Garrison, Dee. (Original work published 1979) 2003. *Apostles of Culture: Public Librarian and American Society, 1876–1920*. Madison: University of Wisconsin Press.

Garvey, Ellen Gruber. 2012. *Writing with Scissors: American Scrapbooks from the Civil War to the Harlem Renaissance*. New York: Oxford University Press.

Gaskell, Philip. 1972. *A New Introduction to Bibliography*. Oxford: Clarendon Press.

Gately, Rachel. 2013. "Black Internationalism in Panama: Sidney Young as a 'Forgotten Editor,' 1928–1950." Senior honours thesis, University of Pittsburgh.

A General Description of all Trades. 1747. London: T. Waller.

Ghosh, Anindita. 2008. "The Many World of the Vernacular Book: Performance, Literacy, and Print in Colonial Bengal." In *Books Without Borders, Volume 2: Perspectives from South Asia*, edited by Robert Fraser and Mary Hammond, 34–57. London: Palgrave Macmillan.

Gilbert, Mark Jason. 2011. "The Collapse of the English Trade Entrepots at Pulo Condore and Banjarmasin and the Legacy of Early British East India Company Urban Network-Building in Southeast Asia." In *The Growth of Non-Western Cities, Primary and Secondary Urban Networking c. 900–1900*, edited by Kenneth R. Hall, 205–39. Lanham, MD: Lexington Press.

Gill, Stephen. 1993. *Gramsci, Historical Materialism and International Relations*. Cambridge: Cambridge University Press.

Gillespie-Needham, Dulcie. 1971. *The Colonial and his Books: A Study of Reading in Nineteenth Century New Zealand*. PhD diss., Victoria University of Wellington.

Gilmore, William J. 1989. *Reading Becomes a Necessity of Life: Material and Cultural Life in Rural New England, 1780–1835*. Knoxville: University of Tennessee Press.

Ginswick, J., ed. 1983. *Labour and the Poor in England and Wales 1849–1851: The Letters to the Morning Chronicle*. 8 vols. London: Frank Cass.

Goldthree, Reena. 2013. "'Just as any other British soldier': Race, Respectability, and Rebellion in the British West Indies Regiment." Unpublished chapter draft.

Gosden, P.H.J.H. 1961. *The Friendly Societies in England, 1815–1875*. Manchester: University of Manchester Press.

Gostwick, Joseph, and Robert Harrison. 1873. *Outlines of German Literature*. New York: Henry Holt and Co.

Goswami, Manu. 2012. "Imaginary Futures and Colonial Internationalisms." *American Historical Review* 117, no. 5: 1461–85.

Gottschall, Rudolf von. 1902. *Die deutsche Nationallitteratur des neunzehnten Jahrhunderts: litterarhistorisch und kritisch dargestellt*. Vol. 4. 7th ed. Breslau: Eduard Trewendt.

Gourmont, Remy de. 1900. *Les Petites Revues: Essai de Bibliographie*. Paris: Librairie du Mercure France.

Grafton, Anthony. 2012. "The Republic of Letters in the American Colonies: Francis Daniel Pastorious Makes a Notebook." *American Historical Review* 117, no. 1: 1–39.

Grand, Sarah. 1897. *The Beth Book*. London: D. Appleton.

Granger, William. n.d. *New Wonderful Museum and Entertaining Magazine*. VI: 3135.

Granovetter, Mark S. 1973. "The Strength of Weak Ties." *American Journal of Sociology* 78, no. 6: 1360–80.

Greenall, R.L. 1979. *A History of Northamptonshire and the Soke of Peterborough*. London, Chichester: Phillimore and Co. Ltd.

Greenwood, Thomas. 1894. *Public Libraries: A History of the Movement and A Manual for the Organization and Management of Rate-Supported Libraries*. London: Cassell and Co.

Greg, W.W. 1932. "Bibliography – An Apologia." *Library* 4, no. 13: 113–43.

Greg, W.W. 1967. *A Companion to Arber*. Oxford: Clarendon Press.

Grenada. 1922. *Blue Book*. Grenada: Government Printing Office.

Griffin, Clive. 1988. *The Crombergers of Seville: The History of a Printing and Merchant Dynasty*. Oxford: Clarendon Press.

Grime, Benjamin. 1887. *Memory Sketches*. Oldham: Hirst and Rennie.

Grojnowski, Daniel. 1996. "Hydropathes and Company." In *The Spirit of Montmartre: Cabarets, Humor, and the Avant-Garde, 1875–1905*, edited by Phillip Dennis Cate and Mary Shaw, 95–110. New Brunswick, NJ: Jane Voorheis Zimmerli Art Museum.

Half A Century of Independency in Ashton-under-Lyne; Together with a Manual of Albion Independent Church. 1867. Ashton: T. Cunningham and Sons.

Hall, Kenneth R. 2014. "European Southeast Asia Encounters with Islamic Expansionism c. 1500–1700: Comparative Case Studies of Banten, Ayutthaya, and Banjarmasin in Wider Indian Ocean Context." *Journal of World History* 25, nos. 2–3 (June/September): 229–62.

Hall, Robert G. 1991. "Work, Class, and Politics in Ashton-under-Lyne, 1830–1860." PhD diss., Vanderbilt University.

Hall, Robert G. 1999. "Creating a People's History: Political Identity and History in Chartism, 1832–1848." In *The Chartist Legacy*, edited by Owen Ashton, Robert Fyson, and Stephen Roberts, 232–54. Woodbridge, UK: Merlin Press.

Hall, Robert G. 2007. *Voices of the People: Democracy and Chartist Political Identity, 1830–1870. Monmouth*. Woodbridge, UK: Merlin Press.

Hall, Robert G., and Stephen Roberts. 2000. "William Aitken, Chartist and Ten-Hour Day Advocate." In *Dictionary of Labour Biography*, edited by Joyce Bellamy and John Saville, 3–6. London: Macmillan Press.

Hall, Robert G., and Stephen Roberts, eds. 1996. *William Aitken: The Writings of a Nineteenth Century Working Man*. Tameside, UK: Tameside Libraries and Heritage.

Hanneken, Jaimie. 2010. "Going Mundial: What It Really Means to Desire Paris." *Modern Language Quarterly* 71, no. 2: 129–52.

Harris, Brayton. 1999. *Blue and Gray in Black and White: Newspapers in the Civil War*. Washington, DC: Brassey's.

Harris, Michael H. 1971. "The Availability of Books and the Nature of Book Ownership on the Southern Indiana Frontier, 1800 1850." PhD diss., Indiana University.

Harrop, Sylvia A. 1983. "Literacy and Educational Attitudes as Factors in the Industrialization of North-East Cheshire, 1760–1830." In *Studies in the History of Literacy: England and North America*, edited by W.B. Stephens, 37–53. Leeds: Museum of the History of Education, University of Leeds.

Haskell, Molly. 1973. *From Reverence to Rape: The Treatment of Women in the Movies*. 2nd ed. Chicago: University of Chicago Press.

Headrick, Daniel R. 2000. *When Information Came of Age: Technologies of Knowledge in the Age of Reason and Revolution, 1700–1850*. Oxford: Oxford University Press.

Heller, Otto. 1905. *Studies in Modern German Literature; Sundermann; Hauptman; Women Writers of the Nineteenth Century*. Boston: Ginn and Co.

Henkin, David M. 1998. *City Reading: Written Words and Public Spaces in Antebellum New York*. New York: Columbia University Press.

Henkin, David M. 2006. *The Postal Age: The Emergence of Modern Communications in Nineteenth-Century America*. Chicago: University Of Chicago Press.

Hess, Earl J. 1988. *Liberty, Virtue, and Progress: Northerners and Their War for the Union*. New York: New York University Press.

Hevel, Michael S. 2011. "Public Displays of Student Learning: The Role of Literary Societies in Early Iowa Higher Education." *Annals of Iowa* 70, no. 1: 1–35.

Hewitt, Martin. 1996. *The Emergence of Stability in the Industrial City: Manchester, 1832–67*. Aldershot: Scolar Press.

Hewitt, Martin. 2000. "Confronting the Modern City: The Manchester Free Library, 1850–80." *Urban History* 27:62–88.

Hewitt, Martin, and Robert Poole, eds. 2000. *The Diaries of Samuel Bamford*. New York: St Martin's Press.

Hill, Robert A. 1991. *November 1927–August 1940*, vol. VII. The Marcus Garvey and Universal Negro Improvement Association Papers. Berkeley: University of California Press.

Hill, Robert A. 2011. *The Caribbean Diaspora, 1910–1920*, vol. XI. The Marcus Garvey and Universal Negro Improvement Association Papers. Durham, NC: Duke University Press.

Hinks, John, and Catherine Armstrong, eds. 2008. *Book Trade Connections from the Seventeenth to the Twentieth Centuries*. New Castle, DE, and London: Oak Knoll Press and the British Library.

Hoare, Peter. 2011. "Some Parochial Libraries in the East Midlands." *Library & Information History* 27 (December): 223–8.

Hobbs, Andrew. 2011. "The Reading World of a Provincial Town: Preston, Lancashire, 1855–1900." In *The History of Reading, Volume 2,* edited by Shafquat Towheed, W.R. Owens, Katie Halsey, and Rosalind Crone, 121–38. Houndmills: Palgrave Macmillan.

Hollinger, David A. 1985. "Ethnic Diversity, Cosmopolitanism, and the Emergence of the American Liberal Intelligensia." In *In the American Province: Studies in the History and Historiography of Ideas*, edited by David Hollingner, 56–73. Bloomington: Indiana University Press.

Hohn, Stefanie. 1998. *Charlotte Brontës Jane Eyre in deutscher Übersetzung. Geschichte eines kulturellen Transfers. Düsseldorfer Materialien zur Literaturübersetzung 13*. Tübingen: Gunter Narr Verlag.

Hollis, Patricia. 1970. *The Pauper Press: A Study in Working-Class Radicalism of the 1830s*. Oxford: Oxford University Press.

Holzer, Harold. 2012. *Emancipating Lincoln: The Proclamation in Text, Context, and Memory*. Cambridge, MA: Harvard University Press.

Hovde, David M., and John W. Fritch. 2005. "In Union There Is Strength: The Farmers' Institute and the Western Literary Union Library." *Libraries & Culture* 40, no. 3: 285–306.

Howe, Glenford. 2002. *Race, War, and Nationalism: A Social History of West Indians in the First World War*. Kingston, Jamaica: Ian Randle.

Howells, William Dean. 1900. "The New Historical Romances." *North American Review* 171:935–48.

Humphreys, John Doddridge, ed. 1829. *The Correspondence and Diary of Philip Doddridge, D.D.: Illustrative of various particulars in his life hitherto unknown ....* London: H. Cloburn and R. Bentley.

Hunte, Keith. 2001. "The Struggle for Political Democracy: Charles Duncan O'Neal and the Democratic League." In *The Empowering Impulse: The Nationalist Tradition of Barbados*, edited by Glenford Howe and Don Marshall, 133–48. Mona, Jamaica: Canoe Press, University of the West Indies.

Hutton, William, and Catherine Hutton. 1816. *The Life of William Hutton, F.A.S.S. Including a Particular Account of the Riots at Birmingham in 1791*. London: Baldwin, Cradock, and Joy.
Igo, Sarah E. 2007. *The Averaged American: Surveys, Citizens, and the Making of A Mass Public*. Cambridge, MA: Harvard University Press.
Jackman, Simon, and Lynn Vavreck. 2011. "Cosmopolitanism." In *Facing the Challenge of Democracy: Explorations in the Analysis of Public Opinion and Political Participation*, edited by Paul M. Sniderman and Benjamin Highton, 70–96. Princeton, NJ: Princeton University Press.
Jackson, H.J. 2001. *Marginalia: Readers Writing in Books*. New Haven, CT: Yale University Press.
Jacob, Margaret. 2006. *Strangers Nowhere in the World: The Rise of Cosmopolitanism in Early Modern Europe*. Philadelphia: University of Pennsylvania Press.
James, Leslie. 2015. *George Padmore and Decolonization from Below: Pan-Africanism, the Cold War, and the End of Empire*. Basingstoke: Palgrave.
James, Winifred. 1913. *The Mulberry Tree*. London: Chapman and Hall.
James, Winston. 1998. *Holding Aloft the Banner of Ethiopia: Caribbean Radicalism in Early Twentieth-Century America*. New York: Verso.
Jennings, Joe. 1929. "Leisure Reading of Junior High School Boys and Girls." *Peabody Journal of Education* 6:333–47.
Jimerson, Randall C. 1988. *The Private Civil War: Popular Thought during the Sectional Conflict*. Baton Rouge: Louisiana State University Press.
J.K. 1858. *History of the Ashton-under-Lyne Mutual Improvement Society*. Ashton: E. Hobson and Son.
Joeres, Ruth-Ellen Boetcher. 1998. *Respectability and Deviance: Nineteenth-Century German Writers and the Ambiguity of Representation*. Chicago: University of Chicago Press.
Johanningsmeier, Charles. 1997. *Fiction and the American Literary Marketplace*. Cambridge: Cambridge University Press.
Johansson, M. Jane, ed. 2000. *Widows by the Thousand: The Civil War Letters of Theophilus and Harriet Perry, 1862–1864*. Fayetteville: University of Arkansas Press.
Johnson, Deidre. 1982. *Stratemeyer Pseudonyms and Series Books*. Westport, CT: Greenwood Press.
Johnson, Deidre. 1993. *Edward Stratemeyer and the Stratemeyer Syndicate*. New York: Twayne.
Jones, Aled, and Bill Jones. 2003. "The Welsh World and the British Empire, c.1851–1939: An Exploration." In *The British World: Diaspora, Culture and Identity*, edited by Carl Bridge and Kent Fedorowich, 57–81. London: Frank Cass.
Jones, Gail. 2007. *Sorry*. North Sydney: Random House.

Jordan, Alice M. 1948. *From Rollo to Tom Sawyer*. Boston: Horn Book.

Jordan, Arthur Melville. 1921. "Children's Interest in Reading." PhD diss., Columbia University.

Jordan, David M. 1971. *Roscoe Conkling of New York: Voice in the Senate*. Ithaca, NY: Cornell University Press.

Joshi, Priya. 2002. *In Another Country: Colonialism, Culture, and the English Novel in India*. New York: Columbia University Press.

Kaestle, Carl F. 1991. "Standardization and Diversity in American Print Culture, 1880 to the Present." In *Literacy in the United States: Readers and Reading Since 1880*, edited by Carl F. Kaestle, et al., 272–94. New Haven, CT: Yale University Press.

Kaestle, Carl F., et al., eds. 1991. *Literacy in the United States: Readers and Reading Since 1880*. New Haven, CT: Yale University Press.

Kaestle, Carl F., and Janice A. Radway, eds. 2009. *Print in Motion: The Expansion of Publishing and Reading in the United States, 1880–1940*, vol. 4. A History of the Book in America. Chapel Hill: University of North Carolina Press.

Kargon, Robert. 1977. *Science in Victorian Manchester: Enterprise and Expertise*. Baltimore: Johns Hopkins University Press.

Kaser, David. 1984. *Books and Libraries in Camp and Battle: The Civil War Experience*. Westport, CT: Greenwood Press.

Kazin, Michael. 2006. *A Godly Hero: The Life of William Jennings Bryan*. Random House.

Kellett, J.R. 1968. "Discussion." In *The Study of Urban History*, edited by H.J. Dyos, 215–30. New York: St Martin's Press.

Kelley, Mary. 1984. *Private Women, Public Stage: Literary Domesticity in Nineteenth-Century America*. New York: Oxford University Press.

Kelly, R. Gordon. 1974. *Mother Was a Lady: Self and Society in Selected American Children's Periodicals, 1865–1890*. Westport, CT: Greenwood Press.

Kemper, G.W.H. 1908. *A Twentieth Century History of Delaware County Indiana*, vol. 1. Chicago: Lewis Publishing Company.

Kessler, M. 1963. "Bibliographic Coupling between Scientific Papers." *American Documentation* 14:10–25.

Kett, Joseph F., and Patricia A. McClung. 1984. "Book Culture in Post-Revolutionary Virginia." *Proceedings of the American Antiquarian Society* 94, no. 1: 97–147.

Khan, M.S. 1961. "William Carey and the Serampore Books." *Libri* 11, nos. 1–4: 197–280.

Kielbowicz, Richard B. 1989. *News in the Mail, The Press, Post Office, and Public Information, 1700–1860s*. Westport, CT: Greenwood Press.

Kimmel, Michael. 1996. *Manhood in America: A Cultural History*. New York: Free Press.

King, Andrew, and John Plunkett, eds. 2005. *Victorian Print Media: A Reader*. Oxford: Oxford University Press.

Klimmt, Christoph, and Peter Vorderer. 2004. "Unterhaltung als unmittelbare Funktion des Lesens." In *Lesesozialisation in der Mediengesellschaft*, edited by Norbert Groeben and Bettina Hurrelmann, 36–60. Weinheim: Juventa.

Klingaman, William K. 2001. *Abraham Lincoln and the Road to Emancipation, 1861–1865*. New York: Viking.

Knight, Charles. (1865) 1927. *Shadows of the Old Booksellers. Reprint*. London: Peter Davies.

Knott, David. 1973–4. "Aspects of Research into English Provincial Printing." *Journal of the Printing Historical Society* 9: 6–21.

Kontje, Todd. 2004. "Marlitt's World: Domestic Fiction in an Age of Empire." *German Quarterly* 77, no. 4: 408–26.

Kopf, David. 1969. *British Orientalism and the Bengal Renaissance, The Dynamics of Indian Modernization, 1773–1835*. Berkeley: University of California Press.

Lamming, George. (1953) 1991. *In the Castle of My Skin*. Ann Arbor: University of Michigan.

Lamond, Julieanne. 2012a. "The Anglo-Australian: Between Colony and Metropolis in Rosa Praed's '*The Right Honourable*' and *Policy and Passion*." *Australian Literary Studies* 27, no. 1: 33–46.

Lamond, Julieanne. 2012b. "Communities of Readers: Australian Reading History and Library Loan Records." In *Republics of Letters: Literary Communities in Australia*, edited by Peter Kirkpatrick and Robert Dixon, 27–38. Sydney: Sydney University Press.

Lamond, Julieanne, and Mark Reid. 2009. "Squinting at a Sea of Dots: Visualising Australian Readerships using Statistical Machine Learning." In *Resourceful Reading: The New Empiricism, eResearch and Australian Literary Culture*, edited by Katherine Bode and Robert Dixon, 223–39. Sydney: Sydney University Press.

Latour, Bruno. 2005. *Reassembling the Social: An Introduction to Actor-Network Theory*. New York: Oxford University Press.

Lears, T.J. Jackson. 1981. *No Place of Grace: Antimodernism and the Transformation of American Culture, 1880–1920*. Chicago: University of Chicago Press.

Leary, Patrick. 2005. "Googling the Victorians." *Journal of Victorian Culture* 10, no. 1 (Spring): 72–86.

Leary, Patrick. 2007. "The Plenitude Effect and the Offline Penumbra." Nineteenth Century Serials Edition Conference, British Library.

Lee, J.M., and R.A. McKinley. "'Kibworth', A History of the County of Leicestershire: Volume 5: Gartree Hundred (1964)." *British History Online*. Accessed 4 September 2013. http://www.british-history.ac.uk/report.aspx?compid=22057.

Leech, Daniel D. Tompkins, and Walter L. Nicholson. 1879. *Post Office Department of the United States of America.* Washington, DC: Judd and Detweiler.

Lees, Lynn Hollen. 2011. "Urban Civil Society: The Context of Empire." *Historical Research* 84, no. 223 (February): 135–47.

LeFebvre, Lucien, and Henri-Jean Martin. (1958) 1976. *The Coming of the Book: The Impact of printing 1450–1800*. London: Verso. Translation of *L'apparition du livre*. Paris: Albin Michel.

Lent, John A. 1977. *Third World Mass Media and Their Search for Modernity: The Case of the Commonwealth Caribbean, 1717–1976*. Lewisburg, PA: Bucknell University Press.

Lester, Alan. 2001. *Imperial Networks: Creating Identities in Nineteenth-Century South Africa*. London: Routledge.

Lindell, Lisa. 2004. "Bringing Books to a 'Book-Hungry Land'." *Book History* 7:215–38.

Lindsay, William. 1898. *Some Notes: Personal and Public*. Aberdeen: W Lindsay.

Lock, Alice. 1981. *Ashton in Old Photographs. Tameside*. Libraries and Arts Committee.

London Topographical Record. 1907. London: London Topographical Society.

Loughran, Trish. 2007. *The Republic in Print: Print Culture in the Age of U.S. Nation Building, 1770–1870*. New York: Columbia University Press.

Love, Harold. 1993. *Scribal Publication in Seventeenth-Century England*. New York: Oxford University Press.

Lovett, William. (1876) 1967. *Life and Struggles of William Lovett, In His Pursuit of Bread, Knowledge & Freedom*. London: MacGibbon and Kee.

Lovett, William, and John Collins. (1840) 1969. *Chartism: A New Organization of the People*. New York: Humanities Press.

Lynd, Robert, and Helen Lynd. (1929) 1957. *Middletown: A Study in Modern American Culture*. Reprint, New York: Harcourt Brace Jovanovich.

Lyons, Martyn. 1997a. "Bush Readers, Factor Readers, Home Readers – Expanding the Australian Reading Public, c. 1890–1930." *Publishing Studies* 5 (Spring): 17–23.

Lyons, Martyn. 1997b. "The History of Reading and Reading Communities." *BSANZ Bulletin* 27, no. 1: 5–15.

Macdonald, Roderick. 1992. "'The wisers who are far away': The Role of London's Black Press in the 1930s and 1940s." In *Essays on the History of Blacks in Britain: From Roman Times to the Mid-Twentieth Century*, edited by Jagdish Gundara and Ian Duffield, 150–72. Aldershot: Avebury.

MacLeod, Anne Scott. 1994. *American Childhood: Essays on Children's Literature of the Nineteenth and Twentieth Centuries*. Athens: University of Georgia Press.

Macleod, David I. 1998. *The Age of the Child: Children in America, 1890–1920*. New York: Twayne.

MacLeod, Kirsten. 2008. "The Fine Art of Cheap Print: Turn-of-the-Century American Little Magazines." In *Transatlantic Print Culture, 1880–1940: Emerging Media, Emerging Modernisms*, edited by Ann Ardis and Patrick Collier, 182–98. New York: Palgrave Macmillan.

Mackal, Mary L., Stevan F. Meserve, and Anne Mackall Sasscer, eds. 2009. *In the Shadow of the Enemy: The Civil War Journal of Ida Powell Dulany*. Knoxville: University of Tennessee Press.

Madden, David, ed. 1968. *Tough Guy Writers of the 1930s*. Carbondale: Southern Illinois University Press.

Makalani, Minkah. 2011. *In the Cause of Freedom: Radical Black Internationalism from Harlem to London, 1917–1939*. Chapel Hill: University of North Carolina Press.

Marshman, J.C. 1867. *History of India from the Earliest Period to Lord Dalhousie*. Vol. 1. London: Longmans, Green, Reader and Dyer.

Marston, E. 1901. *Sketches of Booksellers of Other Days*. London: E. Martson.

Martin, Tony. 1976. *Race First: The Ideological and Organizational Struggles of Marcus Garvey and the Universal Negro Improvement Association*. Westport, CT: Greenwood Press.

Martino, Alberto. 1990. *Die deutsche Leihbibliothek: Geschichte einer literarischen Institution, 1756–1914*. Wiesbaden: Harrassowitz.

Maslen, Keith. 1993. *An Early London Printing House at Work: Studies in the Bowyer Ledgers*. New York: The Bibliographical Society of America.

Maslen, Keith, and John Lancaster, eds. 1991. *The Bowyer Ledgers: The Printing Accounts of William Bowyer and Son*. London: The Bibliographical Society, and New York: The Bibliographical Society of America.

Maxted, Ian. 1982. "4 rotten cornbags and some old books." In *Sale and Distribution of Books from 1700*, edited by Robin Myers and Michael Harris, 37–76. Oxford: Oxford Polytechnic Press.

May, Lary. 1980. *Screening Out the Past: The Birth of Mass Culture and the Motion Picture Industry*. Chicago: University of Chicago Press.

McGann, Jerome. 2008. "Pseudodoxia Academica." *New Literary History* 39, no. 3: 645–56.

McKelvey, Blake. 1961. *Rochester: An Emerging Metropolis, 1925–1961*. Rochester, NY: Christopher Press.

McKenzie, D.F. 1986. *Bibliography and the Sociology of Texts, The Panizzi Lectures, 1985*. London: British Library.

McLachlan, Herbert. 1931. *English Education Under the Test Acts*. Manchester: Manchester University Press.

McMurran, Mary Helen. 2013. "The New Cosmopolitanism and the Eighteenth Century." *Eighteenth-Century Studies* 47, no. 1: 19–38.

McPherson, James M. 1997. *For Cause and Comrades: Why Men Fought in the Civil War*. New York: Oxford University Press.

McPherson, James M. 1998. "'Spend Much Time in Reading the Daily Papers': The Press and Army Morale in the Civil War." *Atlanta History* 42, nos. 1–2: 7–18.

Mellen, Joan. 1977. *Big Bad Wolves: Masculinity in the American Film*. New York: Pantheon.

A Memorial and Biographical History of Northern California. 1891. Chicago: Lewis Publishing.

Middleton, Bernard C. 1963. *A History of English Craft Bookbinding Technique*. London: Hafner.

Middleton, Thomas. 1932. *The History of Hyde and Its Neighbourhood. Hyde*. Higham Press.

Miller, Willis Harry, ed. 1955. *Postmarked Hudson: The Letters of Sarah A. Andrews to Her Brother James A. Andrews, 1864–65....* Hudson, WI: Star Observer.

Mintz, Steven. 2004. *Huck's Raft: A History of American Childhood*. Cambridge: Belknap Press.

More, J.B. Prashant. 2004. *Muslim Identity, Print Culture, and the Dravidian Factor in Tamil*. Delhi: Orient Blackman.

Moretti, Franco. 1998. *Atlas of the European Novel, 1800–1900*. London: Verso.

Morris, Jan. 1973. *Heaven's Command: An Imperial Progress*. New York: Harcourt Brace Jovanovich.

Morrow, James, ed. 1819. *The Poetical remains of the late Dr. John Leyden, with memoirs of his life*. London: Strahan and Spottiswoode for Longman, Hurst, Rees, Orme, and Brown.

Mott, Frank Luther. 1941. *American Journalism: A History of Newspapers in the United States Through 250 Years, 1690–1940*. New York: Macmillan.

Murr, Sylvia. 1977. "Nicolas Desvaulx (1745–1823) veritable auteur de Moeurs, intitutions et ceremonies des peupls de l'Inde, de l'abbe Dubois?" *Purusartha* 3:245–67.

Nackenoff, Carol. 1994. *The Fictional Republic: Horatio Alger and American Political Discourse*. Oxford: Oxford University Press.

Needham, Paul. 1986. *The Printer and the Pardoner: An Unrecorded Indulgence Printed by William Caxton for the Hospital of St Mary Rounceval, Charing Cross*. Washington, DC: Library of Congress.

Nelson, Claudia. 1989. "Sex and the Single Boy: Ideals of Manliness and Sexuality in Victorian Literature for Boys." *Victorian Studies* 32 (Summer): 525–51.

Nevin, David. 1974. *The Expressmen*. New York: Time-Life Books.

Nevins, Allan. 1959–71. *Ordeal of the Union*. Vols. 5–8. New York: Scribner.

Newcastle Family History Society. 1994. *Mechanics Institute Elder Street, Lambton: A Short History and List of Borrowers' Cards*. Newcastle, NSW: Newcastle Family History Society.

Newell, Stephanie. 2009. "Newspapers, New Spaces, New Writers: The First World War and Print Culture in Colonial Ghana." *Research in African Literatures* 40, no. 2: 1–15.

Newell, Stephanie. 2011a. "Articulating Empire: Newspaper Readerships in Colonial West Africa." *New Formations* 73:26–42.

Newell, Stephanie. 2011b. "Local Cosmopolitans in Colonial West Africa." *Journal of Commonwealth Literature* 46, no. 1: 103–17.

Nichols, John. (1812–15) 1966. *Literary Anecdotes of the Eighteenth Century*. 9 vols. Reprinted New York: Kraus Reprint Corp.

Norris, Frank. 1986. *"An Opening for Novelists," Novels and Essays*. New York: Library of America.

Nuttall, Derek. 1969. *A History of Printing in Chester*. Chester: Printed for private circulation.

Nuttall, Geoffrey F. 1977. *New College, London and Its Library*. London: Friends of Dr Williams's Library.

Nuttall, Geoffrey F. 1979. *Calendar of the Correspondence of Philip Doddridge DD (1702–1751)*. London: Her Majesty's Stationery Office.

Nye, Russell. 1970. *The Unembarrassed Muse: The Popular Arts in America*. New York: Dial Press.

Ohmann, Richard. 2009. "Diverging Paths: Books and Magazines in the Transition to Corporate Capitalism." In *A History of the Book in America: Volume 4: Print in Motion: The Expansion of Publishing and Reading in the United States, 1880–1940*, edited by Carl F. Kaestle and Janice A. Radway, 102–15. Chapel Hill: University of North Carolina Press.

Ohmann, Richard. 1996. *Selling Culture: Magazines, Markets, and Class at the Turn of the Century*. London: Verso Books.

Oldham, J.B. 1958. "An Ipswich Master-Stationer's Tiff with his Journeyman." *Transactions of the Cambridge Bibliographical Society* 2:381–4.

Olver, Thomas, and Stephan Meyer. 2004. "Introduction: African Shores and Transatlantic Interlocutions." *Current Writing: Text and Reception in Southern Africa* 16, no. 2: 1–17.

Orton, Job. 1766. *Memoirs of the life, character and writings of the late Reverend Philip Doddridge*. London: D.D. of Northampton.

Parascandola, Louis J., ed. 2005. *Look for Me All Around You: Anglophone Caribbean Immigrants in the Harlem Renaissance*. Detroit: Wayne State University Press.

Parker, Irene. 1914. *Dissenting Academies in England: Their Rise and Their Place Among the Educational Systems of the Country*. Cambridge: Cambridge University Press.

Parker, Jason. 2004. "'Capital of the Caribbean': The African American-West Indian 'Harlem Nexus' and the Transnational Drive for Black Freedom, 1940–1948." *Journal of African American History* 89 (2): 98–117.

Parry, Marc. 2010. "The Humanities Go Google." *Chronicle of Higher Education* 28 (May): Accessed 26 May 2015].http://chronicle.com/article/The-Humanities-Go-Google/65713/.

Pawley, Christine. 2001. *Reading on the Middle Border: The Culture of Print in Late Nineteenth-Century Osage, Iowa*. Amherst: University of Massachusetts Press.

Pawley, Christine. 2009a. *Reading on the Middle Border: The Culture of Print in Late Nineteenth-Century Osage, Iowa*. Amherst: University of Massachusetts Press.

Pawley, Christine. 2009b. "Beyond Market Models and Resistance: Organizations as a Middle Layer in the History of Reading." *Library Quarterly* 79, no. 1: 73–93.

Pawley, Christine. 2010. *Reading Places: Literacy, Democracy, and the Public Library in Cold War America*. Amherst: University of Massachusetts Press.

Pennybacker, Susan. 2009. *From Scottsboro to Munich: Race and Political Culture in 1930s Britain*. Princeton, NJ: Princeton University Press.

Perry, Jeffrey B., ed. 2001. *A Hubert Harrison Reader*. Middletown, CT: Wesleyan University Press.

Petree, Barbara Joanne, ed. 1994. *David and Rebecca: Their Lives and Letters*. Kansas City: B.J. Petree.

Pickford, Christopher. 1982. "Bedford Stationers and Booksellers." *Factotum* 15 (Oct.): 21–7.

Plummer, John. 1860. *Songs of Labour, Northamptonshire Rambles, and Other Poems*. London: W. Tweedie.

Pochmann, Henry A. 1957. *German Culture in America: Philosophical and Literary Influences 1600–1900*. Madison: University of Wisconsin Press.

Polsgrove, Carol. 2009. *Ending British Rule in Africa: Writers in a Common Cause*. New York: Manchester University Press.

Prais, Jinny. 2008. "Imperial Travelers: The Formation of West African Urban Culture, Identity, and Citizenship in London and Accra, 1925-1935." PhD diss., University of Michigan.

Prashad, Vijay. 2002. *Everybody was Kung Foo Fighting: Afro-Asian Connections and the Myth of Cultural Purity*. Boston: Beacon Press.

Pred, Allan. 1973. *Urban Growth and the Circulation of Information: The United States System of Cities, 1790–1840*. Cambridge, MA: Harvard University Press.

Pred, Allan. 1980. *Urban Growth and City-Systems in the United States: 1840–1860*. Cambridge, MA: Harvard University Press.

Prendergast, Christopher. 2004. "The World Republic of Letters." In *Debating World Literature*, edited by Christopher Prendergast, 1–25. London: Verso.

Pressnell, L.S. 1956. *Country Banking in the Industrial Revolution*. Oxford: Clarendon Press.

Price, D.J. de Solla. 1965. "Networks of Scientific Papers." *Science* 149:510–5.

Price, Leah. 2004. "Reading: the State of the Discipline." *Book History* 7, no. 1: 303–20.

Putnam, Lara. 2009. "'Nothing Matters But Color': Transnational Circuits, the Interwar Caribbean, and the Black International." In *From Toussaint to Tupac: The Black International since the Age of Revolution*, edited by Michael O. West, William G. Martin, and Fanon Che Wilkins, 107–29. Chapel Hill: University of North Carolina Press.

Putnam, Lara. 2013a. "Provincializing Harlem: The 'Negro Metropolis' as Northern Frontier of an Interconnected Greater Caribbean." *Modernism/Modernity* 20, no. 3: 469–84.

Putnam, Lara. 2013b. *Radical Moves: Caribbean Migrants and the Politics of Race in the Jazz Age*. Chapel Hill: University of North Carolina Press.

Putnam, Lara. 2014. "Citizenship from the Margins: Vernacular Theories of Rights and the State from the Interwar Caribbean." *Journal of British Studies* 53, no. 1:162–91.

Putnam, Lara. (Forthcoming). "Sidney Adolphus Young." In *Dictionary of Caribbean and Afro-Latin American Biography*, edited by Henry Louis Gates, Jr, and Franklin W. Knight. New York: Oxford University Press.

Pyrhönen, Heta. 2010. *Bluebeard Gothic: Jane Eyre and Its Progeny*. Toronto: University of Toronto Press.

Quelch, Lorenzo. 1992. *An Old Fashioned Socialist*. Reading: Lorenzo Quelch Memorial Group.

Rabbitt, Mary. 1997. "Lambton Mechanics' and Miners' Institute." In *Science, Success and Soirees: the Mechanics' Institute movement in Newcastle and the Lower Hunter*, edited by Barbara Heaton, Greg Preston, and Mary Rabbitt, 53–79. Newcastle, NSW: Newcastle Region Library.

Radice, William, ed. 1991. "Introduction." In *Selected Short Stories by Rabindranath Tagore*, 1–28. New York: Penguin.

Rao, Velcheru Narayana. 2004. "Print and Prose: Pundits, *Karanams*, and the East India Company in the Making of Modern Telagu." In *India's Literary History: Essays on the Nineteenth Century*, edited by Stuart H. Blackburn and Vasudha Dalmia, 146–66. New Delhi: Permanent Black.

Rao, Velcheru Narayana, David Shulman, and Sanjay Subrahmanyam. 2001. *Textures of Time: Writing History in South India 1600–1800*. Delhi: Permanent Black.

Raven, James. 1986. "Print and Trade in Eighteenth-Century Britain." Thirlwall Prize Dissertation, University of Cambridge.

Raven, James. 1996a. *Judging New Wealth: English Popular Literature and the Image of Business, 1750–1800.* Oxford: Clarendon Press.

Raven, James. 1996b. "Imprimé et transactions économiques: représentation et interaction en angleterre aux XVIIe et XVIII siècles." *Revue d'Histoire Moderne et Contemporaine* 43, no. 2: 234–65.

Raven, James. 2007. *The Business of Books: Booksellers and the English Book Trade 1450–1850.* New Haven, CT: Yale University Press.

Raven, James. 2009a. "The Book as a Commodity." In *The Cambridge History of the Book in Britain, Volume 5, 1695–1840*, edited by Michael Suarez S.J. and Michael L. Turner, 83–117. Cambridge: Cambridge University Press.

Raven, James. 2009b. "London and the Central Sites of the English Book Trade." In *The Cambridge History of the Book in Britain, Volume 5, 1695–1840*, edited by Michael Suarez S. J. and Michael L. Turner, 291–308. Cambridge: Cambridge University Press.

Ray, Angela G. 2013. "How Cosmopolitan was the Lyceum, Anyway?" In *The Cosmopolitan Lyceum*, edited by Tom F. Wright, 23–41. Amherst: University of Massachusetts Press.

Read, Donald. 1961. *Press and People, 1790–1850: Opinion in Three English Cities.* London: Edward Arnold.

"Refutation of the Letters of Abbe Dubois." 1825. *The Friend of India.* Calcutta.

Regis, Pamela. 2003. *A Natural History of the Romance Novel.* Philadelphia: University of Pennsylvania Press.

Reuveni, Gideon. 2002. "Reading Sites as Sights for Reading. The Sale of Newspapers in Germany before 1933: Bookshops in Railway Stations, Kiosks, and Street Vendors." *Social History* 27 (Oct.): 273–87.

Ridley, Hugh. 2007. *"Relations Stop Nowhere": The Common Literary Foundations of German and American Literature 1830–1917.* Amsterdam, New York: Rodopi.

Rinehart, Anne C. 1931. *What Pittsburgh Junior High School Pupils Read.* Pittsburgh: Henry C. Educational Commission.

Riney-Kehrberg, Pamela. 2007. "New Directions in Rural History." *Agricultural History* 81, no. 2 (Summer): 155–8.

Risely, Ford. 2001. "The Confederate Press Association: Cooperative News Reporting of the War." *Civil War History* 47, no. 3: 222–39.

Rivers, Isabel. 1982. "Dissenting and Methodist Books of Practical Divinity." In *Books and their Readers in Eighteenth-Century England*, edited by Isabel Rivers, 135–70. Leicester: Leicester University Press.

Rivers, Isabel. 2003. *The Defence of Truth Through the Knowledge of Error: Philip Doddridge's Academy Lectures.* London: Friends of Dr Williams's Library.

Rivers, Isabel. 2009. "Religious Publishing." In *The Cambridge History of the Book in Britain, Volume 5, 1695–1840*, edited by Michael Suarez S.J. and Michael L. Turner, 579–600. Cambridge: Cambridge University Press.

Rivers, Isabel, and David Wykes, eds. Forthcoming. *A History of the Dissenting Academies in the British Isles, 1660–1860*. Cambridge: Cambridge University Press.

Roberts, Kyle. Forthcoming. "Congregational Libraries." In *A History of Dissenting Academies in the British Isles, 1660–1860*, edited by Isabel Rivers and David Wykes. Cambridge: Cambridge University Press.

Roberts, Stephen. 1995. "Who Wrote to the *Northern Star*?" In *The Duty of Discontent: Essays for Dorothy Thompson*, edited by Owen Ashton, Robert Fyson, and Stephen Roberts, 55–70. London: Mansell.

Robertson, Mary D., ed. 1986. "Northern Rebel: The Journal of Nellie Kinzie Gordon, Savannah, 1862." *Georgia Historical Quarterly* 70 (Fall): 477–517.

Robertson, Mary D. 1994. *Lucy Breckinridge of Grove Hill: The Journal of a Virginia Girl, 1862–1864*. Columbia: University of South Carolina Press.

Roche, Daniel. 1997. *Histoire des choses banales: Naissance de la consommation des les sociétés tradionnelles (XVIIe–XIXe siècles)*. Paris: Fayard.

Rocher, Rosane. 1983. *Orientalism, Poetry, and the Millennium: The Checkered Life of Nathaniel Brassey Halhed, 1751–1830*. Delhi: Motilal Banarsidass.

Rodger, Richard. 2000. "Slums and Suburbs: The Persistence of Residential Apartheid." In *The English Urban Landscape*, edited by Philip Waller, 242–68. Oxford: Oxford University Press.

Rodgers, Daniel. 1974. *The Work Ethic in Industrial America, 1850–1920*. Chicago: University of Chicago Press.

Rogers, J. Guinness. 1903. *An Autobiography*. London: J. Clarke.

Romero, Lora. 1997. *Home Fronts: Domesticity and its Critics in the Antebellum United States*. Durham: Duke University Press.

Roosevelt, Theodore. 1900. "What We Can Expect of the American Boy." *St. Nicholas* 27:571–4.

Rose, Jonathan. 2001. *The Intellectual Life of the British Working Classes*. New Haven, CT: Yale University Press.

Rosenstein, Doris and Helmut Kreuzer, eds. 2005. *Deutschsprachige Literaturkritik 1870–1914: Eine Dokumentation,* edited by Helmut Kreuzer with the assistance of Doris Rosenstein, 1:40–8. Frankfurt am Main: Peter Lang.

Ross, Catherine Sheldrick. 2009. "Reader on Top: Public Libraries, Pleasure Reading, and Models of Reading." *Library Trends* 57 (Spring): 640: 632–56.

Runstedtler, Theresa. 2013. "The New Negro's Brown Brother: Black American and Filipino Boxers and the 'Rising Tide of Color." In *Escape from New York: The New Negro Renaissance Beyond Harlem*, edited by Davarian Baldwin and Minkah Makalani, 105–26. Minneapolis: University of Minnesota Press.

Sachsman, David B., S. Kittrell Rushing, and Roy Morris, eds. 2008. *Words at War: the Civil War and American Journalism*. West Lafayette, IN: Purdue University Press.

Sachsman, David B., S. Kittrell Rushing, and Debra Reddin Van Tuyll, eds. 2000. *The Civil War and the Press.* New Brunswick, NJ: Transaction Publishers.

Said, Edward W. 1978. *Orientalism*. New York: Pantheon Books.

Samito, Christian G., ed. 1998. *Commanding Boston's Irish Ninth: The Civil War Letters of Patrick R. Guiney, Ninth Massachusetts Volunteer Infantry*. New York: Fordham University Press.

Sanders, Mike. 2009. *The Poetry of Chartism: Aesthetics, Politics, History*. Cambridge: Cambridge University Press.

Savage-Smith, Emilie. 1988. "John Channing: Eighteenth-Century Apothecary and Arabist." *Pharmacy in History* 30, no. 2: 63–80.

Schaeffer, Satu Elisa. 2007. "Graph Clustering." *Computer Science Review* 1:27–64.

Schaffer, Talia. 2002. "The History of Richard Calmady." *The Literary Encyclopedia.* Accessed 14 February 2013. http://www.litencyc.com/php/sworks.php?rec=true&UID=595.

Scharnhorst, Gary. 1980. *Horatio Alger, Jr*. Boston: Twayne.

Scharnhorst, Gary, and Jack Bales. 1985. *The Lost Life of Horatio Alger, Jr.* Bloomington: Indiana University Press.

Schmitthenner, Peter. 2001. *Telugu Resurgence: C.P. Brown and Cultural Consolidation in Nineteenth-Century South India*. Delhi: Manohar.

Schneirov, Matthew. 1994. *The Dream of A New Social Order:Popular Magazines in America, 1893–1914*. New York: Columbia University Press.

Secord, James. 2000. *Victorian Sensation: The Extraordinary Publication, Reception, and Secret Authorship of Vestiges of the Natural History of Creation*. Chicago: University of Chicago Press.

Shackleton, Robert, and M.L. Turner, comps. 1971. *The John Johnson Collection: Catalogue of an Exhibition*. Oxford: Bodleian Library.

Shaw, Charles. (1903) 1977. *When I Was A Child. Reprint, Firle*. Sussex: Caliban Books.

Shaw, Mary. 1996. "All or Nothing? The Literature of Montmartre." In *The Spirit of Montmartre: Cabarets, Humor, and the Avant-Garde, 1875–1905*, edited by Phillip Dennis Cate and Mary Shaw, 111–58. New Brunswick, NJ: Jane Voorheis Zimmerli Art Museum.

Shifflett, Crandall, ed. 2008. *John Washington's Civil War: A Slave Narrative*. Baton Rouge: Louisiana State University Press.

Shilling, Maree, ed. 2009. *The Story of Lambton: A Suburb of Newcastle, NSW*. Newcastle, NSW: Newcastle Family History Society.

Shorter, Alfred H. 1966. *Water Paper Mills in England*. London: Society for the Protection of Ancient Buildings.

Shulman, David, and Velcheru Narayan Rao. 1998. *A Poem at the Right Moment:Remembered Verses from Premodern South India*. Berkeley: University of California Press.

Sicherman, Barbara. 2002. "Reading and Middle-Class Identity in Victorian America: Cultural Consumption, Conspicuous and Otherwise." In *Reading Acts: U.S. Readers' Interactions with Literature, 1800–1950*, edited by Barbara Ryan and Amy M. Thomas, 137–60. Knoxville: University of Tennessee Press.

Sinha, Mrinalini. 2000. "Introduction." In *Katherine Mayo, Selections from Mother India*, edited by Mrinalini Sinha, 1–62. Ann Arbor: University of Michigan Press.

Sklar, Robert. 1992. *City Boys: Cagney, Bogart, Garfield*. Princeton, NJ: Princeton University Press.

Slate, Nico. 2012. *Colored Cosmopolitanism: The Shared Struggle for Freedom in the United States and India*. Cambridge, MA: Harvard University Press.

Smith, J.F. 1859. *Redmond O'Neil; or, The Substance and the Shadow*. New York: Dick and Fitzgerald.

Smith, Charles Manby. 1857. *The Little World of London*. London: Arthur Hall, Virtue, and Co.

So, Richard Jean, and Hoyt Long. 2013. "Network Analysis and the Sociology of Modernism." *Boundary 2* 40, no. 2: 147–82.

Sparanese, Ann C. 2002. "Service to the Community: A Public Library Perspective." *Library Trends* 51, no. 1: 19–55.

Stallybrass, Peter. 2007. "'Little Jobs': Broadsides and the Printing Revolution." In *Agent of Change: Print Culture Studies after Elizabeth L. Eisenstein*, edited by Sabrina Alcorn Baron, Eric N. Lindquist, and Eleanor F. Shevlin, 315–41. Amherst: University of Massachusetts Press.

Stanford, Charles. 1881. *Philip Doddridge, D.D.* New York.

St Clair, William. 2004. *The Reading Nation in the Romantic Period*. Cambridge: Cambridge University Press.

Steinberg, Marc W. 1999. *Fighting Words: Working-Class Formation, Collective Action, and Discourse in Early Nineteenth-Century England*. Ithaca, NY: Cornell University Press.

Stephens, W.B. 1987. *Education, Literacy and Society, 1830–70: The Geography of Diversity in Provincial England*. Manchester: Manchester University Press.

Stepp, John W., and Isaac William Hill, eds. 1961. *Mirror of War: The Washington Star Reports the Civil War*. Englewood Cliffs, NJ: Prentice-Hall.

Stern, Madeleine B. 1956. *Imprints on History, Book Publishers and American Frontiers*. Bloomington: Indiana University Press.

Sterenberg, Alan. 1983. "The Spread of Printing in Suffolk in the Eighteenth Century." In *Searching the Eighteenth Century*, edited by M. Crump and M. Harris, 28–42. London: British Library.

Stevenson, Brenda L., ed. 1988. *Journals of Charlotte Forten Grimke*. New York: Oxford University Press.

Stevenson, Louise L. 1991. *Victorian Homefront: American Thought and Culture, 1860–1880*. New York: Twayne.

Stewart, Charles W., ed. 1910. *Official Records of the Union and Confederate Navies in the War of the Rebellion. Ser. 1*, vol. 23. Washington, DC: Government Printing Office.

Stewart, David Marshall. 1978. "William T. Berry and his Fabulous Bookstore: Nashville's Literary Emporium without Parallel." *Tennessee Historical Quarterly* 37, no. 1: 36–48.

Stiffler, Stuart A. 2011. "Books and Reading in the Connecticut Western Reserve: The Small-Settlement Social Library, 1800–1860." *Libraries and the Cultural Record* 46, no. 4: 388–411.

Stoker, David. 1977. "The establishment of printing in Norwich." *Transactions of the Cambridge Bibliographical Society* 7, no. 1: 94–111.

Stoddard, Lothrop. 1920. *The Rising Tide of Color against White World Supremacy*. New York: Charles Scribner's Sons.

Stolte, Carolien, and Harald Fischer-Tiné. 2012. "Imagining Asia in India: Nationalism and Internationalism (ca. 1905–1940)." *Comparative Studies in Society and History* 54, no. 1: 65–92.

Stonehouse, Merlin. 1965. *John Wesley North and the Reform Frontier*. Minneapolis: University of Minnesota Press.

Stouder, Nellie M., Nettie Wood, and John Rollo Marsh. 1905. "Brief History of the Muncie Public Library. Jan. 1 1904." In *Catalogue of Books in the Muncie Public Library*. Muncie, IN.

Suarez, Michael. 2009a. "Introduction." In *The Cambridge History of the Book in Britain, Volume 5, 1695–1840*, edited by Michael Suarez S.J. and Michael L. Turner, 1–36. Cambridge: Cambridge University Press.

Suarez, Michael. 2009b. "Towards a Bibliometric Analysis of the Surviving Record, 1701-1800." In *The Cambridge History of the Book in Britain, Volume 5, 1695–1840*, edited by Michael Suarez S.J. and Michael L. Turner, 37–65. Cambridge: Cambridge University Press.

Sullivan, Frances Peace. 2012. "Radical Solidarities: U.S. Capitalism, Community Building, and Popular Internationalism in Cuba's Eastern Sugar Zone, 1919-1939." PhD diss., New York University.

Sweetman, Will. 2004. ""The Prehistory of Orientalism: Colonialism and the Textual Basis for Bartholomaus Ziegenbalg's Account of Hinduism." *New Zealand." Journal of Asian Studies* 6, no. 2: 12–38.

Switzer, Les. 1990. "The Ambiguities of Protest in South Africa: Rural Politics and the Press during the 1920s." *International Journal of African Historical Studies* 23, no. 1: 87–109.

Tatlock, Lynne. 2012. *German Writing, American Reading: Women and the Import of Fiction (1866–1917)*. Columbus: Ohio State University Press.

Tatlock, Lynne. 2014. "'The One and the Many' *The Old Mam'selle's Secreet* and the American Traffic in German Fiction (1868–1917)." In *Distant Readings: Topologies of German Culture in the Long Nineteenth Century*, edited by Matt Erlin and Lynne Tatlock, 229–56. Rochester, NY: Camden House.

Tebbel, John. 1969. *The Compact History of the American Newspaper*. New York: Hawthorn.

Teed, Paul. 2003. "Race Against Memory: Katherine Mayo, Jabez Sunderland, and Indian Independence." *American Studies (Lawrence, Kan.)* 44, nos. 1–2: 35–57.

Thernstrom, Stephan. (1973) 1999. *The Other Bostonians: Poverty and Progress in the American Metropolis, 1880–1970*. Cambridge, MA: Harvard University Press.

Thompson, Jerry D., ed. 2011. *Tejanos in Gray: Civil War Letters of Captains Joseph Rafael de La Garza and Manuel Yturri*. College Station: Texas A&M University Press.

Thompson, W. Fletcher, Jr. 1961. *The Image of War: The Pictorial Reporting of the American Civil War*. New York: Yoseloff.

Thomson, Alistair G. 1974. *The Paper Industry in Scotland, 1590–1861*. Edinburgh: Scottish Academic Press.

Throne, Mildred. 1951. "'Book Farming' in Iowa, 1840–1870." *Iowa Journal of History* 49, no. 2: 117–42.

Tiffany, Daniel. 2009. *Infidel Poetics: Riddles, Nightlife, Substance*. Chicago: University of Chicago Press.

Tillott, P.M. 1972. "Sources of Inaccuracy in the 1851 and 1861 Censuses." In *Nineteenth-Century Society: Essays in the Use of Quantitative Methods for the Study of Social Data*, edited by E.A. Wrigley, 82–133. Cambridge: Cambridge University Press.

Todd, Emily B. 2001. "Antebellum Libraries in Richmond and New Orleans and the Search for the Practices and Preferences of 'Real' Readers." *American Studies (Lawrence, Kan.)* 42, no. 3: 195–209.

Traue, J.E. 2007. *The Public Library Explosion in Colonial New Zealand*. Austin: University of Texas Press.

Trautmann, Thomas R. 1997. *Aryans and British India*. Berkeley: University of California Press.

Trautmann, Thomas R. 2006. *Languages and Nations: The Dravidian Proof in Colonial Madras*. Berkeley: University of California Press.

Trautmann, Thomas R. 2009. "The Missionay and the Orientalist." In *Ancient to Modern, Religion, Power, and Community in India*, edited by Ishita Banerjee-Dube and Saurabh Dube, 236–58. New Delhi: Oxford University Press.

Trautmann, Thomas R., ed. 2009. *The Madras School of Orientalism, Producing Knowledge in Colonial South India*. New Delhi: Oxford University Press.

Trivedi, Harish. 2008. "The 'Book' in India: Orality, Manu-Script, Print (Post) Colonialism." In *Books Without Borders, Volume 2: Perspectives from South Asia*, edited by Robert Fraser and Mary Hammond, 12–33. London: Palgrave Macmillan.

Tucher, Andie. 2006. "Reporting for Duty: The Bohemian Brigade, the Civil War, and the Social Construction of the Reporter." *Book History* 9:131–57.

Turner, Joyce Moore, with W. Burghardt Turner. 2005. *Caribbean Crusaders and the Harlem Renaissance*. Urbana: University of Illinois Press.

Twyman, Michael, and William Rollinson. 1966. *John Soulby, Printer, Ulverston: A Study of the Work Printed by John Soulby, father and son, between 1796 and 1827 with an account of Ulverston at the time.* Reading: Museum of English Rural Life.

Tylecote, Mabel. 1957. *The Mechanics' Institutes of Lancashire and Yorkshire before 1851*. Manchester: University of Manchester Press.

United States, Post Office Department. 1863a. *An Act to Amend the Laws Relating to the Post-Office Department, Approved March 3, 1863, Together with Instructions Predicated Thereon by the Postmaster General for the Government of Postmasters*. Washington, DC: Government Printing Office.

United States, Post Office Department. 1863b. *An Act to Amend the Act Entitled "An Act to Reduce and Modify the Rates of Postage in the United States and for Other Purposes," Passed March Third, Eighteen Hundred and Fifty-One*. Washington, DC: Government Printing Office.

United States, Bureau of the Census. 1902. *Abstract of the Twelfth Census of the United States, 1900*. Washington, DC: Government Printing Office.

United States, Bureau of the Census. 1913–14. *Thirteenth Census of the United States, 1910, Volume 1: Population*. Washington DC: Government Printing Office.

United States, Bureau of the Census. 1976. *The Statistical History of the United States; From Colonial Times to the Present*. New York: Basic Books.

Unwin, George. 1924. *Samuel Oldknow and the Arkwrights: the Industrial Revolution at Stockport and Marple*. Manchester: Manchester University Press.

Uricchio, William. 2003. "Historicizing Media in Transition." In *Rethinking Media Change: The Aesthetics of Transition*, edited by David Thorburn and Henry Jenkins, 23–39. Boston: MIT Press.

Van der Walt, Lucien. 2007. "The First Globalisation and Transnational Labour Activism in Southern Africa: White Labourism, the IWW, and the ICU, 1904-1934." *African Studies* 66, nos. 2–3: 223–51.

Van Tuyll, Debra Reddin. 2000. "Gray Ladies of the Confederacy: Newspaper Culture in the Old South, 1860–1865." PhD diss., University of South Carolina.

Van Tuyll, Debra Reddin, ed. 2005. *The Southern Press in the Civil War: American Wars and the Media in Primary Documents*. Westport, CT: Greenwood Press.

Vincent, David. 2000. *The Rise of Mass Literacy: Reading and Writing in Modern Europe*. Cambridge: Polity Press.

Vinson, Robert. 2009. "Providential Design: American Negroes and Garveyism in South Africa." In *From Toussaint to Tupac: The Black International since the Age of Revolution*, edited by Michael O. West, William G. Martin, and Fanon Che Wilkins, 130–54. Chapel Hill: University of North Carolina Press.

Von Eschen, Penny. 1997. *Race against Empire: Black Americans and Anticolonialism, 1937–1957*. Ithaca, NY: Cornell University Press.

Wadsworth, Sarah. 2006. *In the Company of Books: Literature and Its "Classes" in Nineteenth-Century America*. Amherst: University of Massachusetts Press.

Wallis, Philip. 1974. *At the Sign of the Ship: Notes on the House of Longman, 1724–1974*. London: Longman.

Washburne, Carleton, and Mabel Vogel. 1927a. "Supplement to the Winnetka Graded Book List." *Elementary English Review* 4 (February): 47–52.

Washburne, Carleton, and Mabel Vogel. 1927b. "Supplement to the Winnetka Graded Book List." *Elementary English Review* 4 (March): 66–73.

Watt, Tessa. 1991. *Cheap Print and Popular Piety, 1550–1640*. Cambridge: Cambridge University Press.

Watts, Duncan J. 2002. "A Simple Model of Global Cascades on Random Networks." *Proceedings of the National Academy of Sciences of the United States of America* 99, no. 9: 5766–71.

Watts, Duncan J. 2004. "The 'New' Science of Networks." *Annual Review of Sociology* 30:243–70.

Waugh, Edwin. 1855. *Sketches of Lancashire Life and Localities*. London: Whittaker and Co.

Waugh, Edwin. 1892. *Lancashire Sketches*. Ed. George Milner. Manchester: John Heywood.

Webby, Elizabeth. 2006. "Not Reading the Nation: Australian Readers of the 1890s." *Australian Literary Studies* 22, no. 3: 308–18.

Wenger, E.L. 1961. "The Serampore Mission and Its Founders." In *The Story of Serampore and Its College*, edited by Serampore College, 1–11. Serampore, India: Council of Serampore College.

West, Michael, and William Martin. 2009. "Contours of the Black International: From Toussaint to Tupac." In *From Toussaint to Tupac: The Black International since the Age of Revolution*, edited by Michael O. West, William G. Martin, and Fanon Che Wilkins, 1–46. Chapel Hill: University of North Carolina Press.

Westcott, A. 1897. *Our Oldest Indian Mission, A Brief History of he Vepery (Madras) Mission*. Madras: Society for Promoting Christian Knowledge.

Wevers, Lydia. 2010. *Reading on the Farm: Victorian Fiction and the Colonial World*. Wellington, NZ: Victoria University Press.

"What 'St. Nicholas' Has Done for Girls and Boys." 1980. *Overland Monthly and Out West Magazine* 16 (Dec.): 666–70.

Whiston, William. 1873. "Our Monthly Gossip. Wilhelmine Von Hillern." *Lippincott's Magazine of Popular Literature and Science* 11, no. 2: 115–16.

White, Kevin. 1992. *The First Sexual Revolution: The Emergence of Male Heterosexuality in Modern America*. New York: NYU Press.

Whitehouse, Tessa. 2011. "Dissenting Education and the Legacy of John Jennings, c.1720–c.1729." 2nd ed. Dr Williams Centre for Dissenting Studies. Accessed 28 May, 2015. http://www.english.qmul.ac.uk/drwilliams/pubs/jennings%20legacy.html.

Wiegand, Wayne A. 2011. *Main Street Public Library: Community Places and Reading Spaces in the Rural Heartland, 1876–1956*. Iowa City: University of Iowa Press.

Wiener, Joel. 1969. *The War of the Unstamped: The Movement to Repeal the British Newspaper Tax, 1830–1836*. Ithaca, NY: Cornell University Press.

Wiles, R.M. 1965. *Freshest Advices: Early Provincial Newspapers in England*. Columbus: Ohio State University Press.

Wiley, Bell Irvin. 1952. *The Life of Billy Yank: The Common Soldier of the Union*. Indianapolis: Bobbs-Merrill.

Wilkie, Jane Riblett. 1976. "The United States Population by Race and Urban-Rural Residence, 1790-1860." *Demography* 13, no. 1: 139–48.

Wilkinson, Rupert. 1984. *American Tough: The Tough Guy and American Character*. Westport, CT: Greenwood Press.

Willan, T.S. 1970. *An Eighteenth-century Shopkeeper: Abraham Dent of Kirkby Stephen*. Manchester: Manchester University Press.

William, M., ed. 1892. *Serampore Letters, 1800–16*. London: G.P. Putnam and Sons.

Williams, Philip Martin, and David L. Williams. 1991. *Extra, Extra, Read All About It: A Brief History of the Newspapers of Ashton-under-Lyne, 1847–1990*. Ashton: History on your Doorstep.

Wilson, Edmund. 1966. *Patriotic Gore: Studies in the Literature of the American Civil War*. New York: Oxford University Press.

Wykes, David. 2002. "'Who shall instruct our youth – fill our Vacant churches?' Philip Doddridge and the Academy at Northampton, 1729–51." Unpublished manuscript.

Young, Robert J.C. 1995. *Colonial Desire: Hybridity in Theory, Culture and Race*. London: Routledge.

Zboray, Ronald J. 1989. "The Book Peddler and Literary Dissemination: The Case of Parson Weems." *Publishing History* 25:27–44.

Zboray, Ronald J. 1991. "Reading Patterns in Antebellum America: Evidence in the Charge Records of the New York Society Library." *Libraries & Culture* 26:301–33.

Zboray, Ronald J. 1993. *A Fictive People: Antebellum Economic Development and the American Reading Public*. New York: Oxford University Press.

Zboray, Ronald J., and Mary Saracino Zboray. 1996a. "Books, Reading, and the World of Goods in Antebellum New England." *American Quarterly* 48:587–622.

Zboray, Ronald J., and Mary Saracino Zboray. 1996b. "Political News and Female Readership in Antebellum Boston and Its Region." *Journalism History* 22 (Spring): 2–14.

Zboray, Ronald J., and Mary Saracino Zboray. 2002. "Cannonballs and Books: Reading and the Disruption of Social Ties on the New England Homefront." In *The War Was You and Me: Civilians in the American Civil War*, edited by Joan Cashin, 237–61. Princeton, NJ: Princeton University Press.

Zboray, Ronald J., and Mary Saracino Zboray. 2005. *Literary Dollars and Social Sense: A People's History of the Mass Market Book*. New York: Routledge.

Zboray, Ronald J., and Mary Saracino Zboray. 2006. *Everyday Ideas: Socioliterary Experience Among Antebellum New Englanders*. Knoxville: University of Tennessee Press.

Zboray, Ronald J., and Mary Saracino Zboray. 2010. *Voices Without Votes: Women and Politics in Antebellum New England*. Durham: University of New Hampshire Press by the University Press of New England.

Zboray, Ronald J., and Mary Saracino Zboray. 2011. "Publishing Freedom on the 'Most Glorious Day This Nation Has Yet Seen': Print Culture, New Year's Day 1863, and the Emancipation Proclamation." Paper presented at the annual convention of the Society for the History Authorship, Reading, and Publishing, Washington, DC. July.

Zboray, Ronald J., and Mary Saracino Zboray. 2012. "Reading Communities: Civil War News Linking Home Front and Battlefield." Paper presented at the annual convention of the American Historical Association, in conjunction with AHA-Affiliate Society for the History of Authorship, Reading, and Publishing, Chicago. January.

Contributors

Patrick Collier, Ball State University

James J. Connolly, Ball State University

Brad Evans, Rutgers University

Frank Felsenstein, Ball State University

Kenneth R. Hall, Ball State University

Robert G. Hall, Ball State University

Julieanne Lamond, Australian National University

Christine Pawley, University of Wisconsin-Madison

Lara Putnam, University of Pittsburgh

James Raven, Cambridge University

Kyle Roberts, Loyola University-Chicago

Joan Shelley Rubin, University of Rochester

Joel D. Shrock, Anderson University

Lynne Tatlock, Washington University-St Louis

Lydia Wevers, Victoria University of Wellington

Mary Saracino Zboray, University of Pittsburgh

Ronald J. Zboray, University of Pittsburgh

Index

Studies in Book and Print Culture

General Editor: Leslie Howsam

Hazel Bell, *Indexers and Indexes in Fact and Fiction*

Heather Murray, *Come, bright Improvement! The Literary Societies of Nineteenth-Century Ontario*

Joseph A. Dane, *The Myth of Print Culture: Essays on Evidence, Textuality, and Bibliographical Method*

Christopher J. Knight, *Uncommon Readers: Denis Donoghue, Frank Kermode, George Steiner, and the Tradition of the Common Reader*

Eva Hemmungs Wirtén, *No Trespassing: Authorship, Intellectual Property Rights, and the Boundaries of Globalization*

William A. Johnson, *Bookrolls and Scribes in Oxyrhynchus*

Siân Echard and Stephen Partridge, eds, *The Book Unbound: Editing and Reading Medieval Manuscripts and Texts*

Bronwen Wilson, *The World in Venice: Print, the City, and Early Modern Identity*

Peter Stoicheff and Andrew Taylor, eds, *The Future of the Page*

Jennifer Phegley and Janet Badia, eds, *Reading Women: Literary Figures and Cultural Icons from the Victorian Age to the Present*

Elizabeth Sauer, *"Paper-contestations" and Textual Communities in England, 1640–1675*

Nick Mount, *When Canadian Literature Moved to New York*

Jonathan Earl Carlyon, *Andrés González de Barcia and the Creation of the Colonial Spanish American Library*

Leslie Howsam, *Old Books and New Histories: An Orientation to Studies in Book and Print Culture*

Deborah McGrady, *Controlling Readers: Guillaume de Machaut and His Late Medieval Audience*

David Finkelstein, ed., *Print Culture and the Blackwood Tradition*

Bart Beaty, *Unpopular Culture: Transforming the European Comic Book in the 1990s*

Elizabeth Driver, *Culinary Landmarks: A Bibliography of Canadian Cookbooks, 1825–1949*

Benjamin C. Withers, *The Illustrated Old English Hexateuch, Cotton Ms. Claudius B.iv: The Frontier of Seeing and Reading in Anglo-Saxon England*

Mary Ann Gillies, *The Professional Literary Agent in Britain, 1880–1920*

Willa Z. Silverman, *The New Bibliopolis: French Book-Collectors and the Culture of Print, 1880–1914*

Lisa Surwillo, *The Stages of Property: Copyrighting Theatre in Spain*

Dean Irvine, *Editing Modernity: Women and Little-Magazine Cultures in Canada, 1916–1956*

Janet Friskney, *New Canadian Library: The Ross-McClelland Years, 1952–1978*

Janice Cavell, *Tracing the Connected Narrative: Arctic Exploration in British Print Culture, 1818–1860*

Elspeth Jajdelska, *Silent Reading and the Birth of the Narrator*

Martyn Lyons, *Reading Culture and Writing Practices in Nineteenth-Century France*

Robert A. Davidson, *Jazz Age Barcelona*

Gail Edwards and Judith Saltman, *Picturing Canada: A History of Canadian Children's Illustrated Books and Publishing*

Miranda Remnek, ed., *The Space of the Book: Print Culture in the Russian Social Imagination*

Adam Reed, *Literature and Agency in English Fiction Reading: A Study of the Henry Williamson Society*

Bonnie Mak, *How the Page Matters*

Eli MacLaren, *Dominion and Agency: Copyright and the Structuring of the Canadian Book Trade, 1867–1918*

Ruth Panofsky, *The Literary Legacy of the Macmillan Company of Canada: Making Books and Mapping Culture*

Archie L. Dick, *The Hidden History of South Africa's Book and Reading Cultures*

Darcy Cullen, ed., *Editors, Scholars, and the Social Text*

James J. Connolly, Patrick Collier, Frank Felsenstein, Kenneth R. Hall, and Robert Hall, eds, *Print Culture Histories beyond the Metropolis*